FIRST
SOCIOLOGY

FIRST SOCIOLOGY

Kenneth Westhues

University of Waterloo

McGraw-Hill Book Company

*New York   St. Louis   San Francisco   Auckland   Bogotá   Hamburg
Johannesburg   London   Madrid   Mexico   Montreal   New Delhi
Panama   Paris   São Paulo   Singapore   Sydney   Tokyo   Toronto*

First Sociology

34567890 DODO 89876543

ISBN 0-07-069466-4 HC
ISBN 0-07-069463-X SC

This book was set in Goudy Old Style by Black Dot, Inc. (ECU).
The editors were Eric M. Munson, Alison Meersschaert, and James R. Belser;
the designer was Joan E. O'Connor;
the production supervisor was John Mancia.
The photo editor was Inge King.
Chapter-opening drawings were done by Hans-Georg Rauch.
The cover illustration was done by Colos.

Quotations on pp. 118–119 from The Human Factor *by Graham Greene.*
Copyright © 1976 by Graham Greene. Reprinted by permission
of the author and of Simon & Schuster,
a Division of Gulf & Western Corporation.

Quotations on pp. 119–120 from Who Has Seen the Wind *by W. O.*
Mitchell. Copyright 1947 by W. O. Mitchell. Reprinted
by permission of the author and of Macmillan of Canada,
a Division of Gage Publishing Limited.

Library of Congress Cataloging in Publication Data

Westhues, Kenneth.
First sociology.

Includes bibliographies and indexes.
1. Sociology.   I. Title.
HM51.W45   301   81-15612
ISBN 0-07-069463-X (pbk.)   AACR2
ISBN 0-07-069466-4

To Olive,
in John's memory

*Only when we realize that there is no
eternal, unchanging truth or absolute
truth can we arouse in ourselves a sense
of intellectual responsibility. The
knowledge that mankind needs is not the
way or principle which has an absolute
existence but the particular truths for
here and now.*
Hu Shih, 1919

Contents

Preface   xiii

1   Discipline   1

Scholars like Comte, Durkheim, Spencer, and Sumner invented sociology in the nineteenth century and found it a place in universities. The discipline proved popular and its practitioners multiplied. It is sometimes viewed today as a promising little science still struggling for maturity. More accurately, sociology has already matured as intensely relevant knowledge of the present shape of social life. Its holistic emphasis, interpretive goal, experiential base, and explicitly social focus distinguish this discipline from other ones and recommend it to every citizen.

In other words: C. Wright Mills, "The Promise"   24
For reflection   31
For making connections   32
For further reading   32

2   Methods   35

The first, most critical step in doing useful sociology is to label experience with carefully chosen words. Then to sort these words out in conceptual schemes. The researcher typically posits some hypothesis or statement of relation among certain distinct concepts, treating the latter as independent, dependent, and control variables. Hypotheses are tested against experience through analysis of historical and contemporary records, fieldwork, demographic techniques, surveys, and other methods. Max Weber's study of the Protestant ethic and spirit of capitalism, along with later tests of his hypothesis, illustrates the research process—and the benefits it yields for understanding social life.

For example: Gerald L. Gold, "Fieldwork in Saint-Pascal"   56

For reflection   67

For making connections   67

For further reading   68

3 Society   71

Among the myriad kinds of groups in today's world, the national society merits scrutiny above all. Sociologists study this paramount reality in four especially helpful ways: (1) as a sociocultural system—composed of action and meaning, roles and norms, with inevitable deviance in both respects; (2) as a structure of demands—the structural-functional analysis of institutions and organizations; (3) also as a structure of rewards—power, wealth, and honor, the inequalities in each giving clues to change and history; (4) finally as contained by international capitalism and other larger structures. With similar conceptual schemes sociologists make sense also of groups on a smaller scale. But the latter, like subcultures and minorities, are best understood in national contexts.

For example: John Kenneth Galbraith, "On Switzerland"   90

For reflection   113

For making connections   114

For further reading   115

4 Person   117

Because societies are made of people, sociology implies social psychology. The person appears as a two-sided being, at once created and creative, predictable and surprising, *me* and *I*, superego and id. Behaviorist psychology illuminates the first side. So do studies of child socialization and experiments that document human malleability. Through primary relationships, modeling, and play, children in Western societies are shaped into go-getters keen on individual achievement. Adults also are pressured to conform, and not just in total institutions. But predictability has limits. People steadily inject newness into social life, insofar as the roles they occupy give power. Symbolic interactionist research highlights this second side of the person. Like history, biography is a reciprocal, dynamic process.

In other words: Martin Buber, "The Reality of Between*"*   124

For reflection   154

For making connections   154

For further reading   155

5 Polity

157

Problems of both anomie and alienation urge primary attention to public order, the commonweal, in the study of a society's insides. Growing human self-consciousness through time has undermined traditional and charismatic types of political authority and encouraged the legal-rational type, the kind social-contract theory requires. Yet constitutional government remains even now insecure. Crippled by lingering traditionalism among women and certain minorities. Plagued by militarism. Weakened by the economic alienation that defines a mass society and fosters demagoguery. Modern, legal polities come in two broad kinds, liberal and socialist, representing two paths toward democracy. The first, traceable to Locke and Jefferson, calls for competing parties and self-interested voters in a market economy. The second, inspired in part by Rousseau, has a single party and a governmentally planned economy.

In other words: Alexis de Tocqueville, "Despotism in Democracies"   182
For reflection   198
For making connections   198
For further reading   199

6 Economy

203

Part One: The Development Process
Every society must somehow adapt to the environment of earth. The more effectively it does so, the more developed it is. Domestication of nature, improvement of technology, refinement of work, spread of literacy and know-how, and harnessing of renewable sources of energy are continuing themes in the development process. With some qualifications, so are the enlarging of societies, progressive division of labor, shift in employment away from agriculture, demise of gift-giving in favor of redistribution and market exchange, cultural modernization, and control of fertility.
Part Two: The Capitalist Strategy
Among all paths of development, capitalism has been remarkable for its success. Its effects through time, however, include monopolization of capital and spread of wage labor; the ascendency of large-scale corporations; governmental expansion and social welfare; a shift in the stratification system away from ownership toward consumer spending; urbanization and suburbanization. Some products of capitalism are invaluable, others of doubtful human worth. Further development by this strategy is likely to require more careful planning by the state.

For example: Robert L. Heilbroner, "Planning Capitalism"   258
For reflection   272
For making connections   273
For further reading   274

7 Religion

277

Functionalist and Marxian outlooks overstress the conservative aspects of religion. This institution is better conceptualized as a celebration of limits, the concrete effects of which are in principle indeterminate and socially contrived. Religion necessarily declines in the course of economic advance. The split of profane from sacred, transformation of magic into science, rise of monotheism, and spread of Christianity signify the decline. Liberal-capitalist development has brought freedom of (and from) religion, reduced churches to denominations, and encouraged secularization. Atheism and anticlericalism are common in nonliberal societies. Nonetheless, the popularity of sectarian religion proclaims the inadequacies of contemporary life. Death, uncertainty, and inequality are continuing realities. Further economic advance is unlikely without respect for limits.

For example: Gary T. Marx's Study of Black Religion and Militancy   314
For reflection   319
For making connections   319
For further reading   320

8 Family   323

To sociologists, the family is a social overlay on biological ties. Illegitimacy, adoption, and variation in rules on lineage, number of spouses, and mate selection demonstrate this institution's socially constructed character. Western civilization has long taken sex seriously and kinship lightly—values which reinforced its general dynamism. The nuclear family is a Western creation, tied to the capitalist economy as oil to vinegar. In this way women came to be excluded from economic life and restricted to family roles. The nuclear family fares poorly outside the West—in utopian communities, on kibbutzim, and in the Soviet Union especially. It declines now also in North America and Europe, as women regain roles in the economic mainstream, as sexual expression escapes the marriage bond, as divorce rates rise, and as parental authority weakens. The amount and kind of family life in the future is a political question.

For example: Philippe Ariès, "The Family and the City"   348
For reflection   374
For making connections   374
For further reading   375

9 Education   379

Education happens in the sharing of ideas—whether in school or out, with children or with adults, but never by one person alone. From Plato on, most scholars have considered knowledge an extrinsic thing, to be dispensed by teachers to learners. Thus the contemporary concern with IQ or learning capacity and with alternative educational technologies. Modern theorists like Dewey, Coady, and Freire conceive of education more humanly and dynamically, and with more complex and rigorous criteria. Schooling overlaps education only partially. Among other functions, universities have immersed students in past realities and thereby symbolized conspicuous waste. Public schools have been important for social control. But increasingly schools of all kinds are drawn into the service of contemporary industrial economies, especially as settings for professional training. Schooling is closely tied to stratification.

For example: Everett C. Hughes, "The Stratification of Teachers"   416

For reflection   424

For making connections   424

For further reading   425

10   Liberation   429

A society grips its citizens so tight that not only conformity is predictable but also much deviant behavior. Whether retreatist or aggressive, individual or collective, mild or severe, dissidence springs in greatest part from existing political and economic conditions. Analysis of rates of crime, suicide, mental illness, drug use, and of the rise and fall of social movements bears this out. Authorities respond to deviance also in patterned ways—ignoring, co-opting, repressing those who misbehave. Nonetheless, history is even now in the making, and on a course not altogether predefined. Evolution makes sense only in the backward glance, not in attempts to shape the future. Certain kinds of deviance, carefully chosen paths of liberation, have genuinely new historical effects. Although less obvious than in some earlier eras, these opportunities for progressive change beckon also in our time.

For example: Jo Freeman's Study of How Women Mobilized   458

For reflection   464

For making connections   465

For further reading   466

Notes   469

Indexes   481
    Name Index
    Subject Index

Preface

In 1883, Lester F. Ward wrote in his preface to *Dynamic Sociology:* "Before the science of society can be truly founded, another advance must be made, and the actively dynamic stage reached, in which social phenomena shall be contemplated as capable of intelligent control by society itself in its own interest."

In 1931, Robert M. MacIver made much the same point in his preface to *Society: Its Structure and Changes:* "Not a single social phenomenon would exist were it not for the creative experience of social beings such as we ourselves."

Today, in a world that baffles and intimidates its citizens, there is no better way to preface this introduction to sociology than by echoing MacIver and Ward: control is possible, creativity is real, responsibility for the shape of life rests with you and me. This book differs greatly from theirs, to be sure. As the structure of life changes so must depictions of it that aspire to adequacy and usefulness. But the most basic sociological insight into that structure remains the same as fifty or a hundred years ago: that it is ours, not a force beyond us but a resource for us, not a static absolute to which people surrender but a history which people make. An effort to get that point across underlies the treatment of every specific topic in this book.

"Sociologists equally sound may differ as to which truths deserve the foreground and which should be relegated to the background." By this prefatory comment E. A. Ross justified his *Principles of Sociology*, published in 1920. His observation justifies this book, too. For in a field so large and varied as sociology, it is out of the question to treat equally in a single basic book all the well-founded ideas currently discussed. To do so is impossible. To attempt it is to compile a catalog, not compose a book. The relevant and tough question is which well-founded sociological ideas to pick out and assemble into the clearest picture possible of contemporary social life. To this question these pages are one carefully constructed answer.

Thus, however much this book relies on other scholars' research, it bears the mark of the one man who pulled widely varied ideas into a coherent whole. I have not tried to hide this fact, to pretend that my own point of view is not evident on every page. This is not a survey of a fragmented field but an integral blend of what I believe are its best elements. No other sociologist could or would have synthesized the field quite this way. Every reader will find something to argue with. That is all to the good. Real life is like that. The worth of a book consists not in its insipidity or inoffensiveness but in how effectively it helps readers develop their own personal geniuses. In this respect I share the sentiment of Franklin Giddings, prefacing the 1913 edition of his *Principles of Sociology:* "I have not at any time supposed that these views would immediately be adopted. Every scholar who is competent to discuss sociological theory has himself arrived at carefully matured conclusions which he must not hastily modify or abandon." Himself or herself, I should say.

The aim of coherence and integrity in this book extends not only to the chapters themselves but also to the learning aids which accompany them. Systematic subheadings and marginal notes should keep readers constantly in touch with the overall logic and perspective. Each chapter ends not only with lists of concepts for reflection and suggestions for further reading but with questions for connecting ideas across chapters and with personal experience. Brief selections from other scholars' work expand points made in the text itself. A bittersweet drawing by Hans-Georg Rauch introduces each chapter, and illustrations offer breathers from the text at regular intervals. In every way the editors or I can imagine, this book conforms capably to the best pedagogical standards for teaching sociology.

But substance is what matters, the beneficial, practical knowledge citizens young and old crave for their personal lives. The knowledge given in this book has dictated three departures from textbook convention which bear mention here at the outset. First, there are ten chapters instead of the usual fifteen or more. The reason is simply that the ideas presented fall coherently into ten divisions. But to offer this book with fewer chapters than the usual number of weeks in a term is also a way of acknowledging a supremely important fact. Textbooks are not merely adopted. They are and should be *adapted* by creative, autonomous professors to their respective teaching situations and personal emphases. I would not even if I could program anyone's course in introductory sociology. All I do here is provide the best resource I can.

Although concepts are defined from page to page, often with diverse formulations and examples, no capsule definitions are listed anywhere in this book. The omission of a glossary is intentional. As MacIver wrote in his preface, "To understand is harder than to memorize, to see the relationships of things than to count their parts. Sociology is not an easy study." The study is in fact not eased but undermined by the provision of capsule definitions that beg to be memorized quickly and forgotten soon. My goal in these pages has been to facilitate the cause of learning in every honest way: to construct the index carefully, to grip readers with vivid prose and not let go, to clarify sophisticated points with homespun examples, occasionally to amuse, often to challenge, always to excite and stimulate. But as for turning sociology into a temporary game, I haven't the heart.

One of the works that gave our discipline its start in the English-speaking world, Herbert Spencer's *Principles of Sociology*, appeared in 1876 devoid of references. "If footnotes are referred to," the author wrote in its preface, "the thread of argument is completely broken; and even if they are not referred to, attention is disturbed by the consciousness that they are there to be looked at." In qualified acceptance of Spencer's reasoning, I have let the principle of parsimony guide the citation of names, books, and articles in these pages. The sacrifice I ask of my colleagues, that of seeing more of their friends' names in print, is for a good cause.

But enough of technical details! Textbook convention will not in the end be the measure of this book. Its measure is the living reality of contemporary experience, whose enduring regularities I have sought to capture in words. With MacIver I have asked, "Why should the misunderstood name of science limit the sociologist to the arid schematism of figures and tables and classifications, so that the student often finds a clearer illumination of the working of society in the fragmentary revelations of the social novelist, dramatist, and the essayist?" These pages are one further effort to correct that misunderstanding.

The desk where I wrote most of this overlooked Broadway in midtown Manhattan. Often I daydreamed of putting up in lights along that street the names of those who so obligingly read all or part of the manuscript at my request, criticized it *con amore,* and offered their advice and encouragement. This page is a far cry from Broadway, but anyway here are their names: Margie L. Boschert, Eleonora A. Cebotarev, Juanne N. Clarke, Dorothy M. Dohen, Jeanne Fortunoff, Marcel Gervais, James R. Kelly, Patrick H. McNamara, James W. Rinehart, Eva E. Sandis, Peter R. Sinclair, Dolores M. Wadle, Jeffrey D. Wadle, Olive Westhues, and O. Kendall White. My work on this book depended also on extraordinary support from administrators at two universities, in particular Joseph P. Fitzpatrick and Gerald M. Shattuck at Fordham, J. S. Minas, Robin K. Banks, and Alfred A. Hunter at Waterloo. The roughly twenty editors and prepublication reviewers who applauded the manuscript and suggested ways of improving it not only helped make this book worthier but strengthened my faith in editors, sociologists, and people generally. Four consultants to McGraw-Hill were especially helpful: Thomas E. Drabek, John Kramer, Samuel F. Sampson, and Everett K. Wilson. The publishing experts whose names appear on the copyright page, Alison Meersschaert above all, not only worked hard and skillfully on this project but patiently suffered an author more irascible and meddlesome than most. More than just reading these pages, Anne Westhues lived them with me daily for a thousand days; there is no debt like mine to her. In conclusion let me simply affirm my awareness that this book belongs to many more people than me: to the authors of sources both cited and uncited, to colleagues at Waterloo, Fordham, and elsewhere, to thousands of magnificent students, to secretaries who double as friends, to stamp dealers, typists, compositors, printers, binders, and booksellers, even to the bag lady on 58th Street near Eighth Avenue, whose friendly mutterings in passing enriched me almost daily for many months and deepened whatever understanding of our common life this book reflects. But responsibility for everything written here is mine.

Kenneth Westhues

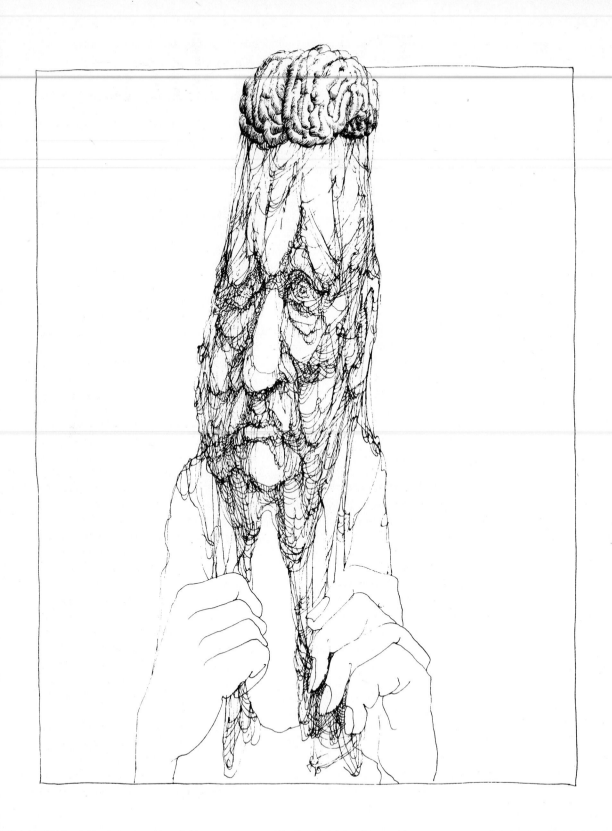

Discipline

Chapter One

*I ask what sociology is
and how it differs from other
fields of knowledge*

*the story of
this book's origin* My parents' farm lay across some hills north of the river, at a point where towering bluffs ease into rolling plains before yielding still farther northward to the prairie. Our house stood high on a ridge and I liked its location. At night I could tell if there was a baseball game in any of the surrounding towns. From my upstairs window I could peer across the darkened hills and catch the lights of their ball parks glimmering on the horizon. More than once I informed my friends on the morning bus to school, "They played ball in Salisbury last night." "Did you go?" someone would ask. "No," I would answer happily, "you can see the lights from where I live." Other kids had their own vantage points. "A tug went upriver just before dark," one would say, "and I counted nine barges it was pushing." That was news to me. From our house you couldn't see the river.

A generation has passed since I left my parents' farm, looking for a place where I could see even more than I could from there. Since 1966, I have been at work and at home in the field called sociology. Three years I spent learning to inspect the world from its particular vantage point. Then I started teaching others the same skill and recording my observations in the scholarly journals sociologists circulate among themselves. This book summarizes the basic perspectives, insights, and ideas of the field. It is not written for specialists but, as it were, for traveling companions who are interested.

Like most young people, I became acquainted with sociology initially through a textbook. Just after fall-term registration in 1964, I stood in line in the college bookstore, waiting to buy the standard compendium of the facts and theories of the field. It was referred to as "Broom and Selznick," after the book's authors, but who wrote it was unimportant to me. Sociology, I imagined, would be a great body of

1

knowledge rather independent of particular people. It would be a stable and coherent set of ideas that would make sense of the tumultuous world of the 1960s just then beginning to explode. I therefore studied the textbook intently. Two years later I carried the same orderly conception of sociology with me as I enrolled in graduate school to study the field full time.

Not long after I enrolled, a prominent American sociologist named Alvin Gouldner (1920–1980) came to campus as a visiting lecturer. I had never heard of him, but one of my professors discussed Gouldner's work in class shortly before the lecture. That professor ventured the comment that in his then-current writings, unconventional by the standards of Broom and Selznick, Gouldner was "defining himself out of the sociological tradition." I remembered the comment but thought no more of it until the evening after Gouldner's lecture, at a dinner we graduate students hosted in his honor. The occasion was a social and intellectual catastrophe. Our distinguished guest, a huge man with ruddy skin and a haystack of red hair, was made to sit at the head of a long banquet table, as if he were Jesus at the Last Supper. There he presided in silence throughout the meal, while we students tried in vain to think of questions or issues for him to address. Perhaps no one had understood any more of his lecture than I had.

"Professor Gouldner," I began unsteadily and in desperation, when even the clinking of knives and forks no longer broke the stillness, "is it true that in your current work you are defining yourself out of the sociological tradition?"

The whole top of the man seemed to have been set on fire. His ruddy skin grew ruddier. His red hair bristled. "Young man," he thundered, "I *make* the sociological tradition."

the basic lesson: sociology is what sociologists make it be

I suppose this was the most important lesson I learned in graduate school. Sociology is what sociologists make it be. It is not like that hilltop of my youth, a vantage point given by nature before recorded time. Better indeed to compare it with a lookout tower constructed by carpenters. The textbook impression is the wrong one. The craft of sociology is not, any more than the craft of carpentry, a static body of tasks, tools, and techniques. It is, above all, people who work, define tasks, invent tools, and conjure up techniques, people who through their work give expression to themselves. Sociology exists only because some number of workers in the eternal quest for knowledge have so influenced one another and combined their efforts that certain commonalities of viewpoint among them can be discerned. These men and women working in concert—some inventing, others copying, some bustling about, others plodding along—they are the ones who make sociology real. And not just make it real but make it change day by day, defining and redefining the sociological tradition with every new book published, every new course taught. Hence to understand sociology, the place to start is with sociologists.

Origins of the Field

Although all fields of knowledge are human inventions, they were not all invented at once. Historians, philosophers, poets, and mathematicians can all trace their ancestry back to the ancient Greeks, and even farther. We sociologists cannot. No one claimed to be a sociologist until little more than a century ago. My grandfather could not have gone to school and studied sociology even had he wanted to; it was not yet taught in the German universities of his day. Sociology is just one of the many inventions of our nineteenth-century forebears in Europe. It is good to recall what its founders had in mind when they first offered it to the world.

The term *sociology* first was used in a book published in 1838 by an ambitious French philosopher from Montpelier, Auguste Comte (1798–1857). By this word he meant the scientific study of the natural laws governing social phenomena. To suggest even that such a science is possible was a novel idea at the time. It was generally believed that there was a natural social law, but one given by reason and revelation, not by the instruments of science. Moreover, people were thought free to abide by natural law or to defy it: this made the difference between saints and sinners. Comte thought otherwise. The natural social laws in which he believed were a matter not of *ought to be* but of *is*. They were not to be found, he judged, in the Bible or in abstract contemplation but in thoughtful, careful observation of the way people actually behave. Once known, these natural laws could be used to predict how people act in different social situations. Comte's natural laws were the kind a person cannot disobey.

Comte's dream of a science of natural social laws

Despite its novelty, Comte's idea was consistent with prevailing intellectual trends. That era, it must be said, was an arrogant one, a time when human beings had learned to take matters into their own hands. The Protestant movement, which had defied the Catholic church's claim to a monopoly on the truth, was centuries old and well-established. The French and American revolutions were already part of history; kings had been deposed and democratic rights proclaimed. Machines had been invented for producing all kinds of goods, and steam engines were hissing their support of early industrialization. Weekly and even daily newspapers proclaimed the unprecedented accomplishments of the human race. The medieval belief that civilization was in a process of decay, that the greatness of Athens and Rome could never be repeated, had gone out of fashion. Indeed, the little capital city of the young American republic had been built as a new and superior Athens, the center of a grander civilization than the earth had yet seen. The educated classes of Comte's day believed in progress, the steady improvement of human life through the methods of science.

On the centenary of his death, the government of the French Republic honored with this commemorative issue the scholar who gave sociology its name.

Comte expressed his own faith in the human mind by renouncing his Catholicism at the age of 13. Thereafter he would prefer to learn through his own human faculties rather than by listening to the voice of church authority. By the time he was 40 he had set forth his law of the three stages, an idea which while not original with him, he was the first to expound systematically. The law posited that every branch of knowledge progresses inevitably through three gradations of increasing worth. In the first or theological stage, events are believed to occur simply because human or superhuman beings want them to. Thus people might pray to God for victory in war. The second or metaphysical stage Comte considered a transitional one. In it there would be awareness of the habitual orderliness of events (that victory in war, for example, depends on the resources and strategies of the opposing sides), but still also a belief that this order could be changed by a miracle, or by what is called even in today's insurance policies an "act of God." The third stage Comte labeled *positive*, with all the overtones of assurance and certainty the word connotes. Now at last people realize that miracles do not happen, that events are governed solely by laws inherent in nature. The positive scientist, Comte believed, knows the rules which control events and can predict them with certainty.

the law of three stages: theological, metaphysical, and positive

This law of evolution through three stages struck Comte as altogether obvious. Already he could see the process nearly complete in a field like astronomy. No respectable scholar of his day still believed that a god or gods pushed the stars around at will; their movements had become predictable through the scientific astronomy begun by Copernicus three centuries earlier. In physics, chemistry, and physiology, Comte observed similar if slower progress toward the discovery of predictive laws. Why, then, he asked himself, should not a positive stage also overtake the study of human social life? If there are natural laws that govern movements of the stars, are there not others that determine the way people behave? Without much modesty Comte took to himself the task of naming the branch of knowledge that would discover these laws. Already the term *social physics* had been suggested; Comte chose *sociology* instead, coining it as a combination of the Latin word for *social* and the Greek word for *idea*.

The label itself did not catch on immediately, but the science did. Karl Marx (1818–1883), a German philosopher who lived his last thirty-five years in England, devoted his entire life to discovering laws of history and social relations. Marx

Marx: a dialectical law of class conflict

thought he had found them in the *dialectical* (that is, contradictory or oppositional) relationship between classes at different stages in history. In every society, he argued, a ruling class lords it over the powerless majority and thereby spawns the forces of its own eventual destruction. The old European aristocracy, for instance, had inevitably bred its own contradiction, a new class of capitalists or bourgeoisie, which in the plan of history eventually seized control of the social order. Looking at Europe in the midnineteenth century, Marx saw these capitalists still in control, using their ownership of productive resources to lord it over the working class, living off profit extracted from the labor of paid employees. This working class or proletariat, he reasoned, is bound to revolt—in accordance with the natural laws of human history. *The Communist Manifesto*, published in 1848 by Marx and his friend, Friedrich Engels, was a call for the revolution they believed was historically inevitable and scientifically predictable anyway. Marx's natural social laws have, of course, turned out to be less inexorable than he imagined. The dialectic of class struggle clearly lacks the predictive precision of Copernicus's astronomy. Nonetheless, and despite the fact that he did not apply to himself the term *sociologist*, Karl Marx ranks easily among the half-dozen cardinal founders of this field of study.

Comte's label might well have fallen into disuse had it not been for two other nineteenth-century thinkers who believed a science of social life was possible, tried to discover it, based their ideas on Comte's, and called their work sociology. One of these was Emile Durkheim (1858–1917), who was the first to occupy a French university professorship formally designated by the word sociology. He taught first at Bordeaux, then at the Sorbonne from 1902 until his death. These prestigious positions gave Durkheim the academic clout to begin to establish the new science as a distinct and legitimate field of study in universities. He performed this task masterfully. His own books on the causes of suicide, the origins of religion, and the process of societal development were widely circulated and continue to be read even today. Durkheim also trained students to be sociologists and founded a regular periodical, *L'Année Sociologique*, for the publication of research findings from the new vantage point. Even so, Durkheim's contribution to the initial establishment

Karl Marx (1818–1883) lived before the study of societies was parceled out among the fields of sociology, economics, political science, social philosophy, and the rest. Nor would such divisions have made much sense to him. In his view social life was all of a piece and deserved to be analyzed as such. The correctness of that view, as well as the insight of his own work, is vindicated by the attention social scientists of all stripes even now give to him. A lawyer's son, Marx studied at the universities of Bonn and Berlin, and earned his doctorate at Jena. But like many other disciples of Hegel at the time, he was denied an academic career in Germany and so spent his life in exile as an independent scholar and writer, also as a news correspondent and organizer of the First International, a workers' organization. Friedrich Engels (1820–1895) was also German-born. Educated in law and commerce, he later helped manage his father's cotton mill in Manchester, England. He and Marx met in Paris in 1844, and found close similarities in their critical diagnoses of the capitalist economy. They later collaborated in political and scholarly activities, and Engels was a frequent visitor at the London townhouse of Jenny and Karl Marx. Vladimir Lenin (1870–1924) was of a later generation and never knew either Marx or Engels. He studied their books, however, and used them as a basis not only for his own writings but for the Bolshevik revolution, which he led to victory in Russia in 1917. But Lenin is only the most famous of the millions of readers who have appreciated Marx's work. No social thinker in modern times has influenced history more than the author of Das Kapital, a man who relished all kinds of knowledge—from Shakespeare to calculus to children's stories—and whose favorite maxim was, "Nothing human is alien to me."

of the field in North America was modest. It was another of Comte's disciples who put sociology on its feet in the English-speaking world.

Spencer: an evolutionary law that the fittest survive

Herbert Spencer (1820–1903) was a British philosopher who shared with his contemporary, Karl Marx, a quest for the laws of society and history. Spencer sought to find them not through dialectical reasoning, however, but through applying directly to human history Charles Darwin's new theory of biological evolution. If physical organisms gradually progress from lower to higher forms of life, said Spencer, so also does the social organism, society. What happens in history is a linear process of natural selection, generation by generation, with the strong and talented steadily winning out over the weak and stupid. It is a process, as he said, of the "survival of the fittest." In the workings of the capitalist marketplace in Britain and America, Spencer could see the process happening. Those with superior intelligence became wealthy and powerful, leaving the less perfect specimens of their generation in the working class.

Herbert Spencer (1820–1903), *depicted above in a thoughtful pose, was in some respects the nineteenth-century capitalists' answer to Karl Marx. It was not that Spencer wrote on their behalf, only that his evolutionary theories seemed to justify their positions. Although quite untouched by formal education, this native of Derby, England, thoroughly mastered the sciences of his day and wrote more than thirty books on subjects ranging from ethics to biology, psychology to politics. For his most original writings, however, those aimed at explaining social change and the differences among societies, Spencer borrowed a label from Comte, sociology. The first such volume appeared in 1873. Entitled* The Study of Sociology, *it caught the attention of William Graham Sumner (1840–1910), the Yale professor whose photograph appears above. Sumner became the major spokesman in the United States for Spencer's theories and based his own research on them. Spencer had other disciples, too, who together were responsible for the establishment of sociology as an academic discipline in American universities. (Spencer: Culver Pictures, Inc.; Sumner: Courtesy of the American Sociological Association.)*

Here, then, was a science of society destined for acceptance in the universities of the day, which then more than now were mainly controlled by the rich and populated by their children. Spencer made no brash prediction that the wage laborers toiling in sweatshops would rise up and overthrow those who owned the factories. On the contrary, he reasoned that the poor were where they deserved to be according to natural law. His writings in the 1860s and 1870s, therefore, enjoyed enormous popularity among the well-to-do. Never was sociology so popular in the American moneyed class as when Spencer was the only sociologist they had heard of. John D. Rockefeller, who had monopolized the oil industry through cutthroat competition and amassed possibly the largest fortune in America, quoted Spencer with deep affection. Andrew Carnegie, whose steel mill near Pittsburgh was the largest in the world, wrote in his autobiography that when first he read Spencer's books, "Light came as in a flood and all was clear."[1] When Spencer visited the United States in 1882, the robber barons feasted and applauded him as if he were some messenger of divine truth. He returned to England with a warm send-off from Carnegie at the dock in New York harbor, secure in the knowledge that his work would be carried on by American disciples.

Charles Cooley (1864–1929), one of the first generation of American sociologists, observed in 1920 that "all of us who took up sociology between 1870, say, and 1890 did so at the instigation of Spencer."[2] Cooley himself had switched from engineering to the new science and begun teaching Spencerian ideas at the University of Michigan in 1894. In the same year, a former journalist named

Franklin Giddings (1855–1931) became Columbia University's first professor of sociology. As early as 1875, William Sumner (1840–1910), a minister and economist, began using Spencer's sociology books in his classes at Yale. Lester Ward (1841–1913), a botanist, took time off from his work to read books by Comte and Spencer, afterward concluding that his own interests actually lay in sociology. In his teaching at Brown University, Ward accepted their name for the field, though he became one of Spencer's leading critics. Ward's good friend, Albion Small (1854–1926), a former Baptist minister, became the first professor of sociology at the University of Chicago in 1892.

Thus did sociology in America begin. Not with young people sent to Europe to get doctorates in the field so that they could return to teach it. It began with mature scholars of varying backgrounds who through Spencer were fascinated by the prospect of discovering the basic laws of a new science. They were original thinkers as well, each proposing new theories, doing original research, writing books, and teaching students. Small founded the *American Journal of Sociology* at Chicago in 1895; it quickly became the medium for exchange of ideas in the community of practitioners in America. About one hundred sociologists met in Baltimore in 1905 to form the American Sociological Association; Ward was elected its first president, Sumner and Giddings the two vice presidents. In the meanwhile, Small had begun to build a sizable department of sociology at Chicago, which became for the field in America its center of gravity throughout the first decades of the twentieth century. Most of the next generation of sociologists would receive their doctoral education there.

The number of sociologists in America grew slowly but steadily until after World War II and then more than tripled during the 1950s and 1960s. By now, well over 20,000 Americans are sociologists by occupation. Some are employed by government or industry but most teach in colleges and universities. Currently, some 300 institutions of higher learning offer graduate degrees in sociology; all but a few undergraduate colleges offer courses in the field. Foundations and governmental agencies spend millions of dollars annually in research grants to sociologists. Now there are dozens of journals in the field and researchers compete with one another, trying to get their work published in the most prestigious ones. Professors of sociology plot out their careers almost routinely, hoping to win appointments at the nation's major centers for research in this field—not just the original centers, like Chicago, Columbia, Michigan, and Yale, but those where sociology developed later, like North Carolina, Harvard, Wisconsin, and Berkeley. Even students majoring in seemingly unrelated fields routinely sample the sociological vantage point in one or a few elective courses. The knowledge sociology offers has become a normal and accepted part of American intellectual life. Even if some scholars in history, literature, philosophy, and other older fields still regard sociology as the new kid on the block, this field has indeed settled into higher education and is not likely soon to be dislodged.

When the new science of Comte and Spencer was brought to America, it was not thereby lost to the European countries where it was born. In both France and England, however, the science of human societies often went by the name *anthropology* (whose root meaning is *ideas about humankind*), especially insofar as it focused on non-European peoples thought less advanced in the evolutionary process. In neither of these countries did sociology flourish to the extent that it did

*sociology in Europe,
Latin America,
Canada, and elsewhere*

in America. In Germany, the new field came to be widely taught, but usually in faculties of philosophy, law, or politics. The work of German scholars like Max Weber (1864–1920) and Georg Simmel (1858–1915) has had a strong influence on sociology on the western side of the Atlantic—an influence which later chapters of this book amply reflect. The new science took root in Latin America as well. Eugenio de Hostos (1839–1903), Puerto Rican by birth, wrote volumes on it and taught it in both Chile and the Dominican Republic. In Argentina, the first course specifically in sociology was taught in 1900, at the University of Buenos Aires. As in Germany, sociology in Latin America was closely tied to law and the study of politics; these ties continue to the present and give Latin American sociology distinctive promise.

The processes by which the new field of study spread around the globe make an interesting chapter in the history of transmission of ideas. Sociology arrived in Canada, for instance, from at least three directions. Scholars who had studied it at Chicago introduced it at McGill University in Montreal; another Chicago alumnus, Harold Innis (1894–1952), fathered at the University of Toronto what is still the most important sociological tradition in Canada. The science of society was imported also from Great Britain, usually in the company of the stronger British field of anthropology. Finally, in the late 1930s sociology was formally introduced into francophone Quebec, mostly by French Canadians who had studied it in France. Chief among them was Georges-Henri Levesque, a Dominican priest who founded the Faculty of Social Sciences at Laval University.

So much success has the field of sociology enjoyed that an International Sociological Association has been thriving since 1948, with members from virtually every nation on earth. The association meets every four years—at Varna, Bulgaria, in 1970; Toronto, Canada, in 1974; Uppsala, Sweden, in 1978; Mexico City, Mexico, in 1982. I should imagine that even Comte, for all his enthusiasm on behalf of the new science, would be amazed to see at such meetings scholars from every corner of the earth seated together, translators' earphones round their heads, sharing ideas they call sociology.

The Meaning of Sociology Today

Given how successfully sociologists have entrenched themselves in contemporary universities, one might think that by now they would have discovered quite a few of the natural laws governing human societies. Knowing these laws, they might now possess scientific remedies for social ills like poverty and war, just as natural scientists offer cures for infection and appendicitis. Procedures might have been devised for vaccinating a society against unemployment and racial strife, in much the same way as individuals receive inoculations against yellow fever and polio. The fundamental orderliness of events in social life would be apparent, at least in rough outline, and sociologists could now concentrate on filling in the gaps of knowledge and implementing what they already know.

Regrettably or happily, depending on one's point of view, this is not the situation. The die was cast for sociology already in nineteenth-century Europe, when Marx and Spencer, for all their honest efforts, could not agree on what was

The London slums in the nineteenth century, from a woodcut by Paul Gustave Doré. Marx attributed squalor like this to an inhumane and exploitative economic system. Spencer theorized that prosperity for the fittest naturally should imply something less for the unfit. Which theorist spoke the social scientific truth? (Bettmann Archive, Inc.)

the elusiveness of true social theories and correct social laws

happening. Each of these men proclaimed that he had discovered the basic laws of society and history, but it would be hard to cite two sets of laws more diametrically opposed. And in the decades that followed, the disagreements among sociologists increased almost as fast as sociologists themselves. Members of the infant profession rode off in all directions in search of *the* correct theories. Still they are searching and they show no sign of arriving ever in the same place. Sociology remains as astronomy would be if astronomers were still unsure whether the earth circles the sun, the sun the earth, or each the other. The field was defined in the first place by agreement on the *possibility* of a science of society, not by agreement on even its basic premises.

Perhaps the clearest evidence that sociology has not turned out as planned is disagreement among sociologists over the important questions of our day. Should the United States begin a process of unilateral disarmament? Would this help prevent war? Should Mexico nationalize the American corporations within its borders? Would this hasten a better life for the Mexican people? Should Great Britain strengthen or weaken its ties to the Common Market? Should divorce be easy or difficult, abortion legal or criminal, schooling open or strict, university degrees expensive or cheap? How should problems like crime, alcoholism, drug abuse, and family breakdown be solved? For every serious social question there are hundreds of sociologists contradicting one another's answers. Consider that Soviet and American aeronautical engineers are so agreed on the nature of space travel that they could arrange in 1975 for their respective astronauts to meet for lunch 140 miles above the Atlantic. One searches in vain for any remotely comparable agreement among sociologists, even in a single country, on the nature of social life. The disagreements proclaim sociology's failure until now to live up to the expectations of its founders. It is a failure which honesty requires be bluntly acknowledged at the outset of this book. The important question, of course, is what meaning should then be attached to the expensive continuing labors of the thousands of sociologists around the globe. If these scholars can still not offer verified scientific truth about the human predicament, why read their books, take their courses, or help pay for their research? The following paragraphs sketch two different answers to this question, two kinds of meaning given to sociology today.

LINGERING FAITH IN POSSIBILITY

positivism: the quest for the highest stage of knowledge

One traditional and still common explanation for the lack of true sociological laws echoes Comte's own assessment a century and a half ago. It is thus sometimes called *positivism*, after his term for the third and highest stage of knowledge. The explanation is in brief that our science has not yet advanced as far as astronomy or physics and needs more time. I remember one of my teachers in graduate school, a sociologist of some note, who reviewed one day in class the theoretical disharmony and then offered us eager students some advice. We should spend our careers in this late twentieth century, he said, just mapping out social facts wherever we could find them, so that some genius-colleague later on might more easily discover the correct principles underlying life in human societies. This would entail, I understood, a lifetime of surveying one population after another with all kinds of different questionnaires, thereby accumulating a file of basic findings which, perhaps in the twenty-first century, a sociologist on whom the light of truth at last had dawned would be able to understand. Whatever the merits of my teacher's advice, it implied faith that somewhere, someday, the correct principles would finally be found. Or consider the closing sentences of a pamphlet entitled *Careers in Sociology* published for student information by the American Sociological Association in 1977: "After all, society knows it needs medicine and routinely interrupts MDs for emergency services. Perhaps sociology will not really have arrived until you hear over the stadium loudspeaker: 'Will sociologist number 26 please report to Community X for emergency consultation.' "[3] These lines nicely capture the lingering faith in possibility still widespread among sociologists: that through our continuing research we will one day find out the truth about social problems and be called upon to solve them, even as today's physicians are thought to know the truth about diseases and are trusted to heal them.

This faith in the possibility of a physicslike science of social life is reflected also in the way the field of sociology has come to be organized. The professional associations, for instance, ask members to state their "specialties," which parts of the body politic they are experts at investigating, in a manner analogous to medicine or biology. One sociologist is said to specialize in the police, another in crime, another in prisons, and so on to dozens of other subfields. And for most of these specialties there are now specialized research journals: the *Journal of Criminal*

How can sociologists most accurately characterize the police: as instruments of the ruling class for keeping people in line, or as defenders of civilized values against riffraff? Might a sociologist's own background affect how he or she answers these questions? (© Bernard Pierre Wolff/Magnum Photos, Inc.)

Law, Criminology and Police Science, the *Canadian Journal of Corrections,* the *Prison Journal,* the *International Review of Criminal Policy,* and so on. Articles in these journals usually run long with citations to earlier articles, in the manner of a steadily progressing, routine, cumulative science. Job advertisements these days seldom ask simply for a sociologist, but almost always for a specialist in criminology, deviance, penology, or some similar area narrowly defined. For graduate education, in fact, whole departments announce specialization in research on various discrete parts of the overall structure of social life. The enterprise of sociology thus appears to the outside observer as if organized in terms of a complex division of labor, as if there were a common framework of sure scientific methods and true scientific principles for researchers to apply to specific subject matters.

But shared faith in possibility does not ensure actuality. Despite the public image there is still no common framework. Cutting across and sometimes underlying a serene division of the field into specialties is fierce debate among theoretical camps. Compare, for example, two specialized researchers on the police. The one, following the drift of Karl Marx's sociology, conceptualizes these men and women in uniform as instruments of the ruling class for keeping everyday life under its control. The other, influenced by Herbert Spencer's kind of theorizing, regards the police as defenders of more civilized values against inferior specimens of humanity. Between these two researchers is a wall of conceptual disagreement that makes it mostly irrelevant that they share a common subject matter. They have less in common with each other than the first has with a specialist on studies of the ruling

specialties—an exaggerated image of orderly scientific progress

class and the second with someone interested in the evolution of civilized values. And so in countless other examples: a fundamentalist Christian and an atheist both specializing in the sociology of religion, a pacifist and a militant cold warrior both studying the U.S. Army, or a male chauvinist and an activist in the women's movement both engaged in the sociology of sex roles. A sociologist with faith in possibility responds, "Let them all continue their research, and the facts will eventually dictate a theoretical position on which all can agree." But indeed study after study is done and research reports accumulate like neckties in a closet. Those who pay taxes and tuition increasingly ask how long they must wait for even one truly natural social law to be discovered, how long before sociologists give birth to the science they have conceived.

ACCEPTANCE OF SOCIOLOGY AS IT IS

Fortunately, there is a value in contemporary sociology more attractive than the traditional positivist one traceable to Comte. From a more modern point of view, the work of today's sociologists has indeed far greater meaning, importance, and relevance than mere groundwork for some eventual discovery of truth. The gist of this more humanist perspective is that the early sociologists had a kind of intellectual false pregnancy. They failed to give birth to a science of society because it never existed even in embryo. Sociologists have failed to discover natural laws of social life not through indolence or incompetence, nor yet for lack of time, but because there aren't any. There has been no Copernicus for sociology because there cannot be one. Modern outlooks on sociology begin with the recognition, at once exhilarating and frightening, that the order in human life derives mainly from the creative actions of human beings themselves. Or to make this point differently, that the laws governing how people behave do not inhere in nature but have been devised and formulated by people. For monks can and do live as if sex were nothing, playboys as if there were nothing else. The Chinese have arranged their economy as if the selfish pursuit of gain were a vice, while in the American marketplace it counts as a virtue. Spain has produced great art, Germany great engineering. Given such wondrous diversity in human social life, the futility of attempting to discover a science that would explain humanity is clear. Such discovery appears as a prospect not only impossible but gloomy, since it would leave nothing new in earthly life, only scientifically predictable events and perhaps random variations upon them.

humanism: recognition that people make their own laws

There is no need here to provide a long list of the social thinkers, both within and outside the formal boundaries of sociology, who have proposed in various ways this more optimistic outlook on social life in opposition to the traditional orthodoxy of positive science. One of the greatest was John Dewey (1859–1952), an American philosopher best known for his ideas on education; Dewey understood history to be constantly in flux, ever in a process of indeterminate, humanly directed transformation. One of his disciples, the Chinese scholar Hu Shih (1891–1962), espoused and summarized the outlook clearly in the brief quotation reproduced at the front of this book. Within sociology proper, Georg Simmel was among the first to insist upon human freedom, the ability of people to make their own rules; Simmel thus directed his field toward making generalizations about historical and contemporary affairs rather than toward the discovery of eternal laws. In the first generation of U.S. sociologists, Lester F. Ward departed perhaps most clearly from the positivist faith, denouncing Spencer and entitling his own first major work *Dynamic Sociology*. Ward's disciple, E. A. Ross, a professor at Wisconsin from 1906 to 1937, sought to ground social research in an active, progressive conception of what life on earth is about. Later in this century C. Wright Mills (1916–1962), an articulate professor at Columbia, argued forcefully that the future is not merely to be predicted but to be *decided* by free, reasonable women and men who have made themselves aware of the status quo and of the options available for transforming it. In 1970 Alvin Gouldner, the thunderous man mentioned earlier, published a lengthy treatise, *The Coming Crisis in Western Sociology*, in which he called for a *reflexive* sociology—one which recognizes the living, reciprocal relation between social researchers and the people they study. Yet as the title of Gouldner's book suggests, the faith in positive science lingers still. Awareness that we humans are responsible for the order in our world can still not be taken for granted even among those whose life's work is to study that order. Modern humanist sociology must still be set forth explicitly and argued for in our time. Indeed, one of the major cleavages in the field today divides those still searching for unchangeable social laws from those who have given up the search, those hoping the field will someday arrive from those who admit that it arrived the day Comte thrust it into Western history.

a humanist view of the sociological task

There is much to be gained by approaching sociology from a humanist rather than a positivist outlook. For even if we humans are not bound by natural social laws, we are quite obviously constrained by something. Each of us can feel an ability and a will to create a world oceans happier and mountains more fun than the one we live in now, but each of us feels also the frustration of trying to improve things even slightly. We know within ourselves that we are free to change our common life for the better, but we also know how hard that is. Marx said it best: "Men make their own history, but they do not make it out of free pieces."[4] The image his line suggests is of a man who would freely, creatively build a new and magnificent house out of bricks, but who has no bricks except those stuck in the mortar of his current home. What is he to do? If he tears down his present house he will die of exposure before the new one is built. He can go on living in his present house, but then his dreams die.

For such a man and for us as human beings history is always a case of remodeling, renovating, changing here and there, inevitably in the context of the present order of things. What stands between us and our dreams is not inherent order but present order. What matters is not *society* in some natural, abstract, timeless sense but *this society*, the one that shelters and confines us here and now. And therein lies the meaning of sociology. From a humanist point of view, what sociology means is simply the analysis of *this society*, the study not of eternal rules governing human behavior but of the actual rules we have to deal with at our particular location in space and time. As luck would have it, moreover, this amounts to much the same thing more traditional sociologists have been doing in their quest for natural social laws. In their mistaken attempts to portray human nature they have indeed sketched out fundamental aspects of the present human condition. The modern humanist outlook does not therefore imply disregard for all the research results derived from the older outlook, but instead a fresh and practically relevant way of inspecting those results. For the goal becomes simply to make sense of the experience of social life today, so that we can make it richer, brighter, more humane in the days to come.

THE MEANING OF FIRST SOCIOLOGY

Against the background of a perspective on sociology that recognizes the awesome reality of human creativity, the purpose of this book can now be more fully understood. In the making of history, just as in the remodeling of a house, the first step is mentally to divide the present structure into the part which will stay the same and the part to be changed. The house renovator says, "This wall we better leave as it is, but that window over there can be enlarged for a door out to the patio." The wall in this case becomes by human decision a context to be relied on, taken for granted in the project as a whole. The window, on the other hand, is defined as malleable, deserving of modification. In much the same way, the first task of sociology and the purpose of this book is to discern which parts of contemporary social structures can best be taken for granted, to analyze those aspects of the present order of everyday life which can be considered a constraint, a context, a framework within which to pursue our varied efforts at social reconstruction. The preeminent duty of the field is to comprehend through reflection and research the basic principles of the present scenario of history, principles which all of us—whatever our respective plans and purposes—had best take seriously if we want to be effective. This book is essentially a summary of such basic principles. That is why it is entitled *First Sociology*.

First Sociology, analysis of enduring regularities in experience

There is more to remodeling a house, even on the intellectual level, than discerning and describing the part of it one is going to take for granted. By the same token there is more to overhauling social life than analyzing the most intransigent aspects of the status quo, the enduring regularities in contemporary structures. Hence, sociology has at least two further purposes. What may be termed *Second Sociology* involves depicting and evaluating alternative plans for those aspects of a society defined as malleable, comparing critically and carefully diverse ways of doing things with an eye to their respective strengths and weaknesses. What are the pros and cons, for instance, of a guaranteed annual income scheme, relaxed abortion laws, various delinquency-prevention programs, or the legalization of marijuana? Sociological answers to questions like these are often taught in courses on social problems, social policy and planning. It is the kind of thinking represented perhaps best of all by the late Richard Titmuss (1907–1973), a professor at the London School of Economics, whose book on the relative merits of different ways of organizing blood-donor services has become a classic. But the same immensely valuable kind of sociology appears also in the work of numerous comparative sociologists, evaluation researchers, policy analysts, and others who weigh the costs and benefits, financial and otherwise, of contrasting ways of arranging our common life.[5]

Second Sociology, critical comparisons of available alternatives

Finally there is *Third Sociology*: analyses of the overall course of change in a given society, attempts to grasp the directionality of social transformation over decades and centuries. This purpose, too, is important, for if we are to make history we

Third Sociology, theories of history and change

need to be able to locate our own efforts in some larger scheme, from the ancient past to the distant future. All the great sociologists have devised such theories of history; already those of Comte, Marx, and Spencer have been suggested in brief. They are often studied in detail in courses in sociological theory and social change. But the present book is not much concerned with sociology's third task and still less with its second one. The goal here is not to encapsulate the entire sociology curriculum. This is a basic book. Its purpose is just to summarize some fairly stable, enduring qualities about the condition of human life as it appears today. And in significant part it relies on research by scholars who conceive of the task of sociology somewhat more traditionally, as one of discovering natural, eternal social laws.

Some readers may question the attention given to positivism and humanism here. But they had best be aware of sociology as it is, a field still divided between the cult of orthodox science and the quest for liberating, practically relevant knowledge of our present social predicament. Only in the context of the latter view, for instance, is it worthwhile even to distinguish First, Second, and Third Sociologies. For with the positivist outlook one tends to neglect all tasks of sociology except the first, to take too much of the status quo for granted, assuming it to be the way things naturally are. One therefore shrinks from social criticism, the pitting of policy alternatives against one another, arguing that only later, when definitive research results are in, is involvement in practical matters appropriate. And nowadays one avoids as well the more speculative enterprise of making theories of history, the inevitably chancy diagnoses of just where we humans are headed and why. It is important that readers know there is more to sociology than what this book concerns—more in the sense not only of greater detail but of additional purposes sociology can and does serve. This book is intended to help readers anchor themselves in certain enduring attributes of social life, and that is where all of us must begin. But no one should imagine that to begin is enough. I hope indeed that later chapters of this book will prompt readers to delve further into all the eminently usable kinds of knowledge the field of sociology offers today.

five benefits of humanism: first, taking personal responsibility for distinctions made

This preliminary discussion is important also because even with respect to First Sociology, it makes a difference whether one takes the traditional viewpoint or the more modern humanist one adopted here. By way of concluding this section, I list below five benefits of the latter viewpoint. The first is that the humanist scholar is aware that it is he or she who distinguishes between what is taken for granted and what is considered mutable. The distinction inheres not in what we see and hear, the phenomena we study, but in the mind of the researcher. A house remodeler can rebuild the porch on its existing foundation or, though it is more difficult, put a new foundation under the existing porch. What is taken as given depends on the remodeler, not the house. Indeed, it is a great architect who comes up with a new distinction in this respect. And so among those who study social life. The trouble is that sociologists who believe they are studying a truly natural, determined social reality too easily conclude that their own distinctions are the real, natural ones, and they thus become close-minded toward alternative interpretations. "We are studying reality," they say, "while those who disagree with us are playing unreal games." But the more we admit, following Hu Shih's advice, that there is no fundamental reality but only that which we choose to regard as such, the more open we can be to new ideas and insights, and thus to the possibility of creative change. Surely a sociology founded on this kind of admission is preferable to one that is not.

second, communicating beyond academic circles

Second, sociologists who believe they are on the way to discovering natural laws feel little obligation to talk to the general public en route. Mostly they are content to converse with one another in the pages of professional journals and in specialized sessions at professional meetings, confident that by themselves they can talk the field into arriving eventually at the truth. Such activities in the relatively closed circle of academic sociologists in fact generally ensure a professor tenure, promotion, and salary increases far more reliably than does writing for magazines that reach hundreds of thousands of nonsociologist citizens. Thus the goal easily becomes not so much to be read as to be published, not so much to communicate as to qualify. And when they do address the outside world, sociological believers in positive science speak mainly at seminars and symposia where they are heard mostly by the government or foundation officials who foot the bill; *The New York Times* has called these junkets "the leisure of the theory class."[6] But once sociologists admit that our field will never arrive as a positive science and that we have even now a place in the making of history, a preoccupation with talking among ourselves quickly loses its appeal. With this admission we become obliged to talk and write at least as much to our students and to ordinary working men and women, since they depend on us now for knowledge they need in their efforts at social transformation. Once the duty to communicate with nonsociologists is acknowledged, moreover, professional jargon is replaced by words chosen to get ideas across as simply and easily as possible.

third, grappling with larger, weightier issues

A third benefit of the modern, humanist outlook is that it forces sociologists to grapple with the larger, more serious issues of our time, even when these resist precise formulation, measurement, and explanation. The journals of past decades and even some major ones today reveal that sociologists have often aimed for indisputability and tidiness in their articles more than for importance and relevance. A typical example is the statistical table, reproduced in dozens of textbooks, showing that by certain calculations from sample surveys the occupation of physician has a prestige rating of 93, as compared to 85 for a banker, 73 for a newspaper columnist, 59 for a truck driver, and 36 for a street sweeper, with about 75 other occupations scored in between.[7] Now there is surely nothing wrong with such findings. Often they are interesting. But the urge to be scientific seems to have bred an inordinate preoccupation with all kinds of ratings, scales and indices, and with explaining scores on one with scores on another, to the neglect of the fuzzier but more crucial public issues. We sociologists, it seems, have been so anxious to nail down social facts that we have often passed by the weightier, more awkward questions in favor of lighter ones that are easier to handle. Just why, for example, is the annual income of a physician in the United States on average about five times greater than that of a skilled industrial worker? How much income inequality must a technologically advanced society take for granted, and how much inequality in property ownership and power? Can the rich and powerful realize their humanity more fully than the poor and powerless? And anyway, what is human life about—money, prestige, power, or what? Questions like these have no tidy answers. Anyone who tries to answer them adequately treads inevitably beyond

This woman sells potatoes in Otavalo, Ecuador. Generals rule her country. At least a quarter of her compatriots are illiterate. Like her, most citizens live close to the land. What kind of sociology do you think would be useful to her? (Barbara Pfeffer/Peter Arnold, Inc.)

demonstrable facts and risks being scorned as unscientific. Sociologists who have come to recognize that every social fact is humanly defined are willing to take that risk. For this reason, they are more deserving of our attention in this book and in the ongoing conduct of public affairs.

fourth, respecting the dignity of people being studied

A fourth advantage to viewing sociology more modestly than was traditionally the case is that we thereby show more respect for the human beings we study and teach. It is an humiliation to tell someone, "I intend to explain you, account for you, demonstrate what a product of natural laws you are." I wonder sometimes how many people have lost their ability to dream, to hope, to love, to create, or to believe in a god because of an encounter with sociology. "These terrible sociologists," Miguel de Unamuno, the great Spanish philosopher, once wrote, "who are the astrologers and alchemists of our twentieth century."[8] Or similarly, when Isaac Singer received the Nobel Prize for literature in 1978, the novelist undertook to state ten reasons why he began to write for children; fifth on his list was, "They detest sociology."[9] But it is only the positivist kind of sociology that has called forth these harsh condemnations. It is no insult to any human being if as a sociologist I analyze the structure of contemporary life, or even if I explain much of his or her behavior in terms of that structure. Far from an insult, it is a *mitzvah*, a dutiful gift. I must only add that there is more, that with work a human being can overcome history, realize dreams, do something new. And if in all this someone presumes to see some kind of divine plan, no sociologist need snicker. God cannot be seen from the field of sociology, but there are other vantage points.

fifth, acknowledging that every truth is limited in space and time

Fifth and finally, if sociology studies not an inherent order but only the present one, there is no need to insist that what is true at one point in time and space is also true at another. Quite the contrary. What counts as good sociology today will not likely be good in 1990 and would not have been good in 1920; the sociological ideas Canada needs would probably be inadequate in Senegal. In the decades after World War II when many countries began to introduce sociology in their universities, they often imported sociologists from the United States, where the field was already strong. I met many such scholars in those days who insisted that sociology is sociology wherever it is taught, and who then expressed surprise that natives accused them of cultural imperialism. While these scholars were indeed in touch with American social reality in that particular era, they unwittingly overlooked the immense differences in the national houses which people around the world are trying to transform.

In summary, no lengthy treatise on the philosophy of social science is required to justify a preference for the newer, humanist outlook on sociology instead of the older, positivist one. Practical reasons are enough. For surely the world today is better served by sociologists who take personal responsibility for the research findings they make, who look for ways to enlighten the public with words easily understood, who tackle big and tough questions head on, who avow human dignity and creativity, and who admit the limits on their own work. *Newsweek* columnist Meg Greenfield described in late 1978 the sad situation of the Washington government as it sits immersed in social scientific information but still seems never to *know* anything. She noted in particular how unexpectedly the Shah of Iran was deposed, despite all the intelligence gathered and processed by social analysts employed to predict such events. "Sooner or later, I have no doubt of it," she wrote, "we are all going to die of terminal social science."[10] The present book is not intended to contribute to our early death. It views sociology not as an arcane science of natural social laws but as an analysis of the historical situation surrounding us here and now. This book seeks to fulfill the first task of sociology in this humanist sense, namely, to discern those aspects of present structures of social life which citizens might best take for granted in their efforts to make history. This task also faces other fields of knowledge in today's university, of course, fields also still divided between ivory-tower detachment and active, aware involvement in the affairs of our day. Hence the remainder of this chapter reviews differences between sociology and the major related fields with which it is commonly confused. Thus will the unique promise of sociology become evident.

Sociology Compared to Other Fields

Sometimes it is imagined that professors in the various fields of the contemporary university sat down one day long ago and divided up the world of phenomena among themselves. Anthropologists took responsibility for nonliterate peoples, botanists staked their claim to plants, economists chose money, and so on. It didn't happen that way. Today's university is not so tidy as that. The first-year student begins to notice overlap on registration day. If students had access to faculty discussions, they would observe heated arguments about which department a particular course belongs to and who has the right to teach what.

Better to understand the contemporary array of fields of knowledge as a throng of tour guides descending upon a visitor to New York. Each one calls out, "I will show you the city," and each offers a map of the major points of interest. One guide, a would-be playwright, has a map of all the theaters, from seedy little ones in the Village to spangled big ones in midtown. "New York," he proclaims, "is Broadway; I'll take you to the shows." But another guide steps in front of him with a wholly different map. "New York is finance," he barks. "I'll show you Wall Street and the World Trade Center." "Nonsense," says a third, producing still another map, "New York is all the different kinds of people." His map shows neither theaters nor skyscrapers but rather Chinatown, Harlem, the Lower East Side, maybe even Brooklyn. And so one map after another is shoved beneath the visitor's nose; a gastronomic guide to restaurants, an atlas of United Nations embassies, a plan of historic sites, and on to the point of sheer bewilderment. All are truly maps of New York, but they scarcely resemble one another.

field of study: plural maps of a singular phenomenon

So it is in the world of knowledge. It is the same wondrous phenomenon that confronts a biologist, a political scientist, a psychologist, an economist, and all the rest. Each only conceptualizes the phenomenon differently, imposes on it a distinctive framework. Gazing upon a single human being, one sees an ailing cardiovascular system, another a disenchanted voter, another a superego at war with an id, another a wage earner on strike. Which truly understands this human being? Obviously none at all and all at once. Experts in disparate fields see the world only as reflected in their variously distorted mirrors. A given field is just a bunch of experts using the same mirror.

The following paragraphs describe how sociology's map or mirror differs from some others. I have in mind mainly First Sociology as here understood but the points made apply relatively well to the field as a whole. I should say in preface that the description offered here resembles quite closely what any other sociologist might write. My definition probably bears some distinctive emphases, but no reader should be fearful on that account—the same is true of any definition penned by a human sociologist. I offer my own depiction of the field with keen awareness of Alvin Gouldner's thunderous assertion years ago, "Young man, I *make* the sociological tradition." My answer now, learned painfully but spoken with confidence, is that I do, too. Not from scratch, not from free pieces, not from new bricks. That cannot be, even in the history of sociology. Instead I rearrange the field a little in order to introduce it in a manner adequate for the present day.

discipline distinguishes sociology from common sense

Sociology is above all an academic discipline. I suppose I called it that long before I connected the scholarly sense of the word *discipline* with its other meaning, namely, training for orderliness. In fact the connection is close and serves to distinguish sociology from one of its most formidable competitors in the realm of knowledge, common sense. People do not learn about social life only from sociologists. The task falls on all our heads, regardless of occupation, to discern the present order of things, for how else shall we realize our particular purposes? The person who discerns well, we say, has common sense. In some respects it is the noblest kind of knowledge.

Common sense is by definition undisciplined. It relies on unarticulated insights and proverbs like "time heals all wounds," which is sometimes true and sometimes not. The purpose of sociology, like other academic disciplines, is not so much to destroy or replace commonsensical knowledge as to refine it and give it order. The goal of higher learning itself, of which sociology is part, is to help students refine their thinking in a systematic and orderly way. Thus will they no longer need to live from proverb to proverb, with only the tools of intuition to guide the realization of their dreams. Careful, disciplined thought often confirms casual impressions, and sociology often confirms common sense. Some other times the reverse is true. The commitment of sociologists is or ought to be not to eliminating common sense, but to systemizing it by the discipline of careful thought. In this way can people gain control of their fate.

HOLISM

But in universities that abound with disciplines we need to distinguish sociology from the rest. Five characteristics are relevant for this purpose, the first of which is sociology's goal of providing holistic social analyses. In the writings of nearly all the founders of the field there is an unmistakable attempt to understand social life as a whole. Marx, for instance, had no intention of writing simply about the economy. He stressed it only because for him it was the basis of political, religious, and all other dimensions of the whole, the society, which ever remained his fundamental concern. When Durkheim wrote about suicide, Sumner about folkways, or Weber about bureaucracy, it was not as specialists in these areas but in order to shed light on the social order in general. An emphasis on the whole, an attempt to integrate knowledge about social life, is almost the hallmark of the discipline.

The lesson of the founders has not been lost on their descendants in the present day. Major contemporary sociologists like Peter Berger at Boston College, Amitai Etzioni at George Washington University, the late Talcott Parsons (1903–1979) at Harvard, or the late John Porter (1921–1979) at Carleton, among many others, have aspired to write holistic analyses of the societies confronting them. The sociology curriculum continues to be wide open, with almost no subject matter excluded in principle. A glance through a few university calendars reveals courses regularly taught in the sociology of art, bureaucracy, conflict, death, education, family, gangs, housing, ideology, Jews, knowledge, law, music, nationalism, occupations, politics, Quebec, religion, sport, technology, values, and youth. If I

Part of the legacy of sociology's founders is a reluctance to specialize, an eagerness to understand the myriad aspects of social life in their relatedness. One giver of this legacy was Eugenio de Hostos (1839–1903), *the first systematic sociologist of Latin America. Born in Puerto Rico and educated in Spain, Hostos later taught at the universities of the Dominican Republic and Santiago, Chile. He authored more than fifty books—not only in sociology but in law, literary criticism, education, and politics. An ardent advocate of independence for his homeland and for other Caribbean peoples, Hostos was a major intellectual influence on Latin American thought. The bust pictured at left sits in the Hall of Heroes of the Pan-American Union Building in Washington, headquarters of the Organization of American States. (OAS, Washington, D.C. Courtesy of the Museum of Modern Art of Latin America. Photograph by Karen A. Doyle.)*

how sociology differs
from economics and
political science

can cite no sociology of something beginning with x or z, probably only my own narrowness is to blame. Surely in southern Africa courses are taught on the sociology of the Xhosa and the Zulu, two important Bantu peoples of the region. Societies as integral wholes are sociology's subject matter, and from this vantage point, any part of the whole merits study.

Its holism distinguishes sociology from economics, political science, and some other fields. Economics limits itself to *that aspect* of a society which concerns the production, distribution, and consumption of goods and services. Political science focuses only on *that aspect* related to governmental institutions and the structure of power. The various "studies"—religious, black, leisure, family, and so on— similarly restrict themselves to a particular part or institution of the societal whole. One need only look at typical curricula in these disciplines to see how much more narrowly than sociology they define their aims. One should also note the anger of economists, for example, when they observe in the sociology syllabus something called "The Sociology of the Economy." Their anger is a price sociologists pay for trying to understand how the whole social enterprise fits together.

In actuality, of course, not all sociologists use their study of particular scenes in the drama of social life to understand the drama in its entirety. Encouraged by the overspecialized organization of the discipline, many researchers look no farther than their specific areas of study, whether drug use or divorce, prostitutes or priests. Thus is created the regrettable misconception that economics and political science study the important aspects of social life, sociology the more piddling ones. But fortunately the overspecialized sociologists are balanced out by those economists and political scientists who exceed the nominal limits of their disciplines, use them instead as windows on the whole, and attempt to write holistic works of social analysis. Economists like John Kenneth Galbraith, Kenneth Boulding, Milton Friedman, or Paul Sweezy come to mind; so do political scientists like C. B. Macpherson, Ralph Miliband, or the late Hannah Arendt. Among the best practitioners, the boundaries separating these latter disciplines from sociology break completely down. Among the rest, however, and in the organization of these disciplines in North America, the distinction between holism and specificity is apt.

THEORY BUILDING

A second characteristic of sociology is its emphasis on interpretation and theory building. Thus is sociology distinguished from journalism and history, both of which share with the first an attentive scrutiny of the events in social life. In the main, journalists chronicle the present, and historians the past. In both cases the emphasis is on accuracy of factual detail, and this is a special strength of both disciplines. There is in journalism an implicit conception of a certain universe of newsworthy events, and reporters are dispatched to city halls, hockey arenas, scenes of crime, and so on for the purpose of "covering" as many such events as possible. For historians the events of the past constitute a comparable universe. One professor is said to "cover" those of the Renaissance period, another those of pre-Civil War America, and so on. Neither journalists nor historians customarily feel obliged, however, to separate rigorously the events of importance from those of little consequence. Doing so is not a high priority for them, nor is tying events together with theoretical glue. Whether for the past or present their goal is to provide, as *The New York Times* puts it, "all the news that's fit to print."

It is a poor sociologist who does not devour newspapers and history books. The facts they provide, though never indisputable and always seen through their authors' mirrors, are the necessary beginnings of good sociology. Journalists and historians provide in a sense the pieces for the puzzle sociologists would solve. Sociology must assume acquaintance with events, for its purpose is to separate the significant from the trivial ones and then to weave the first kind together into a picture of how and why things happen in social life. The goal of sociology is not to chronicle but to interpret, not to record but to analyze, not to describe but to explain. Inevitably the pursuit of this goal entails disregard for some well-documented facts. Historians often complain that sociologists overgeneralize and fail to make room for exceptions. They voice the same complaint against members of their own discipline, like Oswald Spengler or R. H. Tawney, who became more interested in analyzing history than in chronicling it. Without doubt the world needs both chroniclers and analysts, but sociology fits better in the latter category.

INTELLECTUAL PRIMACY

A third and critical quality of sociology is that its purpose is knowledge, not action. This is not to say that sociology is irrelevant to action, only that it remains distinct from it. It is one thing to come up with ideas about the structure of a society, ideas even which imply that something should be done, and quite another actually to set about doing it. The former is the task of sociologists and other social scientists, the *sociology versus social work and other active professions* latter that of social workers, legislators, lawyers, planners, reformers, community organizers, and anyone else who takes up the challenge of acting upon the status quo. If sociologists distill history into theories, people in the active professions distill theories into plans of action and into action itself. An undergraduate major in sociology is a common route to professional schools of social work, law, and planning, but the business of making the ideas that make change is nonetheless distinct from making change directly.

A sociologist is or ought to be an intellectual, one who reflects on the experience of contemporary life and tries to put into words its enduring regularities. A certain detachment from immediate social concerns is for this reason a necessary part of the sociologist's work. In order to perform well the task of the intellectual, he or she stands a little to one side of the class structure and the arena of conflicting interests in the society at large. The more sociologists can emancipate themselves from indebtedness to particular class and ethnic interests, including those of their personal backgrounds, the better their work becomes. Contrariwise, sociologists who do their work in the interests of particular groups cannot thereby fulfill the mission of their discipline. Hired-hand intellectuals, even those engaged by the underprivileged, are not intellectuals at all.

Standing apart is not, of course, the same as running away. The sociologist need not act in order to be concerned with action. Indeed, the sociologist has to be concerned because even in our time people suffer. All kinds of them. Dependent mothers whose husbands have disappeared but whose children still need to eat. People laid off from their jobs and left wondering whether they are good for anything. Adolescents who doubt that the world or even their own parents need them. People made to feel ashamed of their language or the color of their skin. Old people vegetating on pensions in the deathly, parasitic quiet of old-age homes and retirement villages. Even prosperous people trapped in the suburban quest for consumer goods, acquiring more but enjoying it less. It is the obligation of the sociologist to speak to them all with compassion and with an analysis that will help them regain control over their lives. In meeting this obligation, sociologists can be sure of opposition from the advantaged classes, those who fear to lose their advantage if history is diverted from its present path. If there were no such opposition, sociologists would surely be failing in their intellectual task.

SENSE EVIDENCE

A fourth characteristic of the discipline is its attempt to ground ideas in the evidence that meets human eyes and ears, in the social world as perceived by bodily senses, in the data given by experience. We never quite succeed, of course. There is wishfulness in anything anyone ever sees or hears—think of an alarm clock or a cry for help. Nonetheless, scholars differ in the extent of their reliance on the data of experience. Theologians begin with certain ideas which they accept by religious faith, ideas drawn from scriptures which they believe to have been divinely inspired. Our goal by contrast is to accept nothing on faith, to justify what we say and write by repeated reference to behavior and events accessible to all, irrespective of their religious or political beliefs. Even when we speculate, we hearken back regularly to "the facts of the matter," as best these can be determined. This is a basic strength of sociology: the quest to discern things as they are, to set judgment aside in favor of awareness, to rely on the ordinary abilities of the human body as a means of knowing the situation of life on earth.

empiricism, a method distinct from religious and philosophic thought

Sociology's reliance on the evidence of the senses, what is sometimes called the empirical method of research, distinguishes this discipline also from certain kinds of philosophy. Jean-Jacques Rousseau (1712–1778), one of the greatest French philosophers, wrote at the start of his *Discourse on the Origin and the Foundation of Inequality among Mankind*, "Let us begin, therefore, by laying aside facts, for they do not affect the question."[11] Rousseau was actually more respectful of facts than this line suggests, but some contemporary philosophers show great disdain for the kind of sense evidence sociologists closely attend to. They seek to create logically coherent systems of ideas, but systems so abstract as to be irrelevant to happenings in everyday life. At many universities one can take a perfectly secular course on ethics, for example, and learn a great deal about how people ought to behave, but scarcely even look at how they actually are behaving. It is a kind of learning that tends to baffle sociologists, except for its value as an exercise in mental discipline. Other philosophers define their goal differently and try to create sets of ideas which are at once logically consistent and relevant to practical affairs. The ties of their work to sociology are quite close.

AN EXPLICITLY SOCIAL FOCUS

To state clearly the last of the five attributes of sociology relevant here, I should recall the analogy of the variously distorted mirrors. Those of religion and philosophy we can set to one side, since they lack the particular warp of evidential

IN OTHER WORDS

C. Wright Mills, "The Promise"*

Both the holistic and interpretive emphases of sociology appear vividly in Mills's depiction of what he called the sociological imagination, a concept he used as the title of his monograph about the field. Not only by his outlook but also by his substantive research—The New Men of Power, White Collar, The Power Elite, and other books—the Texas-born Columbia professor embodied the best of what sociology stands for. The three tasks of the discipline distinguished earlier in this chapter do not precisely correspond to the three sorts of questions Mills frames in the selection below, but their spirit is similar.

The sociological imagination enables its possessor to understand the larger historical scene in terms of its meaning for the inner life and the external career of a variety of individuals. It enables him to take into account how individuals, in the welter of their daily experience, often become falsely conscious of their social positions. Within that welter, the framework of modern society is sought, and within that framework the psychologies of a variety of men and women are formulated. By such means the personal uneasiness of individuals is focused upon explicit troubles and the indifference of publics is transformed into involvement with public issues.

The first fruit of this imagination—and the first lesson of the social science that embodies it—is the idea that the individual can understand his own experience and gauge his own fate only by locating himself within his period, that he can know his own chances in life only by becoming aware of those of all individuals in his circumstances. In many ways it is a terrible lesson; in many ways a magnificent one. We do not know the limits of man's capacities for supreme effort or willing degradation, for agony or glee, for pleasurable brutality or the sweetness of reason. But in our time we have come to know that the limits of "human nature" are frighteningly broad. We have come to know that every individual lives, from one generation to the next, in some society; that he lives out a biography, and that he lives it out within some historical sequence. By the fact of his living he contributes, however minutely, to the shaping of this society and to the course of its history, even as he is made by society and by its historical push and shove.

The sociological imagination enables us to grasp history and biography and the relations between the two within society. That is its task and its promise. To recognize this task and this promise is the mark of the classic social analyst. It is characteristic of Herbert Spencer—turgid, polysyllabic, comprehensive; of E. A. Ross—graceful, muckraking, upright; of Auguste Comte and Emile Durkheim; of the intricate and subtle Karl Mannheim. It is the quality of all that is intellectually excellent in Karl Marx; it is the clue to Thorstein Veblen's

*From The Sociological Imagination by C. Wright Mills, Oxford Univ. Press, New York, pp. 5–7. Copyright © 1959, by Oxford University Press, Inc. Reprinted by permission. Dr. Mills died in 1962, at the age of 46.

brilliant and ironic insight, to Joseph Schumpeter's many-sided constructions of reality; it is the basis of the psychological sweep of W. E. H. Lecky no less than of the profundity and clarity of Max Weber. And it is the signal of what is best in contemporary studies of man and society.

No social study that does not come back to the problems of biography, of history and of their intersections within a society has completed its intellectual journey. Whatever the specific problems of the classic social analysts, however limited or however broad the features of social reality they have examined, those who have been imaginatively aware of the promise of their work have consistently asked three sorts of questions:

1 What is the structure of this particular society as a whole? What are its essential components, and how are they related to one another? How does it differ from other varieties of social order? Within it, what is the meaning of any particular feature for its continuance and for its change?

2 Where does this society stand in human history? What are the mechanics by which it is changing? What is its place within and its meaning for the development of humanity as a whole? How does any particular feature we are examining affect, and how is it affected by, the historical period in which it moves? And this period—what are its essential features? How does it differ from other periods? What are its characteristic ways of history-making?

3 What varieties of men and women now prevail in this society and in this period? And what varieties are coming to prevail? In what ways are they selected and formed, liberated and repressed, made sensitive and blunted? What kinds of "human nature" are revealed in the conduct and character we observe in this society in this period? And what is the meaning for "human nature" of each and every feature of the society we are examining?

Whether the point of interest is a great power state or a minor literary mood, a family, a prison, a creed—these are the kinds of questions the best social analysts have asked. They are the intellectual pivots of classic studies of man in society—and they are the questions inevitably raised by any mind possessing the sociological imagination. For that imagination is the capacity to shift from one perspective to another—from the political to the psychological; from examination of a single family to comparative assessment of the national budgets of the world; from the theological school to the military establishment; from considerations of an oil industry to studies of contemporary poetry. . . .

methods. The mirrors of economics and political science we can set to another side, since they have the empirical warp but are not, as it were, full-length. To still another side should be placed those of history and journalism, since they reflect the empirical world but in the manner of a set of dots in a child's coloring book—the dots have still to be connected before a picture of something emerges. Social work and planning we shall not count as mirrors, since they are plans of action abstracted from various mirrors. At last we are left with the full-length, interpretive mirrors bent by the evidence of the senses. In contemporary universities only two such mirrors are in common use. Sociology is one, psychology the other. Distinction between them is important because for all their closeness they are immensely far apart.

Students often think that these two disciplines must be nearly the same since both study people. This is a serious mistake for two reasons. First, it fails to distinguish the one discipline from the other. Second and more important, it implies that fields of knowledge differ only on the basis of which part of reality they look at. Above all, we must be mindful that no discipline displays reality directly, not even the present reality, but only through the mirror of its conceptual frame. Or to put it differently, no visitor ever sees the totality of New York, only New York as reflected in some map or guide. Psychology and sociology are both full-length mirrors, interpretive maps of the whole city, but their differences are striking.

sociology is to psychology as groups are to individuals

When a psychologist looks at people, what he or she sees in the mirror of that discipline is so many individual persons. A group or society appears only as a collection of these individuals and can be understood according to the kinds of personalities they have. Psychologists assess individual personality through a vast array of tests, measuring intelligence, aptitude, vocational interest, self-concept, motivation, moral development, creativity, insight, adjustment, leadership, machiavellianism, impulsiveness, authoritarianism, and hundreds of other qualities they have conceptualized. Indeed, I think psychology has more tests than sociology has specialties. Some psychologists reject testing, however, preferring simply to record individuals' behavior in laboratory settings or to interview them one by one. In any case an understanding of the regularities in how individuals act remains the basic goal of the discipline. It is as if the psychologist's mirror reveals the human person as what is fundamentally real; people may join together in groups but the individual always comes first.

In sociology it is exactly the other way around. For us the group is prior. The reality displayed in our mirror is always some kind of social system, whether a dyad (two-person group) of lovers, a family, a nation, or at the most general level the human community. In a sense sociology does not focus on individuals at all, but only on the roles they play in groups. We sociologists spend little time testing personalities. When confronted with an individual our first inclination is to ask which groups the person belongs to: which class, ethnic group, sex, occupation, religion, marital status, age category, income category, civic associations, community of residence, place of origin, and so on. We in sociology approach the individual through the mediation of the roles he or she plays in groups. Qualities of personality, insofar as they are independent of social order, escape our attention. For me at least there are no such qualities, only those many which derive from participation in groups and those few which will leave their mark on social life in the future.

Like all reform movements, the campaign for passage of the equal rights amendment to the U.S. Constitution rests on an outlook more sociological than psychological. Activists like these share an awareness that "getting oneself together" is not enough, but only working with others toward improving the structure of life in common. © Christina Thomson 1978/Woodfin Camp & Assoc.

The difference between psychological and sociological perspectives appears most clearly in their practical applications.[12] For what the detached scholar conceptualizes as the object of analysis, the corresponding applied practitioner regards as the object of change. Applied psychologists therefore use knowledge about individuals to help individuals change. The market for their services is large. Clinical psychologists try to help their clients overcome excessive shyness, aggressive tendencies, anxiety, dependency, depression, or other disorders of personality. Personnel psychologists design employee training programs and try to boost workers' motivation and morale. Counseling psychologists help individuals cope with the transition from youth to adulthood and later from adulthood to old age. In all these and many other applications of the academic discipline, the problem is located in the individual and the solution requires some kind of individual transformation. Success is measured by the degree to which the client becomes able to adapt to life in the society at hand.

the practical difference: working for a better society versus helping individuals adapt to the one at hand

In the eyes of an applied sociologist it is not the individual who needs to change. The problem inheres in the structure of social life and only social change can solve it. The shift in perspective has occurred in the life of many social activists who once considered that something must be wrong with *them* and who later concluded otherwise. Allen Ginsberg, for instance, a poet-hero of the 1960s youth movement, sought psychological counseling in his youth, trying to help himself adapt to the world around him. The therapy did not work, and Ginsberg shifted the blame angrily to his society: "I saw the best minds of my generation destroyed by madness, starving hysterical naked."[13] Betty Friedan, the noted American leader of the women's movement, recalls a similar shift in perspective in her life. Eventually she concluded that her frustration in the conventional woman's role called not for better coping on her part but for change in the social role assigned to women.

As might be expected, the job market for applied psychologists is much larger than for those who would apply sociological knowledge. The latter are more interesting, however, and the impact of their work lasts longer than a lifetime. People educated in sociology, for instance, were well represented in the socialist and separatist government which gained power in Quebec in the elections of 1976. David Barrett, the reform-minded premier of British Columbia from 1972 to 1975, had been trained as an applied sociologist. "This job is just an extension of social work," he told a reporter. "Social workers have more business in politics than lawyers do."[14] It bears mention also that two leftist contenders for the American presidency in recent times, former senators George McGovern and Eugene McCarthy, both have backgrounds in sociology. The application of sociology almost invariably involves political action, because it is not individuals but the society itself which is to be acted upon. Those who use sociology in a practical way do not ask whether people are coping with their milieu but whether their milieu is bringing out the best in them.

The contrast between psychology and sociology is nowhere more apparent than in the field of social work, which draws on both perspectives in devising concrete programs for the alleviation of human suffering. Not surprisingly, both as students and as practitioners, social workers tend to be divided into two camps. The majority adopt a psychological perspective and become caseworkers; each person or family is a "case," to be interviewed, counseled, and helped to adjust to the conditions of contemporary life. A minority of social workers (like Mr. Barrett) adopt instead a more sociological perspective, avoid the casework routine, and apply themselves to community organizing, social policy formulation, and the design of preventive social programs. Their goal is to modify the conditions of contemporary life in such a way that coping comes naturally. Between them and the caseworkers or clinicians there is an inevitable tension, but one which must be expected in light of the divergent theoretical postures with which they approach the task of helping people.

mixing sociology and psychology in social work

Like any distinction, of course, that between psychology and sociology admits of exceptions. Especially is this so in the United States, where popular culture is on the side of psychology, enshrining individualism as a national value. As a result there is an individualistic bent to sociology in the United States, where the discipline's ties to psychology are much closer than elsewhere in the world. An important movement in American sociology, led by George Homans at Harvard University, has even built a conception of society on the principles of behaviorist psychology. But this movement is clearly aberrant in the context of sociology more generally. It is balanced, moreover, by a contrary trend in social psychology toward the adoption of a more sociological outlook. Albert Pepitone, a psychologist at the University of Pennsylvania, has criticized his discipline sharply. In a 1976 article in the *Journal of Personality and Social Psychology*, he argued that "the social behavior we observe in the real world and laboratory . . . is normative, in being more characteristic of definable groups, organizations, and other socio-cultural collectives than of individuals observed at random."[15] Pepitone's point is as novel in psychology as Homans's writings are in sociology; each documents in a backhanded way the distinctive perspective of his discipline.

SUMMARY

A fear sometimes voiced in sociology is that the progressive demise of positivism has left the discipline too much up in the air, too nebulously defined, without coherence or a sense of unified purpose. But the five characteristics reviewed above show that the field is indeed distinctive and coherent, even as it is actually practiced today. For sociologists after all differ from other thinkers by their unique combination of five qualities: an integration of economic, political, and other social insights; emphasis on theory; commitment to the intellectual life; reliance on sense evidence; and focus on groups rather than individuals. Sociology can therefore be defined in summary as the disciplined, intellectual quest for holistic, empirical interpretations of the structure of social life. As the basic strategy in this quest, *First Sociology* is concerned with those aspects of social structure which can most usefully be taken for granted in efforts at social transformation in a given time and place. Thus portrayed, the very uniqueness of this discipline should be clear. It can still be confused with anthropology, but such confusion is itself best understood as an enduring regularity of contemporary life. These two disciplines are, I believe, but a single creature under different names. In many universities they are joined in a single department. Despite the fact that anthropologists more often (though not always) study nonliterate societies, and sociologists industrialized ones, the distinctions in outlook and method between them are so fine as to make discussion of them here unnecessary.

Concluding Words

The origins of sociology and its modern, humanist meaning should by now be clear, as also that part of the field which later chapters of this book summarize. Equally clear, I suppose, is my conviction that sociology is important. For we live in a world in which the division of labor has been carried to too many places. Today's humans gaze upon and treat one another from the secure but lonely solitudes of specialized expertise. Each of us lives surrounded by whole armies of righteous experts, their respective diagnoses wrenching from us control over our collective fate. Physicians, nurses, psychologists, lawyers, counselors, consultants, therapists, nutritionists, engineers, and dozens of other professionals all have their say in how we citizens ought to behave. In New York there are even trained advisers who for a fee will sort through your closet and tell you which clothes may legitimately, by current norms of fashion, be worn. Now no one need begrudge all these experts their varied bits of advice, much of which is indeed worth following. But in this situation should not a little effort be spent also on that discipline which builds on common sense and tries to pull things together? And does not that discipline deserve our time if, far from asking us to cope with life and adapt to change, it equips us to understand life and create change? Is sociology not worthwhile when it offers ideas by which you and I can put ourselves on top of our lives?

sociology: pulling things together and getting on top of life

No one should think that the discipline as depicted here is a myth, a fanciful portrayal that overestimates what sociologists actually do in North American universities. Some departments, of course, publicly proclaim the promise of modern sociology more forcefully than others. The holism, the concerned intellectual stance, and all the other attributes apply more strictly, for example, to the programs in sociology at the Colegio de Mexico in Mexico City, most of the French Canadian universities, and those schools in the United States and English Canada deeply rooted in the ethos of liberal education. In many other colleges and universities, sociology departments are still divided into discrete specializations, enthralled by debates of little practical relevance, and thus isolated from the urgent challenges of social transformation. But in an overall appraisal of sociologists' efforts on this continent and elsewhere, a picture emerges of an immensely valuable orientation to the creation of knowledge, a picture the preceding pages have briefly sketched. This picture includes, I should emphasize, not only research and theory formally labeled sociology but also many books and articles written by economists, historians, political scientists, journalists, philosophers, psychologists and others. This is no cause for dismay. Our guiding principle is not to master a reading list but to understand what can be learned from a particular vantage point. Surely this is the important thing.

Nonetheless, candor obliges me to repeat that many sociologists, reluctant to give up the positivist faith, go a step further than this chapter has proposed. They prefer to ground sociology in a kind of ultimate social reality. Far from admitting that we make our ideas out of nature, they insist that we find them in nature. Instead of saying that we relate parts of the present order, one to another, they argue that we uncover causal relations in an inherent order. Our propositions, they assert, concern not enduring regularities but natural laws. Their view elevates the status of our discipline by the same strategy I saw once in a newspaper advertisement for a speed-reading technique. "This method was not invented," the ad announced, "it was *discovered*." Even some sociologists who do work of obvious practical importance seem to think that their own security and prestige require a public claim that science is the One True Mirror, the Unbiased Guide, the Supreme Vantage Point, a claim that we are Scientists of Society.

A basic purpose of this chapter has been to point out that sociology need not rest on so grandiose a claim, that the discipline means more and is worth more once the wish to become like physics is abandoned. For in the spirit of Dewey, Hu Shih, Simmel, Ward, Mills, and many others, sociology does not merely remove itself from the centuries-old and hurtful quest for absolutes and certainties. It also exposes the hopelessness of that quest in all its forms and liberates citizens from its treadmill tyranny. A humanist outlook does more than forbid sociologists to behave like scientific high priests, pronouncing magical formulas that remove doubts and assuage anxieties. This outlook enables sociologists to help free human history from reliance on high priests of whatever kind. The central insight of the discipline becomes indeed the knowledge of freedom and the admission of responsibility. A hard insight, to be sure. To learn that doubting is legitimate exhilarates but also terrifies. To learn not to be ashamed of anxiety in one sense eases the feeling but in another sense makes it worse. All the same, if an acknowledgment of human freedom seems best to fit the data of experience, we had best assent to it and make

the central insight is the knowledge of freedom and admission of responsibility

our awareness of it the first lesson of sociological study. Then we can proceed with confidence to detailed inspection of the structure of contemporary life, taking advantage even of the work of those scholars who consider this structure more natural than it is.

Lest I myself be accused of pretentiousness, I should end this chapter with one final point. This book reviews what seem to me, on the basis of hundreds of sociologists' research, to be those concepts and principles which best capture the shape of organized social life at this moment in history. But also at a particular point in geography. What is written here does not apply equally to all societies. No book can do that, none ever has, and even in the distant future none will. We humans are organized into separate, often interdependent but still distinct societies. Our history is multiple. Each of us works and lives in a personal context composed at most of a few experiments in human social order. For me these are mainly the United States and Canada, with only occasional forays for study and research to societies in Latin America and Europe. This book aspires to relevance

some limits of this book

for readers only in the degree to which I have learned something of their circumstance. My portrayal of basic social knowledge would surely be different had it been created out of the study and experience of life, for instance, in Pakistan. It would be different, too, were it fashioned of Urdu or Russian words—languages which I can neither read nor speak. I would be pleased if some citizens of Karachi or Kiev found this book useful, but their own books would better fit their social realities.

The next chapter, like this one, is prefatory. It offers an outline of methods and techniques of doing sociological research. I suspect some readers will be tempted to skip it, especially since it uses some technical and even statistical terms. I sympathize with their reluctance. Eating cookies is more fun than learning how to make them. But learning the craft of baking means never having to run out of cookies. The same goes for sociology. I would have my readers never run out of ideas that make sense of the life we share.

For Reflection

vantage points
positive science
law of the three stages
class struggle
survival of the fittest
natural social laws
inherent order, present order
positivist versus humanist outlooks
history as remodeling
First Sociology
Second Sociology
Third Sociology
leisure of the theory class
common sense
disciplines as mirrors

holism
economics
political science
theory
journalism
history
relation between history and biography
an intellectual
social work
evidence of the senses
empirical
theology
philosophy
the facts of the matter
social planning

psychology
qualities of personality
~~applied psychology~~
applied sociology

caseworkers or clinicians
preventive social programs
enduring social regularities

For Making Connections

With personal
experience:

You undoubtedly had some idea of sociology before you read this chapter. Did your initial idea, vague as it might have been, come closer to the positivist or to the humanist outlook discussed here? Did this chapter confirm your earlier impression, change it, or have no effect?

Recall some first-rate courses you have taken in disciplines other than sociology, maybe even courses from high school. Which ideas that you learned in those courses might qualify as sociological ideas? Which ones would not?

Write down two or three basic principles about social life which, by your own common sense and experience, you are inclined to take for granted. Then ask yourself how, through disciplined sociological research, these principles could be refined and improved upon.

Until now have you personally taken a more sociological or psychological approach to life? What do you see as the relative merits of these two approaches?

Just from what you have read in this chapter, how do you think studying and learning sociology will affect your personal life—your religious and political beliefs, for example, or the way you relate to other people?

Suppose you decided to major in sociology for a bachelor's degree. How would you explain this decision to someone majoring in history, economics, or philosophy? Have you ever held ideas you believed were absolutely true? Where did you learn those ideas? Have you ever given up ideas you had earlier taken for certain? What would Hu Shih say about your answers to these questions?

For Further Reading

One way to become familiar with sociology is to glance through the journals in the field, pausing to read any articles that seem relevant and intelligible. The three major journals in the United States are the *American Journal of Sociology*, the *American Sociological Review*, and *Social Forces*; Canada offers the *Canadian Review of Sociology and Anthropology*, the *Canadian Journal of Sociology*, and in French, *Recherches Sociographiques*; the *British Journal of Sociology* is highly respected on both sides of the Atlantic; from Mexico comes *Estudios Sociales* and from Argentina the *Revista Latinoamericana de Sociología*. There are about fifty more regularly published journals in sociology; they are usually grouped together in university libraries. Following are ten further basic references, each of which I have drawn upon in writing this chapter:

1 Peter Berger, *An Invitation to Sociology*, Doubleday, New York, 1963. A little book that brims over with clarity and cordiality.

2 Tom Bottomore, *Sociology as Social Criticism*, Allen & Unwin, Winchester, Mass., 1975. A leading British scholar's diagnosis of the social role of the discipline.

3 C. Wright Mills, *The Sociological Imagination*, Oxford Univ. Press, New York, 1959. A little dated by now, but still a must for anyone who would do sociology carefully, passionately, and compassionately.

4 David Sills (ed.), *International Encyclopedia of the Social Sciences*, Macmillan, New York, 1968. A magnificent 17-volume compendium with articles both on topics and on individual scholars. Biographies of most of the early sociologists may be found here, and also in the earlier *Encyclopedia of the Social Sciences*, R. A. Seligman (ed.), Macmillan, New York, 1935.

5 Talcott Parsons et al. (eds.), *Theories of Society*, Free Press, New York, 1961. Two volumes later published as one. A useful compilation of selections from the work of the founders of the discipline.

6 Richard Hofstadter, *Social Darwinism in American Thought*, Beacon, Boston, 1944. A splendid though unflattering analysis of the origins of American sociology.

7 Thomas S. Kuhn, *The Structure of Scientific Revolutions*, Univ. of Chicago Press, Chicago, 1962. This little book by an historian of science at Princeton goes far toward dispelling pretentious ideas of science, whether social or natural. Numerous sociologists have applied Kuhn's perspective specifically to our own discipline. Robert W. Friedrichs' *Sociology of Sociology*, Free Press, New York, 1970, is the best-known example, albeit one which I have argued against in my article, "Class and Organizations as Paradigms in Social Science," *The American Sociologist* 11:38–49 (1976).

8 Peter Berger and Thomas Luckmann, *The Social Construction of Reality*, Doubleday, New York, 1967. An easy-to-read but systematic theory of how human beings create their societies and what happens then.

9 H. H. Gerth and C. W. Mills (eds.), *From Max Weber: Essays in Sociology*, Oxford Univ. Press, New York, 1946. A very useful compilation of writings by the great German scholar. Part I includes Weber's essay on science, a good statement of the classic orientation to sociology.

10 Alvin Gouldner, *The Coming Crisis in Western Sociology*, Avon, New York, 1970. A long and formidable assault on positivist sociology. Even more interesting is the author's response to his critics in the *American Journal of Sociology* 78:1063–93 (1973). More serious and more worthwhile is his later, shorter, and more tightly argued book, *The Future of Intellectuals and the Rise of the New Class*, Seabury Press, New York, 1979.

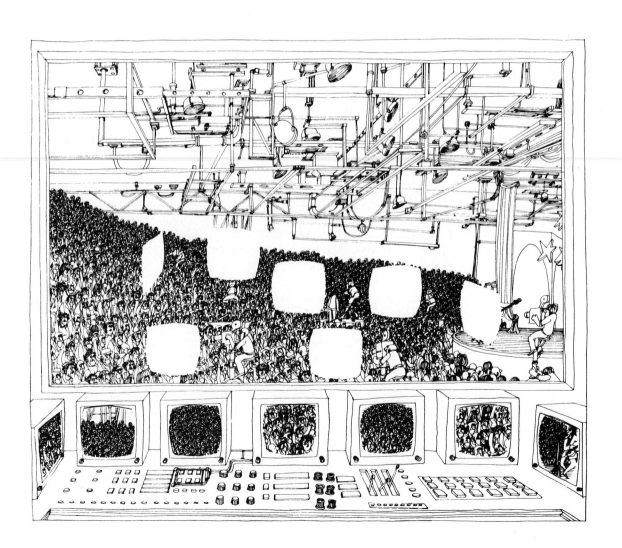

Methods

Chapter Two

*I ask how sociologists come up with
their ideas and how they test them
against the realities of social life.*

Imagine yourself seated in a concert hall. The concertmaster and the conductor enter to applause. The audience falls silent. And then you begin to hear for the first time a symphony orchestra perform. Before you a hundred musicians are arranged in semicircular order. Their playing impresses upon your eyes and ears a sense of order, an interrelatedness, a harmonious fitting together of diverse movements and sounds. Still, being unschooled in music you cannot claim to understand what is happening. And so perhaps you whisper to a knowledgeable companion, "Please tell me what's going on." The answer you get (provided it is not "Be quiet!") probably begins with naming parts of what you see and hear. "There, that's the bassoon. It's playing the theme. See the violins, there in the string section? They'll repeat the theme in a moment." *Bassoon, theme, violins, string section*—your friend is putting labels on parts of the phenomena in front of you, showing you what they mean, and connecting them one to another. Thereby the musicians become for you no longer a single blur, the music no longer a baffling, undifferentiated sound. Concepts give these phenomena order and the symphony begins to make sense.

Sociologists make social life make sense in much the same way: by putting labels on parts of the noisy blur of human movement all around us, pointing out what these labels refer to, and then suggesting connections among them. "There," says a sociologist, "that's the economic elite, voicing the prevailing ideology. See that church, in the religious sector? It will repeat the ideology in a minute." *Economic elite, ideology, church, religious sector*—these are nothing but concepts, names, labels applied to the phenomena of a human society and then connected in sentences. The sociological method begins with just such labels, as the following section explains in more detail.

deciding on key concepts, the least routine and most important aspect of research

Concept Formation

Finding words for a symphony is easier than for a human society, and not only because the latter is larger and more complex. The big difference is that everyday interaction is mostly not performed from a written score, much less from one composed long ago in a quiet chamber in a burst of creative genius. Citizens play their parts in a society partially from notation, from written laws and regulations, but in greatest part because they once watched adults through children's eyes and tried to grow up like them. What is more, people in each generation have nourished their own dreams, rebelled against established practices, revised their parts, and thus forced other people to revise their own. For all these reasons we cannot explain a society just by calling forth the words for it used by its founders. Even if Tchaikovsky's concepts serve well for understanding a contemporary performance of the *Pathétique*, George Washington's words fail miserably to grasp the meaning of today's United States. A term like *slave market* no longer gives insight into the economy of the South, and it only confuses things to call Ohio the *Northwest*. It is also fair to say that *Loyalists* have ceased to be a significant national minority.

The choice of words for good sociology is thus inevitably an uncertain process, one for which no formula exists to guarantee genuinely useful and relevant knowledge. Nonetheless, the selection and formation of concepts is clearly the most fundamental and important facet of the entire research enterprise. For in a sense, the conclusions of a study are already predetermined by the key concepts with which it begins. One researcher might start analyzing Canada by saying, for instance, "There are basically two groups, *French speakers* and *English speakers*." With equal accuracy another might insist, "There are basically three groups, people of *French origin, British origin,* and a *third force* composed of everybody else." A third scholar might like the idea of two basic groups but distinguish a *property-owning class* and a *working class.* Now all three of these conceptual starting points are perfectly legitimate, clearly observable in the Canadian population, and useful for making sense of the society. It is not hard to see, however, that these alternative conceptual beginnings would lead the three scholars to quite different research conclusions, to different kinds of enduring regularities about social life in Canada. The same point applies to studies of any society. And this makes for a problem, since the goal of modern sociology is not just to make accurate statements but, among all possible accurate statements, to make the ones most useful, most relevant, most needing to be said. Hence no step in sociological research should be taken with more care than the choice of basic concepts. The paragraphs below list seven principles sociologists customarily follow in taking that first step.

seven principles of concept formation: first, reviewing previous research

A first and basic principle is to read books and articles reporting previous research and to reflect critically upon the worth of the concepts used therein. Many sociologists, for instance, have approached the United States and many other societies with the concept of *shared values*, trying to discern in each case which common priorities and purposes bind citizens together. By contrast, many other sociologists have studied the same societies with the concept of *interclass conflict*, seeking to understand the opposing interests of different classes of citizens and how these are kept in check for the sake of social order. A young scholar trying to decide what kind of research to do might well review both sets of studies and ask questions like these. Which of the conceptual beginnings has had the most payoff farther down the road when research results are in and published? Which has yielded the more satisfying, enlightening, or useful set of findings about the society at hand? Or perhaps does one conceptual beginning only seem more promising because more studies have taken off from it? Answering such questions is never easy, and most conceptual starting points rest finally on some kind of hunch or gut feeling. All the same, gut feelings are most trustworthy when they follow a thoughtful, careful perusal of many kinds of previous research.

second, being wary of terminology used by elites

A second principle of concept selection is to be wary of the terminology used by people in positions of power and privilege. The reason is that people on the top tend to conceptualize things in a way that justifies their advantage. A good example is the word *fittest*, as used by the robber barons of the nineteenth century in happy confirmation of the justice and rightness of their overweening positions. Or one may recall that those in power in Eastern Europe today studiously avoid the word *class* in describing their societies and refer simply to the people, as in *people's republic*. In the early 1950s, a Yugoslav scholar named Milovan Djilas freed himself enough from this terminology to label the bureaucratic elites of his society a *new class*. He made this concept the title of a fine little book about the social structure confronting him, a book so popular for its relevance and insight that Djilas himself was later silenced by the government. Or to cite another example, if the American military elite divides the planet into the *free world* and the *communist world*, this distinction may be more useful for enlarging the defense budget than for enlarging our understanding of the current realities of international affairs. As a general rule, it seems, the greater one's vested interests the more one depicts social structures in a way that protects those interests and inhibits creative change. We sociologists must therefore look skeptically at the analytic concepts better-off citizens use.

third, learning the native vocabulary

The third principle would seem almost to contradict the second. It is that sociologists must be sensitive to the words and distinctions used by people in the group or society under study, especially those people in positions of power. W. I. Thomas (1863–1947), one of the second generation of U.S. sociologists, wrote a classic line in 1928: "If men define situations as real they are real in their consequences."[1] If, for example, the American government defines a number of nations as constituting the *communist world* and then treats them all with equivalent unfriendliness, these nations may indeed begin to act as a bloc, even if they would not otherwise do so. Or similarly, black Americans did not share a common culture or identity when they arrived from Africa. Quite to the contrary, they came from diverse and sometimes antagonistic tribes. But because white, power-holding Americans defined blacks as a social category and placed most of them in slavery, the blacks came eventually to act as a group with a distinct identity. The language and vocabulary citizens use in any society are indeed primary instruments by which they establish the structure of their lives. Serious scholars must therefore become intensely familiar with the words, idioms, and distinctions used in the population being studied, even while declining to accept indigenous concepts as necessarily most useful in research.

fourth, taking time for playful thought

A fourth principle for deciding with which words to begin is to relax and let one's mind wander a bit after carefully considering the various terminologies used by other scholars, by powerholders in the group or society under study, and by the public at large. When it follows the hard work of reading and study, fanciful reflection often yields an otherwise unobtainable flash of insight. C. Wright Mills put it this way: "An attitude of playfulness toward the phrases and words with which various issues are defined often loosens up the imagination."[2] This may be hazy advice, but it comes from the man who conceptualized the *new middle class* of white-collar employees, distinguishing them for the *old middle class* of independent farmers and shopkeepers, who were their own bosses. This distinction, popularized through a book Mills published in 1951, has become a standard part of the sociological lexicon and has stimulated valuable research. I suspect it was through a similar sequence of laborious study and reflective play that John Kenneth Galbraith conceptualized the *technostructure*, the *mature corporation*, and the *new industrial state*, words now widely used far beyond the community of professional economists. All worthwhile research is necessarily creative, and the creative choice of words requires occasional breaks from routine.

The fifth principle for deciding which words to use, like the sixth and seventh still to come, imposes a constraint on the process of concept selection, to ensure that the words chosen are sociological ones and not part of some other discipline. It *fifth, filtering out* is that the words be as free as possible of the researcher's private, particular values *private judgments* and preferences. If I tell you the United States has two main political parties, *clearheaded Republicans* and *addlebrained Democrats*, I have counterproductively tied a party preference to an empirical distinction. The goal of sociology requires deleting such adjectives and choosing words that simply and clearly indicate some phenomenon, without judging it as good or bad. For the desired outcome of research is not a polemic but an intellectual analysis. We want not to make fun of anything but to make sense of as much as possible. We want to permit our readers and listeners, no matter on which side of political, religious, and other fences they sit, to gain a better understanding of the social structures confronting and embracing them. Thereby they can more freely and effectively pursue whatever purposes they prefer.

Sixth, since sociology relies on empirical methods of knowing, the concepts *sixth, using words* chosen at the outset must refer to the data of our sensory experience, social life as it *which can be measured* can actually be seen and heard. One must be able to measure or operationalize any concept used—that is, to spell out the procedures by which anyone can decide, "Yes, this woman belongs to the *upper middle class*," or "No, this woman is *lower-middle-class*." Not all words therefore qualify for sociology. Believers in predestination, for instance, often divide humanity into the *elect* and the *damned*, readily admitting that only by faith can one know to which category a particular person belongs. This distinction is thus useless in sociology. Similarly, Freudian psychology is sometimes accused of using words without clear operational referents. If a male patient on the couch asserts, "I hate my father," the analyst nods sympathetically and diagnoses an Oedipus complex. And if the same patient protests to the contrary, "I love my father," the analyst concludes that this is a case of reaction formation and then diagnoses an Oedipus complex. Our goal in sociology is to be as clear and unmistakable as possible in the analysis we offer of human societies. This goal requires using words whose meaning can be specified in concrete, measurable terms—that is, words which can be operationalized.

seventh, abstracting
from genuinely social
experience

The seventh and final principle I would offer for concept selection is to choose words abstracted from social life as such rather than from individual human beings. This makes the difference, as Chapter One pointed out, between sociology and psychology. Freudian concepts like *reaction formation* and *Oedipus complex*, and such other psychological terms as *authoritarianism, impulsiveness,* and *happiness*, are therefore peripheral to the discipline of sociology even when they are clearly measurable. For they apply not to groups but to the members of groups. By contrast, words like *divorce rate, level of industrialization, democracy, bureaucracy, social class,* and *hierarchy of authority* can scarcely be used at all except in the context of the organization of many people into larger structures. It is this latter kind of vocabulary which defines sociology's explicitly social focus.

In summary, the first requirement for a worthwhile liberating piece of sociological research is that the basic concepts for labeling parts of social phenomena be chosen with utmost care. To fulfill this requirement, sociologists must as a matter of course review previous studies of diverse kinds, be wary of the vocabulary of people fearful of change, and be sensitive to the words by which the people under observation themselves describe their world. Some time must be spent in playful reflection on the concepts available from these varied sources. And the concepts chosen must in any case be as free as possible of the researcher's own biases, able to be measured or operationalized, and focused on the social rather than the individual aspect of human experience. Following these seven principles does not lead to some "correct" set of words, for no such words exist. These principles have in fact led sociologists to sharply divergent conceptual beginnings—differences which account for most of the debates in the discipline today. It sometimes happens even that a researcher works for years with one set of concepts, finds few interesting or useful results, and then launches almost a new career with a different set of concepts. For all its uncertainty, nonetheless, the process of concept selection and formation is by far the most important facet of research in sociology, or indeed in any other discipline. The words with which a project begins set crucial limits on where it will end.

The Structure of Sociological Ideas

As defined in Chapter One, the purpose of First Sociology is to discern enduring regularities in social life, persistent patterns which can be taken as a context for our varying schemes of creative action. Choosing concepts carefully is the first step toward fulfilling this purpose. The second is putting concepts together, relating them one to another, making connections among labeled social phenomena, or in grammatical terms forming sentences. This step is the topic of the second section of this chapter. It is divided into two parts, conceptual schemes and hypotheses, corresponding to the two complementary ways of connecting words in the sociological enterprise. Now I realize that a discussion like this easily becomes boring and dull, rather like a cooking class held in an empty kitchen. Hence in this section and throughout the remainder of this chapter, a concrete research question will be used as an example, the question of how religion and economics are related

two ways to connect
words: conceptual
schemes and hypotheses

39

"A chained titan whom evil, envious gods were plaguing." Thus did Marianne Weber describe her husband, Max, shown above as he appeared in 1917, three years before his death at the age of 56. They had married in the fall of 1893: she an energetic young feminist, he like his father a Berlin lawyer. Their marriage was close but difficult. Max hesitated to turn from law and practical affairs to academic life. "Nothing is more horrible to me," he wrote in 1893, "than the arrogance of the 'intellectual' and learned professions." Yet he was drawn to the study of political economy, and he was good at it. Probably more than any scholar of his time, he captured in words the tragicomedy of Western civilization. But repeatedly Max Weber pressed his mind to exhaustion and would then slump into months, even years, of depression and inactivity. Marianne sustained him during these periods, often at the expense of her own scholarly career and her activities in the women's movement. The two of them traveled to America in 1904, where Max presented a paper at an academic conference held at the St. Louis World's Fair. He spent most of his remaining years in Heidelberg, dividing his time among writing, intermittent teaching, and political involvements. He helped organize a German sociological society in 1909 but withdrew from it in 1912, judging that it had become overtly political and thus betrayed its intellectual purposes. At the time of his death in 1920, he was lecturing at Munich and serving on the executive committee of the German Democratic Party. His wife survived him by thirty-four years. Marianne Weber's account of him and their life together is available in English under the title Max Weber: A Biography *(Wiley, Interscience, 1975). (The Granger Collection)*

in Western civilization. Max Weber wrote a systematic, illuminating answer to this question some eighty years ago, a book widely read even today as a classic of sociology. The story of how Weber did his project, and how later scholars have continued the line of inquiry he began, will be used repeatedly to illustrate and clarify the conduct of sociological research in general. Thereby the methods of the discipline should become more understandable, just as learning to cook comes easier in a kitchen full of tempting delicacies.

CONCEPTUAL SCHEMES

The first way of putting concepts together is to assert that one includes, is included within, or is the same as another. Weber made the simple point, for instance, that Protestantism is one kind of religion, capitalism one kind of economic system. In each case he was declaring only that the phenomenon labeled by the first word falls within the phenomenon named by the second. It was like saying that violins are part of the string section of an orchestra. Such statements, integral to every attempt at sociological explanation, are an invitation to readers or listeners to adopt what is called a conceptual scheme or framework. One can accept or decline the invitation but not prove it false. It is a matter of definition of terms. A sociologist may define religion in a way that excludes Protestantism if he or she thinks fresh insights can thereby be gained, though anyone who departs too far from conventional usage of words risks being ignored or taken for a pedant or lunatic. But ultimately we must agree with Lewis Carroll's Humpty Dumpty: "When *I* use a word, it means just what I choose it to mean—neither more or less." "The question is," said Alice, "whether you *can* make words mean so many different things." "The question is," said Humpty Dumpty, "which is to be master—that's all."[3]

A major part of sociology consists in nothing more than spelling out conceptual frameworks. The same is true of other disciplines—think of biology, with its lists of phyla, genera, species, orders, and so on. Max Weber set forth his basic verbal scheme at the outset of his classic essay, first published in 1904. He was already 40 years old then, well-schooled in philosophy, religion, and law, well-traveled and multilingual, and sensitive to the conceptual distinctions underlying earlier scholarship and popular culture. Thus did he divide the concept *religion* into two basic categories, *Protestant* and *traditional*. Following convention, Weber included in the first category Lutheran, Calvinist, Methodist, Baptist, and other groups resulting from the Reformation of the sixteenth century. But more important, he identified Protestantism with a particular ethic, an attitude toward life, a way of relating to both the supernatural and the natural. This ethic, Weber said, is the idea that each person stands alone before God, without a priest to forgive sins or provide some assurance of salvation. The Calvinist believer, whom Weber said epitomized the Protestant ethic, is not even sure he or she belongs to the elect predestined for heaven. Thus must each person be as faithful as possible to whatever duties he or she feels called to perform in everyday life. Protestantism, as Weber conceived of it, is a lonely and even stern kind of religion, requiring a disciplined and ascetic way of life, but one of active involvement in worldly affairs rather than of otherworldly withdrawal into monastic contemplation and prayer.

Weber could have divided religion into three, five, or twenty different categories, but he anticipated greater intellectual value from lumping all except Protestantism together under the label of *traditionalism*. Roman Catholicism, Judaism, and the

Weber's two categories of religion: Protestant and traditional

various Eastern religions, he said, can all be grouped together because, like the various Protestant churches and sects, they share a common ethic. All portray the individual less as standing alone before God than as part of a religious community. They thus attach importance not so much to the private, individualistic working out of one's salvation in worldly affairs as to the customary and faithful observance of the rules of the particular community. The Catholic, for instance, enjoys a sense of security that the Protestant does not. The sins of the former can be forgiven in the confessional through the mediation of the church, while those of the latter add up through a lifetime of waiting in fear for the day of judgment. Traditional religion, morever, disdains involvement in the affairs of this world. The highest calling is not to any worldly duties but to detachment from all earthly affairs as a monk, nun, mystic, or holy man.

By inviting readers to distinguish Protestant and traditional categories of religion, Weber was merely sorting out labels for phenomena in a clear and sociological way. It was not his purpose to side with either of these two categories nor with any particular set of religious beliefs. "Whoever wants a sermon," he wrote, "should go to a conventicle. The question of the relative value of the cultures which are compared here will not receive a single word."[4] Then in a similar way, Weber elaborated his conceptual scheme further by distinguishing two basic categories of economy.

Weber's two categories of economy: capitalist and traditional

The first was capitalism, and Weber followed convention once again by defining it in terms of private property, free enterprise, and a division between people who have money to invest and people who must sell their labor for a wage. But as he did for Protestantism, Weber pointed out for capitalism also a cultural attitude, a spirit or mentality, and not just the mentality of wanting to get rich. Peasants, adventurers, gamblers, and speculators may all be after money, he admitted, but they lack the spirit of capitalism. For this spirit is the steadfast pursuit of profit by continuous rational enterprise. It is the subordination of one's whole life to the desire to make money, to invest it and make more money, so that the desire becomes in fact a duty, an end in itself. In contrast to other economic systems, capitalism separates business from family affairs and requires the carefully calculated organization of paid labor, the technical utilization of scientific knowledge, meticulous bookkeeping, and rational administration—all for the sake of profit. But it was the hunger for profit and the relentless chasing after it that was Weber's main interest: the *spirit* of capitalism, on which the system as a whole depended. He explained what he meant especially by quoting the American statesman and inventor, Benjamin Franklin: "time is money," and "money can beget money."

Weber defined his second category of economic life to include everything except capitalism—peasant agriculture, barter, trade controlled by medieval kings, none of which rest on moneymaking as an end in itself. For this reason, he grouped them all under the general label *traditionalism*. In such economies there is a more leisurely attitude, more joy of life, without the worry of trying constantly to calculate and work one's way to wealth. The guiding principle is custom. Barring a windfall, some unexpected stroke of luck, people expect to live only the way they are used to living. So long as there is money enough for that, it is in the normal course of events enough. To illustrate this spirit of traditionalism, Weber offered the example of a man who mows 2½ acres of hay per day, for which he is paid 1 mark (the German unit of currency) per acre. If the rate of pay is increased to 1.25 marks per acre, the man does not work harder, spurred on by the prospect of making more money, but instead slackens his pace, since now he can earn the money he needs for his accustomed way of life by mowing only 2 acres per day. Piece rates increase productivity in capitalist economies, where people try constantly to get ahead, but not in traditional economies. The latter lack not only places to invest the extra money one might make, but also a cultural value on deviating from one's customary lot in life.

This brief outline of Weber's conceptual scheme illustrates not only the first of the two ways in which sociologists connect words but also the fact that such connections need not be complicated or hard to understand. Indeed, at the core of every memorable piece of sociology is a conceptual distinction equally as clear and simple as Weber's two kinds of religion or two kinds of economy. Useful sociology does not result from multiplying words, much less abstruse words, but from working up the effort and imagination to pinpoint those precise distinctions that shed light on the shadows of our experience. I should repeat also that conceptual schemes cannot be proven right or wrong. A critic might complain that there is a big difference between Catholicism and Judaism, a difference Weber glossed over by placing them both in the *traditional* category. "You are right, of course," Weber might answer, "but bear with me, for with my conceptual scheme as a foundation, I will show you important regularities in the order of contemporary life." Weber exposed these regularities by making a second kind of connection between words.

HYPOTHESES

In the second and equally important way of putting concepts together, the sociologist asserts some kind of link between two distinctly different ones, neither of which is included in the meaning of the other. This amounts to positing a relationship between two identifiably separate aspects of social life, two phenomena which can be imagined apart from one another but which in fact, according to the researcher, tend to go together. A connection of this kind is usually called an *hypothesis*, especially insofar as it has been logically deduced from some theoretical line of reasoning. It may also be called a *proposition*, since the researcher is proposing that two (or more) conceptually distinct social things are related. It is like saying that the violins repeat the theme first played by the bassoon: two different instruments joined in sequence by a common melody. Weber, in the same essay cited above, offered such an hypothesis out of words defined in his conceptual scheme. Religion, he proposed, is related to the economic order. More specifically, Protestantism and capitalism, though conceptually distinct, are empirically joined. The Protestant sense of calling to a worldly duty, Weber wrote, has an affinity with the capitalist obligation to pursue profit. The individual's lonely uncertainty about salvation leads to hard, sober work and individual striving for private economic reward. Worldly success, especially to the Calvinist, is indeed understood as a sign of possible membership in the elect.

the hypothesis: Protestantism and capitalism are conceptually distinct but empirically joined

In Weber's hypothesis, as in any other, there is the idea of variation, that the kind or amount of one thing is associated with the kind or amount of another. To say that religion is related to the economy, for instance, implies that both religion and the economy come in different kinds but that one kind of the first is somehow linked to one kind of the second. For this reason, concepts joined in hypotheses are called *variables*. In the specific formulation of Weber's hypothesis, Protestantism can be taken as one variable, since it may be present or absent, strong or weak. Capitalism is the other variable, since the same applies to it. But Weber did not propose simply that when and where Protestantism is present, so also is capitalism, and vice versa. He hypothesized that in Europe originally, and even more clearly in America, Protestantism came first and *led to* the development of capitalism. He considered his religion variable the source of his economic variable. For this reason religion (or Protestantism, depending on how the hypothesis is phrased) is not just a variable but the *independent* variable, the one that comes before, influences, or helps bring about the other. And the economy (or capitalism, to be more specific) is called the *dependent* variable, since Weber proposed that it comes after, follows from, or is dependent upon the first. The title of Weber's essay, still available in English as a book, simply listed in order the independent and dependent variables of his main hypothesis: *The Protestant Ethic and the Spirit of Capitalism*.

independent and dependent variables in hypotheses

There is still a third kind of variable in most hypotheses, one only slightly harder to understand. In the course of his essay, Weber formulates his general proposition still more specifically, hypothesizing that more Protestants than Catholics study capitalist fields like commerce and industry in German higher education. Religious affiliation is here the independent variable, higher studies in commerce and industry the dependent variable. But this dependent variable might also be explained, he says, just by differences in school attainment. Perhaps Catholic youth, coming from generally poorer families, are less able to afford advanced studies of any kind. Maybe Catholic youth would eagerly enroll for commerce and industry if they could afford to enroll at all. And so, Weber continues, look only at students who make it to higher studies, compare Catholics and Protestants in this one category, and you will see that the former choose more traditional, classical fields while the latter elect those related to capitalist economics. In making this argument, Weber was adding to his specific two-variable hypothesis what is called a *control* variable—in this case, school attainment. A control variable is an alternative explanatory factor, another possible independent variable, one which might somehow affect the basic two-variable relationship under discussion. Hence, in order to observe the basic relationship, to defend it against a competing explanation, the researcher acknowledges and seeks to control the effects of the extraneous factor. This requires, to use technical language, *holding the control variable constant*, inspecting the relationship between independent and dependent variables only within categories of the control variable. Thus Weber specified a single category (higher studies) of his control variable (school attainment), and argued that among youth in this category, Protestants more than Catholics would be found studying commerce and industry.

control variables: additional factors for more detailed explanation

For making and understanding hypothetical connections between aspects of social life, control variables are no less important than independent and dependent ones. In grammatical terms, the control variable is a phrase or clause that modifies the relationship between the subject (independent variable) and its object (dependent variable). Control variables make explicit the conditions under which a basic proposition is expected to help explain the world, or competing explanations which the researcher has considered but rejected. Often, for example, a sociologist will preface some two-variable hypothesis being made with such qualifying phrases as: "except in France," "only in the working class," "among both men and women," or "whatever the age of employees." Each of these phrases introduces a control variable (nation, class, sex, age), a third factor. The purpose is either to limit the hypothesis and make it more specific (like the phrases above about nation and class) or to acknowledge a possible alternative explanation which the researcher is willing to discount (like the phrases about sex and age). Weber introduced a control variable for the latter purpose. He was proposing that even though taking advanced schooling in commerce and industry depends in the first place on making it to advanced schooling, it also depends on one's religious affiliation.

SUMMARY

to understand a work of sociology, one must search out key concepts and hypotheses

Virtually any report of research in sociology, whether article or book, can be analyzed and understood in precisely the terms so far outlined in this chapter. For each offers inevitably some kind of conceptual scheme, a vocabulary with which to view some part of social life, and most posit as well some number of hypotheses or propositions. Often the title itself is a clue to the central concepts or hypotheses being proposed. A famous article entitled "Subculture and Contraculture," published in the *American Sociological Review* in 1960, turns out to be a systematic distinction between these two labels and an application of them to observable groups. An article called "Sex Differences in the Educational Attainment Process" sounds as if some relationship between sex (independent variable) and amount of schooling (dependent variable) will be suggested. A title like "Political Democracy and Social Inequality" hints that variation across societies in the first attribute will be linked with variation in the second. When three variables are named in a title, as in "Race, Achievement, and Delinquency," it is a fair guess that one will be treated as a control variable for the sake of illuminating an hypothesized connection between the other two.

It is not always so easy, of course, to pick out the central conceptual distinctions and the key hypotheses. Many book titles consist of only the most important single concept being treated (Marx's *Capital* or Durkheim's *Division of Labor*) or even of just the general subject matter (Weber's *The City* or Galbraith's *New Industrial State*). And in the text of their articles and books, few sociologists worth reading are content to spell out mechanically their conceptual frameworks and propositions. Quite the opposite. They leave no stylistic or grammatical stone unturned in their search for ways to communicate with precision and clarity. They construct from their readers' language as diverse and carefully nuanced a vocabulary as is necessary to get ideas across. But at root every piece of research comes down to a coherent structure of basic concepts distinguished from one another in conceptual schemes and ordinarily also joined as subjects, objects, and qualifying phrases in hypotheses. Every sociologist who writes an enlightening publication necessarily begins with such a structure, even if only sketched on the back of a file card or a scrap of paper. And no reader of a work of sociology comprehends it except by discerning what the basic structure is.

To conclude this section I should reemphasize the link between sociology and common sense, between the ideas of disciplined intellectuals and those of people who think less systematically. Thousands of American travelers to Catholic Mexico have returned saying things like, "No wonder the Mexicans never get ahead; most of them don't have the drive to work hard." Similarly, thousands of Mexican travelers to the Protestant United States have carried home the impression that "Americans have more money than feelings; they're not *simpático*." Catholic French Canadians have often accurately observed, "We work in factories, but the English own them." And the owners of factories in Quebec have not infrequently taken the view that "you make a French Canadian a boss, and all he does is hire his relatives." What separates statements like these from Weber's hypothesis is the discipline of formulating ideas carefully and of filtering out personal likes and dislikes. Sociology must be preferred to common sense not as an alternative to it but as a more rigorous and reliable extension of it. Understood in this way, the discipline is one which invites everybody to take part, if only to refine and strengthen the insights of everyday life.

again, the discipline of sociology improves on common sense

Testing Hypotheses

The discipline of sociology does not stop with the formulation of statements about social life but extends to the rigorous testing of those statements against the diverse data of human experience. This further distinguishes sociology from common sense. For if the most successful merchants in my city are all Catholics and most local Protestants are poor and working-class, common sense tells me to reject the idea that Protestantism and capitalism are favorably connected. But if my relatives are mostly rich Presbyterian industrialists and my wife is from a family of left-wing Jewish intellectuals, common sense by itself may well suggest this connection to me. That is to say that everyday social knowledge rests mainly on the little bits of data that constitute one's personal circumstance. Work situations, interactions at home, friends' recollections, front-page headlines, television dramas, and chance encounters all contribute in an unsystematic way to our casual, commonsensical impressions of how the world works. These are the bases on which we conjure up homespun hypotheses and hold them until further events in our experience force us to change. Then we say, "I used to think thus and so, but that was before I went off to school (or took this job, or got married, or moved here)." The method of knowing called common sense, so heavily reliant on the people, the happenings, the data closest to us, is not a bad method at all. Anyone who fails to use it lives in ignorance.

The goal of sociology, however, is to reduce ignorance even more than common sense is able to. Having formulated an hypothesis, a sociologist is not content to evaluate its worth merely on the basis of personal circumstance. The researcher instead actively enlarges the body of data (that is, evidence given by the senses) on which the hypothesis will be tested. He or she systematically finds out about many people's experiences, gathers many and diverse impressions of as many events as possible, and reflects critically upon the limitations, biases, and distortions inherent in his or her own private circumstance. And once having collected a store

systematic sifting
through large and
diverse bodies of data
of relevant information (whether a file cabinet full of notes, a stack of completed questionnaires, a computer tape of coded interviews, or a crate of documents), the researcher sifts through this store not casually or haphazardly but systematically and in fine detail. The aim is to use for testing hypotheses procedures which are not tied to anyone's particular identity or experience but which are in principle available to all researchers. Sociologists are willing to accept an hypothesis only when it has been shown to fit large and diverse amounts of data analyzed with explicit, orderly techniques. The journals and books of the discipline are a record of hypotheses offered, tested, revised, retested, and so on back and forth for the sake of capturing ever more adequately the enduring regularities in our common experience.

The techniques for testing hypotheses are numerous and often complicated. The undergraduate curriculum in sociology normally includes at least one course specifically concerned with such techniques, which weighty textbooks describe at length. Almost all the rest of this chapter is concerned with procedures for testing hypotheses. But it is important to keep this matter in perspective. The crux of the research enterprise is creating an important and insightful hypothesis, one that pinpoints a pattern in social life which is not already fairly obvious and which, if shown to be supported by data, will have an enabling effect on the process of social change. Any sociologist with common sense can guess with fair accuracy which propositions the data will substantiate and which ones not. The hard part is to choose from among all plausible hypotheses a relevant and useful one for thorough discussion and testing. It is therefore a case of misdirected enthusiasm when (as not infrequently happens) beginners in sociology run hastily into the streets imposing crudely constructed questionnaires on random individuals, all in order to test silly or trifling hypotheses. Far better, even for more experienced sociologists, to spend lots of time reading serious books and talking seriously with different kinds of people, reserving the rigors of hypothesis testing for those ideas one believes the world can simply not do without.

three initial decisions in
testing hypotheses: first,
specifying a level of
analysis
Before reviewing the main strategies in common use for testing hypotheses, I should note three prior decisions which every sociologist implicitly or explicitly makes at the outset. First is at what *level of analysis* the research is to be done. That is, one must decide on the kind of social entities which are expected to display the hypothesized connection between variables. The relationship between Protestantism and capitalism, to return to Weber's example, may be tested at several different levels of analysis. At the *individual* or *social-psychological* level, one would expect as Weber did that proportionately more Protestants than Catholics should be found studying commerce and industry. At the *regional* level, one might investigate (as Weber also proposed) how much capitalist enterprise appears in the northern part of Germany, which is mainly Protestant, as compared to Catholic Bavaria. At the *societal* level, the task would be to see if Protestant societies like Sweden are more capitalist than Catholic ones like Spain or Islamic ones like Egypt. At the *world-history* level, which was Weber's main interest, the entity to be investigated is the overall course of past events, to see if Protestantism gave rise to capitalism. Even though Weber meant his hypothesis to apply at all these levels of analysis, it is important to consider them separately, since empirical evidence may support the hypothesis at one level but not at another. It turns out, for example, as will be explained later in this chapter, that within a society founded on and grounded in

the Protestant ethic, both Protestant and non-Protestant individuals share about equally in the spirit of capitalism.

Some hypotheses, of course, are meaningful at only one level of analysis. Since individuals but not regions or societies are divided into male and female, an hypothesis relating sex to amount of schooling or to anything else can be tested only at the individual level. Similarly, a proposed connection between the parliamentary form of government and a high rate of inflation could only be observed at the level of national societies, since smaller units lack autonomous governments and distinct currencies. Most propositions, however, can meaningfully be applied to several different classes of phenomena, and thus require a choice of one class or another at the commencement of any investigative effort. An hypothesis relating size to the rate of crime could be tested at the level of the city (big cities have more crime), the nation (big countries have more crime), the organization (there is more white-collar crime in large companies than in small ones), or even the university class (students cheat more in large classes). Levels of analysis can be thought of as a special and broad kind of control variable, specifying conditions under which an hypothesis is expected to gain empirical support. A careful researcher is therefore explicit about the particular level or levels to which the hypothesis in question is intended to apply.

second, deciding how much data to gather on how many cases

A second decision the researcher must make is whether to gather rich and diverse data on a small number of cases or summary data on a large number of cases. Sometimes this decision can be quick, as when the variables under study are concrete and easy to measure. The variables of sex and life span are both good examples. Hence, to test the hypothesis that women on average live longer than men, it is clearly preferable to observe as many individuals as possible, recording in each case simply the person's sex and longevity. For variables more abstract and full of social meaning, however, and for levels of analysis beyond the individual, it is harder to decide how best to proceed with research. How, for instance, might one most usefully test Weber's hypothesis at the societal level? Should one find out for each society on earth the percentage Protestant of its population and then relate this to some summary measure of capitalism, like the proportion of national income derived from private enterprise? Or might this be too shallow a test? Is not a society where Protestants control industry and government *more Protestant* than one where the Protestants live in isolated enclaves, even if they constitute the same percentage of each national population? Hence, might it not be better to choose just two or three societies but to study them in detail? For nearly all hypotheses and at nearly all levels of analysis, the hard decision must be made concerning how many cases to look at in how much depth. At the highest level of analysis, of course, that of world history, there is but a single case and the question does not arise.

third, devising valid measures, the kind that capture conceptual meaning

A third decision made at the start of every project of hypothesis testing concerns how to measure or operationalize the variables at the chosen level of analysis, for the chosen number of cases, and within the constraints of time and money. For the researcher wants to exhaust as completely as possible the meaning of the concept by the way it is measured in the scoring of cases. This is what is technically called the problem of *validity*: how to define words operationally for the actual inspection of data in a way that exactly coincides with their conceptual meaning. An example will clarify this exceedingly important point. In one test of Weber's hypothesis on individuals in the United States, Protestant and non-Protestant college students were "scored" on their commitment to the spirit of capitalism according to how much interest each expressed in making a lot of money. This measure of the capitalist spirit quite obviously had low validity. It failed to tap the meaning of the term, which Weber himself had described as more than just wanting to get rich, but rather as hard work calculated toward the end of getting rich. This study might perhaps have been testing how Protestantism was related to the spirit of greed, but not to the spirit Weber defined in his conceptual scheme. And so for all sociological hypotheses. The desire for valid results compels the hard work of spelling out an operational meaning for each variable, a set of procedures for judging each case high or low, strong or weak, in the particular attribute or quality, that matches as precisely as possible what the researcher originally had in mind.

These three preliminary decisions—which level of analysis, how much breadth versus depth, and how to measure the variables—by themselves reveal how far from cut and dried the testing of hypotheses is. And there is more: depending on how these three decisions are made, depending also on the researcher's talents, interests, and resources, a choice must be made among at least five different strategies for testing an hypothesis. The following paragraphs review these strategies in turn, each of which has actually been used by various sociologists to inspect the relationship between religion and the economy, thus continuing Weber's line of inquiry. Repeated reference is therefore made in the pages that follow to studies by these sociologists, scholars who considered Weber's hypothesis important enough to test further, or at least to discuss in connection with their own investigations. In this way three purposes will, I hope, be served. First, to familiarize readers with these different methods of testing hypotheses. Second, to suggest the substantive empirical merits for contemporary life of Weber's hypothesis about Protestantism and capitalism. But third and most important, to demonstrate that tying lofty propositions to the actual phenomena of social life, testing whether they illuminate those phenomena, calls forth just as much creative effort from the researcher as does formulating the propositions initially.

ANALYSIS OF HISTORICAL RECORDS

Many teenagers react with surprise when they hear stories about how their parents behaved when they were young: "You mean they did that, too?" This is not to say that all of history repeats itself, only that most of it does. Hence one of the best ways of testing hypotheses is to inspect the events of the past, as preserved in manuscript collections, archives, museums, and history books. This method is especially congenial to research at the societal level of analysis, since historians offer chronicles of social life on this same level. One can also test hypotheses at the level of community history, organizational history, or even individual history. A standard technique of anthropologists is the *life history*, a simple biography by an ordinary man or woman of a lifetime of personal experiences. This method may be

life histories, case studies, and comparative historical research

applied to one or many cases, but very rarely does the researcher find exactly comparable historical data available on many different societies or communities. For this reason, historical research requires a lot of ingenuity in operationalizing variables and testing connections between them with the information at hand.

"One of the best ways of testing hypotheses is to inspect the events of the past, as preserved in manuscript collections, archives, museums, and history books."

Most often, historical researchers do *case studies* of individual societies, or *comparative analyses* of two or three.

The British historian, R. H. Tawney (1880–1962), was one of the first to repeat Weber's own study of European history, but this time from a critical point of view. In his book *Religion and the Rise of Capitalism*,[6] Tawney did not deny the link between Protestantism and capitalism, but found little evidence that the former was the independent variable giving rise to the latter. Rather, Tawney said, Protestantism and capitalism both sprang from more general changes in Renaissance Europe. Weber's hypothesis appears more plausible, however, in C. T. Jonassen's analysis, published in 1947, of the history of Norway.[7] He traced the rise of capitalism in that country in the late nineteenth century to Protestant revivalist movements in earlier decades. Similarly, in trying to explain industrial growth in England, Herman Israel observed an historic conflict between "Puritan-Parliamentarians," who were rigorously utilitarian and disciplined, and "Anglican-Royalists," who favored tradition, aesthetics, ceremony, and hierarchical authority.[8] Only because the Puritan, Protestant side won, Israel argued, did industrial capitalism develop. From inspecting the historical record of still another country, Canadian historian A. R. M. Lower offered additional evidence in support of Weber's contention. The "primary antithesis of Canadian history," Lower wrote in 1943, is conflict between traditional, rural Quebec Catholicism and acquisitive, materialist, commercial English-speaking Protestantism.[9]

It is fair to say that no one who has systematically observed the historical record has failed to find a certain affinity between Protestantism and the rise of capitalism.

Protestantism and capitalism in U.S. history

This point applies to U.S. history as much as to any other. In a 1975 article destined to become a classic, Edward A. Tiryakian not only traced capitalism in the United States to its Puritan origins, but pointed out numerous reflections of the Protestant ethic in the contemporary American organization of business, education, scholarship, and the arts.[10] Probably more than any other country, the United States embodies those attitudes with which Weber defined the capitalist spirit: relentless striving to get ahead, hard work on behalf of capital accumulation, unending technical applications of scientific knowledge, and meticulous administration of labor for the sake of widening the profit margin. More supportive of Weber's hypothesis than anything else is the simple fact that the edifice of American capitalism was built by hardworking, severe, individualist Yankee Protestants.

Weber acknowledged, even from his vantage point at the turn of the century, that once Protestantism had made it possible for the capitalist spirit to arise, that spirit could survive even without formal religious nourishment. This clearly has happened in the United States, where a Protestant religious outlook has become far more common than attendance in Protestant churches. Even more striking is the acceptance of the capitalist creed by Catholic immigrants to America, whose descendants now constitute fully one-quarter of the population. In a detailed historical study of the ideas of American Catholic bishops, Dorothy Dohen analyzed the extent to which they had been influenced by their Protestant and capitalist milieu.[11] Their loyalty to American society, she argued, has made them ready to defend its economic order in a manner quite uncharacteristic of the Catholic hierarchy in other countries. In another historical study, this one of the American Protestant elite, E. Digby Baltzell observed its defensive response to Jews, Catholics, and not least, black Protestants, as these latter groups have tried to jump on the bandwagon of capitalist success.[12]

There are plenty of other historical works which could be reviewed, but those listed should suffice to illustrate this particular research strategy. By looking at past events in Western civilization as a whole, in specific countries like Sweden, or in specific groups like America's Catholic hierarchy or Protestant elite, scholars have shed the light of further data on Weber's hypothesis. As a result of their research, various qualifications have been placed on the original proposition. The capitalist spirit has been shown to be no longer confined to believers in the Protestant ethic, but shared also by Catholics and Jews, and what is more, no longer much dependent on religious faith of any particular kind.

ANALYSIS OF CONTEMPORARY RECORDS

Published accounts of the present are no less useful than those of the past. On the level of the society, the community, the ethnic group, or whatever, information is readily available in libraries and on the streets. All the researcher need do is systematically analyze it in a disciplined way, as a means of testing hypotheses. Sources of such data include newspapers; newsmagazines; laws and other acts of legislatures; transcripts of legislative proceedings, like the *Congressional Record* in the United States; directories of prominent people, like *Who's Who* compilations, social registers, and biographical dictionaries; governmental reports on crime, migration, housing, industry, public health, social welfare, and all aspects of public administration; novels, magazines, plays, television serials, and similar artifacts of contemporary culture; budget reports of both public and private organizations; graffiti; advertising billboards; political campaign literature; and public statements by major figures, as published in journals like *Vital Speeches*. Through all these readily accessible media, the present order of social life makes itself audible, visible, and tangible (sometimes also smellable and tastable) to anyone trying to discern a pattern in it. Or to put it differently, each source provides rich and diverse measures of sociological variables; what is missing is only an imaginative sociologist who can relate such information to important hypotheses.

In 1965, the late John Porter published *The Vertical Mosaic*, a book which remains the best-known sociological analysis of the class structure of Canadian society.[13] His research was based almost entirely on imaginative use of published

the wealth of data at first hand, waiting to be analyzed and understood

religion and social class
in Canada and the
United States

information about contemporary life. As part of his study, he analyzed characteristics of the 985 Canadians who held directorships in the country's dominant corporations, banks, and insurance companies. He pieced together his list of companies, and then his list of directors, from government statistics, corporate financial statements, and the *Financial Post*, the national newspaper of the business community. Then he gathered biographical data on members of this economic elite, using *Who's Who* and clippings from various newspapers. Among the myriad things Porter learned from analyzing these data was that only 10 percent of the members of the economic elite were Catholic. From census records he knew that 43 percent of the population were Catholic. He thus concluded, in a manner paralleling the judgment of the historian A. R. M. Lower, that Weber's hypothesis is supported by inspection of the present reality of Canadian capitalism.

Comparable studies in the United States do not show, as the story of the Kennedy family alone might suggest, that Catholics are by now well-represented in the American economic elite. In a book published in 1970, *White Protestant Americans*, Charles H. Anderson summarized a number of studies of top business and corporate executives. None was so detailed as Porter's Canadian study, but they were based on analysis of the same kinds of public records and together constitute the rough U.S. equivalent of Porter's work. In concluding his review of these studies, Anderson wrote that "white Protestant control of the 'command posts' of the corporate economy is nearly as secure today as it was in the late nineteenth century."[14] Anderson also presented systematic evidence of white Protestant overrepresentation in the political and scientific elites of the United States. He showed, too, that Jewish Americans, who are more prosperous than Protestants in general, have no more than proportionate representation in the upper echelons of American capitalism. Careful and disciplined analysis of contemporary public records thus suggests that while, as Dohen, Baltzell, and others have pointed out, non-WASPs have jumped on the capitalist bandwagon, they do not yet often occupy its main positions.

FIELDWORK

Neither of the research strategies described so far requires the sociologist to get personally close to the people being studied. One can analyze published information of the past and present while sitting in a library. Fieldwork, however, means leaving the academic hideaway and immersing oneself in the everyday social life under investigation. It is similar to the analysis of records in that a variety of different kinds of data present themselves to the researcher. Here, however, the data are more immediate. The fieldworker interviews at length people who are in good positions to acquaint him or her with how things happen in the particular social setting. The researcher also observes *nonverbal indicators* of group life: how people dress, arrange their day, decorate their homes, behave at parties, and so on. Sometimes the researcher actually assumes a role in the group being studied, in which case the technique is usually called *participant observation*. The major benefit of fieldwork is the immense variety of impressions, indicators, or measures it offers for the variables with which the researcher is concerned. The major cost is that fieldwork takes time, and thus limits the number of cases that can be studied.

Usually, fieldworkers do intensive case studies of single communities or organizations.

Fieldwork is, I suppose, the most bewitching of sociological research methods. To enter the life of an unfamiliar community and to watch at close range people chasing their dreams can scarcely fail to be a deeply moving personal experience. One is impressed by how laughable, how lovable, how magnificent human beings are. Of all techniques, fieldwork is also the most arduous. It is stressful to spend months at a time in unaccustomed social settings, trying to blend in naturally. It is all the more stressful when one is constantly observing, analyzing, and taking the mental notes which one must spend hours every day recording in notebooks.

The merit of observational techniques rests on the fact that connections among variables in a society can only be understood in the context of how people in that society define their world. Proponents of fieldwork might well complain that the first two methods reviewed here are inadequate, that in order to understand the difference between Protestantism and Catholicism, one has to live for a while with people of both religious traditions, understand their divergent ways of looking at life, try to get a feel for the data instead of just handling them. The complaint is not unfounded. Surely many readers of this book have read my words about the difference between capitalist and traditional economic orientations, but the words have remained fairly empty abstractions. This is understandable. Most of us North Americans have grown up taking capitalism for granted, assuming that savings accounts, stock markets, insurance policies, working for pay, and trying to better oneself are normal, natural aspects of human life. They are not. The writings of field researchers go far in fleshing out the bare-bones conceptual distinctions regularly employed in other methods of research.

Fieldwork gained credibility as a method of social research mainly through the writings of those who used it in the study of nonliterate peoples. Its earliest major exponent in North America was a German immigrant named Franz Boas (1858–1942), who published in 1899 his classic field study of the Kwakiutl Indians of British Columbia. Boas taught the method of fieldwork to his students at Columbia University, among whom were Ruth Benedict (1887–1948), Margaret Mead (1901–1978), Ashley Montagu, and many others who have shaped the field of contemporary anthropology. If nonliterate societies deserve to be understood from the inside, however, surely the same applies to literate societies. Both sociologists and anthropologists have thus used fieldwork as a method of research on small towns, city neighborhoods, delinquent gangs, the urban poor, large corporations, and numerous other communities and subcultures of mainstream, industrialized societies.

field studies of religion and economic life in little communites

Robert Redfield (1897–1958), whose education at Chicago was in sociology but who later taught there as professor of anthropology, used fieldwork for his study in the 1930s of Chan Kom, a Mayan village in Mexico's Yucatán peninsula. His first book on the village, authored jointly with his Mexican colleague, Villa Rojas, was followed by another sixteen years later, based on a second stint of fieldwork in Chan Kom. In the second book, entitled *A Village That Chose Progress*, Redfield described how the value in village culture on industry, frugality, and productive effort had led to the accumulation of capital and greater participation in the Mexican economic order.[15] Such a value, Redfield noted, was quite similar to what

Weber had described as the Protestant ethic. It had been reinforced, moreover, by Protestant missionaries in Chan Kom who preached the virtues of sobriety and thrift. Thus did Redfield's field research, while not planned as a direct test of Weber's hypothesis, lend support to it nonetheless.

A number of field studies of communities in the United States outline the mutually supportive relationship between American Protestant denominations and the capitalist milieu in which they exist. Perhaps the classic example is Liston Pope's *Millhands and Preachers*, a detailed analysis in the late 1930s of the role of churches in Gastonia, a North Carolina milltown.[16] His book is especially valuable for its portrayal of the variety in American Protestantism, with some churches like the Presbyterian appealing mainly to those whom capitalism benefits most, and others like the Baptist and Holiness sects serving mainly the disadvantaged. Nonetheless, and despite a certain otherworldliness in the latter, these highly diverse Protestant bodies all join in sanctifying the American economic order, seeking to transcend its inequalities by assuaging equally the guilt of the rich and the afflictions of the poor.

For a depiction of a traditional Catholic community from which both Protestantism and the capitalist spirit are equally absent, none better can be found than Horace Miner's book about St-Denis, a French Canadian parish about a hundred miles northeast of Quebec City, along the south shore of the St. Laurence River.[17] Miner, then a graduate student at Chicago, lived in St-Denis for a year in the mid-1930s. His book, based simply on careful observations of daily life, is a valuable documentary of a folk-peasant society, one in which living in the customary way is nearly all that matters. Since Miner's research was done, however, Quebec Catholics have awakened to the capitalist reality of anglophone North America. In the late 1960s, Gerald Gold did fieldwork in St-Pascal, a town only a few miles from St-Denis.[18] What Gold observed was far from a traditional order. St-Pascal was alive with change, factories were thriving, an elegant new bank stood across from the parish church, and the people displayed a disciplined quest for profit. Gold ascribed this capitalist development, moreover, not to Protestant initiatives from the outside, as has often been the case, but to the efforts of a group of hometown Catholic entrepreneurs. Gold's field research suggests that in Canada, as in the United States, Catholics have in many respects espoused the Prostestant ethic and come to partake of the capitalist spirit.

DEMOGRAPHIC TECHNIQUES

Unlike the three techniques outlined so far, demography sacrifices richness of data for abundance of cases, and diffuse, comprehensive indicators of variables for specific, precise measures. The term itself derives from the Greek *demos,* meaning people, a population, a collection of persons living within the boundaries of a society. Accordingly, the usual level of analysis in demographic research is the individual. The principal source of data is the population census taken by most national governments at five- or ten-year intervals. Typically, the census provides a precise characterization of each person in terms of age, birthplace, education, marital status, ethnic background, occupation, number of children, and so on.

*analysis of census data
for understanding
fertility, mortality, and
much else*

Each of these items, in the hands of an imaginative demographer, can be used to operationalize some conceptual variable. Moreover, relationships between variables can be tested over all the individual cases within a population.

The hypotheses which demographers can test are inevitably limited to those composed of variables which can be measured by information available in census records and similar population surveys. Hence, the field of demography is best known for research on fertility (birth rates), mortality (death rates), and rates of population growth and migration. Emile Durkheim, cited earlier as a founder of sociology in France, used official population records to demonstrate in 1897 that suicide is not at all a free, private act, but instead is related to a variety of social and economic conditions. Census data also permit, for example, tests of hypotheses linking educational attainment to the kind of job one has. The demographer simply divides the individual cases in a population into the categories of the independent variable (those with elementary school education, high school education, and so on), and then looks within each category at the distribution of individuals across categories of the dependent variable (well-paid occupations, poorly paid occupations, and so on). In order to control for a third variable, one repeats this analysis separately within each of its categories—separately, for example, for men and for women.

More than half the governments of the world include in their censuses a question about religious affiliation, thus permitting hypotheses about religion to be tested. No census provides a valid measure of the spirit of capitalism, although most offer indirect measures of the concept like income and occupation. John Porter, for example, in the same study as was cited earlier, reported an analysis of Canadian census data for 1951, which showed what is called a strong *positive correlation* between Protestantism and personal income. That is, Canadian Protestants earn significantly more than their Catholic compatriots. A similar income differential appears in virtually every country where there are large numbers of both Protestants and Catholics in the population.

*the correlation between
Protestant religion and
personal income*

I say *virtually* every country because in the United States this is no longer the case. American population censuses have rarely included a question about religion, but one conducted by the federal government in 1957 was a fortunate exception. In a 1969 article, Sidney Goldstein reported an analysis of these data, showing that American Catholics scored only slightly lower than white Protestants in income and occupational status.[19] They also scored markedly lower than Jews, and markedly higher than black Protestants. Moreover, when Goldstein controlled for education (that is, did the analysis separately for people with much and little schooling), the incomes of Catholics and white Protestants differed hardly at all. Although different in method from the historical studies cited earlier, Goldstein's report suggests quite a similar portrayal of the United States: a society founded on Protestant principles, but one where Catholic immigrants have melted into the capitalist economy, so that except in the elite strata Catholics are by now proportionately spread across the various levels of income and occupational prestige. This fairly distinctive finding for the United States also reinforces the general point that the enduring regularities of one society do not necessarily apply to other societies.

FOR EXAMPLE

Gerald L. Gold, "Fieldwork in Saint-Pascal"*

Social research is shot through with adventure and surprise, however cut and dried the formal published reports might make it seem. Scholarly investigation involves flexibility as well as planning, ingenuity no less than calculation. Qualities of both these kinds appear in Gerald L. Gold's Saint-Pascal, a report of his field study of industrialization in a small Quebec town. Most of the book is meticulous, systematic analysis of how kinship and capitalism intersect in this community and how elites wield power through local and regional networks. In the first chapter, however, Gold gives a personal account of just how he executed the research. He recalls his early interest in French Canada, how he pored over the available articles and books, and then discussed his plans with sociologists and anthropologists well known for their writings on Quebec. He describes the harried, chancy process by which he settled on this particular town for detailed study. The selection below is Gold's recollection of the beginnings of his stay in St-Pascal.

Fieldwork began in June, when we took a hotel room and looked around for a field headquarters. A week later I signed a lease on a small basement apartment in what was then Saint-Pascal's only suburban apartment block. I was ready to do research, although the Pascaliens I had met earlier and anybody else I wanted to see were away on vacation. Even those who were around town hardly came knocking at our door. It was not long before Rosaire Gagnon gave us a quick tour of the countryside and invited us to his home. Shortly afterward his cousin, Maltais the television dealer, took me golfing in Rivière-du-Loup. Not a very exciting way to begin but we were determined to set up an everyday routine: we selected a grocer, tried the butchers, purchased a bed and some canvas folding chairs from Maltais and visited our neighbors and our landlord.

It was one of the neighbors who first involved me in the social relations between townsmen and the business community. Unemployed Paul Letellier and his common-law wife were, like everyone else in the building, strangers to Saint-Pascal who took the only housing available to them. It did not take long for Letellier to discover that "English" next door had nothing better to do than type. He decided to take me in hand and fill me in on his illustrious career and on his unfortunate experiences working first for Gagnon and then for Maltais. . . . A more helpful neighbor was Michel Cloutier, a provincial government employment officer from Quebec City, who moved in upstairs with his wife, a secretary at a nearby college. Through Cloutier I obtained a list of businesses in the county with more than three employees and information on the relatively high employment in the town of Saint-Pascal. . . .

By the end of July fewer people would ask me, "Do you live here?" or "What do you plan to do in Saint-Pascal?" Building on Cloutier's list, I had completed

*From G. L. Gold, *Saint-Pascal*, Holt, Rinehart & Winston, Toronto, 1975, pp. 10–13. Reprinted by permission of the author. Dr. Gold is currently a professor of anthropology at York University.

a survey of the businesses and institutions in the community. Other leads came from chats with the postmaster, the hotelkeeper, the grocer and any other townspeople who would strike up conversations during the daily rounds through the town. . . . From a total of 84 enterprises, ranging in size from a hotdog stand in a school bus hulk to the largest factories, I selected a sample of 44 business families. Using earlier contacts such as Rosaire Gagnon and several others selected from my survey who I thought would be cooperative, I pretested the interview and made some last-minute changes. I was still apprehensive. Would a structured interview only turn the welcome into antagonism and estrangement?

In a first visit I explained to each business manager my interest in the economic base and community life of a growing Quebec town. I promised confidentiality (most of the names in this volume are pseudonymns), but few were ready to share private information with a stranger. Wherever possible, questions became conversation, and were not necessarily presented in a sequential order or during the same visit. If someone wished to tell me about the early history of the town, the behavior of a competitor, a philosophy of French-English relations or a reflection on the landing of the astronauts on the moon, I listened and noted or recorded everything, occasionally steering the conversation back to my chosen topic. The strategy was to open myself to continuing social relationships. I soon realized that relentless interviewing was not a primary goal. . . .

As the interviews proceeded some clear differences emerged between family-oriented enterprisers and about a dozen men in their thirties, including Rosaire Gagnon, who had built the new factories and regional entrepôts for consumer goods. As I coded several hundred pages of interview notes, I found that those who were responsible for the operation of the new businesses belonged to the same voluntary associations and expressed similar viewpoints on the future of their town. An exciting finding was that the new entrepreneurs had once been active in an unusually successful local chapter of the Rural Catholic Youth Movement.

In another way, the interviews were discouraging and I often regretted that I had ever begun them. They were no more than bottled slices of staged behavior, usually without very much depth. Already my interest had been diverted to those families which were more cooperative than others, and I repeatedly invited myself back for long discussions in their living rooms and offices. These meetings served to interrelate the cast of the local scenario and interpret or validate information that others had given me without further elaboration.

This last category of research methods is founded on the same principles as demographic research: a preference for precise measures of variables and a large number of cases. It differs from demography, however, in two important respects. First, instead of relying on governmentally collected census data, survey researchers devise questions of their own, arrange them in questionnaires, and either administer these to respondents in interviews or ask respondents to fill out the questionnaires themselves. Survey research thereby permits information to be obtained on many more variables than the census is concerned with, and in a way that operationalizes sociological concepts much more adequately. The second difference between social surveys and the census is that the former are based usually on only a *sample* of members of some population, rather than on every individual within it. The use of samples requires some explanation because many people legitimately wonder how statements can be made, for example, about 220 million Americans on the basis of a sample of 2000.

probability theory, the foundation of sample surveys

The technique of the sample survey relies completely on a mathematical theory, called the theory of probability, devised centuries ago but not widely used in sociological research until the last fifty years. This is the same theory which, when applied to an honest poker game, informs me that I am twice as likely to be dealt two pairs as three of a kind. It is only a matter of calculating the odds, the chances, the probabilities. The theory, which has become immensely useful in many fields of inquiry, rests on a conception of a population of equal and independent units. It works in poker, for instance, only if each card has the same size and shape, and if none of the cards are stuck together. The theory also assumes that a *random sample* of units is drawn from the population—that is, a sample drawn such that each unit has one and only one chance of being selected (that is why cards are shuffled before being dealt). If each of these conditions is met, the formulas of probability theory can then be used to calculate the odds of being right and the odds of being wrong, in making statements about the population on the basis of sample results. In the poker game, for instance, if my opponent is dealt a royal flush, I can use probability theory to calculate the odds of this happening by chance (once in 649,739 deals of the cards).

a sample is random if all individuals in the population have an equal chance of being selected

In applying probability theory to sociology, survey researchers conceive of some human population, like that of a particular country, as being composed of equal and independent individuals. First, they draw a sample, making sure that each individual has one and only one chance of being included. Then, all individuals in the sample are interviewed or asked to complete self-administered questionnaires. From this point on, analysis proceeds in the same way as for census data: dividing cases into categories of the independent variable, then looking within each category at the distribution across categories of the dependent variable. Once such a table is constructed, however, the formulas of probability theory must be applied to it in order to calculate the odds of being wrong if one treats the findings as if they were based on census data and applies them to the population as a whole. If, for instance, analysis of the random sample shows that 18 percent of men are college graduates but only 10 percent of women, what are the chances of being wrong if one accepts this finding as an accurate description of the whole population? The

*statistically significant
results are those which
could not easily have
occurred by chance*

formulas give an answer based on the size of the population, the size of the sample, and the magnitude of difference between categories (18 percent versus 10 percent). Normally, survey researchers do not accept a finding unless in doing so, they have less than a 5 percent chance of being wrong—or to use the more common terminology, the result is *significant beyond the .05 level*. It turns out as well, by the intricacies of probability theory, that a random sample of 1000 or 2000 individuals is large enough to make inferences to the population, no matter how large it is, with a very high degree of accuracy. For this reason most survey research, including that of public opinion polls, is based on samples no larger than that.

The technique of the sample survey has proven immensely popular for studies at the individual level of analysis. Newspapers, magazines, and television networks routinely report results of the latest public opinion poll by Gallup, Roper, or some similar company that specializes in survey research. Often such polls are intended simply to estimate the population distribution on a single variable, like party preference or support for the government in power. But as reported in the media, such survey results are often also "broken down" by sex, age, region, or education—the latter being in effect independent variables by which some preference or attitude is partially explained. Academic sociologists regularly analyze the results of such polls in much greater detail than appears in the public press and keep the interviews stored in computers for possible further analysis later on. By now many universities in the industrialized societies maintain *databanks* (those at Chicago and Michigan are especially well known, as is the one at York University in Canada), where the results of hundreds of surveys of the national and foreign populations give sociologists the opportunity to test innumerable hypotheses at the individual level. Survey research is also sometimes employed in studies at the organizational, school, county, city, and other group levels of analysis. The researcher simply discerns the "population" of all groups of a given kind, selects a random sample of groups, gathers identical information about each group in the sample, and then proceeds to test hypotheses on these data, using probability theory as a basis for generalizing the results.

*Lenski's Detroit survey
of the Protestant ethic
and its correlates*

The best-known test of Weber's hypothesis using survey methods was done by Gerhard Lenski in a study of the Detroit population in the late 1950s.[20] Lenski chose to work at the individual level, comparing Catholic and Protestant Detroiters in their acceptance of the capitalist spirit. He wanted, moreover, to measure the dependent variable more adequately and validly than is possible with census data on income and occupation. Remembering that Weber had stressed the *spirit* of capitalism, Lenski chose to operationalize this concept in terms of people's attitudes toward life, work, and money. After carefully designing a questionnaire, Lenski used city directories to choose a random sample of 750 adult Detroit residents. He and his colleages succeeded in interviewing 686 of those in the sample.

Numerous items in the questionnaire measured the spirit of capitalism. The following one was typical: "Some people tell us that they couldn't really be happy unless they were working at some job. But others say that they would be a lot happier if they didn't have to work and could take life easy. How do you feel about this?" On the basis of answers to this question, respondents could be placed in one of three categories: those with positive, neutral, or negative attitudes toward work.

Table 2-1 *The relationship between religious preference and attitude toward work among Detroit males, with race as a control variable.*

ATTITUDE TOWARD WORK	JEWS	PROTESTANTS		CATHOLICS
		WHITE	BLACK	
positive	42%	30%	24%	23%
neutral	50%	50%	54%	57%
negative	8%	20%	22%	20%
total	100%	100%	100%	100%
N	12	111	41	106

Source: Adapted from Lenski [20].

how questionnaire data are organized in percentage tables

Further, these could be regarded as the three categories in this measure of the dependent conceptual variable, capitalist spirit. The categories of the independent variable were defined simply as the respondent's stated religious preference: Jewish, Protestant, or Catholic.

Table 2-1, adapted from the study Lenski later published as a book, shows how the connection between independent and dependent variables was tested in analysis of data from the survey. The table reports analysis only for men; thus it controls for sex. The table also controls for race, so that data are presented separately for white and black Protestants (black Catholics and Jews were too few to report). The first step in constructing the table was to divide the respondents into all categories of the independent and control variables; the N figures at the bottom represent the number of male individuals in each of the four resultant categories. The second step was to divide respondents in each column according to how they scored on the dependent variable; this meant placing them in one of the three rows, corresponding respectively to positive, neutral, and negative attitudes toward work. The third step was to calculate what percentage of the column total each row accounted for; these percentages are reported in the table, those in each column summing to 100 percent.

With the data sorted out in this standard format, the test of Weber's hypothesis involves simply observing percentage differences between Protestants and others. The table shows that Jews express the most positive attitudes toward work (42 percent), then white Protestants (30 percent), with black Protestants and Catholics scoring about the same (24 percent and 23 percent). The last three categories differ hardly at all in the percentage reporting negative attitudes toward work. Now this is weak evidence indeed for Weber's hypothesis: more Jews manifest the spirit of capitalism than Protestants, and white Protestants display that spirit only slightly more than Catholics. But before drawing any conclusion, we should follow Lenski in more detailed analysis. For a critic could argue that white Protestants voice more positive attitudes toward work than Catholics do because the former have better jobs. Perhaps it is not religion that explains a person's love for work but the kind of work that person does. This possible alternative explanation can be tested by controlling for the social class of the respondents, as measured by what occupations they reported in the interviews.

Table2-2 *Differences between white Protestant and Catholic Detroit males, with social class as a control variable.*

ATTITUDE TOWARD WORK	WHITE PROTESTANTS		CATHOLICS	
	MIDDLE CLASS	WORKING CLASS	MIDDLE CLASS	WORKING CLASS
positive	34%	26%	18%	24%
neutral	55%	47%	57%	58%
negative	11%	27%	25%	18%
total	100%	100%	100%	100%
N	44	66	44	59

Source: Adapted from Lenski [20].

how control variables are used in survey analysis

Table 2-2 shows an analysis of the same white Protestants and Catholics as in Table 2-1, but this time controlling for social class. Note how this is done. The 106 Catholics have been divided into two categories (44 in the middle class and 59 in the working class, the remaining 3 omitted presumably because they did not state their occupations). The 111 white Protestants are broken into the same two categories of the control variable. Thus Table 2-2 permits the relationship between religion and attitude toward work to be inspected while the effects of social class are controlled. The second and fourth columns show that among working-class respondents, white Protestants and Catholics differ hardly at all in their attitude toward work. The first and third columns, however, show that a much larger proportion of middle-class Protestants (34 percent) than of middle-class Catholics (18 percent) appear to have the capitalist spirit. Thus only partially does the table lend support to Weber's hypothesis. In order to test other alternative explanations and to specify still more exactly the connection between Protestantism and capitalism in the Detroit population, Lenski repeated this same kind of analysis with other questions that measured the dependent variable, and with other control variables. The details of his work need not detain us here. The important thing is to understand the procedures he used for testing his hypothesis with survey data, roughly the same procedures as are used by all survey researchers. In this way Lenski was able to discern small but relatively consistent differences between white Protestants and Catholics in their economic attitudes. And most of these differences were statistically significant by the formulas of probability theory, beyond the .05 level. Laying aside Jews and black Protestants, therefore, Weber's hypothesis still seemed to explain differences among Detroiters, and Lenski reported this conclusion in his book *The Religious Factor*, published in 1963.

Survey research done in the United States in the twenty years since Lenski's book appeared has generally failed, however, to provide further evidence in support of Weber's hypothesis. In Andrew Greeley's survey of American college graduates in 1961, the Catholic respondents seemed no less inclined to economic rationality than Protestant students.[21] Greeley suggested that the particular ethnic composition of Detroit might have made Lenski's findings unrepresentative of the American population as a whole. In a 1965 article, J. D. Photiadis reported survey results for a sample of Minnesota businessmen; the Catholic ones seemed to have adopted the business creed as strongly as their Protestant counterparts.[22] In an article published in 1967, Norval Glen and Ruth Hyland reviewed a number of national surveys and reported that during the preceding two decades, Catholic-Protestant differences with respect to their economic roles in and attitudes toward American capitalism had largely disappeared.[23] Thus do the conclusions of survey research complement and reinforce those of historical and demographic studies. Catholics and Jews in the United States, though not in all other countries, seem to have come gradually to accept the spirit of capitalism and to share in its benefits.

Concluding Words

The five strategies described above for testing sociological hypotheses do not exhaust all those sociologists regularly use. Some departments of sociology even include small-group laboratories, where hypotheses are tested using the experimental methods usually associated with the discipline of psychology. And for survey and other data in quantitative form, statistical techniques are now available which are far more efficient, albeit also more complex, than those Lenski used in his Detroit study. But the preceding pages have sketched at least the most common ways in which sociologists bring together their ideas and the phenomena of social life. Each of the strategies discussed has its own merits. At the world-history and societal levels of analysis, *historical and contemporary records* offer rich and abundant indicators of innumerable variables. *Fieldwork* is not practical for whole societies, but in a representative town, neighborhood, or organization it offers a multitude of subtle impressions at first hand, a wealth of evidence relevant to all kinds of concepts, if only the researcher is adroit enough to make the necessary connections. *Demographic and survey methods* permit a precision of measurement unmatched by the first three methods, and they are especially useful for studies at the individual level of analysis. Ultimately, of course, each researcher setting out to investigate some promising hypothesis fashions an original research design, perhaps using several sources of data at several levels of analysis, depending on his or her abilities and imagination, how much time and money can be spent on the project, and the details of the hypothesis itself.

the various methods for testing hypotheses and their respective merits

But having reviewed these various methods, I should caution readers not to forget the earlier discussion of concept selection and conceptual schemes, the basic structure of sociological ideas. If someone set out to explain to you a symphony but failed to distinguish strings and woodwinds as separate sections of the orchestra, or identified the trumpet as a flute, or picked out some minor variation as the dominant theme of the composition being played, this person's explanation—however detailed—would only befuddle and bewilder you. The same goes for sociological explanations. The worth of any project of research can be no greater than that of its basic framework of concepts and hypotheses. No matter how rigorously a silly proposition is tested, it is still silly. The thing to look for in perusing sociological journals and books, and the thing to strive for in writing one's own sociological papers, is not a clean, tidy test of an hypothesis but an illuminating, liberating idea. The idea is not enough, of course. Disciplined analysis of diverse data must show that the idea fits the experience of social life in our time. But the idea is the important thing.

above all, the idea is still the most important thing

The caution just given is especially apropos for two reasons. The first is that as any discipline becomes established in university life and begins to attract a steady stream of students, the work being done easily slips into a routine. Part of the routine is often a kind of mindless, monotonous gathering of data according to some method that has become conventional. In some anthropology departments, for example, graduate students go off routinely year after year on digs or to do fieldwork, but as a requirement for getting degrees rather than in an excited, thoughtful attempt to relate theoretical ideas to human experience. Contemporary sociology faces a similar danger in the case of survey methods. For by now we sociologists have become so famous for administering questionnaires that beginning students sometimes imagine sociology to be simply a routine of sample surveys, quite irrespective of topic or purpose. This is especially the case in the United States, a society and culture rooted in the assumption of equal, independent individuals competing in an open market. As was noted earlier, the probability theory underlying survey research makes this same assumption: equal, independent units in a population. Given this affinity between survey research and American culture, given also how successfully established American sociology now is, it is easy to be tempted into identifying sociological research as a ritualistic routine of drawing up, administering, and analyzing questionnaires. The temptation deserves to be resisted. Our first priority in sociology is the structure of ideas by which we explain our society. Serving that priority, we should feel free to use whatever methods are most useful—perhaps a survey, perhaps studying history books or newspapers in the library—for relating our ideas to the data of contemporary life.

the promise and the danger of quantitative skills

The caution against overemphasis on hypothesis testing is appropriate also because of the immense improvements made since World War II in the technology of data processing. Percentage tables like those Lenski and his colleagues spent weeks preparing two decades ago are done today inexpensively and with lightning speed on computers whose physical smallness belies their wondrous capabilities. Many sociology professors already have computer terminals in their offices and homes, which they use to analyze quantitative data and test hypotheses more rapidly than anyone even imagined in the recent past. There is no reason to fear such advanced machinery, which is easy enough to learn to use. Beginning students in sociology, who often dread the thought of statistics and programming, are properly encouraged to master these skills thoroughly. But the danger is that once having learned the skills of quantitative research, students become fixated upon them. Indeed, sometimes so do professional sociologists. The glamour and mystique of science surrounding computers easily distract scholars not only from equally valuable methods like fieldwork but what is worse, from the incalculably more difficult task of reading, reflecting, and then formulating important concepts and hypotheses. A word has even been coined for this excessive determination to think in numbers rather than words, and to play at data processing instead of practicing serious sociology. It is *quantophrenia*, and a recent president of the American Sociological Association has criticized it sharply. In his presidential address in 1976, Alfred M. Lee warned that "this common emphasis on quantophrenia and other intellectual rituals turns away many persons who might develop into sensitive observers and literate recorders and interpreters of social behavior."[24] Lee's warning is well taken. The proper focus of sociology is not any particular method or

Among the first sociologists to use quantitative methods systematically in research was a French admirer of Comte and Spencer named Emile Durkheim (1858–1917). Born near Strasbourg and educated in Paris, Durkheim embarked early on an academic career. Two universities attracted his service as professor of sociology and education: Bordeaux from 1887 to 1902, the Sorbonne from then until his death. The third of his four major works of sociology was entitled Suicide. In it he methodically analyzed the French government's official records of suicide, district by district, testing hypotheses about how this phenomenon varies by economic status, sex, age, religion, and other social factors. One of his major findings was that Protestants take their own lives at a higher rate than Catholics. Much like Weber but independently, Durkheim argued that Protestantism forces its adherents to bear individual responsibility for the conditions of their respective lives. The detailed theory of suicide Durkheim proposed has since been qualified in various ways, but most of his basic findings have been confirmed time and again. Still more important, his now classic research provides inspiration to contemporary sociologists in the analysis of numerical data for the sake of understanding social life. (Bibliothèque Nationale, Paris)

technique, but the concepts and hypotheses useful to citizens in their efforts at progressive social transformation.

Having stressed the importance of the intellectual substance of sociology, I had best conclude this chapter with a summary evaluation of that substantive hypothesis about Protestantism and capitalism to which this chapter has so frequently referred. This hypothesis will have served only its secondary purpose if readers can now envision the general process by which sociological ideas are created and tested. For the primary purpose of the hypothesis, the purpose Weber and later investigators hoped to serve above all, was to capture an important enduring regularity of social life. The following paragraphs suggest what conclusions we might draw from their varied investigations.

Protestantism and capitalism: a summary evaluation

If Weber came back from the dead and looked at the literally scores of different tests of his hypothesis, I suspect he would admit that within the United States his hypothesis no longer explains very much. He would see this society as one founded by mostly Protestant bearers of the spirit of capitalism and tied by constitution and law to the principles of a free-enterprise market economy. But he would observe that gradually through time, the economic child has outgrown its religious parent—that the desire for profit has flourished far more than has the Protestant faith. He would see as well that in the United States, the descendants of Catholic and Jewish immigrants and also of African slaves have learned the attitudes and behaviors appropriate to a capitalist economy and are by now almost indistinguishable in this respect from the Protestant sons and daughters of the American Revolution. Weber would find much insight, I believe, in Dwight Eisenhower's statement that "our form of government has no sense unless it is founded on a deeply felt religious faith, and I don't care what it is."[25] This is to say that particular religious beliefs, except those of bizarre cultic minorities, have come to be mostly irrelevant to the workings of the American economy. What matters is deeply felt faith in the American way, in the virtues of capitalist development, a faith which Americans of almost all denominations seem to share. Non-WASPs may not yet have gained proportionate representation in the society's economic elite, but they appear to be well on their way.

On the level of the societies on earth rather than the individuals in the United States, however, I suspect Weber would cling to his hypothesis, though in modified, reconceptualized form. For the world of the late twentieth century is no longer divided into capitalist and traditional economies. The capitalist ones remain, to be sure. Two world wars, the great depression, and the loss of their empires have not diminished the disciplined commitment of the United States, Great Britain, France, West Germany, the Netherlands, and other capitalist societies to the profit motive. These societies remain entrenched by law and culture in values of private property, wage labor, competitive markets, and other economic principles, much as was the case in Weber's time. They are wealthier now than before, their corporations are larger and less vulnerable, and governments in all these societies now temper the harshness of capitalism with various kinds of social welfare. Wealth in these lands continues to derive, nonetheless, from the individualistic pursuit of profit by private economic concerns.

the demise of traditionalism in Africa, Asia, and South America

It is in that part of the world where Weber could see only custom and tradition that the biggest changes have occurred. Almost all the traditional societies of Africa, Asia, and South America have adopted more disciplined ways of life, utilized scientific knowledge in a practical way, and begun to build industrial economies. The factories and department stores of what Weber knew as backward czarist Russia are today as large as those of Britain or the United States. Superhighways and skyscrapers spread across the landscapes of Japan, Brazil, Italy, and Mexico. But just from reading the newspapers, a resurrected Weber would observe that only one of these new industrial giants, Japan, has allied itself firmly with the capitalist, free-enterprise form of internal economic organization. Weber would read with delight a book by sociologist Robert Bellah on Tokugawa religion, wherein Bellah traces Japanese capitalism to qualities of Japanese religion quite similar to the Protestant ethic.[26]

In the rest of what was at the turn of the century the traditional part of the world, Weber would see now mostly some form or other of socialism. In virtually none of these societies would he find the quest for private profit enshrined as a national value. Instead he would find state regulation and ownership of the society's productive resources. He would see the persistence of communitarian, collectivist thinking even in the midst of industrial advance. Many of the once traditional societies (like Russia, China, Cuba, Angola, Vietnam) now rest squarely on the principles of Marx and Lenin, principles which make profit an obscene word. Many others (like Tanzania, Mexico, Egypt, and Pakistan) have fashioned new nationalist ideologies, not communist but hardly capitalist, given their emphasis on state planning and control for the sake of the common good. Weber would undoubtedly be fascinated with the question of why capitalism did not spread, why the United States, that greatest exponent of free enterprise, now must watch in puzzlement as the rest of the world industrializes on a different set of principles. These would be the two new categories of Weber's dependent variable, I believe: not capitalism and traditionalism, but capitalist and socialist kinds of industrial economy.

a more contemporary formulation: capitalist versus socialist forms of industrial economy

For explaining this difference, I suspect Weber would still rely heavily on religious factors in the various national histories. No matter that the capitalist societies have mostly severed their religious roots and that their churches stand mostly empty. No matter that the same is true in many of the socialist societies. Notice, Weber might well point out, where communism or socialism is creeping at the fastest pace. Not in the old Protestant lands like Sweden, the Netherlands, Britain, or the United States, but in Catholic Italy, Catholic Portugal, and even Catholic France. It has already crept forward, moreover, in Catholic societies like Cuba, Nicaragua, and Chile, though in the last-named country the old capitalist powers helped turn it back by force. I think Weber would be especially fascinated to look at Canada, where Catholic Quebec has fled religion in favor of industry but where the provincial government pressures strongly for the autonomy necessary to build a distinct socialist economy. Weber would laugh, I believe, at the idea that a society can abandon its churches and thereby escape its religious and cultural heritage. Differences of just these kinds simply explain too much of the economic differences and divisions across nations of the contemporary world.

Finally, I should say that in the course of explaining how the music of sociology is composed, I have called on a number of colleagues to perform one composition. This has involved sprinkling more names and footnotes in the text than is appropriate in a general and basic book, and more than readers will find in the chapters to come. But the purpose here has been to illuminate the process by which living, working scholars create a sociological idea and test it against the data of human experience. That same process is only implicit in the eight chapters to come, since their focus is not so much on the "how" of the discipline as on the "what." People have a right to expect more of us than techniques. They can legitimately demand results. The remainder of this book summarizes the best results I can find of research done so far.

For Reflection

concepts
how sociologists choose words
playfulness
words free of personal feelings
measure, operationalize
properties of group life
conceptual schemes
Protestantism
individualism
traditionalism
capitalism
hypothesis
variable
independent variable
dependent variable
control variable
hypothesis testing
data
level of analysis
number of cases, amount of data
validity
historical records

life history
case study
comparative analysis
contemporary records
fieldwork
nonverbal indicators
participant observation
demography
census data
correlation
survey research
random sample
probability theory
statistical significance
data banks
questionnaire
interview
relative merits of different methods
quantitative research
quantophrenia
socialism

For Making Connections

With personal
experience:

Suppose you were going to undertake a sociological analysis of your family, as compared to other families you know. Write down the basic conceptual distinctions with which you would begin.

Write down some hunch or hypothesis about contemporary life that you consider genuinely important. At what level or levels of analysis do you mean it to apply? How would you operationalize the variables in it? How would you go about testing it sociologically?

If you answered the two questions above, now ask yourself where you got the conceptual distinctions and the hypothesis you wrote down. How much came from reading, how much from tuning in to the words used by your own family and friends, how much from common sense?

If one of your friends told you that sociology is nothing more than common sense, what kind of answer would you give?

If Weber knew your religious background and beliefs, do you think he would be able to tell anything about your attitudes toward work and money?

With Chapter One:

How would you suppose the making and testing of hypotheses differ between sociology and psychology?

Do you think any hypotheses can be proven absolutely true? If so, how would you do that? If not, where does this leave you?

Do you think the modern humanist outlook on sociology is more or less likely than the positivist outlook to lead to quantophrenia? Why?

For Further Reading

There is no better way to learn how to do sociology than to choose from the journals the most insightful and compelling pieces of past scholarship one can find and then pick them apart, analyze and reflect upon them. This exercise is not just for beginners. Even seasoned practitioners of my discipline, like accomplished architects, profit from inspecting the handiwork of their most talented colleagues. Among questions to be asked of any article chosen for this exercise are the following: what its key concepts are; what kind of conceptual scheme it draws; which propositions or hypotheses it suggests, and which independent, dependent and control variables; what its unit of analysis is, and the level on which arguments are made; what its overall research strategy is, how it brings data to bear upon ideas; how variables are operationalized, and how validly; to which other articles or books this particular one relates, and in what ways; its general theoretical implications on the one hand and its practical political ones on the other; what alternative concepts, hypotheses, strategies, and levels of research might have helped illuminate still more the events and behavior on which this article is focused. But for learning sociological research methods, textbooks are important, too. Listed below are seven which I especially recommend. None of these says much of statistics, a fact which should be taken to imply not that quantitative techniques of analysis are unimportant but only that they are hard to learn through independent study. Instead of seeking to read statistics on their own, the uninitiated are better advised to enroll formally in a course on the subject.

1   Sanford Labovitz and Robert Hagedorn, *Introduction to Social Research*, McGraw-Hill, New York, 1971. This little book reads smoothly and clearly; its approach is somewhat more formalistic and technical than my own.
2   Claire Selltiz et al., *Research Methods in Social Relations*, rev. ed., Holt, Rinehart & Winston, New York, 1977. A comprehensive and thorough treatment of the subject, respected through two decades of widespread use.
3   Matilda Riley, *Sociological Research I: A Case Approach*, Harcourt, Brace & World, New York, 1963. Another tried and true survey of the field, with 34 selections from classic pieces of research along with detailed commentary on each.
4   J. B. Williamson et al., *The Research Craft*, Little, Brown, Boston, 1977. A well-done collaborative effort, especially valuable for its focus on social science in general, not just sociology. Easier to read than either Selltiz or Riley.
5   B. J. Franklin and H. W. Osborne, *Research Methods: Issues and Insights*, Wadsworth, Belmont, Calif., 1971. A fairly balanced collection of 41 essays on different kinds and aspects of social research.
6   Nan Lin et al., *Conducting Social Research*, McGraw-Hill, New York, 1976. A clear and understandable guide to conducting survey research and analyzing the results, though nothing about other methods is included.

7   Abraham Kaplan, *The Conduct of Inquiry*, Chandler, 1964. A remarkably thoughtful and intelligible exposition of the logic which guides social science research by a philosopher of science.

Society

Chapter Three

*I ask what a society is, how
it differs from other kinds of
group, and what it is made of.*

Chapter One sketched the history and character of sociology, promising that later chapters would summarize the first and basic part of the discipline: knowledge of enduring regularities in the structure of our common life. Chapter Two discussed the methods by which sociologists create and test such knowledge, offering as example Weber's idea about Protestantism and capitalism. This chapter begins a report of that knowledge itself, the substance of sociology, the ideas it offers for making sense of the human predicament here and now. And this beginning is much like the one home buyers make when they inspect a house: first, a quick run through the structure as a whole. For if our purpose is to understand our social abode, the edifice of rules and roles within which we live, then we might appropriately first survey the whole thing once over lightly, saving for later a close inspection of the most important parts. Thus the present chapter presents an overall conceptual scheme, a vocabulary with which to approach the varied sights and sounds that constitute contemporary human experience.

Even everyday experience raises the first question: *Which* abode, *which* edifice, *which* social structure? For it seems that each of us lives in houses within houses within still larger ones. Structures of family life embrace most of us, but families are contained by local communities, communities by cities, and cities by larger forms of organization. A professor and students work within the structure of a course, but the course belongs to a department, and the department to some kind of school, which is itself part of the whole system of higher education. In a broad but hardly irrelevant sense the world itself is our community. Could any American or Vietnamese, left still with the scars of the Indochina war, doubt that every living person is somehow locked into an international, even global structure of events? A sociology equal to today's world must sort out these levels and kinds of social order and specify which can most usefully be its main focus. The discipline quite properly includes research on groups of every size, from single-parent families to world religions. But the question is, Which kind of group is the appropriate object of the present overview?

an adequate sociology must be neither too narrowly nor too broadly focused

An intellectually sound and politically liberating conceptual scheme must be focused on neither too low nor too high a level of social structure. To concentrate too much on some small-scale kind of group, like the family or the friendship clique, is to indulge in the pretense that it is somehow self-contained, independent of the constraints of larger groups. This is like studying just one room of a house, as if an overhaul of its size and shape would not affect the other rooms. Or to cite a more social example, the lingering domination of women by men cannot usefully be understood through research on families and friendship groups alone. As activists in the women's movement know well enough, the status of women at home and in informal groups is closely intertwined with their status in the labor force, in churches and schools, in the law, even in the grammar of pronouns of the English language. Thus, although it is easier to think only of little groups at first hand, a desire for adequate knowledge obliges us to think of them mainly in a larger context. A sociology with too narrow a focus reflects intellectual myopia and leads to an ineffective politics, the kind that results only in confusion and uproar.

But sociologists who aspire to relevance avoid also too intense a concentration on social order at its highest and broadest level. Overemphasis on global patterns of social life, overinsistence on "one world and one humanity," implies the pretense that events on this planet are or ought to be harmoniously orchestrated. This is like worrying overmuch about the neighborhood instead of one's own house. Such an all-encompassing perspective leads easily to an attitude of irresponsible timidity, an unnecessary feeling of being trapped in a vast maze of external expectations from which there is no escape. What is worse, too broad an outlook can induce its bearer to assume the stance of the domineering busybody who would have every house on the block be remodeled to fit some single image of a neighborhood. Surely one lesson of the Indochina war, as of other entanglements of world powers in foreign lands, is that there is much to be said for minding responsibly one's own business and admitting to others the same right. A sociology with too wide a focus frightens readers and listeners away from creative action or tempts them to impose alien dreams on people who ought to dream their own.

The National Society

The evidence of the late twentieth century argues that the paramount focus of contemporary sociology be the national society. By this term is meant, to be concrete, the roughly 150 members of the United Nations, from tiny Bhutan high in the Himalayas to the gigantic Soviet Union, spread from the Baltic to the Bering Sea. Three national societies can thus be discerned on the North American continent: at the northern end Canada, the largest in area but the smallest in population, embracing about 24 million people in 1980; in the middle the United States, with only slightly less territory and a population almost ten times as large as

Canada's; and at the southern end Mexico, about one-fifth the geographic size of either northern neighbor but with some 70 million people, making it the most densely populated of the three. But all of these are relatively large as societies go. The smaller South American continent is divided into a dozen national societies plus one department of France. Sprinkled across Central America and the islands of the West Indies are a dozen more.

To center sociology today on the national society does not at all imply disregard for either smaller or larger kinds of group, for either microlevel or macrolevel research. For just as a house is composed of various and often ill-fitting rooms, decor, and furniture, so also does a society contain diverse and often conflicting smaller groups, all of which deserve to be studied and understood. And just as houses are never immune from their neighborhoods, so also are societies influenced by one another and by many kinds of transnational structure. But in our time the national society itself is the structure of overriding social significance, the one that demands our attentive focus above all. The following paragraphs list seven reasons why this is so.

seven reasons to focus on the national society: first, its sovereignty

The first is that the government of a national society, its ruling body or highest authority, claims sovereignty. A national government repudiates the idea of any larger earthly structure within which it is obliged to be integrated, and of any higher earthly authority to which it must answer. Unlike a corporation's board of directors, a social club's executive committee, a city council, union boss, or head of a family, a national government publicly assumes absolute, final, supreme authority. It may interact with other governments, make treaties, sign agreements, and permit international trade, but all this is understood to be voluntary. The rule now followed almost everywhere on earth, that no flag may fly above the one symbolizing the local national society, suggests the import of this particular kind of group. By the assertion of its own rulers, a national society is an autonomous and independent structure of human life, one which can be modified on its own terms and without prior approval from any outside agency. It deserves to be taken at its word in sociology.

second, its monopoly on force

Second, the national government claims and tries to maintain a monopoly on the resources of violence. Now all the social order in human experience, whatever groups it is part of, endures only through various techniques of enforcement and control. Moral suasion, sheer enjoyment, monetary rewards, and threats of hellfire are among the techniques commonly used, and they are available to the authorities in nearly all kinds of group. But when all else fails, order is maintained only through some kind of physical force: fists and elbows, nightsticks and knives, bullets and guns, tear gas and tanks, missiles and bombs. And it is these resources of violence, the control techniques of last resort, which national governments reserve to their own agencies, the national armed forces and police, and to similar agencies of subsidiary governments. And not only within its own borders does a national government feel free to enforce its will by violent means. Almost alone of social entities, it claims the right to extinguish human life in war. The gravity of that action suggests how seriously we students of social life must take the national society.

third, its inescapability

Third, the national government refuses individuals within its borders the right to opt out of participation in the society it governs. All citizens and residents are obliged ultimately by force to obey its laws. One cannot simply withdraw, as is possible from a country club, factory, church, city, or marriage, insofar as the laws of the relevant national regime permit. Moreover, physically departing one national society implies entering another, with its own claim to sovereignty and monopoly on force. Even ships in international waters customarily fly national flags. More vividly than any kind of social structure, the national society attests to Marx's point that we do not make history out of free pieces. The national government confronts us as an inescapable reality, one which we cannot ignore, whatever our respective plans or goals.

fourth, its broad responsibility

Fourth, the national government claims to act for the common good of its citizens and thus assumes responsibility for ensuring that all their purposes can be served. It is not a specialized kind of authority, limiting its purpose to the provision of food, tools, earthly love, or divine grace. Instead it trumpets itself as the guardian of an overarching framework within which all the more particular human wants can be satisfied. While few national governments themselves try to organize the satisfaction of all their citizens' purposes, they nonetheless define the rules within which other kinds of group are organized toward these ends. Thus to summarize these first four points: because of the sovereign, violent, inescapable, and all-embracing power the national government claims the right to exercise, the national society over which it presides is in a class apart from other kinds of social structure and deserves to be the chief focus of a sociology adequate for the present day. Three more reasons why this is so may be discerned, each of which concerns not the government so much as the society itself.

fifth, the boundaries it sets on social life

Fifth, the physical, geographical boundaries of the national society tend in fact to coincide with major boundaries of human interaction. In most cases, that is, the claims of national governments are not empty; they do indeed rule relatively distinct and cohesive subsets of the human population. More than 90 percent of people within the boundaries of the United States, for example, are native-born and have never been part of any other society, except fleetingly as tourists or on military assignment abroad. The figure is almost as high for Canada, higher for Mexico, and still higher for most other national societies. As a result, family relationships, educational experiences, employment, leisure, and other aspects of life are organized for the most part within national borders. Not only do governments assert the autonomy and independence of national societies, but these qualities are more or less evident in the societies themselves.

sixth, the collective identity of its citizens

Sixth, unlike larger forms of social organization, the national society endows its membership with a sense of peoplehood, a feeling of closeness to one another and distinctness from human beings elsewhere. This more than anything is what is meant by the concept of *nation*: a large group of people who interact mostly with one another and whose collective sense of identity transcends differences in family, class, occupation, religion, region, and other small-scale groups. Societies vary, of course, in the extent of their national integration. And at least one transnational religion, the Roman Catholic Church, can in some settings seriously challenge the national society's hold on the allegiance of its citizens.[1] But in general, no larger kind of group breeds such a feeling of togetherness as does that defined by national identity. Indeed, Australians, for example, who prefer to be called subjects of the British Crown or citizens of the Commonwealth are thought eccentric. So were

Patriotic themes in music, literature, and art nourish a collective sense of national identity, thereby strengthening the national society as a form of social organization. The drawing above by John James Barralet is one example for the United States. Done in 1802 and entitled "The Apotheosis of George Washington," it depicts the first president's ascension into divine company. Graphic art like this complements the marches of John Philip Sousa ("The Stars and Stripes Forever"), the songs of Irving Berling ("God Bless America"), John Wayne's movies, Bob Hope's humor, and Theodore H. White's books about making presidents. In this age of national societies, most culture is national culture. (The Metropolitan Museum of Art, Gift of William H. Huntington, 1883)

those young Americans abroad during the hippie era, who sometimes proclaimed themselves citizens of the world. Because humans have defined national citizenship as real, it is real in its consequences, and sociology must take it seriously.

seventh, the prevalence of linguistic unity

Seventh and finally, most national societies are integrated by a common language, often distinct from that spoken elsewhere. Italy, Norway, Sweden, Poland, and some other European societies are prototypical examples of linguistic distinctiveness. The United States, Mexico, Peru, and Brazil represent the most common pattern among societies of the Americas: a single national language of European origin, with some indigenous and immigrant minorities speaking languages of their own. Having separate anglophone and francophone populations, Canada is in that minority of national societies where no single language serves as a unifying mode of common national expression. Belgium, Switzerland, Nigeria, and South Africa also fall in this category. The internal conflicts and cleavages that plague all societies which lack a common tongue demonstrate the prominence of language in the formation of national identity. So does the general historical trend toward making national and linguistic boundaries coincide.

Enumeration of United Nations members is thus not the only way to define what is meant by a national society. Nor is it the best way, since a few societies—like Switzerland—have never joined. More meaningfully defined, a national society is that inescapable kind of large group whose government claims sovereignty, a monopoly on the use of force, and responsibility for setting the overall framework of life, and whose physical boundaries enclose a population with a common way of life, a sense of peoplehood, and usually a common language. It is this kind of contemporary reality our sociology must teach us to understand above all if we are to gain control of our fate and exercise the creativity in each of us. No matter that it is easier to think only about one's family, workplace, and friends, ignoring the wider structure of social life except to affirm helplessly now and then, "The world is getting smaller every day." We are dust in the wind if we do not master with our intellects the basic historical reality facing and embracing us. Only then can we master it with the sweat of creative action and shape it to fit our aspirations for a brighter day.

the national society defined

That the national society should command our primary attention today is especially remarkable because this was not the case even 150 years ago when Comte named our discipline. In the early nineteenth century the most significant forms of human organization were at once larger and smaller. The relevant larger structure was still the empire, as it had been for millennia. This was a loose system of control over often far-flung and disparate tribes, achieved by military conquest and designed to enrich the rulers of the conquering tribe. The Persian, Greek, and Roman empires were early examples in southern Europe, Africa, and Asia Minor, the Mayan and Incan empires in the Americas. In Comte's day, the process by which empires would later be shattered into national societies had only just begun. Thirteen of England's colonies in North America had declared their independence, but the British Empire still embraced Canada, Ireland, India, Australia, and New Zealand, plus nearly half of Africa and parts of eastern Asia. The Spanish and Portuguese empires had only begun to crumble in Latin America. France, Russia, Holland, and Denmark all had empires, too, and the imperial ventures of Germany and the United States had not yet begun. Not until after World War II did the sun begin to set for the last time on the reality of empire itself. More than fifty new national societies were created from colonies and recognized as independent between 1950 and 1980. The few colonial remnants left today—like Puerto Rico for the United States, Northern Ireland for Great Britain—have become white elephants to their overlords.

The old imperial powers used to enjoy shading in their colonies on maps of the world. As late as 1940, "overseas France" still included most of northwest Africa plus Madagascar and Vietnam. By 1980, it had shrunk to French Guiana on the South American coast, Martinique and Guadeloupe in the Caribbean, St. Pierre and Miquelon south of Newfoundland, and a few other islands of meager significance.

Nonetheless, the empire was an exceedingly loose kind of social structure—necessarily so, since the technology of transportation and communication was until recent decades too inefficient to permit easy penetration by conquerors into the everyday lives of the conquered. Vanquished tribes, unless killed by the invading army or its foreign bacteria and viruses, usually continued their customary ways of life with only modest and occasional intrusions by the imperial authorities. The most immediately relevant kind of structure for them was the *little community*—to use the label proposed by the American anthropologist Robert Redfield. By this word he meant a distinct, homogeneous, and largely self-sufficient group of people, like a farming or fishing village or a tribe of hunters. Within the narrow physical and social boundaries of such little communities the vast majority of people a century and a half ago lived from rough cradle to early grave, producing and consuming their own goods, sharing a sense of peoplehood, and reproducing themselves in their children. The hundreds of anthropologists who have done fieldwork in communities of this kind chose as their focus what has been indeed for most of history the preeminent basis of human organization. Progressively in the nineteenth and twentieth centuries, however, our ancestors on this planet not only toppled empires but uprooted little communities, creating thereby a new and intermediate kind of social structure, the national society that faces us today.

empires crumbled into national societies, and little communities were swept up into them

Throughout the rest of this book, the term *society* is used in the specific sense of the national society. In everyday language and the popular press, the word often indicates a vague conception of social behavior in general ("life in society"). Sometimes it also refers to particular organizations ("Society for the Prevention of Cruelty to Animals," "learned societies") or to the leisure activities of the rich ("society columns," "high society"). It is important to keep these common and usually less disciplined uses of the word separate from its meaning in these pages. Usage here reflects the historical truth that what our generation must make sense of more than anything else is the organization of life under the rule of national governments. What Americans need to understand above all is the United States of America, for Japanese it is Japan, for Peruvians Peru, and for others the respective societies in which they lead their lives. This by no means justifies ignorance of societies other than one's own. One's own is indeed best understood by how it differs from the rest and relates to them. That is why comparative references dot the pages of this book. But such references themselves reinforce the point, I trust, that the context of discussion is not *society* in some ghostly, intangible sense but a world full of terribly real *societies*.

this book concerns not society but societies

The remainder of this chapter sets out the major concepts with which sociologists approach societies and try to make sense of them. The first section below portrays a society as a sociocultural system, a structure of action on the one hand and of meaning on the other. The next section views it as a structure of demands, a complex of institutions and smaller-scale groups which exact from individuals a variety of necessary behaviors. Then a society is inspected as a structure of rewards, compensating its members for their participation. Finally it is analyzed in the larger context of international and global structures. These four sections, extending all the way to the chapter's conclusion, provide the basic vocabulary with which anyone can begin to sort through the data of experience and then piece it together in a coherent, satisfying, and useful way. The following pages, I should note in preface, rely loosely but extensively on the writings of Talcott Parsons, a Harvard professor and the most influential American sociologist in the 1950s and 1960s. By the time he died in 1979, Parsons' influence had long since begun to wane. But he was a master of conceptual distinctions and definitions, and I am indebted to him in the pages that follow.

The Society as a Sociocultural System

Like all types of human group, a society is a sociocultural system composed, as the compound adjective indicates, of two related facets or dimensions. A society is not one but two sets of entities, connected and arranged into wholes. The first or social one is the order visible in events and behavior, the structure of interaction as citizens engage in it. The second or cultural dimension is the order present in citizens' thoughts and feelings, the structure of meaning they carry inside of them. Both these facets are necessary to a society's existence. The social order directly breaks down if citizens do not nourish in their heads and hearts a supporting body of knowledge, a collective symbolic system, a shared mythology, in sum a common culture. When Pakistan, for instance, became an independent society in 1956, it had two geographically separate parts, one on either side of India. The hope was that their common Islamic religion would be sufficient basis on which to forge the two parts into a common national culture, especially since predominantly Hindu *a society exists only* India sat between them. But the common culture died aborning, the social order *insofar as structure and* dissolved into war, and the eastern part proclaimed its independence as Bangladesh *culture are joined* in 1971. Just as social structure alone does not make a society, neither does culture. The myth or dream, the culture of Lithuania lingers even now in the minds of aging emigrants in North America and of aging residents in the homeland who have managed to resist russification. But Lithuania has not existed as a society since 1940, when it was incorporated by conquest into the U.S.S.R. A society is necessarily two things, both something people do together and something they collectively know and believe in.

The worth of distinguishing cultural and social facets is that sociologists can then investigate in particular societies the degree to which the two facets coincide, how symmetrical or congruent they are. For a major concern of the discipline is to shed light on the shadow that everywhere falls between the idea and the act. Yet there would be no shadow were not the idea and the act everywhere drawn to each other. Hence our prior concern is simply to grasp whatever congruence exists between the two facets in a particular case, the symmetry without which no society can exist. Let me illustrate this point with reference to the most elemental units of the social and cultural systems. The smallest unit in the social system is usually taken to be the *role*, an orderly bit of behavior enacted by various people and joined to other bits in patterned interaction. Among the thousands of roles constituting U.S. society is that of the national president. Its behavioral content includes signing and vetoing bills, preparing legislation for the Congress, shaking lots of hands, smiling frequently, and so on. In January of 1981, Ronald Reagan became the fortieth person to play this role. Like his predecessors he has performed the role in a unique way, but the role itself remains distinct. It is part of a social structure that

*"Each society has its own mythology of government and hence its own governmental roles."
Here Margaret Thatcher, prime minister of the United Kingdom, faces the press alongside
Helmut Schmidt, chancellor of the Federal Republic of Germany. The date is 1979. (United
Press International)*

*role is to norm as
action is to idea*

transcends personalities. But it could not be performed at all without *norms* that
correspond to it in U.S. culture, without commonly accepted rules about how any
president should behave. Norms are the basic units of culture, defining and
reinforcing the behavioral content of social roles. Ronald Reagan could act in the
role of president only because he, his cabinet members, the joint chiefs of staff,
newspaper reporters, and the public at large share and respect a set of norms or rules
about what the office entails. When the actual performance of a role grossly
contradicts the norms attached to it, when the shadow lengthens between idea and
act, as happened during the Nixon presidency, a condition of crisis results. The
sociocultural system is thrown out of kilter and remains disjointed until symmetry
between role and norms is restored—in that instance by Nixon's resignation and
the switch to a new role player, Gerald Ford.

Although every society consists of these two related facets of social structure and
culture, roles and norms, the specifics differ from case to case. No norms in
Canadian culture dictate what the national president is or is not supposed to do.
The very concept is meaningless in Canada, except in discussions of life in the
United States or some other foreign land. And because the norms are missing, so is
the presidential role. On the other hand, Canadian culture includes the ideas of
governor-general and prime minister, and many norms surrounding each of these
roles. Such cultural properties make it possible for individuals actually to *be*
governor-general and prime minister. In January of 1979, Jules Leger stepped out of
the first of these roles and Edward Schreyer began to act in it. Five months later,
when the Liberal Party lost its majority in Parliament, Pierre Trudeau quit behaving
as prime minister and Joe Clark started to do so—only to be replaced by Trudeau

again in February of 1980. It would be inaccurate to say that Canadians call their president a prime minister or that the American president is "just like" a governor-general. Better to admit that each society has its own mythology of government and hence its own governmental roles. Our purpose in sociology is not to project the social and cultural attributes of one society onto another but first to see how attributes of these two kinds hang together in the distinct dramas of particular societies. Only after this is done can we usefully try to formulate more general insights.

CONCEPTS FOR ANALYZING CULTURES

Sociologists can fairly be said to attend more to social structure than to culture: to analyze what people do in their accustomed roles rather than what they know how to do and think they ought to do according to prevailing norms. Most of the concepts discussed in this chapter reflect this common social or behavioral emphasis. But the two dimensions of life in a human society are so closely intertwined that one can hardly speak of one without implying the other. For unlike the behavior of mere animals, human action is filtered by complex ideas. A human society differs radically and qualitatively from a pack of hounds or a family of baboons. It is not just a constellation of movements fueled by natural, instinctual drives, but also an intentional creation propelled by willfulness. The movement of a human arm or leg seldom makes much sense except with reference to something going on inside a human mind. Hence, culture is no less valid a point of entry into the study of a society than is social structure, its more or less symmetrical counterpart. Accordingly, five important but clearly cultural concepts are reviewed below.

of five key cultural concepts, the first is law, the official norms enforced by governments

First is the notion of *law*, which refers to any and all of those norms in a society which are formalized, officially written down, explicitly spelled out and enforced by governmental authority. Law in this sense includes all norms enshrined in public policy, from constitutional framework to procedural regulation. Contemporary societies concretize in law thousands upon thousands of norms concerning nearly all the roles citizens play. The United States Constitution and diverse federal statutes detail what the nation's president is required, permitted, and forbidden to do. Canadian laws set forth the behavior expected of a governor-general and prime minister. And so in other societies for their respective roles of governmental leadership. But no contemporary society limits the law to leading roles. A glance at the books on the average lawyer's shelf reveals formally defined, written norms governing the roles of wife, husband, father, mother, daughter, son, taxpayer, student, employer, nurse, landscape architect, electrician, tenant, landlord, homeowner, house builder, hotel guest, bus traveler, pedestrian, stockholder, welfare recipient, professor, child, voter, adult, pensioner, nonresident, and countless others. Few roles any of us has ever played are immune to the public legal code of our respective societies, not to mention the regulations laid down by smaller-scale groups and organizations. This makes the study of law an integral part of the sociological enterprise, a major source of insight into the culture underlying, urging, and justifying the orderly behavior of citizens.

Notwithstanding its singular importance, the law does not encompass the entirety of culture in any society. It embodies only the basic outline, the outer limits of required, accepted, and proscribed behavior. A society where citizens obeyed only those norms written into law would directly fall apart. A social structure supported only by legislation, litigation, and law enforcement would not hold together. The greater part of culture anywhere consists not in law but in *custom,* the unwritten encyclopedia of dos and don'ts which citizens carry inside their heads, their common understandings, tastes, and manners, the meanings they share of even subtle gestures and slight inflections of speech. Custom can be understood as a residual category, embracing all those norms and ideas in a culture which have not been formalized as law. Custom surrounds every structural component of a society, from the simplest role to the most complex organization. In contemporary industrial societies, whose lawbooks and procedure manuals tend to be voluminous, some roles of undeniable import remain largely untouched by law and fixed only in custom: football star, hero, intellectual, neighbor, lover, date, and friend, for example. The method of field research is especially useful for studying the customs of a society, just as the analysis of official documents is most congenial to the study of its laws.

the second is custom, the unwritten encyclopedia of dos and don'ts

A third basic concept for the study of culture is *language,* the set of verbal and written symbols by which citizens communicate with one another and incorporate within themselves the structure of their common life. Sometimes beginners in the Berlitz schools imagine that the foreign language they hope to learn is an undistorted mirror image of their own, except that the mouth and vocal chords must be twisted a little differently. But this is not at all the case. Languages are meant to reflect not one another but their respective structural or behavioral milieux. Each language, as it is spoken and written in a given society, is cultural underpinning for that society's way of life. For this reason, learning and analyzing a society's language is a necessary and integral part of understanding the society itself. Translations are never enough. The more different life is in any two societies, the less possible it is to translate their tongues. To cite an obvious example, one cannot say *telephone* in the language of a society that does not know what a telephone is. But language also clarifies differences among quite similar industrial societies. Contemporary Christians and Jews in English-speaking societies often begin their prayers "O Lord," calling God by a title they otherwise almost never use. But Spanish speakers say, "O Señor," the same respectful title they give to an ordinary man. *Lord* and *Señor* are therefore not quite the same word, however often they are treated so by translators of prayers. Still further, the English language differs even from one anglophone society to another. In a British context, for instance, the following sentence is meaningful enough: "My solicitor tells me the barrister should go before the magistrate tomorrow with my application to open a public house." But this sentence is noise to most American ears and rightly so. Court proceedings are arranged differently in Britain and the United States, and so are the roles of functionaries within them. And English pubs are as foreign to the United States as American bars are to England. The point is that language is part of culture and thus intimately tied to social structure. No sociologist could hope to understand any society without learning the words and grammatical constructions by which its own citizens make sense of it.

the third is language, citizens' own symbols for shaping and understanding their experience

the fourth is values,
guiding principles
especially useful in
cross-cultural research

The analysis of law, custom, and language puts sociologists in touch with a culture from the inside, helping them learn the system of meaning which bolsters a corresponding organization of life. For interpreting this sytem of meaning and comparing it to others, the concept of *value* has proven useful. It means a general orientation, priority, or criterion of choice in a culture, a guiding principle in the arrangement of social life. A value is a general norm, the kind of basic rule or belief often articulated in a constitution or national creed. The study of values has flourished in sociology especially since 1949, when a research project began at Harvard under the title "The Comparative Study of Values in Five Cultures." Navaho, Zuñi, Spanish-American, Mormon, and Texan communities were studied intensively during the next few years. More than fifty scholars eventually took part, including Talcott Parsons and Clyde Kluckhohn (1905–1960), a leading anthropologist and student of Navaho life. The value differences participants in that project conceptualized continue to be used in comparative cross-cultural research. Does a given society orient itself mainly to the past, for instance, to the present, or does it live for the future? Is it mainly concerned with individual rights or with the common, corporate good? Does it encourage citizens to express their feelings or to show emotional restraint? Must citizens behave toward one another universalistically, that is, according to explicit general standards, or are they free to form particular attachments irrespective of general rules? The answers to questions like these clarify how people in a society think of themselves, with what kind of meaning they invest their common life. The preceding chapter has already provided an example of how useful such questions can be, the example of Weber's linkage of the value on individualism in Protestant cultures to the capitalism of their economic structures. Values can be studied by all the research techniques discussed in connection with Weber's hypothesis.

One might infer from the past couple of pages that in a certain sense, analytically if not temporally, the cultural aspect of a society precedes the social one. It is tempting to say even that citizens behave as they do *because of* the laws, customs, language, and values they carry within them. But culture is not necessarily the independent variable and social structure the dependent one. The opposite argument can be made as well, as a fifth cultural concept implies. It is *ideology*,

the fifth is ideology, the
theory that justifies a
given way of life

which the German-British sociologist, Karl Mannheim (1893–1947), defined as a set of beliefs put to the service of an existing social order, a theory or system of ideas which justifies or affirms the way life in some society is organized. The social-Darwinist books of Herbert Spencer, for example, became part of the ideology behind the ruthless capitalism of Britain and America in the late nineteenth century. Similarly, Marx's theories have formed part of the ideological foundation for life in the Soviet Union since the 1917 revolution. Now obviously, this last of the five cultural concepts offered here is pricklier than any of the first four. The direction of the relationship it connotes between action and idea is less flattering to our human nature. It rankles a little to admit that we do not just behave in accordance with our beliefs but also latch onto beliefs that justify our behavior. By including *ideology* in this basic list, I want to emphasize that culture and social structure are *mutually* reinforcing aspects of any society, that we human beings both act as we think and think as we act. On the one hand a change of mind or of heart seems to precede a change of carriage. On the other hand the reverse seems to be the case. Careful sociology requires thinking on both hands at once.

The cultural dimension of a society embraces much more, of course, than norms, laws, customs, language, values, and ideology. It includes also the kind of tonalities and rhythms citizens find beautiful in music, the forms and subjects they enjoy in the visual arts, the way they dance and how often, their styles of clothing and cookery, which god they worship and how much—in sum, all the preferences and tastes they nourish in their thoughts and feelings. But the concepts reviewed here should be enough to make the point that understanding a society involves not only inspecting its social structure but getting into its culture. One of my best professors in graduate school described once in class certain unusual practices in some factory and then asked us students how we would go about investigating why these practices were followed. I forget all the complicated, detached, and arcane research strategies we proposed in response. At last our professor suggested simply, "Why wouldn't you begin by asking the people who work there?" His advice was sound. For human interaction does not happen in the absence of human thought and feelings. One of the best ways of understanding any structure of events is to study the structure of meaning attached to those events.

DISORDER AND DEVIANCE

The concept of sociocultural system has been shown to be of use for analyzing the congruity between citizens' external behavior and internal attitudes, congruity which helps explain the order apparent in human life, specifically as organized in national societies. But the data of our experience include not only order but disorder. Nixon's misbehavior as U.S. president is but one example of that common phenomenon sociologists call *deviance*: actions people take or ideas they hold which nonetheless do not fit into the society at hand. Deviance comes in many kinds. *Deviant behavior* is that which fails to conform to the roles constituting a given social structure. *Deviant beliefs* are those which violate the norms of a given culture. Deviance may be as mild as a smiling face in a society where grave expressions are preferred—in which case it is usually ignored. Or it may be as severe as a married woman's adultery in a society where wives are considered their husbands' property—in which case the misdeed is probably *criminal*, that is, contrary to written law and punishable by public authority. Deviance may be done or thought individually, as when a solitary American citizen preaches communism on a street corner, or collectively, as when a group of Soviet citizens circulate procapitalist books among themselves. But whatever its kind, deviance disrupts some specified order established in human life. Thus it is necessarily and by definition relative, discernible only with reference to a particular sociocultural system. What counts as disorderly conduct or abnormal views in one society may fit perfectly well in another.

deviance: actions and ideas which do not fit

The present chapter is not the place to treat deviance in detail. Nor indeed is the present basic book, which is properly concerned more with the army of regularities in our experience than with the scattered gang of abnormalities. (Only the final chapter attends much to the latter concern.) But here at least should be noted how useful the concept of sociocultural system is for the study of deviance. For the evidence suggests that deviant ideas and acts arise mostly out of the shadows

"The cultural dimension of a society embraces much more, of course, than norms, laws, customs, language, values, and ideology. It includes also the kind of tonalities and rhythms citizens find beautiful in music, the forms and subjects they enjoy in the visual arts, the way they dance and how often, their styles of clothing and cookery, which god they worship and how much—in sum, all the preferences and tastes they nourish in their thoughts and feelings." This dancer lives in Burundi, a central African society where 90 percent of citizens are illiterate. He belongs to the Watusi tribe, whose style of dance has been copied in the Western world, but not very authentically. (Thomas D. W. Friedman/Photo Researchers, Inc.)

citizens perceive between conventional ideas and conventional acts. That is, it is contradictions within the sociocultural order at hand that induce citizens to think and behave in disorderly ways. Let an example illustrate this possibly difficult but exceedingly important point. Sociologists have long sought to explain why poorer, less advantaged youths are more likely to commit robberies, thefts, assaults, and other deviant acts than better-off young men and women. For indeed such is the case in the United States and most other Western societies, even granting that poorer delinquents are more likely to be caught and prosecuted. Robert K. Merton, a Columbia professor and Talcott Parsons' most eminent student, has given probably the best-known explanation for this finding. Poorer youth, he argued, have learned to accept the cultural goals of their society—goals like getting rich—but they lack institutionalized means for achieving these goals—means like the role of inheritor of daddy's stocks or the role of student in a leading business school. They confront, in other words, an inconsistency between the dream they have learned at school and from the media and the social structure they experience in everyday life. For them the shadow is long between their society's symbolic mythology and its behavioral reality. They therefore concoct innovative schemes

contradictions between culture and social structure, goals and means, meaning and experience, breed deviance

for reconciling this contradiction, using whatever resources they have—and thereby often end up in jail. Richer youth, by contrast, experience less contradiction in their lives. The ideals their society holds out seem more attainable through the roles they themselves can reasonably expect to occupy. Lived experience is for them more meaningful in conventional terms and they are thus less likely to deviate.

An adequate explanation for deviance in general and for particular kinds of it in particular societies requires to be sure much more than Merton's general proposition. The relevance of his proposition here is mainly just to show that an analytic separation of a society into social and cultural dimensions helps makes sense not only of social order but of social disorder. Research evidence on the whole suggests that the tighter and more symmetrical the fit between culture and social structure in citizens' own experience, the less likely the occurrence of deviant thoughts and acts. The more closely the established order of life corresponds to established expectations, the more secure is the society against dissidence, innovation, and change. The trouble comes, that is, the novelty in earthly life, out of the contradictions within the established order itself. Immigrants still wrapped up in a culture that conflicts with the social structure at hand, children taught ideas at home that clash with their experiences away from home, youth from poor societies sent to study in North America or Europe and now returned home—these are the kind of humans to whom explosive ideas usually occur and from whom unseemly behavior often springs. The contradictions they experience make life interesting for more settled citizens.

OTHER KINDS OF SOCIOCULTURAL SYSTEMS

For reasons outlined at its beginning, this chapter is focused on the national society, today's preeminent kind of human organization. But in concluding this section I should note that the concept of sociocultural system can be usefully applied also to any other kind of group—basketball team, church, city, insurance company, university, or whatever. For every group, regardless of its size or purpose, displays a social structure, an orderly arrangement of roles. And every group consists also of a culture, a structure of thoughts and feelings which members share. Indeed, beginners in sociology might well find it worthwhile to apply the notion of sociocultural system to some small-scale group in their immediate experience, gaining thereby a pointed lesson at first hand in the usefulness of the concept. Thus encouraged, they can raise their eyes with greater confidence to the level of the national society and begin to master it with essentially the same vocabulary. As an example, the paragraph below suggests the kind of analysis which could be made of a family, any family, as a sociocultural system.

analysis of smaller groups and organizations is a good place to start

For a start, a family's existence implies both social and cultural dimensions, both interaction and meaning shared among its members. A family where people live together but without shared feelings inside is incomplete, an empty shell, a situation of living in the same cage. A family of feelings but no interaction is likewise incomplete, broken perhaps by separation or divorce, one which failed to work out in spite of good intentions. But provided the family is integral and alive, its structure can be analyzed: what concrete behavior constitutes the roles of wife, mother, husband, father, son, brother, sister, daughter, mother-in-law, grandson, niece, and so on. One can spell out in words on the basis of empirical observation how these roles fit together both in single individuals (father-husband) and between individuals (mother-daughter). And in relation to social structure, one can sketch the family culture: what rules or norms the parents have laid down, what the unspoken customs around the house are, which words and symbols used in the family capture especially well what this family is about, what values underlie interaction in this family as compared to others, and what excuses members of this family give for the way they live together. Then once both social structure and culture are outlined, a serious student of this family looks for contradictions between the two dimensions. Does the father himself exemplify the advice he gives his children? Does the mother act the way members of this family think a mother is supposed to act? Does anyone experience role conflict, that is, the situation of occupying two roles at once (like sister and daughter) that are governed by incongruent or opposing norms? Have the contradictions within this family as a sociocultural system resulted in deviance, perhaps the lies a son tells his father, a mother's dependence on tranquilizers, or a daughter's withdrawal?

role conflict: the predicament of trying to perform at once roles with contradictory norms

Questions like these provide a disciplined framework for reflection about the data of family life. In this way one can begin to make sense of one's own family. Inevitably, of course, such an exercise reveals how deeply affected most families are by other groups and organizations. The demands of work roles, leisure roles, and roles in school must somehow be meshed with the expectations attached to family roles. The rules and customs in most families today can hardly be independent of more general cultural trends. Thus a serious analysis of one's own family leads easily to similar analyses of larger-scale sociocultural systems, even to the level of the national society. To follow such leads is to be seized by the sociological imagination and to begin to get on top of the realities of contemporary life—which is after all the point of all this.

The Society as a Structure of Demands

The preceding section identified a society as a *system*, a useful concept for commencing also this second part of our overview of the social order at hand. For basic to the idea of system is that the parts serve the whole. Whatever kind of system we imagine—heating, automotive, public transportation, data-processing, digestive, circulatory, or some other kind—the implication is that the various parts must perform their respective tasks, otherwise the system begins to break down. Drawing upon this conception, many sociologists have analyzed the national society as a structure of demands, a social system that requires citizens to play various roles, exacts various kinds of behavior from them, in order that the benefits of life organized in this way may continue to be secured. This kind of analysis basically involves studying which tasks or *functions* different parts of the social *structure* serve for the survival of the society as a whole. Researchers begin with a particular function and ask how a particular society arranges for it to be accomplished. Or they start with some component of the structure, some group or organization, and study what functions it performs for (or possibly against) the whole. Thus this kind of analysis is appropriately labeled *structural functionalism* or simply *functionalism*. Articulated most explicitly by Talcott Parsons and his disciples, it underlies much of the best sociological research yet accomplished. And it has intrinsic common-sensical appeal. If nothing else, the regular strikes in most Western societies by postal workers, air-traffic controllers, sanitation workers, police, schoolteachers, and other employees pointedly remind us all that the established order critically depends on an immense number of groups fulfilling the varied demands placed upon them.

Probably the most ticklish part of doing structural-functional analysis is specifying which functions are necessary to a society's existence. Does every society vitally *need* some kind of arrangement for worshipping a god, or for terminating unwanted pregnancies, or for deploying nuclear weapons? Societies differ immensely in the demands they feel obliged to make on their citizens. The demands constantly change, moreover, as each society makes and remakes its own history. Nonetheless, functionalist sociologists have formulated four broadly defined tasks or functions served by some kind of component in every contemporary society. These four functions can properly be counted as enduring regularities, things unlikely to change in the decades to come—though the precise arrangements for fulfilling them will continue to vary across societies and over time. First is that every society must establish, maintain, and defend its own internal order. Chaos contradicts the very definition of a society. Hence there must be some kind of political regime, a government with its associated agencies. Second, every society must adapt itself to its physical environment, come to terms with its space on this planet, and provide its citizens with some range of earthly goods: food, housing, and clothes inevitably, and lots of other things possibly, from hockey pucks to electric toothbrushes. The economy can be understood to serve this function. Third, every society must nourish a feeling of collective worth among its citizens, a sense of cultural well-being, a belief that their life in common has meaning. Religion and the arts are usually associated with this task. Fourth and finally, every society must reproduce itself over time by creating new citizens and shaping them to fit its various roles. The family and education are considered to serve this function. These four functions seem so intrinsic to the idea of a society that they can be taken for granted in all our discussions of social life.

But if these functions can be taken for granted, so can the functionally defined components which serve them. That is, whatever society we study or seriously hope to create, it is a safe guess that within it can be found some kind of polity, economy, religion (with which the arts and leisure are often grouped), family, and education. For this reason each of the latter can properly be called an *institution*, an arrangement of roles (with corresponding norms) so enduring and essential that one cannot imagine a society without it. This term is sometimes applied more loosely to other groups, organizations, and practices that have lasted for generations and have been accepted as a routine part of life in a particular society. Thus can the monarchy be termed a British institution, bullfighting a Mexican one, and the drinking of wine a French one. In everyday language even schools or hospitals considered part of the long-standing order of life are referred to as institutions. But none of these loosely defined institutions is so important or universally relevant as the five basic ones listed first. Indeed, these five—polity, economy, religion, family, and education—are the titles of half the chapters in this book. These chapters treat the institutions from more points of view than the functionalist one, but the latter offers a useful initial way of understanding what they mean.

To study a particular society as a structure of demands is therefore to analyze how it organizes its citizens in the service of basic functional needs. It is to ask how the necessary tasks are accomplished, to sort out roles and groups according to which institutions they belong to, and then to investigate how the parts fit together for accomplishing the common good, however defined in the society under study. Or more simply, to inspect the structure of demands is to get to know how the system works. The following pages, organized by the basic institutions, outline the major kinds of groups by which contemporary societies satisfy their basic needs. And to help readers relate personally to some fairly general concepts, I make occasional reference in these pages, as indeed through the rest of this chapter, to a real human being, John Angus McDougald. Any reader of this book, with his or her own collection of roles, could illustrate these same concepts, but the choice of this man is especially apt. Unlike most of us, he acted in two societies, Canada and the United States, and could easily have passed for a citizen of either one. And he played an unusually interesting set of roles, one which illuminates important features of contemporary life in North America. He was 67 years old in 1975, the year a journalist named Peter Newman described him at length in a popular book.[2] When John McDougald's name appears from time to time in coming pages, readers might well ponder their own roles in relation to his, for he was part of the same show in which we and millions more have our exits and entrances.

POLITY

political subdivisions: microcosms of the larger society

Like all the rest, the political institution consists of groups and organizations, subsystems of the society as a whole. And beyond the national government itself, the *political subdivision* is the most important subsystem of this institution in contemporary societies. It is a geographically delimited social order within which all four basic societal purposes are to be served, but only for people within its boundaries and only within limits imposed by the national government. The largest political subdivisions may be provinces (as in Canada), states (as in the United States, Australia, West Germany, or Mexico), republics (as in the Soviet Union), departments (as in France), or some similar unit. These subdivisions comprise cities, towns, villages, and sometimes regions, counties, districts, and townships. Each such subdivision is legally recognized by the national government as a kind of microcosm of the society at large. Thus did John McDougald play the roles not only of Canadian citizen but of resident in the borough of North York, the city of Toronto, and the province of Ontario. Like everyone else, he was assigned these roles simply by virtue of where he lived. His home was nicer than most, a 19-acre estate valued at more than $2 million in 1975. He had a second one, too, a villa with eighteen bathrooms. Its location gave him roles in a second hierarchy of political subdivisions: the city of West Palm Beach, Palm Beach County, Florida, U.S.A.

Although political subdivisions are among the subsystems of all societies today, their significance varies widely. Many smaller societies whose populations are culturally quite homogeneous keep subdivision governments on a relatively tight leash and reduce them mainly to local administrators of national policy. Ireland,

Finland, Paraguay, and Japan exemplify this pattern of *unitary* structure. The United States, the U.S.S.R., and Canada, by contrast, accord their largest political subdivisions considerable autonomy and permit them to pass their own laws and nourish distinct structures of social and cultural life. They illustrate the pattern of *federal* structure. For John McDougald, as for most Canadians and Americans, his roles in political subdivisions were a matter of some importance. He once had to persuade the North York Borough Council to exempt him from its laws so that he might keep his horsebarn within the borough's boundaries. And he must have been pleased that the Florida government encourages Ontarians to own vacation homes within its boundaries, even though the Ontario government imposes a discouraging tax on the sale of vacation properties to Floridians.

The political institution includes a second kind of societal component, one established not for fulfilling in microcosm the four broad purposes but for accomplishing a particular facet of public order. Subsystems of this kind are *public bureaucracies*, organizations created and controlled by a national or subdivision government and organized for the achievement of some specific objective. Military and police forces are the best examples, existing for no other purpose than to maintain and defend the order imposed by law. Among other public bureaucracies are the postal system, public school systems, social-welfare agencies, prisons, and the organizations responsible for highways and public works. Like most of his compatriots, John McDougald played no active roles in any of these; he was not a public employee or civil servant. On the other hand he played numerous more passive political roles as a law-abiding citizen, adapting his behavior to the public order established in the societies where he lived and worked. As a taxpayer, he was assessed as much as $1 million annually in income tax alone. Every time he voted, paid even a sales tax, walked along a city sidewalk, drove down a public highway, flew into a public airport, mailed a letter, visited a public park, or even drank water from a tap linked to a municipal utility, he thereby affirmed and reinforced the basic political order of the society at hand.

public bureaucracies: specialized instruments of public order

Societies founded on capitalist principles, as outlined in the preceding chapter, limit the national government, subdivision governments, and public bureaucracies to the task of setting only a basic order or framework. That is, societies of this kind display narrow definitions of the polity. About the farthest their governmental mandates extend is to the *infrastructure*, the systems of transportation, communications, and energy allocation upon which other institutions depend. In Canada, for instance, public bureaucracies run the major airline (Air Canada), railroad (Canadian National), television network (the Canadian Broadcasting Corporation), and most hydroelectric utilities (like Ontario Hydro). The societies of Western Europe and South America are similar in this respect. The United States, the archetype of capitalist organization, stops its policy short even of most infrastructural purposes, holding it to a regulatory role in air and rail transport, the broadcast media, telecommunications, and the production and distribution of energy.

capitalist governments tend to control directly only the infrastructure

ECONOMY

The more capitalist a society is, the more it seeks to shift the achievement of its purposes away from the political institution toward the economic one, to translate

FOR EXAMPLE

John Kenneth Galbraith, "On Switzerland"*

Although never immune to outside influence, each national society is a reality of its own. In the selection below, a regular visitor to one of the more admirable societies on earth offers a capsule description.

The Swiss example has always encouraged me to believe that there is power and effectiveness in democracy. It is the Swiss instinct that problems can be solved by the collective responsibility and intelligence of the people themselves. It is that responsibility and intelligence that count. Accordingly, the solution lies with the citizen, not the leader. The Swiss citizen does not delegate to the great in the belief that they have the answers. He seeks the answers. In a few of the 22 (very recently 23) cantons, all voters still meet as a legislative body. The initiative and referendum—a direct vote on issues—are much used. In consequence, many more elections are to resolve issues than to choose leaders. In further consequence, the Swiss have had few noted leaders, few heroes. The most famous Swiss was Calvin, who was French. After Calvin comes William Tell, whose distinction rests only on a somewhat perilous approach to parental duty.

One winter day a few years ago a telephone message was relayed to me from a man in Bern whose name seemed familiar; he wanted me to come over for lunch to discuss economic problems. I sought out my very intelligent Swiss neighbor to find out who he was. "He might have been last year's President." she said. "Anyway, I'm quite sure he isn't President now."

Small countries are far from being masters of their people's destiny. Inflation and recession come in from abroad. In a nuclear war these countries would be no less the victims than the nuclear powers themselves. But for questions within the power of the Swiss democracy—protection of the environment; ethnic reconciliation between those who speak German, French, Italian; a tolerant relationship between religions; provision of good housing and public services; sensible support to agriculture and industry; education that nurtures the democratic idea—it has found solutions, brilliant solutions on the whole.

It is common, even there, to dismiss this democratic accomplishment by saying that Switzerland is a small country that also has had no wars. Perhaps it was the good sense of Swiss democracy that kept it out of Europe's internecine wars, as some have called them. To say that a small country has no problems

*From John Kenneth Galbraith, *The Age of Uncertainty*, Houghton Mifflin, Boston, 1977, pp. 325–27. Copyright © 1977 by John Kenneth Galbraith. Reprinted by permission of the author and of the Houghton Mifflin Company. Dr. Galbraith is professor emeritus at Harvard University and a former U.S. ambassador to India.

shows only an instinct for error. Ulster is a small country. So is Lebanon. So is Chile. The Belgians quarrel dutifully over language. Small countries may feel especially obliged to assert their capacity for self-destruction. It is a form of compensation.

For the task of governing themselves, the Swiss have three sources of strength. Each participant in the democracy has a personal concern for the result. Small size and the continued protection of the authority and autonomy of the canton and the responsibilities of the commune or local government—the celebrated Swiss federalism—is a help. One person's vote and voice can have an appreciable bearing on the outcome. So they are worth using and worth careful thought. Important issues are submitted to the people in referendum. Indeed, as noted, most Swiss elections are to pass on issues (new taxes, new spending, votes for women, limits on the number of foreign workers) and are not, as elsewhere, to select between parties and politicians.

The next source of strength is the Swiss sense of community. The Swiss, one need hardly say, have a keen sense of personal pecuniary interest. But they recognize the greater loss if the community is sacrificed to the special interest. Meeting politicians, businessmen, trade union leaders, even bankers in Switzerland over the years, I've always been impressed by the feeling, implied or expressed, that the interest of the commune, canton or country has precedence over the interest of the individual, part or organization and that this is not generosity but good sense.

Finally, I've always thought that the Swiss were far more interested in results than in principle. In economics and politics, as in war, an astonishing number of people die, like the man on the railway crossing, defending their right of way. This is a poorly developed instinct in Switzerland. No country so firmly avows the principles of private enterprise but in few have the practical concessions to socialism been more numerous and varied. When in Switzerland, we bank at a publicly owned cantonal bank, ride the national railroads, pay our bills through the Post Office *giro*, talk on a publicly owned telephone system, send telegrams over state-owned wires, look at public television, get news from the public radio, which can be heard over public telephone wires.

We do not live while there, as do many deserving Swiss, in clean, bright, publicly owned housing, access to which is considered a public right. But we do not pay private insurance on our house because the local government considers it cheaper for the individual and better for the community just to replace a house in case of fire. This is also thought to discourage arson, a risk that is not extreme. Swiss farmers are massively supported by the government, partly because they are thought cheaper for keeping the countryside in condition than a parks service. No industry is so uniquely Swiss as watchmaking. For around half a century the movements of most Swiss watches, a not unimportant feature, have been made by a firm that initially was sponsored by the Swiss government. Only the cases, watchbands, boxes and advertising have their origins in the realm of strict private enterprise. In other countries such arrangements would be thought inconsistent with the fundamental principles of free enterprise. The Swiss do not worry about such trifles.

the commonwealth into the maximization of *utility*—a concept which deserves brief explanation here. First of all, as many goods as possible—including transportation, telephones, oil, electricity, food, housing, and medical care—are defined simply as commodities, useful things. Machines, land, and even the labor of citizens are defined in the same way. Then, all these commodities are hurled, as it were, into a market economy in which the worth of each is measured in precise monetary terms, according to how much citizens are willing to pay for it. By current prices, for example, twenty copies of *Playboy* magazine are worth as much as a week's food for a family of four. The idea of capitalism is to let citizens' acquisitive impulses play against one another in an apolitical economy, in such a way that more and better commodities are steadily produced at ever-diminishing cost. The richer the society becomes, the more utility is being maximized. The capitalist society measures its success not so much by the excellence of the public order its government establishes as by the amount of money in the marketplace over which its government presides. The most common indicator is the gross national product (GNP) per capita, the total monetary value of everything bought and sold in a given year, divided by the number of citizens.

under capitalism, the maximization of utility is the measure of success

In a capitalist society, therefore, the most important roles most people play are defined as economic and apolitical, as part of the process of production, sale, and consumption of commodities. Virtually all citizens play roles as consumers, of course, since there is almost 'no other way to get access to the necessities of life. And on the production side some citizens participate directly in the market economy: doctors, architects, hair stylists, lawyers, and other professionals in private practice, who sell their skills; self-employed artisans like some tailors and cabinetmakers, who sell their handiwork; independent farmers, who sell the products of agriculture; and small merchants and shopkeepers, who relay commodities toward final sale to consumers. It was learned long ago, however, that there is money to be made from buying the labor of other people, organizing and managing it efficiently, and then selling for profit whatever is thereby produced. Thus was created the cardinal component of capitalist economies: the *corporation, company, economic firm*, or *private bureaucracy*. Most citizens now play their productive economic roles not directly in the market but only through this kind of subsystem. They do not so much work *at* a particular job as *for* a particular company. Contemporary capitalist societies are brimming with such private bureaucracies, each with its own strategy for returning profit to its owners, just as socialist societies overflow with public bureaucracies, each charged by public authority with some facet of the national plan. Currently about 1000 corporations own more than half of all the productive resources in the United States; the number is smaller for Canada.

private corporations: the cardinal components of capitalist economies

It was in the economy, and more precisely in corporations, that John McDougald played his most important roles. In Canada he was chairman of the board of the Argus Corporation, Massey-Ferguson, and other firms, and a director of radio station CFRB and the Canadian Imperial Bank of Commerce, among others. And he also played roles in U.S. firms. He was a director of one of America's largest corporations, Avco, headquartered in Connecticut. In each of these private organizations, Mr. McDougald's role dovetailed with thousands of others in order that marketable commodities could be produced for profit. At plants in Detroit,

Des Moines, and elsewhere, Massey-Ferguson employed roughly 75,000 people in 1975, which made it one of the world's leading manufacturers of tractors, agricultural implements, and various kinds of industrial machinery. Avco, on the other hand, was making money by loaning money (through its subsidiary, Avco Finance), handling charge accounts (the Carte Blanche credit card), and also developing land, conducting defense and space research, and selling insurance, among other ventures. Although they differ widely by size, product line, technology, and internal structure, private corporations share a common purpose: to provide at a profit some commodity by which a capitalist society can fulfill its second basic purpose.

RELIGION AND OTHER CULTURAL INSTITUTIONS

A society maintains public order by creating political subdivisions and public bureaucracies, and then supporting them with tax revenues. It provides goods and services either by establishing additional public organizations with economic purposes (the socialist model) or by recognizing in law private companies in a market economy (the capitalist model). But how shall a society ensure a sense of collective well-being? One option is to entrust this purpose to the polity. The government can maintain a national church and establish governmental agencies for music, arts, sports, and similar activities that provide citizens with a common feeling of uncommon worth. But capitalist societies tend to choose a second option: to entrust most cultural purposes to the market economy. Baseball players are regularly bought and sold in the United States, for instance, in the quest for profit of firms which make a commodity of spectator sports. Most motion pictures are handled in the same way: Avco Corporation makes part of its money from the production of Hollywood films. Television viewing in America is treated as a commodity, too: economic firms buy time on the screen and then intersperse the entertainment with advertisements for their products. John McDougald contributed in a profit-making way to the cultural commonweal of Canada and the United States not only as a director of firms involved in leisure but also more directly as an owner of racehorses.

voluntary associations: nonprofit, nongovernmental vehicles for citizens' collective action

A collective sense of honor is also achieved, especially in capitalist societies, by a kind of societal component not yet mentioned in this discussion, the *voluntary association*. This subsystem is not part of public administration since membership is not compulsory, governmental control is minimal, and financing comes mainly from private funds. Neither is it part of the market economy; it does not produce commodities for a profit. The voluntary association instead serves for its own sake some purpose left unfulfilled by both governmental organizations and private firms. The purpose may be a redefinition of public order (as in the case of political parties and pressure groups), or sometimes the provision of goods and services outside the market (John McDougald led fund-raising drives for hospitals and other voluntary charities). Most often the purpose is to nourish a sense of well-being among members and the citizenry at large. In the United States and to some extent in Canada, churches are legally recognized as voluntary associations, optional activities for those who care to join. John McDougald belonged to the Roman Catholic Church, thus demonstrating that this religion is not unequivocally hostile

Fire protection is among the specific purposes a society must accomplish. The question is, How? In times past voluntary associations of citizens often performed this task. Fire departments today are more often organized as public bureaucracies under the jurisdiction of municipal governments. More than a quarter of a million Americans fight fires for a living as public employees. In this as in many other aspects of life, capitalist development has brought a decline of voluntarism. (J. P. Laffont/Sygma)

to capitalists. The category of voluntary association also includes private clubs. Mr. McDougald held memberships in the New York Yacht Club, the Toronto Club, the Everglades Club, and numerous others. The YMCA, masonic lodges, bowling leagues, labor unions, and professional associations are also properly regarded as voluntary associations.

FAMILY

The fourth basic institution of human societies is the family, the group which joins marriage partners with their parents, children, and other blood relations. The family serves the goal of a sense of well-being and is a unit of economic consumption if not production, but the primary purpose it is thought to serve in a society is the creation of new citizens, new role players to replace those whose lives are at an end. In capitalist societies the family is especially important, since through it the ownership of capital and commodities is transferred from generation to generation. John McDougald, like the vast majority of the super-rich, was the son and grandson of wealthy men. And not only did his family background provide him with a financial start, it also gave him a network of friends and relatives and perhaps most important, a cultural definition of himself as a person destined to go places. In 1934, Mr. McDougald married Maude Eustace Smith, an Olympic figure skater, but theirs was a childless marriage and thus deviates from the main functional role defined for marriages. Governments build family groupings into the structure of social life by requiring that marriages be contracted before someone duly certified, that they be legally recorded, that they continue for life unless ended by governmental divorce decree, and that family members behave in accordance with family law.

EDUCATION

Also part of the creation of new role players are those organizations in a society directed toward educational purposes. It is not enough that children be born and grow to maturity. They must also learn the culture, the ideas, norms, and values, the entire mythology which will enable them to play productive roles as adults. Basic education is defined in virtually all contemporary societies as a primary means of maintaining public order. Hence governments create public school systems. More socialist societies go further, defining colleges and universities also as public bureaucracies, albeit relatively autonomous ones. This is the case in the Netherlands, where there are no purely private degree-granting institutions. In the United States, by contrast, alongside public colleges and universities are private ones organized in a voluntary, nonprofit way, and supported mainly by their endowments and tuition fees. The United States has thousands of primary and secondary schools organized in the same private way.

An obvious conflict exists between public education and wealthy families, insofar as the latter seek to give their children exceptional advantages and to guard them from slipping into the hoi polloi. For this reason, wealthy families almost universally seek to enroll their children in schools organized as voluntary associations of the rich. Thus did John McDougald receive his high school education at St. Andrew's and Upper Canada colleges in Ontario, probably the two most exclusive private schools in Canada. He also undertook to enroll at Sidney Sussex College of Cambridge University, but the 1926 general strike by British wage laborers intervened, and young John returned home to a job his father had arranged for him in Dominion Securities, a large investment corporation. Had John McDougald grown up in the United States, he would almost certainly have attended Groton, St. Mark's, Choate, Shattuck, or one of a few dozen other schools organized privately by the American rich.

STUDYING THE STRUCTURE OF DEMANDS

summary: perspective and concepts for functionalist research

The preceding paragraphs have sketched a rough outline of how the United States, Canada, and similar societies appear to sociologists studying them as structures of demands. They appear first as a national government, subdivision governments, and public bureaucracies engaged in the work of defining, maintaining, and defending public order. They display secondly all kinds of economic roles, mostly in private, profit-seeking companies producing useful commodities from the raw materials of nature. Third are the public bureaucracies and private firms, but also churches and other voluntary associations, serving the cause of cultural well-being. Fourth are the families, and public and private schools of every level, extending the society's life by creating and educating new citizens. These paragraphs have suggested the contributions one man, through his roles in groups of these various kinds, was recently making to the overall functioning of Canadian and American societies. Readers of this book can similarly review their own contributions, and those of their relatives and friends, toward making the system work. Having made such a review most people modestly conclude, "My contribution sure doesn't amount to much." Probably not, but then neither does anyone else's—not even John McDougald's. The vast wheels of contemporary societies turn from the concerted effort of millions of little role players, even as giant hydroelectric plants run by the combined force of millions of individually insignificant drops of water.

Important as it is to sort out roles and groups by the functions they serve and thus learn how the social system works, one must guard against expecting or hoping that everything will fit. National societies are not timeless, static utopias running smoothly and unproblematically. Each one is just a tentative human creation, an experimental design which no citizen fully approves and many deeply oppose. Consider that more than 40 percent of Quebecois voted in a 1980 referendum that their provincial government should negotiate Quebec's removal from the Canadian federal system, its reorganization as a sovereign, separate society. Note how much in dispute is the public order of the United States with respect to governmental control of private companies, the legal rights of minority groups, abortion, energy policy, environmental protection, capital punishment, and a host of other major issues. Within every society's borders can be found an abundance of deviant behavior and belief, at least a little of which is done or voiced by every citizen. And recall that national societies are relatively recent inventions, and that none has yet integrated all the former little communities into an overall national system. Thus

dysfunctional words and deeds are not necessarily undesirable, just unfitting

any society inevitably displays all kinds of *dysfunctional* roles and groups: phenomena which do not serve national purposes as currently defined. The task of sociology is not at all to ignore or condemn dysfunctional data, but to explain why and how unfitting phenomena do not fit, bearing in mind that some deeds and thoughts empirically dysfunctional for the status quo are the components of social systems far preferable to what we have now. But we are unlikely ever to implement a more humane system for our lives without first understanding the present one—and that is the worth of structural-functional analysis.

The preceding section concluded, you recall, with the point that not only societies but also smaller-scale groups and organizations can be studied as sociocultural systems. This section concludes with a similar point: that the component or constituent groups within a society can also be studied as structures

an example: functionalism applied to a complex organization

of demands. Especially is this the case for public and private bureaucracies, large purposive groups which sociologists often join under the label *complex organization*. Each of these has the same four basic functional needs as a society, and each can usefully be studied in terms of its political, economic, cultural, and reproductive components. The Avco Corporation can serve as an example. Certain roles within it are and must be assigned to the formulation of company policy, to the establishment, maintenance, and defense of its own internal order. Members of the board, executives, and managers occupy such roles, and at a lower level the maintenance staff and security guards. John McDougald's affiliation with Avco was thus in the political sector of what is overall an economic organization. Most roles in Avco, as in most organizations, are in its internal economic sector—assigned to the task of procuring raw materials, processing them, and transforming them into the prescribed products. Borrowing agents, lending agents, debt counselors, secretaries, and clerks are all examples in Avco Finance. But still other roles in Avco are assigned to the nurturance of collective well-being, what is usually called employee morale—personnel relations officers and psychological counselors, for example. Lastly, certain members of the Avco organization must spend their time recruiting and training new emplotees, lest the company disappear as workers die, retire, quit, or are fired. Structural-functional analysis is not the only way to analyze complex organizations, just as it is not the only way to study societies. But it is one useful way. Employees in any firm or agency know by their own experience the reality of the system with which they must contend from day to day. The trick is to understand that system in detail; only then can it be improved upon.

The Society as a Structure of Rewards

The first two conceptualizations offered in this general depiction of national societies rest admittedly on a rather static outlook. To view a society as a sociocultural system or as a structure of demands is to take a still photograph of it and then study the order apparent in that single frame. It is to take much the same approach as engineers do when they inspect the diagram of a heating system or the sketch of an automotive system, the approach of home buyers poring over the floor plan of a house. But we know from our experience that a human society is more than a mechanical system or physical structure. And not only because a society's human components have thoughts and feelings inside of them. For social systems are constantly in a process of change, steadily on the way to becoming radically different. While most movement within them is routine—citizens circulate daily from home to work and back again much like water circulating in furnace pipes—other movement is new, deviant, dysfunctional, and what is more, creative of change in the system itself. No society hovers endlessly in static equilibrium. Each is in the midst of its own history, its own self-transformation. A society is at best a *moving* equilibrium, often with occasional lapses into civil war and anarchy. Let me suggest still another analogy. A play called *The Mousetrap* has been running in London (as of 1980) for over thirty years, its performances enduring almost unchanged through multiple generations of actors. Real-life societies are not like that. Their scripts of law and custom are rewritten a little every day, and actors are forever inserting new lines, new plots, and whole new characters into the reality of lived experience. Hence an adequate sociology cannot rest on static outlooks alone—on the image of a still photograph, a mechanical system, a lifeless building, or an unchanging play. Somehow our sociology must capture social *process*, the fact of history.

static outlooks alone cannot capture the process of history

As one means of achieving this end, this section of the present chapter offers a third conceptualization of the national society, a third way of analyzing the data of our experience: as a structure of rewards. This perspective rests on the simple recognition that unlike mechanical systems, social systems have a peculiarly reflexive quality: they are made not only out of people but for people; they both use human beings and are used by them. The leviathan of our common life not only takes; it gives. In the drama of real life, we actors are collectively the audience. Hence a basic question in the case of any society is what benefits the citizens together produce and how these benefits are distributed among them. To answer that question is to study the structure of rewards. Such study complements research on the structure of demands and strengthens greatly our intellectual grasp of the social order at hand. The following paragraphs discuss the three principal rewards sociologists normally distinguish, rewards which correspond roughly to the first three functional needs described in the preceding section.

POWER

Few concepts are so central to sociology as the concept of power. A couple of paragraphs here can hardly define the word adequately, much less review the dozens of articles and books devoted to distinguishing its numerous meanings, types, and bases, and the variety of techniques for using it. But power is best understood initially as the foremost reward a society can give. It is the opportunity to hold a little of the present social order in one's own human hands and decide what to do with it, the opportunity to change in some degree the society itself. Just as the basic achievement of a society is the structure it imposes on human life, so the basic reward it offers is the action of deciding how that structure shall change. To take such action is to exercise power: to choose whether to keep things the same or overhaul them in some way. Power can be thought of as something attached to roles, a paycheck that comes with performing them, a chance to define or redefine the content of the role itself, of other roles, and of events in general. Power is the ability inherent in today's world to make a difference in tomorrow's.

the ability inherent in today's world to make a difference in tomorrow's

Power that is publicly held according to the norms of the prevailing culture, power recognized as legitimate in the social order at hand, is called *authority*. In this respect John McDougald's roles in the various corporations were their own reward. Attending board meetings is work, to be sure: there are reports to read, arguments to make, and strategies to devise. But through his roles on corporate boards of directors John McDougald was publicly and legitimately able to make decisions whose concrete effects would soon be felt by literally millions of other people. Never was he elected to public office, nor was he even an American citizen. Nonetheless, by law in the United States as well as in Canada and elsewhere, the structure of human life in the 1950s, 1960s, and 1970s bore the imprint of this man. Would the new shopping center include a Dominion supermarket? What would be the terms of a consumer loan at Avco Finance or the Bank of Commerce? Would there be layoffs soon at the Massey-Ferguson plant, or would they instead be stepping up production of some new kind of tractor? The answers to these and similar questions could be traced in part to the boardrooms where John McDougald occupied a chair. His authority, moreover, did not exhaust his power. Like all of us and more than most of us, he had the chance to make a difference also in unofficial, nonpublic ways—by taking advantage of his information networks of friends and acquaintances, for example, and by seizing opportunities inherent in his particular constellation of familial, recreational, religious, and other roles.

a person's power is sometimes greater than his or her authority, sometimes less

In one sense all law-abiding adult citizens in contemporary Western societies enjoy equal authority: each may cast one and only one ballot in the voting booth. But the role of voter is virtually the only one governed by a norm of equality with respect to authority in particular or power in general. That is, roles vary widely in the amount of power attached to them. Among economic roles in capitalist societies the key determinant of power is how much investment money or capital a person owns. John McDougald literally bought his powerful roles on corporate boards, holding them by virtue of the stocks he held in the companies. About 90 percent of American or Canadian adults, by contrast, lack the money to buy any significant share of the land, materials, and machinery of their workplaces. They occupy roles in economic production only by selling their labor to corporations. How much power they exercise as employees depends on numerous factors: how "high up" their roles are, how easily they can be replaced on the labor market, how strong the relevant union or professional association is, how hard they work, how much they know, how well they get along with their bosses, how helpful their personal contacts are, and how assiduously they milk their roles for the power inherent in them. Power also comes with roles in voluntary associations—that of bishop, for instance, churchgoer, artist, or patron of the arts. And certainly the roles of parent, grandparent, older sister, or rich uncle give their performers some chance to leave a mark on the next generation. So, too, the roles of teacher and counselor in the institution of education.

In sum, it is impossible to play any role in the structure of demands without deriving from it some modicum of power. Even one whose job is "to shut up and do as you're told" has the opportunity to act to the contrary—otherwise such advice would not have to be screamed in that person's ear. Nonetheless, we know just from our own experience and newspapers that some roles give much more power than other ones. To study such variation systematically and thus to discern the structure of power is an integral part of understanding any society. Researching the structure as culturally prescribed, that is, the structure of authority, is part but not all of this task, since the power actually exercised to accomplish change is more often shrewdly seized than formally bestowed. (Who would you judge has made more difference in the world, businessman McDougald or economist John Kenneth Galbraith, both of whom were born in 1908? The question has no easy answer.) In any case, the structure of power remains one of the best ways of coming to grips with social process in a society, for by knowing the distribution of a society's preeminent reward we can sense the direction of that society's history.

to understand a society's structure of power is to sense the direction of its history

WEALTH

Corresponding to the second function a society must serve in its structure of demands is the second reward it returns to its citizens: the goods and services produced in the economy, all the items that constitute a standard of living, or in a word, wealth. In capitalist societies like our own, economic goods are defined as commodities and distributed mainly in the form of money, that intrinsically worthless but instrumentally necessary means of acquiring things, what Marx unkindly called "the pimp between man's need and the object."[3] Goods and services are attached to roles also in the form of perks, short for perquisites, meaning any extra tangible benefits which accrue to a role performer. But money is the main thing, and it, too, is distributed unequally. Currently in North America, families in the richest fifth of the national population have annual incomes about eight times as large as families in the poorest fifth—a degree of inequality which has changed very little at least since World War II. In most of the less industrialized societies the gap between rich citizens and poor ones is even greater. No society exists where citizens are not sharply divided by the quality of their food, the fineness of their clothes, the size and comfort of their homes, and their overall access to the pleasures of earthly life.

Money can normally be spent in two ways, either for the ownership of productive property (and other means of exercising power) or for the consumption of goods and services (thus the enjoyment of wealth). Hence with money as a common denominator, the structures of power and wealth tend to converge especially at the top. Powerful people tend also to be rich and vice versa. But the convergence is far from complete. The role of U.S. president, for example, though the highest authority in the land is attached to it, yields a salary ($200,000 per year as of 1980) smaller than thousands of corporate executives receive. Further, the ownership of productive property in the United States and in Canada is far more unequally distributed than is spendable income; it is estimated that about three-quarters of all the resources in North America, apart from those owned by governments, are owned by fewer than 20 percent of the continent's population. Or to cite a more specific example, line workers at Massey-Ferguson and other industrial plants may be obliged to follow orders more or less blindly on the job, to behave as cogs in a machine with minimal chance to exercise economic power. But if their unions have been successful, these workers may draw paychecks large enough to support quite a comfortable living after hours. In this and other cases, role performances may be rewarded with spending money actually as a substitute for the reward of power. Similarly, the affluent suburbs around North American cities almost overflow with women who live in luxury as wives of wealthy men, but with little power over either themselves or others, except perhaps some children, servants, and family pets. Examples like these point out the importance of keeping the structures of power and wealth distinct in our sociology, being attentive to points of both convergence and divergence between them.

inequalities in power, income, and property overlap

HONOR

The third kind of reward is honor, the personal good feeling a person can be made to have, the moral approval dispensed among citizens in varying amount. One can imagine almost that the pool of warmhearted cultural sentiment, the sense of collective worth achieved through citizens' work together, is then divvied up among them and distributed in the form of prestige to the roles they play. That the structure of honor coincides at the top with those of power and wealth was a major thesis of Thorstein Veblen (1857–1929), a brilliant rogue of a scholar who was thrown out of Chicago, Stanford, Missouri, and other univerities for irreverence and loose living. In his book *The Theory of the Leisure Class*, Veblen wrote: "The basis on which good repute in any highly organized industrial community ultimately rests is pecuniary strength; and the means of showing pecuniary strength, and so of gaining or retaining a good name, are leisure and a conspicuous consumption of goods."[4] John McDougald is a case in point. His Toronto home had a thirty-car garage, where he kept his collection of Rolls-Royces, Cadillacs, and

Veblen's insight: conspicuous consumption is the basis of good repute

other classic automobiles. He also had his racehorses, Florida villa, and similar items of conspicuous consumption. Hence, it is not surprising that he was honorary president of the Royal Agricultural Winter Fair, that his portrait graced the halls of St. Michael's Hospital in Toronto, that the British royal family did him the honor of staying at his home, or that the likes of Dwight Eisenhower and Francis Cardinal Spellman favored him with their friendship.

Farther down in the structure of honor, where the bulk of people live, it diverges from the structures of power and wealth. In particular, those in religion and the arts who give citizens their sense of collective well-being are often repaid mostly in kind. Great pianists and stage actors are often overwhelmed with applause and flowers, but their bank accounts seldom overflow and their power often extends only to their own performances. Priests are also honored more than they are paid, and the reverse is true for prostitutes. Housewives, rewarded with little money and less power, usually precede their husbands through doorways. And lately in America, a number of prominent citizens jailed for felonies have recouped their loss of honor with royalties from their best-selling exposés. All these examples illustrate the need to keep honor analytically distinct among a society's rewards.

THE RELATION BETWEEN DEMANDS AND REWARDS

Having been informed first of four general functions every society must serve, and then of the rewards corresponding to three of the functions, some readers might now wish in the name of scientific tidiness to read about a fourth compensation for citizens, one which reciprocates the reproductive and educational tasks their society enjoins upon them. But no such fourth reward is commonly conceptualized in sociology and I see no need to invent it here. Its absence may indeed be a useful reminder that in a sense every society takes more than it gives. Notwithstanding cosmetic surgery and all the other magic of medical science, and though the rich do generally live longer than the poor, no society rewards anyone with eternal life. Power, wealth, and honor, or variants of them, exhaust the sack of presents a society can dispense. Anyone offended by the inequitable distribution of these three resources can take comfort from Thomas Gray's Elegy: "The boast of heraldry, the pomp of pow'r,/And all that beauty, all that wealth e'er gave,/Awaits alike the inevitable hour:/The paths of glory lead but to the grave."[5] John McDougald died in 1978. His roles and the rewards attached to them were parceled out to other, younger actors. His principal responsibility, the Argus Corporation, passed into the hands of Conrad Black, 33 years old, fifty times a millionaire, son of a wealthy financier, bachelor, history enthusiast, director of the Canadian Imperial Bank of Commerce, Massey-Ferguson, Carling-O'Keefe, and other firms. Within some number of years, if he performs his roles well, Mr. Black will probably also be befriended by British royalty and U.S. presidents. The harsh fact is that humanity is more real than any human, that the curtain never falls on history, that the show goes on eternally beyond our individual exits. The most anyone can ask of the society at hand is to make a little difference in its future.

Our list of four basic functions but three basic rewards bears a general lesson for good scholarship, a lesson especially relevant in the present context. It is that the spinning of genuinely useful sociological yarns requires an avoidance of excessive scientific tidiness. To be sure, sociology means imposing a coherent, disciplined, orderly structure of words and numbers on the data of experience. But it means also acknowledging the disorder in experience and steadfastly refusing to create analytic schemes tidier than the data themselves. Let me give one famous example. In the *American Sociological Review* in 1945, two earnest practitioners of structural-functional analysis published what became one of the most widely debated articles in U.S. sociology for the next twenty years. Kingsley Davis and Wilbert Moore proposed as a principle that what is called here the structure of demands is symmetrical with the structure of rewards, that roles are compensated with money and prestige in the same degree as they contribute to the satisfaction of a society's functional needs. "Social inequality," they wrote, "is thus an unconsciously evolved device by which societies insure that the most important positions are conscientiously filled by the most qualified persons."[6] By this reasoning each role performer gets what he or she deserves. It was presumably in the national interest that John McDougald be able to afford his thirty-car garage and the cars within it. The million-dollar salaries some presidents of U.S. corporations currently draw are necessary for the survival of American society. By knowing how much reward a person receives, one can tell how important are the demands that person fulfills.

a caution against too much tidiness in social thought

Davis and Moore's proposition is clearly not entirely wrong.[7] Certain kinds of inequality enhance the functioning of certain kinds of social system—as Weber pointed out, paying farmhands according to how much hay they mow is useful for increasing their productivity, provided they have the capitalist spirit. Indeed, one strategy of labor management is to encourage competition among employees, try to compensate each in proportion to his or her contribution, and thus bring the structures of rewards and demands into symmetry. But everyday experience abounds with evidence that such symmetry is seldom achieved even in single organizations, much less in a society as a whole. The biggest gaps in income and prestige derive not from differences in people's jobs, talents, or the scarcity of their skills but just from the accident of birth. Like John McDougald, most millionaires inherited wealth from the start—they did nothing more important to gain this reward than be born to the right parents. Inequality results also from blind luck (not just in lotteries but in the marketplace) and from all kinds of political infighting (think of workers who unionize, strike, and thereby get a raise while doing the same jobs as before). Just reading the newspaper teaches us all that squeaky wheels do often get more grease, and that the performers of some roles are indeed screwed by the system. How much inequality is functional for a society therefore depends on the kind of inequality and the kind of society. It is a matter for specific description rather than general principles. And we should hope that the inequality may nowhere and never be completely functional: there could be no social change if money were not sometimes spent, power exercised, and prestige utilized in ways currently defined as dysfunctional. In sum, it is no less useful to study the structure of rewards than the structure of demands. But to propose that these two structures fit is too much tidiness. No good purpose is served by letting our minds run in symmetrical abstract circles that frustrate rather than aid the cause of knowledge and the movement of history.

the reasons for inequality are multiple

"Status is a person's overall rank in the structure of rewards, taking into account the various roles that person plays and how much power, wealth, and honor is attached to each. It is one's social position, whether high or low, a summary statement of how an individual fares in the apportionment of what his or her society has to give." (Ray Ellis © 1976/Rapho/Photo Researchers, Inc.)

STUDYING THE REWARD STRUCTURE

Partially to discern the direction of a society's history but also just to diagnose the quality of human life here and now, sociologists have long given high priority to research on the structure of rewards. Such research has most commonly begun with conceptualizing for every citizen in the society under study the attribute of *social status,* one of the key terms of the discipline. Status is a person's overall rank in the structure of rewards, taking into account the various roles that person plays and how much power, wealth, and honor is attached to each. It is one's social position, whether high or low, a summary statement of how an individual fares in the apportionment of what his or her society has to give. Needless to say, the measurement of social status (or *SES,* short for socioeconomic status) is difficult. Assessing rank on even a single scale of reward, especially that of power or honor, poses problems enough, but combining possibly incongruous ranks on three distinct scales is still more challenging. Who ranks higher, for instance, a call girl rolling in riches or a penniless social reformer, a low-level executive or the unemployed wife of a top executive, the governor of California or a physician with twice the governor's income, a ski bum supported by an inherited trust or a small-town

status: overall rank in the structure of rewards

undertaker with the same income? Nonetheless, for the sake of depicting and analyzing the reward structure as a whole, sociologists have sought to measure social status as validly as possible.

In most research on the reward structures of the United States, status or SES is measured simply by adding or otherwise combining an individual's "scores" on income, education, occupational prestige, and sometimes the reputability of his or her parentage. Having calculated these combined scores, researchers can then place people into relatively continuous layers or *strata* in the reward structure—strata typically labeled the upper-upper, lower-upper, upper-middle, middle, lower-middle, lower, and lower-lower classes. Accordingly, this kind of research on the reward structure is usually called social *stratification*: the study of how people are arranged in higher and lower strata. Other sociologists, however, especially those who take a Marxian view, criticize the conventional scales as distracting jumbles of disparate indicators which skirt the major issue, namely, power. The key reward, they insist, is the chance to make a difference, a chance that comes mainly from control over productive resources in the society at hand. Hence scholars of this orientation define class more precisely. They are less concerned with income itself than with *source* of income, whether it comes from investing one's own capital (which places an individual in the property-owning class or bourgeoisie) or from selling one's labor for a wage or salary (the mark of membership in the working class or proletariat). There is no need here to discuss in detail these divergent outlooks, social stratification versus class analysis. Chapter Six of this book, which is concerned with the economy, treats the matter further. It is enough to remember here that by any measure some citizens of every society seem to bask in clover while others scratch in the straw of powerlessness, penury, and disrepute. John McDougald is a case in point—sociologists of all stripes would agree that his status and class put him far above nearly all his compatriots.

Most students of the reward structure would agree further that Mr. McDougald belonged to a special group within the upper-upper or bourgeois class, the economic elite. The word *elite* is reserved for those citizens at the top of some institutional sector, people who not only share a category but constitute a group, a network of powerful, wealthy, and reputable friends who mix together at private clubs, share common and distinctive tastes, and often come from similar backgrounds. The single most famous work of sociology in Canada, *The Vertical Mosaic* by John Porter, mentioned in Chapter Two, was a detailed analysis of the economic, political, religious, and other elites of that society, and of the links among them. But sociologists debate how best to conceptualize and analyze also this highest level in the structure of rewards. In a book published in 1975, a young Canadian scholar named Wallace Clement repeated and updated Porter's research.[8] Clement, however, saw so much overlap among the various elites that he was willing to identify them almost as a single group. His analysis implied that a man like John McDougald belonged to Canada's and maybe also the United States' *ruling class*, a conceptualization for which Porter had no use. Indeed on both sides of the border this term continues to have both staunch defenders and steadfast abstainers. But before deciding through reflection and study which concepts to use and which ones to disregard, the first task is just to learn the major ones available.

social stratification versus class analysis

Finally, I should note that not only whole societies but also smaller-scale sociocultural systems can be analyzed to good effect as structures of rewards. Part of understanding a state or province, city or town, is learning what it takes in this microcosm to gain power, wealth, and honor, what the status symbols are and on what basis some citizens qualify for membership in the elite. A complex organization, being purposefully and formally structured, usually spells out publicly its authority structure, pay scale, and honorific distinctions—one can measure even the size of offices, the presence or absence of carpeting, the size of employees' names on business cards, and who must make appointments with whom. But every bureaucracy has also informal structures that sometimes compete with formal ones—think of the poorly paid but long established secretaries who know the ropes more surely and can cut red tape more swiftly than their bosses. In organizations as elsewhere, power does not accrue so much as it is seized. Families, too, can be analyzed by how they dispense power, perks, money, and affection among their members. There is no marriage wherein the relative power of wife and husband, their respective access to enjoyable commodities and their probably unequal regard for each other, cannot be assessed. Every kind of group, in short, rewards its members even as it makes demands on them—though seldom in direct proportion. By surveying one's own rewards from the various groups in which one occupies roles, any reader of this book can get a sense of his or her own status in each one and in all combined—that is, in the society at large. To understand one's status is to know one's position in history.

The Society as Contained by International Structures

This chapter began with a description of the national society as the most independent and sovereign form of human organization in the contemporary world, a kind of group which therefore has first claim to the attention of sociologists. Then the chapter moved to an analysis of a society's insides: first its social and cultural dimensions, then its structural-functional components, and in the section just concluded its manner of apportioning rewards. I have illustrated topics repeatedly with the roles of John McDougald, and perceptive readers probably wondered if this ambitious, active gentleman was not discrediting the idea with which the chapter began. For did he not play roles in both the United States and Canada? And does not this very fact cast doubt upon the independence and sovereignty of these national societies? Should I not rather have chosen for illustrative purposes some all-American role player or a compleat Canadian, someone whose behavior falls totally within a single national boundary? But no, John McDougald was a better choice. This section, the fourth and final part of our overview of the national society, explains why.

INTERNATIONAL CAPITALISM

The description in earlier pages of the United States and other societies as capitalist itself implied that these societies are joined in a larger system, international capitalism. Since the 1960s, the inspection of societies in this broader context has

105

become one of the major pursuits of social scientists throughout the Western world. This outlook has been propagated above all by Fernand Braudel, an historian at the University of Paris, who has traced the international capitalist system's origin to the Mediterranean region in the sixteenth century. Probably the best-known world-system analyst in North America is Immanuel Wallerstein, who left McGill University in 1975 to chair the sociology department at the state university in Binghamton, New York. The system exists because the relevant national governments share, though with varying degrees of enthusiasm, a policy of permitting money and commodities to flow freely across national borders in a market relatively free of intervention by national regimes. This chapter has already described how capitalist societies keep their polities small and give free rein to private profit-seeking in their economies. Thus the Canadian government, for instance, defines tractor production as outside its political domain and relinquishes this task to the Massey-Ferguson Corporation and to similar firms. The international capitalist system comes into being by the application of this same economic orientation across national borders. The U.S. government, for instance, also regards tractors as a fairly apolitical commodity and thus permits even a foreign company like Massey-Ferguson to produce tractors in and for the United States. The guiding premise behind international capitalism is that all societies in the long run will benefit if natural resources, manufactured goods, and anything else that can be priced are allowed to cross borders according to where and how the most profit is to be made, almost as if the borders did not exist.

the multinational corporation: product of acquiescence by capitalist governments

The acquiescence of the various capitalist governments has permitted a special kind of private bureaucracy to arise and flourish, especially since World War II. This is the multinational corporation, a profit-seeking firm with units of supply, planning, production, sales, or maintenance in more than one national society. Massey-Ferguson, for instance, has subsidiaries and sales offices in more than a dozen societies; its annual income from all its enterprises around the globe is roughly the same as the gross national product of some societies themselves, like Bolivia, Paraguay, or Tanzania. From his Toronto office (and West Palm Beach retreat) John McDougald presided over this domain. Massey-Ferguson is not large enough, moreover, to rank even among the hundred largest multinational corporations. Exxon, General Motors, Ford, IBM, ITT, General Electric, Chrysler, United States Steel, Procter and Gamble, Dow Chemical, Goodyear, Eastman Kodak, RCA, Kraft, and Xerox, all U.S.-based multinationals, are much larger. So are Royal Dutch Shell (Netherlands), British Petroleum (Great Britain), Renault (France), Volkswagenwerk (West Germany), Toyota (Japan), Nestle (Switzerland), and scores of other corporations, each of them an empirelike organization spread across many national societies.

To John McDougald it seemed completely natural that a Canadian owner of capital should control in significant measure the working lives of thousands of American employees in Massey-Ferguson or Avco. It seemed right that he should in return be granted a measure of American power, wealth, and honor. "Governments," he said, "should just run the affairs of the country. . . . They shouldn't be trying to kill off the people who are creating the nation's wealth."[9] This is the ideology of international capitalism, an ideology usually voiced and defended also by the governments of the United States, Canada, and similar societies. Nonetheless, U.S. citizens need not be fearful on this account, despite the occasionally

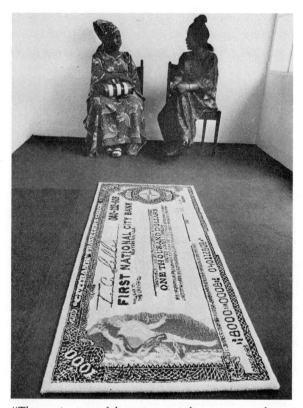

"The acquiescence of the various capitalist governments has permitted a special kind of private bureaucracy to arise and flourish, especially since World War II. This is the multinational corporation, a profit-seeking firm with units of supply, planning, production, sales, or maintenance in more than one national society." The carpet pictured here is in the waiting room of Citibank's branch office in Kinshasa, Zaire. Since its independence in 1960, this former Belgian colony has vacillated between capitalist and socialist forms of economic organization, moving generally toward the latter. Floor coverings of native design may one day replace carpets like this one. (Erich Hartmann/Magnum Photos, Inc.)

frantic press reports that oil-rich Arabs and other foreigners are buying up America. For the United States has made vast contributions to the international capitalist system—natural resources, know-how, management skills, inventiveness—and the system has rewarded the United States generously, at least with power and wealth. One can say that the United States got in on the ground floor of the system, or even better, that it built the foundation. Only a tiny part of the U.S. economy is owned by foreigners like John McDougald, while U.S. firms own a sizable part of natural and productive resources in numerous societies. Besides, the people of the United States enjoy as a group almost as many commodities as any national population.

In the same way, however, that domestic capitalism distributes its rewards unequally across roles, its international variant spreads them differentially across societies. Of the hundred largest industrial corporations in Canada, more than half are majority-owned by foreigners, and almost all of the latter have one or more U.S. directors on their boards. Thousands of commodities produced in Canada are

inequality in the international capitalist system

of American design, and production workers often follow personnel policies decreed by some parent company to the south. This is to say that international capitalism does not reward Canada with a great deal of power over its own future. Canada appears instead like the employee who gets a healthy paycheck in return for submissiveness. In a wider perspective, however, Canada joins the United States, Japan, the societies of Western Europe, South Africa, Australia, and New Zealand in the elite of the international system. Among proletarian societies, those which receive little power, less wealth, and still less honor in relative international terms are South Korea, Taiwan, Singapore, Hong Kong, Paraguay, Chile, Bolivia, and some societies in Africa and Asia that are still worse off.

Important though the international capitalist system is, its existence does not warrant retreat from the emphasis placed in these pages on the national society. The most basic reason is that the system is mainly an economic one and thus is incomplete. No multinational corporation, not even Exxon or IBM, assumes sovereign power over itself. None has soldiers, tanks, and missiles for its own defense. Each exists only with the sufferance and support of those national governments willing to use their resources of violence to defend foreign interests within their borders. But not only does international capitalism lack its own political institution. It also wants for a culture of its own. Workers on General Motors assembly lines do not pledge allegiance to a GM flag. The employees of Eastman Kodak have nothing that even approaches a sense of nationhood. No giant corporation successfully persuades its employees that God loves it more than its competitors. The structures of global capitalism must instead ground themselves in the norms and values of their national environments. GM must argue in Detroit, for instance, that what is good for the company is good for the United States, but in Oshawa, Ontario, it must apply the argument to Canada. And finally no multinational corporation alone can reproduce itself. Training programs begin with adults who have already been raised and educated in the families and schools of their national society. In sum, the evidence suggests that the international capitalist system is rather like poker with strangers: just an economic game. The stakes in it may be high but only fools take it to heart. The main focus of our sociology must be on that sociocultural system where political, economic, religious and cultural, familial and educational functions all are served in a sovereign, integral way. For better or worse, that system in the present day is mainly the national society.

A second reason why the international capitalist system should not be overblown is that national politics intrude upon it in innumerable ways. U.S. corporations are forbidden by law from doing business with societies defined by Washington as enemies. All capitalist governments restrict the international trade of selected commodities by means of tariffs, import quotas, export quotas, embargoes, and their own internal economic policies. Wealthy capitalist governments provide less industrialized societies with various kinds of loans and grants, which often cannot be justified in profit-making terms but only on political or cultural grounds. The international capitalist system is modified also by the special agreements that exist among various factions of its societal members. The European Economic Community (EEC) is probably the most important. Formed in 1958, it comprised ten members in 1980: Belgium, Denmark, France, Greece, West Germany, Ireland,

three weaknesses of international capitalism: first, its narrowly economic character

second, the persistent intrusion of national politics

Italy, Luxembourg, the Netherlands, and the United Kingdom. The EEC represents the coordination under the Brussels government of various policies of member states, thus enabling them to act as a kind of bloc vis-à-vis other capitalist societies. The League of Arab States (created in 1945), the Organization of Petroleum Exporting Countries (founded in 1960), the Organization of American States (founded in 1948), and a host of bilateral agreements exemplify as well how the overall system is tempered by special ties between national governments.

third, the nonparticipation of numerous societies

Third and finally, it bears remembering that international capitalism does not embrace the world. Most nation-states do not open their borders to multinational firms and permit foreigners to seek profit from the labor of their citizens. This does not mean, of course, that noncapitalist societies are uniformly isolationist and self-contained. Under the sometimes coercive leadership of the Soviet Union, the communist societies of Eastern Europe have formed since World War II a highly integrated economic bloc. And also outside the region of the Warsaw pact, socialist societies trade with one another on a variety of terms: China, for instance, with North Korea and Tanzania; the U.S.S.R. with Finland and Cuba; Algeria with East Germany. Substantial commerce also flows between capitalist and socialist societies; the United States' repeated sales of wheat to the Soviet Union are a case in point. But outside the network of international capitalism, trade almost inevitably occurs in an overt and unashamed political context. The simple rules of profit maximization do not apply. It is a matter of one nation-state dealing with another, each being mindful not only of market value but of whatever other factors may be defined as relevant. Roughly two-thirds of the earth's population live in national societies that fall outside the international capitalist system. This alone suggests which of the two kinds of social order should receive the higher priority in sociological research.

THE WORLD AS AN INTEGRAL WHOLE

At the highest and most general level, the world itself since the late 1940s has often been portrayed as a kind of sociocultural system—a system not in the sense of cooperative effort toward common purposes but of a tug of war between capitalist and communist ways of life. Politicians and scholars in the United States and the U.S.S.R. have been most inclined to depict the world in this way, viewing their respective societies as leading protagonists in the two-sided global game. Because powerful actors have defined the game as real, it has had real effects. It gave rise to the space race. It led to the deployment of terminally destructive weaponry. Most important, it induced many small societies to align themselves with one side or the other, capitalist America or communist Russia, to accept military and economic patronage from its chosen leader, and thus to shape its own history in light of the bipolar division of the planet. Each of the two superpowers, moreover, has felt free to enforce loyalty upon the societies within its own bloc. The Soviet Union did this successfully in the case of Hungary in 1956, of Czechoslovakia in 1968, and of Afghanistan in 1979. With similar success the United States suppressed the anticapitalist rebellion in the Dominican Republic in 1965, though later military efforts on the Indochinese peninsula met with failure. One of the cruelties of this most dangerous game is how it has been played out in poor, confused, strife-torn

the game of nations—capitalist versus communist

societies, where the superpowers have armed and financed competing factions in internal wars, thus enabling greater numbers of people to be killed. Angola, Chile, Laos, Vietnam, Cambodia, Ethiopia, Iran, Greece, and Nicaragua are all examples.

It is not hard to guess why Russian and American thinkers have been especially involved in the depiction and analysis of the cold war, as Bernard Baruch labeled the bipolar competition. Thinking about the world in this way has reinforced the hegemony or dominance of these two societies over others in their respective blocs. Even as I write these lines the American media report nostalgia for the 1950s and early 1960s, the Kennedy era, the heyday of American supremacy, when the dollar was strong and gas was cheap. Other societies have been involved in the cold war, too, but seldom with such deadly seriousness. Canada, while clearly a capitalist society, never felt obliged to sever its ties with the Castro government in Cuba. And it has never been strong enough to challenge the Russians militarily, nor rich enough to race them to the moon. It therefore took them on in hockey. The seven-game series in 1972 remains to this day the single major event in Canadian sports history. The president of Brock University said afterwards, "Team Canada probably did more to create a Canadian identity by defeating Russia by four games to three than did ten years of Canada Council fellowships."[10]

the lesson of the nonaligned societies

In 1961, at the height of the cold war, Josip Tito of Yugoslavia, Gamal Abdel Nasser of Egypt, and Jawaharlal Nehru of India led in the creation of the movement of nonaligned nations. The continuing existence of this movement, which had nearly 100 members in 1980, bears an important lesson for sociology. Most nation-states in the late twentieth century would like to define the world as a collection of autonomous and independent societies, linked to one another by cultural ties, criss-crossing agreements, international trade, and the United Nations, but not locked into a global game in which Mother Russia and Uncle Sam are the two team captains. Poland, Yugoslavia, Albania, and China are among the communist societies which have successfully asserted their independence of Soviet domination. Within international capitalism, Japan and the European Economic Community have grown wealthy enough to challenge the preeminent position of the United States. The new societies in Africa and Asia, those which emerged from empires only in the last few decades, prefer almost anything to the status of pawn of a superpower. Thus not only accuracy in scholarship but respect for human aspirations counsel caution in the portrayal of transnational social structures. Those structures are real. So are such global religious structures as the Roman Catholic Church, about which later chapters of this book have much to say. But no

More than ever in history, we humans live in an integrated world. One of France's contributions to such integration is the metric system of measurement, the use of which increases steadily all around the globe. The United States government set up procedures for switching to metric in 1975. Among other reflections of world order are the calculation of time by the Gregorian calendar and the 24-hour clock, the spread of belief in democratic politics, and the common use of technological innovations like electricity, radios, televisions, telephones, and automobiles. One of the pressing questions of our time is how far the trend toward social and cultural standardization should be allowed to proceed. Far enough to prevent major wars, certainly. Opinions differ as to how much farther.

form of human organization is so important or central to contemporary social life as the national society.

Concluding Words

No one could be more aware than I of the concepts skipped in the preceding review. Sociologists have invented so many technical words and given so many technical meanings to ordinary words that if even a tenth had been mentioned here the result would be not a chapter but a glossary. And few readers would ever have finished reading it. My purpose therefore has been to discuss just fifty or sixty axial concepts, the few words which, as Humpty Dumpty said, deserve to be paid extra for the illuminating work they do. For the important thing is not to memorize a list of textbook definitions but to learn to use words for making sense of one's own experience. If this chapter has succeeded in its aim, readers will have taken time out repeatedly from reading it to reflect on their own lives, to lift a word from these pages and see if it fits what they themselves have seen and heard, and thus to deepen their personal understandings here and now of the shape of human life in our time. That is why this chapter has focused not on the ghostly abstraction of "society" but on the concrete national societies within which we humans today have no choice but to arrange our lives. This chapter has offered four reasonably coherent outlooks, four sets of concepts by which not just professional sociologists but any citizen can climb intellectually on top of the society confronting him or her. And can discern not only the present order of life but also, through inspection of the reward structure, the direction of contemporary history. Now admittedly the conceptual scheme given here is general. As Chapter One made clear, sociology is a generalizing discipline. But the scheme is not so general that it cannot be applied to any individual's own life. If John McDougald has driven this point home, he deserves a posthumous word of thanks.

a test of whether this chapter has succeeded in its goals

Among concepts neglected in this discussion one category deserves a brief word. It is a category of labels for all those subgroups of a national population in which people are bound together on the basis of sex, language, race, sexual preference, religious tradition, health condition, age, ethnicity, or some similar personal quality. Such groups are seldom intentionally designed or tightly organized. They are often called *subcultures*, or sometimes *minority groups*. No analysis of American society could possibly be complete without reference to the racial division between blacks and whites or to such ethnic minorities as Puerto Ricans, Mexican-Americans, or WASPs. Similarly, the French-English split in Canada is of fundamental importance for understanding that society, and so are the Ukrainian, Jamaican, East Indian, Italian, Portuguese, British, Inuit, and other ethnic subcultures. And whatever the society under study, a sociologist would surely be interested in the status within it of women, men, children, youth, the aged, homosexuals, young marrieds, the blind, diabetics, slum dwellers, school dropouts, short people, adherents of offbeat religions, and so on. These groups are real, too, as anyone in one or more of them—that is all of us—can attest. They are "additional factors" which every society and every attempt to understand it must take into account. Survey researchers often refer to them as background characteristics and use them as intervening or control variables in their analyses.

subcultures and minorities in the context of national societies

But if subcultures are so important, why are they mentioned only now at this chapter's tail end? Because they are most usefully studied and understood in the context of the laws, customs, institutions, bureaucracies, voluntary associations, power structure, and the other systemic attributes of societies reviewed in the body of this chapter. The black-white cleavage in the United States, for example, is meaningful mainly because it is institutionalized in law and custom (think of desegregation policies and affirmative-action legislation), linked to the stratification system (blacks are concentrated in the lower strata), and embodied still in separate schools, colleges, churches, neighborhoods, and social clubs. Or similarly, the French-English division in Canada is real mainly because each language group enjoys legal rights; or more precisely, the threat of separation springs not from French Canadians (an ethnic subculture) but from the voters of Quebec (a predominantly francophone political subdivision). By the same token, Protestantism (a religious subculture) would have little meaning in either the United States or Canada except that it is embodied in Protestant *churches* and other voluntary associations. The same point applies to any religious or ethnic subculture, each of which merits study mainly through the medium of its concrete, organized expression.[11] So also for other subcultures. Homosexuals became a socially significant minority only when they publicized their identity and formed gay-rights organizations. The aged came to constitute a meaningful social category mainly when compulsory retirement laws, urban migration, homes for the aged, and retirement villages removed people over 65 from the social and economic mainstream. In sum, the intention here has not at all been to neglect subcultures but to put first things first: to sketch the overall framework of social life within which subcultures can best be analyzed.

Sociologists in decades past often showed a preference for studying subcultures, gangs, friendship groups, cliques, factions, and other informal groups to the neglect of the public, institutional order. Indeed, they sometimes portrayed the whole discipline as an effort to uncover a hidden order of roles and statuses, norms and values, an order thought more helpful for explaining events than the more obvious order evident in government, constitutions, public policy, and formal organizations. Their orientation is apparent in the concept of *folkways*, a classic term coined by William Sumner and defined as the little customs and habits widespread in a population.[12] Sumner regarded folkways as the underlying determinant of what happens and how people behave; he gave scant attention to the actions of legislatures and other policy makers. A similar orientation appears in a classic definition of sociology's subject matter given by Robert MacIver (1882–1970) while a professor at Columbia University: "A system distinct from the state; a system revealing internal principles of coherence and change of a different order from the prescriptive rules of morality . . ."[13] Many sociologists have cherished concepts like *subculture* and *ethnic group*, while showing disinterest in terms like *state, corporation, law,* and *bureaucracy*. Sometimes they have regarded the latter as epiphenomenal, obviously visible but one step removed from the "real" order of things.

It was Howard Odum (1884–1954), the founder of sociology at the University of North Carolina, who insisted that in the course of history folkways have become less important than *stateways*, the formal norms of public authority.[14] For understanding the America of his day, Odum stressed the importance of social planning,

folkways have yielded to stateways and custom to law

the intentional, conscious creation of sociocultural systems and subsystems by the various levels of government. I believe that the direction in which Odum pointed the discipline is the correct one. We live, moreover, decades after Odum wrote. Written rules and regulations have multiplied in the meanwhile, custom has yielded steadily to law, and humans have become more able to make their common life a conscious creation. If we are to understand the contemporary world and even more the direction in which it moves, we need to conceptualize the society not as a system apart from the state but as one over which the state exercises sovereign power. The state may choose, as capitalist ones do, to unleash private corporations from both inside and outside national boundaries, but such a choice is itself an exercise of sovereignty. The formal structure of what we are together must be viewed not as a reflection of something else but as a reality of its own, a reality that we deny or discount at our peril.

overview of the remaining chapters

The substance of this book, its main course if it were a meal, is a series of five chapters which consider in turn the major institutions: polity, economy, religion, family, and education. Each of these chapters offers a conceptual scheme relevant to its title and a statement of enduring regularities in social life surrounding the particular institution. Other topics, from shifts in the class structure to women's liberation and the energy crisis, are addressed in the framework of these chapters. They are, I believe, intrinsically more interesting than the necessary but necessarily general overview just concluded. From among the trends and countertrends, themes and variations on themes, evident in the contemporary world, I try to let the data guide my choice of the ones most worth talking about. But before commencing the analysis of particular institutions, there is still one more preliminary topic—in some respects the most appealing one of all, namely the human person. To it I turn now, hoping that it may enrich my readers without satisfying them.

For Reflection

society	contradictions	family
nation	structure of demands	education
resources of violence	structural functionalism	private schools
empire	functional needs	dysfunctional
little community	institution	complex organization
sociocultural system	subsystem	social process
social structure and culture	polity	structure of rewards
role	political subdivision	power
norm	unitary versus federal structure	investment money
law	public bureaucracy	wealth
custom	infrastructure	structures of power and wealth
language	economy	honor
value	commodity	conspicuous consumption
universalism	GNP	structures of demand and reward
ideology	corporation	scientific tidiness
deviance	religion	status, SES
criminal	voluntary association	class, stratum

social stratification	multinational corporation	movement of nonaligned nations
bourgeoisie, proletariat	incomplete social systems	subculture
elite	EEC	minority group
ruling class	cold war	folkways
international capitalist system	superpower	stateways

For Making Connections

<table>
<tr>
<td>With personal experience:</td>
<td>Systematically compare your personal life to the lives of your parents, grandparents, and great-grandparents. To what extent have succeeding generations in your family been progressively less enclosed by little communities and more integrated into national social patterns?

Even dyads, two-person groups, can usefully be analyzed as sociocultural systems. What roles, norms, values, and linguistic phrases constitute your relationship with your closest friend?

What are the main contradictions you yourself perceive between your society's public culture and the way life actually goes on? How do you handle these contradictions?

How much power do you get from the roles you play? What do you do with the power you have? Could you seize more power than you do?</td>
</tr>
<tr>
<td>With Chapter One:</td>
<td>How might an overview of social life given by a political scientist differ from the one presented in this chapter? How about an overview offered by an economist?

In what ways has this chapter fulfilled the promise of First Sociology, as explained initially? In what ways has this chapter failed?

Think of some nonindustrialized society in Asia, Africa, or South America that you know something about, even if only from reading a magazine article or watching a television documentary. How would the present chapter be different if it had been written in the context of that society?</td>
</tr>
<tr>
<td>With Chapter Two:</td>
<td>The first way of putting words together in sociology is to state that one is the same as, is included within, or includes another. List ten or twenty concepts that have been put together in this way in the present chapter.

Try formulating an important hypothesis about the structure of rewards in your society as a whole or in your local community. How could you go about testing your hypothesis systematically?

Make a survey of all the economic goods in whatever room you are reading this. How many of these goods were produced by people in independent economic roles, by public bureaucracies, by local corporations, and by multinational corporations? And laying aside the question of who made each item, which ones did you purchase or obtain from each of these same four sources? What conclusions can you draw from this survey of data available to you? Would making the same survey in a very rich or very poor person's room yield the same conclusions?</td>
</tr>
</table>

114

For Further Reading

The foundation for the sociological analysis of any contemporary society is detailed factual knowledge of its way of life. My chief recommendation here is therefore the newspapers, legislation, novels, biographies, census reports, and political and social commentaries which regularly appear in any national context. For making sense of such raw information, consult the following more analytic treatments:

1 Talcott Parsons, *The System of Modern Societies*, and *Societies: Evolutionary and Comparative Perspectives*, Prentice-Hall, Englewood Cliffs, N.J., 1966. These two little books are not Parsons' major ones but they are more intelligible than most and convey an outline of their author's conceptual scheme.
2 Robert K. Merton, *Social Theory and Social Structure*, Free Press, New York, 1957. A classic work of general structural-functional theory by Parsons' most eminent student, now professor emeritus at Columbia University.
3 Arthur J. Vidich and Joseph Bensman, *Small Town in Mass Society*, Doubleday, New York, 1960. A study of the process by which a small American community is incorporated into the national mainstream. A similar but more modest study in Canada is a book which I coauthored with Peter Sinclair, *Village in Crisis*, Holt, Rinehart & Winston, Toronto, 1974.
4 Robert Redfield, *The Little Community*, and *Peasant Society and Culture*, Univ. of Chicago, Chicago, 1960. A lucid theoretical and conceptual frame for researching small-scale societies.
5 Clyde Kluckhohn, *Mirror for Man*, Fawcett, New York, 1964. The kingpin of the Harvard Values Study summarizes his perspective. One of the best research articles to come from the Harvard project is Evon Z. Vogt and Thomas O'Dea, "A Comparative Study of the Role Values in Social Action in Two Southwestern Communities," *American Sociological Review* **18**:645–54 (1953).
6 Karl Mannheim, *Ideology and Utopia*, Harcourt Brace Jovanovich, New York, 1936. To my mind the best single source for the study of ideology. For a different perspective see Edward Shils' article on the topic in the *International Encyclopedia of the Social Sciences*, Macmillan, New York, 1968.
7 James E. Curtis, "Voluntary Associations Joining: a Cross-National Comparative Note," *American Sociological Review* **36**:872–880 (1971). A little article that nicely documents the greater importance of voluntary associations to social organization in some societies than in others. Also relevant is the compilation *Social Stratification: Canada*, 2d ed., James E. Curtis and W. G. Scott (eds.), Prentice-Hall, Toronto, 1979; many of the articles they include, Raymond Breton's not least, are relevant to the study of the reward structure of numerous societies.
8 John Porter, *The Vertical Mosaic*, Univ. of Toronto Press, Toronto, 1965. Splendid example of holistic analysis at the societal level, winner of the American Sociological Association's MacIver Award.
9 Amitai Etzioni, *The Active Society*, Free Press, New York, 1968. A big book offering general perspectives for the analysis and planning of societies, written by an exceptionally creative American sociologist.
10 Daniel Chirot, *Social Change in the Twentieth Century*, Harcourt Brace Jovanovich, New York, 1977. A lively and well-written textbook on the international capitalist system. See also Immanuel Wallerstein, "The Rise and Future Demise of the World Capitalist System: Concepts for Comparative Analysis," *Comparative Studies in Society and History* **16**:387–415 (1974).

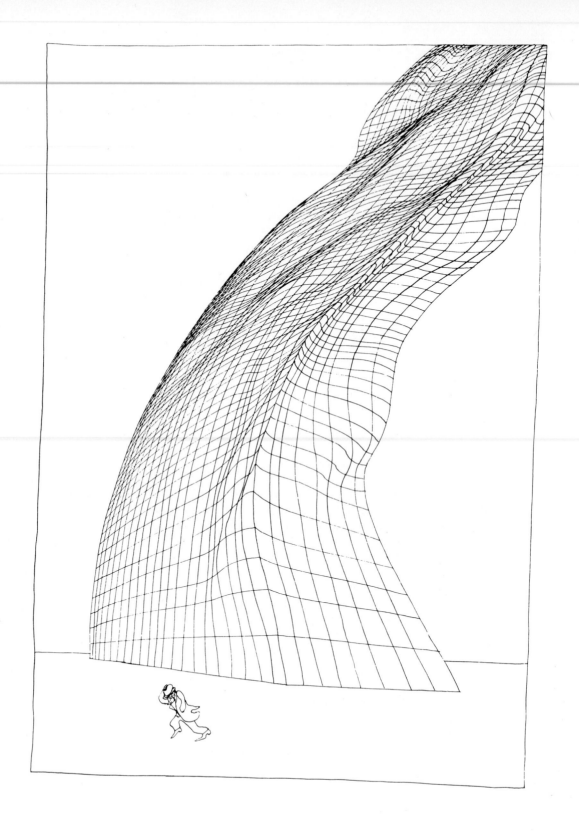

Person

Chapter Four

*I ask whether people create their
society or it creates
them and what this question's
answer implies for social research.*

No matter how deeply engrossed in research on societies and other sociocultural systems, no sociologist ever escapes the question of just what the human person is. Strictly defined, the discipline gets no closer to people than the scattered bits of them called roles, which are assembled into groups. But the study of groups inevitably sets the mind to wondering about the mysterious beings out of whom groups are made. One cannot gaze long upon a floral display in a summer's boulevard or park, some splendid symmetrical mélange of petunias, begonias, mums, marigolds, and plants with unremembered names, without shifting focus in a blink to the flowers one by one, the individual blooms which at first were lost in the arrangement as a whole. So in the study of human life. One cannot do sociology without lapsing now and then into social psychology, the study of the person as involved in groups. For there can be no role without a person to fill it, nor any idea without someone to believe in it. Social psychology is the topic of this chapter. The goal here is to outline some major sociological perspectives on the ablest of the earth's inhabitants.

social psychology: the study of the person as involved in groups

The Dialectics of the Person

first, a story of calm predictability

This inquiry might best begin with two characters from fiction, two exemplars of humanity chiseled out by novelists in their own quest for understanding of the species. The first is Emmanuel Percival, a physician by training, but by occupation an officer of the British Secret Service in London—this as given by Graham Greene

117

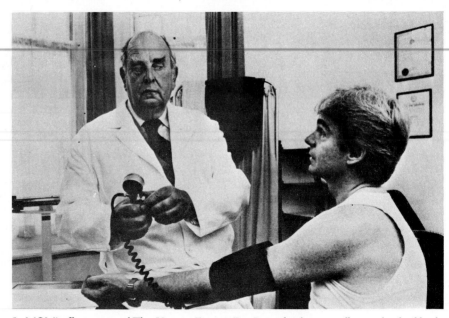

In MGM's film version of The Human Factor, *Dr. Percival informs a colleague that his blood pressure leaves much to be desired. "In the meanwhile I enjoy the game we're all playing. Enjoy. Only enjoy." From the MGM release* The Human Factor © *1979 Metro-Goldwyn-Mayer, Inc.*

in his 1978 spy story, *The Human Factor.* If you have not yet read the novel, do not fear. These few paragraphs will not spoil the plot for you. But I must tell you that it opens on a scene where Dr. Percival learns from his boss that someone in their office is apparently a double agent, a traitor to his country and a servant of Russian communism. Security leaks have been discovered and traced to their unit. The problem is to find out who is to blame, which of their colleagues is a liegeman of the other side. The further problem, once the culprit's identity is ascertained, is how to remove him without either generating publicity or giving him the chance to flee abroad. Dr. Percival solves both problems with consummate skill while his boss is away in Washington. By a little trickery he settles on the man to blame. Then he simply ends the man's life by poisoning his whiskey. The death is attributed to an ailing liver, and Her Majesty's Government is spared the embarrassment of public scandal. Dr. Percival sits bored but quiet through his deceased colleague's funeral.

The afternoon of that same day finds Dr. Percival lunching with his boss at the Travellers Club—an occasion for Graham Greene to present the core of the doctor's character. The two gentlemen regret that smoked trout is temporarily off the menu. Emmanuel reluctantly accepts smoked salmon as a substitute. They ponder the wine list. Emmanuel prefers claret. But his superior, beneath it all, is shaken and upset. Not just by the thought of having had a Russian spy in his employ, or even by the manner of the man's dispatch. What baffles the boss is Emmanuel's dispassion, his composure after doing what most would call murder. "Don't look shocked, John," Dr. Percival tells him. "You think I'm a cynic, but I just don't want to waste a lot of time. The side that wins will be able to build the better hospitals, and give more to cancer research—when all this atomic nonsense is abandoned. In the meanwhile I enjoy the game we're all playing. Enjoy. Only enjoy. I don't pretend to be an enthusiast for God or Marx. Beware of people who believe. They aren't reliable players. All the same one grows to like a good player on the other side of the board—it increases the fun."

"Even if he's a traitor?"

"Oh, traitor—that's an old-fashioned word, John. The player is as important as the game. I wouldn't enjoy the game with a bad player across the table."[1]

So much for Dr. Percival. The question is whether Graham Greene does not expose with bruising candor through this man some primary attributes of the human species. Above all, perhaps, responsiveness to role expectations, compliance with the claims of social structure, willingness to behave as situations require. For when you think of it, Dr. Percival was only doing his job. His behavior was just what the situation called for. He performed not only capably but with such initiative and finality that even his employer was shocked. Maybe what distinguishes Emmanuel from most people is just his courage to admit that people are only players in games, that they act only as their roles require them to—provided, of course, that they are up to the task. If we would be expert social psychologists, should we not take Emmanuel's advice and beware of people who believe? Enthusiasm for God, Marx, and other causes may be just a subterfuge for hiding a poor performance, concealing squeamishness or disguising self-interest, even to a point where people deceive themselves. Perhaps the way to commence a sociological theory of the person is by laying aside romantic wishful thinking and acknowledging that human beings, though sometimes pretentious, are nonetheless quite predictable. Then to those who disagree we can apply a quote from Max Weber's lecture on science as a vocation: "To the person who cannot bear the fate of the times like a man, one must say: may he rather return silently, without the usual publicity build-up of renegades, but simply and plainly. The arms of the old churches are opened widely and compassionately for him."[2]

now, a story of restless energy

But the likes of Dr. Percival are not the only possible inspiration of a sociological theory of the person. For an alternative we might recall a second character from fiction: Brian O'Connal, the hero of W. O. Mitchell's classic novel, *Who Has Seen the Wind*, first published in 1947. Brian in that tale did nothing so urbane as snuffing a spy or lunching at a club. A typical episode in his rustic life was to empty a sofa pillow of its feathers, which then might be fashioned into wings for flying around Saskatchewan. Or to crawl into bed on Christmas night with one hand clenched around the runner of a new tube skate. Brian for a while was on speaking terms with the Almighty, whom he described as wearing rubber boots and riding a vacuum cleaner, and whom he called by the more familiar name "R. W.," as in "Amen, R. W." He also let himself be drawn in wordless friendship to the Young Ben, a wild thing whom Mrs. Abercrombie said belonged in an institution of correction.

Brian O'Connal was just a little boy growing up on a prairie where "every grass-blade and leaf and flower seemed to be breathing, or perhaps, whispering—something to him—something for him."[3] He could find himself awestruck even by

From the film production of Who Has Seen the Wind. Brian O'Connal was just a little boy growing up on a prairie where "every grass-blade and leaf and flower seemed to be breathing, or perhaps, whispering— something to him— something for him." (Courtesy of Souris River Films)

drops of Sunday-morning dew on the leaves of a spirea bush. "Within him something was opening, releasing shyly as the petals of a flower open, with such gradualness that he was hardly aware of it. But it was happening: an alchemy imperceptible as the morning wind, a growing elation of such fleeting delicacy and poignancy that he dared not turn his mind to it for fear that he might spoil it, that it might be carried away as lightly as one strand of spider web on a sigh of the wind." But Brian's life was not unreal. For his mother called him to breakfast and "the feeling broke; it broke as a bubble breaks. Once it had been there; and then, with a blink, it broke." W. O. Mitchell's tale is of a boy with a universe inside of him, with a tingling awareness of himself and death, and in the end an ambition to be a "dirt doctor" for farmers like his Uncle Sean. Brian wrote a composition, "Why People Should Raise Cows in Southern Saskatchewan." "Let me have a look at the goddam thing," said Sean.

The question now is whether there is not in Brian O'Connal, as Mitchell painted him in words, some inherent, universal quality of the human race. Not least an energy, an unconquerable will to express oneself, an urge to realize in experience some still intangible reality seething in a person's thoughts and feelings. For nowhere in the novel is Brian observed just to be doing his job. The expectations attached to his childhood roles did not include calling God "R. W." or maintaining that the Supreme Being transports himself by vacuum cleaner. No teacher or parent mandated Brian's attraction to the strangest lad at school. Far from playing by the rules, Brian filched the paring knife used to disembowel the feather pillow. What makes the story so encouraging is that Brian did the *unexpected*, *illogical* new things, which Mitchell traces not to the claims of social structure but to the effervescence of the boy himself. Therefore should we not let Dr. Percival sink into oblivion and build a social psychology upon the model offered by this little boy? Perhaps our first premise ought to be that people are essentially creative beings, each unique and unpredictable, each with a natural claim to the adjective *special*. Such a starting point would probably delight not only W. O. Mitchell but most other creative writers, Graham Greene included. The "human factor" of Greene's book was not, after all, Emmanuel Percival. The cynical doctor was but a foil for the novel's hero, a man whose qualities were not unlike those of Brian O'Connal.

social psychology requires a dialectical starting point

But no adequate social psychology can rest upon the principle of either-or. Neither Emmanuel Percival nor Brian O'Connal can alone inspire much understanding of the human person. These characters have been presented here to indicate not alternative starting points for a theory of humankind but a single point of departure: the dialectical nature of each of us. Perhaps this word *dialectical* requires a word of explanation. Coming from the ancient Greek, it combines the word for *between* with the word for *discourse*. The image it evokes is of conversation traveling back and forth between two people. Hence as a term in sociology, *dialectical* refers to movement to and fro between two opposing ideas or principles. In the present context, the point is that human nature can be understood only by means of two divergent propositions. The first, the one which Percival asserted both in word and deed, is that people behave simply according to the roles they play in groups. The second, the one young Brian acted out, is that people have minds of their own and behave accordingly. Or to make the point differently, the human person has two dimensions, the one programmed and predictable, the other one free and full of surprise. The first is labeled in this chapter the *dimension of humility*, since it debases our race, strips it of dignity, and portrays it as almost beastly. The second is called here the *dimension of pride*, since it flatters the human species and attributes to it an almost divine creative power.

LOPSIDED VERSUS DIALECTICAL THEORIES

Every theory or research report in social psychology can be inspected for how much emphasis it gives to one or the other of these two dimensions. Some scholarship, however, so much denies or neglects one or the other dimension that its portrayal of the human person is grossly unbalanced, lopsided, distorted, and therefore inadequate. Perhaps the best contemporary example is the work of Harvard psychologist B. F. Skinner and his numerous disciples. The focus of their interest has been *operant conditioning*, the process by which people learn to act on their milieux in a way that obtains for them rewards. Skinner and his colleagues have pursued their work, moreover, by concentrating simply on human behavior, without regard for thoughts or feelings (hence their approach is sometimes called *behaviorism*). Thus they have portrayed people, pigeons, and various animals in quite a common way: as products of learning, creatures of external stimuli who do

the imbalance in Skinner's behaviorism

whatever yields rewards and avoid whatever does not. For decades Skinner and his students experimented with different reinforcement schedules (that is, different rates and patterns of dispensing rewards) and with varying mixes of rewards and punishments. Sometimes they used people for research, sometimes pigeons, sometimes rats. And they achieved clearly memorable and useful results. They showed that creatures generally learn better and faster through rewards for performing well than through punishments for performing poorly. And further that once a creature connects a certain behavior to a certain reward, a schedule of random intermittent reinforcement (occasional rewards given in no fixed pattern) will elicit more of that behavior than a pattern of invariant reward each time the behavior is performed. An example of this principle is how frequently students (and professors, too) check their mailboxes when mail delivery occurs at varied and irregular hours, hoping that "maybe *this* time the letter will be there."

Such principles as these are obviously worth knowing but they are rooted in a one-sided conception of the person as beast, a humble product of external forces, a creature of habit equally as much as a pigeon. Hence a social psychology built of such principles alone necessarily cheapens and demeans its subject matter. This is precisely the kind of social psychology Skinner built. He went unwisely further than suggesting how behavior is affected by its consequences; he insisted that behavior is *determined* by its consequences. Not being content to portray people partially as instruments of forces beyond their control, Skinner claimed people are nothing more than that. His 1971 book, entitled *Beyond Freedom and Dignity*, was a put-down of the human race, a snickering negation of that proud dimension of ourselves that sets us apart from and above mere animals. Derision of so noble a race should not be heard among its students. It should not be voiced even against animals. John Kunkel, himself a leading behavioral sociologist, has quite correctly diagnosed the Skinnerian error: "Behavioral philosophy, finally, attempts to describe and reconstruct all of man and much of society on the basis of operant principles, instead of viewing these principles as describing only one aspect of individuals."[4]

imbalance also on the side of human spontaneity

While behavioral and social scientists remain fixated on the humble side of the human race, other authors overstate the free, unfettered aspect of that race. Scholars of the latter kind often work apart from academe in an intellectual underground and publish outside the college divisions of the leading houses. Literary anarchists are one example, a loose chain of scholars from Pierre Joseph Proudhon (1809–1865) and Peter Kropotkin (1842–1921) to their present-day biographer, George Woodcock, whose engaging writings have continued and enlivened this tradition.[5] The anarchists' confidence in the spontaneous human will is unmitigated. In their view, if only all corrupting and inhibiting structures of authority were abolished, people could live up to their own essential goodness. The existentialist movement in philosophy, especially as represented by Albert Camus (1913–1960) and Jean-Paul Satre (1905–1980), represent in the judgment of most sociologists another kind of disregard for the inherent createdness, the mundane predictability that we humans cannot escape. During the late 1960s in America, numerous gurus of the hippie generation also propounded social psychologies neglectful of the pliant, passive, conditioned aspect of our being. In *The Greening of America* Charles Reich proposed "Consciousness III," a state of being in which "the individual is free to build his own philosophy and values, his own life-style, and his own culture from a new beginning."[6] The trouble is that our individual and collective past permits us no new beginnings, that we never can be free to be ourselves. This humbling fact marks anarchic, existentialist, and other utopian views of the human person as no more adequate than Skinner's behaviorism.

A social psychology worthy of its subject matter must rest instead on recognition of the twofold character of every woman or man, who on the one hand passively submits to outside expectations and on the other actively defines what those expectations shall be. If we would understand ourselves, we must appraise each other in the way folksinger Gordon Lightfoot wrote that he saw his fellow man: "as a creature of infinite grace, bound by natural law to create, yet controlled by his own creations."[7] In a variety of different ways the best social psychologists have

Freud, Weber, Simmel, Maslow: examples of two-sided thinking

taken this dialectical view. The Austrian psychiatrist Sigmund Freud (1856–1939) deserves applause on this account, however much he may be faulted for his inattention to the sociocultural systems wherein individuals play roles. For the Freudian superego clearly describes that humbler dimension of the person, the one bound by a set of rules or a conscience received from parents and other people. Contrariwise, the id is but a label for that chaos of energy propelling people to act independent of the superego's constraints. It is not one or the other but superego and id conjoined that result in the ego, the acting self.

Among other examples of integral, two-sided social psychology might be recalled the work of the aforementioned Max Weber, who carefully analyzed the rational, predictable, bureaucratic orientation to life but juxtaposed against it the charismatic orientation, "which knows only inner determination and inner restraint."[8] Charisma was Weber's id, his dimension of pride, and he mourned what he thought was its demise in the course of Western history, its surrender to the force of calculated social order.[9] Weber's compatriot in German sociology, Georg Simmel, even more forcefully set forth the logically contradictory facets of the unity of the person. Or in quite a different but still dialectical vein, the late Abraham Maslow of Brandeis University repeatedly contrasted the existential, subjective, personal, private aspect of individuals with their logical, objective, impersonal, aspect—not in order to discount one aspect or the other but to recognize both in his psychology of becoming and being. Concordia University sociologist Anton Zijderveld has grounded his writings in the *Homo duplex* theorem, which posits a double nature of humankind, at once creative and created. The two dimensions of the person are handled skillfully as well in Edward Tiryakian's first book, *Sociologism and Existentialism*, published in 1962. Tiryakian there tries to reconcile the supreme predictability in human life (sociologism) championed by Emile Durkheim with the mystery of life celebrated by such existentialist philosophers as Søren Kierkegaard, Martin Heidegger, and Sartre.

There is neither space nor need in the present context to review all the variations on this basic dialectical theme which the best students of our humanity offer in their work. Only one more such scholar I feel obliged to mention here: George Herbert Mead (1863–1931), a popular professor at Chicago who fathered a

Mead and symbolic interactionism

movement in American sociology which Mead's foremost disciple, Herbert Blumer, was later to call *symbolic interactionsim*. The importance of Mead's work was that it challenged then-prevalent depictions of the person as nothing more than a follower of instincts, a humble creature of external pressures. Mead argued by contrast that the person has two sides, a *me* and an *I*. The first he understood to

IN OTHER WORDS

Martin Buber, "The Reality of 'Between' "*

Like every serious social psychologist, Martin Buber (1878–1965) sought to reconcile the two sides of the person, dimensions he identified as individualistic (proud, assertive) and collectivistic (humble, dominated). The human reality is neither of these alone, he argued, but the dynamic, reciprocal relations humans form with one another, the sphere of "between." The paragraphs below conclude a lecture Buber gave in 1938 at Hebrew University, where he later served as first chairman of the department of sociology.

As life erroneously supposes that it has to choose between individualism and collectivism, so thought erroneously supposes that it has to choose between an individualistic anthropology and a collectivist sociology. The genuine third alternative, when it is found, will point the way here, too.

The fundamental fact of human existence is neither the individual as such nor the aggregate as such. Each considered by itself is a mighty abstraction. The individual is a fact of existence in so far as he steps into a living relation with other individuals. The aggregate is a fact of existence in so far as it is built up of living units of relation. The fundamental fact of human existence is man with man. What is peculiarly characteristic of the human world is above all that something takes place between one being and another the like of which can be found nowhere in nature. Language is only a sign and a means for it, all achievement of the spirit has been incited by it. Man is made man by it; but on its way it does not merely unfold, it also decays and withers away. It is rooted in one being turning to another as another, as this particular being, in order to communicate with it in a sphere which is common to them but which reaches out beyond the special sphere of each. I call this sphere, which is established with the existence of man as man but which is conceptually still uncomprehended, the sphere of "between." Though being realized in very different degrees, it is a primal category of human reality. This is where the genuine third alternative must begin. . . .

In a real conversation (that is, not one whose individual parts have been preconcerted, but one which is completely spontaneous, in which each speaks directly to his partner and calls forth his unpredictable reply), a real lesson (that is, neither a routine repetition nor a lesson whose findings the teacher knows before he starts, but one which develops in mutual surprises), a real embrace

*From M. Buber, *Between Man and Man*, Beacon, Boston, 1955, pp. 202–5. Reprinted by permission of the Macmillan Publishing Co., Inc., and of Routledge & Kegan Paul Ltd. First published in 1947.

and not one of mere habit, a real duel and not a mere game—in all these what is essential does not take place in each of the participants or in a neutral world which includes the two and all other things; but it takes place between them in the most precise sense, as it were in a dimension which is accessible only to them both. Something happens to me—that is a fact which can be exactly distributed between the world and the soul, between an "outer" event and an "inner" impression. But if I and another come up against one another, "happen" to one another (to use a forcible expression which can, however, scarcely be paraphrased), the sum does not exactly divide, there is a remainder, somewhere, where the souls end and the world has not yet begun, and this remainder is what is essential. . . .

This reality provides the starting point for the philosophical science of man; and from this point an advance may be made on the one hand to a transformed understanding of the person and on the other to a transformed understanding of community. The central subject of this science is neither the individual nor the collective but man with man. That essence of man which is special to him can be directly known only in a living relation. The gorilla, too, is an individual, a termitary, too, is a collective, but *I* and *Thou* exist only in our world, because man exists, and the *I*, moreover, exists only through the relation to the *Thou*. The philosophical science of man, which includes anthropology and sociology, must take as its starting point the consideration of this subject, "man with man." If you consider the individual by himself, then you see of man just as much as you see of the moon; only man with man provides a full image. If you consider the aggregate by itself, then you see of man just as much as we see of the Milky Way; only man with man is a completely outlined form. Consider man with man, and you see human life, dynamic, twofold, the giver and the receiver, he who does and he who endures, the attacking force and the defending force, the nature which investigates and the nature which supplies information, the request begged and granted—and always both together, completing one another in mutual contribution, together showing forth man. Now you can turn to the individual and you recognize him as man according to the possibility of relation which he shows; you can turn to the aggregate and you recognize it as man according to the fullness of relation which it shows. We may come nearer the answer to the question what man is when we come to see him as the eternal meeting of the One with the Other.

be the objective, external phase, "the attitudes of others which one assumes as affecting his own conduct" or "a definite organization of the community there in our own attitudes."[10] Mead used the example of a baseball player who has fielded a ball. In the instant in which the ball is in hand, the player knows what the team and crowd expect, to whom the ball should be thrown and how. In the flash of a moment, all the norms of the game of baseball bear down upon a person, a *me*, who has a role to play.

In that same moment, however, what the player will actually do remains uncertain: perhaps overthrow first base or make some other error, perhaps live up to expectations, perhaps exceed them by making a spectacular double play. For the self is not just a *me* but also an *I*, an active, free being who takes the initiative and *does* something. "It is because of the I that we say we are never fully aware of what we are, that we surprise ourselves by our own action."[11] For Mead, the self "is essentially a social process going on with these two distinguishable phases. If it did not have these two phases, there could not be conscious responsibility and there would be nothing novel in experience."[12]

THE DIALECTIC AND THE DATA

Social psychology does not end with the conceptualization of the person in terms of the dimensions of humility and pride or some similar dialectical formulation. This is only a promising starting point. What remains is to analyze within this conceptual frame the attitudes people voice and the behavior they demonstrate, to operationalize the two dimensions in the concrete evidence of everyday experience. Researchers of the human person must examine exactly what people do, how much they do by rote and how much freely, by what techniques they are humbled and by what means they rise above external constraints. Work like this requires social psychologists to ground themselves in the data of particular societies at particular points in time. For only in the most general sense is human nature constant across geography and history. Theories cannot remain at a universal level. The process of human identity is realized only in the context of real societies and the groups and organizations within them. The content of conformity varies from one social order to another. So do the methods by which it is enforced. So also the actions that constitute creativity and the opportunities to do them. The crucial question anywhere and anytime is precisely how people are made to behave by the institutions surrounding them, or, conversely, how in the midst of severe constraints they still manage to assert themselves.

The two following sections of this chapter, focused respectively on the dimensions of humility and pride, sketch an answer to this question in the context of the United States and the Western world in general during this last quarter of the twentieth century. But in preface to those sections I should note two common *mis*applications of the basic dialectic of the person to the data of human experience, mistaken ways of operationalizing our twofold character in concrete terms. The first is the "noble-savage hypothesis," the idea that in the long haul of history people have sacrificed their freedom on the altar of civilization, that they have become more and more like mindless cogs in a machine, *me*'s instead of *I*'s. Rousseau became famous for this hypothesis. He began the first chapter of his

the noble-savage hypothesis: history dehumanizes

Paul Gaugin's Day of the God, *a Tahitian image. "Neither the pill nor penicillin was available." (Courtesy of the Art Institute of Chicago)*

masterwork of 1762, *The Social Contract*, with a line that has since been quoted often: "Man was born free, and everywhere he is in chains."[13] The nostalgia Rousseau voiced echoes among the disenchanted even now but it was popular also at that time. And just seven years after Rousseau's book appeared, Captain James Cook dropped anchor off Tahiti in the South Pacific, bringing to European light what came to be considered the last vestige of ancient unchained freedom. Some 40,000 people inhabited the island then, wore jasmine and hibiscus in their hair, and worked but seldom, since the fertile tropics abounded with yams, bananas, breadfruits, coconuts, and wildlife. Cook thought it an idyllic, truly human life. Herman Melville and Robert Louis Stevenson later celebrated it in print, and Paul Gauguin on canvas.

What the eyes of foreigners mostly overlooked was that Tahitian society in its own way subdued and brutalized its citizens even more than did England, the United States, or France. Human sacrifice, intertribal warfare, the strangling of newborn infants of the priestly class, and rigidly unequal structures of power, wealth, and honor marked the organization of island life. Captain Cook may not have noticed, but the girls who bedded down with his sailors were mostly servants and serfs. Pregnancy meant marriage in Tahiti, marriage meant fidelity, and neither the pill nor penicillin was available. In sum, Tahiti was not at all a primeval paradise where people flourished in the freedom to be themselves.[14] Indeed, history gives up no evidence anywhere of savages more able than we to express their nobler side. Perhaps the reason we humans sometimes wax nostalgic is only that we imagine all the great things we would do if, knowing what we know and feeling as we do, we could act in and on the simpler social structures of the past. How creative and liberated we would be! But such imaginings are too partial. If we want to project ourselves into the past it should be into not only the roles but also the mentality of our ancestors: mostly illiterate peasants who never traveled farther than a few days' journey walking, whose heads reeled under the weight of ineffectual superstitions, and who firmly expected hell and an earthly beating if they departed from tradition. And then we should guess just how many surprises we would give to our compatriots. The sobering fact is that never in the data of history have human beings been more able to realize their magnificent nature than we are today. We should not pine for nonexistent Edens in our collective past.

A second misapplication of the dialectic of the person is to identify the early years of the life cycle with the dimension of pride, and adulthood with that of humility. This may be called the "child-of-nature hypothesis." It portrays boys and girls as balanced human beings who, like wild and spirited young mules, are broken by professional trainers and harnessed to burdensome roles. By this hypothesis Graham Greene's Dr. Percival is W. O. Mitchell's Brian O'Connal plus thirty years in a corrupting world. Humanity is something a child outgrows. An implication sometimes drawn (as in North America in the late 1960s) is that children should be spared the cruelty of constraint as long as possible and permitted to express themselves in an open, unstructured environment of self-expression. But neither this implication nor the hypothesis itself sits well with empirical evidence. The fact is that for all their beauty and simplicity children are fundamentally incomplete adults. The creative energy they display seldom results in anything of public worth. Brian O'Connal's plan to shape feathers into wings was after all a failure, like most creative childish schemes. Children, let the truth be said, neither perform adequately in conventional adult roles nor successfully act back upon such roles in an innovative way. Hence the main thing any and every child must do is grow up: learn how to behave as a competent and creative adult as quickly and smoothly as biology permits, aided in this process by the loving discipline of parents, teachers, and other adults who are seriously concerned for the future of our human race. The dialectic of the person applies to children but only in an imperfect way: both conformity and creativity are skills they must learn.

In summary, both the noble-savage and child-of-nature hypotheses are inadequate. Neither history nor biography necessarily represents the dwindling of those qualities about ourselves that make us proud. The living of a human life consists, whatever the era and whatever one's personal age, in mastering the roles to which one is assigned and then rising above them with a little novelty. The first of these tasks bespeaks humility, submissiveness to the status quo, docility in the face of the objective, external world, a readiness to learn. The second implies pride, confidence in one's own unique worth, the boldness to leave one's imprint on the earth, a willingness to teach. The self of each of us is a dialectic, a process back and forth between these two dimensions: a superego and an id, rationality and charisma, *me* and *I*, a humbled creature of the society outside and a proud creator of surprise.

the child-of-nature hypothesis: humanity is something a child outgrows

here as there and then as now, a human life consists in mastering roles and rising above them

The Dimension of Humility

Sociology by definition is mainly a humbling discipline. The reason is that our focus on societies, groups, and organizations requires us to assume that people more or less conform to the expectations attached to the roles they play. One cannot analyze Mexico, for instance, without taking for granted that Mexicans by and large obey the laws of their governments, observe national customs, work faithfully in their economic roles, and in general abide by the norms of their society. And one can make a study of Massey-Ferguson or some other corporation only because the employees generally follow company policy. The study of any sociocultural system presupposes its domination of the people within it. Any group that cannot control its members in their roles ceases to be a group. Sociologists sometimes offend their students and listeners by seeming to deny that people can do otherwise than conform. Sociological explanations seem harsh and one-sided to those of a more existential frame of mind. But so be it. For only by realizing the extent of their domination can people begin to liberate themselves.

child socialization: the process of being shaped into a competent adult

Thousands of social psychologists have made the prime focus of their research the first and most basic process by which every society dominates its citizens. It is child *socialization*, the action of transforming an infant expression of universal human nature into an adult role player for a particular sociocultural system. Notwithstanding parents' protestations to the contrary, one baby is fairly much like any other; in birth we humans partake of a commonality, a unity that is repeated only in death. In between these two moments we mostly grow apart, as each submits to the socialization process in a specific social context. For in order to extend itself through time every society must overpower its children, impose its own order on the movement of their bodies and minds. No society ever achieves anything quite so splendid as this, the transmission of its social structure and culture from one generation to the next, the socializing of impressionable children to the roles and norms, the actions and ideas, of adults. Both the content of this process and the techniques by which it is accomplished vary widely across societies and groups within them. The following pages successively summarize in these two respects the major emphases of contemporary Western societies.

CHILD SOCIALIZATION: CONTENT

The cognitive or intellectual content of socialization depends mainly on what kind of tools a society uses for putting the earth into the service of humanity. Children everywhere must learn the skills necessary to operate and make the utensils, instruments, or machines with which adults are equipped in their productive economic roles. What is remarkable about advanced industrial societies in this regard are the complexity and variety of the tools and the consequent abstractness of the requisite skills. There is simply more to learn—more technical words, more scientific theories, more mathematical formulas—than in nonindustrial societies. One need only compare a scythe to a combine, a surrey to a jet aircraft, a windmill to a nuclear generating plant, or the doctor's bag of yesteryear to today's

If the arrow was propelled so far that neither man nor boy could see it land, then no longer were they man and boy, but man and man. The sculpture was done by Harmon Atkins MacNeill in 1889. (The Metropolitan Museum of Art, Rogers Fund, 1919)

four hallmarks of cognitive learning in industrial societies

pharmaceutical cornucopia. Because of the kind of tools in use, child socialization in any industrial society bears four inevitable hallmarks. First, universal literacy comes to be taken for granted as a necessity for the maintenance of the social order: few productive roles can be found in a technologically complex society for adults who cannot read and write. Second, a high proportion of youth must gain proficiency in mathematical and scientific reasoning: most key positions require some kind of engineering skills, including an ability to manage other people in a calculated, goal-oriented way. Third, the socialization process becomes increasingly varied, as young people split into training groups or scholastic streams according to their occupational destination in an intricate division of labor; the pattern of peasant societies, where nearly all children of the same sex are taught a common body of skills, steadily disappears. And fourth, mental ability gains in priority over motor skills and manual dexterity; with the spread of electricity and other nonhuman energy sources, fitness for a job is measured mainly in intellectual terms and physical fitness becomes mostly a matter of general health and recreation.

The content of socialization is not, however, merely cognitive. Despite the bewildering number of books in libraries and courses in curricula, the most problematic aspect of what children even today must be taught is not cognitive but emotive, not intellectual but moral, not of the brain but of the heart. The successful performance of adult roles requires more than technical knowledge. It demands also the recognition and acceptance of the laws, customs, values, and ideology that underlie the structure of the relevant society. Children must learn their society's distinction not only of truth from falsity but of goodness from evil. They must be led to affirm the cultural and political order within which their

the moral content of
socialization in the
Western world

economic know-how will one day be put to use. Thus have students of socialization asked in their research what distinctive kind of emotive, moral, and political orientation the United States and similar societies inculcate in their young.

The empirical answers to this question fill many books and are not easily condensed into a few paragraphs. But if these studies must be summarized, an American neologism perhaps does it best. The word is *go-getter*, meaning an alert, energetic, enterprising, resourceful person who seizes opportunities and gets what he or she is after. There are other values to be sure: honesty, respect, kindness, politeness, patriotism, generosity. Goodness everywhere is multifaceted. Moral socialization varies, moreover, across the societies of the Western world and across classes and ethnic groups within them. But in all of them, and especially in the American middle class, the child who is a "real go-getter" has the making of adult success. A major body of research evidence in support of this point concerns what Harvard's David McClelland and others have labeled *achievement motivation*.[15] By this they mean a psychological need to succeed, to perform well against high standards, to excel in the attainment of goals even in the face of obstacles and risks. Achievement motivation has been operationalized in numerous ways, including the analysis of what children say when asked in experiments to make up stories about pictures shown to them. McClelland and his associates have found that American children, much more than their age-mates in nonindustrial societies, conjure up tales of people applying themselves assiduously to tasks, overcoming problems, pursuing goals, seeming to *need* to achieve. In a similar vein, Stanford sociologist Alex Inkeles has found through survey research that people in Western industrial societies score relatively high in "individual modernity," a concept that includes a sense of human efficacy in the face of nature, the idea that through science and calculated effort people can achieve their goals.[16] Scholars do not agree how best to label or measure this basic and distinctive value that Western societies instill in their children, and this is hardly the place to resolve such disputes. But the central conclusions of most of their research seem awfully close to what plainspoken parents and teachers mean when they call a child a go-getter and then smile approvingly.

The moral content of socialization in the mainstream of Western societies bears an even more distinctive attribute: that exactly what children are supposed to go and get is left relatively undefined. They are not asked to give their resourcefulness and energy unselfishly to some collective national plan or to accept a preselected status in the emerging socioeconomic order. Parents, teachers, and others offer guidance, to be sure, but the burden of deciding the object of achievement falls increasingly on the individual child inching toward adulthood. At the legal age of maturity, now eighteen years in most jurisdictions, the individual becomes morally free to reside, work, study, marry, enter into contracts, and form associations wherever and however he or she pleases within the broad constraints of law. Children are therefore expected even from an early age to be surveying the existing order of things, formulating occupational and career goals, and letting these private, even secret ambitions guide the choices and decisions they make. In other words, children are taught to be self-centered, to look out for Number One, to seize advantageous opportunities quickly as they arise. The market economy in which the child will work and live is premised on self-interest. Only by learning this general moral posture can the child one day accumulate wealth and be said by

learning the self-interest
required in a market
economy

This young American appears well-socialized to the go-getter ideal. Competitive sports like baseball, arranged in a way that lets individuals star, are an important socializing technique. In societies less keen on individual achievement children play games of a different kind. Pygmy boys and girls in Africa, for instance, make a game of climbing a tall but pliant tree. Six or more go up at once to the very top, their combined weight bending it steadily within jumping distance of the ground. Then all at once they leap off and laugh—especially if one of them fails to cooperate and soars back skyward. (© Sylvia Johnson 1980/Woodfin Camp & Assoc.)

admirers to have "done quite well." This value is actually forced upon the child. In a system that rewards self-interested effort, the effect of thinking in collective, altruistic terms is to fall behind and fail. Thus are children also taught to be competitive, to enjoy winning even when this implies another's loss, even to define success as one person outdoing another. In sum, children in the Western world are not taught just to be go-getters. They are made to understand that no matter what they choose to go and get, others have probably chosen it as well, and the important thing is to get there first.

Some of the most telling evidence on this point comes from experimental research by Millard Madsen, a psychologist at UCLA.[17] Since the 1960s he has been inviting children to play the Marble Pull Game, a contraption he devised for studying cooperative and competitive behavior. Two children play it at a time, seated at opposite ends of a rectangular table. There is a hole at the edge of the table with a cup beneath in front of each child. And each child holds a string attached to a little frame around a marble in the middle of the table. As the experiment is typically staged, Madsen first shows the children how, when the frame is pulled over the hole at either of the two opposite edges of the table, the marble falls through the hole into the cup. He then explains that he will put ten marbles one by one into the frame, that in each instance they may then pull the frame across the table, and that each child will get to keep however many marbles fall into his or her individual cup. What the children discover as they begin to play is that this game has a hitch. When they compete for a marble, pulling against one another as in a tug of war, the frame comes apart, the marble rolls off to the side, and both players lose. Only through some kind of cooperative strategy can any marbles at all be won. If they take turns, for instance, each letting the other win successive rounds of the game, no marbles are lost and both players in the end win equally. The purpose of Madsen's research is therefore to know what kind of children are relatively more and less successful in a game that requires cooperation.

achievement through competition is the American way

Two of his findings are especially noteworthy. First, mainstream white American children perform progressively worse with age; pairs of 4-year-old players won more marbles than children three to seven years older. Second, the more children have been influenced by urban-industrial Western culture, the more likely they are to fail; children from a rural Mexican village did better than their urban, middle-class compatriots; a similar pattern was found in Israel; and white middle-class American children scored at or near the bottom.

Madsen's research documents the fact that children in the United States and similar societies are socialized to an ethic not just of achievement but of individual achievement through competition with other people. This, the evidence suggests, is the single cardinal virtue that best distinguishes our children from their age-mates in non-Western societies. It is the quality of nourishing an active sense of *self*—and this is a word almost embarrassing for its prevalence in our English language. Our children are taught self-confidence, self-discipline, self-reliance, self-respect, self-sufficiency, and self-control. They learn that it is good to be a self-starter and a self-made person, to be self-educated, self-employed, self-willed, self-directed, and self-supporting. They should become so sure of themselves that they need not be self-conscious. And they should take such good care of themselves that they never fall prey to self-contempt, self-hatred, self-despair, or other self-defeating ills. Each should develop a strong self-concept. But despite the urgings of philosophers like Ayn Rand, we stop short of urging selfishness itself upon our children. For already we have organized our societies near the brink of narcissistic chaos. The harsh, uncaring, dog-eat-dog character of urban-industrial life could easily get out of hand. We therefore seek to temper our stress on competitive achievement in the socialization process with a qualifying emphasis on fair play, kindness, charity, and compassion for those who have met defeat (think of the high school awards for good sportsmanship or the title of Miss Congeniality in beauty contests). By instilling a sense of the commonweal drawn from our traditional past, we hope to moderate sufficiently the self-interested aggressiveness at the core of what we teach our young.

the content of socialization varies by class and other social categories

The few preceding paragraphs have barely scratched the surface of the cultural path down which youth in contemporary Western societies are led. Much more could be said of the cognitive content of socialization: the linguistic, mathematical, and engineering skills which children learn in their varying courses of study. Much more could also be reviewed of moral education; only its most distinctive qualities in the capitalist, urban-industrial societies have been suggested here. In particular I should note the variation by social class. The sketch offered here applies mainly to the middle strata. The children of the rich can often afford a more relaxed upbringing; destined to inherit wealth, they are not so much obliged to achieve it through pragmatic study and competitive effort. Similarly, impoverished parents who have themselves achieved little seldom instill much self-confidence in their children; the latter are more likely to be underachievers, school dropouts, and in later life dispirited laborers. The values on competence in technical knowledge and competitive achievement are but general qualities of Western societies. And there is wide variation across these societies, too, and across the subdivisions and subcultures within them. Each such grouping communicates to its young its own sense of patriotism or pride, its own folklore, customs, beliefs, and history—so deeply even that decades often are required for an American to feel at home in Canada, a New Yorker in California, or a Protestant husband at the family reunions of his Catholic wife. Each reader of this book can reflect upon the particular conspiracy of social forces that bequeathed an identity on him or her. I recommend such reflection especially to those inclined to say, "I am a self-made man," or "I am my own woman." For these readers are the ones on whom the content of socialization in the Western world has been most successfully impressed.

CHILD SOCIALIZATION: TECHNIQUES

The other aspect of child development to be considered here is just how the transmission of a culture from one generation to the next occurs. Social psychologists interested in socialization study not only what is taught to children but who does the teaching and what kind of techniques the teachers use. Later chapters on the family and education review the various agents of socialization in the contemporary Western world and discuss the diminishing power of parents over their children's upbringing and the growing authority of professional educators, media personalities, and adolescent peer groups. Here it will suffice to list five general techniques of child socialization, all of which apply no matter who the socializing agent is. The first and most basic is to control the child's environment, the structure of daily life as the child experiences it. If some mythical society removed its young from the governing presence of adults and permitted them in some barbaric sense to "grow up on their own," that society would terminate its own history. Its social and cultural order would forthwith disappear. Children learn only from people who make a difference in what happens to them. They mature in the image of those on whom they depend for food, warmth, and protection from the dangers lurking in the darkness of earthly experience. Hence the fundamental means of transforming a child into a conforming, competent adult is to gain control of everyday events in the child's life, to be there when the child is hungry, hurt, frightened, or otherwise in need, to decide what kind of books, toys, playmates, TV programs, clothing, and schedule of life should constitute the child's milieu. Adults pass on their culture to the younger generation by taking command of children's energy, taking advantage of their vulnerability, and setting the conditions under which their wants are satisfied. The maintenance of such control is a prerequisite for everything else.

A second technical principle is to establish in the child's experience a firm and consistent connection between how the child behaves and how completely the child's desires are fulfilled. This means rewarding the child for conforming to the norms of the society at hand and withholding rewards when the child acts to the

five techniques: first, controlling the child's environment

second, dispensing rewards only for conformity

contrary. This is a basic principle of learning theory, as documented by social scientists like B. F. Skinner; it deserves to be taken seriously, along with such related principles as the one about intermittent reinforcement mentioned earlier. Such research findings by and large vindicate the common sense of millions of parents in thousands of societies, both ancient and contemporary. Anyone who can remember being sent to bed without dinner, grounded for a week, treated to a movie, or applauded at a school performance—all in consequence of particular misdeeds or good behaviors—is well acquainted with the principle of selective reward. So essential is it to the child-rearing process that neglecting it almost guarantees failure. Parents and teachers, for example, who through misguided love reward and reinforce children no matter what they do, both handicap these young citizens and compromise their society's future. Indiscriminate indulgence prevents children from learning the difference between what is true and false, good and bad, in their society. Even worse is the predicament of children who are rewarded and punished inconsistently, who are given conflicting messages from one day to the next about how they should behave, or who encounter one set of rules at school, another at home, and still another in their peer group. Such children grow up profoundly confused, unsure of who they are or ought to be. One of the greatest gifts any child can receive is clear and consistent reinforcement of the behavior that qualifies as normal and good in the society at hand. Such a child can approach the challenges of adult life with confidence.

third, drawing the child into loving primary groups

A third technical principle is to rely insofar as possible on the reward of love, expressing it with cuddles, kisses, and words of praise for good behavior, withholding it in response to misconduct. For children want more than food, drink, and the material necessities of life. Like other human beings, they crave the security of belonging to a group, the safety of participation in a common effort. Hence they first must be assured that the community of people in their milieu has room for them, wants them, loves them, and places in them its hope for the future. But increasingly as time goes on children must learn that their acceptance in this community is not unconditional, that they must abide by the rules or risk rejection and exclusion. This is the meaning of such timeworn socializing tactics as a parent telling a child to leave the dinner table, a teacher standing a pupil in the corner facing the wall, or schoolmates informing an errant friend, "We won't play with you anymore." In this way the people in the child's milieu become not just impersonal dispensers of material rewards and punishments but a *primary group,* to use the term coined by Charles Cooley, one of the first generation of American sociologists and an early student of socialization. According to Cooley, this kind of primary, intimate, face-to-face entanglement of the child with other people results in "a certain fusion of individualities in a common whole, so that one's very self, for many purposes at least, is the common life and purpose of the group.[18] In Western societies the family is the first primary group for most children, though gradually it gives way to the child's collection of friends, the peer group. Through these groups the child gains what Cooley called a "looking-glass self," an identity that reflects the judgment of those on whom the child depends for acceptance and love. Or to make the same point differently, conditional participation in a primary group enables the child to *internalize* its norms and values, become so immersed in it that to violate its rules, even secretly, causes remorse and guilt. Only to the extent that a child can muster such feelings is the socialization process having its effect.

Scouting has provided millions of North American youth with their first important primary groups outside the home—intimate, face-to-face entanglements in the lives of other children, personal involvements that foster in each child a "looking-glass self."

fourth, offering appropriate models to the child

The fourth technique in this brief review is to provide the child with models of the kind of adult he or she should become, especially models similar in age to the child. However rich a child's imagination, it is not the major source of the novel and varied behaviors which appear from day to day, beckoning for selective reinforcement. Most of them the child has simply picked up from watching other people and observing how others gain social approval. Albert Bandura of Stanford University and the late Richard Walters (1918–1967) of the University of Waterloo achieved academic fame in the 1960s for their repeated and diverse documentation of the influence of models on what children do.[19] These psychologists were able, for instance, to induce normal, well-adjusted children to perform aggressive and hurtful acts, just by letting them view as if by accident another person behaving in this way, or even by showing them film portrayals of people engaged in violence. But if aggressiveness is learned in part by imitation, so also is gentleness. And so, too, all the other qualities which children might be taught. Like apprentices in smithies, mills, and other workshops years ago, children spend much of their time watching, following the actions of others with their eyes, and absorbing what they see into their own identities. Adults guide the future of their children and of their society by deciding which other people their children shall have opportunity to peer upon. For the company children keep lingers in their own behavior into adult life.

fifth, encouraging the child to play at adult roles

Fifth and finally, adults socialize children by monitoring their play activities and providing them with the necessary props. For child's play is never pointless; it is rehearsal for adult roles. That is why little girls in Western societies often find dolls inside birthday packages while little boys almost never do. Similarly, American department stores stock dozens of monopoly boards for Christmas, but this is a game few Russian children know exists. Or could anyone imagine Ecuadorian youngsters playing cowboys and Indians? Parents sometimes account for their children's toys and games in terms of their children's preferences: "It's what Angelica wanted." But an understanding of play requires going one step farther back in the sequence of events. Angelica wanted what she was taught to want by her parents, friends, teachers, or some other relevant person in her milieu (a "significant other," in the language of social psychologists). However much children might seem to have minds of their own, their minds are mainly a gift from adult upbringers, the ones who influence the way children rehearse for later life.

Formulated in general terms, the five techniques of socialization outlined here can be discerned in the child-rearing practices of all societies, classes, and ethnic groups. Specific applications vary, however, depending on precisely which ideas, skills, and attitudes are to be inculcated. Modern industrial societies, for example, inject progressively larger doses of uncertainty into their children's environment, but a kind of uncertainty that young minds and hands can resolve through creative effort. Such societies are noteworthy for their jigsaw-puzzle portrayal of life to children—as a problem to be enjoyed in the act of solving it. They nourish the value of achievement in their young by placing them in a milieu of answerable challenges and overcomable obstacles. More specifically, Western capitalist societies pit children against one another in little-league sports, spelling bees, examinations graded "on the curve," and similar competitions. Children are rarely permitted to win rewards except at the expense of other children; thus are their games a rehearsal for the adult economy. And the primary groups in which Western children are encouraged to invest themselves are groups which welcome and praise the member who "stands on her own feet," "holds his own," "takes care of himself," and "keeps up her end of things." Children in our societies must learn love at a distance, lest they be smothered by it and rendered incapable of negotiating their way as individuals through the harsh realities of the market economy. They are given baseball, football, and hockey stars as heroes, people whose team spirit never seems to interfere with individual success. All these, of course, are general statements applicable to the middle more than to the upper or lower strata, to anglophone Protestant majorities more than to immigrant Catholic minorities, and to boys more than to girls. There is variation, too, across households and individual children within them. Thus does it behoove each of us to reflect upon the particular techniques of socialization our respective parents, teachers, peers, and other upbringers used on us. Such reflection illuminates how well each of us fits into the structure of mainstream national life and how successfully each of us plays by its rules.

the Western way: a milieu of answerable challenges and surmountable obstacles

ADULT LEARNING

This chapter's initial statement of the dialectics of the person warned against facile identification of youth with iridescent pride and of age with leaden humility. Discussion of the what and how of child socialization has pressed the same point further: socially even more than biologically children are made, they do not make themselves. Now must be added a still more humbling proposition: adults are also for the most part creatures of their milieu. Not only the milieu of their childhood, which no one ever quite outgrows, but also the here-and-now social structures which compound the constraints of the past. We humans are humbled at all stages of the life cycle. External forces bend and shape us not only as children but also as adults. Our plasticity does not harden magically with age. Indeed, among the prime values every society teaches its children is lifelong allegiance, loyalty, fidelity, and obedience to its own structure of authority, its own way of deciding who should have power over whom. A grown-up in a sense is only a successfully socialized child, one who knows how to do and does as he or she is told, who seldom falls down on a job or fails to adapt to the changing demands of established power holders. In our contemporary Western societies this means conforming to laws as

human plasticity does not harden magically with age

they are passed by national and subdivision governments, following doctors' orders and other professional advice, responding to hard-sell advertising, absorbing the networks' definition of the news, and above all acquiescing to the dictates of employers who have bought our labor for a wage or salary. The form and content of adult malleability in the present day could occupy a score of books. Here I want only to recall some evidence of just how malleable we are.

In the early 1960s a Yale professor named Stanley Milgram undertook a series of experiments which have been widely discussed ever since for their documentation of the extent to which average, normal adults fall prey to the pressures of authority.[20] His first step was to advertise for people willing to spend a few hours taking part in a scientific research project. By offering standard rates of pay he attracted more than enough participants. It was arranged that subjects should arrive two at a time for what was explained to them as an experiment about the effect of punishment on memory. Randomly, so it appeared, one subject was assigned the role of memorizing a list of word pairs, so that from hearing the first word of any pair he would be able to recall the second word. Then this subject was strapped into a kind of electric chair; it would give him a shock each time he failed to remember the second word of a given pair. The other subject was told to sit in an adjacent room, there to operate the device for administering the shocks. Its dial showed a range of from 15 to 450 volts; at the upper end, bold lettering announced, "Danger: Severe Shock." In the course of having the experiment explained to them, both subjects were given a sample shock at low voltage, lest they doubt the reality of the punishment to be administered.

As in many psychological experiments, there was more to this one than met the eye. The subject assigned to memorize the word pairs was in fact Milgram's confederate, a collaborator in the experiment, and he would purposely fail to remember. Moreover, he would not actually receive the severe shocks indicated on the dial but would only pretend to suffer pain. The purpose of the research was not, after all, to learn the effects of punishment on memory, but to see how much pain the unknowing subject would inflict on a fellow human being, when assigned to a pain-inflicting role in the little sociocultural system of a psychologist's laboratory. The experimental results were a demonstration of human docility. More than half the subjects conformed to role expectations. When the confederate failed to recall word after word and the experimenter directed an increase in voltage, the majority of subjects complied even to the maximum indicated on the dial. Nearly half laughed nervously during the experiment and many talked back to Milgram ("Aw, no. You mean I've got to keep going up with the scale? I'm not going to kill that man!"), even while they physically conformed to expectations and administered the shocks. In variations on the experiment, Milgram directed the confederate to cry out in pain, to sit within view of the subject, even to try to escape, so that the subject would be asked to help hold the forgetful victim physically in place. Even then Milgram found high percentages of subjects willing to perform the brutal task assigned to them.

Whenever I have lectured on these experiments in university classes, students without fail have responded with all kinds of objections. One leans back skeptically and allows that surely the subjects must have guessed what was going on. A second asks for more methodological details, venturing that maybe Americans are "like

Puppets worshipping their puppeteer in a Munich cafe, 1933. At its worst, life on earth is sheer humility, the abnegation of responsibility and power to forces outside oneself. (United Press International)

that" but surely not Canadians, maybe men but surely not women, perhaps ill-educated laborers but never members of the higher classes. A third student has an ethical complaint, that Milgram should be ashamed for having tricked people into revealing how weak they are, how easily they can be led. Never do my students seem so attentive to the fine points of research techniques and ethics as when they are faced with the results of these experiments. But their technical objections are quite unfounded. Milgram discounted from his results any subjects who became suspicious or caught on to the experimental ruse. And dozens of other studies on both women and men in various societies and classes have confirmed the basic point of Milgram's project. With my students' ethical objections I am inclined to sympathize, though I believe that queasiness in this respect springs from the same source as skepticism on technical grounds. The source is simply our common unwillingness to admit how much adults are creatures of the sociocultural systems within which we play roles. The seamier side of the dialectic of the person offends us. It is more flattering to our race to imagine that every man and woman has at root the courage of a single flower in a fire-parched land.

> the lesson of Milgram's research: adults are mostly creatures of the roles they play

Milgram and others through their laboratory research have sought to measure the burden of social order that weighs on human beings. Their answer is unmistakable: as heavy as a millstone. Most of the things most people do most of the time are traceable to authority overriding them, to cultural and structural characteristics of the established groups bearing down on them. Only rarely is this cause for horror or alarm. Indeed, all of us routinely *demand* that others confine themselves to their assigned roles. "Mind your own business." "Act your age." "This is your job, so do it." "If you don't perform your duty, I'll see you in court." "If you're my friend (mother, colleague, neighbor, or other role incumbent), why don't you act like it?" By making comments like these and by dispensing our various rewards appropriately we keep one another in the line marked out by our particular customs and laws. Hence we should not be surprised when people burdened by vicious authority and crushed by a fiendish social order behave in vicious and fiendish ways. The German people in the Nazi era by and large just minded their own business, did their jobs, performed their duty, stayed out of court, and acted like good citizens. So did the roughly 15 million soldiers and 35 million civilians who were killed in World War II. So, too, the millions of other soldiers who killed them. War is the real-life counterpart of Milgram's laboratory, for as Jefferson correctly observed, "Breaking men to military discipline, is breaking their spirits to principles of passive obedience."[21]

Nonetheless, normally peaceable adults are not easily induced to play military roles that imply killing and a substantial risk of being killed. Governments therefore establish special agencies of resocialization for new recruits—boot camps, military academies, and suchlike—where the uninitiated can be taught the special norms and values required in the exceptional roles they are destined to play. Such *in total institutions, adults are resocialized toward unaccustomed purposes* agencies are one kind of what sociologist Erving Goffman has called a *total institution*, an organization whose main purpose is to transform the identities of novices, to induct them into a radically different social order.[22] Another example is the novitiate of Christian monasteries, where newcomers are purified of their worldly selves and urged to "put on the Lord Jesus Christ, and make no provision for the flesh, to gratify its desires."[23] A further example is the prison, where new arrivals are socialized to the identity of convict, criminal, pariah of the human race. Goffman's generic term for agencies like these is apt, for their success depends on total control of the adult learner's environment. Neophytes are figuratively if not literally stripped naked, divested of their previous habits, and deprived of contact with their former family and friends. Often their heads are shaved. They are outfitted in the uniform of their new identity and subjected to long hours of indoctrination. Their free time is kept to a minimum lest in moments of idleness the organization lose its grip upon time. They eat, work, play, and sleep amid myriad tangible reminders of the new roles imposed upon them. Rewards accrue only to "model" soldiers, monks, or prisoners, not to those who still show signs of former statuses. Only after months of intense resocialization can the order of their days be relaxed a little, but by then conformity is almost second nature.

Commentators in recent years have had much to say, most of it negative, about the severe resocialization practices of movements like the Unification Church and the Hare Krishna cult. Neophytes are said to be forcibly indoctrinated, propagandized, and brainwashed to such an extent that they "are no longer themselves." But the techniques such groups employ differ little from those deemed generally appropriate for military, monastic, and penal institutions. The crucial difference is only how alien and threatening to conventional culture is the content of what is taught and learned. Nor is it the case that those of us who live outside total institutions of any kind are somehow "free to be ourselves," immune to external pressures of adult socialization. The conditioning techniques of mainstream life are subtler and less direct, and they do not aim for so radical and fast a personal

even everyday adult life is an ongoing process of resocialization

transformation. Nonetheless, anyone who reflects can feel employers, coworkers, friends, and kin urging conformity to "the way things are done here," "everyday good manners," "what is expected of someone in your position." Any kind of mobility in adult life—a new job, promotion, or demotion, a new house, spouse, or social club—implies new norms to be learned, a change of clothes, a more or less different identity to be assumed. And for the most part we do not resist. Like converts to dissident religions, monastic postulants, and military recruits, also like little children running to their mothers' arms, we crave belongingness and submit to environmental demands. Who we are, even as adults, is mostly who our favorite people would have us be.

SUMMARY

Social psychologists come in diverse theoretical shapes and sizes, but they share a basic supposition: that a human being is for the most part a puppet dangling on the stage of some social order. The common scholarly goal is to know which strings to pull and how to maneuver them in order to make the puppet dance this way or that. From various pieces of research the preceding pages have drawn a summary conclusion: Western societies create their diverse kinds of scientifically minded, achievement-oriented, competitive breed of humanity by the way they structure the environment of children, reward and love them selectively, provide them with models and permit them to play. It has been shown further that the puppetry extends into adult life—if not dramatically in the intense resocialization processes of total institutions, then at least by the routine subjection of citizens to the authority structure prevailing in their milieu. Hence it is erroneous to think that any child grows up naturally or that adults can ever truly be themselves. Each one of us is mostly a creature, a product, an artifact, an outcome of external social forces. It is these forces, much more than we ourselves, that give us our identities and make us come alive. Without them we are like puppets unstrung, crumpled in a lifeless heap.

While acknowledging the point of Stanley Milgram's research, some readers might still insist that people *know* better even when they are persuaded to behave in ways that seem strange or out of character. Might it be that group domination of individuals stops short of perception, that human beings at least see and hear for themselves, whatever they might do? The answer is no: even perception is socially induced. This section of the chapter might appropriately conclude with a classic *Asch's experiments:* psychological study that points this out. It was done in the early 1950s by Solomon *even perception is* Asch, then a professor at Swarthmore College.[24] Asch invited between seven and *socially induced* nine students at a time to take part in his experiment, and showed each group at the start two large white cards. On one was a single vertical line. On the other were three numbered vertical lines, two obviously longer or shorter than the line on the first card, the third exactly the same length. The researcher then explained to the subjects that they would be shown a series of such pairs of cards and that in each case each student should simply pick out the line on the second card that matched the length of the line on the first card. When each pair of cards was shown, the researcher would ask each student in turn to say aloud his choice of the matching line. The experiment proceeded through eighteen pairs of cards.

What Asch did not explain at the outset was that all but one student in each group had been instructed beforehand to choose some obviously shorter or longer line instead of the one of equal length for twelve of the eighteen sets of cards. There was thus just one actual subject in the experiment, the person who was honestly trying to choose the matching line. What Asch wanted to find out was what effect on this subject's perception the obviously mistaken answers of other people would have. For this reason the unknowing student was positioned in such a way that he would answer only after the others had done so. More than a hundred such students went through the experiment, each of them being subjected unknowingly to group pressure from six to eight other students.

The results confirmed a humbling diagnosis of the human person. About a third of the subjects refused to believe their own eyes and yielded to group pressure in half or more of their choices. Or perhaps we should better say that these students believed their own eyes but that their eyes saw what other people wanted them to see. Asch also found, in variations on the basic experiment, that what was most critical was the unanimity of the group. If some of Asch's confederates chose the correct line and others an incorrect one, almost all the experimental subjects saw correctly. If even one other student confirmed his perception, the subject was unlikely to choose the wrong line. A united front of peers answering incorrectly, however, caused about one of every three subjects to miss or to deny even so obvious a fact as the length of a black line on the card in front of him. This research suggests a revision of the old adage that in the land of the blind the one-eyed are kings. We might hypothesize that in such a land even some of the two-eyed would not see a blessed thing.

The Dimension of Pride

the power to surprise is the measure of humanness

The active, creative side of the human person is harder to discuss than the passive, socially constructed one, especially from the sociological vantage point. For a person has cause for pride only insofar as he or she defies scientific explanation. People distinguish themselves from machines and demonstrate their dialectical nature only by doing something unforeseen and unforeseeable, unpredicted and unpredictable, unprogrammed and unprogrammable: by giving surprises to the status quo. Such inventiveness is hard to analyze because by definition it occurs outside the boundaries of sociocultural systems. It is a part of the person that roles do not encompass. One of my nephews was often seized as a boy by seemingly uncontrollable urges to disobey, act up, defy somehow his father's expectations. On such occasions my brother would stand the squirming lad in front of him and say directly, "Pinch that little worm." To illustrate this command my brother would press together the tips of his thumb and forefinger and hold them to his forehead, as if the mischief-making worm dwelt somewhere just inside a person's head. But wherever it resides, that worm is the dimension of pride. Even daily pinching in the socialization process fails to kill it. The worm wiggles in every living woman or man. It is the *I*, the id, charisma, the quality that separates people from machines and makes them beautiful, like gods.

"The I, the id, charisma, the quality that separates people from machines and makes them beautiful, like gods."

But perhaps for some readers such sentences as these are too much. "Enough," they respond. "What has sociology to do with cerebral worms? This is preposterous!" The section below therefore reviews some empirical evidence for a dimension of the human person beyond the passive, created one. Two further sections focus respectively on the conditions under which a person's effervescent side can be asserted and on the context in which this inevitably occurs.

THE LIMITS OF BEHAVIORAL SCIENCE

Much has been made in this chapter of the results of social-psychological experiments, each of them showing in some way how malleable human beings are. Given the will and enough pages I could review countless more experiments and innumerable pieces of survey research to reinforce the same point. I could even make it a kind of taunt, taking one human attribute after another and demonstrating how much it is socially conditioned. That would be the ultimate insult—to claim that a person's life is beyond his or her control.

The evidence warrants no such insult. Study after study does indeed demonstrate that people's actions and ideas are influenced, conditioned, shaped, affected, taught, manipulated, and otherwise accounted for by the social structures surrounding them. But never completely. Not a single piece of research has ever shown that even one human attribute is utterly determined by external factors. It bears remembering that some Anglo-American children won lots of marbles in Madsen's experimental game and that some of Milgram's subjects defied their employer's authority and refused to administer the electric shocks. The conclusions of social-psychological research are always probabilistic: given such and such conditions, the odds that such and such kind of person will engage in such and such behavior are 10 to 1, 20 to 1, or some other ratio. Articles and books in psychology and sociology are full of qualifying phrases like "more likely," "less likely," "tended to," and "slightly fewer." Many researchers today use available statistical techniques to calculate what percentage of variation in a set of people's scores on some quality or attribute is accounted for by one or more explanatory variables. Even with half a dozen or more independent variables, typical studies are able to explain no more than 10 percent, 20 percent, or in rare cases 50 or 60 percent of the variation. The more interesting and important the quality under study, moreover, the less variation can ordinarily be explained. There is, in sum, plenty of room amidst the findings of social-psychological research for an unpredictable worm, an existential self, a free will—for the dimension of pride, however it is named.

But might it not be that social psychologists just need more time to expose the utterly predictable nature of human action? As their science matures will it not discredit more and more those defeatists who insist on the basic indeterminacy, the inexplicability of the human species? Will social psychologists not eventually be able to predict people's actions as accurately as astronomers today predict the movement of planets and stars? The answer is no. Unlike celestial bodies, human bodies talk back. So mischievous are they that as subjects in laboratory experiments they often spoil the results if they know what the researcher is trying to prove. People are most predictable when they are unaware of predictions others make of them. Once they become aware, they often change their minds. For if Jane finds

the less aware experimental subjects are, the more predictable

143

out what Dick is expecting her to do she now has the advantage, since she can predict what he will do in response—unless, of course, he knows that she knows what he was predicting in the first place. So back and forth it goes between people, even when one is in the experimenter role and the other is merely a subject. Astronomers have no such problems with their subject matter. The moon never changes its course in response to somebody's prediction. But people often do, and that makes almost all the difference in the world.

This is not to say that social psychology cannot progress or that further research will be in vain. Quite on the contrary. We can hope that with more careful theorizing, more refined measurement, and more powerful analytic techniques social scientists will increase the amount of behavior we can predict and explain. No one need fear this prospect or flinch from knowing more about how people are conditioned and shaped by present structures of social life. Indeed, if even 99 percent of me is programmed by external forces I want to know all about it: every role expectation, every socializing technique, every aspect of my unfreedom. For the other 1 percent of me, my charismatic active self, can use that information to turn the table on my milieu, as Jane did in the example of the preceding paragraph. That is, the more thoroughly people understand the content and manner of the constraints upon them the farther they leave behind the miserable condition of Milgram's or Asch's experimental subjects, who through ignorance of the pressures placed upon them were all the more likely to succumb to those pressures. The more human beings become aware of their humility the more able they are to assert their pride: to act freely and creatively. Thereby people further the process of social change and transformation, revamping present structures of domination and forcing social psychologists to overhaul their theories in accordance with later moments in the histories of human societies.

POWER, PRECONDITION TO HUMANNESS

Ontario sociologist Richard Henshel has studied with much care the matter of prediction, pondering why natural and physical scientists are so much better at it than students of human behavior.[25] One reason he offers is that, compared to our colleagues in other sciences we social scientists can exert little control over the environment of our subject matter. A beaker full of some chemical compound, for instance, is not much more predictable than a man or woman if it is left sitting in *ability to predict* an untamed forest, exposed to the vagaries of wind and weather, insects and *depends on control of* animals. The compound might expand, contract, explode, gasify, solidify, spill, or *the relevant* who knows what—its environment is uncontrolled. In the laboratory, by contrast, *environment* where the chemist can precisely regulate temperature, light, humidity, and other external influences, an accurate scientific prediction becomes much more possible. Our trouble in social science, Henshel argues, is that numerous ethical and legal constraints prevent us from controlling the environment of humankind. Men and women continue to wander in the untamed forests of their own societies. Predicting what a human person will do tomorrow or next week becomes for this reason a far chancier, riskier task than that normally faced by chemists, physicists, botanists, and zoologists. But suppose social psychologists could incarcerate human beings in university laboratories from the moment of birth and meticulously regulate every external influence on every subject. No boy or girl in the experiment would be allowed to see, hear, or touch anything except stimuli programmed in advance by the scientists in charge. They would not be permitted to move even an eyelash except on command. It is easy to imagine that after twenty or thirty years the products of such an experiment would behave so utterly predictably that those who had engineered them would literally jump for joy.

Granted that such an experiment is at least conceivable, especially in the dawning age of electronic surveillance and computerized social control, three implications deserve to be drawn from it—and from Henshel's basic line of argument. The first is that whatever predictability a person manifests inheres not in the person but in his or her environment, past and present. People behave this way or that not because of some inner compulsion beyond their control, some kind of natural social laws, but because of external forces brought to bear on them. The subjects of the imaginary experiment might presumably be programmed as murderers or pacifists, capitalists, communists, or Jehovah's Witnesses. It would be a matter not of drawing out some essential nature inside of them but of feeding into them a desired mode of conduct. The albatross that humbles people is therefore not buried within them; it is hung around their necks. People have to be *made* predictable; they are not that way naturally.

three implications: first, people are not born predictable, but made that way

But who could make people predictable, manipulate their environment so carefully and thoroughly that none would do anything surprising? Neither elephants nor leprechauns, obviously enough, but only other people. This is the second implication of Henshel's argument, that people's predictability reflects the control of their environment by other people. It is human beings who have to do the training, conditioning, and programming if other human beings are to be completely humiliated. In the experiment above, it is the social scientists. They would indeed have demonstrated that people can be rendered incapable of doing anything new, but thereby they themselves would have done something new. That is why they would jump for joy and feel proud. They would proclaim their own creativity in the very act of depriving other people of theirs. They might object, I suppose, that they were forced to do their experiment by subtle, unknown stimuli in their respective backgrounds. But no actual evidence would support their objection. And in any case the striking aspect of their work would not be any alleged commonality between them and their subjects, both being passive objects of external forces. No, the noteworthiness of the event would consist in the *difference* between the researchers and their subjects, that the former had actively accomplished something surprising upon the latter. The researchers, not the subjects, would be congratulated (or condemned) for their achievement. Indeed, such is already the practice in social psychology. Madsen, Milgram, Asch, Bandura, and Walters do not get their names in books like this one by demonstrating their own predictability as passive, manipulated subjects in experiments. Such researchers win acclaim by *designing* experiments, by actively and creatively controlling the environment of some other human beings in such a way as to obtain unprecedented research findings. Albatrosses that weigh people down have therefore a mainly human origin: they are set in place by other people.

second, people are made predictable by other people

Now to the last and concluding implication of Henshel's argument: that people can be active and creative, assert their pride and realize their dialectical nature,

third, power is a precondition for creativity and surprise

only to the extent that their environment is outside the control of other people. In other words, power is a precondition for a fully human life.[26] Only when the existing order of things is in some way entrusted to a person can that person generate surprise and leave his or her uncopied mark upon the planet Earth. People become human only when they are not only acted upon but acting, making a difference in what happens in their milieu. Such an experiment as that described above, were it ever proposed or carried out, would therefore be an abomination, a cruelly perverse and dehumanizing attack upon the subjects involved. No matter if they were programmed to the most civilized mode of conduct the researchers could imagine, housed in luxury, and permitted the most complete gratification of their various appetites. Because their environment would be controlled by others, they would be denied the one reward to which every person is by nature entitled: power, the chance to act back on one's milieu in an unpredicted and unpredictable way, the opportunity to change things and make history.

Much more than their behaviorist colleagues, symbolic interactionist scholars have recognized in their research the active, reality-defining dimension of the human person. The social-psychological disciples of George Herbert Mead and Herbert Blumer have by and large avoided the experimental laboratory. Their energies have gone instead into first-hand field observation of citizens' everyday life. Their focus has been on *relationships*, the process of people giving and receiving identities from one another, acting and being acted upon, responding back and forth to one another's ever-shifting expectations. Symbolic interactionist research, through its diverse analyses of intimate, face-to-face conduct, demonstrates that even the everyday roles of ordinary citizens have a little power attached to them. Two strangers, a suicidal man and a pretty woman, sit bored in the crowded anonymity of a bus station; their eyes meet for the briefest moment; she smiles the slightest smile; and he decides to wait one more day. Or an office worker pointedly ignores a colleague when they pass in the hallway and thereby spoils the colleague's day. Or a restaurant cashier slaps an aged woman's change down on the counter, disregarding her outstretched hand and making her feel old. Or a mother tapes her son's paper, graded A, to the refrigerator door, and that night he skips TV to work on his homework. To have even a lowly status in the society at hand is to enjoy a little power, the chance to make a difference in what goes on. For no role player ever duplicates exactly the performance of any other role player. Every *I* inevitably transcends the *me* to which it responds. Thus in a certain sense every human life is an unprecedented and unique intrusion of a human will upon the world.

donkey power: the ever-present opportunity to say no

The human person shares with the jackass, moreover, a kind of power which no group or society, no other people, can possibly take away. When a donkey is pressed too far, and sometimes just when the mood strikes, this humble beast of burden proudly, majestically, triumphantly stops in its tracks, brays defiantly, retires to its haunches, and refuses to budge. There are few sights in the world more splendid. The almost powerless animal, crushed by the weight of indecent demands, responds firmly and creatively in the only way left open. Human beings deprived of other kinds of power can respond in much the same way. A wildcat strike is one example. Wage laborers unable to affect the conditions of their work by other means simply walk off the job. Or a housewife feeling hopelessly abused and

146

helpless runs to her car and drives away. An office worker otherwise unable to get out from under the boss's thumb quits on the spot. White South Africans convinced that events in their country are beyond their control catch a plane and leave. During the Indochina war, thousands of American draftees dropped out of the United States and moved to Canada. History books record numerous examples of the extreme case: suicide, self-inflicted death in lieu of submission to the will of other people. All these are cases of donkey power, the desperately creative act of the almost powerless. It by no means represents the zenith of human creativity. To quit is to play one's final card, to relinquish any further chance to change the organization, marriage, group, or society left behind. All a quitter can do is assume a role in some other social order, hoping to gain therein something more than donkey power. This option nonetheless remains eternally open to every human being regardless of situation: the power to say no and thus to feel the pride of liberation.

There is more than withdrawal, of course, to the creative dimension of human existence. There is also more than the casual messages sent in passing encounters of everyday life. An adequate social psychology must analyze more than the common denominators of power inherent in all social roles and available to all citizens. It *inequalities of power* must study and dissect the power structure in the society at large, the unequal *imply unequal chances* distribution across roles and statuses of the chance to make a difference. For what is *to become fully human* at stake in the power structure is nothing else than the opportunity to become fully human, to be more than a cog in the machinery of social order. Consider the difference, for example, between two seamstresses with identical technical skills and equivalent incomes. The one does piecework in a garment factory. She owns neither the materials nor the machines with which she works. Others have decided the fabric, color, and design of her products. She is expected to sew whatever is assigned: today collars, tomorrow sleeves. She can scarcely vary even a single stitch without receiving a reprimand. About all she controls is the speed of her work. The other seamstress is a self-employed dressmaker. External factors impinge on her as well: the policies of textile mills and the tastes of her customers. But much more than her colleague in the factory she has power over her work. She can influence her customers' choice of pattern, fabric, and color. She can decide which parts of a dress to make first and how best to assemble them. She can decorate her sewing room as she pleases. If she wants, she can work evenings this week and take next week off. She can cater to customers she likes and discourage others from ever coming back. In all these ways she can put herself into her work, actively shape the conditions and products of her labor. Now whatever the pros and cons of these two modes of clothing manufacture, it must be admitted that the independent dressmaker *has more chance to be human in her work* than the pieceworker. The latter is little more than an extension of the sewing machine. The former is a dialectical being; her work is humanizing.

The social-psychological study of human creativity requires above all an analysis of the differences in power attached to the work roles citizens occupy. The *the differences in power* significance of any citizen to any society depends mainly on the work that person *attached to economic* does within it. Hence the crucial question is how much of a chance a person has to *and other kinds of roles* generate surprise in the actual course of performing his or her accustomed

Pigeons and people have a lot in common, else Skinner could not have used experiments with pigeons to make sense of how people behave. But this photograph trumpets a contrary emphasis, a truth our generation needs to hear. People have beauty, creativity, and power that pigeons cannot touch. These boys in the South Bronx have trained a "stack" of birds to fly at their command. It is a nimble, grandly human sport in a brutalizing slum. The boys have dignity. Even the pigeons seem pleased. (Marcia Weinstein)

occupation. For most line workers, keypunch operators, stenographers, typists, file clerks, supermarket checkout clerks, and mail sorters the answer is painfully obvious: they live as human beings mostly after hours. Even worse is the condition of the unemployed, people altogether cut off from the making of economic history. Self-employed artisans and professionals, by contrast, along with professors, journalists, building superintendents, independent farmers, shopkeepers, members of producer cooperatives, and owner-managers of firms all have greater chance to be more than one-dimensional, to realize the dialectical nature within themselves. The same question can be asked of noneconomic roles. Can a wife affect her husband as much as he affects her? How creatively can consumers do their shopping, or how completely have their options been predefined? To what extent can people in their leisure roles express themselves in music, dance, sports, and hobbies, or how much are they expected just to let themselves be entertained? How much say do citizens have over who is elected to national and local political office and over the content of governmental legislation? Such questions as these are fundamental to social psychology in any society. For a role or status is humanizing only insofar as it implies a relationship of countervailing power between the role player's internal self and his or her external milieu, so that the person's behavior is in some way a trade-off between what others require and what the self prefers.

why people fail to use their power to improve and innovate Many people, nonetheless, do not use the power attached to their roles for any purpose except to repeat the past and perpetuate the status quo. Why do they not create, improve, innovate, change for the better the situation of earthly life? There are some empirical answers. The person may not yet be adequately socialized to the role; just learning and trying to meet conventional expectations may exhaust his or her energies. Or perhaps the person has experienced too little variety on earth to be aware of how much beneficial novelty the human species can effect. Or maybe the person lacks the time to reflect, to assume the mental attitude of playful thought that sparks new ideas. Or still further, the person may have been taught a one-sided view of humankind: that humility is a virtue and pride a vice. But empirical answers necessarily fall short. Creativity and surprise cannot be predicted; if they could they would not be what they are. No one can look inside another and see all the burdens that person carries, all the pressures to conform that inhibit free expression, all the agony of moral choice. No one can say with certitude to another, "You could have chosen to do otherwise than you did," though each man may say that to himself, every woman to herself. Thus in the design of our societies we cannot guarantee that every citizen will drink the water of active, creative change. We can, however, lead ourselves to that water by teaching each other all we can and then giving each other power. This, I believe, is the practical implication of Martin Luther King's words of acceptance of the Nobel Peace Prize in 1964: "I accept this award with an abiding faith in America and an audacious faith in the future of mankind. I refuse to accept the idea that the 'isness' of man's present nature makes him morally incapable of reaching up for the 'oughtness' that forever confronts him."

CREATIVITY IN CONTEXT

The discussion earlier in this chapter of the dimension of humility emphasized that the empirical meaning of conformity varies from one society to another. The content of child socialization is not the same in India as in France, nor are the techniques by which it is achieved. The United States and the Soviet Union have each a distinct definition of what constitutes competent, routine, normal adult behavior. The same point applies to the dimension of pride. Creativity does not consist in expressing oneself "with total honesty" in verse, song, painting, or some other kind of art. Even the intense self-assertion of fine art is relational. Unread poems and songs never sung are but sad expressions of donkey power. Artists realize human nature in their work by agonizing over the same two questions that confront the seamstress making a dress, the student writing a term paper, the homeowner redecorating the den, the legislator amending a bill, and everyone else in their various roles: what do others expect of *me* here and now, and what do *I* think I should do? The first question alone is too much humility; it is surrender or prostitution to external forces, and its answer is purely commercial art. The second question by itself is too much pride, and the response to it is an unintelligible, unmeaningful product of conceited selfishness. The truly human artist is one who manages to solve in some orgasmic moment the contradiction between humility

creativity means to walk from where you stand

and pride. And so in all other roles. It is a profound mistake to imagine that we can walk except from where we now stand. Every contradiction of an order is also its extension. Recall Marx's words: "not out of free pieces." Thus if anyone should choose to be creative it can only be in the context of the existing order of things. A person has cause for pride when he or she rises a little above the structure of life as it empirically appears at a given point in time and space.

This contextual imperative explains why the dimension of humility necessarily precedes the dimension of pride. Not by denying the present order but only by scaling it, not by refusing to grow up but only by growing beyond conventional maturity, does a person become free to invent, act upon the status quo, do something new. A seamstress who cannot sew a straight stitch is unlikely to produce a masterpiece of *haute couture*. Adults in the industrialized Western world who cannot read and write fluently and scientifically can hardly help prolong the status quo, much less improve on it. Indeed, we in history's most technologically advanced societies can easily become discouraged. The magnificent achievements of our ancestors can easily overwhelm us and frighten us into an attitude of excessive meekness. The present order sometimes appears as a giant of human ingenuity from the past, a colossal product of a bygone heroic age. Who in the present generation should dare to innovate still more, to press even farther the human shaping of the earth? The answer is all of us, albeit carefully and thoughtfully. Humility alone does not make life human. And we can take courage from the metaphor offered by the Roman poet Lucan, who lived just after Jesus: "Pygmies placed on the shoulders of giants see more than the giants themselves."[27]

The same contextual imperative has a further implication, with which this section can conclude. It is that no person behaves proudly without in some way humbling other people. At least for practical purposes, no one can say anything new unless someone else is listening, nor generate surprise unless someone else is watching. We are social beings. Each citizen of a society forms part of the external forces that weigh on other citizens. Innovation by one citizen challenges the order in the lives of all the rest. Hence it should not be thought that a person becomes more and more human the more he or she chooses oughtness over isness, creativity over conformity. Machiavelli's power-hungry prince is a monstrosity, no less than Caspar Milquetoast. It is the balance that makes a person fully human, not the triumph of one dimension of a person's nature over the other. Exercising too much creativity means seizing too much power, and this can happen only at the expense of other people. The husband who proudly imposes his will upon his wife does not thereby become more human but less so. Adolf Hilter and Josef Stalin were undeniably proud, powerful, and creative men but hardly exemplars of humanity; they perverted their own nature and that of their victims. The sociocultural system that spreads power around is the one that brings out the best in all its members, permitting each to discover the essentially human happiness of at once acting and being acted upon.

the society that spreads power around brings out the best in all its members

Concluding Words

How much tidier life and scholarship would be if a dialectical view of human nature could be avoided! If everything about us were predictable we could join Dr. Percival and just "enjoy the game we're all playing. Enjoy. Only enjoy." Or if we were free like gods we could weave feathers into wings with all the confidence of Brian O'Connal. But the reality of who and what we are is twofold. Under the heading of humility this chapter has outlined some social-psychological evidence of our domination: the content and techniques of child socialization, the continuing pressures of adult learning. And under the heading of pride this chapter has pointed to the limits of scientific prediction, the meaning of power, and the context in which people can after all create. An adequate theory of the person has to incorporate both these dimensions: *me* and *I*, superego and id, rationality and charisma, essence and existence, being and becoming. Be sure that I would have painted a simpler, neater picture if the data had permitted it. These pages even now are dross beside the complicated splendor of the human race. But they have offered at least a framework within which to consider and reflect upon the variety of specific social-psychological essays and research reports available today.

The dialectical conception of the human person offered here should illuminate not only ourselves and other people but also some disputes within the community of sociologists. For every sociological theory, every analysis of events in societies and smaller groups implies some kind of social psychology, some suggestion of the nature of the human beings out of whom groups are made. The question is what kind of social psychology, one that emphasizes people's humble, malleable dimension or their proud, creative one. An emphasis on humility is fairly obvious in structural functionalism, the outlook taught by Talcott Parsons at Harvard which dominated American sociology in the 1940s and 1950s. This approach, as Chapter Three explained, calls for sorting out the components of a sociocultural system (the structure) in terms of the purposes they serve (functions) for the system as a whole. It continues to be a popular orientation in research and its roots run deep in Western thought generally. But from this point of view people are mainly just role players. About everything they do seems more or less to fit into the overall picture. Even behavior which serves no *manifest* or obvious function may be serving a *latent*, unrecognized function—to cite a major insight of Robert Merton at Columbia, one of Parsons' most illustrious students. Reading the books of structural functionalists one begins to wonder just what a person could do that would be new, exciting, and good. The sociocultural system seems rather closed and mechanical. Social change is portrayed mainly as the transition from disorder to order, the process of institutionalization by which a society dominates its citizens so completely that they take the status quo for granted as legitimate, sacred, natural, inevitably, really real.

structural functionalism emphasizes people's humble side

Scholars in this tradition tend not to think of the human person as the kind of noble savage Rousseau described, a being whose blissful freedom is shackled by social order. They draw their inspiration more from the seventeenth-century English philosopher, Thomas Hobbes, who took the view that people are not so noble, that if uncontrolled they would gobble each other up in a war of everyone against everyone. In a purely natural state there would be "no arts; no letters; no society; and which is worst of all, continual fear and danger of violent death; and the life of man, solitary, poor, nasty, brutish, and short."[28] For Hobbes the key question is how social order is possible, how the destructive wildness of human beings can be contained for their own common good. The answer he gave was the absolute and sovereign authority of the state. Hobbes's intellectual descendants still wrestle with the same question, though the answers they give are more complex: intricate analyses of how a society is institutionalized, its parts fitted together, and its citizens socialized to common values. But the image of the person remains much the same as in Hobbes's own writings: an image of potentially destructive pride and

worry about Hobbes's question bespeaks a humble view of our species

of very necessary humility. Genuine and surprising creativity would be dysfunctional, a discomfiting intrusion upon a fragile social order whose preservation is of paramount practical and intellectual importance. The charismatic, idlike qualities of the human race should therefore be ignored, or suppressed.

In an oft-reprinted article first published in 1961, New York University professor Dennis Wrong pointedly attacked what he called the "oversocialized conception of man in modern sociology."[29] He accused the structural functionalists in general and Parsons in particular of being one-eyed, of neglecting the proud, active dimension of the person. Wrong allied himself by contrast with scholars who took a more dialectical view, sociologists who came to be generically labeled *conflict theorists*. What distinguishes their work is a conception of the social fabric as something which not only unfolds across a human landscape but is woven by human beings themselves. The present order of American society or any other is not the be-all and end-all of human existence but one of many possibilities. History is not a long, single process of institutionalization but movement back and forth between institutionalization and change. One of the leading conflict theorists in America is Lewis Coser of the State University of New York at Stony Brook, the president of the American Sociological Association in 1975. A contemporary disciple of Georg Simmel, Coser by no means denies the fact of social order or the need for it. Indeed, he has exposed latent functions which conflict and deviance often serve. But the title of his 1974 compendium of articles is significant: *Greedy Institutions*. Chapters of the book demonstrate the incredible capacity of sociocultural systems to swallow up human beings and refuse their attempts at creative change. Coser at least calls this greed, warning proud people to be wary. Parsons would regard it as a normal societal appetite and recommend humility.

conflict theorists sought a more balanced view

Today, two decades after Wrong's article appeared, sociologists no longer divide themselves so much into structural-functionalist and conflict categories. New theoretical perspectives have come to the fore and old ones have been repackaged and relabeled. The variety of competing factions and fashions in the discipline today is bewildering, but they continue to differ in part according to which dimension of the person they emphasize.[30] Sociological behaviorism, the building of social theory on the principles of operant conditioning in the spirit of B. F. Skinner, implies fascination with people's predictability. So does sociobiology— the explanation of social order in terms of genes, chromosomes, body chemistry, and other aspects of human physiology. So, too, at least some brands of general systems theory. Still further, many rather atheoretical articles appearing regularly in the journals seem to rest on a deterministic view of social life: a belief that once our science comes of age we will be able to predict with certainty. On the other hand, symbolic interactionists continue to analyze the reciprocity in small-scale human relationships, thereby affirming people's creative side. Such affirmation fairly leaps from the pages of work in that specific outgrowth of symbolic interactionism called ethnomethodology. One also reads these days of existentialist, radical, Buddhist, phenomenological, and other kinds of sociology, whose titles at least suggest attention to the unprogrammable side of humankind. Finally and most important, is the growing number of sociologists in nearly all societies, the United States included, who ground themselves in the ideas of Hegel and Marx, drawing from these men a dialectical conception of our species. The Frankfurt Institute in Germany nourished many influential scholars of this orientation from the 1920s to the 1960s; Erich Fromm, Max Horkheimer, Theodor Adorno, Herbert Marcuse, and Jurgen Habermas are perhaps the best-known. Many other Marxian scholars unrelated to the Frankfurt school also stress the creative potential of contemporary role players.

This chapter has by no means disguised the kind of social psychology its author finds most fruitful: a dialectical one that fully respects both the humble and proud sides of our nature. My dissatisfaction with scholars who implicitly or explicitly humiliate people—B. F. Skinner, Talcott Parsons, or whomever—should by now be more than clear. All the same, a sociology adequate for today must seize on *any* insights into the structure of our common life, whether they be offered by dialecticians in love with the human race or by one-dimensional thinkers estranged from it. The goal of First Sociology is to grasp the enduring regularities of the status quo, the predictability in social order here and now, the conditioning to which we role players are subject at this historical moment. Fundamentally, it makes no difference who can explain the cage in which we now find ourselves. It is not quite to the point that some analysts believe the cage is unbreakable and inescapable. The important thing to anyone with hope is the analysis of the cage. Coming chapters, like preceding ones, draw freely from scholars of diverse persuasions, mostly irrespective of the social psychologies underlying their work. These pages are not designed to entangle readers' minds unnecessarily in the academic quarrels among exotically named factions of sociologists, quarrels often tangential to the actual work of our discipline. The nonsociologists we serve care little about matters of professional housekeeping anyway. The sociology they seek is one that directs attention away from itself toward the pressing economic, political, and other social realities of our day. Their expectations are the ones this book attempts to satisfy.

adequate sociology takes its insights wherever they can be found

Besides, the usefulness of sociology is mostly as a guardian against excessive pride. Grand utopian adventures in social change that try too hard to leave the past behind have a way of resulting in the worst kind of misery. There is a lesson in the People's Temple, so innocently begun by Jim Jones in Indiana, then carried off to California, and finally transplanted to Guyana's jungles, where it was thought the good life could blossom at last, away from the strictures of American society. On November 18, 1978, an estimated 911 citizens of that utopia fell upon each other in willful death. The lesson of the Jonestown suicides is this: for all its problems the status quo is the only resource we humans have with which to approach the future. There is no escaping who we have been taught to be, only the prospect of becoming something more. Our generation inherits an order no less fragile than the finest porcelain. Our task is above all to understand what we hold and to handle it gently, only thereafter to be bold enough to try to enhance its quality. No reader should be disheartened if in the institutional analysis to come the stress is on the way things are. Everything written here takes for granted the truth of Dante's warning six centuries ago: "To a greater force, and to a better nature, you, free, are subject, and that creates the mind in you, which the heavens have not in their charge. Therefore if the present world go astray, the cause is in you, in you it is to be sought."[31]

"therefore if the present world go astray, the cause is in you"

For Reflection

dialectics	moral socialization	environment control and power
dimension of humility	achievement motivation	power and creativity
dimension of pride	go-getter	study of relationships
operant conditioning	individual modernity	donkey power
intermittent reinforcement	competitiveness	power in work roles
anarchism	primary group	surprise
existentialism	internalization	contextual imperative
superego, id	models	being, becoming
rational, charismatic	play	manifest, latent functions
me, I	adult learning	institutionalization
symbolic interactionism	total institutions	Hobbes's question
noble-savage hypothesis	limits of behavioral science	structural functionalists
child-of-nature hypothesis	probabilistic explanation	conflict theorists
cognitive socialization	percentage of variation explained	

For Making Connections

With personal experience: Recall the two or three most important decisions you have made in your life. If a sociologist were aware of the socialization processes you went through and all the external influences upon you, how well could he or she have predicted those decisions? Don't flatter yourself in answering this question.

How well socialized would you judge yourself to be to the go-getter type of person favored in Western societies, especially in the United States? What concrete evidence can you offer for your answer? How do you explain your conformity or lack of it?

Reflect on the models that have been available to you, the adults who controlled the environment of your upbringing, the toys they gave you, the behavior you were rewarded for, and the kind of primary groups you were brought into. Have you turned out as a knowledgeable observer might have predicted? Do you have cause for pride?

With Chapter One: The present chapter has offered sociological perspectives on the person. How would you expect psychological perspectives to differ?

Would you expect a correlation between the outlook a sociologist takes on the discipline (more positivist or more humanist) and the dimension of the human person most emphasized in that sociologist's work (humility or pride)? If so, what kind of correlation and why?

With Chapter Two: Madsen used experimental methods to test hypotheses about cross-national differences in moral socialization. What other methods might be used to test his hypotheses?

Which three or four concepts in this chapter strike you as most enlightening or useful? How would you operationalize them? Could you do it simply by observing behavior or would you have to talk to people, too?

With Chapter Three: On the basis of your reading so far, how would you expect socialization procedures to differ between the capitalist and socialist societies of the contemporary world? What does the structure of rewards in a society have to do with citizens' respective chances to realize their human nature? How so?

154

For Further Reading

Social psychology journals proliferate. *Psychology Today* is trendy and readable. The *Journal of Personality and Social Psychology*, the *Social Psychology Quarterly*, and the *Journal of Cross-Cultural Psychology* are among the more technical, professional periodicals. Below are some varied books which I have found useful.

1   Edward Evans-Pritchard (ed.), *Peoples of the Earth*, Grolier, Danbury, Conn., 1973. Twenty magnificent volumes of beautifully illustrated articles on diverse contemporary cultures. Books like these instill not only understanding but a sense of awe, and that, too, is appropriate.

2   Colin M. Turnbull, *The Forest People*, Simon & Schuster, New York, 1962. Descriptions of the Pygmies of the Ituri Forest by one of the profoundest living anthropologists. Note his depiction of cooperative values and how they are taught to children. Only after reading this book should one go on to Turnbull's later ones, *The Mountain People* and *The Lonely African*, from the same publisher.

3   George Herbert Mead, *On Social Psychology*, Anselm Strauss (ed.), Univ. of Chicago Press, Chicago, 1964. Collected papers by the man who inspired a major school of American sociologists. See also the collection by Mead's student, Herbert Blumer, *Symbolic Interactionism*, Prentice-Hall, Englewood Cliffs, N.J., 1969.

4   Sigmund Freud, *The Standard Edition of the Complete Psychological Works*, 24 vols, Macmillan, New York, 1953–1964. No normal person would read all these books, but Freud's influence is too great to ignore them completely. Volume 19 includes *The Ego and the Id*, his model of the human psyche. One might also be content with a summary of Freud's work, like *An Outline of Psychoanalysis*, W. W. Norton, New York, 1933.

5   Erich Fromm, *Marx's Concept of Man*, Ungar, New York, 1961. Through selections from Marx's writings and the author's lucid analysis, this book puts to shame both Russian communism and Western capitalism. See also Fromm's *Heart of Man* and *Revolution of Hope*, Harper & Row, New York, 1964 and 1968 respectively.

6   Herbert Marcuse, *One-Dimensional Man*, Beacon, Boston, 1964. A social psychology for the contemporary Western capitalist world by one of the leaders of the Frankfurt school and long-time professor at the University of California at San Diego. See also Marcuse's dialectical theory of art in *The Aesthetic Dimension*, Beacon, Boston, 1977, published two years before his death.

7   The *American Sociological Review*, which published most of the major articles for and against structural functionalism. Those by Harry Bredemeier (1955), Kingsley Davis (1959), and Harold Fallding (1963) argue in favor of this approach; those by Dennis Wrong (1961), Pierre van den Berghe (1963), and George Homans (1964) are critical.

8   Erving Goffman, *Asylums*, Doubleday, New York, 1961. The most frequently cited work of a leading symbolic interactionist, though not his best. See also his *Presentation of Self in Everyday Life*, Doubleday, New York, 1959, and *Stigma*, Prentice-Hall, Englewood Cliffs, N.J., 1963, among others.

9   B. F. Skinner, *About Behaviorism*, Knopf, New York, 1974. A mature statement by the dean of behavioral psychologists, author of *Walden Two*, Macmillan, New York, 1948 and *Beyond Freedom and Dignity*, Knopf, New York, 1971. For a more sociological, humanistic, restrained, but still behavioral conception of humankind see John H. Kunkel, *Behavior, Social Problems, and Change*, Prentice-Hall, Englewood Cliffs, N.J., 1975.

10 W. Peter Archibald, *Social Psychology as Political Economy*, McGraw-Hill, New York, 1978. A refreshing analysis of human behavior in the context of differences in social class. See also his article, "Face-to-Face: The Alienating Effects of Class, Status and Power Divisions," *American Sociological Review* 41:819–37 (1976).

Polity

Chapter Five

I ask on what bases governments hold power, when and how they hold it legally, and how far their power extends into citizens' lives.

Chapter Three commenced with the question of which level of social organization deserves to be the main target of theory and research in sociology today. On the basis of the data of contemporary life I proposed in answer the national society and spent the rest of that chapter sketching out a society's internal components and external milieu. The present chapter begins with an analogous question, that of which component should get first attention in the analysis of a society's inner workings. Five main institutions were distinguished, you recall, through a structural-functional kind of analysis. But with which must an adequate sociology begin? With the economy, as materialist writers suggest? Is the mode of production of goods and services the key to understanding everything else? Or should we enter the society as scholars where we arrived as infants, in the family? Could not a case be made for starting with religion and agencies that serve cultural ends, defining what counts for goodness and truth? Or even for beginning with educational institutions, since they cradle our hopes for a brighter day? Numerous kinds of group are essential to a society's existence. Which shall we study first?

If a choice must be made, it might best fall on that single institution which defines a society's identity and delimits its social and geographical boundaries. This is the polity, the set of roles which constitute public order, the structure of citizens' life in common, the overall framework to which everything else is tied. A political starting point for a sociology of national societies is recommended first of all by the humble side of human nature. For from the outlook of Hobbes and his intellectual descendants in the present day, the paramount social task is to hold the potentially dangerous human species in check. Without a political, governmental agency to lay down the law and enforce it, a society would slip into a condition of *anomie* or normlessness, becoming a libertine jungle wherein citizens might prey upon one

fear of anomie urges first attention to politics

157

another in internecine war. Once free of public authority human life would become a page from William Golding's *Lord of the Flies* or James Dickey's *Deliverance*. The anomie these novels illustrate is the ghost that perennially haunts structural-functional sociologists. And while many sorcerers are required to keep the ghost away, surely a sovereign political regime must be chief among them, as it was in Hobbes's own view. If many of his disciples in the United States have given the polity short shrift in their research, I suspect this is mainly because the American government is stable enough to be taken for granted. Political affairs are more problematic in most other societies and hence more closely attended to by social scientists. Rightly so. Without action to ensure public order human life is surely but civil war, screams of terror in the anarchy of night.

But a political point of departure suits equally well a more optimistic view of humankind, one that stresses our creative side, our right to outgrow the status quo and to transform ourselves into something more. For history teaches that creativity and freedom depend in great part on governmental permission. A tyrannical regime can hold people down, deny them their right to laugh and talk back, prevent them even from humanizing themselves through autonomous work. Oppressive rulers

abhorrence of alienation also urges a political starting point

press the ruled into a condition of *alienation* or powerlessness, wherein citizens are estranged from one another, cut off even from their own creative selves. Such was the plight of Vyry, the heroine-slave of Margaret Walker's *Jubilee*: "She was dull to all feeling and nothing seemed new. The same years were passing without hope. The same seasons were arriving on the heels of each other. From Randall Ware she asked nothing anymore, and she expected nothing. He was like everything else around her and everybody else she accepted. He was part of the scenery. There was no joy in her life."[1] For scholars who take a dialectical view of our race, alienation like Vyry's is the number-one demon to be exorcised from social life. And if bad government is the witch responsible, good government is the exorcist. Indeed, a regime that urges people to become more themselves, to act back on their milieu, even to help shape public life, is an incantation of divinity upon them.

Thus both the humble and proud dimensions of human nature warrant that we students of national societies commence our studies with the polity. Whether our biggest worry be normlessness or powerlessness, anomie or alienation (and we should properly concern ourselves with both), the basic framework of our common life matters fundamentally. This is to say that no serious social analyst can afford to ignore politics. Politicians cannot be tossed into an academic basket with plumbers, pianists, and priests as just another occupational category, one among many optional subject matters. Holders of political office spell out in law the context for everything we do. They are the guardians of present order and the gatekeepers of alternative futures. The buck stops on their desks. Hence we sociologists are obliged above all to inform ourselves of what they do and to make sense of it.

key terms for political sociology: polity, government, state, public order

Here at the outset I should clarify four terms that are central to the work of political sociology. *Polity* is the first and most general. It includes all roles and organizations in any way involved in the definition, implementation, or maintenance of public order. The roles of voter, legislator, soldier, tax collector, lobbyist, civil servant, and law-abiding citizen fall within the polity; so do such organizations as parties, parliaments, pressure groups, and citizens' action committees. In a cultural sense the polity consists of constitutional and legal premises, along with the popularly held norms and values underlying public order: the idea that citizens should elect public officials, for instance, or a value on citizen participation in legal reform. The terms *government* and *state* refer to subsets or categories of roles and organizations within the polity. The first applies to those which formally bestow on their holders the overriding power and responsibility over the national public order or some subdivision within it. At the national level the government may be a despot, a military junta, the ministers and ruling party of a parliament, or in the United States, a tripartite group of President, Congress, and Supreme Court. At the city level the government usually consists of a mayor and council. And so on to the other levels of government. In the United States, Mexico, Brazil, and some other societies, one of these levels is called by the word *state,* but in political sociology this word usually means something quite distinct: it refers to those political roles and organizations which are entrusted with the task of administering and implementing governmental decisions. Thus the military and police forces, the courts and prisons, and all public bureaucracies and positions in civil service are considered part of the state, as sociologists use the term. The British queen, for instance, or the president of the Federal Republic of Germany is properly called a *head of state*: one who presides over the whole apparatus of a society's public administration. The prime minister of Great Britain, by contrast, and the chancellor of West Germany are *heads of government*—unlike the heads of state, their job is to lead in the exercise of power. In the United States, of course, the president is head of both state and government.

The polity as a whole and the government and state more specifically are all concerned with *public order*, the fourth term that requires clarification here. It refers to all those patterns of social life within a society which are formally recognized as common, collective concerns. It consists of all those ways of behaving which are decreed by the government, spelled out in its constitutions and laws, administered by its state bureaucracies, and enforced by the resources of violence it controls. A particular marriage, for example, is part of the private order, outside the concern of government; few regimes dare to mandate who should marry whom. The limitation of marriage to two spouses, however, one wife and one husband, is part of the public order in the vast majority of contemporary societies. Or similarly, retail beer and liquor stores in most parts of the United States are part of the private order, owned and operated as competing businesses in a market economy, though subject to governmental regulation. In most parts of Canada, by contrast, retail outlets for alcoholic beverages are under the direct ownership and control of a public, provincial bureaucracy and thus form part of the public order of Canadian life. However a society defines it, the public order constrains private life, providing the legal, governmentally ordained outline which citizens may fill in as they please.

three basic questions this chapter addresses

Of all the political questions ever asked, surely the most basic is who shall rule—who shall form the government, manage the state, and have the last word in the determination of public order. One thing is sure: it will not be everybody. Even a government "of the people, by the people, for the people" inevitably consists of only an infinitesimal proportion of citizens. Hence the more precise question is how rulers are decided upon, on what cultural or ideological basis a government rests, with what kind of ideas the rulers' power is clothed, justified, and made legitimate, so that it properly can be called not just power but *authority*. But by now in the history of our race one basis of governmental power, one definition in political culture has come to outstrip all others in attractiveness. It is the one Lincoln described in the quotation above, a government of law, one that is bound by written norms and procedures to respond to the will of citizens and serve their interests. Hence the second crucial question is how this kind of government can be strengthened. Finally is a third question: how broadly the public order may be defined, into how many facets of life national and subdivision governments may intrude, and to what extent contrariwise they leave private individuals and organizations free to pursue their particular purposes. These are the three questions with which this chapter is concerned: on what basis rulers rule, under what conditions they do it legally, and how far their rule extends into citizens' lives. The three following sections consider these questions in turn, constituting the substance of the present chapter.

Three Bases of Political Authority

The tone of the United States Declaration of Independence is confident and matter-of-fact. Governments, it says, derive "their just powers from the consent of the governed." Indeed, it calls this a self-evident truth. Equally so, according to the Declaration, is the idea that whenever a government becomes destructive of the inalienable rights of man, "it is the Right of the People to alter or to abolish it, and to institute new Government, laying its Foundation on such Principles, and organizing its Powers in such Form, as to them shall seem most likely to effect their Safety and Happiness." Today, more than two centuries later, such ideas are generally accepted around the world, even if they are but feebly realized in practice. We take it for granted that some few of our fellow human beings are going to govern, and the only question is how seriously they take into account the consent of the rest of us, our right to partake of political power. The issue for us is not *whether* people will rule, but *which ones* and *how*.

TRADITION

To understand past political realities and present political problems, we might best admit that the idea of government by human beings neither was nor is half so self-evident as the Continental Congress tried to make it seem in 1776. We have to walk in the wooden shoes of a tenth-century French peasant—or better still, go barefoot over cobblestones. In order to comprehend the polity in human societies we should begin by inspecting the world through the nearsighted, unbespectacled eyes of a Russian serf or from the uncushioned, straight-backed throne of a medieval Spanish king. We must, in short, put ourselves in the place of our ancestors twenty or so generations in the past. To them it seemed preposterous that *the idea that humans* mere mortals should alter, abolish, or institute government, much less that they *govern themselves is* should fabricate the form it takes or the principles it embodies. What was *relatively new* self-evident to them was that they had been born into an order of life that had been

Three examples of traditional authority: Nicholas Romanov II, czar of Russia, executed in 1918; Norodom Sihanouk, prince of Cambodia, exiled in 1970; Jigme Singye Wangchuk, king of Bhutan, still reigning in 1980.

around for as long as anyone could remember, a structure that would last for incalculable time to come. Our distant forebears did not imagine that public order belonged to them. They might inhabit it for a while, pass it on to their children, but they could not fathom that it was *theirs*. They attributed the structure of their empires, kingdoms, and communities to God, nature, or fate—timeless forces outside of human reach. The public order was not, from their vantage point, a human invention but a divine imposition, in some respects a blessing but mostly a curse. The task of kings, princes, and government in general was not to decide the framework of common life but to administer a framework decreed from beyond the human will long ago in the unknowable past. And the task of ordinary men and women was simply to submit.

It was to describe this kind of political mentality that Max Weber labeled the first of his three types of governmental authority *traditional*: the kind grounded in "the belief in the everyday routine as an inviolable rule of conduct," the kind that rests upon respect for "what actually, allegedly, or presumably has always existed."[2] Traditional rulers did not think of themselves as exercising the active, creative power suggested in the preceding chapter. Nor did they conceive of themselves dialectically. They felt obliged to knuckle under almost as much as their subjects. It was only that, in the nature of things, they happened to have been invested with responsibility for keeping the lid on human pride and preserving intact the legacy of the past. The question of who shall rule was not asked, at least not in the sense in which we ask it today. The question was rather who shall be entrusted with rule by forces beyond human control. It was answered most often by recourse to heredity: the king's son inherited the crown, just as the son of a serf eventually took his father's place. The question was sometimes decided by selection or election, as in the case of the popes of Rome. In the latter case, however, the criterion of choice was above all fidelity to the traditional and customary order, and God was believed to have rigged the election anyway. No cardinal would dare to announce his candidacy or campaign for the job. Such arrogant actions would have implied a man's appropriation of power that belongs to God.

Some of the most eloquent, thoughtful, and influential theories of traditional authority were articulated by the classical Greek philosophers, especially Plato (427–347 B.C.) and his student Aristotle (384–322 B.C.). For Plato, the source of

traditionalism in the
political theory of
ancient Greece

most social problems was deviation from the traditional, patriarchic state, and his principal solution was to strengthen the ruling class and educate it well, so that it could fulfill the changeless task entrusted to it. Similarly, Aristotle believed that the Greek city-state was not just a desirable form of political organization but the *natural* form, imposed from outside human volition. Its government should thus be entrusted only to substantial citizens, to men of quality and merit, who could therefore administer the state in the way *nature* intended. Aristotle could conceive of rule by a single person (kingship) or by many (polity), but rule by a few meritorious men (aristocracy) seemed to him ideal. Nature would only be perverted if government were handed over to the small number of rich people (oligarchy) or worse still, to the large number of the poor (democracy). For Plato and Aristotle, as for most people for most of human history, civil authority properly belongs to those who exercise it in the traditional way.

Our vantage point of the late twentieth century tempts us to accuse ancient proponents of traditionalism of speaking with forked tongues. Surely so bright a philosopher as Aristotle must have known better. Medieval kings must have been aware that it was they, not God or nature, who held responsibility for the way things were. The evidence suggests to the contrary. Until the last few centuries life on earth was overwhelmed by the experience of constancy instead of change, being instead of becoming, stasis instead of movement. The intransigence of the status quo left scant room in human consciousness for faith in human ability or belief in the possibility of progress. The vast bulk of people lived from cradle to grave in the same community, walked the same roads, plowed the same fields, and endured the same monotony as their parents before them and their children afterward. Until my grandfather moved away in 1892, my forebears had subsisted on the same little patch of earth in Münsterland for at least the preceding five centuries. Most readers of this book have exactly the same ancestry, with only the names, dates, and places changed. In a condition of such timeless stability why should people have imagined that they were the architects of their social abodes? Over the long haul of history, certainly they were. But unlike us they could not read history: less of it had yet been made, much less written down, and anyway they mostly were illiterate. Hence the awareness we take for granted escaped them. Even Innocent III, pope from 1198 to 1216 and the most powerful man in Europe at that time, felt obliged to write a treatise on the misery of the human condition, its hopelessness save for the promise of heaven. Innocent was convinced that the human life span had shortened over time, that so had the human body, and that everything else had become generally worse. In his quite representative medieval view the worst sin was to expect that earthly life could be other than vile, painful, filthy, and base. Such expectation would amount to pride, the last and worst of Solomon's seven abdominations, the sin of doubting that "every power is from God."[8] This being the case, anyone who might challenge the customary structure of political power would be doomed to hell. This is the meaning of traditional authority.

CHARISMA

Nonetheless, moments of change occasionally punctuated the stability of traditional societies. History was after all in the making even then. And few if any ancient

Three examples of charismatic authority: Louis Riel, leader of the Métis rebellion in Manitoba in the early 1880s, hanged in 1885; Mohandas K. Gandhi, champion of self-rule for India, assassinated in 1948; Martin Luther King, civil rights leader in the United States, murdered in 1968.

peoples were more aware of it than that tribe of Semitic wanderers who, along with the Greeks and Romans, laid most of the foundation of Western civilization. The Jews did not believe that they created their own public order or government, but neither did they regard the polity as inherent in nature, in the manner of the classical Greeks. The order of Jewish life was thought instead to be the will of Yahweh or Elohim, the god of the chosen people, who let them know from time to time how they should behave. His will was normally made known through the traditional authority of kings and high priests, those entrusted with power by divine anointment. These rulers tended mostly to perpetuate the status quo in God's name. At times, however, especially when the Jews were troubled by such uncustomary disasters as famine or foreign conquest, Yahweh would send to his people a special messenger, a prophet like Ezekiel or Daniel. These messengers called the Jews to do something new, not by virtue of their traditional authority for they had none—Jeremiah was still a boy, and Daniel a servant to King Jehoiakim. The basis of the prophets' authority was instead charisma, a seemingly superhuman personal manner which by its intensity and force commanded people's attention and attracted followers.

the ancient Jewish prophets' basis of authority

The example of these prophets provided Weber with the name of his second type of authority, *charismatic*, the kind of governance "to which the governed submit because of their belief in the extraordinary quality of the specific person."[4] The charismatic leader disrupts the traditional order and calls followers to adopt a new one. Freeing people from the bonds of custom, the one with charisma holds them spellbound. Jesus is the prime example. Although only a carpenter's son and a poor cousin in the royal line, he gained a following by virtue of attributes inherent in his own individual self. Other examples are Muhammad (establishing the Islamic order in seventh-century Medina and Mecca), Joan of Arc (leading the French to victory at Orléans in 1429), Joseph Smith (founding the Mormon Zion in nineteenth-century America), Louis Riel (attempting a sovereign French state in nineteenth-century Manitoba), Adolf Hitler (creating the German Third Reich from 1933 to 1945), and the Ayatollah Khomeini (commanding Iranians to overthrow the shah in 1978). On a lesser scale charisma has also been the basis of the authority of warlords, military chiefs, *caudillos*, demagogues, and populist leaders, whose exceptional personal abilities have overpowered other men and women, won their obedience, and induced their self-surrender. In all these cases the claim to power has rested not on timeworn patterns of social life but on the allegedly superhuman qualities of a human being.

Although we today can readily understand charismatic authority as a burst of creative human energy, it appears differently to the leader and followers involved. Charisma is indeed an assertion of human pride, but one without much self-consciousness. Like traditional authority it is grounded in a one-dimensional, humble view of humankind. Charistmatic power holders do not think of themselves as mere human beings but as mysteriously chosen delegates of superhuman authority, specially designated instruments of divine power, earthlings seized by forces from the beyond and therefore compelled to act. Equally as much as one who inherits a crown, the prophet typically refuses to accept personal responsibility for his or her power, attributing it instead to some almighty being. Thus the prophet does not hesitate to demand of everyone else total obedience, unquestioning surrender, prostration no less complete than that expected by those who rule on the basis of tradition. Neither Jesus nor Muhammad nor anyone else who has held their kind of authority has urged followers to think for themselves, innovate, create, or talk back. The message has been rather, "Follow me: and let the dead bury their dead."[5] For this reason, if a charismatically inspired order persists at all it quickly passes upon the leader's death into a condition of stasis and stability wherein custom once again becomes the guiding norm of conduct. Weber called this the routinization of charisma, the process whereby life settles down into a new routine, becoming established and institutionalized. Being replaces becoming once again, and prophetic novelty gives way to priestly repetition. The postcharismatic leader comes to power not "by virtue of purely personal qualities, but by virtue of acquired or inherited qualities, or because he has been legitimated by an act of charismatic election."[6] Government becomes again a matter of preservation of the past.

similarities between tradition and charisma

LAW

The rhythmic movement back and forth between tradition and charisma did not end suddenly. Only little by little have human beings become convinced that there is more to life on earth than conforming to customs and surrendering to saviors—millions of our contemporaries in nonindustrialized societies are doubtful even now. The awareness that *people* form governments has overtaken our race but gradually. A Greek historian named Heraclitus (575–480 B.C.) argued in his day that governments are a matter of convention rather than of nature, but his voice was mostly drowned out by those of Plato and Aristotle. At various points in medieval times the monarchs of France and Spain were compelled to grant *fueros*, bills of collective rights, to various provinces and districts, thus accepting limitations on their power. In 1215, England's King John signed the Magna Carta, curtailing under duress his domination over nobles and freemen. But such events as these did not signify a mentality among rebellious subjects that the king derived his right to rule from them. Nor did the kings who acknowledged certain rights of citizens thereby admit that their governments were obliged to follow the desires of

the strengthening awareness that people form governments

Three examples of legal-rational authority: Winston Churchill, prime minister of the United Kingdom during World War II; Dwight D. Eisenhower, president of the United States, 1952–1960; Lester B. Pearson, prime minister of Canada, 1963–1968.

mere men and women. The significance of *fueros* and charters was that they narrowed the domain of traditional authority and permitted some citizens to innovate without direct challenge to government. Long before people felt themselves free to impose the human will on the polity, there gradually arose the idea that it might legitimately be impressed on the physical world.

Our forebears in the late Middle Ages and the Renaissance began to be aware of the creative potential within themselves more through economic than through political behavior, more through acting innovatively upon the earth than through changing the norms of public order. Michelangelo Buonarroti (1475–1564) had no intention of challenging the God-given authority of kings or popes when he sculpted the Pietà or embellished the Sistine Chapel. Nor did Leonardo da Vinci (1452–1519) when he painted the Mona Lisa, Marco Polo (ca. 1254–1324) when he trekked to China, Christopher Columbus (1446–1506) when he sailed to the Indies, Galileo Galilei (1564–1642) when he invented the telescope, Johann Gutenberg (ca. 1400–1468) when he began to use movable type, or Isaac Newton (1642–1727) when he formulated laws of gravity and motion. These were not meant to be political acts, but they all shouted out the same message: "People, look what people can do!" Much more than any political events, it was the art, explorations, inventions, and discoveries of the fourteenth through seventeenth centuries that brought the dawn of the modern world. For they nourished a self-consciousness among human beings that humanly effected novelty is possible and good. The innovations of that era had a compounding effect, moreover, spawning still further innovations, and this process continues to the present day.

social-contract theory: political effect of apolitical invention

It was only a matter of time before the apolitical innovations would have large-scale political effects. Once the written word could be mass-produced on printing presses, more people could learn to read and write. Having this ability, they found it easier to put the status quo inside their heads, ponder it, and think new thoughts. In a sense, Gutenberg fathered the Protestant Reformation, with its insistence that each person could interpret the Bible and approach God directly, independent of the mediation of traditional authority. For such a doctrine assumed the availability of Bibles and an ability to read them. And the Reformation in turn loosened the political imagination of the entire northern part of Europe. Against its background there arose in the seventeenth and eighteenth centuries a revolutionary new conception of government. John Locke (1632–1704), an English Protestant philosopher, and Jean-Jacques Rousseau (1712–1778), who was raised a Calvinist in Geneva, were its major proponents. The new idea was that the polity results from a *social contract*, that government rests upon an agreement among citizens, that public order in some sense belongs to the human race. The state is not a divine imposition but a human invention. Locke made the point succinctly in his *Second Treatise on Government*, published in 1690: "But I shall desire those who make this Objection, to remember that Absolute Monarchs are but Men."[7]

The new theories of politics permitted even sovereign political power to be understood in terms of Weber's third and final type of authority, the one he labeled *legal-rational*. In this case power is held not simply by virtue of age-old tradition or charismatic gifts but "by *rationally established* norms, by enactments, decrees, and regulations, in such a manner that the legitimacy of authority becomes the legality of the general rule, which is purposely thought out, enacted, and announced with formal correctness."[8] Law as a basis of authority was well-accepted, of course, even centuries before Locke and Rousseau. Functionaries in state bureaucracies, royal emissaries and underlings routinely exercised power throughout the medieval era on the basis of legal prescription. But not kings themselves, not the heads of government. These were taken as given, above and outside the domain of lawmakers. France's King Louis XIV (1638–1715) expressed the common traditional view when he insisted, "I am the state." But social-contract theory thoroughly undermined such a view. If the political order itself is a matter of agreement among human beings, none of them can be above or outside the law. The corpus of law in fact spells out the social contract. By no means etched in the stone of custom, government exists simply on paper. This was the awareness that Jefferson and his coconspirators shared when they declared America's independence. Most of them had studied Locke's theories and they meant only to apply them to the case at hand. By taxing the colonists without their consent, restricting their trade, denying them trial by jury, and committing dozens of other offenses listed in the Declaration of Independence, King George III had failed to live up to his end of the social contract. The colonies were therefore "absolved from all Allegiance to the British Crown" and could make a new government on their own.

the U.S. example of legal-rational authority

As much as any existing national government, that of the United States exemplifies the legal-rational kind of political authority and epitomizes the idea of social contract. It is grounded in a written document, the Constitution of 1789, and it feels obliged to act within the constraints of that document, at least as it has subsequently been amended and interpreted by due process of law. Within constitutional limits, moreover, the social contract in the United States is regularly renewed, renegotiated, and reinforced by the periodic election of most members of the government. The 100 senators are elected for six-year terms, two from each state; a third of them must face the voters every two years. The 435 members of the House of Representatives must all stand for election every two years, each in a geographically defined district. Thus are constituted the two houses of the Congress, the government's legislative branch. The president and vice president are elected for concurrent four-year terms by an electoral college committed to the results of a nationwide popular election. The president proposes legislation to the Congress, signs or vetos the bills Congress sends him, oversees the state's execution of its laws, and is commander-in-chief of the military forces. State, city, and county governments in the United States are grounded in the same kind of political culture, one that unashamedly assumes human ownership and control of political life.

During the past 200 years, authority in the American system of government has become steadily more concentrated in the presidential role. Theodore Roosevelt, Woodrow Wilson, Franklin Roosevelt, and all the presidents since Dwight Eisenhower have successfully defined the role far more broadly than anyone could have imagined in 1789. The Indochina war, for example, although it involved millions of United States soldiers and caused an estimated 2 million deaths, was never declared by Congress, as is constitutionally required. And in the midst of contemporary crises the citizenry tends to wonder what the president will do, not what the Congress will direct the president to do. Nonetheless, the near-impeachment of Richard Nixon, his resignation under duress, and the orderly resolution of that critical period are strong evidence of the continuing legal-rational foundation of the U.S. government. Further evidence is the constitutional amendment, enacted in 1951 in the wake of Franklin Roosevelt's exceedingly active presidency, that limits service in the presidential office to two terms.

The American war of independence was revolutionary not only because it defied the British king and gave new government to the thirteen colonies, but more importantly because it defied the *idea* of traditional authority and embodied with unprecedented clarity the *idea* of constitutional government. Separated by an ocean from the hoary customs of Europe and unfettered by strong indigenous traditions, the United States almost deserved the title Stanford sociologist Seymour Martin Lipset has given it, *The First New Nation*. But it was not the last. After 1789, society after society began to embrace the theory of uncustomary government and to place the polity on a contractual, constitutional, legal-rational basis. Monarchs resisted, to be sure, and that is why France's King Louis XVI was beheaded in 1793, Mexico's Emperor Maximilian was executed in 1867, and Russia's Czar Nicholas II was shot in 1918. Other traditional rulers abdicated or fled in the face of demands for constitutional rule: Portugal's King Manoel in 1910, China's Manchu emperor in 1912, Germany's Kaiser Wilhelm in 1918, Spain's King Alfonso in 1931, Italy's King Victor Emmanuel in 1946, and Ethiopia's Emperor Hailie Selassie in 1974. In some societies, those who ruled by birthright were allowed to keep their thrones once the rug of authority had been pulled from under them; Great Britain, Denmark, Belgium, the Netherlands, Norway, and Sweden all maintain the trappings of monarchy to this day.

One of the few societies which gained constitutional rule without paying the price of revolution was Canada. Its population in 1789 consisted mainly of two groups: English-speaking Loyalists, who clung to the authority of the British Crown, and French-speaking peasants, over whom the traditional rule of the king of France had been replaced, in 1763, by that of the king of England and the Catholic church. But the stirrings of constitutional politics soon appeared, and there were minor rebellions in both Upper Canada (Ontario) and Lower Canada (Quebec) in 1837. Nonetheless, when these two colonies were joined with Nova

constitutional government found favor also beyond the first new nation

the unusual case of Canada

Scotia and New Brunswick to create Canadian society in 1867, the new government in Ottawa was by no means defined like that in Washington. It was thought to "derive its just powers" only in part from the consent of the Canadian people, and more fundamentally from the consent of the British government. Its legal-rational basis was not an indigenous constitution but an act of the Parliament in London. The British North America Act established a parliamentary government for Canada, but one whose powers were limited by the imperial center.

Gradually as time went on, London doled out sovereignty to Ottawa piecemeal. The process is by now effectively complete. No single constitution but a long succession of legal precedents has come to define the Canadian polity as resulting from contractual agreement. In a manner similar to that in the United States, the Canadian social contract is periodically renewed by the popular election of members of government. The 282 members of the House of Commons are chosen by voters in as many parliamentary districts, or ridings. The leader of the party which wins the most seats is invited by the governor-general to become the head of government and to appoint a cabinet. The defining of Canadian public order proceeds as legislation proposed by this government makes its way to passage by the House of Commons. Whenever the Commons refuses to give majority support to this government, or in any case before five years have passed, the prime minister must call a new election, and the process is repeated. There is also a Canadian Senate, whose 102 members serve from the time of appointment until the age of 75; the prime minister appoints new members as vacancies occur. The Senate, however, has little power and can at most delay legislation passed in the lower house of Parliament. As in the United States, the governments of political subdivisions (provinces, cities, regions, and counties) are rooted in the same kind of political culture as underlies the federal regime.

SUMMARY

the humane awareness underlying contemporary political debate

Not only in the U.S.A. and Canada but in most contemporary societies, the everyday political process now comes down to unashamed debate over which words shall be written into law, which norms shall be defined as public policy, which human ideas shall set the framework of life in common. The purpose of this first section of the chapter has been to identify the assumption underlying such debate: the assumption that mere human beings can indeed write lawbooks of their own and use them to organize social life. The great majority of national cultures by now take for granted this principle, that people can and must decide in what their commonweal consists. It is a principle that contrasts sharply with those underlying the traditional and charismatic types of authority. Government of both these latter kinds is thought to come from outside human capabilities, from the security of a god-given past in the case of tradition, from the certainty of a superhuman savior in the case of charisma. Only gradually has the idea of government by law, polity by common human agreement, caught on in the human race. Only in recent centuries have men and women become so aware of themselves, so reflective on their own condition, as to be able to admit their own human responsibility for the political structure within which they pursue their respective private purposes. This awareness, so it seems, is traceable mainly to the inventive, creative schemes in the

The human movement toward legal, constitutional government has been long, painful, and slow. This nineteenth-century engraving shows a reluctant King John of England about to sign the Magna Carta at Runnymede in 1215. (The Granger Collection)

physical arts and sciences that came to fruition in the late Middle Ages and the Renaissance. Human mastery of the earth became in that era so obvious that our ancestors began to harbor a belief that they could master even themselves. Thus was born the theory of social contract, a little later the American republic, and since then a host of other experiments in what is now routinely called self-government.

yet legal-rational politics does not imply democracy

Dramatic as the shift in political culture has been, it must not be misunderstood. Legal-rational government by no means implies democracy, if the latter is understood to require an equality of political participation and power. The American, British, Canadian, and all other constitutional regimes are quite obviously more responsive to some groups of citizens than to others. And officeholders in every contemporary society tend on average to hail from the wealthier and more prestigious social strata. Many voters cast ballots for one or another political party purely for traditional reasons: "I *always* vote Republican, just like my father and grandfather." Many others vote for charismatic superstars, ignoring concrete issues in favor of candidates' personal styles. There is, in sum, plenty of thoughtlessness and inequality left in the political process. But the residue of premodern politics lingering still throughout the world should not obscure the change that has occurred. Self-conscious political activists have become so numerous in our race that few rulers anywhere can any longer rule without at least the semblance of a constitution, laws, and elections. The unexpected fall of the shah of Iran in 1978 held a lesson for the few remaining monarchs and emperors still exercising power: the days left to them are short. No polity in the contemporary world can long survive simply on the basis of custom. Too many people are thinking about politics, and too much change is in the wind.

Notwithstanding the overall trend toward rational government, more immediate problems still remain. Political sociology cannot yet limit its attention to variation across societies and their subunits in the terms of the social contract, the kind of agreement that governs social life. It cannot study merely the contemporary issues of debate, the shifting configurations of political antagonists, and the dynamics by which conflicting viewpoints are resolved. All this diversity is appropriate grist for sociological analysis, especially as it confronts scholars in their own respective societies, provinces, states, counties, cities, and similar contexts. The journals are full of results of such research, and newspapers give daily reports and commentary. But the section immediately below had best address a more fundamental question, that of what conditions in any society facilitate government according to some kind of social contract, whatever its terms and concrete issues, and even granting the incompleteness of its democratic base. The idea of legal-rational political authority is not yet secure on our planet. Our first interest must be in how this idea can be nourished.

Three Enemies of Legal-Rational Authority

If the works of Locke and Rousseau found their way upon publication into the hands of God, I suspect they induced a smile of divine pleasure. For at last the leading political thinkers of a human society were recognizing, as John Kennedy phrased it much later, that "here on earth God's work must truly be our own."[9] It is not too much to say that the human race was coming of age. No longer would conformity to a traditional past or a charismatic present be the measure of human worth. At last people might reckon virtue by the excellence of the societies they themselves, thoughtfully and self-consciously, would create. But alas, the path to self-government has been slow. Cromwell's revolutionary forces set foot upon it in England in 1649, and cut off the head of King Charles I. Eleven years later, Charles II was sitting on the British throne, merrily restoring the traditional order. In France, the republic formed in 1792 surrendered itself later to the Emperor Napoleon, and then more kings. Even two and a half centuries after Locke published his treatises on government, the German people let themselves be captured by a charismatic madman, their Weimar republic disappeared, and history had its darkest hour. Even today, the retreat from constitutional government goes on. Every one of the South American societies was at one time a republic, yet current governments in most of them rule by military force. What has gone wrong? Why cannot people limit their squabbles to the *terms* of social-contract government? Why is the very *idea* still in jeopardy? The answers to such questions are not easy. There are dozens of books on each major instance of retreat. Still, three very general factors that appear and reappear in many explanations might at least be mentioned here in brief, since they continue to threaten in the present day.

the slow and torturous path to self-government

LINGERING TRADITIONALISM

Historically, the idea of the social contract arose in Europe after a period of unprecedented invention, exploration, discovery, and artistic expression. People came to believe they could create polities only after they saw with their own eyes the novelty they could make out of physical matter. Self-conscious action upon the public order was an extension of self-conscious control of wood, metal, ocean waves, flowing streams, the wind, and the printed page. But this historical process was felt by only a minority of the population. The vast majority of Europeans in the eighteenth and even nineteenth centuries remained peasants, living and working in the customary manner of their ancestors. The technical and artistic achievements were not quite real to this majority; hence neither was the idea of self-government. Until a person is drawn into the experience of a modern economy, that person's allegiance is likely to remain at the feet of traditional authority. This, then, is the first enemy of legal-rational authority in any society: the persistence of certain sectors of the population in a backward economic condition, isolated from the experience of innovation in work and other aspects of everyday life.

being uninvolved in modern work, peasants tend not to accept the legal-rational ethic

The aversion of Marx, Engels, and many other progressive intellectuals for the peasant class can best be understood from this perspective. For so long as peasants' tedious and customary routine of life is not disrupted, they tend to submit to whatever government is in power—not out of rational conviction but as an unthinking matter of course, as a natural human obligation. This class can thus constitute a base of power for kings and others who claim to rule by divine right. Consider, for instance, the case of Quebec. Between roughly 1615 and 1760, the old regime of France established on the shores of the St. Lawrence a traditional society. Feudal lords (*seigneurs*) ruled in the name of the king, and peasants (*habitants*) worked the land and worshipped God with the same age-old fidelity as their forebears in France. Quebec was founded, in effect, as an extension of France. And when Britain completed its conquest of the colony in 1763, nothing much changed. The *seigneurs* and other nobles returned to France, leaving behind 70,000 illiterate *habitants*, 138 priests, and one bishop. The British colonial regime won the clerics' allegiance by leaving them free to practice Catholicism and then used the traditional religious authority of the latter to transfer the *habitants'* loyalty from the French crown to the British one. Life went on fairly much as usual for the common people, and the French Canadians behaved with general docility. Isolated linguistically, geographically, and economically from the frenzy of industrial progress to the south and west, the people of Quebec were incorporated into Canada and then watched it gain self-government without themselves having much part in it—indeed without believing very strongly that they *should* have power over it. To be sure there were exceptions like Wilfrid Laurier, Canadian prime minister at the turn of the twentieth century, but the bulk of the Quebec population remained literally and figuratively on the farm.

Quebec: stronghold of traditionalism until recent decades

As late as 1956, a church-sponsored radio broadcast on the eve of a general election in Quebec expressed the still-prevalent political view: "Sovereign authority, by whatever government it is exercised, is derived solely from God, the supreme and eternal principle of all power. . . . It is therefore an absolute error to believe that authority comes from the multitudes, from the masses, from the people, to pretend that authority does not properly belong to those who exercise it, but that they have only a simple mandate revocable at any time by the people."[10] Such ideas, however, were soon to be forgotten. Quebecois were conscripted for service in World War II, and after 1945 economic development spread throughout the province. Literacy rose and an ever-larger proportion of the population came to be concentrated in urban areas and mechanized occupations. Against this background there has arisen since the 1960s a whirlwind of political change. Encouraged by experience in creative action upon the inanimate world, Quebecois have now turned their eyes consciously upon themselves and upon the public order of their life. Twenty-one years after the radio message quoted above, the newly elected Quebec premier, René Lévesque, flew to New York for a speech before a club of elite American business executives. He repeated the self-evident truths of America's Declaration of Independence and proudly reaffirmed the intention of his government to make Quebec as sovereign and self-governing as the United States.

Traditionalism lingered longer in Quebec than in the United States for several reasons. The most important is that most settlers in the American colonies, like the Puritans at Plymouth Rock, had already challenged traditional authority by their Protestantism. They came to the New World not to replicate the feudal order of Europe, as did the French settlers and those from Spain and Portugal to the south, but to create a *new* kind of society. This more than anything explains why the United States became the first new nation. Most of the 20 million immigrants which the United States accepted during the nineteenth century were of peasant origin, it is true, but they came to join an industrial labor force, surrounded by the fruits of American invention. Besides, Puritan culture had already defined the style of American politics, and the message to the immigrants was unequivocal: either become assimilated or go home.

Vestiges of political traditionalism nonetheless persist in America, and precisely in those sectors which have remained most detached from the experience of creative economic activity. Chief among them, as in most societies today, is that composed of women. Long after the vast majority of men were immersed in industrial activity, most women were still at home in the roles of wife and mother, roles which had changed very little through the centuries. Thus only quite gradually has the idea of government "of the people, by the people, for the people" been understood to include the female half of the species. Not until 1920 could women vote in American federal elections (the year was 1918 for Canada, but 1940 for the provincial elections of Quebec). But only after the requirements of a wartime economy in the early 1940s had brought more women into the labor force, and contraceptives and household conveniences reduced their subjection to household duties, did self-conscious political action by women become widespread. Even now, women are generally less likely than men to vote, to run for office, and to be elected. They account for fewer than 4 percent of the U.S. Congress. Thousands belong to voluntary associations which proclaim, often with Biblical justifications, that the total woman is a political puppet. Full participation by women in government must inevitably await their realization, through achievement in uncustomary work, that their power to create is no less than men's.

the traditional roles of wife and mother have delayed women's involvement in modern politics

The culture of traditionalism lingered long among the descendants of slaves in the United States. But as their participation in the industrial labor force increased, so did their self-awareness, and then their insistence on political power. In Plains, Georgia, in 1976, a Baptist church served as a polling place. (J. P. Laffont/Sygma)

exclusion of U.S. blacks from participation in the first new nation

The other sector of the American population which was excluded from normal participation in an industrial economy was the black minority. America was not a new nation in all respects. While it jettisoned monarchy, it clung to slavery for the first ninety years of its existence. Generation after generation of blacks worked in the traditional cotton fields of the South, and most remained there even after Congress abolished slavery by constitutional amendment in 1865. Migration to northern industrial cities did not become large-scale until after World War I, and even in the cities blacks were largely restricted to menial jobs, often in traditional domestic service. Not until the 1950s did the exercise of black power in the industrial economy become sufficiently widespread to give birth to a black political consciousness. The voter-registration drives, freedom marches, sit-ins, and demonstrations of the 1950s and 1960s were the result. By now, a much smaller proportion of blacks than of women in America still prefers to regard government as a fact of life outside its control. This is reflected in the Congress, where black representation is much less disproportionate to their numbers in the population than is that of women. The current racial problem in the United States is no longer one of bringing black Americans into the national political culture. That goal has largely been achieved. The task now is to complete the integration of the black minority into the political *structure*.

The first major audience to which the idea of social contract appealed was that composed of economic entrepreneurs, the people in eighteenth-century England, America, and France who were involved in action upon the world, organizing little factories, risking their money in long-distance trade, pitting their ingenuity against the intransigence of nature. In the first instance, government "by the people" meant mainly this kind of people. Only gradually has participation in the modern economy embraced a larger proportion of the population. But the more this has occurred, the more broadly the word *people* has come to be defined. In societies where 25 percent or more of the population even today is involved in peasant agriculture, the idea remains widespread that "sovereign authority, by whatever government it is exercised, is derived solely from God," or from some other superhuman force. In such societies, it is difficult to imagine what "free elections" might mean. In North America, Europe, and much of the rest of the world, free elections are more possible, but the prospects of constitutional government continue to be weakened by the vestiges of traditionalism which remain.

MILITARISM

Widespread participation in an industrial economy is not, however, enough to ensure constitutional government. An active economic life does indeed break the bonds of traditional authority, but it does not guarantee the legal-rational alternative. The latter has legions of enemies. A second one is militarism, the substitution of armed force for authority of any kind. The word *authority*, as Weber used it, implies a joining of culture and social structure, so that the bulk of citizens *believe* that their government's exercise of power is legitimate. Weber's interest was in three alternative bases for popular acquiescence to government, three different ideological ways by which power becomes authority. But if a government controls sufficient weaponry and armaments and if it is ready to use them against large numbers of people, it can rule without authority. This prospect properly occurs only in modern times, and there are two reasons. First is that in traditional societies most people most of the time accepted as legitimate whatever government was in power, whether it got there by heredity or force of arms. The accustomed loyalty of the Quebec people to the British Crown is a case in point; they mostly acquiesced to incorporation into even a non-Catholic and anglophone empire. The second reason illegal and illegitimate government is a problem particular to our age is that military technology has been made so effective. The same worldly action and involvement that has nourished a belief in political self-determination has resulted in machine guns, tear gas, tanks, bombs, techniques of torture, and other instruments by which a few people can deny self-determination to the rest with unprecedented effectiveness. Power can more easily run naked today; it needs less ideological clothing than it used to. When a nuclear bomb is hovering overhead it becomes quite irrelevant by what kind of authority, if any, it was deployed.

military power without authority—a problem almost unique to our times

The very societies which were the first to establish constitutional government for themselves have been among the most steadfast in denying it to others. The various European governments used their technical achievements to impose colonial rule on whatever societies they could conquer. Initially they played upon indigenous respect for traditional authority. Later, as colonized peoples began to learn the ideas of legal-rational government the imperial rulers readily used their military prowess to hold onto power, even long after their regimes had lost all semblance of legitimacy. They justified their imperialism to themselves by a variety of doctrines summed up in Rudyard Kipling's phrase, "the white man's burden," the supposed responsibility of pale-faced people to govern those with tawnier complexions. What is remarkable is how fiercely the imperial powers fought to keep the burden on their shoulders: Britain against East Indians until 1948, and even against the pale-faced Irish until 1922; France against Vietnamese until 1954, against Algerians until 1962; the Netherlands against Indonesians until 1949; Portugal against the peoples of Angola and Mozambique until 1974. For the most part, however, by the 1950s and 1960s, the European governments were willing to lay the burden down. British royalty kept themselves busy flying off to preside willingly over colonial independence days.

new native military regimes in Latin America and elsewhere

Most contemporary military regimes are not foreign to the populations they rule. Latin America provides some of the most tragic examples. Most of these societies proclaimed their independence from Spain or Portugal in the 1820s, fought wars of liberation, and established constitutional governments. For a variety of reasons, however, political stability eluded most of them. Their populations had carried traditional notions of authority with them from Europe, and these melded with similarly traditional notions in the indigenous cultures. Industrial advance was slow, the majority of people remained on the land as peasants (*campesinos*), and the Catholic church entrenched itself as a guardian against human pride. As a result, governments vacillated between law, tradition, charisma, and naked power. There were exceptions, notably Uruguay, Chile, and Mexico, which developed relatively stable social-contract forms of government in the early twentieth century. Optimistic observers predicted that the other societies would follow suit, and that legal-rational political authority would become ever more secure in Latin America, as ever-larger proportions of the population became literate and involved in urban-industrial economic life.

Indeed, by the 1950s and 1960s, the idea of government by the people had taken root as never before in Latin American national cultures. The demand for an end to rule by the traditional elites was heard from more and more sectors of the population. But instead of constitutional governments, nearly all the Latin societies got military dictatorships, generals who simply put themselves in power without regard for authority. This happened in Paraguay in 1954, in Argentina in 1955, in Bolivia and Brazil in 1964, in Peru in 1968, and in Ecuador in 1972. At last, in 1973, the two exemplars of constitutional government in South America both fell to the armed forces. In Chile, President Slavador Allende went to his death rather than surrender. In Uruguay, President Juan Bordaberry cooperated with the generals, who then ousted him three years later. Any observer has to ask what went wrong. These were not the first coups d'état (*golpes* or military takeovers) in these countries, but they were unprecedented in their harshness. They contradicted, moreover, the steady movement of the whole continent toward stable, constitutional government. Indeed, Chile had had such government for forty-six years. Why should groups of generals reverse so promising a trend?

The sociology of military takeovers is a complicated area of study and varies across the national settings where such takeovers have occurred. Some general points, however, can appropriately be noted here. There are in principle two prerequisites for a coup against a legal government. First, the military has to learn not to care about what the legitimate regime or the people as a whole prefers. Second, the military has to be so large, well-trained, well-equipped, and well-organized that it can rule without legitimacy, that is, irrespective of popular preference. In other words, given the will and a way, the military forces can at any time and in any society take over the government. Tragically enough, both these conditions were met in postwar South America. For by that time, the United States and the U.S.S.R. had squared off against one another in the cold war. It became a major goal of each of these governments to increase its influence throughout the world and to curtail the influence of its opponent. Accordingly, the United States launched a massive foreign-aid program in Latin America (and elsewhere), in order to keep the continent loyal to the American side of the conflict. The United States earnestly hoped to strengthen the cause of constitutional government in Latin America, confident that it would thereby secure the Latin republics' allegiance to American leadership of the noncommunist world.

Even in the early 1950s, a substantial proportion of the grants and loans given to the Latin American societies was for military purposes. The idea was to arm them against possible Soviet invasion. But their armies lacked training in advanced warfare and understanding of the nature of the alleged communist threat. The American government therefore began to bring Latin American officers and men to study on military bases in the United States and in the Panama Canal Zone. By 1972, the number of Latin American alumni of these training programs had reached 230,000. These men had been dazzled by the sight of sophisticated tools of warfare unheard of in their own societies. They had learned to use such armaments. Most important of all, they had learned a reason to use them: to combat communism. After Castro's success in Cuba, moreover, they had learned that communism could arise from the inside, that even people within their own societies could not be trusted. Thus was the first precondition for a coup fulfilled: the Latin American military commanders had learned to think of themselves as agents less of their respective governments than of the American-led crusade against communism. Henceforth they would justify their exercise of power less in terms of the laws of their respective societies than by their own self-serving interpretations of the anticommunist crusade.[11]

During the 1950s and 1960s the weaponry and matériel available to the Latin American armed forces also increased steadily. Between 1946 and 1968, American grants and loans to Brazil totaled $3.8 billion, to Chile $1.6 billion, to Colombia $1.1 billion, and similar amounts to the remaining societies of the continent. To be sure, only a small part of these moneys was earmarked for military purposes, but even the purely economic aid enabled the Latin American governments to spend more of their own money on armaments. Through the Foreign Military Sales Program established in 1962, moreover, the United States dispatched hundreds of salesmen to Latin America, whose goal was to sell these governments weaponry made in America. Between 1962 and 1965 alone, their purchases amounted to more than $100 million. Thus was the second precondition for a coup fulfilled: the

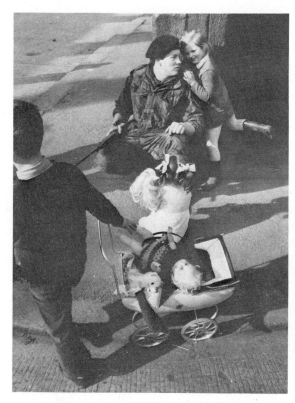

The more a government rules by military force, the less it rules by law. A social contract that endures only so long as troops patrol the streets is not a contract at all, but tyranny. That is the tragedy of Northern Ireland, where children by now accept soldiers as part of life's everyday routine. (Gilles Peress/Magnum Photos, Inc.)

availability of the hardware necessary to keep people under control, whether they liked it or not.

An excerpt from U.S. history may help to clarify the present plight of millions of Latin Americans, as well as people elsewhere living under military regimes. The founders of the United States were well aware of the danger that their new federal government might one day fall into the hands of the armed forces. For this reason, "the right of the people to keep and bear Arms" was set down in the second amendment to the Constitution. Consider what this meant in 1791. Not only were there no nuclear bombs, submarines, fighter planes, bombers, or intercontinental missiles. Not even dynamite had yet been invented, nor tear gas, nor the machine gun. It was the age of the single-shot rifle. If citizens could keep such a weapon in their homes, their collective resources of violence were almost on a par with those of the army. Without legitimacy in popular culture, government was virtually impossible. The military forces lacked the technology to control the population by force, even if they wanted to.

Now consider the Latin American societies in the 1960s, and picture tanks rolling down cobblestone streets amidst oxcarts and donkeys, machine guns pointed at demonstrators still in peasant dress, tear gas hurled into crowds of students who memorize lectures because books cost too much, and fighter planes strafing shanty towns of illiterate urban immigrants. The people literally do not have a chance

the original significance of citizens' right to bear arms

against armies trained and equipped by a foreign superpower. And when the army has been taught not to trust the people it is supposed to defend, the likelihood of success for constitutional government is extremely small. Those who rebel against military rule resort to terrorist tactics and guerrilla warfare, the effect of which is to undermine further the public order of social life. Economic production slows down, the faith of people in themselves is shaken, and the human spirit wavers. One can hope that out of this experience, the Latin American governments might yet be established on legal-rational bases. At this writing, Venezuela, Colombia, and Peru appear to have moved decisively in this direction. Mexico, whose government rests on a constitution adopted in 1917, has created a strong and vibrantly self-conscious political culture. Farther to the south, the prognosis is less optimistic. Pessimism also clouds the political horizon of Africa, where most governments also rule by force rather than by law. Much of the military weaponry and expertise in Africa is of Russian, Chinese, or Euorpean rather than American origin, but the effect on native populations is much the same as in Latin America.

the rightful role of military force under a government of law

The paragraphs above are not meant to suggest that a government has no need for an army or police. There are always dissenters against political authority, whatever its basis, and only anarchists and utopians could doubt that the maintenance of public order regularly requires in all societies the occasional use of force. Beyond some point, however, the reliance on force is so complete that one can no longer speak of authority, but only of power. When generals take over a government, that point has surely been passed. In Canada, the United States, and those other societies which have not yet suffered coups d'état, the means of preventing them are the obverse of their preconditions. First is careful education of military personnel and their integration into the natural culture of constitutional authority, so that the ideas they think are those of loyalty to government, not to ethereal, self-serving ideologies. Second is the steady process of disarmament, thus eliminating the tools by which constitutional government can be destroyed. It should be some comfort to Canadians to know that with their current (1980) troop strength of about 80,000 men and women and with their limited weaponry, the nation's armed forces would find it difficult to rule the citizenry. In the United States, by contrast, there are about 800,000 men and women in the Army, 500,000 in the Navy, 200,000 in the Marines, and 600,000 in the Air Force. They are equipped with weaponry that defies human imagination. Americans and everyone else on earth can only hope that these soldiers and their officers remain loyal to a government of law.

ALIENATION IN EVERYDAY LIFE

Surely some readers must have recoiled from even the brief description given above of militarism in Latin America. More repugnant still is the idea that through its aid program the United States actually facilitated the military takeovers. Human eyes tend to glaze over at the sight of contemporary kinds of naked power. We often prefer not to think of such horrors but retreat into the private world of friends and family. "I can't do anything about it anyway," people often say. But if today's uses of armed force tend to overpower the human intellect, so also do other aspects of life in the advanced industrial societies. The sheer size of the corporations and bureaucracies we work for and deal with seems to defy efforts at understanding them. Our cities, too, are huge. We can grasp their bigness only from the tops of towers and skyscrapers, vantage points that leave a sense not of understanding but of awe. As if size were not enough there is also the complexity of this world created by our hands. Our supermarket shopping carts are crammed with items made by unknown workers, in distant factories, with strange machines, and of ingredients outside our personal experience. Even the experts seem not to know what is going on. Nuclear power plants spring leaks for no apparent reasons; skylabs and satellites crash to earth at spots of their own choosing. Consider how economists contradict one another in their discussions of inflation rates, stock-market ups and downs, oil shortages, and the prospects of economic growth. Faced with the complicated bigness of contemporary social life, many people throw up their hands. "It's all beyond me," they say. The average American adult spends almost thirty hours a week watching television, but no wonder sports events and situation comedies get higher ratings on the whole than does the news. Games and fantasies seem often to make more sense than real events.

lack of control in work and little things: the gravest threat to self-government

In such an attitude lies the third and most menacing enemy of legal-rational authority: engulfment or mystification in the process of mechanized production and high consumption, lack of control over everyday life, powerlessness at work and play, economic alienation. Citizens cannot enter into a reasonable contract with one another about a social order that is beyond them. The point cannot be stressed too strongly: a person's belief in his or her ability to help create the polity depends utterly on the experience of acting creatively in small matters. People seize political power only when their confidence in themselves has been bolstered by the exercise of other kinds of power. Only when people are on top of the goods and services surrounding them will they believe that they *can* get on top of their government. The political eyes of peasants open when peasants learn to read and write, to do their work a little differently, to make blueprints for a house and then build it, to take apart a car and put it back together, to choose their own marriage partners, to change the style of their clothing, to carve their own niches in the larger economy—in sum, to decide in a very practical way how to run their daily lives. It is then that they defy traditional authority, ignore charismatic gurus, and assert their right to a reasoned voice in governmental affairs.

But consider the world of peasants' great-grandchildren. And suppose that generations of action upon the earth have created economic firms and cities so large as to escape human comprehension, a world where radios, televisions, and telephones permit citizens to get by without reading or writing much, where houses are built mainly by expert developers, cars repaired mainly by professional mechanics, clothing worn according to the whims of distant designers, marriage partners chosen sometimes even by computers, and jobs taken wherever they can be found—in sum, an economic milieu in which most people most of the time are inactive objects, passively living out their days in response to forces outside their control. When daily life in industrial societies becomes mainly an experience of being acted upon, the political eyes of peasants' descendants become as closed as those of peasants' forebears. Like everything else, government seems to happen off in the distance. The public order becomes just part of the scenery. One can follow the preelection opinion surveys and wait in suspense for the election returns, but the idea of *deciding* who will win is left to anonymous others. In the 1978 American elections, nearly two-thirds of the eligible voters did not bother to go to the polls. The population staying home has been hovering around 30 or 40 percent even in presidential election years.

a mass society is the breeding ground for demagoguery

A society in which people cease to believe that government is their creation and no longer involve themselves in the definition of public order is what many scholars have called a *mass society*. Citizens lose their grip on government and the will to regain it. They quit thinking seriously about political issues and instead place blind faith in existent authority, expecting government to take care of them, to safeguard their accustomed way of life. They give up trying to understand politics, confident that people more talented than they will keep things running smoothly. In its initial stages, a mass society may not seem to bode ill for its members. So what if most of them are passive, unconcerned, and uninvolved politically? Does it really matter that voter turnout is low and political discussion both rare and cynical? Perhaps professionals in government—economists, accountants, policy analysts, military experts, and the sons and daughters of prosperous old political families— know better anyway how to maintain the basic framework of the commonweal. Indeed, a mass society may be marked by a carefree, happy-go-lucky ambience, the giddy euphoria of a disco or carbaret. Citizens may just be enjoying life as a kind of game. But therein lies the danger. For what happens when sooner or later a crisis erupts: a shortage of food or fuel, the prospect of war, a nuclear accident, mass unemployment or anything that prevents citizens from continuing to enjoy their accustomed way of life? How do alienated citizens react, once deprived of the public order they have come to take for granted? They react like the unknowing powerless of past generations. They cry like mindless sheep deprived of pasture and then follow whichever shepherd sings the most compelling song. The culmination of a mass society is rule by some charismatic demagogue, a ranting savior whom followers believe can magically set things right. Politics is reduced to personalities, and there is less concern for law than for faith.[12]

the Nazi case

The theory of mass society provides a partial but still powerful explanation for the rise of Adolf Hitler and the Nazi party in Germany in the 1930s. The roots of the Third Reich, that is to say, seem to lie in great part in the everyday powerlessness of German citizens who therefore lacked the will to exercise their political power seriously and thoughtfully. Hitler was supported, it is true, by most of the German peasantry, simple, unaware farmers who would have pledged allegiance for traditional reasons to almost anyone in authority. As the Nazi era progressed, moreover, the governmental will was enforced steadily more by the naked force of weaponry. But no explanation of that horrible chapter in human history can ignore the fact that Germans working in the industrial economy and living in cities found in their everyday lives little experience of autonomous, creative action. In his *Theory of Stable Democracy*, Harry Eckstein wrote that the Weimar republic of 1919 to 1933 "was superimposed upon a society pervaded by authoritarian relationships and obsessed with authoritarianism. . . . German fami-

It is rare for a single stamp to celebrate at once two distinct threats to legal-rational politics. On the left is Alfredo Stroessner, the general who seized power in Paraguay in 1954. On the right is Juan Perón, the populist demagogue who was elected to the Argentine presidency in 1946. Not surprisingly, Stroessner and Perón were fast friends. The stamp commemorates a visit between them in 1955, shortly before Perón's ouster in a military coup.

ly life, German schools, and German business firms were all exceedingly authoritarian. German families were dominated, more often than not, by tyrannical husbands and fathers, German schools by tyrannical teachers, German firms by tyrannical bosses."[13] To the extent that Eckstein's depiction is adequate, no one should have expected legal-rational authority in Germany to last. By virtue of their powerlessness in everyday life, the citizens lacked the self-confidence to make it last. Thus could Hitler capture them with a sweet-sounding song and lead them out of the euphoria of the early 1930s into the horrors of war and genocide.

other examples of demagogic appeal

Powerless people everywhere seek saviors and willingly subvert even legal-rational, constitutional government out of rapturous enthusiasm for demagogues. This happened in Argentina in 1946, when a citizenry suffering from more than a decade of military rule and class exploitation wasted a chance for constitutional government by electing an irrational demagogue, Juan Perón, who then ignored the very principles of law by which he had come to power. Perón was ousted by the military in 1955, but his charismatic grip on voters remained so strong that in 1973, eighteen years later, he returned from exile to be elected again. The United States and Canada, by contrast, have until now escaped demagogic rule; they deserve to be counted among the world's best examples of legal-rational, constitutional politics. And one of the main reasons is undoubtedly that the proportion of voters in these societies lacking control over their personal lives has never yet been sufficiently large to hand government over to demagogues. In the depression era, nonetheless, rabble-rousers like Huey Long, a Louisiana Senator, Charles Coughlin, a priest and radio commentator from Michigan, and William Aberhardt, the Alberta premier, gained huge followings with vague but impassioned calls to "come follow me, and let the dead bury their dead." In the late 1940s and early 1950s, millions of Americans applauded Wisconsin Senator Joseph McCarthy's irrational witch-hunt for communists. In the 1960s, George Wallace's populist crusade had a significant impact on American federal politics; so did Réal Couette's in the 1970s in the case of Canada. More conventional political leaders, moreover, those committed to a government of law and grounded in coherent ideologies, seem often to have garnered more votes by their personal mannerisms than by their political doctrines. Franklin Roosevelt and John Kennedy in the United States and Pierre Trudeau in Canada are good examples. The third enemy of legal-rational government, the everyday alienation that leads to demagoguery, is hardly absent even from the societal exemplars of rational politics in the contemporary world.

IN OTHER WORDS

Alexis de Tocqueville, "Despotism in Democracies"*

France gave two memorable gifts to the United States in the nineteenth century. One stayed in New York harbor, symbolizing liberty. The other gift, a social commentator named Alexis de Tocqueville, traveled the country in 1831–1832 and wrote a classic appraisal of what kind of liberty the American way of life permits. In the selection below, de Tocqueville describes what he sees as the major threat to freedom in the American kind of political system. Would you judge that his point has gained or lost relevance over the last century and a half?

I think, then, that the species of oppression by which democratic nations are menaced is unlike anything which ever before existed in the world: our contemporaries will find no prototype of it in their memories. I seek in vain for an expression which will accurately convey the whole of the idea I have formed of it; the old words despotism and tyranny are inappropriate: the thing itself is new, and since I cannot name, I must attempt to define it.

I seek to trace the novel features under which despotism may appear in the world. The first thing that strikes the observation is an innumerable multitude of men, all equal and alike, incessantly endeavoring to procure the petty and paltry pleasures with which they glut their lives. Each of them, living apart, is as a stranger to the fate of all the rest,—his children and his private friends constitute to him the whole of mankind; as for the rest of his fellow-citizens, he is close to them, but he sees them not; he touches them, but he feels them not; he exists but in himself and for himself alone; and if his kindred still remain to him, he may be said at any rate to have lost his country.

Above this race of men stands an immense and tutelary power, which takes upon itself alone to secure their gratifications, and to watch over their fate. That power is absolute, minute, regular, provident, and mild. It would be like the authority of a parent, if, like that authority, its object was to prepare men for manhood; but it seeks, on the contrary, to keep them in perpetual childhood: it is well content that the people should rejoice, provided they think of nothing but rejoicing. For their happiness such a government willingly labors, but it chooses to be the sole agent and the only arbiter of that happiness; it provides for their security, foresees and supplies their necessities, facilitates their pleasures, manages their personal concerns, directs their industry, regulates the descent of property, and subdivides their inheritances: what remains, but to spare them all the care of thinking and all the trouble of living? . . .

After having thus successively taken each member of the community in its powerful grasp, and fashioned him at will, the supreme power then extends its

*From A. DeTocqueville, *Democracy in America*, Richad D. Heffner (ed.), New American Library, Mentor, New York, 1956, pp. 301–5. First published in 1835 and 1840.

arm over the whole community. It covers the surface of a society with a network of small complicated rules, minute and uniform, through which the most original minds and the most energetic characters cannot penetrate, to rise above the crowd. The will of man is not shattered, but softened, bent, and guided; men are seldom forced by it to act, but they are constantly restrained from acting: such a power does not destroy, but it prevents existence; it does not tyrannize, but it compresses, enervates, extinguishes, and stupefies a people, till each nation is reduced to be nothing better than a flock of timid and industrious animals, of which the government is the shepherd.

I have always thought that servitude of the regular, quiet, and gentle kind which I have just described might be combined more easily than is commonly believed with some of the outward forms of freedom, and that it might even establish itself under the wing of the sovereignty of the people.

Our contemporaries are constantly excited by two conflicting passions; they want to be led, and they wish to remain free: as they cannot destroy either the one or the other of these contrary propensities, they strive to satisfy them both at once. They devise a sole, tutelary, and all-powerful form of government, but elected by the people. They combine the principle of centralization and that of popular sovereignty; this gives them a respite: they console themselves for being in tutelage by the reflection that they have chosen their own guardians. Every man allows himself to be put in leading-strings, because he sees that it is not a person or a class of persons but the people at large, who hold the end of his chain. . . . It must not be forgotten that it is especially dangerous to enslave men in the minor details of life. For my own part, I should be inclined to think freedom less necessary in great things than in little ones, if it were possible to be secure of the one without possessing the other.

Subjection in minor affairs breaks out every day, and is felt by the whole community indiscriminately. It does not drive men to resistance, but it crosses them at every turn, till they are led to surrender the exercise of their own will. Thus their spirit is gradually broken and their character enervated; whereas that obedience which is exacted on a few important but rare occasions, only exhibits servitude at certain intervals, and throws the burden of it upon a small number of men. It is in vain to summon a people, who have been rendered so dependent on the central power, to choose from time to time the representatives of that power; this rare and brief exercise of their free choice, however important it may be, will not prevent them from gradually losing the faculties of thinking, feeling, and acting for themselves, and thus gradually falling below the level of humanity.

Of all the threats to a political process based on reason and law, three especially serious ones have been considered briefly in this section. First is the lingering traditionalism, the isolation of some sectors of a national population from the reality of an industrial economy, and their consequent inability and unwillingness to assume an active and thoughtful role in the definition of public order. This threat hovers especially over many societies of Africa and Asia, where the majority of citizens remains illiterate and trapped in peasant agriculture. But it menaces also even the most highly industrialized societies insofar as women and various ethnic or racial minorities are excluded from thoroughgoing participation in modern kinds of work. The second threat in this review is militarism, the control of government and the state by armed force, irrespective of either legal or traditional authority. Militarism also weighs most heavily on the poorer societies, especially given the extent to which foreign superpowers have trained and equipped the armed forces of members of their respective blocs. But this enemy of constitutional government looms over the United States and the U.S.S.R. as well, and indeed over the human race as a whole, as long as professional armies possess the weapons and know-how necessary to subdue at once large numbers of people. All the same, it is the third threat to a government of law that deserves closest attention in the advanced industrial societies. Only to the extent that their citizens exercise power in small matters, have opportunities for creative self-expression at work and at play, can they be expected to claim their rightful roles in political decision making and to renew and renegotiate the social contract governing their common life. Citizens who are not on top of their everyday lives sooner or later ask to be beneath the thumb of demagogues.

how the future of constitutional government can best be secured

Political analysts have been pointing out for decades that the future of constitutional government in any society depends on a literate, active, and aware citizenry. Scholars generally agree that people can vote intelligently and otherwise take reasonable part in legal-rational agreement about their commonweal only to the extent that they are educated in the principles and procedures underlying this kind of political system. Thus do most contemporary governments make school attendance mandatory, and within the schools specific courses on civics, citizenship, and national and local government. Thus also are newspapers and television networks expected to give substantial attention to public affairs. Without gainsaying the importance of such forms of political education, the preceding paragraphs have emphasized a prior safeguard for a government of law. It is the experience of power and creativity in the concrete, everyday experience of citizens: in their jobs mainly, but also in their families, neighborhoods, cities, and similar, more immediate settings. For the evidence suggests that the lofty confidence in oneself that reasoned political activity requires must itself be reinforced from day to day in the practical conduct of life. Otherwise, newspaper editorials remain unread, television documentaries unwatched, civics courses forgotten, voting booths unvisited, and the citizens themselves incapable of managing their political affairs. Only when people have the chance to leave their personal marks upon their private lives do they feel enough pride to leave their respective marks upon collective public life. If people are given such a chance, a chance that is rightfully theirs, they can be trusted by and large to attend to their own political education.

Two Conceptions of Democracy

So far this chapter has steered shy of the word *democracy*, loaded as it is with more meaning than any contemporary political reality can match. For the idea of true democracy would require that every citizen have not only equal voice in defining public order but also the full knowledge and awareness necessary for rational decision making. No society today even comes close to meeting these requirements. Even in societies where every adult is allowed to cast one and only one vote in elections, wealthy and well-connected citizens have obviously more chance to make their political voices heard than do poor and powerless citizens. None of us, moreover, has the time or opportunity to become so thoroughly acquainted with current issues and to think them through so completely that our respective political acts can be fully rational. Traditionalism still lurks in our thinking—in the form of every action we take unthinkingly, every norm or value we take for granted or accept by blind faith. No politician today can succeed, moreover, without relying to some extent on looks and oratory, the stuff of demagoguery. Democracy, in short, is a big word for which all too little evidence exists. When we call a society democratic, the most we can mean is that it tends in a democratic direction, that it is founded on legal-rational, contractual principles of government, that it at least is working toward such ideals as political equality and enlightenment. Societies differ in how democratic they are, and each has problems particular to its own historical situation.

a hard lesson: democracy varies not only in degree but also in kind

But if societies vary in the *degree* of democracy they manifest, they differ also in the *kind* of democracy they hope to achieve. For us in the Western world this is a hard point to grasp but an immensely important one. Our systems, based on multiple political parties and competing interest groups, are not the only kind with a claim on the word democracy. The contract among men and women by which public order is laid down and government invested with the legitimacy of reason can be drawn up with as many different terms as any other contract. But this point was generally ignored in the West after World War II, especially in the United States. The U.S. government included in its definition of the free world only those societies whose regimes were similar enough to the one in Washington to condone relatively free trade on international capitalist principles. Thus its attitude even toward military dictatorships in Latin America, South Korea, Taiwan, Iran, Greece, and elsewhere was benign, so long as they welcomed U.S.-based multinational corporations wanting to do business within their borders. Such societies were said to be on the right road to democracy, but a few decades behind the politically advanced Western societies. The U.S. government was hostile, by contrast, toward the Soviet Union, China, the societies of Eastern Europe, and postrevolutionary Cuba. Communist and socialist governments in these lands were considered not just less democratic than the one in Washington (an accurate observation), but basically and inherently *un*democratic. The United States failed to see that in most of the world outside its own borders, and even within them, a different kind of democracy was and is in the making. This unfortunate misapprehension did not cause the cold war, but it has been a major part of the ideological foundation for that war even to the present day.

Such an error, however, has been made many times before in U.S. politics. Perhaps its was inevitable that the first new nation would suffer from a little too much pride and exaggerate the extent to which it is an exemplar for human beings everywhere. In 1812, U.S. Secretary of War William Eustis confidently declared: "We can take the Canadas without soldiers; we have only to send officers into the provinces, and the people, disaffected towards their own government, will rally round our standard."[14] Secretary Eustis was genuinely surprised when this did not happen. The same arrogance underlay the spirit of manifest destiny in the 1840s, and the conquest of the Philippines and the Spanish West Indies at the turn of the century. In light of these events, it is easier to understand how the United States could imagine after World War II that people living under communist governments would welcome liberation by American power. In 1961, President Kennedy and his advisers were sure that mass uprisings against the Castro government would follow the invasion they sponsored at the Cuban Bay of Pigs. The joint chiefs of staff were shocked when 80 percent of the invaders were taken prisoner instead. It was much the same story in Southeast Asia less than a decade later. Each instance of rebuff, moreover, has left many Americans angry and perplexed. Both sentiments could be reduced by the simple recognition that the United States is for the world a beacon of democracy only in degree, not in kind.

legal-rational authority may be narrowly or broadly understood

Legal-rational authority, as exercised by contemporary national governments, differs most basically according to how broadly the public order is defined, how much of social life is placed under the polity's legitimate control. The social contract can be limited to the barest essentials necessary for the maintenance of order, or it can be understood to embrace almost the totality of social life. The possibilities are similar to those available in the marriage contract. Husband and wife may agree to maximize each other's individual freedom, and thus maintain separate careers, bank accounts, titles to property, beds, bedtimes, religious affiliations, vacations, hobbies, and circles of friends. In the ideal open marriage, the partners would be expected to check with one another about only a small number of well-defined activities, their sex life, presumably, and the care of their children. At the other extreme, the woman and man might give themselves fully to the marriage, enclosing within it all their money and property, their work, their leisure activities, and their friends. They would prefer to do everything "as a couple." Bear in mind that democracy can be the goal in both kinds of marriage. Both can be self-conscious creations by reasonable human beings. It is a question not of the *degree* of legality or rationality in the marriage, but the *kind*.

classical liberalism—the social contract narrowly defined

The societal analogue to an open marriage seeks democracy through the principles of *classical liberalism*: the government is established through competitive elections and serves as a referee over the interaction of self-seeking individuals in a largely uncontrolled market economy. The measure of this kind of democracy is how much personal freedom citizens enjoy, how much chance each one has to apply his or her privately owned capital and privately held talents to private purposes. The government exists mainly to safeguard freedom in this individualistic sense. Hence politics is not supposed to occupy much of anyone's attention.

Freedom is exercised mainly in the ever-changing and ever-growing economy and in one's private life. For the relatively small number of issues that require action by some level of government, citizens freely cast their votes in elections according to their private interests and form various parties, interest groups, and other voluntary associations. Great Britain and the United States have produced most of the proponents of this kind of legal-rational government. John Locke, Thomas Jefferson, and Herbert Spencer have already been mentioned. Others include Adam Smith (1723–1790), John Stuart Mill (1806–1873), and in the present day, Milton Friedman.

socialism—a broadened legal base for government

The societal counterpart to a marriage of togetherness seeks democracy through the principles of *socialism*: the government is established through some kind of expression of the general will and then assumes control over the economy, managing it for the common good. The measure of democracy in this case is how much chance citizens have, not to pursue their private purposes—indeed, such selfishness is considered undemocratic and antisocial—but to join creatively with others in achieving an ever more humane common life. The government is expected to safeguard this right of participation, freedom in a collective sense. Hence politics is supposed to penetrate nearly all facets of life—neighborhood associations, workers' councils, schools, and on to the highest levels of government —in each of which individuals have the right and the duty to further the public good through cooperative decision making and unselfish work. Non-Protestant and especially non-Anglo-Saxon societies have produced most theorists of this more inclusive kind of social contract, among them Jean-Jacques Rousseau in France, Karl Marx in Germany, Vladimir Lenin in Russia, Mao Zedong in China, Ho Chi Minh in Vietnam, Jacques Maritain in France, Julius Nyerere in Tanzania, Fidel Castro in Cuba, Robert Mugabe in Zimbabwe, and Eduardo Frei and Salvador Allende in Chile. There is obviously much more variety among socialist than among liberal thinkers, and among socialist governments than among capitalist ones, simply because the former *act* more than the latter do. But notwithstanding the variety of different actions socialist thinkers recommend and socialist governments take, they are united in their conception of the state as manager or coach instead of referee, in a broad definition of what constitutes public order.

To dwell at length on the relative merits of liberal and socialist forms of government would go beyond the purposes of this book. Here it is enough to note that in a liberal society, as in an open marriage, a person often seems to die of loneliness in a crowd of lonely friends. In a socialist society, by contrast, as in a marriage of togetherness, one seems to gasp for air beneath a smother of mutual solicitude. Each route toward democracy has its strengths and weaknesses. But surely neither represents a fundamental perversion of humanity. And surely citizens living more or less democratically in the one kind of political system have no need at all to be liberated by those living more or less democratically in the other kind. C. B. Macpherson, the dean of Canadian political theorists, now emeritus at Toronto, has argued strongly for thinking of world politics today in terms of competing types of democracy. His conceptualization illuminates the data far better and facilitates creative thinking much more than one which finds democracy only on the liberal right or the socialist left. The following paragraphs, which consider these two sides in turn, owe much to Macpherson's writings.

The most important question in the present context is under what conditions these two conflicting tendencies emerged in history and continue to win adherents in the present day. The answer must begin by assessing how broadly traditional governments defined their scope, that is, how much of social life kings and princes could legitimately include under their public power. When we make such an assessment of medieval Europe, or indeed of almost any other premodern civilization, it is clear that the domain of traditional rule was culturally defined to include almost all of social life. Very little value was placed on privacy, secrecy, individual freedom, personal initiative, or inalienable human rights. The society rather than the person was the primordial fact of human existence. Before anyone did anything new, it was thought essential to check first with the political authorities. Such an outlook is reflected in *mercantilism*, the economic doctrine which prevailed in Europe even as late as the eighteenth century. This theory placed the exchange of goods under close governmental control, especially across the borders of fledgling national societies. Each ruler sought to accumulate gold and silver, and each economic transaction by subjects of the realm was expected to contribute to this goal.

mercantilism and other static outlooks in medieval Europe

It is worth recalling that in a traditional society, the amount of wealth is thought to be more or less fixed, as changeless as everything else about life. Hence if one person gains, another inevitably loses. Such a static conception of the economy, a conception which fits the reality, accounts for the medieval condemnation of usury, the lending of money for interest. For if the amount of money (and hence the goods which money can buy) remains constant, the moneylender who takes interest is simply enslaving the borrower. Using somebody else's money can only mean exchanging present consumption for future want, and the creditor who also demands interest is taking completely unfair advantage of the debtor. For the same reason, it was thought sinful to sell something for as high a price as one could get. In a fixed economy, this could only be commercial exploitation. The seller should rather charge no more than the *just price*, the normal, generally accepted, customary price in the local context. Medieval theologians like Albertus Magnus (ca. 1193–1280) and Thomas Aquinas (1225–1274) never doubted the right of political authority to announce what the just price of an item would be and to punish those who charged more. The purpose of government, after all, was to see that the customary order was preserved, that human avarice not interfere with the God-given nature of social life.

It was the all-embracing quality of government much more than its undemocratic character that most annoyed the early inventors and entrepreneurs, those who first gained self-consciousness of the extent and goodness of human inventiveness. From their point of view, it was mainly the intrusion of political authority into economic matters that prevented the ball of human ingenuity from beginning to roll. They envisioned a society essentially dynamic instead of static, one in which the amount of wealth would constantly increase. If individuals who applied themselves to the creation and production of needed goods were only free to sell them wherever they could get the highest price without regard for political authority, commodities yet undreamed of would be invented, and also more

restraining government's visible hand and letting individuals be possessive and free

efficient ways of producing them. In other words, as Adam Smith argued strongly, human avarice should be counted not a vice but a virtue. Give everyone the freedom to be selfish, let prices be set freely in an open market, forget about usury and the just price, encourage competition, and let the invisible hand of capitalism replace government as the guiding force on economic affairs. If only this were done, one person's gain would no longer require another's loss. All could grow wealthier at once. As people pulled against one another, money would be made like taffy.[15]

The creative action of Renaissance Europeans on the physical world thus had a political effect beyond the idea of social-contract government. It urged that government be limited, that it serve mainly to referee a market economy. The *kind* of legal-rational polity it engendered was the one Macpherson has labeled *possessive individualism.* In forming a government, individuals give up only parts of themselves, retaining their inalienable right to own commodities and the means of producing them. The founders of political liberalism sought to invert what had previously been considered the natural priority of society over individuals. They argued that individuals are the fundamental reality. Individuals create societies only in order to protect the private property they own at the start. The state can require individuals to relinquish only so much of their autonomy as is necessary to protect the rest of it. The important aspects of life are what people do in the marketplace. That is where the action is. The task of government is to step aside and let it happen.

the liberal way of deciding on governments

In devising the procedures by which people choose members of government, classical liberals relied on the same principles as they favored in the economy. Political entrepreneurs should have to compete for voters, just as economic entrepreneurs should compete for purchasers. There should be at least two political parties, since a monopoly in the business of government would threaten the common good as surely as a monopoly in any economic sector. Individuals should be free to form pressure groups and other voluntary associations for their selfish political ends, just as they might form companies for their selfish economic ends. The national legislature should be the scene of political horse trading, and its vitality should be measured by the extent to which conflicting voices are raised in parliamentary debate. There should be freedom of the press, with numerous newspapers slanting their reportage and editorials to competing constituencies. But above all, government should realize that it is not the most important part of a society. Constitutions and precedents should prevent it from trying to replace the market in the definition of what constitutes the good life. Unlike the polity, the capitalist economy has within it a dynamic force. The former can only redistribute wealth; the latter can increase it.

the United States: ideal setting for liberal politics

It was this kind of legal-rational government which the United States adopted in 1776, and to which it rigorously adhered until the early decades of this century. America was the ideal setting for the realization of the liberal ideal. Not only was it relatively unencumbered by premodern political values, but it also had an immense amount of sparsely settled land and natural resources on which enterprising individuals could engage in creative economic action. Its citizenry, moreover, was ethnically, regionally, and religiously diverse. Better to have a weak government than one which Protestants might use against Catholics, the Northeast against the

"In devising the procedures by which people choose members of government, classical liberals relied on the same principles as they favored in the economy. Political entrepreneurs should have to compete for voters, just as economic entrepreneurs should compete for purchasers. There should be at least two political parties, since a monopoly in the business of government would threaten the common good as surely as a monopoly in any economic sector." (© John Chao/Woodfin Camp & Assoc.)

South, or citizens of British ancestry against those from central Europe. The best government would be one that governed least. It was a theory that worked to the benefit of the vast majority of citizens. The only ones who lost out completely were the indigenous peoples, who were driven from the land in order to make way for immigrants. For immigration was congenial to the liberal ideal of an open society. Let all those willing to work enter and make a place for themselves; thereby the national wealth could only be increased. In 1900, more than 95 percent of the American labor force worked in the private economy, and less than 1 percent for the federal government. That government's annual budget was less than 3 percent of the gross national product. There was no income tax. The federal government got three-quarters of its revenue from taxes on imported goods, alcohol, tobacco, and luxury items for which a hard-working nation should anyway have little use.

The United States became the best example of political liberalism, but not the only one. Great Britain preceded it, limiting political authority to the role of referee long before removing it from the clutches of royalty and nobility. The same was true in France, the Netherlands, Germany, Canada, Australia, and New Zealand. In all these societies, governments gave a relatively free hand to the marketplace and safeguarded the rights of their citizens to own property, worship as they pleased, and move freely from place to place. Gradually as well, as ever larger numbers of people demanded a political voice, these societies distributed the franchise more broadly. They were rewarded for their liberalism, moreover, by steady and rapid increases in wealth. If one removed from the contemporary world all the inventions and discoveries made in just three countries—the United States, England, and Germany—life today would probably bear close resemblance to that of medieval Europe. It was not socialism that stretched the length of human life from thirty-five or forty years to seventy or seventy-five. Nor was it concerned government that made today's high standard of living possible. It was cold, lonely capitalism, protected by liberal regimes that seemed not to care at all.

SOCIALISM

Why, then, has government in all the capitalist societies veered away from the liberal ideal during the past few decades? Why have most of these governments curtailed immigration, put controls on their economies, and created so many public bureaucracies? Why does 16 percent of the American labor force now work for some level of government? Why does the revenue of the American federal government alone now account for some 18 percent of the gross national product? And why is almost half of that revenue derived from personal income tax?[16] Why even has the meaning of liberalism shifted from political unconcern to governmental action? These are questions of supreme importance, for they suggest that the kind of government which has done the least (and thus the most) for human betterment is being abandoned. These questions are reserved for the next chapter, however, so that in the remainder of this one we can consider an equally puzzling political event. This is the refusal of most of the rest of the world to embrace the principles of classical liberalism. Does it not seem strange that the societies outside North America and Western Europe, the ones which have won their independence only during the last half-century and have only now begun to industrialize, have almost uniformly adopted socialist kinds of government? Why should they not want to follow the path to liberal democracy?

three reasons for socialism's popularity outside the West: first, a cultural sense of the general will

In solving this latter puzzle, three factors deserve at least brief mention. The first one is cultural. Few if any cultures in Asia, Africa, or South America value individualism to the extent that it is valued in Great Britain, northern Europe, North America, and Australia. Without an idea of the goodness of privacy, secrecy, and individual initiative, political and economic liberalism is hard to practice. It is fair to say that the European tribes among which this ideology first took hold were predisposed to it from the start. The success of Protestantism, liberalism, and capitalism in Holland and Scotland, for example, but not in Portugal and Greece is hardly accidental. The culture of limited government took centuries, moreover, to win out over traditional corporatist (that is, group-minded or communitarian) values even in Great Britain. Hence even if the citizens of Somalia, Rwanda, or some other new African nation can be persuaded that government should be in the hands of the people, they are unlikely to think of the people as a collection of individuals. The word for them is more likely to be a singular noun. The notions that political self-interest is a good thing and that citizens should cast selfish ballots in elections, notions taken for granted in WASP cultures, are altogether foreign to most cultures of the world.

Non-Marxist, noncapitalist, nonmilitant, and nonaligned, Julius Nyerere has led the African nation of Tanzania down a socialist path since the mid-1960s. The keystone of the new political and economic order is ujamaa, the development of village communities wherein citizens work and act cooperatively for the common good. Village meetings like the one pictured above help build a modern but collective consciousness. Progress in Tanzania has been slow, despite massive infusions of foreign aid, mainly because of the society's traditional poverty, illiteracy, and intertribal rivalries. Nonetheless, Nyerere was reelected president in October of 1980 with 93 percent of the vote. (Marion Kaplan/Photo Researchers, Inc.)

Much more likely is that legal-rational politics, once it reaches a newly modern population in the twentieth century, will be understood along the lines suggested by Rousseau. For the French-Swiss theorist of the social contract differed with Locke in a number of aspects. He agreed that people create public order and government, but in his view the very act of creation implies near-total surrender of every individual to the collective whole. Good government should be responsive to the *general will* of the people, but this is not something discernible simply in the view of the majority. The preferences of 51 percent of citizens are by no means a credible or legitimate basis of political decision. For Rousseau, the general will is voiced by the overwhelming majority of citizens, once they have set their respective selfish interests aside. It quickly wins their common agreement, once they sit down and direct their discussion toward common ends. Rousseau saw no value at all in Locke's frenetic scramble for the votes of competing factions and interest groups. Rousseau called such groups *partial societies* and warned that they could easily obscure the general will. "The more that harmony reigns in the assemblies," he wrote, "that is, the more the voting approaches unanimity, the more also is the general will predominant; but long discussions, dissensions, and uproar proclaim the ascendancy of private interests and the decline of the State."[17] Such is the kind of political democracy that appeals most to contemporary cultures outside Western Europe and North America. In practice it normally implies a single political party and a government that does not hesitate to manage the economy and to assume a directive role in numerous aspects of social life.

As compared to American political culture, even that in Canada tends toward Rousseau's model, and this even despite Canada's formal grounding in liberal democratic principles. For of Canada's two founding peoples, one was composed of French peasants and the other of dissenters from Jeffersonian politics. Canada's federal political system during the twentieth century has been multiparty, but not quite as multiparty as in the United States; during sixty of the century's first eighty years, the Liberal party was in power. By the standards of either the Democratic or Republican parties in the United States, the Canadian Liberals have involved the federal government in economic matters to a decidedly illiberal extent. None of the other parties, moreover, neither Progressive Conservatives, New Democrats, nor Créditistes, stands for governmental disengagement from economic affairs. With reference to Canadian politics, I should note also that landslide elections are far more common in francophone Quebec than in anglophone Ontario. French Canadians know what Rousseau meant by the general will, a fact that troubles English Canadians and defies the imagination of Americans.

second, a low priority on indigenous technical innovation

A second factor that explains the popularity of socialism outside the societies where liberalism first took root is technological. It is the lower priority attached to indigenous technical invention outside the capitalist core. Remember that for Adam Smith, the problem was how to free the entrepreneurs, how to unleash their creative powers. By contrast, from the vantage point of a society just emerging from traditionalism in this century, the problem is not a lack of invention. A fantastic array of novelties, from refrigerators to jet planes, has already been invented. The pressing problem is instead how to incorporate these innovations into societies that until now have not known them. Few contemporary impoverished societies see any need to turn loose the dynamics of capitalism within their borders. The challenge they see is rather to gear up their own production processes in order to achieve a level of living already available elsewhere. This challenge warrants an active government, not one that maintains a posture of unconcern. In addition, the leaders of new legal-rational governments in the so-called third world have been educated for the most part in the industrialized West and desperately want for their own people the prosperity they themselves have seen in Europe and America. Lenin, Mao, and Ho Chi Minh were all examples, but there are many more. Unlike traditional rulers, such leaders are not threatened by advanced technology; they themselves are in the modernizer role and they want to *act*.

From the point of view of most governments in today's poor societies, it would be silly to try to replicate the process of economic development which Britain and

The government of Grenada paid homage to Jean-Jacques Rousseau during International Educational Year, 1970. But Rousseau's ghost haunts not only the island's school system but also its politics. A leftist revolutionary government seized power in 1979 and immediately set about curtailing market forces, planning the national economy, and forging close ties with Cuba. The U.S. government was deeply distressed. Whatever the future holds for this smallest of societies in the Western hemisphere, its polity is more likely to reflect Rousseau's theory than Locke's.

America required centuries to undergo. What would their people do, reinvent the refrigerator in 1998? Governments and citizens in such lands are usually reluctant, moreover, to accept as a model the crass materialism they perceive in the wealthy capitalist societies. They want wealth with a human face, wealth that does not depend upon the selfish exploitation of people and the natural world. They would like to preserve the humane values of their traditional past, even as they add the benefits of industrial technology. They display scant ambition ever to have a higher economic level of living than the United States has at this moment. Their concern is rather to formulate and follow a plan of economic development over the coming years, one which will make them wealthier without their having to measure their worth solely in terms of wealth. For this purpose, a strong, well-managed, active government is a necessity.

third, the high cost of arriving late for the capitalist game

But perhaps most important is a third, explicitly political factor which discourages the adoption of classical liberalism in the societies which modernized later than Western societies. It is resentment against exploitation in the international capitalist system. Ever since they embraced liberalism themselves, the core capitalist governments have behaved like spouses involved in a very open marriage. Such men and women desperately want other marriages to be as open as theirs; otherwise they have no one to relate to freely as individuals without regard for marital authority. In much the same way, liberal governments have earnestly tried to spread liberalism all over the world. This indeed was necessary for the long-run survival of their own market economies. As the Czech-American political economist Joseph Schumpeter (1883–1950) observed, capitalism "is by nature a form or method of economic change and not only never is but never can be stationary."[18] In order to support their citizens' creative material action, the advanced capitalist societies have needed ever greater supplies of raw materials, more and more places to invest profits from their industry, and steadily larger markets for the sale of their products. If the rest of the world were closed to capitalist initiative, liberalism would collapse as surely as an open marriage surrounded by men and women who do everything as couples.

This, fundamentally, is why Britain extended its imperial rule over much of the world, why the United States has supported military dictatorships in Latin America and elsewhere, why the Cuban invasion was launched at the Bay of Pigs, why the CIA helped the Chilean junta overthrow President Allende, and why the war in Indochina took place. The wealthy capitalist societies have tried earnestly to keep the rest of the world open to capitalist development, lest the dynamics of their own economies in the long run break down. But such openness is a mixed blessing for the society just beginning to industrialize. Like an impoverished gambler invited to play poker with a rich one, the society just emerging from traditionalism lacks the wherewithal to play the capitalist game. The rich society generously offers to send its own corporations into the poor one, often in mining, oil, and other extractive industries, which export raw materials needed for manufacturing in the rich society. Accepting such *direct* investment from abroad means that the profits are controlled by foreigners. If these profits are sent back to the rich country, the poor one loses out. If they are reinvested in the poor country, thus expanding its industry, that country finds that the wealthier it gets, the more it is owned by foreign interests and the less control it has over its own future. A better alternative for the poor society is simply to borrow money from the rich one and thereby start its own industries—this is called *indirect* investment.[19] But rich societies are disposed to provide money on this basis only when doing so is clearly in their own interests; often they require the poor society to use such loans to buy equipment and other goods which the rich society wants to export, even if these are not the goods the poor society needs most.

Lenin and the Soviet strategy

Lenin, the Russian intellectual who led the revolutionary Bolshevik government from 1917 to 1922, understood very well what lay in store for his country if it adopted a liberal stance and opened itself to the corporations of Britain, Germany, and the United States. It was Lenin, in fact, who offered the most detailed classic analysis of the reasons behind never-ending capitalist expansion.[20] Lenin therefore advocated that Russia close itself off, repudiate liberalism, set up a strong and centralized government, and let the government manage Russia's transition from peasant agriculture to modern industry. Since 1917, the Soviet Union has invented relatively little. What it has done is take technical ideas from Germany, the United States, and Britain, and establish by governmental authority the machinery for putting them into action. By now it is the second strongest military power in the world. On a per capita basis, its level of wealth is higher than that of most societies in South America, where governments have generally supported liberal principles. In addition, the Soviet Union is master of its own destiny. It need not ask for American foreign aid. Virtually all of its people can read and write, as compared to about 66 percent of Brazilians, 35 percent of South Africans, or 74 percent of Colombians. The Soviet Union is the best example in the contemporary world of the incredible wealth and power which can be gained through socialism.

It is no less possible for a socialist than for a liberal society to lose its legal-rational foundation and come under the sway of tyrannical government. The socialist world is no prouder of Lenin's successor, Josef Stalin, than the liberal world is of Adolf Hitler. Nonetheless, the 1950s, 1960s, and 1970s have seen one society after another outside the capitalist core opt for a socialist definition of its political system. Marxian ideas have often played a major part in the political ideology chosen, as in China, Ethiopia, Angola, Mozambique, Cuba, the Congo, and Benin. The communitarian theology of the Catholic church, updated to take account of industrial progress, has played a part in some societies, Tanzania and Nicaragua most clearly. Some other societies have grown steadily more socialist, but without identifying themselves with any detailed political and economic theory; among them are Mexico, Algeria, Portugal, Peru, Bangladesh, and Guyana. All have moved steadily in the direction of one-party states, with active and interventionist governments, and a close watch on foreign economic activity within their borders.

socialism's appeal is a measure of liberalism's success

It is a measure of the success of liberalism that today, only two centuries after the capitalism it safeguarded got underway, this political ideology can be rejected by societies which have not yet shared its benefits. For by now, so much action has been taken on nature that there is little enthusiasm outside the capitalist core for the invention of still more commodities. As the supply of fossil fuels diminishes, moreover, there is fear that the planet cannot tolerate much more capitalist expansion. No longer is American technical genius held in such high regard. When the premier of Quebec spoke in New York in 1977, he got little applause.

His audience was well aware that René Lévesque agrees with the degree of democracy Jefferson espoused, but not the kind. Lévesque did not even try to hide his socialism. His government had already shown itself ready to expropriate foreign-owned corporations in Quebec. His audience of business executives shuddered to think that Cuba's controlled economy might soon be balanced by a northern counterpart. "Where will we get the raw materials needed for U.S. economic growth," they must have wondered, "the markets for our new products, and the places where profits can be invested for the sake of more profits?" Upon questions like these the next chapter will shed further light.

Concluding Remarks

Two qualities of this chapter may well have surprised some readers. The first is its neglect of many important topics that regularly come up in political discussion. No analysis has been offered of how political parties work in America or anywhere else, or why citizens vote for one or another of them. Major issues of current debate have scarcely been mentioned—issues like capital punishment, abortion, tax cuts, gasoline prices, and welfare reform. The mechanics of the legislative process have been ignored, moreover; so has the complex issue of how much power should be at the federal level in societies like the United States, and how much at levels of government closer to the people. And the emphasis here has been on formal structures of government, not on the wheeling and dealing behind the scenes that both supplements and subverts due process of law. But this one chapter could not address the whole range of political topics nor review all the careful work published in political science and political sociology. The goal here has not been to offer a comprehensive portrayal of the polity in any one society, much less in two or three. The purpose has been rather to put first things first: to outline the modern culture upon which legal government rests, and the economic conditions upon which that culture rests. More particular issues assume a reasonable, contractual foundation for the structure of life in common. I have judged that that foundation should get most attention in this basic book.

A second characteristic of these pages that might have caused puzzlement is the recurrence of economic matters in a chapter focused on politics. But in fact these two institutions are inextricably intertwined. It was the absence of economic innovation and change that permitted political authority to vacillate so long between traditional and charismatic poles. Similarly, it was action upon the physical world by Renaissance inventors and explorers that gave rise not only to the modern economy but to the modern polity. For *modernity* is nothing more than self-conscious human creativity. Modern government is only that which is intentionally created by human beings through some kind of social contract, a government in which even the sovereign rulers are subject to laws devised and written down on the basis of human reason.

the meaning of modernity, upon which constitutional government depends

The second section of this chapter, concerned with the conditions under which a government of law can prevail, dwelt also on economic considerations. For only people involved in a modern economy appear to be willing to reject traditional attitudes toward authority and to demand a voice in political affairs. The evidence also suggests that certain products of the modern economy, namely those of warfare, constitute an ever-present danger to a government of law. Finally, the data of history direct our attention to the way individuals participate in a modern economy. If they cannot exercise power at work and in their everyday lives, they tend to despair of governing themselves and to fall prey to the charismatic powers of tyrants. In sum, a government of law can survive and move steadily toward its democratic ideals only insofar as it ensures that goods and services are produced in a way that convinces ever more people ever more surely that Dante's words apply to them: "Therefore if the present world go astray, the cause is in you, in you it is to be sought."

In the last section of this chapter, the scope of government was also shown to have an economic basis. It was to stimulate action upon the world that the theory and practice of political liberalism came into existence. And that, indeed, has been its effect. By doing little except defend private property and by playing its role on the sidelines, perhaps even more like a cheerleader than a referee, the United States government has used its sovereign power to let the wealthiest nation on earth create itself. Now that the products of human avarice abound, societies outside the liberal capitalist core have generally rejected the theory and practice of this kind of social-contract government. Societies outside Western Europe and North America tend to take politics more seriously. Socialist governments rest on a different kind of legal-rational foundation, one in which avarice is just as much a vice as it was traditionally, one on which a less individualistic and more communitarian kind of democracy might directly be built.

Since economic factors explain political ones so well, might this sociological review of institutions better have begun with the former than the latter? The answer is no. If action upon nature first permitted societies to come of age, it is action upon their own public orders that enables them to grow beyond maturity. For we are now modern men and women, all of us, liberals and socialists alike, who are conscious of our abiliity to define the order of our common life. Through our industry we have assured ourselves of the necessities of life and more. There is no need any more for anyone, at least in Western Europe and North America, to be hungry or deprived of medical care, adequate clothing, and shelter. The mastery of nature which writers just a century ago could only dream of has occurred. No longer do we in North America need to be slaves of material want, dependent variables accounted for by economic independent ones. Today, in a manner unprecedented in history, we can reflect as free people and ask ourselves what kind of societies we want to create for ourselves. That question is a political one.

It will be asked and answered anyway, because the instruments for the effective use of governmental power are now available. Norman Cantor, the American medievalist, has observed that despite the breadth of their definition of authority, medieval kings could not actually control very closely events in their realms. As late as 1500, "the under-developed character of the communications network still meant that royal government, no matter how authoritarian its ideology, could do very little to affect the daily lives of the vast majority of the population."[21] Today, with all manner of industrial technology, national governments *can* exercise control over their citizens. As time goes on, increasingly they *will*. The question is only the degree and kind of democracy governmental action will reflect and pursue.

politics and economics are closely intertwined, but politics comes first, especially in modern times

For Reflection

anomie
alienation
government
state
public order
power
authority
tradition
charisma
prophets
routinization of charisma
law
social contract
rationality
renegotiation of the polity
the first new nation
lingering traditionalism
peasant mentality
God-given power
free elections
militarism
white man's burden
coup d'état
American military aid

right of people to bear arms
disarmament
economic alienation
mass society
Third Reich
demagogues
democracy
degree of democracy
kind of democracy
liberalism
Locke's theories
mercantilism
usury
just price
possessive individualism
socialism
Rousseau's theories
privacy, secrecy, individualism
general will
partial societies
indigenous invention
direct versus indirect investment
capitalist imperialism
modernity

For Making Connections

With personal experience:
How much lingering traditionalism can you detect in your own political mentality and in your attitude toward authority?
How vulnerable are you to being caught in the sway of a demagogue? How could you make yourself less vulnerable?

With Chapter One:
What enduring regularities about politics and government have you learned from this chapter?
What political principles are you willing to take for granted?
In what way has this chapter confirmed ideas you already held through common sense, and in what way has it challenged or refined common sense?

With Chapter Two:
Probably the main hypothesis of this chapter is that legal-rational government depends on citizens' everyday experience of power and creativity. What evidence for this hypothesis was offered here? How might the hypothesis be tested further? List three or four valid indicators of the variable *degree of democracy*.

With Chapter Three:
How would you expect the reward structure of a society to change during a fifty-year period in which the society was moving steadily closer to the democratic ideal?
This chapter has emphasized the culture of legal-rational politics. Which structural

attributes of your own society reinforce this kind of culture, and which ones contradict it?

With Chapter Four: Which of the three types of authority—traditional, charismatic, and legal-rational —gives citizens the most chance to realize their dialectical nature? Why?
How would you expect the citizens of a liberal democracy to differ in their moral and political values from citizens of a socialist democracy?

For Further Reading

Each reader of this book lives and works in a particular national society and in particular political subdivisions within it. No treatises on government can substitute for reading the political news, editorials, and commentary in one's own local newspapers, thereby acquainting oneself with ongoing political process in the public order at first hand. The first responsibility of each of us is to our own respective political milieux. But a broader perspective is important, too. The mainline journals in political science deserve attention: the *American Political Science Review*, the *Western Political Quarterly*, the *Canadian Journal of Political Science*, *World Politics*, and similar publications. Of no less value are journals of political commentary like *The Nation, Dissent,* or the *New York Review of Books*. Also relevant are standard textbooks on the political systems of the various national societies. The following are ten sources in political sociology which have been especially helpful to me in writing this chapter:

1   C. B. Macpherson, *The Political Theory of Possessive Individualism*, and *Democratic Theory: Essays in Retrieval*, Oxford Univ. Press, New York, 1962 and 1973 respectively. Two major works by Canada's premier political theorist, invaluable for grasping the underpinnings of political life in liberal societies. The uninitiated may prefer to start with Macpherson's easy-to-read pamphlet, *The Real World of Democracy*, CBC, Toronto, 1975.

2   Richard Hofstadter, *The American Political Tradition*, Random House, Vintage, New York, 1973. Hofstadter (1916–1970) contributed more to the understanding of American politics in his fifty-four years of life than most scholars could contribute in two centuries. He described this book, first published in 1948, as "a kind of intellectual history of the assumptions behind American politics." Of equal importance are his *Anti-Intellectualism in American Life*, and *The Paranoid Style in American Politics*, both published as Vintage paperbacks in 1964 and 1968 respectively.

3   Seymour Martin Lipset, *The First New Nation* (published in a Norton edition with a new introduction, 1979). Lipset, perhaps the leading contemporary political sociologist in America, here depicts the public order of his native land in comparative context. His first book, *Agrarian Socialism*, Univ. of California Press, Berkeley, 1950, a study of postwar Saskatchewan, is also worth reading. So is his more general theory, *Political Man*, Doubleday, New York, 1960.

4   Max Weber, *The Theory of Social and Economic Organization*, Macmillan, New York, 1964. Translated and edited by Talcott Parsons, this book is heavy reading; it remains, nonetheless, the most coherent, integrated, and extensive volume available in English of the eminent German scholar's work.

5   John Locke, *Two Treatises on Government*, Cambridge Univ. Press, New York, 1960, and

Jean-Jacques Rousseau, *The Social Contract*, Pocket Books, New York, 1967. A comparison of these two classic works is an excellent means of getting insight into the two conflicting directions in which democratic theory has gone over the past hundred years.

6 C. Wright Mills, *The Power Elite*, Oxford Univ. Press, New York, 1956. A still relevant depiction of how undemocratic America remains; in the same vein are G. William Domhoff's *Who Rules America?* and *Who Really Rules America?*, Prentice-Hall, Englewood Cliffs, N.J., 1967 and 1978 respectively. For an opposing view see the numerous pieces of research by Robert Dahl, Nelson Polsby, and others reviewed in John Walton, "Substance and Artifact: The Current Status of Research on Community Power Structure," *American Journal of Sociology* 71:430–38 (1966).

7 Pierre Trudeau, *Federalism and the French Canadians*, Macmillan, Toronto, 1968. Canada's prime minister, an ardent advocate of liberal democracy, here analyzes and criticizes the lack thereof in Quebec during the 1950s and 1960s. Quebec-style democracy is defended, on the other hand, in Fernand Dumont's *Vigil of Quebec*, Univ. of Toronto Press, Toronto, 1974; Dumont is a sociological mentor of the separatist movement.

8 Michael Harrington, *The Twilight of Capitalism*, Simon & Schuster, New York, 1976. Harrington is one of America's most thoughtful and articulate socialists, a reasoned critic who combines academic life with political organizing. This book, like his earlier *Accidental Century*, Macmillan, New York, 1965, and *Socialism*, Saturday Review, 1972, represents left-wing political economy at its best.

9 Ben Agger, *Western Marxism: An Introduction*, Goodyear, Santa Monica, Calif., 1979. An excellent collection of the writings of contemporary Marxian political economists, interwoven with Agger's illuminating commentary. The book demonstrates how helpful the Hegelian-Marxian tradition remains for understanding current polities and planning future ones.

10 Norman Cantor, *Medieval History*, Macmillan, New York, 1969. This readable survey of medieval social and political life illuminates what traditionalism empirically meant in that era. Everyone should gain acquaintance with some political culture of this kind; Richard Pipes's *Russia Under the Old Regime*, Scribner's, New York, 1974, is useful for this purpose, as are the field studies by Redfield and Miner cited in Chapter Two.

Chapter Six

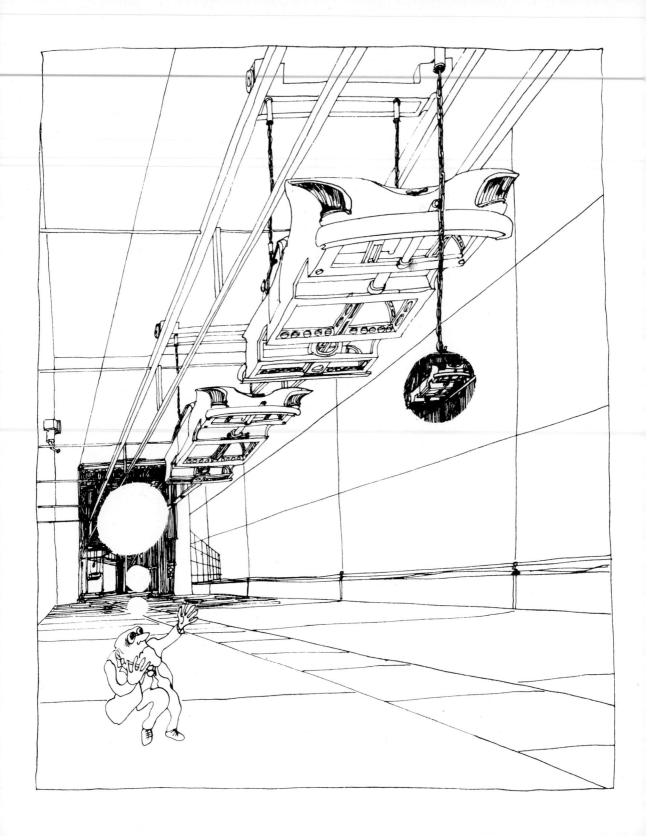

Economy

Chapter Six

*I ask how a society improves on
its relationship with the earth
and how capitalism has contributed to such improvement*

Of all the precepts in the Judeo-Christian scriptures, few have enjoyed more faithful, literal observance than the Creator's direction to Adam and Eve to subdue the earth and "have dominion over the fish of the sea and over the birds of the air and over every living thing that moves upon the earth."[1] The ancient Hebrew god could hardly ask a more tangible sign of obedience to that command than the industrial economies of the late twentieth century. That particular god's pleasure with today's landscape of earth exceeds, I suspect, the pleasure of Lao-zi, the ancient Chinese philosopher whose stock has fallen even in China. "To produce things and to rear them," Lao-zi advised, "To produce, but not to take possession of them,/ To act, but not to rely on one's own ability,/ To lead them, but not to master them—/ This is called profound and secret virtue."[2] This sixth chapter of *First Sociology*, concerned with the economic institution, explains what humans have found by walking down the Judeo-Christian path instead of the way of Lao-zi.

*economy: the way a
society adapts to its
natural milieu*

Defined generally, the economy is the set of roles and procedures, the organized activity by which a society relates to fish, birds, and all the rest of nature, the whole physical environment. It is the means by which a society faces up to the reality of this planet and adapts to it, the barrier a society constructs against the extinction of our species, the techniques a society invents for enhancing the quality of life. Obviously enough, the economy is an institution no society can do without. For if politics concerns how humans treat each other, economics investigates how they treat the earth. This chapter summarizes basic and timely results of such investigation. It is long, nearly twice as long as most other chapters, and for that

An umbrella factory on Kyushu Island, Japan. "The means by which a society faces up to the reality of this planet and adapts to it, the barrier a society constructs against the extinction of our species, the techniques a society invents for enhancing the quality of life." (George Holton/Photo Researchers, Inc.)

reason it is divided into two distinct parts. Part One, "The Development Process," answers the question of how societies in general can improve over time their relation to nature, make it more beneficial and salutary. Part Two, "The Capitalist Strategy," describes and explains the particular path of development followed by the United States and kindred societies. This outline parallels that of the preceding chapter, which considered first *how much* democracy and then *what kind.* Our interest here is first in degrees of development, then in the particular kind evident in our own experience.

Both parts of this chapter draw heavily from the discipline of economics, but no reader need be fearful on that account. The economic research which baffles most citizens and justifies its being called the "dismal science," consists mainly in the technical analysis of money, a substance with which this chapter is only secondarily concerned. There is no denying, of course, the usefulness of concepts like inflation, recession, rate of economic growth, stock-market average, profit margin, and interest rate, all of which are normally defined and discussed in terms of what is happening to money in the marketplace. But such concepts are one step removed from living persons and tangible goods. Our discussion here is of the latter more directly and thus need not be any more dismal or baffling than any other part of sociology. This chapter is rooted in the kind of sentiment set down in the Arusha Declaration of 1967, the document by which Tanzania's ruling party outlined the economic challenge facing that African society. The declaration criticized at length a preoccupation with money: "What we are saying, however, is that from now on we shall know what is the foundation and what is the fruit of development. Between *money* and *people* it is obvious that the people and their *hard work* are the foundation of development, and money is one of the fruits of that hard work. From now on we shall stand upright and walk forward on our feet rather than look at this problem upside down. Industries will come and money will come but their foundation is the *people* and their hard work."[3]

the analysis not of money so much as of real people and tangible goods

Money, after all, is just a medium for exchanging goods, as the telephone is a medium for exchanging words and the highway a medium for changing places. Much can be learned from studying the flow of traffic, whether in dollars, words, or automobiles, but this is not the heart of the matter. The medium is *not* the message. Marshall McLuhan correctly discerned a current tendency to identify the two, but the tendency deserves to be resisted. Surely what people say by telephone is more important than the wires and waves by which their words are transmitted. And I should rather know where and why people travel than which road they take. Similarly, more important than money is what one must do in order to have it, what things one can spend it on, and the effect of all this on the quality of human and nonhuman life. The intent of economic sociology as presented here is to answer crucial questions of the latter kind, to inspect contemporary economies more directly than is possible in facile terms of dollars, pounds, pesos, marks, or some other medium of exchange.

the intellectual sources of this chapter

The following pages, accordingly, rely on the work of those economists who have looked *through* money to observe the actual work people do, the goods they produce, and the way they distribute these products. Five groups of scholars are especially relevant. First is the so-called institutional school in the United States, a collection of economists united mainly by their respect for Thorstein Veblen, the roguish critic of the leisure class mentioned in Chapter Three, and by their efforts to understand the economy in relation to other institutions. The major contemporary spokesman for this school is John Kenneth Galbraith, a Harvard emeritus, president of the American Economic Association in 1972. The disciples of the late Harold Innis constitute a second group. Innis was also a Veblen admirer, and had the distinction of being elected president of both the Canadian Political Science Association (in 1937) and the American Economic Association (in 1951). The kind of economics made use of here was called *substantive* by Karl Polanyi (1886–1964), an Hungarian émigré who taught at New York's Columbia University. Along with his coworkers, Polanyi is a third source of substantive, as opposed to formal, economic analysis. In a loosely defined fourth category are such Marxian political economists as Paul Sweezy, Harry Braverman, William Leiss, and James Rinehart, who have similarly refused to deal in monetary abstractions to the neglect of more tangible human concerns. Finally is a disparate coterie of political economists abroad, including Celso Furtado of Brazil, E. J. Mishan, Joan Robertson, Ralph Miliband, and the late E. F. Schumacher in Britain. The ideas of this chapter derive in great part from economists in these five categories, though also from scholars usually called sociologists. If this chapter is true to its origins, its effect will be not to bewilder but to inform readers, not to muddy but to clarify the present economic situation.

Part One: The Development Process

from hunting and gathering to advanced industrialization

Across the creek and up a little valley from the house where I was raised there was a spring which trickled faithfully even during the driest summer months. My friends and I spent countless Sundays walking the fields around it, scanning the ground for arrowheads, knives, and other flintstone tools which Sioux Indian tribes had centuries earlier left behind when they visited the spring for water. The Sioux provide as good an example as any of the most ancient form of human relation to the physical environment: the hunting and gathering economy. The Sioux's action upon the earth did not go much beyond appropriating certain items available in nature for their own use. They did not drill for water but looked for it in creeks and springs like the one on what became my parents' farm. They did not domesticate animals or harness them but roamed across the plains in search of herds of bison. With skins and antlers to disguise themselves as deer, they would mingle with the herd and then seize an animal. They ate its meat, wore its fur, and slept beneath its hide stretched across saplings cut from the forest. They ate fruits, berries, fish, and small game mostly as they ran across them in their travels. Their tools were simple ones of stone, the ones I found as a boy and hoarded in cigar boxes.

Until ten or twelve thousand years ago, hunting and gathering were the economic foundation of all human societies. People related to the earth in the manner of an unborn child to its mother. Even the term *relation* is scarcely appropriate, since both were joined as a single, living organism. Primitive peoples did not set themselves apart from their milieu but immersed themselves in it. Unlike us, they dared not imagine themselves superior to animals, the sun, or the seasons. They sought to understand other creatures in the passionate, respectful way that lovers (and also enemies) try to understand one another. Human knowledge was full of anthropomorphic imagery, the projection of human qualities onto nonhuman entities: Mother Earth, angry skies, the whispering of reeds in the wind. The very name of the Aleutian Eskimo meant, in their native tongue, Brothers of the Sea Otter. Societies differed greatly, of course, in language, mythology, diet, clothing, and customs, but the diversity could be accounted for mainly by differences in their natural physical environments. Whatever the setting in which these nomadic peoples wandered about in search of sustenance, they lived with the earth more than against it.

Although my friends and I would lie on our bellies and drink from the same spring as the ancient Sioux, we were different from them in a fundamental way. Already we had learned to relate to nature as something separate, distant from us. Like a growing child who inspects its mother from across the gap of generations, we could stand apart from the earth, observe it with a calculating eye, and act upon it aggressively with unfeeling purpose. We knew how to pull the trigger of a gun, to kill wildlife just for sport. We could stoke our basement furnaces and slam the door in winter's face. Like economically developed peoples everywhere, we had skills and tools for cutting away from us the encircling cords of the physical world. Not for us was the idea of submitting to nature. We had studied in school and at church our god's command that we subdue the earth, a precept far more meaningful to us even than to our ancient Hebrew forebears. Although we did not use the word, we approached nature in a *dialectical* relationship: while admitting its power over us, we claimed authority over it. Putting this dialectic in force is what economic development means. It is the process by which humans break loose from nature and set about controlling it, become less the creatures and more the creators of their environment, thus making their relation to the earth a reciprocal, two-sided affair.

development is the process by which humans break loose

The process of economic development is varied and complex, and there is no inherent order in it. Half a millennium before Columbus's voyage, the predecessors of the Sioux in North America had created an economy markedly more advanced than hunting and gathering. A city half the size of medieval Rome had flourished on the Mississippi floodplain opposite today's St. Louis. Farmers, traders, potters, and priests had lived in tidy rows of thatched houses and had met for play and marketing in spacious plazas. The citizens were so well-organized that together they built earthen pyramids and cones high as Missouri hills. Yet by the time French explorers came upon the site, the gigantic mounds were overgrown with brush, the city long gone, and the Amerindians dispersed into wandering tribes. Many Europeans doubted that natives of the region, peoples by then become so primitive, could once have designed and raised these huge dusty monuments from the bottomlands. As late as 1920, some professional geologists argued that the mounds were "erosional remnants," natural formations rather than human handiwork. But current evidence decisively dispels such incredulity and points up the disorderliness of human history.[4] Societies have not moved steadily forward. They have not irreversibly progressed. Economic development has happened mostly in fits and starts, here then there. One innovation has not guaranteed other ones, nor ruled out stagnation. Egyptian, Greek, Roman, Spanish, British, and Chinese societies have all, in the judgment of various historians, taken their respective turns over the centuries in leading the world in economic excellence. United States superiority in this regard has of late been unquestioned, but this, too, shall pass. The process of economic development is at root a quest for the happiest kind of interplay between people and their milieu. If we knew where it will end, we would be there already. What faces us for now is magnificent diversity across time and place, as humans apply themselves to all kinds of earnest but uncertain schemes for reversing nature's tyranny over them.

historicist scholars avoid the idea of progress altogether

The diversity is great enough to persuade a minority of social scientists, even a growing minority during the last decade, to resist the very concept of economic development. No empirical evidence, they rightly claim, compels the conclusion that the process even exists, that one society is somehow better than another, or that humans have indeed progressed through time. Were the ancient Sioux, drinking from open streams, *really* less developed than we who poison our streams with pesticides and acid rain? Or which is farther along the path of progress, a Polynesian tribe that eats an occasional enemy or an industrial nation that keeps nuclear missiles poised to annihilate whole continents of humanity? Rather than contriving theories of development, many scholars argue, we should just study history: the inventions, invasions, investments, and all the other concrete empirical events that have marked the shape of life on earth. Thus this point of view is accurately called *historicism*: an insistence on staying close to the facts of social change and cross-societal difference, without trying to fit them into an overall directional theory, without pretending that the human race is marching down some natural course. Probably the most articulate proponent of such a view today is Robert Nisbet, a sociologist-historian at Stanford University, who has meticulously debunked conventional Western definitions of progress and economic growth.[5] Nisbet has criticized in particular the theories of development promulgated in the 1950s by Talcott Parsons and many others, theories which seemed to portray the United States as trailblazer for the world, the most developed society, with all the others, the so-called developing nations, following naturally along in Yankee footsteps.

the worth of theories of progress and history

But the historicist position must not be pressed too far. A useful sociology is not buried in the secure harbor of fact-finding; it drifts elusive on the chancy open seas of theory building. Even if the diverse events of human life bear no inherent order, we scholars are properly obliged to *give them order*, to discern creatively in history some pattern we today can assume and build on in our attempt to make more history. This obligation falls on our generation with special heaviness, now in the wake of the Indochina war and in the midst of energy crises, inflation, crime epidemics, and most ominous of all, widespread cynicism and doubt. For if we cannot chart systematically where the human race has been, to be sure we will get no farther. Denying that history leads somewhere will get us nowhere. We need not return to the conceptions of progress popular in the 1950s, conceptions which overgeneralized from the U.S. experience, took too much of Western capitalism for granted, and thus served mainly as ideological props for the status quo. It did our human race no good to portray North America and Europe as developed, the rest of the world as developing. But it does even less good today to disavow development altogether and retreat from purposive history. Our responsibility today as always is to get our bearings as best we can, to conjure up theories for locating ourselves in time, to formulate enduring principles of development that will stimulate beneficial change. The following paragraphs present eleven such principles gleaned from many scholars' writings, ten plus one critical elements in the eternal human quest to turn the table on nature.

SETTLING DOWN

Human beings asserted their economic potential first and foremost when they refused any longer to camp on nature's trail and learned instead to make nature come to them. This is the significance of the shift from hunting and gathering to animal husbandry and agriculture. Between 12,000 and 5000 years ago, scattered societies on every continent made this shift, entering what is often defined as the

domestication of
animals and plants in
the neolithic age

neolithic age. They ceased to stalk their prey like wolves; instead they taught sheep and cattle to follow the human voice, even to the day of butchering. They quit foraging for food like rabbits; instead they cultivated cereal grains and vegetables, making them grow according to human design. The first great distancing of people from animals was accomplished: people could stay in one place, producing their food and clothing on purpose at first hand, while animals were left behind, prowling about wherever the fruits of nature could be found. This was economic development in its primordial sense: domesticating animals and plants, arranging them around a human home, taming them, controlling them, subjecting them to the human will.

Even today, it is a sign of power when a man can oblige others to come to them, and a sign of weakness that he must go to them. Who should crawl to whom is regularly a matter of dispute, but only *among* human beings. Between human and nonhuman beings, there is no longer any doubt in principle and progressively less in fact. Steadily through the centuries, people have made more and more of nature available at their own doorsteps. Consider the triumph, for example, of the ancient aqueducts, carrying water where people wanted it. In the garden of the Escorial, a royal palace in central Spain, giant New World sequoias still grow, brought back as seedlings by the explorers of the sixteenth century. In the contemporary era, what do pipelines and high tension wires symbolize if not the assumed right of humans to live where they choose, and the duty they impose on nature to come to them? Central heating puts summer in our homes during winter, and air conditioning transforms summer into spring. Coal, Emerson once wrote, is a portable climate. No longer is people's diet in the developed part of the world dictated much by the seasons or by geographic location. The fruits of the earth are brought to citizens according to their tastes. All this is part of the most ancient and basic element of the process of economic development, that which involves ever more movement in nature for the sake of making it serve people in their chosen locations.

MAKING TOOLS AND MACHINES

Abandoning the chase after nature, bringing it to heel, does not happen simply by an act of the human will. It requires shaping bits of nature in such a way that they can be used to control the rest of it. Without tools, the instruments for acting upon the world, we gangly, furless beings are among the weakest and most vulnerable of earthly creatures. A naked man against a bull is doomed to die, but even with such simple tools as a cape and a sword, Mexican and Spanish men daily put ferocious

bulls to death for the sport of it. Even hunters and gatherers used tools, of course: bows and arrows, stone knives, spears, hand-held millstones, traps, levers, fishing nets, various concoctions for poisoning game and preserving meat, and so on. The neolithic age was marked, however, not only by a shift to more sedentary living but by the perfection of stone implements. Later came the invention of tools made from such metals as copper, tin, zinc, lead and iron, and such alloys as bronze. The greater strength and plasticity of metal, as opposed to wood and stone, vastly increased the number of tools humans could make. With a metal saw or axe, a man could fell a tree in minutes. With a metal plow he could easily overturn the earth and ready it for planting. And so on to all the more effective tools invented by various societies in later centuries. Those with moving parts are normally called machines, or collectively, technology.

*industrialization:
machine technology and
further separation from
nature*

Industrialization is commonly understood as the process by which a society increasingly uses machines in approaching and operating upon its natural milieu. It bears mention, nonetheless, that until little more than a century ago, economic development was sustained by only a small array of relatively simple tools and crude technology. Machines for carding wool, ginning cotton, spinning the raw materials into thread and weaving the thread into cloth were invented only in the eighteenth century. Simple grist mills beside fast-flowing streams provided the flour for much of North America even into the present century. There were no railroads a century and a half ago, no motorcars a century ago, no useful aircraft even seventy years ago. Large-scale production of steel for making tools began only in the late 1800s, and of synthetic plastics only since World War II. It is only in the last fifty years that technology in a few societies around the globe has become mind-boggling in its complexity. This is a problem to which we shall return later in this chapter.

One further point should be made about tools and machines. No less dramatically than the shift to domestic life, technology enlarges the separation between people and the rest of nature. Technology is by definition a go-between, an intermediary, a device that prevents the active human subject from having to encounter directly the object acted upon. Desiring to cross a river, a man without tools has to swim, immersing his body in its waters, feeling its currents against his skin, hearing, smelling and tasting it as he moves. With a boat as a tool, the man can paddle across without getting wet. With a bridge and a car, he can ride across as if the river were not there. In a plane on a cloudy day he crosses the river without even seeing it, much less giving it a thought. This same sequence of technological development, multiplied by a thousand other examples, inevitably widens the gulf between people and their milieu. There is no escaping this progressive widening in any effort at development. The process happens only as the human species, the one to which you and I belong, pulls farther and farther away from other species and the inanimate world, and then manipulates this divorced environment for human purposes. People have come a long way from the time they were flattered to call themselves Brothers of the Sea Otter or some other beast. By means of tools we have set ourselves apart from nature, broken our kinship with it, and given ourselves a history.

HARNESSING NONHUMAN SOURCES OF ENERGY

Even armed with tools and machines, we humans are still no match for nature. However well primed by jogging and exercise, our bodies have too little strength. Giraffes can run faster than we; kangaroos can jump higher; the lifeless wind and rain can move mountains more easily. Hence economic development necessarily

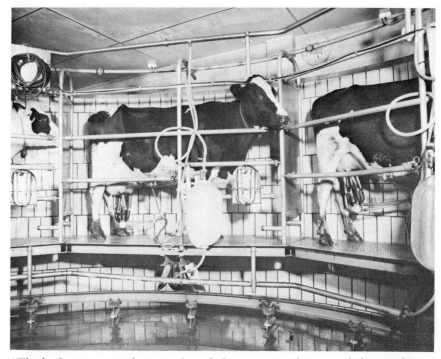

"The development process happens only as the human species, the one to which you and I belong, pulls farther and farther away from other species and the inanimate world and then manipulates this divorced environment for human purposes." Above, a Holstein bears the brunt of human enterprise. (Grant Heilman Photography)

implies a third element: the capturing and harnessing of strength outside ourselves, the trapping and training of movement or energy available in our milieu. Thereby we compel one part of nature (the energy source) to move another part (the tool or machine), usually in order to transform still a third part (the raw material) into something we want (the product). Our planet abounds in energy sources and there is no need trying to sort them all out here. Some, I suspect, have so far escaped human attention and many others remain as yet uncontrolled. Nonetheless, one distinction between types of energy source is so crucial to development at our point in history that it must be considered here. It is the difference between *renewable* and *nonrenewable* resources, between those which can in principle be made to last indefinitely and those which cannot. This distinction is important because until about a century ago no society anywhere ever fueled its action on the earth mainly with nonrenewable resources. Today the most powerful and active societies on earth are actually doing so. The change is ominous.

The renewable resources most commonly harnessed in history have been animals of superhuman strength. Oxen, horses, burros, camels, yaks, elephants, water buffaloes, llamas, dogs, and reindeer, according to local availability, have all been enslaved for millennia and trained to move in accordance with human purposes. As beasts of burden they have transported people and people's products. As draft

renewable resources: animals, wind, water

animals they have pushed and pulled all manner of tools and machines. At the beginning of this century they were the primary source of non-human energy everywhere in the world. As late as 1920, there were 20 million horses and 5 million mules in the United States alone, nearly all of them regularly in harness, about one for every four citizens. And they were an easily re-newable resource. Given the chance, all animals instinctively eat, drink, and copulate, producing further generations of their kind to serve further generations of our kind.

Also in the renewable category are numerous inanimate forces inherent in nature: the blowing of wind, the rush of rivers toward the sea, the ebb and flow of tides, the powerful rays of the sun. Since the natural climate of earth replenishes these forces unceasingly, they exceed even animals in their usefulness. But they are less easily harnessed. Medieval Europeans nonetheless learned to dam up streams and create waterfalls for turning mill wheels. These wheels were then geared to giant stones whose rotation could grind cereal grains into meal and flour. Windmills like the ones Don Quixote mistook for giants in sixteenth-century Spain had been used for both grinding grain and drawing water in the Middle East even 900 years earlier. By capturing wind in the sails of ships, Europeans managed to travel amost all the earth by 1800, and to conquer and colonize most of it.

Contemporary industrial societies do not completely ignore renewable sources of energy. Rivers are controlled now more than ever, though the old mills have mostly degenerated into heaps of rubble or trendy restaurants. For in 1895, a U.S. inventor named George Westinghouse succeeded in converting motion from Niagara Falls into alternating electric current, a medium of energy which could be made to travel by metal wire almost anywhere people wanted it. Here at last was instant power, domesticated energy, stronger than a thousand mules, more versatile, more dependable, cleaner, nearly free of maintenance, and with a life span of untold millions of years. Hydroelectric power therefore proved popular in societies all around the globe, wherever there were waterfalls or the possibility of making them by damming streams. The huge hydroelectric projects of the early 1980s at James Bay in northern Quebec and on the Paraná River between Brazil and Paraguay testify to the continued value placed on this source of energy. But the industrial societies of North America and Europe rely little any more on the other renewable sources. Windmills have gone the way of sailing ships. The wind blows freely now almost everywhere, fueling only pleasure craft and weather vanes. Although techniques have been devised for harnessing the sun and tides, these remain little used. As for animals, they are now just for eating and playing with. The U.S. horse population is less than one-tenth what it was in 1920, while this society's human population has more than doubled.

The difference between the renewable sources of energy reviewed so far and nonrenewable ones is more than a difference of objects: a horse versus a lump of coal, for example, or a river versus a barrel of oil. For in the former case harnessing energy means overtaking motion inherent in the earth, channeling and directing it toward human ends; it means plugging into nature. In the latter case, by contrast, harnessing energy means creating motion by destroying some of the earth, burning

the mentality underlying use of nonrenewable resources

up or exploding physical matter; it means abolishing part of nature, the better to control what is left of it. All human societies have taken this latter approach to some extent and fed their progress on nonrenewable resources. Wood is the oldest and best example—sent up in smoke for the sake of clearing land (what anthropologists call slash-and-burn agriculture), cooking food, heating homes, smelting and forging metals, or firing earthenware, glass, and bricks. By any standard fire has been a boon to economic development. Besides, wood is a partially renewable resource, since most terrain can support repeated crops of timber. The same goes for vegetable matter processed into gas and burned as fuel.

Increasingly during the last 200 years, however, Western societies have relied for energy on the utterly nonrenewable fossil fuels: coal, oil, and natural gas, and more recently the mineral sources of uranium. These substances exist in finite supply. The earth yields them but once. Burned up today, they are gone forever. But they were plentiful enough in the nineteenth century, humans were still few enough, and the human ability to destroy nature was so limited that to let minerals lie untouched seemed silly romanticism. And so machines were invented for transforming fossil fuels on a large scale into energy: efficient steam engines in the late eighteenth century, internal combustion engines about 100 years later, nuclear reactors during World War II. It was a short step, moreover, from hydroelectric power to the generation of electricity from the burning of fossil fuels. And as the years passed people built more and larger engines and invented more and more tools and machines for these engines to run. On this basis, the ever-growing wastage of nature, development has proceeded in North America, Europe, and to a lesser degree, the rest of the world. Societies have come to be arranged in such a way that their citizens' whole way of life depends on the steady and massive consumption of coal, oil, and gas. Currently, for example, only about 13 percent of the electricity generated in the United States derives from renewable sources; about half is from coal, the rest from oil, gas, and nuclear fission.

Geologists differ in their estimates of how much coal, oil, and gas the earth still contains, but they agree that the supply is dwindling rapidly, that the short run is over and the long run is now. By conservative estimates it appears that the supply would be completely depleted within the next five years if all societies burned these minerals at the same rate per capita as the societies of North America are burning them. Since this is not the case, we have more time. But for us to take comfort in *massive consumption of* having ten, twenty, or even eighty years left is to live in a fool's paradise. A man *oil and gas is a fool's* who heats his house by throwing one wall after another into the stove, and who *paradise* brags that his fuel supply will last easily two years more, is obviously deranged. So are we when we measure development, as economists often do, simply in terms of the consumption of energy, without consideration of its source. We humans cannot at once have dominion over the earth and incinerate it. Progress means mastering this planet, not destroying the only environment we have. Hence the large-scale use of nonrenewable sources of energy can by no means be counted an enduring principle of economic development. It is instead a costly mistake our particular societies have made along the way—costly for its irreparable waste and for its pollution of the atmosphere. Now that the mistake is made, our generation is faced with a choice. We can bring development to a halt, perhaps voluntarily or more likely just by carrying on as we are until our wells are dry, our telephones dead, our lights off, our planes grounded, and our cars stalled. Then our children and grandchildren, if they survive, can pick up the pieces and begin anew on a less mistaken course, cursing us with every breath. On the other hand, we ourselves could speed up the process of development here and now and carry it to unprecedented heights—by training our minds economically and politically on ways of shifting our reliance swiftly from nonrenewable to renewable resources. Electric wires may symbolize development or its contradiction, depending on the source of the energy within them.

LEARNING TO WORK

Animals and plants cannot be tamed, nor tools manufactured, nor energy harnessed unless people impose structure also upon their own behavior. This is the fourth element in the process of economic advance: the application by humans of their own activity to the earth in a planned, purposive, systematic, orderly way, or

more simply, work. Our everyday language is confused about this word. Work often refers simply to paid employment and is distinguished from leisure, what people do after hours and on weekends. But as experience demonstrates, paid positions differ in how much work they require and employees vary in how much they do. Moreover, most citizens of today's industrial societies work quite a lot under the label of leisure: battling expressway traffic, scrutinizing supermarket shelves for weekly specials, planning and preparing meals, tending gardens, washing clothes, and vacuuming carpets. Hence work is most usefully understood as any sustained, disciplined

sustained, disciplined effort, the opposite of play

effort—whether mental or physical, paid or unpaid, forced or voluntary, engaging or repulsive—aimed at accomplishing something upon the earth. Work in this sense is the opposite of play, relaxation, rest, setting one's mind and body at ease, as in dawdling over lunch, unwinding with friends, cutting loose at a party, meandering through a park, or losing oneself in a film. It can also be distinguished from those sports and games which demand systematic effort but lack economic purpose, serving mainly to entertain, amuse, and refresh. Work is to play as shaping up is to letting go, as serious purpose is to silliness and fun, or as fighting the earth is to loving it.

Intrinsic to economic development is a shift from play to work both with regard to how much time each occupies in daily life and as a change in general outlook. This point may be difficult to grasp, especially since we easily imagine our impoverished ancestors to have spent their lives in unceasing toil. But anthropologists who have lived with economically primitive tribes report almost without fail a playful orientation to life, an unhurried joie de vivre, an easygoing acceptance of events even in the midst of harsh circumstances. Hunters and gatherers accomplish things and make products, to be sure, and they may seldom seem idle. But their economic activity appears by our standards halfhearted, casual, and unmethodical, lacking the intensity, concentration, discipline, and rigor definitional of work. In the course of development humans necessarily abandon such nonchalance and lessen the whimsy in everyday life. Probably nothing symbolizes this so well as the mechanical clock, introduced throughout most of Europe in the fourteenth and fifteenth centuries. Clocks permitted what had otherwise been impossible, the imposition of detailed structure upon time, the regulation of human conduct in the context of minutes and hours. Timepieces in a sense are the measure of work itself. The more humans live by the clock, the more they assume a working orientation toward the earth. In less developed societies one can readily wander through villages and countryside, finding most citizens with time to spare for relaxed conversation with a stranger. In the industrialized world the stranger finds most people checking their wristwatches fitfully, finely calculating just how many minutes (if any) they can give to unscheduled interruptions. Such is the workaday culture of developed societies, a culture which penetrates nearly all of nearly every day.

the clock: sign and measure of work

In the course of economic development people work not only more but also differently. The huge amounts of unskilled labor required in nonmechanized agriculture and simple factories (as in nineteenth-century America or the Soviet Union in the 1930s) cease to be necessary at later stages of the process. Ability to operate complex tools and machines counts steadily for more than sheer physical prowess and endurance. Mental effort gradually supplants bodily force. These trends intensify, moreover, as nonhuman energy is brought under control. The burden on humans shifts increasingly from doing things directly to thinking about how gasoline, electricity, and other forms of energy can be made to do them. By now most of the physical work required of most citizens in the advanced Western world happens at home: carrying groceries and packages, doing dishes, caring for infants, wallpapering bathrooms, and suchlike. At least two-thirds of gainfully employed citizens have occupations which in a physical sense are simple and almost identical: walking, standing, sitting, exchanging messages verbally or in written form, and pushing buttons on some kind of machine, whether cash register, typewriter, keypunch, truck, bulldozer, telephone, dictaphone, computer console, switchboard, or whatever. Most jobs today in North America differ mainly in which messages are exchanged and which buttons on which machines are pushed. Only about a third of workers, including surgeons and some mechanics, line workers, and tradespeople, still do something physically arduous and complex. The advanced societies can scarcely find any job at all for a person who has only the strength and vigor of a horse, the kind of person who was the mainstay of primitive economies.

the shift toward skilled, mental labor

It should not be thought that the development process requires that people work eternally more and more and more. This clearly is impossible. Without play, sleep, rest, and other experiences of nature in control, people become physically or mentally ill and die. Further, time for reflection and silliness is prerequisite to conjuring up new ideas for advancing the development process. Nor does development at any point imply that some citizens should force others into the misery and drudgery of powerless, uncreative work, the kind that permits little or no personal expression. But it is an enduring principle of development at all advanced stages that the vast bulk of citizens must work steadfastly and productively. There is simply no point imagining that computers and automated production technologies will engender in coming decades a society of women and men all taking it easy and spending their lives in play. Improved machines can indeed diminish the amount of routine, tedious work humans must perform. But there will be no improved machines unless humans engage in the hard mental work of inventing, designing, perfecting, building, programming, and maintaining those machines. Nor will our complex industrial economies endure, much less will they advance, unless citizens as average as you and I set our minds systematically to making sense of what is going on. Apathy among citizens, the cessation of motivation to work, is indeed a prime condition for the physical extinction of a society itself, and there are historical examples of this happening.[6] The point needs to be stressed in an era like ours, when absurd ideas circulate and citizens suffer from lack of confidence: economic progress depends utterly on systematic, purposeful, rigorous human effort. Our species has come this far only because our ancestors learned to work. We today can move history forward, but only by imposing comparable discipline upon ourselves.

ANALYZING NATURE SYMBOLICALLY

The prevalence of mainly cerebral kinds of work in contemporary industrialized societies is vivid evidence of a fifth element in the development process, the

progressive incorporation of nature into the human mind through the media of words and numbers. Integral to the four principles of development listed so far, and to all those reviewed below, is people's generally increasing ability to put nature symbolically inside their heads, rearrange it there, and then impose that rearrangement on nature itself. This ability expresses

the economic significance of naming things

itself above all in everyday language, the primary tool for asserting human authority over nature. Thus in the Genesis creation story, the Creator brings newly formed beasts and birds to Adam "to see what he would call them; and whatever the man called every living creature, that was its name."[7] Adam's first technique for subduing and having dominion over nature, and the continuing basic technique of humans ever since, has been to inflict words upon it, symbols for taking nature apart and manipulating it mentally. And this is only the beginning. For carrying development farther, language must be set down in written form. This first occurred some 5000 years ago in certain tribes of present-day Iraq, but the practice both spread in all directions from there and arose independently elsewhere. Especially in recent centuries, spoken and written languages have become more ample in vocabulary and more complex in grammatical form, in tandem with increased variety and sophistication of tools and machines. And for good reason. The richer the language, the more it can capture the earth.

The development process entails more, however, than enlarging and enriching vernacular languages. Higher stages of the process imply the decline of mythical, poetic ways of depicting nature in favor of more detached and abstract vocabularies, the lexicons of science. A science is at root a *working* language, one devised for analyzing nature with greater precision, discipline, and rigor than everyday words permit, thus for controlling nature with greater success. Closely related to scientific languages are the mathematical ones, composed of the most abstract symbols of all: numbers, standard units of time, space, and motion contrived to reduce nature to the most manageable categories possible. Mathematics is the paramount symbolic tool for the human domination of earth, empty as it is of feelings and so utterly disciplined in its handling of the data of human experience. Both science and mathematics were enormously advanced in England and France during the sixteenth and seventeenth centuries, with Galileo, Descartes, and Newton among the chief architects of the new symbol systems. This was the same period when many instruments for precise measurement, like the thermometer and micrometer, first were invented. Steadily since that time, systems of quantitative science have been improved. Contemporary industrial economies rely vitally on these systems as embedded in human intellects. For this reason the term *pure science* is a misnomer. When governments today grant money for so-called pure research, they are banking on the hope that scientists who stand still farther back from nature and reduce it to even more abstract symbols will think up ways for extending still farther the frontiers of action on the earth.

the working languages of science and mathematics

Because the symbolic analysis of nature is so central to economic development, one of the more common contemporary measures of a society's level of development is the percentage of its adult citizens who can read and write. It is a measure that dramatically exposes the abysmal chasm of difference between nations by now relatively advanced in mastery of their milieux, and nations still intensely vulnerable to nature's caprice. In the African societies of Chad, Niger, Ethiopia, and Mali, fewer than 10 percent of citizens are literate—a percentage smaller than that of the United States in 1776. In 1975, the literacy rate in India was 36 percent and in Bangladesh 25 percent, while in Mexico it was 82 percent. In Canada, the United States, Europe, Japan, Australia, and the Soviet Union, more than 95 percent of adult citizens are literate. The human species has indeed a curious history, when some of its specimens can know and do so much but at the same time allow so many other specimens to suffer nature's tyranny in ignorance. The species seems to lack a sense of solidarity.

literacy rates—a basic measure of economic development

Literacy rates do not, of course, tell even half the story of economic development, especially given the diverse relationships among societies within international capitalism. Quite a small corps of foreign-educated scientists, engineers, and technicians can apply advanced technology to native resources, sell them abroad, and amass great wealth in their society, even while the bulk of their compatriots remain illiterate and uncomprehending. By virtue of its oil wells Kuwait is an extreme case. On a per capita basis in 1980, this small society south of Iraq had more cars than Great Britain, a higher income than the United States, and a medical system that rivaled Canada's. But more than half its citizens were illiterate. South Africa, Saudi Arabia, Iran, and to a lesser extent many other societies of Asia and Africa display similar imbalance between the diffusion and implementation of scientific knowledge within their borders. So indeed do the advanced Western societies, where millions of youthful products of ineffective schools are barely able to read and write, yet live amidst the fruits of wonderfully sophisticated science-based engineering. Any such imbalance makes for a problem. As the preceding chapter suggested, the inability of a large part of a national population to master intellectually the national economy bodes ill for that society's political future. Without a grasp of abstract language and mathematics, citizens can hardly get a grip on an industrial economy, much less on the government presiding over it. The society with the brightest future is the one whose citizens, collectively to be sure but also individually, possess symbolic instruments for making sense of their present economy.

ENLARGING SOCIETIES

The five principles of development so far reviewed extend back into the unrecorded past and forward into the indefinite future. They can be taken for granted as

interminable. Domesticating nature, contriving technologies, harnessing energy, setting to work, and analyzing experience necessarily continue, intensify, and become somehow more excellent, whatever the society and whatever the level of progress toward which it moves. The six remaining principles are more problematic, more time-bound, integral to development in only limited degree or at particular stages of the process. The first

of these is the expansion of political authority over greater numbers of people, the incorporation of small-scale societies into larger ones. Had our human race remained forever divided into thousands of discrete little communities, a few hundred hunters and gatherers or peasants in each, significant reversal of nature's oppression of our race would never have occurred. For such reversal is accomplished only by sizable classes of active but initially unproductive innovators, people who experiment, toy with new ideas, and seek to realize fantasies of unprecedented human accomplishment. Such classes can support themselves only by expropriating food and other goods from many thousands of conventional producers. The system resembles a protection racket. For fear of being molested, a large number of hard-working plebeians hand over some fraction of the fruits of their labor to a powerful elite. The plebeians consider this a tax they must pay to keep their health. But to the elite these taxes are a surplus available for investment in something other than routine work. Like bosses of organized crime, many elite classes in history have spent this surplus only on their own idle amusement. Their societies therefore failed to develop. But other elites have used the surplus to support citizens engaged in diverse and novel schemes of action on the earth. The Egyptian pyramids (ca. 2700 B.C.), the Athenian Parthenon (447–432 B.C.), the Great Wall of China (begun ca. 400–200 B.C.), the Mayan temples of the Yucatán (begun ca. 100 B.C.), the cathedrals of medieval Europe, and the "research and development" of our own day rest on just this economic foundation.

That economic development historically required the enlargement of societies, the extension of sovereign power over many thousands and even millions of taxable citizens, seems obvious enough. The question is how far such expansion of social

the advantage of expanding political authority

order needs to go. England, for example, commenced the industrial revolution in the eighteenth century with a population quite modest by today's standards—about 6 million in 1750. The English capitalist innovators accomplished this feat, of course, not only by keeping the mass of English workers in poverty but also by using productively the large surpluses extracted from British colonies, which then covered much of the globe. The great age of American invention, the late nineteenth century, blossomed in a highly self-sufficient population numbering 50 million in 1880. Russia industrialized late but rapidly, transforming the poor, agrarian economy of the turn of the century so remarkably that it could launch the first humanly constructed satellite into space in 1958. Russia achieved such admirable advance, it appears, only by bleeding severely a large population (125 million in 1896) for the sake of supporting an innovative class of scientists, engineers, and technicians.

the optimal size of societies today

The question is an intriguing one: How many citizens need a society comprise in the present day in order to develop economically, and with a high degree of autonomy and self-sufficiency? There is, in answer, no magic number, but a number clearly smaller than was required in the past. For the challenge facing societies not yet industrialized is to gear up their own productive resources, to educate people in scientific knowledge, and to adapt innovations from outside to their indigenous economic plans. A hard task, to be sure, but certainly no harder in a society of 6 million like Bolivia than in one of 650 million like India. In the advanced societies, by contrast, production already so far exceeds subsistence levels that an entire citizenry can live in relative luxury while a third of workers or more is engaged in some kind of study, research, or experimentation for the sake of extending development still more. In 1977, the economies of Australia (14 million people), Switzerland (6 million), Norway (4 million), and even Iceland (220,000) seemed to be keeping pace well enough with that of the United States (215 million). Large-scale projects can often be undertaken as productively by several smaller societies jointly (Britain and France, for example, in making the Concorde aircraft) as by large ones going it alone (the United States or the U.S.S.R. in their respective space programs). Besides, there is no evidence that the most salutary economic advances possible today can only be achieved through such large-scale projects as these.

Much contemporary economic discussion seems grounded in the empirically unwarranted assumption that further development on our planet requires humans to be grouped in ever larger sociocultural systems—until, one supposes, some parliament of 100 humans should be allowed to rule all the rest of us. Such an assumption disparages and insults human abilities. There is in principle no reason why 2 or 3 million literate men and women, organized with purpose and located in a territory of average natural endowment, could not create even on their own a way of life richer, more civilized, more humane than any yet known. And with regular exchange of ideas and goods by voluntary agreements, a planet full of small sovereign societies might well elevate the quality of life to unprecedented heights. Hence there is no cause to scoff on basic economic grounds at the continuing prospect of Quebec seceding from Canada. Nor at the possibility of Puerto Rico declaring its national independence. Nor at the proposals regularly made that

Soviet republics, American states, Canadian provinces, or such territories as Scotland and Wales should have greater autonomy. All these are political questions much more than economic ones. They concern not so much how people live with the earth as how they live with one another. Our language offers us a good word, *balkanization*, for division of people into groups too small to be efficient—something the goal of development clearly precludes. But in an era when bigger is often unthinkingly assumed to be better, the opposite danger of social *elephantiasis* deserves our attention still more. Discussions of the optimum size of societies might even take note of San Marino, that proud republic near the Adriatic coast whose population is less than 20,000.

the contrary dangers of balkanization and elephantiasis

MAKING A DIVISION OF LABOR

The progress of our species historically required the enlargement of societies not only to provide tax bases sufficient to support innovative classes but also more generally to permit the division of labor. Such differentiation of work into separate tasks spread across various individuals constitutes the seventh element or principle of the development process. Ancient primitive economies had almost all their workers, at least those of the same sex, doing almost identical jobs. Men's work typically differed from women's, and specialists performed magic and witchcraft, but most children learned in the course of growing up nearly all

the skills by which their society related to its natural milieu. Birds flying over tenth-century France, for example, looked down upon little communities where the vast majority of people worked in the common and relatively simple routine of peasant agriculture. Out of such a circumstance development did not occur by a sudden collective focus on the common challenge of managing nature to greater human benefit. It happened instead as individuals set their minds to diverse and specific challenges like grinding grain, cutting stone, or making cloth—perfecting discrete parts of the overall production process. This led to the invention of new and more complex tools, many of which required years to master. Lengthy periods of study and practice came to be necessary for understanding and operating just some tiny fraction of the snowballing technology that defined industrialization. The advanced Western societies today distinguish thousands of job titles, corresponding to the varied and specialized tasks that constitute their economies. The fundamental reason for specialized work is nothing other than the intransigence, the limitations of any single human mind and body. No one is able to learn more

*Durkheim's theory of
mechanical and organic
types of solidarity*

than a few of the mental and physical skills by which an advanced industrial society relates to the planet Earth.

In his first major book, published in 1893, the French sociologist Emile Durkheim seized upon occupational specialization as the key element not just for economic advance but for the development of civilization itself. Under the title *The Division of Labor*, the book was published in English in 1933, and came to have major impact on sociology in the United States. Durkheim portrayed the primitive society as a communistic horde of like individuals, all sharing common beliefs and sentiments, joined in a collective conscience and controlled by a system of repressive law. Such a society, he said, is held together by *mechanical solidarity*: lacking individuality, people conform for fear of the penalties attached to nonconformity. Specialized work, Durkheim argued, sets people free from the oppressive and stultifying aspects of primitive economies, letting each person contribute his or her particular talents, skills, and inclinations. In an occupationally diverse society repressive law yields to cooperative law, a vast array of agreed-upon rules, contracts, and procedures to which people conform because they *want* to. A society enriched by a complex division of labor resembles a living organism, each of its varied parts accomplishing an almost unique purpose for the whole. Thus *organic* rather than mechanical solidarity holds it together. This kind of society won Durkheim's earnest approval. He admitted that specialized workers sometimes feel alone, isolated, unrelated organically to compatriots in other jobs, to the unknown consumers of their products, and to the society as a whole. He called this a "state of anomie" and deplored it as an unnatural, pathological condition of the social organism. Durkheim nevertheless scorned the idea of giving workers general education and he disdained governmental interference with what he took to be the natural progress of the division of labor. This division, he concluded, would have ill effects only in exceptional circumstances. "It is necessary and it is sufficient for it to be itself, for nothing to come from without to denature it."[8]

*two qualifications on
Durkheim: first, the
value of individual
enrichment*

With the benefit of hindsight, however, we today must place two qualifications on Durkheim's almost rhapsodic portrayal of occupational specialization. First is that only a limited degree of it need or should be taken for granted in the development process. The division of labor may well affect a society the way absence affects a romance: a little seals and strengthens it, too much breaks it up. Specialized work roles are necessary, after all, only because the human mind is too puny to grasp all the knowledge in an advanced economy and the human hand too clumsy to learn all the corresponding skills. But the mind must not be thought punier than it is, nor the hand clumsier. Surely no one would argue that learning to operate a drill press, microwave oven, chain saw, or typewriter exhausts the mental or physical capacities of a human being. The development process requires no such argument nor does it insist that some citizens spend their lifetimes in routine, repetitive, specialized tasks that undervalue human potential. Indeed, the process is more complete, the more thoroughly a society is mastered by its citizens—not just as an organic collectivity but also as proud individuals. Alexis de Tocqueville, the French social commentator who traveled America in 1831, observed from his travels that while "the art progresses, the artisan retrogresses." Such need not be the case. In the course of economic advance the art (that is, the sum total of know-how) does indeed progress, and far beyond any individual artisan. But the artisan need not retrogress. Today's so-called developed societies could develop themselves further by encouraging the rotation of jobs, by permitting citizens to enrich themselves individually throughout their lives, adding new skills year by year to their occupational repertoires and putting these skills to use. As a facet of the development process, the division of labor by no means implies the infinite regression of the human person, but only some limits on individual mastery of the economic whole.

second, division only of labor, not of power

A second qualification on Durkheim's enthusiasm concerns not the extent or degree of division of labor but the kind. Much of the difference among occupations in contemporary Western societies is in how much autonomy or creativity each permits, the difference between boss roles and hireling roles. On the one hand are professionals, managers, and independent tradespeople, who enjoy considerable power over the timing, techniques, and quality of what they do. Workers in this category can put themselves into their work and innovate if they choose. On the other hand are orderlies, sales clerks, file clerks, line workers, and other employees, whose jobs consist in following externally given directions. The division of labor necessary for development does not at all imply or justify this *kind* of division, much less an increase of it over time. For examples of the kind of division we must assume as inevitable, we can compare a seamstress to a blacksmith, a novelist to a pianist, a bricklayer to a pharmacist—comparisons grounded in diverse productive tasks, each of which requires distinct knowledge and skill. Comparisons like that between owner and employee, barker of orders and listener, are of a different kind. They refer to a division more precisely of power than of labor, a kind of apartness among humans which genuine economic development reduces rather than intensifies.

TOWARD GOVERNMENT, MARKETS, AND MONEY

The eighth principle of economic development offered in this review applies not so much to the way goods are produced as to how they are distributed among citizens.

For our discussion so far makes it clear that economic advance means increased productivity, greater quantity and variety of items available for human use and enjoyment. This in turn calls for reorganization of the procedures for moving these goods from producers to consumers. From his studies in economic history, Karl Polanyi distinguished three such procedures or modes of exchange, which in varying combination describe the way every society

gift giving: exchange as interpersonal communication

allocates its goods. Most tribes of hunters and gatherers rely mainly on the first mode, *gift giving*. Primitive tribes are so small that everyone knows everyone else, and thus none of the few available goods can be thought of apart from the particular person who seized it from nature or fashioned it by hand. The exchange of an object is therefore bound up in the identities of the people involved. Transfer of something is interpersonal communication, an extension of the giver's own being into the life of the receiver—every object is a gift. Marcel Mauss (1872–1950), a

Federal laws against potlatching failed to prevent such celebrations among the Kwakiutl, and the potlatch was legalized again in 1951. Ironically, the gifts exchanged in more recent times have often been products of the Western market economy. The enamel bowls shown above are an example. (Courtesy of the American Museum of Natural History)

disciple of Durkheim and also his nephew, made the classic analysis of this form of exchange. In his *Essay on the Gift*, he wrote that in archaic societies, objects "are never completely separated from the men who exchange them: the communion and alliance they establish are well-nigh indissoluble."[9] The most celebrated example was the potlatch of the Kwakiutl Indians in nineteenth-century British Columbia. This was a joyous ceremonial festival where the host reduced himself to virtual poverty by giving away his possessions to his guests. But he had not at all made himself poor in the context of Kwakiutl culture, for his friends and kin had accepted the host's very self into their lives along with his gifts. The norm of reciprocity in gift giving would ensure, moreover, that others would soon invite him to partake of their own possessions.

When the Canadian government outlawed the potlatch in 1883, it furnished thereby a poignant symbol of the fate of gift giving in more economically advanced societies. This mode of exchange does not completely disappear, of course, as birthday and Christmas customs in mainstream North America amply demonstrate, but it is greatly depersonalized, relegated to special occasions and engaged in with awkwardness. Gifts come to be considered bribes, and received reluctantly. The reason is that as groups grow larger, as production becomes specialized, and as goods proliferate, the immersion of economic exchanges in interpersonal relationships becomes cumbersome—too time-consuming in a culture of minutely measured time. More developed societies need modes of exchange which separate objects from specific people, procedures which detach products culturally from their producers. One alternative is the second mode or procedure Polanyi distinguished, what he call *redistribution*. This means that the society's economic goods are identified with citizens collectively and placed under public, governmental authority, to be allocated or redistributed across citizens by political decision. Who gets what depends upon some kind of announced policy carried out by agencies of public administration. The ruler or government sets economic priorities and goals and then mobilizes resources appropriately. Virtually all the major accomplishments of the early empires resulted from shrewd and relatively impersonal management by governments of tools, people, raw materials, and products. One can still inspect today the irrigation and terracing systems, roads, and public buildings constructed in antiquity by innovative and aggressive governments. The subways, satellites, and superhighways, the nuclear power plants and hydroelectric installations in the contemporary Western world also reflect the redistributive mode of exchange: the enforced public allocation of goods toward politically defined economic purposes.

the redistributive mode of exchange: public ownership

Polanyi's third mode of exchange is a further alternative to gift giving as societies progress. This is the *market*: trade, barter, buying and selling of goods according to the possessive desires of the parties involved. Even more than the redistributive procedure, the market depersonalizes economic objects. For in the former case goods are still tied to people, albeit in a collective rather than an individual sense. But in the latter case, goods are understood in relation only to one another. What is taken or handed over is not a gift from a friend, nor a grant from public authority, but a *commodity*—an important word, since it illuminates the very core of a market economy. Etymologically it means something which can be measured against something else. An economic object becomes a commodity at that moment when its possessor imagines trading it for another object. The market mentality is an ethic of supreme detachment, an owner's definition of his or her possessions as so extrinsic and foreign that they can be sold or bartered away out of purely private inclination. Literally foreign objects, those produced in distant, alien societies, were among the first to be exchanged on market principles. Europeans in the late Middle Ages and early Renaissance engaged in vigorous trade for pepper and other spices from the East, silk and other imported fabrics, ivory from Africa, tobacco, gold, and furs from America. These items could easily be defined as commodities and marketed precisely because they came from afar and were not personally identifiable. Among other items marketed in many preindustrial societies are common and ordinary agricultural products, fruits and vegetables, the relatively natural, impersonal fruits of the earth.

the market: exchanging mere commodities

For estranging people from goods, encouraging a definition of goods as commodities, and thus facilitating the market mode of exchange, the widespread use of money is a necessity. For money is but an abstract standard, a neutral quantitative measure for assessing the worth of one item versus another. And the more deeply entrenched market procedures are in a society, the more abstract and neutral the money used will be. The perfection of money in the Western world owes much to John Law, a British thinker and opportunist who wrote a treatise in 1705 spelling

These bowls in an Egyptian market are neither gifts nor grants but commodities—things measurable in terms of other things. (© 1977 John Ross/Photo Researchers, Inc.)

metallic, paper, and now informational money for the marketplace

out the main qualities a substance used as money ought to have. It should be of recognizable and undisputed quality, he argued, easy to deliver, easy to transport, amenable to storage without loss or maintenance, and able to be divided without losing any part of it.[10] These criteria accounted quite well for the preference in ancient and medieval times for silver and gold coins as money instead of livestock, grain, iron, or other available commodities. But Law proposed that paper currency, backed by a nation's wealth in land, would satisfy these criteria still more. And he sold the French government on his idea. Although that first experiment failed and John Law had to flee for his life, the popularity of paper over metallic forms of money has increased steadily in the Western world ever since. Coinage has by now been reduced to small change. In recent decades, moreover, improved communication technologies have yielded forms of money even better—more neutral and abstract—than paper. Increasingly, money exists only as information stored in bank computers; it is the balance in an account, a number of standard units of exchange value attached to a person's name. More and more transactions involve no physical handing over of money at all but only a formal, ritualized declaration, a signature on a check or credit card, subtracting units from one account and adding them to another. So popular has informational money become that the prestige of safecracking has declined among sophisticated thieves in favor of skills in computer programming.

Among these three modes of exchange—gift giving, redistribution, and the market—the first inevitably declines in the course of development. But the optimal mix of the latter two in the advanced industrial societies of our day cannot be determined simply on economic grounds. It is a cultural and political matter, admitting of wide variation across the multiple social realities coexisting now on this planet. Clearly, nonetheless, development requires some combination of redistributive and market procedures, some mix of grants and merchandise, rather than a choice between them. All developed societies, for example, subject a wide range of household items to a common monetary standard and allow citizens to spend their money on whichever ones they prefer. Workers in socialist societies receive paychecks, go shopping, and maintain savings accounts much as workers in capitalist societies do. Economic advance would undoubtedly cease anywhere a government sought to eliminate the market completely, deny the variety in individual preference, and enforce a totally planned economy. On the other hand, not even the most market-oriented society treats everything as merchandise. The Liberty Bell in Philadelphia is not for sale. Students in capitalist societies are pleased to receive nontransferable, nonexchangeable, nonmarketable scholarships and grants for their higher schooling, in much the same way as in socialist societies. Development would be sure to flounder anywhere a government defined all goods as foreign objects and let them all be measured by a standard financial yardstick. Whatever its formal ideology, every contemporary society confronts two challenges in its effort to develop further. One is to devise more careful and disciplined political plans for allocating resources in a way that will improve citizens' collective relation to the earth. The other is to augment citizens' bank accounts and increase the ways each can spend his or her money, thus permitting individual inclinations as much expression as is consistent with the common good. The last half of this chapter considers how these challenges are met in the advanced capitalist societies.

DOING WITH FEWER FARMERS

As readers are by now well aware, this chapter avoids depicting the development process in terms of particular economic projects. The reason is that human history has been and remains plural. Different societies contrive immensely different

schemes for improving earthly life; principles underlying such improvement must therefore be formulated in fairly general terms. Who can say which society is more advanced, one that uses trucks and cars to transcend space (the United States) or another that relies more on trains (Switzerland)? One that cultivates delightful food and drink (France) or another whose citizens eat more crudely but live in larger, finer homes (Australia)? Which signals a higher level of development, well-attended private clubs or well-maintained public parks, big cities or small ones, inexpensive television sets or inexpensive medical care, a few big machines or lots of little ones, the production of pianos or of deodorants? A portrayal of development built on answers to questions like these is bound to be inadequate. Our purpose is not to encourage our own self-righteousness, to project our particular history onto others, or to imply that the wonderfully diverse societies of earth should all march down some common, narrow path. Our purpose is instead to study carefully the disparate histories so far made on this planet and to expose the kind of enduring regularities which will guide effectively our own efforts to press development further. This purpose disallows any effort to tie the process in principle to specific projects.

understanding development in terms of the primary task to be solved

But no matter what new projects a society undertakes, it has to have citizens available to work on them. Hence even if we cannot specify the content of development in a positive sense, we can more easily do so negatively. The process necessarily involves freeing up the citizenry from the basic tasks of biological survival. This can be taken as the ninth principle of development: that a society must reduce the proportion of its labor force devoted to agricultural production, the growing of crops and animals for food and clothing, the necessities of survival. As late as 1870, half the U.S. labor force worked on farms. By mechanizing cultivation and the harvest, perfecting plant and animal hybrids, fertilizing the soil, rotating crops, increasing the size of farms, and imposing stricter discipline on agricultural work, this figure was reduced to 4 percent by 1976. Nearly all the advanced Western societies, including Canada, Great Britain, Australia, West Germany, the Low Countries, and those of Scandinavia, recorded comparably low percentages in the same year. Japan, France, East Germany, Italy, Czechoslovakia, Austria, Trinidad, Uruguay, and Argentina had each between 10 and 19 percent of its labor force in agriculture. In the 20 to 29 percent range were Spain, Portugal, the Soviet Union, and Cuba. Between 30 to 39 percent were Mexico, Poland, and South Korea. At the other, underdeveloped extreme are those societies with precious little labor to spare for projects beyond survival needs. In 1978, 72 percent of India's labor force worked in agriculture, 76 percent of Vietnam's, 78 percent of Laos's, 80 percent of Kenya's, 74 percent of Mozambique's, 67 percent of China's, 58 percent of Bolivia's, 85 percent of Ethiopia's, 85 percent of Botswana's, and 70 percent of Bangladesh's. With certain exceptions like China, these are the same societies which score low on other measures of development—literacy, for example.

proportion of the labor force in agriculture—a basic measure of economic advance

Without overspecifying how citizens of a developing society occupy themselves as progressively fewer are obliged to farm, I might note that at least in Western history manufacturing has not proven to be a major employment alternative. Shrinkage in agricultural work has not increased the proportion of citizens engaged in processing raw materials into finished products. In 1900, for example, 22 percent of the United States labor force was engaged in manufacturing; the figure was 21 percent in 1975. Other advanced Western societies report similar constancy. The reason is that the same innovations in technology and energy which permitted the mechanization of agriculture (the Bessemer process and open-hearth steel, steam and internal combustion engines, electricity and so on) had the same effect on manufacturing. Hence although the quantity and range of manufactured goods increased, the human labor required to make them did not. Nor has construction taken up the slack, so to speak, in employment—again for the same reason. The proportion of the U.S. labor force accounted for by the building trades has held steady for the last century at roughly 6 percent. Nor has the proportion employed in transportation changed much—the range has been between 4 and 9 percent. The majority of American workers today spend their time not directly in production at all but in the distribution and exchange of goods (trade, finance, real estate) and services (as in hotels, restaurants, hospitals, schools, repair shops, recreation centers, and social welfare agencies). High-growth occupations include law, accounting, consulting, security, and bookkeeping—fields which amount to economic housekeeping. The same is true in varying degree for European societies.

an apparent case of doldrums in the advanced Western world

Although today's advanced Western societies obviously do with fewer farmers, exactly *what* they do is hard to say. Having learned to feed, clothe, house, and transport their citizens with less than half their labor forces, they seem rather at a loss as to what to do next.[11] They accomplish the classic projects of development effortlessly enough but seem unable to decide upon new projects, new targets for the effort of their citizens. Consider, for instance, that Mexico classed 70 percent of its men 65 years old or older as economically active in 1970; the figure was a mere 19 percent for the United States in 1976. Further, from 6 to 8 percent of workers in the latter society have typically been unemployed during the last decade—that is, able-bodied and actively seeking productive economic roles but unable to find them. And it is not as if Americans are just barely fed, clothed, and housed. Pockets of poverty still exist, to be sure, but the bulk of women and men have so much to eat that obesity is a constant worry. We seldom wear clothing until it is threadbare, and even more rarely wear it patched. Our dwellings are warmer in winter than necessary, cooler in summer, and larger year-round. It is not unusual to travel the length of a continent—to Hawaii, Florida, California, or the Caribbean —for a week's holiday. Much of the work for which citizens are paid well seems awfully close to paper shuffling. In sum, it is hard to escape the conclusion that the advanced Western societies, the United States perhaps most of all, are very nearly spinning their wheels, treading water, moving without going much of anywhere. The space exploration, which captured popular imagination for a while, seems to be in its denouement. Technological advances in electronics and computerized information systems seem to have left more and more people searching for something to do. The great danger when development is stalled is that societies will turn to war, destroying one another's accomplishments in a frenzy of disciplined effort. The fact is that Western Europe and North America have millions upon millions of potentially productive humans to spare for whatever new designs upon the earth they might choose to contemplate.

MAKING CHANGE A MATTER OF COURSE

The preceding nine elements or principles all imply activity, the application of human ingenuity to the earth—whether by fencing in a cow, tinkering with a machine, hoisting a power line, sweating to get work done on time, analyzing a chemical compound, expanding the size of societies, dividing up tasks, regulating monetary policy, or increasing the yield of a harvest. We today take such creative action for granted. We discern it even in the simplest tribe of hunters and gatherers

and trace it even to the day—July 20, 1969—when astronauts first walked on the moon. That humans can shape their natural environment is as obvious to us as their ability to establish governments of law. But as Chapter Five of this book explained, humans have become willing to acknowledge and admit openly the latter idea only since the seventeenth and eighteenth centuries, when thinkers like Locke and Rousseau first articulated theories of the social contract in the Western world, and when politicians like Jefferson first put those theories into practice. The former idea began to take root only a little earlier and in roughly the same setting. Until that time and place in history humans had never made change fast or steadily enough to become unashamedly aware of their own creative power. But that cultural breakthrough, or more accurately a process continuing even now, is an integral part of development. Hence a tenth element may be set down for economic as well as for political advance: modernization, the growing recognition of the fact of human power, the spread and deepening of awareness of human creativity, or more briefly the rise of human self-consciousness. This is the change in economic culture that accompanies structural innovation: an awakening to the truth and goodness of work and the overhaul of nature that results from it.

the all-important process of modernization

Premodern societies can be imagined as a row of lonely frogs sitting motionless on the landscape of earth. Occasionally one would feel itself seized by the force of charismatic leadership and make a great leap forward in economic advance. Such leaps account for the heroic achievements of ancient peoples. But then the frog would sit motionless again, as if frozen in tradition, even while others leapt in front of it. By contrast, modern societies are defined by the constancy of their motion, by so much leaping to, fro, and sideways that self-directed, experimental change comes to be assumed as part of human nature. Indeed, modernity means feeling more oneself in the leap than in the landing. In the words of the intensely modern Lebanese poet, Kahlil Gibran, "Man is happy only in his aspiration to the heights; when he achieves his goal he cools and longs for other distant flights."[12] This is the value which underlies what is often called the Renaissance conception of work, that represented perhaps best of all in the diverse innovative achievements of Leonardo da Vinci. A different variation on the same value appears in the teachings of Luther and Calvin, the Protestant notion of work as duty. It is this value as well which the spirits of entrepreneurship, adventure, invention, and discovery imply. The capitalist's relentless pursuit of profit and the socialist's persistent efforts at economic reform share a grounding in this fundamental principle: that the mission of the human species is not to be, but to become.

Since Chapter Five has already pointed out the link between modern politics and modern economics, between the thoughtful exercise of power in public affairs and the everyday experience of power in work, there is no need to repeat that discussion here. But I should emphasize that movement sustains a belief in movement, and vice versa. Self-confidence gets results, even as results build self-confidence. Continued economic advance depends on a society's ability to keep citizens aware of their responsibility to understand and control the economic status quo. Among individuals it is apparent that those who experience change without also experiencing control over it lose rapidly their will to work assiduously and creatively. They turn away from their own abilities toward lotteries and games of chance for their economic well-being, even as they turn to demagogues for political safety. So also among societies. The surest way for any society to doom its own future is to let its economic status quo get out of hand, that is, escape the intellectual mastery of its citizens. The ethic of modernity disappears when economic change does not reinforce a society's belief in its own power to control change. This ethic cannot survive, given a preoccupation with adapting to change rather than directing it. Among other reasons, that is why the sociological outlook is so important today: it nourishes our awareness that we make our world.

LIMITING THE HUMAN POPULATION

As an element or principle in the process of economic development, birth control is appropriately reserved for last in this review. For throughout the long and impressive history of human progress, a certain reluctance to tamper with nature has persisted in counterpoint. Every innovative step, every substitution of human genius for the natural course of events, aroused in our ancestors a gnawing fear. This time are we going too far? Are we tempting fate? Might we be better off leaving this aspect of experience free of human meddling? Such fear struck deep when people first sought to limit pregnancies and reduce the number of babies born—thereby intruding their own schemes upon the mysteries of sex and procreation. For most of history contraception and abortion have been unmentionable, shameful practices engaged in rarely, secretly, and usually ineffectively. Preventing births was something few people seriously thought about, much less tried to do. Even now the largest of the organized religions, the Roman Catholic Church, officially condones birth control only by the most "natural" method, that is by restricting intercourse to those days of a woman's menstrual cycle when she is unlikely to conceive. But traditionalism has yielded to modernity by now also with regard to reproduction. Condoms and diaphragms have been perfected and mass-produced since the early decades of this century. Contraceptive pills and intrauterine devices have become popular since World War II. Numerous governments in underdeveloped societies, Indira Gandhi's in India most famously, have launched mass campaigns for sterilizing men (by vasectomy) and women (by salpingectomy or tubal ligation). Many governments have formally removed the stigma from voluntary abortion during the early months of pregnancy. The United States Supreme Court ruled to this effect in 1973.

Economic development has necessarily implied some form of birth control simply because its other implications reviewed earlier in this chapter otherwise multiply too much the number of living humans. Predictably enough, our ancestors directed their increasingly skillful economic efforts toward prolonging their own lives. And the more they succeeded, the more the human population snowballed. It swelled from about 300 million in Jesus' time to 700 million in 1750, then to 1.1 billion in

230

1850, 2.5 billion in 1950, and more than 4.3 billion today. To appreciate this increase, suppose that in 1980 every person alive in North America, South America, Europe, Australia, and Africa perished in a single blow. Even if such a catastrophe had occurred, wiping out humanity from two-thirds of the earth's terrain, there would still have been as many people left as there were altogether in 1950, a mere thirty years before. Now obviously, humans could not go on multiplying as fast as they did during those three decades. The finite earth cannot support the infinite increase of our race, particularly if we humans should learn to live in peace. We cannot intentionally reduce our death rate without at some point intentionally reducing our birthrate. Thus are contraceptive or abortive measures integral to the development process. Even so, the evidence shows that individuals and couples invent and take such measures seldom out of generalized humane concern. They do so mainly when their own personal and working lives offer opportunities for creativity beyond the biological kind, and when these alternatives seem more rewarding and less costly than having another child. Thus have many governments established programs not just for informing citizens of contraceptive and similar techniques but also for adding incentives to use them—even such incentives as transistor radios dispensed free in a poor society to men who undergo vasectomies.

variation across societies in the smoothness of the demographic transition

The severity of the problem of overpopulation varies sharply among contemporary societies, depending mainly on how early each began to industrialize. For as the figures given in the preceding paragraph demonstrate, the human population increased quite slowly until the nineteenth century. Uncontrolled birthrates were high, hovering around 50 births per year per 1000 citizens. But death rates were also high, routinely 25 or 30 per year per 1000 citizens, and even higher than the birthrate in times of famine or plague. In the societies which industrialized first the death rate fell gradually to 9 or 10 per year per 1000, in tandem with a long series of improvements in sanitation, diet, and medical care. The birthrate also fell gradually, as more and more ingenious city dwellers chose to plan their families small; the U.S. birthrate had dropped to about 30 in 1900 and 21 in 1930, standing now at about 15. Thus the population of the industrialized Western world increased only slowly and is now increasing hardly at all. These societies had a relatively smooth demographic transition, from high to low rates of birth and death. Elsewhere this has not been the case. Most of the underdeveloped societies have imported during the last fifty years sophisticated technology for reducing infant mortality and the death rate as a whole: techniques like sanitary childbirth, immunization against contagious diseases, purification of drinking water, and general standards of diet and health. But their citizens have not experienced much reason to limit their progeny. Thus birthrates have remained high while death rates have precipitously declined. These rates for Mexico were 42 and 9 per 1000 respectively in 1975; for Bangladesh 50 and 28; for Bolivia 47 and 18; for Thailand 43 and 11. It is to societies like these that the term *population explosion* most accurately applies, since their populations are increasing at the rate of even 2 or 3

population explosions and how to stop them

percent per year (as compared to almost zero populaton growth in the industrialized societies). And what is worse, the Asian continent had a larger population to start with, that is, before industrialization anywhere began. China, for example, has a territory almost as large as the United States, but a population four times larger.

Hence with respect to population problems, there is a sharp split between the advanced industrial societies and the underdeveloped ones. What strike us as unnecessarily harsh strong-arm methods of encouraging couples to practice birth control may therefore be vitally necessary in other social contexts.

The sociology of population extends, of course, far beyond the brief discussion here. Demographers have devised a wealth of refined measures for studying how populations increase, decrease, and change in various ways. Explanations for why and how citizens in a particular society practice birth control must look toward numerous economic, political, and religious factors. But these few paragraphs should at least make clear how drastically in the course of progress death rates do decline, and how necessarily therefore birthrates must also decline—by some method or other. This brings us to one final point. While surgical sterilization, condoms, diaphragms, intrauterine devices, pills, jellies, foams, and abortion have all the common effect of limiting births, they are not equally desirable. They vary in their effectiveness and in the amount of expense, bother, and medical risk implied by their use. And most important, to prevent a child from being conceived is obviously quite a different way of limiting births than to abort a child already conceived but not yet born. Development is a process designed by humans for the sake of humanity. Birth control techniques which prevent conception from occurring therefore satisfy the goal of development intrinsically better than techniques which extinguish the life of a human fetus. Whether and under what circumstances abortion should nonetheless be permitted or encouraged in a particular society at a particular point in time are difficult and debatable issues. I know of no way to resolve the debates here. I should think they could end most happily with such widespread knowledge and use of contraceptive techniques that no need for abortion would any longer be felt.

IN SUMMARY

The eleven principles of economic development outlined above by no means exhaust the rich literature in this area. The discussion here has inevitably glossed over the myriad variations on the process that constitute the distinct histories of the societies of earth. Some readers might even wish that I had offered instead of abstract principles a graphic narrative of how some specific society had moved from peasant agriculture to advanced industrialization. But too much specificity would have confounded the purpose of this first half of the chapter, namely, to list ingredients of human progress so basic as to be reflected in *every* society's history, so essential as to deserve to guide us in our own efforts here and now to advance our race. The first five elements or principles can be taken as interminable, never-ending, to be perfected, extended, and improved upon as far into the future as we now can see. These are the domestication of nature, the fabrication of tools and machines, the capture of nonhuman energy, the discipline of work, and the symbolic analysis of experience. The last six elements or principles do not inexorably increase but still must be taken for granted to some degree in any effort at development: sufficient size of the economy, a division of labor, governmental regulation and the marketing of goods, the shift from agriculture to other occupations, the spirit of modernity, and control of the birthrate.

principles of economic development are cautions against retreat

These principles are not so general, nor are they so widely understood, that they can safely be shunted to the back of our minds and forgotten. For do not many young men and women today wistfully contemplate a "return to nature," a retreat from the "artificial world" of human engineering into a world "just the way God made it"? And are there not parents who think that to go easy on their children, to hesitate with discipline and demands for work, is an act of love? Have not many professors in recent years relaxed their course requirements, made it easier to get high marks, and thereby permitted students to get by with woefully inadequate analyses of the world in front of us? To such compatriots as these the well-read student of development is obliged to say, "The evidence of history is not on your side. Your attitude is likely to send our human race backward into misery." Or to cite another example: millions of couples gratefully accept "however many children God sends." So powerful and in many ways admirable a church as the Roman Catholic all but fosters such acceptance by its proscription of contraceptives. And literally millions of citizens of the United States, a society by some measures the most advanced on earth, passionately assert a naive trust in fundamentalist dogmas, Christian or otherwise, seeming to believe that a supernatural power will take care of us humans even if we do not. The principles summarized here are therefore hardly irrelevant. By careful and critical thought each reader of these pages can draw practical, everyday applications for his or her own life. A hard task, to be sure, but one with far more promising results than a refusal to think empirically about what progress requires.

these principles are also standards for assessing current trends

The relevance of the principles outlined in this review consists also in the doubt they cast on various aspects of Western economies as currently organized. Most important of all, the large-scale burning up of nonrenewable fossil fuels has been shown not to advance the development process, as is often erroneously assumed, but to divert it down a mistaken course. And none of the eleven principles has suggested that development requires building more high-rise apartments, lengthening and widening expressways, expanding suburbs, or replacing small businesses with chain stores. The evidence reviewed here has not implied that bigger is always better, that governmental intervention in market economies is bad, that dividing labor ever more minutely is virtuous, or that dividing it into jobs permitting creativity and jobs inflicting powerlessness is necessary. In short, much of what today passes for economic development has been conspicuously absent from these pages. For good reason. This book concerns enduring principles. We neither need nor should tie ourselves to specific recent trends as inescapable determinants of what we do next. Indeed, we *cannot* take for granted any trend that relies on cheap and abundant oil, gas, and coal. In other words, development in the next thirty years will necessarily take a different direction than it has in the last thirty, if indeed we are to escape economic stagnation and the general regress of our civilization. The principles offered here are intended as loose guidelines for charting that new direction. Or better to say, in broader context, directions. The paths of economic development in the future can be just as plural, just as diverse as they were in the past. Each national society in our day deserves to make its own marriage with the earth; like man-woman marriages, every earth-nation marriage deserves some privacy and the chance to work itself out.

But underlying all eleven principles given here is the idea that the human race has indeed progressed in the course of its history, that economic development has after all occurred, that our ancestors and we have in fact managed somehow to weaken nature's hold on us and strengthen ours on it. The process has not always been steady or cumulative. It is neither irreversible nor inevitable. It has happened only because groups of human beings in various times and places chose to make it happen. And the societies on earth today reveal variation in how far they have taken the process, how economically developed they are, how much they have progressed. From these pages may be gleaned at least three even quantitative measures of this variation: the percentage of adult citizens who are literate, the percentage freed for nonagricultural work, and how far the rates of death and birth have been reduced. Using these measures and other more qualitative ones we can rank societies, albeit crudely, according to their respective levels of development. To do so is not at all arrogant, contemptuous, or ethnocentric–symptomatic of undue intoxication with the virtues of our own society. For if it is wrong to pretend that all societies will model themselves on those of the West, it is no less wrong to deny the monstrous differences in how far societies have progressed. Claiming that no way of life excels any other is not intellectual sophistication but cruel, inhumane indifference. The 30 percent of babies in some parts of Africa who die before their second birthdays do not need to be told we find their culture interesting. They need our carefully planned help to stay alive, to grow up literate, laughing, and aware. And if then they turn on us, sneer at our particular path of development, and choose to walk their own, that is the moment for us to affirm cultural relativism and respect for national autonomy. Human history, in sum, is a little bit singular and a whole lot plural. To separate the bit from the lot is one task of sociology, a task the first half of this chapter has been intended to fulfill in brief.

Part Two: The Capitalist Strategy

To come to grips with the concrete economic conditions prevailing in the West today, it is not enough to ponder such general principles of development as were summarized above. These principles help illuminate the heights to which various societies have risen; they broadly point the way still higher, but they do not explain precisely how we humans in this part of the world have made it as far as we have. And if abstract principles help expose the mess, the fix, the pickle into which we of the Western world seem to have gotten ourselves—with overconsumption of nonrenewable fuels, underutilization of labor, stifling excess of government rules, all kinds of unwieldy bigness and so on—such principles still fail to account for our predicament. Hence the remainder of this chapter focuses on the *kind* of development pursued in the societies grounded in classical liberalism—a value discussed in Chapter Five. It was these societies—England, the United States, France, Germany, and the Netherlands in particular—which industrialized first. These same societies are today in many respects the most economically advanced. We need vitally to know what it was and is about their economies that has enabled them to achieve so much. No less urgently, we need to understand what problems flow from their particular kind of economy. Both the achievements and the *capitalism, not as stage of development but as strategy*

problems are enduring regularities in the lives of most readers of this book and define the conditions of everyday life over much of the globe.

Only gradually during the last 100 years has the economic system of these societies come to be called capitalism. When this label first was applied, moreover, it was meant to describe not one among many paths of economic advance but the single, inescapable path. For in the world of the late nineteenth century, it was clear that things were happening in northern Europe and North America, that people in these areas were on the move toward industrialization, while the rest of the world was stuck, more or less, in an agrarian, peasant economy. Thus despite his criticisms of the capitalist kind of economic organization, Marx saw it as an inevitable stage in the development process. Only *after* reaching it could a society move still farther ahead, to the stage of communism. Similarly, when Weber wrote his classic essay at the beginning of this century, he could unscrupulously identify all the dynamic, developing societies as capitalist and lump all others together under the rubric of traditionalism. It was taken for granted that any society seeking to industrialize would have to adopt capitalism, that is, learn to behave toward the earth like the British, Americans, French, and Germans.

We know by now that this is not the case. The communist revolution which Marx thought was about to break out in Germany, France, or England, happened in Russia instead. During the last fifty years, the Soviet Union has created an advanced industrial economy without ever having passed through a capitalist stage. So have the smaller societies of Eastern Europe. Societies elsewhere are rapidly industrializing, too, but few of them in the manner of those which industrialized first. Hence from the present vantage point, we are obliged to regard capitalism as one among many paths of industrial advance. It was the first path, the one that initially spawned complex technology, scientific expertise and a modern consciousness, but it is no longer the only one. Present evidence obliges us to study capitalism not as a stage in the process of development but as a strategy for advancing the process to ever-higher stages. It is a set of principles which have guided the development process with incredible effectiveness in certain locales. The United States still clings to this strategy and adheres to these principles—though in much modified form, as we shall see presently. With but minor reservations, the other societies of the so-called free world also remain faithful to the capitalist game plan. The plan guides economic relations *among* these societies, too, and to some extent *between* them and others grounded in socialist principles. It is in this light that capitalism deserves our attention.

the useful pretense of denying nature's power

At the heart of the capitalist strategy is a denial of the dialectical relation between people and nature. It is a useful pretense, but a pretense nonetheless. For two fundamental truths are obvious: that people dominate the earth and that it dominates them. The development process makes the first truth truer and the second one less so, but it by no means negates the dialectic itself. Just one moment of evidence is enough to make this point—the moment of death. However much we have divorced ourselves from the earth, made it foreign and exploited it, in the end it embraces every one of us. However hard we work while the tide is out, inevitably it comes in again to wrap itself around our sand-castle selves. Even while the tide is out, moreover, there are innumerable things people cannot do. But the capitalist strategy is to refuse to admit the power of the earth, to keep on planning and plotting as if death could be escaped, to push all attitudes of submissiveness aside and ponder only the potentiality of humankind. The strategy has worked well precisely because of its uncompromising, relentless one-sidedness. This is the secret of its success and the source of its problems. The following paragraphs outline five major empirical reflections of this unidimensional posture toward the earth, five qualities which set capitalism apart from other economic strategies.

THE MEANING OF CAPITALISM

five definitional qualities: first, radical detachment from the earth

The first basic quality of capitalism is how radically it detaches people from virtually all tangible goods—by permitting almost anything to be priced, measured in money terms, defined as interchangeable, handled as salable merchandise. It is not detachment itself that distinguishes capitalism, since development is inconceivable except as people hold themselves aloof from nature and define it as an object of human manipulation. Nor is money by itself distinctive, since higher stages of development everywhere assume that people relate to some range of goods in the distant, uncaring manner that money permits. What is unique about capitalism is how totally people are detached from goods, how broadly the range of marketable commodities extends. Almost all objects are identified as foreign, divested of moral meaning, and evaluated in precise comparison, one with another. No matter that food and shelter are necessities of life, while perfumes and jewelry are luxuries. All are plugged into the same monetary equation. Renewable parts of the earth (hydroelectric power), nonrenewable parts (oil, coal), tools for transforming the earth (bulldozers, air conditioners), products of purely artistic worth (paintings), and items for consumption (green beans or socks) are all assessed by the same financial yardstick. Whatever the good, it is imagined that you can "always buy another one" or "try to get your money out of it." Not even capitalism's most ardent defender, of course, claims that all goods are in fact interchangeable—that televisions can be eaten, for instance. But the system requires treating them as if they were. Almost the entire economy is reduced to a set of procedures for producing, trading, and consuming commodities. Indeed, this is a common textbook definition of the economy in capitalist societies.

second, few restrictions on private property

A second attribute of capitalism, and a second reflection of its one-sidedness, is how broad a range of these commodities individuals are permitted to hold as private property. Now property, too, is intrinsic to all strategies of development: to own something means to feel free to dominate it, control it, decide what happens to it, and economic advance requires that humans arrogate to themselves such freedom. But capitalism gives to the ideas of ownership and property their fullest possible expression. Any citizen is allowed to own almost anything *privately*, thus to decide its fate on the basis of individual inclination, without having to consult others beforehand. Ownership is legally defined, moreover, as virtually total domination. Whatever the item, the owner can try selling it for money, moving it, modifying it, wasting it, sitting on it, burning it into energy, or whatever else comes to mind. Political restrictions are few and minimal. Other citizens' objections can be dismissed with the silencing comment, "It's mine. It belongs to me. Mind your own business." And if need be, the police can be called upon to enforce the prerogatives of private ownership. Indeed, the capitalist conception of government is as defender of private citizens and their respective possessions, and as enforcer of the contracts citizens enter into with respect to what they own. The more it allows private property, the more political authority removes itself from the center of action and relegates itself to the sidelines, keeping only the job of blowing the whistle when citizens steal or cheat.

third, a rule of selfishness for enforcing hard and innovative work

The third basic and peculiar quality of capitalism is how hard, steadily, and inventively it compels citizens to work. Like money and a dominative attitude, work is also integral to the development process. The problem in any society is how to persuade citizens to keep at it and involve their imaginations in it. Capitalism solves this problem by allowing prices for all commodities to be set by the rule of selfishness. The rule is that no one is obliged to part with anything for free and can in fact charge the highest price someone else is willing to pay. This is called the market price. The effect of this rule is that everything becomes scarce, even the necessities of life. Not even a loaf of bread, not even a hamburger can be bought for less than the market price. Without money a person could starve to death in a McDonald's drive-in, and no living person would be held responsible. Once the rule of selfishness is in place, the only way to stay alive is to become part of the capitalist system: to work, produce something somebody wants, sell it at the market price, and thus obtain the money one needs in order to eat. A large number of producers and consumers, buyers and sellers, all behaving by this rule, all having to serve one another in order to serve themselves, together constitute the capitalist free market. The price of any item, say hamburgers, depends on how urgently hamburger makers want to sell their product (hence, the supply on the market) and how hungry consumers are to purchase hamburgers (hence, the market demand). Prices are set where a supply curve meets a demand curve, each of them being shaped by the same rule of selfish accumulation of commodities.

But hard and steady work is not enough. Under capitalism, persistent effort alone cannot assuage one's sense of insecurity. For fear of being left behind, citizens must not only keep running, but running constantly in new directions. For inevitably some hamburger producer sets out to make more money, to enlarge his or her share of the market, and therefore devises new tools, techniques, or materials for reducing the per unit cost of production. This is what McDonald's and Burger King have actually done during the last two decades. Such inventive producers can thus lower the market price, undercut the competition, sell in greater volume, and thereby increase profits—that is, the difference between production costs and money taken in. But entrepreneurs like these do more than improve themselves. They also cripple old-fashioned producers who continue to work hard and steadily in their customary way. The latter lose business and find themselves being squeezed out of the market into poverty. Thus the only way to make it in a capitalist economy is to keep one innovative step ahead of all competitors, even while they are trying to do the same thing. Survival requires never looking back, taking it easy, becoming attached to anything, loving the earth or one's own handiwork, for fear that in a moment of dalliance some competitor will seize the advantage. A lifetime under capitalism is a series of leisurely tomorrows.

A fourth reflection of the single-minded aggressiveness in capitalism is the lopsided kind of relationship it permits between citizens for the sake of economic advance. To be sure, no society ever manages to keep everyone equally on top of its economy. Whatever the development strategy, some people will have more economic power than others. But the capitalist strategy requires some people literally to sell themselves to others in order to make a living. This is the only means of survival for those who cannot get their hands on capital—that is, on enough money to buy the land, tools, and raw materials necessary to produce something for the market. People who lack capital are obliged to detach themselves from the very movement of their bodies and working of their minds, to treat their own labor as a foreign object, for sale to the highest bidder. To the capitalist employer, hired labor is a commodity, measurable in the same units of money as land, raw materials, and tools. Its worth depends on how much profit can be gained by training the labor, managing it, and harnessing it to machines in the production process. What the worker gets is a wage or salary, the amount of which depends upon supply and demand in the labor market.

In the United States until the 1860s, the right of some people to own others was total. The ancient institution of slavery had been adapted to the money economy and to the capitalist definition of private property, so that the entire lives of captured Africans and their descendants could be measured in standard units of currency, purchased and possessed. Seldom if ever in history have people in a single society been so radically estranged from one another as U.S. slaveholders were from their human property. Since 1865, however, when the Thirteenth Amendment to the Constitution was passed, the U.S. government has permitted only the *working* lives of people to be placed as commodities on the market. Each person retains ultimate control over his or her activity, only the economically productive part of which may be sold for money. Nonetheless, few limits are placed on actions that can be sold—or from the employer's point of view, on tasks to which hired labor can be assigned. Most capitalist jurisdictions exclude sexual intercourse from the realm of legitimate commerce, though other forms of erotic stimulation (striptease performances, for instance) fetch a high market price. Americans are not legally allowed to sell themselves as mercenaries to foreign military commanders—or at least to make the deal within American borders. The law also forbids buying or selling electoral votes, though it permits hired labor to be used to promote particular candidates. And no one is allowed to hire another to perform a criminal act. All in all, however, limitations on the uses to which hired labor can legally be put are exceedingly broad in the culture of capitalism. In the United States and some other societies, a citizen is even allowed to buy blood from other citizens (in small quantities) and then sell it for profit to accident victims, cancer patients, and others in need of it.

The fifth and final attribute of capitalism in this preliminary review is how easily and fully it recognizes groups and organizations as persons under the law—or more simply, as corporations. Once having been incorporated or chartered, these artificial persons are allowed to own property, hire and fire employees, enter into contracts, lend and borrow money, earn profits, file lawsuits, and so on, much as if they were flesh-and-blood citizens. According such rights to corporations is a kind of ultimate step in estranging people, distancing them from nature and even from

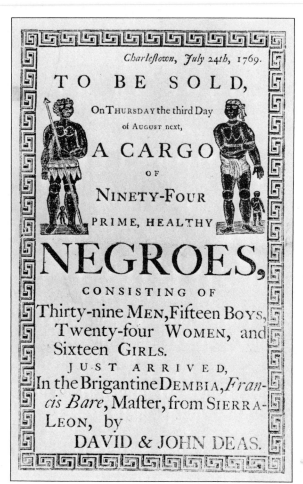

Charleftown, *July 24th*, 1769.

TO BE SOLD,

On THURSDAY the third Day of AUGUST next,

A CARGO

OF

NINETY-FOUR

PRIME, HEALTHY

NEGROES,

CONSISTING OF

Thirty-nine MEN, Fifteen BOYS, Twenty-four WOMEN, and Sixteen GIRLS.

JUST ARRIVED,

In the Brigantine DEMBIA, *Francis Bare*, Mafter, from SIERRA-LEON, by

DAVID & JOHN DEAS.

"The ancient institution of slavery had been adapted to the money economy and to the capitalist definition of private property, so that the entire lives of captured Africans and their descendants could be measured in standard units of currency, purchased and possessed." (The Granger Collection)

their own working lives. Contemporary law permits a man to invent a corporation in his mind, give it a name, describe it on paper, register it with the appropriate governmental agency, then use his ownership of the corporation to hire himself as an employee, thus selling his work for a specified price to a figment of his imagination. Such mental and legal gymnastics, nonsensical except in capitalist cultures, illustrate the extent to which corporations are defined as real. But for capitalist development corporations are also necessary. The need for them appeared first in seventeenth-century Britain, as the early capitalists began to contemplate massive, potentially lucrative enterprises in international trade—like sending ships to North America to acquire furs from indigenous tribes. No one however, wanted to risk all of his capital on the high seas, even if he had enough to finance the venture personally. And to ask the Crown for financing from tax revenues would have implied public ownership and thwarted hopes for private gain. The solution was therefore for a group of men each to contribute to a joint fund or pool of capital and then ask the Crown to recognize this fund as a legal entity by granting it a charter. The contributions were understood as stocks in the new entity. As a group

"Once having been incorporated or chartered, these artificial persons are allowed to own property, hire and fire employees, enter into contracts, lend and borrow money, earn profits, file lawsuits and so on, much as if they were flesh-and-blood citizens." A Sony Corporation workshop in Japan. (Sony Corporation)

or through an elected board, the stockholders then hired a manager and from that point on the company's work proceeded much as if it were an individual's own enterprise. The Hudson's Bay Company in Canada (now mainly urban department stores called "The Bay") and the Great Atlantic and Pacific Tea Company in the U.S.A. (now supermarkets labeled "A & P") are contemporary survivors of that earliest era of corporate capitalism.

As might be expected, capitalist entrepreneurs initially faced opposition from governments to the formation of corporations. Kings, lords, and parliaments were threatened enough by the innovative, money-making schemes of real persons; they were loathe to recognize in law chimerical persons whose power and wealth might challenge political authority still more. Then as now, corporations were not easily pinned down. In 1720, the British government under George I discouraged them formally by passing what is known as the Bubble Act, "An Act to Restrain the Extravagant and Unwarrantable Practice of Raising Money by Voluntary Subscriptions for Carrying on Projects Dangerous to the Trade and Subjects of this Kingdom." Nonetheless, by the early nineteenth century governments in both Europe and the United States were steadily relenting, and the corporation became entrenched in law. Today in the United States it is designated by the suffix *Inc.* In the Spanish-speaking world the symbol is *S.A.*—for *Sociedad Anonyma*, nameless group. But the British symbol *Ltd.*, is the most meaningful of all. It stands for

a definition of
capitalism

"limited liability," meaning that unlike an individual entrepreneur, corporate shareholders are not liable for more than their investment in the corporation. An entrepreneur is by law personally accountable for business contracts and debts and may be financially wiped out if the business fails. If a corporation goes broke, by contrast, even with a mountain of debts unpaid and contracts unfilfilled, shareholders lose no more than the money they initially put in. As a means of reducing the risks of investing capital, therefore, a means also of amassing the large sums necessary for market success, the corporation is an economic actor of immense and ever-growing power in all capitalist societies.

In summary, capitalism can be defined as that strategy of economic development which turns almost everything, including human labor, into a commodity, which places commodities under private ownership, which treats corporations as legal persons, and which lets prices be set freely in a market guided by the rule of selfishness. Capitalism is no more natural a kind of economic organization than any other, only the one that has evolved since the eighteenth century in British, American, and collateral societies. But it is without doubt the most successful strategy ever devised for the human conquest of this planet. It keeps people energetically at work, forever rankled by the monkey of the market on their backs. The practice of wage labor allows successful capitalists to skim a surplus off workers' productivity and call it profit. The reinvestment of profits is entrusted to the very people who have already proven their ability to manage money wisely. Despite how preposterous it may seem to reduce almost everything to a common monetary standard or to translate the common good into the virtues of selfishness, no one can fail to be impressed with the results. Because they are so deeply impressed, most economists and many citizens make money the measure of the economy itself. Development is just economic growth. Happiness is a higher income. A society's relation to the earth improves, the greater the market value of all the commodities it produces. Such market value is the society's gross national product, the single most commonly used index of level of development.

But that is too narrow a view. The capitalist strategy does more than just advance the development process. It also gives the process particular qualities which cannot be understood in monetary terms, and which development itself by no means requires. Even the definition of capitalism suggests as much. For development in principle is a two-sided thing, implying innovative action that somehow takes note of the earth's reaction, a relationship between humanity and nature not as gladiators fighting to the death but as dancers straining to improve their joint performance. But in the one-sided theory of capitalism the earth is even less than an enemy; it is just the target at which humans take aim. So indeed is one human being in the eyes of another, since each is a potential competitor for scarce commodities, a potential hireling to be employed. Even so, the capitalist strategy of development merits study less as theory than as practice. For no national economy has ever followed this strategy except with qualifications of its own. And the concrete social consequences of capitalism have varied greatly across societies and over time. Already the preceding chapter has suggested the fairly dire consequences of capitalist development for colonized peoples—results which help explain why so many latecomers to industrialization have rejected both capitalism and the associated liberal kind of politics. The remainder of this chapter reviews six important results capitalism has had in the United States over the past century, six effects of this economic strategy unfolding year by year in the land of its fullest expression. Most of what follows applies also to Canada, Australia, and the societies of Western Europe, whose economic histories have in general run apace with that of the United States.

THE SPREAD OF WAGE LABOR

For development to occur, even by one-sided definitions, human beings must increasingly control the earth. It is to serve this goal that capitalism turns the earth into privately owned commodities upon which citizens must act creatively in order to earn their living. But the capitalist strategy does not put all citizens in control, only those with enough capital to establish themselves as owners of land, raw materials, or some kind of productive machinery. Only citizens who hold title to some means of producing marketable goods are economically part of a progressing humanity. Citizens without capital are obliged to join animals, plants, and machines in the category of what is controlled, manipulated, used, acted upon by owners of property. Possessing no capital means having to put one's working life on the labor market, to be bought and employed for profit by somebody else.

the late nineteenth century: era of small-scale capitalists

Fortunately, relatively few people in North America during the late nineteenth century were forced into the latter alternative. Capitalism in that era inflicted pain on Indians, who were driven onto steadily smaller reserves, but if life was painful for other citizens, the cause lay more in nature and tradition than in the strategy for transforming nature and breaking tradition. The reason is that land was abundant and cheap, even free to those willing to homestead in the western regions of the continent. The tools needed to set up most enterprises were simple, few, and also cheap: a mule, a chilled-iron plow, a wagon, a blacksmith's anvil or shoemaker's last, a cabinetmaker's lathe, a barber's razor, or a dressmaker's sewing machine. Almost anyone willing and able to work could accumulate enough capital to go into business. Not surprisingly, roughly 80 percent of all economically active people did so. They earned their living as independent, self-employed farmers, professionals, and shopkeepers, or as family members working alongside such autonomous producers and merchants. Only a small proportion of citizens sold themselves for a wage, and those who did often hired out to a neighbor or relative. Factories were small and corporations few. The idea of a labor market was but feebly realized in practice. The bulk of citizens were on top of the economy, in control of themselves and their work, in charge of their market destiny.

To be sure, growing industrial cities like New York, Philadelphia, Boston, Chicago, and St. Louis embraced several million wage laborers. The railroads employed thousands by the hour or day. Black sharecroppers were all but bled white by landowners in the South. But citizens who made a career of selling themselves for pay were still a relatively insignificant minority, and even they could realistically nourish dreams of saving some money and starting out on their own, probably by heading west. Indeed, the U.S. Congress had passed the Homestead Act of 1862 with keen awareness that the opportunities it offered would keep the capitalist system credible. One congressman affirmed his support for the act "because its benign operation will postpone for centuries, if it will not forever, all serious conflict between capital and labor in the older free states."[13] In some respects the late nineteenth century was capitalism's purest and finest moment. The number of independent economic actors (firms, enterprises, farms, production units, businesses) came closer to the number of economically active citizens than ever it has since. It was like the first round of a sports tournament, when all the players still have a chance to play. The lively spirit of the age can be grasped still today in the rags-to-riches stories of Horatio Alger, the frontier depictions of novelist Willa Cather, the rendition of history given by Frederick Jackson Turner, and the humor of Mark Twain. Twain wrote in 1883: "The world and the books are so accustomed to use, and over-use, the word 'new' in connection with our country, that we early get and permanently retain the impression that there is nothing old about it."[14] Visually, this heyday of U.S. capitalism appears best in the buoyant murals and paintings of Missouri artist Thomas Hart Benton. What must be kept in mind is that the cultural optimism of the late nineteenth century had an economic base—not prosperity so much as the economic power widespread among citizens over their everyday working lives.

the process of monopolization of capital

But the optimism did not and could not last. The Homestead Act did not postpone even for half a century, much less a whole one, serious conflict between capital and labor. For like athletes in a tournament, capitalist actors are obliged by the system to compete, to try to eliminate one another from the game, and the number of active players declines steadily as decades pass. In the course of time, whichever of two competing enterprises has the most capital will drive the other one out of business. This does not always happen, since capital cannot substitute for intelligent hard work. But capital in a market economy is like size in a boxing ring—it makes stupidity less of a handicap. The large enterprise can ordinarily standardize its production, thereby reducing its per unit cost below that of a smaller enterprise. Thus can the former undercut the latter in the market. Further, having more reserves to draw on, the larger firm can usually win a price war. And because it has more money it has more room to be inventive. It can spend on advertising, on lobbyists engaged to persuade legislatures to pass laws in its favor, and on research and the development of new products. There is thus built into the capitalist strategy of economic advance an inexorable tendency for capital to become concentrated in progressively fewer hands, for a shrinking number of ever larger enterprises to own the means of production and control the earth. Economists call this the trend toward monopoly, and it appears wherever the capitalist game is played.

why self-employed workers are steadily squeezed out

The principle that large businesses steadily triumph over small ones has an important corollary. It is that a person who hires wage labor will, in general, accumulate more money than an independent, self-employed producer working alone. The capitalist game thus favors the man or woman who buys control of some competitor's working life and subjugates it, over another man or woman who practices the norm of "live and let live." No successful entrepreneur hires wage labor out of generosity, but only to increase the amount of money the enterprise takes in. And the increase cannot all be returned to the employee—if it were, there would be no point in having hired the person in the first place. The idea is instead to pay the employee only his or her price on the labor market, and keep the rest of the increase as profit. If there is no profit the laborer is fired or laid off. The laborer is retained only if the employer ends up with more money than he or she would have working alone. In effect, the employer is supplementing the money earned by his or her own work with some part of the money derived from the work of the employee. The employer thus accumulates more profit than the solitary producer. But what shall be done with the profit? Like any other money, it can be spent for personal enjoyment or reinvested in some kind of business expansion. But to choose the former is risky, since some competing employer may seize the advantage by foregoing self-indulgence, reinvesting profits and enlarging his or her enterprise. Thus to stay on top of the capitalist kind of development, a citizen must subject to himself or herself steadily more and more employees, lest that citizen soon be subjected to and employed by someone else.

It was this process which gained momentum in the late nineteenth century. It happened to some extent in agriculture, as large farmers bought out small ones. Mainly, however, it happened *because* of agriculture, for farming was becoming a less and less likely way to make a living. Through both natural increase and immigration, the population was growing steadily, and land was becoming more scarce and hence more expensive. Forced by the market to stay abreast of competitors, more and more farmers adopted new varieties of grain (like hard wheat) and new implements (like the cord binder and sulky machinery). As their productivity and profits increased, the proportion of the population required for agriculture declined. The remainder had to find something else to do. Despite a plenitude of the agricultural products which are the necessities of life, people without money couldn't obtain them, and the only way to get money was to work.

the concentration of capital in ever-fewer firms

The growing number of people who settled in cities found it more difficult with each passing year to go into business for themselves and stay on top of the economy. For the relative anonymity of urban life gave free rein to the forces of cutthroat competition. There the struggle had already advanced beyond the point of pitting self-employed entrepreneurs against those who hired wage labor. Now it pitted those with only fifty or seventy-five workers against those who employed hundreds. As the system required, the larger firms were steadily winning out. During a single decade, the 1880s, the number of woolen mills in the United States dropped from 2000 to 1300, the number of farm-implement manufacturers from 1900 to 900. The same pattern was repeated in other manufacturing sectors and in Canada. It appeared in retail sales, with the founding of Woolworth's chain of department stores and the big mail-order houses. This was also the period of huge—and hugely profitable—ventures in railroads, oil refining, and steel production. The industrial magnates who owned and controlled such enterprises lived to see their names become household words: Arden, Carnegie, Dow, Eaton, Firestone, Ford, Fuller, Guggenheim, Heinz, Hill, Hilton, Kaiser, Kellogg, Morgan, Rockefeller, Sears, and Vanderbilt, among others. And where did all this leave citizens required to work in order to live? It left them with steadily less hope of ever controlling their own work or the profit derived from it. It left them trying to sell their labor to large companies. By 1931, only 29 percent of the gainfully occupied population of Canada owned their own enterprises and enjoyed the status of freeman in the market economy. The percentage was even lower in the United States, but in the frenzy of capitalist advance no one seems to have given the figure exact calculation.

Sometimes it is argued that big corporations prosper and small businesses fail because the former somehow do a better job or serve their customers more capably. Yet it is hard to see why barbers and stylists should cut hair more skillfully once they can no longer afford their own shops and equipment and are reduced to employment by chains of hair salons. All the same, self-owned shops like this one are steadily disappearing. The business of cutting hair is increasingly under corporate control. The reason is that the trend toward monopolization of ownership is intrinsic to capitalist economics, quite apart from questions of efficiency, productivity, and quality of workmanship. (© Chester Higgins, Jr./Rapho/Photo Researchers, Inc.)

acceleration of the trend during recent decades

The dual trend—concentration of capital and spread of wage labor—has accelerated still more during the last half century. In 1980, fewer than 10 percent of citizens who worked in either the United States or Canada owned the land, machines, and materials with which they worked. Roughly nine of every ten economically active citizens are employees, commodities on the labor market, structurally defined not as dominators of the earth but as part of what is dominated. Most of the self-employed farmers and shopkeepers who are left work many more than forty hours per week and have relatively low income—sacrifices made in return for a degree of independence. No one can point, however, to some small group of latter-day Rockefellers and Carnegies, wealthy capitalists controlling the contemporary economy. For the stakes in the competitive game have become too high for individuals. Fictional persons have priced flesh-and-blood persons out of the market. The largest corporations in the United States as of 1980, General Motors and Exxon, are each worth at least three times as many dollars as *any* living American. In the heady world of high finance, corporations own one another and sometimes even themselves. Most stock in most corporations is distributed across numerous shareholders. No one knows exactly who owns what, since personal wealth is a legally guarded secret. Most students of the topic estimate that half of one percent of the population owns the vast bulk of shares in corporations, but most of the super-rich work very little, except to place their money wherever it promises to yield the highest return.

The concentration of capital has progressed so far that in 1979, the ten largest corporations in the United States (GM, Exxon, Ford, Mobil, Texaco, Standard Oil of California, IBM, General Electric, Gulf Oil, and Chrysler) had combined revenues of about $325 billion, about one-seventh of the gross national product. The concentration has had international effects as well. Since Canada has been faithful enough to capitalist principles to permit foreign ownership of its productive resources, the larger American corporations have steadily bought out their smaller Canadian competitors or driven them out of business. Thus the three largest Canadian companies (GM, Ford, and Imperial Oil) are mere branch plants of giant U.S. companies (GM, Ford, and Exxon). On the other hand, in those economic sectors where Canadian firms got an initial edge up on U.S. competitors, they entrenched themselves in the United States as well as in Canada. Massey-Ferguson is one example, as described earlier in Chapter Three. Among others are breweries like Molson and Carling-O'Keefe, and distilleries like the Seagram Company and Hiram Walker. There is little overtly political in such goings on. The U.S., Canadian, and some other governments simply required their citizens to play that economic game called capitalism. Their enforced competitive efforts have transformed the earth as never before, but with an exceedingly awkward result: the vast majority of citizens have been eliminated from the game. Dispossessed of capital, they now must sell themselves to fictional persons who hold title to most of the land, raw materials, and technology.

Given their mandate to serve the good of the people, the national governments of the Western world have worried increasingly in recent decades about the monopolistic tendencies of the capitalist strategy of development. For the longer this strategy is pursued, the fewer citizens own anything productive, and the less democratic the economy becomes. But what to do is the problem. Governments have hesitated to expropriate large corporations and place them under citizens' collective ownership, for fear of subverting the whole capitalist strategy and bringing development to a halt. Besides, employees of large complex enterprises are unlikely to exercise much power at work even if they themselves as citizens share ownership. About all most governments in the capitalist world have done is pass antitrust, anticombines, and antimonopoly legislation, the effect of which is to forestall the final play-offs of capitalist competition. In the United States, for example, the automobile, oil, computer, household appliance, cheese, farm machinery, steel, and aerospace industries are each currently dominated by a handful of huge corporations which have by now eliminated most smaller competitors but which are prevented by law from eliminating one another. Compelled by the market to keep growing, however, these dominant corporations now seek to eliminate firms in industries other than their own: oil companies buy movie theatres, chain stores buy real estate developers, and hydroelectric utilities buy breweries. This is called *diversification,* the process by which a successful corporation uses its profits to take possession of firms in relatively unrelated fields. If political authority does not intervene, we can expect within a couple of decades to

As Marx had predicted, the workers did in fact revolt. Above, an engraving of the strike at Pittsburgh's Carnegie Steel in 1892. (Archives of Labor and Urban Affairs/Wayne State University)

see but two corporations left in the entire Western world, and all working citizens will be employed by one or the other. But, of course, intervention will occur and that day will not arrive.

LABOR RIGHTS AND SOCIAL WELFARE

Marx's prediction of revolt by an impoverished working class

Marx predicted in the midnineteenth century not only that the proportion of citizens employed by others would increase but also that their wages would be kept just above the starvation level. Since a hireling's labor is no less a commodity in the capitalist economy than that of a horse, Marx saw no reason why the one could expect to be better compensated than the other. Each would be priced according to its supply and the demand for it. In the case of human labor, a high birthrate among the poor and an open immigration policy would keep the supply ample and the price low. Capitalist development would leave the working class farther and farther behind until at last this class would revolt, demanding communistic or collective ownership of the land, materials, and machinery which constitute the means of production.

For a while, the sequence of events in the United States and the other capitalist societies seemed to bear out the Marxian prediction. Wage slavery was revealed to be almost as cruel and exploitative as black slavery had been in the Southern states. Frederick W. Taylor (1856–1915), an advisor to the owners of factories, became famous for his theories of scientific management—theories which suggested how employers could control their workers' movements in ever more minute detail, in order to increase productivity. For the sake of living in squalor, people had to work unspeakably long hours in miserable conditions without holidays or hope. Even children were used in this way. Upton Sinclair entitled his novel about the lot of wage laborers in Chicago *The Jungle*. And the workers did in fact revolt. The Haymarket riot in Chicago in 1886, the strike against Carnegie Steel in Pittsburgh in 1892, and the Pullman strike of 1894 are among the best-remembered instances of rebellion by the U.S. working class during this period. The Socialist Labor party was formed in 1877 and in 1899 the more successful Socialist party led by strike leader Eugene Debs. As Marx had predicted, moreover, governments initially responded with violent suppression of workers' discontent, dispatching troops to force strikers back to work on company terms and imprisoning organizers like Debs. This tactic of dealing with rebellious wageworkers is part of what is meant by the word *fascism*, since the police states of Hitler in Germany, Mussolini in Italy, and Franco in Spain relied on it so heavily. It means using the state's monopoly on the resources of violence to keep workers down.

Had governments in North America persisted in their reliance on fascist techniques, a revolution would undoubtedly have ensued. Instead they have opted, especially since the 1930s, for a more creative response to workers' dissent and consequent civil strife. In basic principle, the response has been to pass and enforce laws which elevate the status of hired labor above that of other commodities used in the production process. These new policies have eased the brutality of capitalism toward citizens who do not own productive property, while preserving capitalism as a basic economic strategy. These modifications have rescued the capitalist game plan from almost assured subversion by wage workers and permitted its survival and evolution more than a century longer than Marx anticipated. Three categories of change can be discerned. First are laws which place limits on how uncaringly hired human labor can be treated. Employers are no longer allowed to hire children less than sixteen years old or some similar age. Employers have to pay a governmentally set minimum wage, even if this exceeds some employee's "market worth." The machines workers operate must be equipped with safety devices, and the work environment must conform to public health regulations. Laws limit the number of hours in the workday and workweek and mandate higher rates of pay for overtime. Time off for holidays and annual vacations is guaranteed. In sum, laws have qualified, restricted, and tempered the prerogatives of ownership when the object of ownership is human labor.

three reasons why the revolution never came: first, protection for labor

second, the right to unionize and strike

In a second category of changes are the laws which recognize workers' right to organize, to bargain collectively, and under certain conditions to strike. Having

this right, workers in a particular craft (like plumbing, carpentry, or baking) or in a particular industry (like textiles, steel processing, or automobile manufacture) can collectively command a price for their labor markedly above its market worth and the legal minimum. Through collective action workers place limits on employers' authority also in other respects. Current labor contracts specify not only pay scales but also a variety of fringe benefits (including pension plans, availability of toilets and lunchrooms, frequency of coffee breaks, sick leave, medical and dental insurance, and so on) and even such conditions as the number of bricks a hod carrier can be obliged to haul at once. As of 1980, about one in four nonagricultural employees in the United States belonged to a union. Most locals are themselves branches of larger unions, like the Teamsters (about 2 million members), United Auto Workers (1.5 million), United Steelworkers (1.3 million), Brotherhood of Electrical Workers (1 million), or Association of Machinists (1 million). Most of these (though not the Teamsters or the UAW) are joined in the largest national federation, the AFL-CIO. Organizational details differ in other capitalist societies but the principle is the same: wage laborers taking advantage of their hard-earned legal right to confront employers and lobby governments collectively.

third, income
supplements

A third set of techniques by which governments have diminished the hardships of life under capitalism include programs which supplement the rewards citizens get from the intrinsic workings of the economic system. Foremost are government-run insurance plans, usually compulsory and subsidized from other tax revenues, which safeguard working people from destitution on account of unemployment, disability, old age, or the disability or death of a supporting spouse. During 1980, for instance, more than 35 million Americans received old-age, survivors, and disability insurance benefits (popularly called "social security"), and a further 10 million received unemployment insurance benefits. Also in this category are governmentally sponsored medical insurance programs. These have been universal for decades in Great Britain and most other capitalist societies, but as of 1980 were still limited in the United States to older, low-income, or disabled persons. Still other programs are organized not as insurance plans but as direct grants of money or service to citizens who fail to qualify for insurance benefits or for whom such benefits are inadequate. Such grants are ordinarily restricted to people who own no productive property, have no source of income adequate for subsistence living, and are unable to sell their labor to an employer because of their child-care responsibilities, illness, old age, or physical or mental handicap. Programs of this kind in the United States include supplementary security income for the aged, medicaid, food stamps, aid to families with dependent children, and general welfare assistance. There are also day-care and job-training programs, aimed at making the unemployed employable. Like the United States, most capitalist societies today display a bewildering variety of sometimes overlapping insurance and aid programs, most of them funded jointly by national and lower-level governments through complicated cost-sharing arrangements, but intended nonetheless to provide some minimum level of living to citizens denied as much by the normal workings of the market economy.

welfare capitalism—the
same strategy, but
adapted to a later stage

The laws which elevate human labor above the level of other commodities, spell out employees' rights in collective bargaining, and establish programs for rescuing from squalor those citizens condemned to it by the market—these laws are generically termed welfare legislation, and the economic system which results from their enforcement is called *welfare capitalism*. And this indeed is the present state of the economy in North America and Western Europe. These advanced societies have by no means jettisoned the principles by which the capitalist strategy of development is defined, such principles as money measurement, private property, competition, and wage labor. Governments have intervened only to protect citizens and prevent revolution as the ownership of the means of production has slipped inexorably into fewer hands, especially corporate hands. The smaller capitalist societies—Sweden or the Netherlands, for example—are uniformly ahead of the United States in the extent of governmental intervention, in the degree to which they exemplify welfare capitalism. One reason is that their cultural, legal, and constitutional adherence to capitalist principles has never been so strict as in Benjamin Franklin's native land. Another reason is simply that the smaller the society, the faster is the progression within it toward monopoly capital and the sooner governments are obliged to intervene. But no amount of welfare legislation, not even a guaranteed annual income, and no extension of the right to strike can put citizens back on top of their economy or restore to them the pride and power of ownership more of them once enjoyed. Therein lies a central problem of advanced capitalist development. The progress and achievements of passing years have nourished not a sense of confidence, importance, and uniquely human worth but instead a feeling of being left out, expendable, on the dole—the attitude of "I just work here." It is remarkable that so many of the most accomplished humans ever to walk the earth feel like, and are, hirelings and pensioners.

STRATIFICATION WITHIN THE WORKING CLASS

A century ago the basic split in the capitalist economies was between those who owned some means of production and those who did not, between capitalists and wage laborers, those on top of the economy and those beneath it, the owners and the owned. This was the crucial division in the structure of reward, though there was variation also within each category. "Little farmers" were not so well off as "big farmers," the lone shopkeeper was poorer in power, wealth, and honor than one who used lots of "hired help," and the industrial magnates presided, of course, at the top of the bourgeois class. The wages of employees varied, too, as did their power and prestige at work, but most were poorly paid and all bore the stigma of not being their own boss. By now corporate capitalism has evolved so far that the stigma of wage labor is borne by nine of every ten citizens in the labor force, so large a proportion that it is taken for granted. Selling oneself for pay on the job market can hardly be counted a disgrace when almost everyone does it. Hence rank in the structure of reward has come to be thought of differently. Massively wealthy capitalists are still at the top, people who can live in luxury off their investments. And the manners and snobbery of those with old money still set them apart from the *nouveaux riches*. But in the bulk of the population, the chief basis of social distinction is how well the stigma of selling one's labor is covered up by the payment received. A high salary, business suit, and private office makes a person *seem* less a hireling than one whose low wages and open blue collar make class position obvious. Thus in both popular culture and sociology the focus has shifted from class to stratum. The object of interest is increasingly the invidious distinctions between higher and lower social strata within the wage-laboring class rather than on the differences between this class and the small, shrinking class of true capitalists. It is much as on plantations in the Old South, where field slaves envied house slaves but took their common master as a fact of life.

from class to stratum in the assessment of status

To depict contemporary structures of reward in this new way, as social stratification instead of as class division, obviously serves the interests of those who

"By now, therefore, to prosper by setting mind and hand to one's own productive property is quite out of the question for the vast majority of economically active citizens. What is in question is how high a stratum among propertyless sellers of labor one can attain." (© Joel Gordon 1979)

multiple layers of managers, skilled workers, and staff experts in large firms

have by now monopolized ownership of the means of production. The more narrowly citizens concentrate on the ladder of income and prestige, and on their private strategies for climbing it, the less they worry about ownership. But the proliferation of social strata does more than deflect criticism from the property-owning class. It is an integral part of capitalist development, and this for three reasons. First, as the number of employees in an enterprise grows, some are increasingly separated out as managers of the others. Thus is born a special category of workers, the ones harnessed to the task of harnessing others to machines. By virtue of their straw-boss power, their status is higher, their wages are called salaries, their hours are more flexible, and their loyalty is usually more with their overlords than with their underlings. In large corporations like General Motors (800,000 U.S. employees in 1978) or Sears, Roebuck (430,000), there are layers upon layers of managers arranged in a hierarchy with which the pay scale roughly coincides. A second reason for multiple strata is the pressure employers feel to replace employees with machines, especially as minimum-wage laws and union pressures drive up the cost of labor. But while sophisticated machinery reduces the total number of employees required, it necessitates the hiring of at least some workers highly skilled in techniques of operation. Being more scarce, skilled labor commands a higher price than common labor and thus makes for a second kind of split within the wage-laboring class. The third and last reason for stratification is that as an enterprise grows and its profits increase, its need for new ideas about what to do with profits intensifies. It tends, therefore, to hire certain employees, usually people with advanced schooling, to do research, experiment with new products and production techniques, and in general point innovative directions. These well-paid staff experts bring still another kind of disunity to the working class.

By now, therefore, to prosper by setting mind and hand to one's own productive property is quite out of the question for the vast majority of economically active citizens. What is in question is how high a stratum among propertyless sellers of labor can one attain. Numerous projects of survey research have documented these strata: executives and higher managers are at the top, researchers and staff experts almost as high, minor managers below them, skilled laborers still farther below, and at the bottom common laborers, who often fail to find a job and remain unemployed. Citizens in all but the lowest strata tend not to think of themselves as working class at all but as middle class, a term which connotes pride at being able to conceal the stigma of selling oneself for pay. But whatever the label people put on themselves, it is mainly size of paycheck that determines to which stratum a person belongs. If it is large enough, the working citizen can own a big house, a big car, a big boat, a big cottage, a big swimming pool, a big television—lots of big things, mortgage-free, with money to spare for dressing in designer clothes, eating out, entertaining and being entertained, vacationing, and saving for retirement. Progressively smaller paychecks imply smaller houses and cars, fewer consumer goods, and larger mortgages. It is a measure of the extent to which capital has been concentrated in fewer hands that most citizens lack full legal title even to their places of residence. They need mortgages to pretend they own their homes. Further, the proportion of citizens who merely rent their homes, without even the appearance of ownership, now ranges as high as 65 percent in the cities of North America. Workers paid at or near the minimum wage, of course, typically own almost nothing outright, having purchased their cars, furniture, and television sets with consumer loans.

today's stratification system is defined mainly by how much consumer spending one's job permits

Like other citizens, we sociologists often survey contemporary economic inequality simply in terms of the enjoyment of commodities, without reference to matters of ownership. We dwell on differences of income and ignore whether it derives from profit on a personal business, from stock dividends, employment earnings, lottery wins, unemployment insurance, or a welfare grant. And invariably we conclude, like everyone else, that some people's incomes are too large, others' too small. But to make sense of the economy facing us, we need to ask why we are so much concerned with income differences. The reason is not, as in ages past, that many citizens starve and freeze to death while others wallow in luxury. Nearly everyone in North America and Western Europe has money enough to eat and keep warm—or could get enough by filling out the proper governmental forms. No, the reason for our fixation on income is that the vast majority of citizens cannot reasonably hope for much, if anything, more. The freedom to decide through one's work the circumstances of personal life, the ability to make some little difference in the world by one's own efforts—such economic self-actualization is by now beyond most people's reach. For in the capitalist mode of development only ownership bestows such freedom, such an ability, such a chance to give economic expression to oneself, and fewer and fewer people own much of anything. The hard truth is that with respect to economic power, the bulk of citizens are in quite similar predicaments. Well-paid and poorly paid alike, executives equally as sales clerks, work not freely but according to corporate policies mandated by some distant committee at head office. Indeed, the common resignation to being economic pawns has progressed so far that a standard textbook in business administration can maintain: "In addition, although self-actualization may be important to all, there is no reason to conclude that that need must be satisfied on the job. Since work consumes only 35 percent of waking hours, we have a good deal of opportunity to be autonomous and self-actualizing in our off-the-job activities."[15] The trouble is that self-actualization is possible only in things that matter. And it is the economy that matters above all. A citizen who cannot make a difference on the job can hardly expect to make more difference off the job. He or she will more likely fall to complaining about being underpaid and spend evenings and weekends in front of the television set.

power-elite theorists and the question of a ruling class

C. Wright Mills, whom readers will remember from Chapter One, was among those many analysts who discern above the strata of wage and salary workers a small and secretive class of wealthy capitalists, millionaires hundreds of times over, who actively wield the power that makes a difference. These analysts, often called power-elite theorists, look beyond corporate management to those who own the corporations. They point in the United States to such incredibly wealthy families as the Du Ponts, Mellons, Gettys, Rockefellers, Fords, Hunts, Bechtels, Phipps, and Kennedys. No one can deny that this class exists. There are, to be sure, people like the late John Angus McDougald who enjoy on a large scale what quite a large proportion of citizens formerly enjoyed in little bits, namely ownership and control of their society's productive resources. And one can safely bet that such people like capitalism and would do all in their power to preserve it. Yet it is a mistake to imagine that the super-rich are keeping everybody else down. Quite to the contrary, they are playing by accepted and time-honored rules of profit seeking. The contemporary problem is not so much inequality of power (some having too much, others too little) as a shortage of power (life is arranged such that nobody seems able to make much difference). The playing out of capitalism has tied the hands of so many citizens that even those still free would be quite unable to free the rest. The pleasures of capitalism are many, moreover, and the standard of living is high. Surely most people, if they were honest, would admit that considering how little they know and how little they work, it is amazing how much they are paid. Pleasureful powerlessness is seductive; it makes people wary and fearful of changing the rules of the game. It is such fear among well-paid wage laborers, much more than the fortitude of the ruling class, that keeps the capitalist system going. And in the meanwhile, each stratum of citizens envies the lifestyle of the one next higher up, much as streetwalkers envy call girls. The envy is understandable: fat monthly checks beat low hourly rates and penthouses must be preferred to flophouses. But the envious and the envied remain both on the market. That is the tragedy.

THE GROWTH OF GOVERNMENT

As previous pages have noted more than once, the liberal theory of politics underlies and complements the capitalist theory of economics. The responsibilities of the national government in the early stages of U.S. capitalism were therefore simple and few: mainly to defend citizens and their property, to enforce contracts,

Propertied elites

W. Nelson Smith, III
CHAIRMAN OF THE BOARD

3-05 World Trade Center
New York, New York

SMITH ENTERPRISES

INVESTORS
Wanted for Texas Oil drilling projects. Investment size $10,800 to $4 Million. For additional information write Great Western Resources, 2100 Tanglewild, Suite 605, Houston, Texas 77063.

WINCHENDON SCHOOL
COED 5 & 7-day bdg., gr. 9-12. Prep for college & enjoy success. 6 students per class; diagnostic tests; counseling. Remedial & tutorial help. Golf course. 65 mi. Boston. Est. 1926.   18 Ash St., Winchendon, MA 01475

AN EXCITING LEARNING PROGRAM IN A SCHOOL THAT CARES
West Nottingham, the 2nd oldest coed boarding prep school in the country (Est. 1744), with young ideas. Accredited MS. Encourages self-reliance. 56 different courses. Grades 9-12. Small classes, athletics, activities. 80 Acres 90 mi. NE of Wash., D.C. Non-discriminatory.
Write or call: Headmaster, Box 31
WEST NOTTINGHAM ACADEMY
Colora, Maryland 21917   301/658-5556

PORSCHE Roadster
teren of Belgium/Nat'l Concourse Ch. Very rare/perfect. $29,500. 703-978-5552

Rolls Royce 1973
Silver shadow, forest green exterior, egg shell interior w/forest green piping. Car has been well maintained and is in overall very good condition. 51,800 miles. Special features include: AM/FM tape-quad system, folding foot rest. $29,000. Contact Chuck Pazman in Atlanta, GA 404-939-6582

ROLLS ROYCE 1950
SILVER WRAITH
Excel. Cond.—Limited Edition
201-687-0726 or 201-678-7060
R.R. '20 Silver Ghost Phaeton

HELD OVER THRU SEPT 5th
ELIZABETH TAYLOR in
THE LITTLE FOXES
by LILLIAN HELLMAN
Mon.-Sat. at 8 & Sat. at 2: $30, 27.50, 25.
Wed. at 2: $28.50, 25, 22.50.
SUN. MATS. BEGIN JULY 19 at 2
CHARGIT: (212) 944-9300
Ticketron: 977-9020/Groups: 398-8383
MARTIN BECK THEA. 302 W. 45 St. 246-6363

installed. $6,500

516-735-4023
FT. LAUDERDALE
FOR THE SELECT FEW...
This Mediterranean 4 bedrm +, 4½ bth residence is loc. in the Las Olas Islands, Ft. Lauderdale area of prominent home owners. Exquisitely custom built W/unrivaled amenities that include an Olympic sized diving pool and a 3-car. A home for the most discriminating buyer, priced at $750,000. For more information contact Joan Rice, realtor associate, M.A. Gregory & Co., 2700 N.E. 14th St. Causeway, Pompano Beach. Fla 33062 (305)942-2700; Eves 943-8475
FT. LAUD-condo 2 BR bath pool, Indry

Persian Rugs
SUPERB PERSIANS & ORIENTALS
WE WILL REPURCHASE ANY RUG YOU BUY FROM US FOR THE PRICE YOU PAID.
WE BUY, WASH & RENOVATE RUGS
OPEN 7 DAYS - 9 A.M. TO 7:30 P.M.
SAFAVIEH CARPETS OF ISFAHAN
DIRECT IMPORTERS OF FINE PERSIAN RUGS
683-8399
153 MADISON AVE. NYC 10016 (CORNER 32nd ST.)
ZURICH ● BERNE ● HEIDELBURG ● TEHERAN ● ISFAHAN

SALISBURY, CONNECTICUT
Alternative to the Hamptons
Complete 27 acre family retreat, a relaxing 2 hour drive from NYC. Charming main residence, in-law or guest house, tennis court, pond, swimpool, trout brooks, views, privacy. Near cultural/athletic activities. $450,000
Appointment and brochure available thru Cynthia White at
Robinson Leech Assoc.
Lakeville, Ct. 06039
203/435-9891   Eves 203/435-9213

Le Select Bistro

Mrs. W. Nelson Smith, III

High-income employees, affluent professionals

William N. Jones, Jr.
GENERAL MANAGER

Smith Manufacturing, Inc,   431 Metropolitan Blvd.
Indianapolis, Indiana
A DIVISION OF SMITH ENTERPRISES

PREUSSAG
Preussag ranks among the major international metal producers and its activities, also extend significantly to transportation, energy, chemical products and construction. Our services have been retained to assist in the recruitment of a
Chief Executive Officer
for one of its metal processing and distribution subsidiaries located in the Montreal area. This is a rare opportunity for the right person. This is a real chance of action

STANLEY H. KAPLAN
Our 43 Years of Experience Is Your Best Teacher
PREPARE FOR:
LSAT · GMAT · GRE
DAT · MCAT · SAT · ACT · CPA
GRE PSYCH · GRE BIO
MAT · PCAT · OCAT · VAT · TOEFL
● Permanent Centers open days, evenings and weekends
● Low hourly cost. Dedicated full-time staff
● Complete TEST-n-TAPE facilities for review of class lessons and supplementary materials
● Opportunity to transfer to and continue study at any of our over 85 centers
MSKP · NATIONAL MED BOARDS

Bayer Cadillac, INC.
ESTABLISHED 1928
"Standard of the World!"
AUTHORIZED
SALES ● SERVICE ● PARTS
● LEASING
Cadillac Certified Service

MAJESTIC THEATRE
ORCHESTRA
GOOD ONLY
SAT. 8:00 P.M.
MAY
V 20 19
1979
$25.00

CRISPIEST DUCK – LUSCIOUS GOOSE
BAR MAGNIFIQUE

2 EXQUISITE SILK ORIENTAL rugs, each approx 4x7, intricate floral pattern w/medallion, gold, white, soft pastel colors, perf cond. $1500 ea. 595-0348
ORIENTAL RUG-Serouk, Mansion size, 12x20, mint condition, Karastan $3500 Cost $8,000 to make (201)445-6794
SELLING 44 sq yds & 16 sq yds of like new blue & bwn cptg. + padding. $600. 212-687-2525 work; 9-5pm wkdys
Furs & Wearing Apparel   3220

SHAUGHNESSY PL. $177,000
Quality-crafted by Vintage in prestigious Beechwood West. Beautifully detailed from the double-entry vestibule to the leaded-glass turreted window and OAK STAIRCASE. 4 bedrooms. Luxurious kitchen. Log-burning fireplace in main-floor family room. MLS 1E025. JOE NEWMAN 886-9482 or 886-5400.

MRS. WILLIAM N. JONES, JR.
PRESIDENT
METROPOLITAN SYMPHONY AUXILIARY
30 City Center

CLUB MED
A GREAT VACATION ESCAPE
CELEBRITY
CLUB MED
AND
CELEBRITY
"PARTNERS IN TRAVEL"
● CALL US DIRECT ●
CLUB MED
RESERVATIONS
NEW YORK (212) 154-1601
ALL OTHER AREAS
1-800-223-7820
CELEBRITY 501 7th Ave. NYC
ONLY CELEBRITY WILL
GIVE $10 FREE BAR BEADS
CLUB MED CELEBRITY
WEEK-END
PARADISE ISLAND
THURS-SUN
$454   ALL INCLUSIVE

Middle-income employees, self-employed artisans

Cabrillo Comm. Coll., Aptos, CA 95003		1959
Caldwell Comm. Coll. & Tech. Inst., Lenoir, NC 28645		1964
Camden County, Blackwood, NJ 08012		1967
Canada, Redwood City, CA 94061		1968
Canyons, Coll. of the, Valencia, CA 91355		1968
Cape Cod Comm., W. Barnstable, MA 02668		1960
Cape Fear Tech. Inst., Wilmington, NC 28401		1964
Carl Albert Junior, Poteau, OK 74953		1934
Carl Sandburg, Galesburg, IL 61401		1966
Carteret Tech. Inst., Morehead City, NC 28557		1964
Casper, Casper, WY 82601		1945
Catawba Valley Tech Inst., Hickory, NC 28601		1958
Catonsville Comm., Baltimore, MD 21228		1957
Cayuga Co. Comm., Auburn, NY 13021		1953
Cazenovia (W), Cazenovia, NY 13035		1824

Low-income employees, unemployed

and to manage the post office. To get a sense of how small the national government used to be we can recall that in 1900, 57 percent of all civilian federal employees worked in the postal service. Indeed, people employed by any level of government were a rare and special kind of worker. That is why they were called *public servants*. They were custodians of the sparse but vital framework within which other citizens could pursue their private purposes. Since stamps covered the cost of mail delivery, moreover, the federal government had little need to tax the citizens. This was indeed thought to be wicked. The collection of taxes on personal incomes was illegal, even unconstitutional, and so it remained until ratification of the Sixteenth Amendment in 1913. Until then taxes were imposed mainly on property. The federal government obtained three-quarters of its revenues from just three sources: customs duties on various imported goods, excise taxes on luxuries like alcohol and tobacco, and estate taxes on the property of the dead. State and municipal governments imposed their taxes mostly on real estate and used the revenues to run schools, pay policemen's and jailors' salaries, and maintain roads, sewers, and other public works. In the era of laissez faire capitalism, governments took little and gave little. The rest was up to private enterprise.

By now capitalist governments both give and take much more. During its 1979 fiscal year, the U.S. federal government appropriated $467 billion, about 19 percent of the gross national product, as compared to 3 percent at the turn of the century. Further, its revenues now derive less from taxes on goods than from taxes on the sale of human labor: 46 percent of its revenues in 1979 came from personal income tax and a further 30 percent from social insurance taxes and contributions. A mere 12 percent came from corporate income taxes, and the remaining 12 percent from what were formerly the only taxes it imposed—customs, estate, gift, and exise. Federal government employees now account for about 3 percent of the civilian labor force. State and municipal governments have grown as well. The 50 state budgets amounted to about $225 billion in 1978, together about 56 percent as much as the federal budget. As of 1980, about 16 percent of all civilian employees in the United States worked for some level of government. And the state and municipal governments have also sought out new sources of funds. All but a few states now tax personal incomes, and so do most large cities. All but a few states collect retail sales taxes. Such practices as these are not, of course, limited to the United States. The size of government budgets and the scope of government activities have enlarged everywhere in the capitalist world. Indeed, citizens of most other advanced Western societies are taxed more heavily than Americans.

It is sometimes argued that the present malaise in the capitalist world is the fault of legislators, who have irresponsibly given in to the demands of a greedy electorate, spoiled citizens with expensive social welfare programs, and obstructed production with minute regulations and red tape, thereby draining capitalism of its earlier dynamism. I suppose every argument contains some truth, but the truth in this one should not be overblown. For when most citizens owned their means of production, their little farms and shops, they demanded less of government. They did not ask for unemployment insurance so long as most were or could be self-employed. They did not clamor for retirement benefits at the age of 62 or 65 so long as most owned their own businesses and were not forced to retire. Nor still did citizens want governments to regulate the production process when most goods

why governments have
grown: to protect
citizens

256

were produced in locally owned and operated establishments. In sum, citizens have demanded that politicans "do something" about this or that, as more and more citizens have been dispossessed of their capital and rendered incapable of doing things for themselves. Lacking more and more the means to stay on top of the economy and manage on their own, voters have turned to politicans as a court of last resort.

The politicians have responded with the kind of social welfare programs detailed some pages back, programs which account for roughly half the U.S. federal budget and for large parts of the budgets of most states. Both federal and state governments spend heavily also to protect citizens in their consumer roles. For as corporations have grown larger and less personal, their pursuit of profit has become more resolute, less tempered by the milk of human kindness, less mitigated by worry for the consumers of their products. Corporations have proven their willingness to advertise and sell cars, drugs, toys, and houses injurious to the health and safety of purchasers. Nor is there anything in the workings of an uncontrolled market to prevent corporations from befouling the rivers, polluting the air, poisoning the soil, destroying the forests, squandering fossil fuels, or exterminating whole species of wildlife. Thus have governments been obliged to intervene with a vast and expensive array of regulatory agencies. Thousands of inspectors are required to enforce building codes, product-safety standards, restrictions on the sale of rotten groceries, and so on. Huge staffs of experts must be employed in research on the various industries which have to be regulated. The capitalist system, after all, is founded upon the idea that economic actors should disregard the public good and serve only their respective selfish interests. Now that most actors are no longer flesh-and-blood people but gigantic, unfeeling corporations, this ethic of selfish disregard for the public good is carried to potentially disastrous extremes. Only an enlarged political authority has a chance of keeping it under control.

the need to respect corporate power

Governments cannot, of course, behave as enemies of corporations, since the latter own and control most productive resources, pay the wages and salaries of most working citizens, and have financial resources sufficient to shape public opinion through advertising and public relations. However much citizens might resent their corporate employers, they detest still more any government that would cause those employers to cut salaries or lay workers off. Hence government must tread softly and try to placate the corporate giants even while controlling them. Consider, for example, that the twenty largest U.S. corporations together spend more each year than the federal government, and the corporations do it without going into debt or annoying people with taxes. In 1978, the Canadian government had a budget of $42 billion; the Canadian branch alone of General Motors had a budget of $6 billion. The Coca-Cola Company, headquartered in Atlanta, Georgia, has annual revenues roughly equal to those of the Georgia government. Small wonder then that governments tax corporations so lightly and compete with each other to attract corporations to their jurisdictions with serviced industrial land, tax breaks, low-interest loans, and promises of cheap labor. The Michigan government was running ads in European business magazines in 1978, seeking to woo foreign firms to set up operations in Michigan. The ads were headlined, "ONE STATE FOR SALE." Another state government entitled its ad in the July 1978, issue of *Canadian Business:* "THE 11TH PROVINCE. KENTUCKY." Comparable ads offering

FOR EXAMPLE

Robert L. Heilbroner, "Planning Capitalism"*

For the sake of preserving capitalism as a development strategy, Western governments will be required to stick the public nose into private life still more in coming years, and in ways far beyond those manifest today. Depletion of the planet's food and energy resources is one reason, Heilbroner argues, but there are more.

And then, of course, the fragility of the atmospheric and liquid mantle pose the last and perhaps most formidable obstacle of all. Human activity, especially in the industrial regions where its effect on nature is most concentrated, is at the verge of creating violent and irreversible effects on the planet. Nothing is more sobering in this connection than the recent scientific debate as to whether fluorocarbons—the propellant gas in hairsprays and underarm deodorants—posed a serious threat to the filtrating properties of the atmosphere. What was sobering was not the outcome of the debate—the consensus was that the danger was not clear and immediate—but the tacitly accepted premise that the volume of these gaseous releases was so large that it might actually endanger human health. The same immense scale of technological assault on the environment is indicated by the ongoing debates over the possibility of carbon dioxide creating a "greenhouse effect" that would alter the temperature of the earth, or the possibility that massed industrial heat could change the patterns of air circulation and rain precipitation, or that the release of chemical waste could contaminate ground water, or that the volume of nuclear wastes would constitute a massive hazard.

All these new realities point in the same direction. They indicate the need for an unprecedented degree of monitoring, control, supervision, and precaution over the economic process. Some of these safeguarding functions can perhaps be performed by the marketplace itself, particularly insofar as the allocation of scarce resources is concerned. But the market will not monitor safety, nor will it impose decisions about the rate of growth, or its sharing within or among countries, that accord with the moral and political, as well as the economic, desires of peoples and nations. Thus the constraints of our time, the need for which will steadily intensify as far ahead as we can see, imply a powerful, and I think irresistible, force for planning the economic process in a way that has never before been necessary.

What is new about the thrust toward planning is its purpose. Some aspects of planning are by now familiar. We plan to develop appropriate transportation networks, whether road or rail or air. We plan to develop rural, or now urban, hinterlands. We plan to carry on the fiscal and monetary and welfare functions on which economic life depends. To be against planning, as such, is to be for chaos, not for laissez faire.

*From Robert L. Heilbroner, *Beyond Boom and Crash*, W. W. Norton, New York, 1978, pp. 182–189. Copyright © 1978 by W. W. Norton and Co., Inc. Reprinted by permission of the author and W. W. Norton and Co., Inc. Dr. Heilbroner is professor of economics at the New School for Social Research.

But the planning that will emerge from the present crisis will be of a different nature. Its essential purpose will not be to remedy the various failures that capitalist growth has brought, but to direct, and at bottom to protect, the very possibility of such growth, as long as that can be. This will certainly require the formulation of strict policies with respect to the use of energy. It must embrace an ever wider range of considerations affecting the environment. The process of scientific development and technological application must likewise fall more and more under the guidance and, where necessary, the veto power of government.

All this will involve allocations of materials, prohibitions against certain kinds of investment or consumption activities, and a general sticking of the public nose into private life, wherever that life, left to itself, threatens the long-term viability of the system.

This sort of planning seems an inescapable direction in which capitalism must move if its work of accumulation is to proceed as long as possible without encroaching suicidally on the carrying capacity of the planet. But the fact that the purpose of national planning will be to assist the continued functioning of the system does not mean that it will be welcomed by the business community, perhaps with the exception of a small advance guard that always sees further than the pack. On the contrary, the steady intermeshing of state and economy will be feared and fought as tantamount to a surrender to socialism. Indeed, that fear and that fight *are* the current crisis, quite as much as the actual blockage of circuits by oil or inflation. It is the vision of an impending "socialism" as one outcome of the present trend, alternating with even more alarming visions of an end to the acceptance of the morality and legitimacy of the system, that account, I think, for the dark and nameless fears that beset the capitalist world in general. . . .

History has shown capitalism to be an extraordinarily resilient, persisting, and tenacious system, perhaps because its driving force is dispersed among so much of its population rather than concentrated solely in a governing elite. In pursuit of the privileges, the beliefs, above all the profits of capitalism, its main protagonists have not only created the material wonders that Marx marveled at, but shown a capacity for changefulness that even he, who never underestimated the self-preserving drive of capital, did not fully anticipate. Thus it is still too soon to write finis to the present era, for in our time capitalism has yet another subchapter within its power to create, and perhaps others after that. But already we can see more clearly than past generations that the chapter cannot go on forever, and that in our own time we will have to live through periods of wrenching change even if the system survives. What comes thereafter is still a closed book.

all manner of foreign jurisdictions for sale to U.S. corporations appear regularly in the *Wall Street Journal*, *Fortune*, and *Forbes*, the business magazine that calls itself the "capitalist tool."

In one sense, the enlarged activity of governments has enhanced the capitalist strategy of development—mainly by assuaging its ill effects on employed citizens and thus preventing violent revolt, also more directly by facilitating corporate investment and profit seeking. But more fundamentally, any active intrusion by governments into economic life undermines capitalism at its core, since the prerogatives of private property are inevitably curtailed. Thus the transition from laissez faire to welfare capitalism has everywhere been reluctant, hesitant, and haphazard, without much sense of direction—a series of stopgap measures taken piecemeal. Those citizens still in possession of productive property—not just big industrialists but independent professionals, farmers, and small business proprietors —at first steadfastly resisted interventionist government, hoping they could manage on their own. Their political voice in the United States, the Republican party, espoused more classical principles of capitalism, as evidenced in the administrations of Presidents Coolidge, Hoover, and Eisenhower. The growing class of employed citizens, by contrast, especially the middle and lower strata, looked to the Democratic party for unemployment relief, income security, and general protection from corporate tyranny. It was during the presidencies of Wilson, Franklin Roosevelt, Kennedy, and Johnson that most social welfare legislation was passed. To some extent even in the 1980 electoral campaign, Ronald Reagan and Jimmy Carter exemplified the longstanding differences between their respective parties.

During the last two decades, however, the ideological foundations of U.S. political parties have steadily weakened. For by now governments at all levels are so much involved in economic life that the relevant question is no longer how much involvement but, more simply, what kind. Each voter seems to ask, "Who will take the better care of me, candidate X or candidate Y? Which one will act more vigorously on behalf of my private special interests?" And the answer to these questions has more to do with the candidates' respective personalities and sources of campaign funds than with their respective party affiliations. This is an unfortunate state of political affairs. The more a constitutional government uses its authority to serve particular and private interests, the more it squanders the allegiance and respect even of those citizens it favors. Only by proclaiming and implementing some strategy for achieving the public, collective good, some plan of economic development open to the creative participation of all citizens, can a constitutional government lead its people anywhere worth going. A century ago laissez faire capitalism qualified as such a strategy in the United States—an imperfect strategy, an unusual plan, but nonetheless one that worked. Today it does not work, and neither do millions of potentially innovative and productive citizens.

URBANIZATION AND SUBURBANIZATION

For every square mile of earth in Italy, there were 486 Italians in 1978. The figure was 252 for France, 398 for Switzerland, 593 for the United Kingdom, 641 for West

Germany, and 976 for the Netherlands. Against this background, the corresponding population densities for Canada and the United States, 7 and 60 respectively, seem artifically low, deflated perhaps by the uninhabitable Arctic wastes of the Northwest Territories and Alaska. Better then to calculate density statistics on only those parts of the earth fit for plowing. There were nearly 5 acres of arable land for every Canadian in 1978, more than 2 acres for every American, but no more than an acre for anyone in the countries of Western Europe. By any measure, North America is one of the least populous continents, Canada and the United States among the least populous countries. Would not some extraplanetary visitor therefore be surprised to find that as of 1976, 42 percent of the entire U.S. population were huddled in a mere 36 urban areas (called Standard Metropolitan Statistical Areas or SMSAs), each embracing more than a million people? Only one of four Americans in that year lived with fewer than 100,000 immediate neighbors. In the same year, 29 percent of Canadians lived in the three metropolitan areas that had passed the million mark, and a total of 56% in urban areas with more than 100,000.

Urbanization in these two countries is recent. In 1900, only 8 percent of Americans and no Canadians at all lived in cities of more than a million population. In all the United States there were but 37 cities with as many as 100,000 people, and these embraced a mere 19 percent of the population. In Canada there were only two, Toronto and Montreal, and 90 percent of Canadians lived elsewhere. The question has to be asked, Why did the cities expand so much? Is this an inevitable facet of the process of economic development? Do people have a firmer grip on the earth if they live in apartments stacked twenty or thirty stories high? There is no evidence to suggest as much. Industrial work requires some concentration of people in urban areas, but hardly to the extent apparent in North America today. The late E. F. Schumacher saw no economic reason why any city needs to be larger than 300,000. Given advanced technology in transportation and telecommunications, even that figure is too high. The growth of cities must therefore be attributed not to the development process itself but to the strategy that has carried it along.

The fact is that urbanization in North America has followed in the wake of the enlargement of production units, which in turn results from the concentration of capital in progressively fewer hands. The successful entrepreneur with profits to invest does not loan them to a friend so that the friend can start a competing enterprise. The profits are more likely invested in the expansion of the profit-making enterprise, thus driving smaller competitors out of business. Thus the size of factories and plants increases. In 1909, for example, 15 percent of U.S. wage laborers worked in establishments employing more than 1000 people; by 1956, the figure was 38 percent. In 1923, 21 percent of Canadian wage laborers worked in establishments with more than 500 employees; it was 47 percent by 1944. Now this trend does not reflect a technological imperative. A factory with 3000 employees does not necessarily produce shirts, refrigerators, or typewriters more efficiently than one with 300. Nor is there any reason why the production process of most goods could not be broken down into parts, with each successive part being performed by distinct, autonomous, smaller firms. The process of capital concentration, however, creates its own technological imperative. Machine manufacturers, knowing full well the direction of the economy, gear their production to the needs of the larger enterprises, since there is no incentive for them to conjure up technology for use by establishments with a few hundred employees. Thus does the playing out of the capitalist strategy make it inevitable that factories and plants will become immense.

But no employer with the capital to build a plant employing 1000 people wants to locate somewhere within commuting distance of only 1000 prospective employees. It is in the interests of the employer to locate in a setting where the supply of labor on the market is many times greater and full of variety. This leaves the employer more free to pick and choose, to hire and fire, and if unions do not intervene, to keep wages low. Thus as a general rule, the larger the firm and the larger it intends to become, the larger is the city in which it needs to be located. In the meanwhile, the growing number of people forced to sell their labor in order to eat have to move wherever they can find a job. Thus has generation after generation made the trek to ever larger cities, hoping to find work. And to find not only work but also the opportunities larger firms afford for promotion and movement up the income ladder. Still further, the larger firms in the larger cities tend to be more profitable and to be obliged to compete with one another for at least certain kinds of skilled or professional labor. Many categories of workers can command in large cities a higher price for the labor they sell. Thus employers lead, employees follow, and cities grow.

More recently, especially since World War II, the cities of the United States and Canada (and to a lesser extent Great Britain and Western Europe) have taken an historically unprecedented shape. Urbanization has continued but in the particular

suburbanization mainly since World War II

form of *suburbanization*: the concentration of people around, rather than in, cities, the expansion of relatively low-density neighborhoods outside the main municipal boundary. Between 1950 and 1980, the populations of New York, Chicago, Philadelphia, Detroit, Baltimore, Cleveland, St. Louis, Pittsburgh, and more than a dozen other major U.S. cities actually declined—in most cases by 15 or 20 percent, in the case of St. Louis by almost 40 percent. At the same time, however, the populations of the metropolitan areas (the SMSAs) surrounding these older cities has, in most cases, increased. Moreover, those U.S. cities which became large only during the last half century resemble, visually and spatially, massive agglomerations of suburbs. Examples are Los Angeles, Houston, Dallas, San Diego, San Antonio, and Phoenix, all located in the so-called Sunbelt. This sprawled form of urban growth has occurred even in the midst of improved techniques for constructing high-rise buildings, techniques which would have permitted higher densities of urban populations than ever in history. But generally lower densities have instead been the rule. Today one often sees thirty-story apartment buildings set in acres of unused grassland forty miles from the nearest city center. Indeed, large parts of many central cities lie in rubble. The question is, Why?

three reasons for suburbs: first, the car

Three factors may be noted in brief answer. The first and main one is the stupendous popularity among citizens of the automobile, an attractive means of transportation especially congenial to liberal-capitalist cultures, since it can be owned and operated privately, according to individual inclination. Until the 1920s and 1930s, urban travel by any kind of private conveyance was in general limited to the rich. Even the bicycle was not perfected until near the end of the nineteenth century. Travel by horse-drawn surrey or carriage was expensive. Most citizens

Henry Ford with his son, Edsel, in a Model F Ford, Detroit, 1905. "The automobile not only permitted but actually required cities to spread out. For streets now had to be widened and space left for garages, driveways, parking lots, and filling stations. Especially after World War II, dependence on cars became a self-reinforcing process." (United Press International)

therefore made their way through urban life mainly on foot. Cities were designed for walking, with narrow streets, and townhouses abutted one another. The norm of high density continued to be followed in the late nineteenth and early twentieth centuries, when municipal governments launched systems of public transportation: first animal-powered and electrical streetcars, later elevated trains and subways. But in 1909, Henry Ford introduced the Model T and began to mass-produce it on his assembly lines in Michigan. Gasoline, by then, was abundant and cheap. By 1920, there was one automobile in the United States for every 12 citizens; by 1950, one for every four citizens; by 1980, one for every three. The automobile not only permitted but actually required cities to spread out. For streets now had to be widened and space left for garages, driveways, parking lots, and filling stations. Especially after World War II, dependence on cars became a self-reinforcing process. As the number of cars increased, the newer parts of cities were laid out to facilitate their use, and pedestrians found themselves waiting longer for buses and walking farther for work and shopping. The growing inconvenience of travel on foot heightened the demand for cars. Affluent suburbs are now often built even without sidewalks, and residents are seldom seen walking anywhere (though they may jog for exercise). This is quite understandable. Many suburban homes are miles away from even so much as a variety store.

*second, spending for
highways instead of
public transit*

The availability of automobiles would not have encouraged urban sprawl, of course, had governments not intervened in the economy to equip the country for their use. Hence a second factor underlying the suburban phenomenon has been the political preference of governments to build streets, roads, highways, and expressways instead of railroads, subways, and other public transportation systems. This preference coincided with the interests of the large automobile manufacturers (even in 1920, Ford and General Motors dominated the industry), but it also enjoyed popular support. As late as 1970, the prospect of an energy crisis had not yet entered public consciousness. The greatest boon to suburban expansion was the construction of expressways from central cities to their municipal boundaries, so that automobile owners could commute to work. In addition, the Interstate Highway Act passed by Congress in 1956 gave federal funding to more than 40,000 miles of expressways, not only around and through cities but between and among them, at a public cost of as much as $8 billion annually. Thus the proliferation of automobiles upon which the new shape of cities utterly depends is not explained simply as an integral part of capitalist development. A further necessary precondition was the active and intentional planning of the appropriate infrastructure by federal, state, and municipal governments.

*third, the role of
suburbs in social
stratification*

The third factor encouraging suburban growth was that cars and expressways permitted a sharp physical split between higher and lower social strata. Never, of course, have the rich shown much interest in chumming with the poor. But as the class of wage and salary earners expanded, the craving for social segregation intensified. Higher paid workers desperately sought to parade their superiority over the lower paid. From the 1920s on, owning a car and living in a suburb became the prime means of such ostentation. Poor families had to live in central cities within walking distance of workplaces and stores or along streetcar, bus, and subway routes. The better-off could flaunt their advantage by moving out to a fashionable suburb. White white-collar workers in the United States seized this opportunity, especially after World War II, as thousands of blacks from the rural South moved north in search of jobs. Like the earlier peasant immigrants from Europe, blacks were looked down upon. Their lack of capital, low-status occupations, alien customs, and accented English placed them in disrepute. Additionally, they suffered from the legacy of slavery, anti-black prejudice woven deep in the fabric of U.S. culture. Differences of skin color accordingly exacerbated the desire of salaried employees in the higher strata to separate themselves by automobile from their financially inferior compatriots. By 1970, for example, Detroit was 44 percent black, Chicago 33 percent, St. Louis 41 percent, Baltimore 46 percent, and Philadelphia 34 percent. With more affluent citizens beyond municipal boundaries, moreover, city governments became less and less able to maintain with tax revenues the public transportation systems, parks, recreational facilities, and social welfare programs necessary for humane urban living. Crime increased. Employers able to relocate their businesses in the suburbs did so. Unemployment increased. Thus did many once-thriving American cities gradually crumble into desolations of poverty and hopelessness, while the suburbs surrounding them prospered.

Continuing urbanization has assumed the suburban form since World War II also in other Western societies, but with effects much less severe than in the United States. Governments in Britain, Canada, Sweden, West Germany, and elsewhere

were less wholehearted in their support of travel by private car and less willing to permit a sharp geographic split between higher- and lower-income strata. Governments in these countries built fewer expressways and continued to promote public transportation. Often they redrew municipal boundaries, so that migrants to the suburbs could not escape city governments' powers of taxation and land-use planning. In the 1950s, Toronto became the first city in North America to be governed as a metropolitan area, an amalgam of city and suburbs under common municipal authority. As a result, suburban residence around Toronto has never indicated or symbolized higher income than an address nearer downtown, and the core area remains easy on the eyes, the ears, and not least the nose. In the United States, by contrast, governments sought to stem the decay of central cities less by regional planning than by subsidized construction of housing and similar projects of social welfare. These efforts at urban renewal for the most part failed. Gas was still cheap, cars popular, suburbs attractive, and an inner-city address symbolic of disrepute. Indeed, government handouts to concentrated core-area populations of chronically unemployed and desperately powerless citizens seemed only to nourish a culture of subordination and dependency. The late 1970s, however, brought scattered signs of a return by higher-income workers to inner-city neighborhoods. The process was dubbed *gentrification*, meaning the displacement of lower strata by the professional and salaried gentry of corporate capitalism. As the energy crisis worsens in coming decades and as citizens rediscover the benefits of public transportation and high-density living, the core areas of U.S. cities may regain the allure other Western cities never lost. But whatever form cities assume in coming decades, the overall urbanization trend is likely to continue so long as citizens feel the pressure of the labor market in a corporation-dominated economy.

THE PRODUCTS OF CAPITALISM

Among the myriad effects of the capitalist strategy of development in and across Western societies, one last category deserves attention here: the products, the actual goods manufactured. For the effects of capitalism reviewed so far concern mainly the organization of the economy, not its output. The preceding pages have outlined the shift from proprietors to corporations, from diffuse to concentrated ownership of productive resources, from small-scale to large-scale modes of production. Explanations have been given for why the class of employees enlarged, why governments intervened on behalf of this class, why it split into strata defined by consumer spending, why public bureaucracies grew, and why citizens clustered in cities of high and then low density. But the question remains, What kind of products are associated specifically with the capitalist mode of production, what kind of tangible goods result from this particular strategy of economic advance? It is a hard question, since few if any noncapitalist societies have yet reached so high a level of development as the major capitalist ones. By the eleven criteria listed in the first half of this chapter, the capitalist societies in general surpass those following socialist strategies. It is difficult to say how much an automobile, airplane, or aerosol deodorant belongs to development and how much to its specifically capitalist variant. This is the case especially since the fruits of capitalist invention have won acceptance in many corners of the earth and by now form part of human history as a whole. We can never know what might have been if the Western world had progressed to its present heights by some strategy other than capitalism. Anyway, what might have been is hardly a fit object of sociological research.

Nonetheless, concern for what can be in years ahead obliges us to discern now as best we can the general priorities of capitalist economics with respect to the goods produced. Four such priorities deserve mention here. The first was implied already in the discussion of urbanization. It is the emphasis on large-scale technology, on the kind of machinery appropriate for large numbers of specialized workers organized under a single chain of command. As we have seen, the route to success in a free-market economy is to drive competitors out of business, subject them to oneself as employees, and manage them well for the sake of high productivity, high profits, and further expansion of one's own business. This trend toward ever larger business establishments permits and encourages technologies that require hundreds and thousands of workers to work together. Hence capitalist societies tend increasingly to produce the kind of goods which can be *mass*-produced in standard shapes, sizes, colors, weights, and styles by armies of corporate employees. Being more easily priced, such goods are also more congenial to market exchange. The incentives are few for the design of production systems usable by five, twenty, or fifty workers, since small firms ordinarily grow, fail, or sell out to larger firms. Inventors and makers of machinery instead direct their thinking to the grand scale, the kind of technology epitomized by Henry Ford's assembly line. As capitalist development proceeds, standardized products made by gigantic companies increasingly predominate. Custom-made, hand-tailored items become ever more expensive, beyond the reach of all but a shrinking minority—and this point applies not just to clothes, houses, boats, furniture, draperies, jewelry, and meals in restaurants but also to less tangible goods like vacation trips and entertainment. For the most part, the music of capitalism is heard on records and tapes. Its houses are picked from a contractor's model homes. Its clothes are bought ready-to-wear. Its holidays are taken as package tours. Its foods come in identical boxes, 3 million or billion already sold. Such standardization flows inevitably from large-scale technologies designed for large firms.

A second priority in capitalist development is on the kind of products citizens can buy for their private, individual enjoyment and use. For capitalism is a system of both production and consumption, a system which collapses without ample markets for its products. One major market is composed of the citizens themselves: employers, employees, and their families, eager to buy the necessities of life plus various affordable extras. The importance of this market has increased since the 1930s, with the passage of minimum wage laws and other social welfare measures, whose effect was to enlarge the purchasing power of wage and salary workers. Capitalist production has thus been aimed in great part at satisfying private consumer demand, or in other words, at providing citizens with an adequate and ever higher standard of living. This means food, housing, and clothes most basically, the goods required for physical survival. But beyond the subsistence level, the standard of living is defined by whatever commodities citizens crave and corporations can mass-produce. One has only to page through a mail-order catalog, scan the newspaper ads, or tour a shopping mall to appreciate the excellence,

four priorities: first, mass production of standardized items

second, private consumer goods

abundance, and variety of things produced under capitalism for purchase by private citizens. This priority on private consumption, of course, implies relative unconcern for public amenities. Capitalist governments spend relatively little on things for people to enjoy collectively, and capitalist citizens tend to abuse what public services and property there are. In the United States, for instance, public parks are fewer, smaller, and less well cared for than the national wealth would lead one to expect. Public transportation tends to be sparse, dirty, and irregular. Public toilets are often hard to find. Public medical and health facilities are meager. Yet the standard of living remains high, since most citizens have private backyards for cook-outs, private cars for travel, often two or three toilets in their private homes, and family physicians for private medical care.

The capitalist system is so productive, in fact, that repeatedly during the last century the availability of goods has outstripped citizens' ability or willingness to buy them. This was what happened during the great depression of the 1930s. U.S. farms and factories "overproduced," turned out more commodities for the market than citizens (and foreign purchasers) could or would pay for. Employers therefore laid workers off. But once deprived of their paychecks, workers could not afford to buy even as much as before, and the economy spiraled downward. Hence, especially since that disastrous decade, a third priority of capitalist development has been to stimulate consumer spending, to incite a craving among citizens for goods they never knew they needed and make it possible for citizens to buy those goods. A principal technique of such stimulation is advertising, which both proclaims new items for consumption and titillates interest in having them. As of 1980, U.S. businesses spent about three times as much on advertising as the U.S. government spent on foreign aid. Providing money as consumer loans is a further technique of stimulating market demand. As of 1979, the average U.S. adult owed about $2000 for consumer goods, not counting home mortgages. But the most crucial means of keeping demand high was been deficit spending on the part of the national governments—a practice encouraged in the 1930s by the British economist John Maynard Keynes (1883–1946) and adopted first in the United States by Franklin Roosevelt. During the 1970s, the U.S. government spent from $30 to $65 billion more each year than it took in through taxes. The effect was to leave more money in consumers' hands than the normal workings of the economy would allow and thus enable citizens to spend more. The joint effect of advertising, consumer loans, and deficit spending has indeed been to heighten citizens' acquisitive impulses and to prevent a repeat of the great depression. But the stimulation of demand has had other effects, too. Almost any novelty, even so silly one as a pet rock, finds willing buyers if it is promoted effectively, especially if it can be identified in popular culture with high socioeconomic status. Many consumer goods which formally raise the standard of living seem to be of dubious substantive worth: designer labels on clothing, for example, sugared breakfast cereals, hugely powerful cars, or swiftly changing styles of furniture and home decor. Many citizens eagerly buy food processors, skis, boats, electronic organs, camping equipment, and many other well-advertised goods, but allow them soon to fall into disuse. Yet the good life under advanced capitalism is defined by what consumers buy, regardless of what prompts their purchases, whether hidden persuasion or more self-willed motives. The inflation that occurs as citizens bid up prices for the goods they want

third, whatever novelties will keep employment high

vindicates, in a sense, the acquisitive concept of a human being upon which capitalism rests.

Even laying aside the danger of runaway inflation, there is a limit in advanced capitalism to how much money wage and salary workers can safely be allowed to spend on themselves. If too many of their wants were satisfied, they might lose motivation to sell their labor and the economy would go into decline. The stimulation of consumer demand is thus only a partial and limited solution to the problem of finding markets for steadily expanding production. Additional markets are necessary in order to stave off unemployment and economic downturn. The major one of these is the fourth and last priority to be mentioned here concerning

fourth, the implements of war

the products of capitalism. It is the production of goods to be bought by both the national government and foreign governments and to be used for noneconomic purposes, namely, warfare. The U.S. Department of Defense currently accounts for about one-quarter of the entire federal budget. U.S. corporations, moreover, export about $5 billion worth of arms annually to foreign regimes, as of the late 1970s. To be sure, there is nothing idiosyncratically capitalist about manufacturing instruments of war. Indeed, the Moscow government spends even more of its budget on weaponry that does Washington. But in the Soviet Union, as in other planned economies, mobilization for war implies reductions and shortages of consumer goods and public amenities. In advanced capitalism, by contrast, military spending tends actually to bolster the economy as a whole. It is a noninflationary stimulant, a technique by now institutionalized for relieving unemployment, quickening the production and trade of all kinds of goods, and speeding the standard of living on its upward course—so long as actual all-out war is avoided. Armaments, of course, are but one example of noneconomic spending by capitalist governments with economically beneficial effects. The U.S. space program is a different example, costing about $4 billion annually during the 1970s. The fact is that the advanced capitalist societies have had trouble coming up with the vitally necessary new outlets for their ever-increasing productive power. Arms have served as the principal stopgap solution, albeit a terribly risky one.

These paragraphs have suggested four priorities of advanced capitalist production: on mass-producible rather than custom-made goods; on consumer commodities rather than public amenities; on sometimes fatuous novelties serving needs artificially induced; and on the instruments of war. I should stress, however, that these are only priorities. Anyone who looks can find plenty of handcrafted items in the capitalist world, lots of public sidewalks, and clearly worthwhile novelties ranging from silicon chips to new kinds of antibiotic. The capitalist societies vary, moreover, in the products they make, depending on their respective national cultures, resource endowments, roles in international trade, and even their locations. Canada spends little on armaments, relying on the United States for defense against other foreign powers and on prayer for defense against the United States. The societies of Western Europe spend far more freely on public transportation, medicine, and recreation than does America. These paragraphs describe only in general terms the products of capitalism. Whatever fault may be found with these products, no one can deny the material riches they signify.

Concluding Words

We humans are forever trying to get on top of things. Thousands of us daily ascend the Empire State Building in New York, the Sears Tower in Chicago, the CN Tower in Toronto, the Gateway Arch in St. Louis, the Eiffel Tower in Paris, the Tower of London, or the Skylon at Niagara Falls. Or if not towers then mountains: Sandia Peak over Albuquerque, Pike's Peak over Colorado Springs, Mount Royal over Montreal, the Sugarloaf above Rio. In other places other heights. Our ancestors the Greeks located their gods on Mount Olympus. Atop Mount Sinai, Moses spoke with the god of the ancient Jews. But physical summits and pinnacles are only symbols of what we humans seek through that infinity of actions that constitute economic development: to rise above the earth and control it for our own purposes. The first half of this chapter set forth eleven principles evident in that effort, in the development process visible in the histories of all types of societies. This chapter's second half concerned more specifically the strategy that has guided the effort and directed the process for the past couple of centuries in the United States and similar societies.

the principles of development and practice of capitalism

Even casual readers undoubtedly sensed in this chapter some discrepancy between its two halves, between the principles of development and the practice of capitalism. Not total discrepancy, of course. The tallest buildings and towers on earth rise up from capitalist lands. Our standard of living is high, our lifetimes are long, and few of us would trade the power and wealth of our economies for anything currently available in the noncapitalist world. But pointing out worse problems elsewhere is no solution for our own. Especially is this so when the capitalist strategy seems to contradict the idea of development more and more obviously, the longer we follow it. The crux of the problem is this: the strategy rests on citizens' private ownership of productive property, but by now only a shrunken minority actually owns anything except consumer goods. By the rights of private property, capitalism sought to put people on top of things. But with the passage of time it has put corporations on top of the vast majority of people. Most citizens today count themselves lucky just to have a secure, high-paying job, that is, to be able to sell their labor for a good price to somebody else. This is hardly the outcome of capitalism that Adam Smith envisioned in the eighteenth century, or that Thomas Jefferson sought to hasten in the first new nation. Our strategy has become one that puts people down instead of helping people up. Citizens increasingly find themselves objects of manipulation, to be fed, clothed, housed, educated, tested, processed, hospitalized, treated, hired, promoted, fired, retired, taxed, subsidized, awarded, loaned money, billed, and otherwise acted upon by impersonal but slickly personalized bureaucracies, the owners of capital and holders of power. This retrogressive quality of life appears not least in how frequently citizens use the passive tense to describe the events in their lives. But what topsy-turvy kind of economic development is this? Where is the pride in oneself, the sense of power and personal dignity celebrated in the literature and art of the American frontier? The goal of development is not to be taken care of, however well, but to care.

Many critics, notably Marx and those who write in the tradition he began, have

"By the rights of private property, capitalism sought to put people on top of things. But with the passage of time it has put corporations on top of the vast majority of people." (© Jim Anderson 1978/Woodfin Camp & Assoc.)

capitalism needs to be studied in terms of how the game is played

condemned capitalism on basic theoretical grounds. They have argued that a world of commodities is by definition alienating, that putting a price on human labor is inherently wrong, and that an economy built on the principle of selfish competition is intrinsically inhumane. In an abstract sense they are right. By utopian criteria, I suppose, about anything anyone has ever done is alienating and inhumane. But a useful sociology of economic life must relate more closely to experience. For development is inconceivable without some distancing of people from goods and even from one another. And whatever we might wish, domination of some humans by others is a fact of life. So is selfishness. The question is what we humans should do with all this apartness in our experience as we devise strategies for economic advance. The capitalist answer is not to deny the apartness, not to pretend that we can reach nirvana overnight, but to use the apartness against itself. Or in other words, to unleash and encourage the selfishness of citizens, and with it their respective creative energies, for the sake of encouraging invention, productivity, and the furtherance of the common good. However offensive capitalism might be in theory, it is often no more offensive in practice than any competitive game or sport. Who has not enjoyed being challenged to a race, a debate, a tennis match, or an evening of chess? Even lovers like to tease one another. Capitalism is no less a game, an assertion of the differences among people; its benefits are all around us.

Any game turns sour when players take it too seriously, fail to keep it in bounds, and treat it as the be-all and end-all of life. Generations of small-scale capitalists, the much maligned petite bourgeoisie, managed to avoid this mistake. They knew the risk in lending money to a friend, splurging on a new house, taking a holiday, indulging personal tastes in the products of work, hiring a neighbor's son because he needed a job, or being a loyal customer to a trustworthy merchant. They knew the penalty for hesitating to make monetary profit their sole purpose in life, for sinning against the legally established virtues of selfishness. But they took the risk and endured the penalty, for they owned their means of production and had the power to treat capitalism as a game. In thousands of ways they injected whimsy and caprice, compassion and sympathy (sometimes also hate) into economic life, thereby asserting the commonality among members of our species. Even Andrew Carnegie, hard man that he was, spent millions building public libraries all across the North American continent. Victory, however, passed year by year to those who took only calculated risks, held sympathy in check, and single-mindedly sought to increase their wealth and expand their businesses. By now victory passes to an ever-smaller number of mighty but fictional game players, corporations conceived and bred specifically to pursue profit, unaffected by compassion or caprice, reluctant to take risks of any kind, and incapable of knowing that capitalism is just a game. The big corporations are like those occasional little-league coaches for whom the game never ends, fanatics who forbid members of the team to laugh, cry, or otherwise betray their humanness. Few citizens today have the capital necessary to rise above capitalism and keep the game in bounds. The most an average employee can do is make fun of the company after hours, cultivate some interesting private hobby, and daydream of winning a lottery and setting up some little business of his or her own.

the need for ground rules, but the problem they cause

When the United States began as a society, it imposed almost no ground rules at all on the capitalist game. More than Britain or Germany, France or Canada, the United States made the game a free-for-all. In the language of the day it was every man for himself. But as citizens themselves became progressively less able to keep the game in bounds, they demanded that the national government do so. And it did, restricting how labor could be used, setting a minimum price for it, protecting unions, providing income security and other forms of social welfare, setting standards for various products, and engaging in deficit spending. With each passing year both national and lower-level governments imposed more and more ground rules—and so have governments in the other capitalist societies. The result has been what any little-league coach could have predicted. Once the list of ground rules gets too long, the time spent squabbling over rules begins to exceed the time spent playing the game. In advanced capitalism this means concretely the prevalence of strikes—in the late 1970s, at least 2 million U.S. workers took part each year in organized work stoppages. It means lawsuits, too, and intense pressures on governments to make additional ground rules in favor of aggressive special-interest groups.

No special genius is required to know that the Western world will either shift in the next decade or two to a new strategy of economic development or else cease to develop. We can safely take capitalism for granted in years to come only as a cultural orientation for our economic plans, not as the present structure of corporate control. For the welter of rules and regulations, forms and red tape, is nearing the point of absurdity. Large firms are buying smaller ones out at such a pace that the final play-offs of the present game cannot be far off. The proliferation of nuclear and conventional arms extends so far that the danger of catastrophic global war becomes daily more severe. Fossil fuels are nearing depletion. Most important of all, citizens are decreasingly on top of their economic lives. Hence the appropriate question is, What alternative strategy of development will soon be guiding history in the capitalist societies of the West. Will Western governments eventually expropriate the large corporations, impose centralized public ownership of the means of production, and set up precisely managed economies similar to those in Eastern Europe? This is indeed a dreary prospect. Not even Marx would approve of it. Or will new ideologies triumph—strategies for dispersing control of resources, dismantling large firms, and encouraging inventiveness in a revitalized market economy, one where planning serves to preserve the economic power of citizens? Not all Western societies need follow the same strategy, of course. We may see a rebirth of variety even within discrete societies. But whatever we see in years to come, if it is good it will have resulted from hard, critical, rational, creative thinking on the part of citizens. This chapter has had no purpose but to encourage such thought. It rests on Thomas Jefferson's faith: "Enlighten the people generally, and tyranny and oppressions of body and mind will vanish like evil spirits at the dawn of day."[16]

For Reflection

money
institutional school
anthropomorphism
economic development
historicism
hunting and gathering
animal husbandry, agriculture
tools, technology
industrialization
renewable sources of energy
fossil fuels
electricity
work
physical versus cerebral work
language, mathematics
pure science
literacy rates
size of societies
balkanization versus elephantiasis
degree of division of labor
mechanical versus organic
kind of division of labor
gift giving
redistribution
market
commodity

from paper to informational money
labor force in agriculture
economic modernization
population control
birthrates and death rates
demographic transition
abortion
progress
capitalist development
capitalism: stage or path?
radical detachment from things
private property
the rule of selfishness
inventive work
wage labor
slavery
limited-liability corporation
economic growth
gross national product
capitalist one-sidedness
the monopolistic trend
diversification
labor rights
unionization
social welfare
from class to stratum

straw-boss power
skilled and unskilled labor
staff experts
middle class
the expansion of government
welfare capitalism
stratification and politics
urbanization
suburbanization

cars and capitalism
suburbs and stratification
gentrification
war and prosperity
standardization of products
overproduction
consumer society
deficit spending
ground rules

For Making Connections

I hope that by now readers are accustomed to connecting the ideas of these chapters to their personal lives, if they had not acquired this habit even before beginning this book. Hence, here and in the remaining chapters, the questions concern only how to connect the various parts of this one book.

With Chapter One: In light of the pages you have just read, are you convinced of the worth of studying the economy from an holistic point of view? Why or why not?
Has the analysis of economic development given here helped you see how much First Sociology and Third Sociology overlap? How so?

With Chapter Two: Capitalism is a major concept for studying economies. How would you go about measuring in concrete, empirical terms how capitalist a particular society is?
Search out in this chapter two or three hypotheses which you personally doubt are supported by empirical evidence. How would you go about testing these hypotheses further?

With Chapter Three: For understanding the reward structure of advanced capitalism, what difference does it make to focus on classes instead of strata?
What specifically cultural aspects of your society tend to reinforce the structure of the capitalist economy?

With Chapter Four: Economic development has been explained here as a dialectical process. The human person can also be understood dialectically. Are these two dialectics related? If so, how?
What emphases in child socialization would you expect to find in a laissez faire capitalist economy? How about in an advanced corporation-dominated capitalist economy?

With Chapter Five: Explain in as much detail as you can the connection between the liberal path to democracy and the capitalist strategy of development.
Has the trend toward monopoly capital increased or decreased people's vulnerability to demagogues in Western societies? How so?

An understanding of contemporary economics requires above all an intimate acquaintance with economic data: the everyday organization of production and commerce, how people work and under what constraints. Hence nothing should be recommended more strongly than the daily newspapers, especially their financial sections and classified ads. Business publications like the *Wall Street Journal, Fortune,* and *Forbes* in America, the *Financial Post* and *Canadian Business* in Canada are still more valuable. Virtually all the descriptive statistics cited in this chapter can easily be confirmed and updated in such sources, if not still more easily in compilations like the *World Almanac.* For almost any city, profession, or trade, and for all the larger corporations, a variety of economic reports and plans can easily be obtained, often without charge. Except for personal experience in the workplace, nothing enhances one's economic awareness so much as steadfast attention to concrete events and processes as reported in public media. Only with such awareness can the numerous journals in the economics sections of libraries be used to advantage. In addition, for interpreting the data of contemporary economic life, I recommend the following twelve more general sources:

1   John Kenneth Galbraith, *Economics and the Public Purpose* and *The Age of Uncertainty,* Houghton Mifflin, Boston, 1973 and 1977 respectively. The first of these synthesizes and rounds out the author's many decades of research on advanced industrial capitalism. The second is a collection of illustrated essays in social and economic history. Both are masterpieces of style and scholarship.

2   Paul A. Baran and Paul M. Sweezy, *Monopoly Capital,* Monthly Review, New York, 1968. Two of America's best Marxian economists, the former now deceased, here analyze the causes and effects of growing concentration of economic power. Their book is a careful documentary of the basic structure of advanced capitalism.

3   Harry Braverman, *Labor and Monopoly Capital,* Monthly Review, New York, 1974. Similar in theoretical outlook to Baran and Sweezy's book, this one offers penetrating insight into the expansion of the wage-laboring class and the decreasing autonomy enjoyed by employees locked into a fragmented division of labor. Monthly Review Press is probably the best publisher of socialist economics in the United States.

4   Milton Friedman, *Capitalism and Freedom,* Univ. of Chicago Press, Chicago, 1962, and with Rose Friedman, *Free to Choose,* Harcourt Brace Jovanovich, New York, 1979. Like the books listed so far, these are both insightful and readable. But in sharpest contrast, Friedman defends the principles underlying capitalism and liberalism, proposing only that the United States should follow such principles more closely. Friedman, winner of the 1976 Nobel Prize in economic science, writes a regular column in *Newsweek* on current affairs.

5   Robert Heilbroner, *The Making of Economic Society,* and with Lester C. Thurow, *Understanding Macroeconomics* and *Understanding Microeconomics,* all from Prentice-Hall, Englewood Cliffs, N.J., Among the more thoughtful and understandable of basic economics textbooks, all three of these are regularly revised and updated. Heilbroner's *Inquiry into the Human Prospect,* Norton, 1974, is a naked and honest portrayal of the problems of economic growth.

6   E. F. Schumacher, *Small Is Beautiful,* Blond and Briggs, London, 1973. A refreshing critique of contemporary capitalist economics, written with a compelling combination of rigor and passion. Schumacher died in 1977, but not before setting down the

philosophical underpinning beneath his social science in *A Guide for the Perplexed*, Harper & Row, New York, 1977. There has to be hope for a world that somehow engendered a scholar like this man.

7 William Leiss, *The Limits to Satisfaction*, Univ. of Toronto Press, Toronto, 1976. A thoroughgoing critique of the kind of economic system that locates human fulfillment in the passive consumption of goods rather than in the active production of them. Leiss is a professor of environmental sciences at York University, an exceedingly reasonable and thoughtful scholar.

8 Harold A. Innis, *Essays in Canadian Economic History*, Univ. of Toronto Press, Toronto, 1956. A posthumous collection of essays on a broad range of topics by the progenitor of most of the freshness in English Canadian economic thought. Innis's salutary influence is apparent today in the work of economists like Abraham Rotstein and sociologists like S. D. Clark.

9 Emile Durkheim, *The Division of Labor in Society*, Free Press, New York, 1933. A theory of capitalist development worth reading mainly for the influence it has had on Anglo-American sociology. Even more worthwhile is the depiction of precapitalist economic exchange by Durkheim's nephew; see Marcel Mauss, *The Gift*, Free Press, New York, 1954.

10 Karl Polanyi, *The Great Transformation*, Beacon, Boston, 1957, and with Conrad Arensberg and Harry Pearson (eds.), *Trade and Market in the Early Empires*, Free Press, New York, 1957. Critical analyses of contemporary and preindustrial economies, respectively.

11 C. Wright Mills, *White Collar: The American Middle Class*, Oxford Univ. Press, New York, 1951. By now a classic analysis of the new middle class in the United States. For a more up-to-date depiction with a focus on Canada, see *The Tyranny of Work*, Longman, Don Mills, Ont., 1975, by James Rinehart, a careful analyst of the class structure, now at the University of Western Ontario.

12 Frances Fox Piven and Richard A. Cloward, *Regulating the Poor*, Random House, New York, 1971. A social history of welfare capitalism by an effective if sometimes reckless team of U.S. sociologists. See also their later paperback, *The Politics of Turmoil*, Random House, New York, 1975, a critique of antipoverty programs in American cities.

Religion

Chapter Seven

*I ask why and how people bow
to gods and what this has to
do with their political and
economic lives.*

Virtually all serious scholars agree that both a polity and an economy are essential to life in human societies. Nor is there much disagreement about how to define these two institutions, at least in broad terms. The same cannot be said of religion, the third of the five institutions of national societies discussed in this book. What religion is and whether anyone needs it are very open questions in contemporary sociology. Hence, the first two sections of this chapter are devoted to the basic issue of how religion is most adequately conceptualized. Only thereafter can the question of its necessity be addressed, by analyzing the variety with respect to religion both in the history of Western civilization and across the societies of the contemporary world.

*the importance of a
clear definition*

Functionalist and Marxian Conceptions of Religion

Nature is unkind along the Peruvian Pacific coast. Sand blows steadily across an arid waste, dusting mouths already parched and stinging eyes already burned by a seldom-clouded sun. Driving south from Lima in 1970, I quickly learned to hate the ashen whiteness and to crave the greenery of those very occasional valleys where Andean rivers have been trained to spill moisture on the earth. The highway faltered briefly in Pisco, where a fine headache whiskey is produced, and in Ica, a university town. Later it traversed for many miles the so-called Nasca lines, gigantic images of insects etched in the desert by ancient neolithic peoples even better known for their erotic pottery.

But it was not extinct religion that lured me. About 300 miles south of Lima the desert covers metallic ore, and there the Marcona Mining Company, a U.S.-based multinational firm, had established a decade earlier what seemed to be the farthest outpost of industrial capitalism. By the time I visited, the mining camp had grown to a population of roughly 20,000. It was spread across barren, treeless plains, which sloped upward toward the coast. At the bottom were thousands of shacks for the Peruvian miners and their families. On terraces of streets a little farther up were modest bungalows for white-collar employees. The lavish homes of executive gringos were at the top, on cliffs overlooking the sea. And off to one side, near the hospital, school, and market, rose the spire of the church of San Juan de Marcona. The company had shrewdly dipped into its profits to provide land for the church, architectural services, and half the construction cost. Protestant company officials had sought out a Catholic bishop in their native land and persuaded him to send priests to the mining camp. The officials had argued, as the bishop later wrote, "that their laborers would be practical Catholics or without any religion whatsoever. In the latter case they would be easier prey for those seeking to sow anarchy in Peru."[1]

The founding of that remote Peruvian parish, its title joining the names of a Christian saint and a profit-seeking corporation, illustrates almost in caricature the most common outlook on religion in contemporary sociology—structural functionalism. This outlook, readers may recall from earlier chapters, is rooted in the problem of order—how the sinister side of human beings is kept in check by the harmonious fitting together of the parts of a society. From this point of view, the special role of religion is to serve as a sacred safeguard against anarchy, a supernatural justification of the natural status quo. Religion serves this function, so it is argued, by spinning ghostly tales that give meaning to the routine of everyday life and by celebrating the goodness of that routine symbolically in ritual, thus furnishing people with a sense of purpose and collective well-being. Indeed, some structural functionalists define religion as whatever beliefs and symbols glue a society together in this fundamental way. Probably the best-known among them is Emile Durkheim; the last of his four books, his magnum opus, was entitled *The Elementary Forms of the Religious Life*. Another classical representative of this tradition is Bronislaw Malinowski (1884–1942), a Polish anthropologist who taught for most of his life at the University of London; his book, *Magic, Science and Religion*, is still widely read. More recent representatives include Talcott Parsons, Elizabeth Nottingham, Robert Bellah, Milton Yinger, G. E. Swanson, and Harold Fallding, whose diverse writings on religion seem to spring from a common functionalist point of view.

the functionalist view: a necessary crutch

Scholars of this orientation seldom express doubts that religion is a necessary part of human societies. They argue that political and economic structures are by themselves unable to get a firm grip on restless human beings prone to misbehavior. For these structures cannot explain to people why they have to die. Nor do they have answers when people are perplexed by the vagaries of weather and climate, and by the unpreventable accidents and unanticipated side effects of well-meant schemes of action on the earth. Nor still can they satisfy the complaints of malcontents who ask why some people flourish at the top of the heap while others languish at the bottom. Death, uncertainty, and inequality are the three enduring problems to which functionalists regularly point in defense of their claim that religion is necessary. Religion appears as a residual category, solving only those problems insoluble by other means, but still a necessary one. Indeed, many functionalist scholars have tried to outline what kind of religion can best relieve the inadequacies of modern industrial societies. Durkheim drew such an outline, as Rousseau, Comte, and Spencer had done before him, and as scholars like Parsons and Bellah would do in later decades. Such scholars, like most authors of textbooks, are more interested in whether some particular religion is functional than in whether it is true. They avoid the issue of whether Jesus was "really" God or indeed whether God "really" exists. This issue is customarily regarded as a personal one, to be left to the faith of individuals or their lack of it.

the Marxian view: false consciousness

But the story of San Juan de Marcona illustrates no less clearly the sharply contrasting conception of religion held by most Marxian sociologists and many others who focus on the proud, creative side of the human dialectic. From this point of view, what the Marcona corporation sought to prevent was not anarchy but transition to a more just and humane economic order. Company officials wanted to ground their desecration of human labor in the symbolic absolutes of Peruvian Catholicism and thus discourage workers from imagining that they could take the company into their own hands. The officials' willingness to buy a religion contrary to their own only demonstrates from this point of view what a fraud religion is. It is false consciousness, a package of beliefs and rituals contrived to keep people unaware of their own abilities, an opiate for dulling their creative sensibilities. Marx and Engels articulated this view of religion in their own writings, drawing inspiration mainly from the German philosopher, Ludwig Feuerbach (1804–1872). The same view is held by numerous contemporary sociologists. It is not, however, often found in textbooks and scholarly articles written in English. The major reason is that once religion is conceptualized as poppycock, an alienating epiphenomenon, there is not much point even in talking about it. The contemporary popularity of the Marxian view of religion is therefore evident not so much in the content of the sociology of religion as in the low priority and prestige attached to it relative to other subfields of the discipline.

Although the functionalist and Marxian outlooks are at odds with respect to the worth of religion, they both portray it as a defender of existing political and economic structures against the threat of change. This common portrayal has colored the thinking of contemporary sociologists, myself included, perhaps more than the cause of careful scholarship warrants. In June of 1972, I was again traveling in South America. An aboriginal bus had transported me deep into the interior of Paraguay, a gentle, verdant country blemished mainly by the longest-lived of Latin American military dictators. The bus left me in a sleepy town devoid of industry, an oversized trading post for peasants who eke out a living on tiny farms nearby. My purpose in being there was not to visit French Canadian nuns, but having learned that five or six were living in the town I thought I should pay them my respects. I clapped at the gate of their house, as is the Paraguayan custom. A servant girl showed me into the parlor, which smelled as clean and starchy as convent parlors are supposed to. Presently the sister superior arrived. She looked and acted the part: a silver-haired woman dressed in black, gracious and with an engaging smile, but exuding an air of serious purpose, too. We exchanged appropriate pleasantries.

"What kind of work do you sisters do?" I asked. "We teach," she said. Of course, I thought to myself, having confirmed a stereotype. "You have your own school?" "No," she replied. "Ah, then you teach in the government school." "No," she replied again, "we teach adults." "Ah, then you have a literacy program," I said with confidence, rearranging my stereotypes and recalling similar programs elsewhere. "Well," she said and hesitated, "not exactly." "Then, Sister," I answered, "please tell me just exactly what kind of teaching you sisters do."

"Of course," she said, "you are a sociologist. You will be interested to know." And with that comment she disappeared into another room, returning moments later with a sheaf of mimeographed pages. Simply but pointedly, she explained more or less as follows, using diagrams on the pages to illustrate her remarks. "You see, our people are poor and powerless. They have nowhere to sell their products except to middlemen who pay them as little as possible. And whatever they need, they have to buy from middlemen who charge outrageous prices. The middlemen get rich, the money stays in the capital or goes to foreigners, and our people continue to be exploited generation after generation. What we try to teach them is awareness of their real economic and political situation. We want them to be conscious as a group of their oppression so that collectively they can demand change. The church teaches that people must liberate themselves from sin, and the worst sin in this country is the alienation of the people, the poverty and powerlessness of all but a small minority." On and on the sister went with her explanation, becoming gradually more impassioned and intense. I listened and nodded, taking mental notes to write down later. But all of a sudden she stopped in midsentence and her face became grim. "Did the CIA send you here?" she asked.

That missionary nun was by no means exceptional. She was indeed following the teaching of her church, as spelled out in the documents of an official meeting of the Latin American Catholic bishops held at Medellín, Colombia, in 1968. There was a story in Paraguay when I was there that so many protesting peasants were quoting the words of Medellín that the military police, hardly renowned for their reading habits, had issued a warrant for Medellín's arrest. Nor have bishops, priests, and nuns in Latin America become generally more well-behaved since 1972. Literally thousands continued their dissidence as the decade drew to a close, steadily pulling more sacred props out from under the established military regimes, demanding recognition of human rights, and demonstrating that if religion is a tranquilizer, it sometimes has the effect of a stimulant. In 1979, the Latin American bishops met again in Puebla, Mexico, reaffirming theological doctrines only slightly less threatening to the political and economic status quo than those of Medellín.

rebellious religion disputes both functionalist and Marxian emphases

The functionalist and Marxian conceptions of religion can handle the church of San Juan de Marcona in Peru but not the French Canadian convent in Paraguay. The latter, like all other instances of rebellious religion, must either be ignored or treated as a fluke. Indeed, textbooks commonly mention such instances as a series of "but sometimes" theoretically detached from the substance of their arguments. This is not good enough. There are too many exceptions to the conservative rule. Every religious tradition in the world today was born as a movement of protest, a harbinger of social change. Weber showed this clearly in the case of Protestantism, but there are countless other examples. The Mormon church, although today a hallowed bulwark of U.S. capitalism, posed such a threat in 1856 that President James Buchanan dispatched an army to subdue it. Methodists, Mennonites, and Moravians were once no more respectful of law and custom than Moonies and Black Muslims have been in more recent history. But it is not only newly formed, pristine religions that make trouble. French Canadian nuns belong to a very old church. Although its role in Quebec has been generally reactionary, the massive support it gave miners in the Asbestos strike of 1949 was the single major reason why the government failed to break the strike. And in the 1960s in the United States, thousands of Protestant ministers, both black and white, defied even their own congregations in the struggle for racial equality. Even more recently, mainstream denominations in both Canada and the United States have angered churchgoers by putting foreign-mission dollars into the hands of African guerrillas. Whatever definition of religion we sociologists contrive has to be able to recognize that Martin Luther King, head of the Southern Christian Leadership Conference, was no less a minister of religion than Francis Cardinal Spellman, vicar of the American armed forces in Vietnam.

Religion as Response to Limitation

An adequate sociological understanding of religion requires for a start that we not build hypotheses into its defintion. It is hardly useful to define government as essentially democratic or the economy as intrinsically capitalist. Neither is it helpful to identify religion with fear of social change. Instead we might more adequately conceptualize religion simply as any set of beliefs, rituals, roles, and procedures by which people respond to the fact of limitation. For this fact, the existence of a beyond, is as empirically obvious as people themselves and their

the reality of the beyond

physical environment. We human beings cannot do everything we wish. An escape from death is beyond us. Certainty is not within our power. A social arrangement in which all are absolutely equal is impossible. Death, uncertainty, and inequality are not just flaws in the present scenario of public order, nor are they residual distractions from the "real" business of politics and work. They inhere in the human condition. They are part of our nature no less than our ability to act. Our real situation is marked equally by humility as by pride. Through economic and political development we have indeed extended the limits of human prowess and put huge chunks of the beyond within the grip of human hands. With luck we in the contemporary world will whittle infinity down still more. But we will not eliminate it—ever. Limitation, the beyond, will always confront us. If you are not convinced, ask me again the day before yesterday, or a million tomorrows after today.

But how can we human beings relate to what is beyond relation? How can we come to grips with our own impending death, our fundamental vulnerability, our ultimate uncertainty, our insurpassable limits? The answer is that we cannot. Every answer contradicts the questions. Answers are composed of words, the supreme instruments for dominating the earth. For questions beyond domination, words fail.

Scholars who have seriously grappled with the problem of religion all agree on this point. Religion ties us intellectuals up in *nots*: it is not natural, not earthly, not rational, not material, not routine, not explainable, utterly nonsensical. Even so, no one who faces the reality of the beyond can quite argue that it is not of serious consequence. And so the same scholars who use *nots* also use superlatives: religion is extraordinary, supernatural, sublime, singular, transcendent, marvelous, wonderful, mysterious, spiritual, holy, sacred, preeminently sane. It is both reassuring and frustrating to come across the same fundamentally useless words in the writings on religion of an American psychologist like William James (1842–1910), a Danish philosopher like Søren Kierkegaard (1813–1855), a German theologian like Rudolf Otto (1869–1937), a Canadian-American anthropologist like Edward Sapir (1884–1939), an American sociologist like Thomas O'Dea (1916–1974), an Israeli social philosopher like Martin Buber (1878–1965), and even of a Zen Buddhist mystic like D. T. Suzuki (1870–1966), or a Catholic one like Thomas Merton (1915–1968). Empirically, we can define religion best as the way people act in their encounter with the limits of action.[2]

the most authentic response: purposeful, silent inactivity

The simplest, most common, and most authentic form of religious expression appears to the observer as intentional transfixion, silent but purposeful inactivity. It may be called meditation, contemplation, recollection, retreat, prayer, or communion with God, but it consists simply in training the mind or in freeing it to dwell utterly on the fact of the beyond. The ardent cultivation of stillness provides the chance par excellence, in William Blake's words, "To see a world in a grain of sand/And a heaven in a wild flower,/Hold infinity in the palm of your hand/And eternity in an hour."[3] It is a way of life in many cultures for those who feel themselves called to practice religion most perfectly: Trappist and Buddhist monks, hermits, cloistered nuns, Hindu holy men, and mystics of diverse social origin. The same religious response is evident in the magnificent emptiness of Quaker meetings, in the periods of intentional silence during most Protestant, Catholic, Jewish, and Islamic liturgies, in yoga exercises, in the practice of transcendental meditation, in the almost catatonic trance into which shamans fall in the rites of numerous tribes, in the moments of silence which legislatures observe upon the death of respected personages, and in other formless forms as well. The purest religious ritual is nonritual, the voiceless cry and motionless gesture of surrender to the mystery of life and death. The most natural response to the beyond is to shout yes to it with all of one's being, but without so much as thinking the word.

the response of wildly expressive art

Almost equally as authentic as silence among forms of religious expression are the chanting and dancing of nonsense, superlative counterparts to the negation of activity in stillness. Words like *alleluia, amen, om,* and *hare krishna* have no empirical meaning. They are utterly insane and, for that reason, holy and sacred. They are what the Nebraska poet, Karl Shapiro, called in his definition of poetry *not-words.* Glossolalia, speaking in tongues, a practice widespread in Christianity and other religions, is similarly nonsensical as conventional language and therefore meaningful as spiritual expression. But if pointless words serve well as responses to the beyond, so also do pointless gestures. The "turning" of the Shakers in nineteenth-century America, the rocking back and forth and clapping in black American Protestant sects, the whirling of dervishes, and the cymbal jingling of those with Kirshna consciousness all have this in common: repetitive, rhythmic

Dervishes are rough counterparts in Islam to monks in Christianity. These ones in Konya, Turkey, are whirling. Their motion is intentionally intentionless, and therefore worshipful. (© Ira Friedlander/Woodfin Camp & Assoc.)

movement without mundane purpose for the sake of celebrating the divine. Poetry, music, dance, and the other expressive arts have inevitably a certain numinous, ethereal quality, of course, even when they are not directed toward an ultimate end. That quality intensifies, however, the more they are created and performed in acknowledgement of the sublime uncertainty of the human condition. Whether or not the jubilant dance of Zorba the Greek, for example, counts as religion is therefore only a question of where one draws the line between ordinary and extraordinary mystery.

religion's inevitable effect on everyday life   Whatever the form of religious response, whether sheer silence, ecstatic frenzy or some more conventional variant, it inevitably affects the routine of everyday life. Empirical and nonempirical awarenesses cannot both inhabit the same human mind without bumping into each other. People cannot acknowledge both a world that meets the eye and an otherness that eludes the senses without seeking to reconcile the two, to relate the now to infinity, the here to eternity, what is beyond human capabilities to what is within them. This is what gives religion its sociological import: not what happened to Moses on the mountaintop but the conclusions he brought down from that journey for the practical conduct of life. Whether religion has disruptive or supportive effects on existing empirical structures depends entirely on the kind of conclusions drawn, the kind of reconciliation or relation made between the beyond and the within. In principle, the more authentic the religious response, the more disruptive its consequences for the status quo. The closer one comes to the ultimate frontier, the more it cavorts in mystery, suspense, freedom, and surprise, by comparison with which the here and now seems to be squatting in boredom and banality. The more purely a person contemplates the fact of limitation itself, the less seriously he or she can take the conventional limitations of current political and economic organization. This is to say that authentic religion is dangerous to the status quo. It liberates people from the tyranny of present order, nourishes creativity, and strengthens the human will. Its precise consequences are indeterminate. They range from monastic withdrawal to intense involvement for the sake of revolutionary change. In any case, the more authentic religion is, the more it contradicts the functionalist and Marxian definitions.

It is to avert the destabilizing, indeterminate effects of authentic religion that societies and groups within them imprison the beyond in words, thus making it less authentic and more accessible. The more such imprisonment takes place, the more religion loses the singular, universal quality to which mystics of all stripes attest, and the more it becomes plural. One group of people calls the beyond God, another Allah, another Brahma, another Manitou, and others still different names. And the imprisonment does not stop there. Any society that can give limitation a name, like "God," can put words in God's mouth. The beyond can then be made to decree rituals of worship, moral laws, explanations for death, reasons for inequality, and excuses for the status quo—all the varied stuff of organized religion. In principle,

the more organized the religion, the less disruptive to the status quo

the more organized a religion is, the better it can play the conservative role functionalists assign to it and the more it is susceptible to the Marxian critique. For once people have been taught to see a reflection of the status quo in their experience of ultimate limitation, that experience not only loses its disruptive qualities but gains supportive ones. If people in a polygamous society believe in gods who practice polygamy, the religion serves not to weaken but to uphold their own purely conventional family organization. Or similarly, divorce in our own society cannot help but be discouraged by those words pronounced often over marriages: "What therefore God has joined together let no man put asunder." The sturdier the religious umbrella a society puts over itself, the less easily do unexpected showers disrupt its plans, and the less likely are its people to be drenched by the liberating waters of uncertainty.

Empirically, of course, no religious response is ever completely simple or totally organized; each falls instead on a continuum between these two extremes. Even mystics have to use props to achieve their experience of ultimacy—a crucifix, for example, a yoga posture, a Hindu mantra, or a Zen dialogue. And for all the rigidity in Roman Catholicism, especially before the reforms of the last two decades, it still had room for the silence and Gregorian chants of Cistercian monks. Within religious groups, moreover, such full-time functionaries as ministers, priests, nuns, and rabbis ordinarily see the beyond more nakedly than most churchgoers and for that reason judge the status quo more harshly. Hence, the social role a particular religion plays in a given setting can only be understood by concrete analysis of where it falls between the poles of authenticity and dogmatism. There are other factors as well. The poor and powerless often contrive religions which, while relatively dogmatic, are nonetheless unfriendly to the mainstream order which

The Jehovah's Witnesses report more than half a million members in the United States, over 2 million worldwide. This religion appeals mainly to powerless, poor, dishonored citizens. That is why this young woman on Upper Broadway in New York offers literature in Spanish. New Yorkers of Hispanic origin, especially those from Puerto Rico, are concentrated in the city's lower socioeconomic strata. (© David Bookbinder, 1975/Peter Arnold, Inc.)

deprives them so. The Jehovah's Witnesses are an example in North America. Those whom a society rewards generously, on the other hand, may espouse religions which combine flexible doctrines and fluid liturgies with blessings on the way things are. Relative to other denominations, the United Church in Canada and the United Methodist Church in the United States illustrate this pattern. In addition, the same religion which supports the social order of one society may threaten that of another. Roman Catholicism cannot easily be considered dangerous to the way of life in Portugal, but it was accurately regarded so in nineteenth-century America. All of this is to say that the social consequences of religion are by no means implied by its definition, but rather by the degree to which it is structured and the particular form that structure takes.

Is religion therefore mere contrivance, a human creation for the sake of human purposes? Insofar as it departs from the rich language of silence, indeed it is. There is no fabrication in admitting that life is a gift or that we are called to surrender ourselves to something beyond the limits of our experience, and thus to realize the plenitude of our being. But any details about that something are no less invented than are national governments, industrial organizations, and scientific theories.

religion's socially constructed character

Moreover, when particular religious myths are regarded as absolutely true and certain, they are fraudulent and deserve to be debunked. Admittedly this comes easier in the case of religions other than our own. We easily laugh at the medieval doctrine of the divine right of kings, for example, and see it for what it was: religious underpadding for regal tyranny, a cushion against the blows of people demanding the right to exercise power. Yet any laughter went unreported at Lyndon Johnson's presidential inauguration in 1965, when a leading churchman intoned the following prayer: "In thy divine Providence, O Heavenly Father, the moral leadership of the world has been entrusted to us: the fate of humanity is in our hands; the nations look to us for survival; western civilization stands or falls with America."[4] Americans find it difficult to read that prayer for what it was: religious underpadding for American hegemony, a cushion against the blows of other nations demanding the right to exercise power.

The plague of disinterested scholarship deserves to fall equally on all houses of worship, even our own. If Muhammad was just a man, then so was Jesus. If the Book of Mormon was conjured up by a human mind, then so were the books of the Bible. If the pope is not infallible, then neither are the gospels. If the Arabs are not God's chosen people, then neither are the Jews. In sum, there are no sacred texts, no moral doctrines, no sacraments, no liturgies, no rituals except those fabricated by people as ordinary as you and I. Sociology textbooks seldom make this point except by innuendo, as if students should be spared the burden of a blunt statement. But so basic an insight from the sociological vantage point should not be left unsaid. For indeed, if it was our very own, merely human, ancestors who wrote the Buddhist Tripitaka, the Hindu Bhagavad Gita, the Islamic Koran, and the Judeo-Christian scriptures, we should not be afraid to speak bluntly with one another. For such books testify to the enormous capacity of the human mind and the everlasting buoyancy of the human spirit. Nor should an awareness of the socially constructed character of particular doctrines and rituals lead us necessarily to abandon all of them. Corporations, currencies, and the rest of our economies are socially constructed, too, transient and contrived, but we do not therefore abandon them. The same goes for religion. We are not complete as human beings unless we act out both our pride and our humility, using the props available in the real historical situation confronting us. But there is no need to claim that any particular kind of acting out, whether economic or religious, is somehow eternally true and infinitely right. I would insult my readers if I allowed them to pretend that we can burst the bubbles of others' absolutes without making our own go poof.

summing up before moving on   We are left, then, with a conception of religion as any kind of mental and physical effort, from stillness to ceremony, created and made in response to limitation, the beyond. Religion is what people do about the fact that they cannot do more. Depending on how it is constructed, it may be either disruptive or supportive of political and economic arrangements. The question remains, however, whether religion is necessary to social life. Can a society survive without a sacred foundation, without some kind of lifeline to a mysterious vessel of beliefs and rituals? Functionalists tend to answer no, while Marxists claim that without religion a society is better off. The three next sections of this chapter address this issue by surveying the empirical status of religion in past and present societies. The first inspects religious change in the broad sweep of history; the next two examine religion, respectively, in contemporary liberal and socialist forms of social organization. In this way can be gained at least a tentative grasp of the enduring empirical regularities with respect to religion, or the lack of it.

Before proceeding, I should acknowledge that this chapter is inevitably narrower and more culture-bound than those on politics and the economy. The reason is not hard to understand. There is more variety in what people imagine goes on beyond the earth than in what actually happens in their experience. Gods can be made to behave in far more diverse and interesting ways than humans are able to themselves. Hence, this chapter can make no more than passing reference to the religions of the East—to Islam, with its roughly 600 million adherents, to Hinduism, with its 500 million, to the 250 million Buddhists, or to the perhaps 200 million Confucianists. Nor can mention be made of the thousands of distinct religious systems among nonindustrial peoples. The following pages are mostly restricted to the Judeo-Christian tradition, whose various branches embrace well over 1 billion people. This tradition predominates in all the national societies in Europe, the Americas, and Australia, and in some of those in Africa and Asia. It is the heritage of capitalist economics and political liberalism. If our focus must be selective, this tradition is the appropriate choice in light not only of the main audience for this book but of the data of world history. It is important, moreover, to include the world's 15 million Jews within the same tradition as the various Christian religions. Judaism spawned Christianity. Almost all Jews outside Israel live in Christian countries today. Israel itself is generally and accurately regarded in the Middle East as an outpost of Western civilization. It is the religion of this civilization that is the principal point of reference in the pages which follow.

Religious Evolution

For understanding how religion has changed over time, we had best begin with the situation of hunters and gatherers—people who live as one with nature, without the know-how and tools necessary to set themselves apart and dominate it. At primitive levels of economic development, people come up against the beyond at every turn. They encounter the caprice of nature with every footstep on a jungle path. They have not learned to delay death. It routinely claims a third or more of babies in their infancy. Those who survive into adulthood have to watch their age-mates die at a rate only people in their seventies experience today in North America. Wild uncertainty pervades daily life with an immediacy we cannot fathom. Doubts about tomorrow nettle people like incessant pins pricking their flesh. Small wonder, then, that our distant ancestors conjured up whole societies of powerful spirits parallel to their own. There were gods of this and gods of that, who together were imagined to control human destiny. No one dared to do anything without first pondering whether the gods would approve or disapprove. People moved in a world in which the differences between them, the creatures of nature and the spirit creatures of their imagination were indistinct. In the absence of economic development, social life was religious to the core because the very stuff of it was limitation. In a sense, religion *was* the primitive economy. People adapted to their milieu by celebrating in myth and ritual their inability to do much about it.

From that point up to the present, religion has generally gone downhill. For as the economy expands, religion contracts. As societies unleash their citizens to act upon the earth, they inevitably curtail the escapades of gods. As the empirical world becomes more interesting, the spirit world becomes less so. As people adopt techniques for doing something in the here and now, they necessarily abstain from procedures for surrendering to the beyond. There is, of course, no universal pattern in how this happens. It is people, after all, who spell out the details not only of their polities and economies but of their religions as well. Hence, we should not be surprised that from the vantage point of the supremely secular present day, the changes in religion that transpired in the ancient past seem to be changes only in kind, not in amount. We tend to think of all premodern peoples as more or less equally religious, differing only in the particular beliefs they adhered to and rituals they practiced. There is some accuracy in this perspective, since not until modern times did people become arrogant enough to flout religion altogether. Nonetheless, a closer look at religious change through the centuries reveals a substantial reduction in the cult of the beyond even before people admitted it to themselves. Four major ways in which this reduction took place are especially important. The following paragraphs review them.

CREATING THE PROFANE

In some rudimentary sense, the first assault on the beyond was to manufacture myths about it. Had our prehistoric forebears allowed themselves to be immobilized by the fact of limitation, frozen spellbound in awe of ultimacy, history would never have happened. Their imposition of words on the beyond was thus an initial, splendidly creative step in the process of getting a grip on the situation of earthly life. But it was also a false step, because stories invented to explain away powerlessness tend to perpetuate it. Better that we trace the beginnings of religion's demise to that point where it is separated out from the rest of life as a distinct set of beliefs and roles. This is, indeed, the first plateau Robert Bellah distinguished in his outline of religious evolution.[5] For once some member of a tribe or village is invested with the specialized role of priest or shaman, other members by definition occupy *less* religious roles. When certain parts of the day or season are reserved for worship, the other parts become less entangled with the cult of limitation. Every place or building designated as sacred implies that space elsewhere is less so. Every idea defined as religious defines other ones as something else. In sum, to identify religion as something special and extraordinary is to make the rest of life ordinary, malleable, and profane and thus to open up an arena for human action on the earth.

The differentiation of religion from the rest of life in the course of economic advance is initially cautious and tentative. Even after religious authority is entrusted to one group while civil authority rests with another, the latter still legitimates its rule by tying it to the spirit world. Even after the gods are physically located in some place of worship, they still lurk behind trees, clouds, and ocean waves, frustrating those adventurers who try to escape from them. And profane ideas are not supposed to transgress the limits of sacred ones, as Copernicus learned in the sixteenth century when he proposed that the earth revolves around the sun,

288

or as Darwin learned in the nineteenth by the reaction of God-fearing people to his theory that our ancestors were apes. Nonetheless, the very existence of the profane gives rise to doubts about the sacred. The profane recognizes the reality of human potential, the possibility of doing something new. In everyday language even today, to call something sacred is to remove it from the domain of legitimate tampering, to deny people the right to work it over. The fewer objects, ideas, places, times, and roles which are defined in this way, and the more clearly the rest are treated as profane, the wider are the opportunities for people to create their own environment. That opportunity first appeared in some prehistoric moment when something was first seized from the sacred and treated as profane.

MANIPULATING THE SUPERNATURAL

It was not only by separating the sacred out from the rest of life that primitive peoples reduced the power of the unknown. They did it also by imagining themselves to be able to harness divine beings and forces, manipulating them for the sake of concrete, immediate human purposes. The rituals, supplications, potions, elixirs, talismans, and fetishes by which they did so are usually called magic. Most scholars distinguish it from religion. The latter implies surrender, a posture of worshipful prostration in the face of the beyond. Magic, on the other hand, is more aggressive. It suggests an attitude of self-confidence. Witches, necromancers, medicine men, and fortune-tellers seek to get on top of the spirit world, to master the forces within it, and to apply them to the solution of specific problems at first hand—like curing someone who is ill, killing an enemy, ensuring a woman's fertility, bringing rain, or strengthening the body for combat. Religion and magic are nowhere very separate, of course. There is an element of magic even in contemporary Christian cultures, when people pray for the health and safety of their friends or light votive candles for special intentions. Nor is the evidence clear as to which came first, the worship of the divine or its manipulation. But it is important to see in the latter the beginnings of boldness and courage in the face of the unknown. That is why ancient peoples always gave more prestige and trust to specialists in worship like prophets and priests than to performers of magical rites. To surrender to the beyond seemed an attitude of obvious propriety. To play with it was arrogant and therefore dangerous.

the aggressiveness of magic versus worshipful prostration in religion

Magic has mostly disappeared from contemporary industrial societies, and the term now ordinarily refers only to sleight of hand. In truth, magic was doomed to extinction from the start, because it sought both to affirm powers beyond human control and to control them. Thus did it threaten both religion (by contradicting its meaning) and profane science (by locating its subject matter in the realm of the sacred). The Roman Catholic Church, for example, has kept a posture of official reserve toward Lourdes, Guadalupe, and other places of pilgrimage where people are thought to be magically restored to health, while the medical profession has been no less skeptical. Economic development, especially in Western civilization, has called for an ever-sharper distinction between the sacred and profane aspects of life on earth. Because magic falls in the middle, it disappears. The shamans of modern societies insist that the forces they manipulate are not supernatural but natural, a legitimate part of the profane world and thus vulnerable to unembar-

"Religion and magic are nowhere very separate, of course. There is an element of magic even in contemporary Christian cultures, when people pray for the health and safety of their friends or light votive candles for special intentions." This little girls lights her candle in the Holy Virgin Mary Russian Orthodox Church in Los Angeles. (© Craig Aurness 1978/Woodfin Camp & Assoc.)

rassed human ingenuity. Scientists and physicians today work with self-assured and confident awareness of their abilities, and their cultures value boldness and courage in the face of a profane unknown. These contemporary practitioners owe a debt, nonetheless, to ancient sorcerers who dared to confront what was then the supernatural and to manipulate it toward precise and concrete ends.

REDUCING THE DIVINE POPULATION

how the shift to monotheism can best be understood

A third characteristic of religion in premodern times reflects even more clearly the growing pugnacity of people toward forces beyond their control. It is the shift from polytheism to monotheism. In 1975 and 1976, the *American Journal of Sociology* published an earnest debate on this topic between two respected scholars, Ralph Underhill from Dartmouth and G. E. Swanson from Berkeley.[6] The first argued, following Marx and Engels, that technological complexity is the key source of belief in a single, supreme god, that the farther a society advances beyond simple hunting and gathering, the more likely it is to abandon polytheism. Through analysis of data on more than a thousand societies, Underhill reported empirical support for his hypothesis. Swanson, on the other hand, a disciple of Durkheim, had earlier attributed the origin of monotheism to the presence in a society of multiple sovereign groups arranged in a hierarchy. He had reasoned that once a society becomes differentiated into a number of distinct subunits based on kinship, age, political administration, or whatever, it needs to believe in one ultimate god as a sacred model for its own integration. Swanson therefore did his own analysis of the same data and concluded that Underhill relied too much on economic factors in the explanation for monotheism. The debate concluded for the nonce in a later issue of the journal, with Underhill challenging Swanson's sample of societies and Swanson doubting the adequacy of Underhill's operational definitions.

It was a shame that the debate ended in bickering about fine points of method, for Underhill and Swanson had more in common than they seemed to realize. In the former's Marxian perspective, the one god emerges as an abstract, alienating, summary symbol of the natural and social constraints on human enterprise—the final religious obstacle to further progress. In the latter's functionalist view, the one god symbolically binds together the diverse parts of a developing society and thus signifies progress already made. But whether one looks forward or backward, the fact is that one god requires less attention than many. Economically active societies reduce their gods to one for the same reason that assiduous individuals consolidate their debts: one overwhelming problem is easier to deal with than a bundle of exasperating little ones, and it leaves more time free for thinking about other things. A vast pantheon of deities demands an exorbitant amount of time and energy. The gods quarrel with one another and each envies sacrifices made to appease other ones. Men and women can keep themselves busy just trying to placate the diverse and cantankerous beings with which they have peopled the beyond. Monotheism, by contrast, means less in the beyond to worry about and more time free for action upon nature. It represents above all the simplification of religion, a shift in attention from what transcends human capabilities to what awakens them. Monotheism can best be understood as one step along the path of economic development, an attack upon the gods that eliminates all but one.

the demise of polytheism is not abrupt nor yet complete

The transition to monotheism is not, of course, abrupt. Only gradually during the thousand years before the birth of Jesus did the Jews abandon other gods than Yahweh. The Christian heaven, moreover, hardly has but one occupant. The one god is composed of three persons, surrounded by angels, archangels, and all the heavenly host and hated by Satan and his followers. The church of Rome permitted the heavens to be populated also with saints—dead people who led exemplary lives and who might now intercede with the one god on behalf of the living. Foremost among them was Mary, the mother of Jesus, whose statue still graces virtually every Catholic church. In nonindustrial parts of the Christian world even today, people still live in close awareness of the numerous personages in the spirit world. They hang their pictures in living rooms, speak to them in prayer, erect shrines to them in fields, and place flowers before their images at church. In more industrialized Christian settings and especially where Protestantism flourishes, the cult of angels, Mary, and the other saints falls into neglect. Modern Christians tend not so much to annihilate these companions of the one god as to ignore them. Instead of praying to St. Anthony when something is lost, they scurry about in search of it. Driving down expressways they think about oncoming traffic more than about St. Christopher. For safety on unlit streets at night they trust police officers more than their guardian angels. Thus do the conditions of an industrialized, developing society shrink the galaxy of sacred personalities and leave but a single god—at most.

MAKING GODS INTO MEN

*the need for caution in
positing social effects of
religious beliefs*

A fourth assault upon the heavens and the last to be discussed in the present context was the creation of Christianity itself, the mythology of Jesus Christ. This is an important point, but one which requires a cautionary note in preface. The connection is always tenuous between particular beliefs about heaven and concrete ways of behaving on earth. Religious knowledge is poetic, suggestive, full of overtones and undercurrents, and therefore congenial to diverse practical implications. No chain of logic ties articles of faith in the beyond to immediate acts in everyday life; at most they are joined by drifting threads of nuance and emphasis. During the 1960s, there was much research and controversy in U.S. sociology over the question of whether Christian beliefs "cause" anti-Semitism.[7] The debate struck me as no less arid than the Peruvian desert described earlier in this chapter. It is hardly impossible to infer from Christian doctrine a political mandate to persecute Jews. Many people did just that in Nazi Germany, to cite but the most glaring example. Yet others in that same time and place deduced from the same Christian doctrine a moral obligation to resist Nazism and defend Jewish rights. Christianity, like all the great religious traditions, is rich and diverse enough to sustain numerous and contradictory interpretations. It does not "cause" anything. At most it lends itself a bit more easily to some practical applications than to others. In light of the diverse data within Christian history, careful scholars think twice before asserting to what kind of political practice the Christian faith is most favorably inclined.

*nonetheless, the
dramatic impact of the
gospel of Jesus Christ*

Even after thinking thrice and four times, however, it is hard not to infer an eminently practical lesson from the doctrine of the joint humanity and divinity of Jesus. It was not unusual in ancient religions for a god to meddle in human affairs, to speak to selected individuals, or even to assume temporarily a human form. But Christian theology was bold enough to pull god out of heaven directly onto earth. What greater honor and distinction could befall people than for the one god to send his only son to be born as a fully human being, to grow up, work, preach, eventually suffer a murderous death, and then come back to life, all for the sake of redeeming them? How better could people assert their majesty than by believing that god had made his own son one of them, and then sacrificed that son in crucifixion on their behalf? Even more than the Jews' belief in their status as the one god's chosen people, the doctrine of the god-man, Jesus, implied an incredibly high appraisal of the human race. It became the most sacred doctrine in all of Christian theology. Early in the fourth century, a Greek priest named Arius attracted a following with his theory that Jesus was not quite divine, but only an exceptionally holy man. The church of Rome vigorously came to Jesus' defense— and the defense of humanity. At the Council of Nicaea in 325, it condemned Arianism as heresy and promulgated a creed often recited in Christian liturgies even now: "Begotten, not made; Being of one substance with the Father; By whom all things were made: Who for us men and for our salvation came down from heaven, And was incarnate by the Holy Ghost of the Virgin Mary, And was made man."

There is no need to insist that industrialization could never have occurred in the absence of Christianity. Any number of religious myths might have flattered people enough that they could make the headlong strides in economic advance of Western civilization. Nor should the pride evident in Christological doctrine obscure other, more depressant aspects of Christian theology. Nonetheless, it was Christian cultures which first reached self-consciousness of human prowess and which have led the world to its present level of development. In the context of historical events, the fundamental myth of Christianity must be seen as an important step in the redirection of human interest away from the heavens toward the earth. No less than monotheism, the Christian religion diminished the divine. The first eliminated all gods but one, the second brought the son of the one remaining down to earth, where he became a sacrifice for the redemption of human beings. Henceforth, when people worshipped and prayed, it could be to one of their own kind—to a man who had walked around Palestine, gone fishing and enjoyed a glass of wine, cherished friends and felt the pain of their fickleness. This was not the only religion even in the ancient world to manufacture gods with exceedingly high opinions of humankind. But it is hard to find earlier myths more unashamed than Christian ones of their celebration of the goodness of the human race.

IN SUMMARY

The four developments just reviewed should be enough to make the point that long before church attendance began to dwindle in North America, Western societies were recoiling from a posture of total surrender to the supernatural and overhauling their religion in a way that diminished it. By carving out ever-larger niches of profanity in the sacred edifice of social life, by manipulating unknown forces first magically and later scientifically, by steadily depleting the heavenly population, and by affirming the doctrine of Jesus' divinity, our forebears curtailed the cult of the beyond even as they enlarged the scope of action upon nature. This fact should not startle us. The preceding chapter made it clear that economic development is far from a recent phenomenon, that it is traceable even to the era of the dog's domestication. It would be anomalous if the demise of religion had not begun equally as long ago. Ours is not the first generation to make history. Neither is it the first to rebel against the gods. For whenever it was that the economy began to brighten, religion started to fade.

religious innovation in premodern times lacked self-consciousness   Nonetheless, religious innovations in the distant past gained acceptance mainly through charismatic outbursts, unself-conscious shifts in belief about the "true" nature of the beyond. Premodern peoples lacked awareness that it was they who invented new beliefs and rituals. The myths they came to adopt affirmed a prouder self-image of the human race, but they did not embrace the myths proudly and thoughtfully. They submitted to them humbly and ecstatically, moved by the extrinsic weight of the experience of conversion, as if seized by uncontrollable alien forces. The books of the New Testament document this process in the case of Christianity. The prototypical example is Paul, who despite his erudition hardly reasoned his way to faith in Jesus Christ. In the biblical account, he was on his way to Damascus in the midst of a campaign against Christians when a light flashed from heaven. "And he fell to the ground and heard a voice saying to him, 'Saul, Saul, why do you persecute me?' And he said, 'Who are you, Lord?' And he said, 'I am Jesus, whom you are persecuting; but rise and enter the city, and you will be told what you are to do.' " Paul found himself blind when he arose. His blindness lasted three days, until the Lord sent Ananias to visit him. "And immediately something like scales fell from his eyes and he regained his sight. Then he rose and was baptized."[8] The tale of Paul's conversion is a paradigm of the way religious evolution happened in the premodern world—a sense of being overpowered by the forces of the beyond, directed by them to espouse a new definition of what they are.

For all its novelty, Christianity therefore represented but one more new certainty. While it solved the problem of human limitation with unprecedented optimism, the solution was offered no less dogmatically than were those of the religions it replaced in the Middle East, Europe, and elsewhere. The early Christians, like premodern peoples everywhere, failed to realize that their myths were their own handiwork and a legitimate object for further modification. Instead they claimed nonhuman authorship for the good news of Jesus. They felt themselves worthy only to believe in it, publish it, preach it, and convert others to it. Thus did Christianity fall prey to the process Weber labeled the routinization of charisma. Its good news became old news. Prophecy yielded to parrotry. An organization gradually emerged, headquartered in Rome, tied to the Roman Empire, and serving to legitimate the mostly unchanging status quo of medieval Europe. In concert with political authorities, the church of Rome successfully squelched most innovative religious movements, like the Donatists in the fourth century and the Waldensians in the twelfth century. Other such movements it co-opted and incorporated into itself. Such religious orders as the Benedictines, Cistercians, Franciscans, Dominicans, and Jesuits were allowed to survive as safety valves, providing a legitimate outlet for the creative energies of those who might otherwise have subverted the stability of Christendom.[9]

the routinization of Jesus' charisma in the medieval Christian church

In the estimation of most historians, the routinization or institutionalization of Christianity reached its apex in the thirteenth century. The papacy of Innocent III (1198–1216) ushered the era in. A skilled bureaucrat and politician, Innocent systematized the organization of the church throughout Western Europe and cleverly bent beneath his will the kings of France, Germany, and England, and lesser ones besides. He was an heroic contradiction of his name. His courts of inquisition routinely tried and convicted heretics, afterwards turning them over to state authorities for execution. His Lateran Council in 1215 decreed that all Jews should wear yellow labels, thus making their pariah status recognizable at first glance. Great Gothic cathedrals rose all over the continent. Those at Westminster, Cologne, Chartres, Salisbury, and Paris remain to remind us today of the tidiness of the High Medieval world. That same order is reflected as well in the tight, logical, all-encompassing books of the thirteenth-century theologians, above all Thomas Aquinas. It was as if everything had at last been made to fit—stones, mortar, Jesus, Aristotle, popes, kings, monks, peasants, the rich, and the poor—everything in a neat Christian bundle. There were answers for all the important questions about the human predicament. The idea of making history seemed preposterous. History had already been made when the one god sent his son to earth. The rest of time was a denouement. Thus was the situation ripe for new plots by eternally restless human beings, fresh attacks on the gods that would open the way for more economic action on the earth. The revolution came with the Protestant Reformation.

Religion under Liberal Capitalism

The unity of Christendom had already been shattered by the time the Reformation broke out. In 1054, the bishops of eastern Europe, what was then the Byzantine Empire, had severed their ties with Rome, thus formalizing a long-standing antagonism and establishing the autonomy of orthodox Christianity. Most of these bishops, moreover, had then come under the sway of various governments and immersed Christianity in their respective national cultures, creating thereby the family of distinct orthodox churches which exists today—Albanian, Armenian, Bulgarian, Greek, Romanian, Russian, Serbian, and others as well. In England, meanwhile, Henry VIII (1491–1547) had defied the pope, subjected the English bishops to his sole authority and laid the foundation of an autonomous Anglican church. The creation of these national churches was a blow to religion in the areas where it occurred, since it implied the supremacy of political over ecclesiastical authority. Nonetheless, this in itself was nothing new—some earlier popes had been mere puppets of Roman emperors. Nor did the fledgling national churches alter substantially the age-old doctrines and rituals. Whether in Moscow, Constantinople, London, Paris, or Rome, Christianity at the dawn of the sixteenth century was more or less equally full of symbolic justification of the traditional order, about equally drained of the humane optimism in its seldom studied scriptures. Against this background, the Protestant reformers voiced new versions of the Christian faith.

Even in so brief a review as this, the impression must be avoided that Protestantism was or is in any sense a doctrinally or organizationally unified movement. Its two most imposing leaders, Martin Luther (1483–1546) in Germany and John Calvin (1509–1564) in France and Switzerland, differed sharply in their ideas. And clearly, despite the prophetic impact of these two men, the Reformation neither started nor ended with them. John Wycliffe (1320–1384), who first translated the Bible into English and encouraged the reforms of the Lollards, foreshadowed Luther and Calvin by a century and a half; so did Jan Hus (1369–1415), a Bohemian prophet whose followers came to be called Moravians. Later religious rebels, too, deserve to be classed as progenitors of Protestantism: John Cotton (1584–1652), who raised Puritan dissent against Anglicanism, George Fox (1624–1691), who founded Quakerism, Cotton Mather (1663–1728), who championed Puritanism in America, and John Wesley (1703–1791), the founder of Methodism, to name but a few. Protestantism is best understood as a storm of dissent against traditional Christianity, a storm which gathered slowly and then swept through central Europe in the sixteenth century. It later infiltrated the Church of England and became the dominant religion of Great Britain, British North America, Scandinavia, and parts of Holland, Germany, and Switzerland. Previous chapters have already described how it encouraged both development and democracy, nourished the liberal-capitalist strategy for achieving these goals, and thereby engendered the first widespread self-consciousness of human capabilities. The task here is to understand Protestantism in the context of religious evolution.

In the very name of this movement lies the key to understanding it. Its name is

negative, not positive. Luther, Calvin, their followers, and other Protestants were not defined as a group by what kind of beliefs and rituals they were *for*. These were varied and conflicting. They are defined by what they were *against*. Unlike the Hebrew storytellers, unlike Jesus, his apostles, and the fathers of the early Christian church, also unlike Joseph Smith (1805–1844), who wrote the Book of Mormon, the leaders of Protestantism were more interested in nullifying established myths than in manufacturing new ones. Their program was not just a reformation of religion but a reduction. Their effect was not so much to reshape Christianity as to simplify it. Both in its beginnings and in later centuries, the Protestant movement was basically a fresh assault upon the gods, an incarceration of religion in a smaller cage than humans had yet devised. Four ways in which the attack was made are especially noteworthy.

not just a reformation, but a reduction as well

First, the Protestants jettisoned the vast corpus of canon law, saints' biographies, papal encyclicals, conciliar documents, and tomes of scholastic theology in favor of a single volume, the Bible, which they defined as the sole authoritative source of knowledge about the beyond. All of a sudden the sacred literature a Christian had to worry about contracted to what could be contained within the covers of a single book. Reformers wrote treatises, of course, and groups of their followers published catechisms and prayer books, but none of these was thought to be divinely inspired, truly sacred, or beyond the jurisdiction of ordinary men and women. Only the Bible enjoyed such status. Second, the Protestants proclaimed that every Christian had the right to read and interpret the Bible personally, without regard for clerical authority. This doctrine, the priesthood of all believers, undermined religious organization not only at the level of the papacy but even at that of the local church. The Protestant clergyman could never be the equal of a priest, that indispensable link to the saving grace of Jesus Christ, but only the leader of a congregation of Christians, each of whom could make his or her own link through personal faith. By permitting as many interpretations of the Bible as there were interpreters, Protestantism challenged not just the Roman church but *any* kind of seriously organized Christianity. A Protestant church can never quite be a public bureaucracy: by the theology on which it is founded, it remains basically a voluntary association.

only the Bible, and even it was opened to private interpretation

Third, the reformers eliminated most of the sacraments, rituals, ceremonies, art, and architecture of the medieval church, thus depriving people of symbols for the cult of limitation. Protestant Christians at worship could not rest their eyes and ears on a rich vocabulary of sacred gestures, words, and artifacts, as Catholic Christians could at mass. Protestants had to work at their religious services, since only their own ardent participation could give meaning and value to the simple liturgies they performed. Fourth and finally, by redefining monastic withdrawal as silliness instead of sanctity, the reformers forced people to evaluate themselves in terms of the political and economic reality at hand. By forbidding disengagement from the status quo, they required people to take it seriously. "This-worldly asceticism" is what Weber called the Protestant style of religion: purposeful, disciplined involvement in empirical life for the sake of working out one's personal salvation.

the simplification of symbols and rejection of otherworldly ideals

296

In these four and in other ways, the Protestant movement enclosed religion more firmly than ever before in the privacy of the individual conscience and thus enlarged the realm of profane action. Specifically, the Protestant kind of Christianity made it possible to think of a political and economic order free of identification with any structure of religious authority. The state might henceforth be Christian without either subjecting itself to the will of popes and bishops or sponsoring particular kinds of ritual and belief. In other words, Protestantism made the separation of church and state a possibility. The significance of this innovation easily escapes us, since by now in northwestern Europe and North America it is a commonplace. What is important to realize is that church-state separation, while it seemed to benefit dissident religious minorities, was the bane of religion itself. It was not a freeing of religion from the polity but the reverse, a wrenching of government from the realm of the sacred, a recognition that mere human beings could make politics on their own. Freedom of religion is in this sense but a euphemistic way of saying freedom *from* religion. Once the state can act on people and they on it without regard for myths about the beyond, once such myths are legally irrelevant to the basic order of social life, they can be forgotten with impunity.

wrenching politics from an untouchable domain

Like most outstanding features of life on earth, church-state separation is a process, not an event. It has been realized but gradually. An initial step was taken with the Peace of Augsburg in 1555, which recognized religious pluralism among cities and principalities in central Europe. The Edict of Nantes was a further step in 1598; it promised toleration to the Huguenots of France. Religious wars broke out again early in the seventeenth century, however, and only with the Peace of Westphalia in 1648 was the pope's authority over international politics effectively ended. By then, the most promising advance against religion had already been made on the other side of the Atlantic. In 1636, Roger Williams had founded the colony of Rhode Island in British North America, grounding its government in only general Christian principles and assuring to all the right to believe and worship as they pleased. A century and a half later, the new American republic adopted as the first amendment to its Constitution: "Congress shall make no law respecting an establishment of religion, or prohibiting the free exercise thereof." By placing its government outside the realm of the sacred, subject only to the democratic will of the electorate, the United States affirmed itself as the first and clearest national embodiment of the principles of the Reformation.

The idea of church-state separation has been implemented only in tandem with the theory of liberal capitalism, of which it is an integral part. By this theory, the essence of a society is profane. It consists in active, innovative, independent individuals producing, exchanging, and consuming commodities for the sake of profit in an unrestrained market. The state is a champion of profanity, safeguarding each person's almost unlimited right to handle property as he or she sees fit. Religion, according to this theory, is legally and structurally an optional pastime, a hobby or diversion, a voluntary, nonprofit respite from the market for those who

the voluntary character
of religious practice
under liberal capitalism

seek to engage in it. People are free to hire ministers, build churches, and send their children to Sunday school in the same way that they can freely build nudist colonies, golf courses, and private clubs. All these voluntary associations cost money, and they require people to forego some of the profit they could make if they invested their money instead. But under liberal capitalism, that is for people to decide themselves, as autonomous individuals. So long as cults of limitation do not directly challenge the limitless growth of a free market, so long as religion does not interfere with the profane economic structure, it is a private matter with which government is unconcerned.

Under liberal-capitalist sovereign states, therefore, organized religion assumes a character categorically different from that in traditional Western societies. Prior to the Reformation, Europe displayed only three kinds of organization specialized in the affairs of the supernatural. There was first of all the *universal church*, Roman Catholicism, with branches in numerous nations and states, in each of which it enjoyed governmental patronage and recognition. There was secondly the *established church*, best represented by Anglicanism and Russian Orthodoxy, which identified itself with a particular national culture and was joined to a single regime. Third was the illegitimate, persecuted, minority *sect*, Jewish or heretical-Christian, an ethnic or voluntary association of dissenters from the official religious and political order. Protestantism, however, and the liberal-capitalist theory it generated, rejected all three of these types of religious organization in favor of a new one: legitimate but not established, voluntary but not persecuted, legal but deprived of

the shift from churches
and sects to
denominations,
especially in the United
States

governmental patronage, secure so long as it lets the economy alone. For want of a better term, sociologists usually call this type of religious organization simply a *denomination*.[10] In the hands of the poor and propertyless, it may proclaim the world as wicked and seem sectlike. Fundamentalist Baptist and Pentecostal groups are cases in point. In the hands of the wealthy, the denomination may build cathedrals as grand as those of an established church. Episcopalians in the United States come to mind. But the formal legal status is the same for the religions of both the rich and the poor in a liberal-capitalist society. They are just denominations, supernatural hobbies for those who are interested.

As the archetype of liberal capitalism, the United States demonstrates with unique clarity the denominational form of religious organization. As of 1978, roughly 60 percent of the population voluntarily belonged to a religious congregation, some participating actively and frequently, others doing little more than keeping their names on the rolls. There were in that year more than 200 distinct denominations, from large ones like the Southern Baptist Convention (13 million members) and the United Methodist Church (10 million) to such small ones as the Pentecostal Fire-Baptized Holiness Church (545 members) or the Primitive Advent Christian Church (514 members). Most U.S. denominations are organized more democratically than the government itself, with local congregations retaining the power of the purse and the controlling voice in the selection of ministers. Aside from tax concessions and a few special prerogatives, these religious associations get no more favors from government than do recreational or political ones. In 1976, Seventh-Day Adventists spent an average of $522 each in support of their denomination; the figure was similarly high for most of the sectlike religious bodies. Episcopalians, by contrast, contributed a mere $186 per person in the same year,

United Methodists only $110. The mainline denominations are generally less energetic than other ones. The latter tend to sponsor a wide range of activities, from summer camps to mission programs, all of them colored by the particular beliefs of the membership, but always in the context of an economic and political order from which organized religion is structurally separate.[11]

Roman Catholicism in America

American-style denominationalism posed, especially in the early years of the republic, a vexing problem for the Roman Catholic Church. As the embodiment of Protestant principles, the United States stood for everything Rome was against. For in response to the Reformation, the Catholic church had dug its heels into traditional turf and secured its age-old position in Spain, Portugal, Spanish and Portuguese America, Italy, Poland, Ireland, Austria, Belgium, Hungary, Lithuania, parts of Germany, Holland, and Switzerland, and to some extent in France. But Catholics from these countries immigrated to the United States, some even before the war of independence, about 35 million of them in the fifteen decades afterward. What was the Vatican to do, betray its principles and establish itself in America in the lowly status of denomination, or abandon the Catholic immigrants and watch them convert to Protestantism? The Vatican chose a middle course. It resolutely condemned the structure of American society; in 1899, Pope Leo XIII damned an assortment of heresies with the label *Americanism*. At the same time, however, Rome appointed bishops in America, let them build seminaries and ordain priests, and encouraged them to create a formally voluntary insular subsociety for Catholics within American borders. Much of this subsociety still exists: about 10,000 private Catholic schools in 1978, with more than 3 million pupils, about 250 private Catholic colleges and universities enrolling 400,000 students, about 800 Catholic hospitals treating 25 million patients annually. There are also Catholic welfare agencies, cemeteries, and homes for senior citizens. Effectively what happened is that American Catholics were persuaded to create inside the United States a partial replica of a genuinely Catholic society, but all in the private sector. In great part they succeeded. As of 1978, the Catholic church was the largest U.S. denomination, embracing nearly a quarter of the population, about 37 percent of all church members.

religion elsewhere in the capitalist world

Australia and New Zealand placed organized religion in a denominational status, much like that in America. Like the United States, the New World societies down under welcomed immigrants to a basically Protestant and capitalist social order and permitted them to practice their various faiths as voluntary associations. Elsewhere in the capitalist world, however, the separation of church and state is not quite as clear. In England, Anglicanism has still not completely relinquished its public, official status and accepted a Protestant definition of itself. It is still an institution of English life, the religion of royalty and the popular majority, and hence integrated into the social order more than any denomination in America. The same goes for the Calvinist Church of Scotland to the north and the Lutheran church in all the Scandinavian societies and in Finland. Nonetheless, all of these societies have defined religion ever more clearly as a private matter, deprived religious authorities of all but symbolic roles, and granted freedom of religious expression to nonconforming minorities.

A separation of church and state as sharp as that in the United States has been still more difficult in those societies where the Roman Catholic Church was already deeply entrenched in a sizable minority of the population by the time a liberal-capitalist government came to power. Four societies in this category are especially noteworthy: Canada, the Netherlands, the Federal Republic of Germany, and Switzerland. In each of these, compromises were worked out which permit the Catholic church to retain some measure of public institutional status, at least in certain locales. The Netherlands is the most interesting case, its population being divided into Protestant and Catholic columns, each one served by distinct, officially recognized systems of education, health, and welfare. Major Dutch political parties also bear religious identification. As for Canada, previous chapters have already described the special status of the Catholic church in Quebec, a status which has been reduced during the last two decades but which has hardly disappeared. In Newfoundland, Ontario, Saskatchewan, and Alberta, moreover, there are two distinct, publicly funded school systems, one for Catholics and the other for everyone else. Nonetheless, it is only by comparison with denominations in the United States that those elsewhere in the liberal-capitalist world seem still intertwined with the public order of social life. In actuality, governments in all these societies are today clearly profane agencies, human creations, markedly separate from organized forms of religious expression.[12]

SECULARIZATION

The Reformation did more than encapsulate Christianity, placing it in a private sphere detached from the public order of government and the market economy. In a sense, Protestantism was the religion to end all religions. For as Chapters Five and Six have already made clear, the capitalist economy to which it gave rise is inherently dynamic, forever growing, relentless in its pursuit of novelty and development. I have already described capitalism as a one-sided strategy of economic advance, a tactical denial of human limitation, an acknowledgment of only the proud side of the dialectic of human nature. Capitalism pushes people into the sea of a competitive market and forces them to swim persistently toward profit as if there were no point of exhaustion, no moment of death. We should not, therefore, be surprised that the social prominence of religion has generally dwindled still further, the longer the capitalist strategy has been pursued and the more it has proven itself as a technique of economic development. This is to say that Protestantism not only reduced and simplified religion but also set in motion an active, aware, arrogant, ever-growing celebration of possible tomorrows, one which makes people forget about infinity more and more.

progress on capitalist principles implies retrogression for religion

The label usually applied to the more recent demise of religion is *secularization*. Among its best-known contemporary analysts are Bryan Wilson at Oxford University in England and Peter Berger at Boston College in the United States. The latter has defined secularization as "the process by which sectors of society and culture are removed from the domination of religious institutions and symbols."[13] Church-state separation, as the legal denial of a political role to organized religion, is an initial and basic part of the process, but there is more. For even after religion has been reduced to a private, voluntary activity, it can still be so popular that it pervades most facets of everyday life. This was clearly the case in the nineteenth century throughout the capitalist world. Christian symbolism and prayer were a routine part of public education, political debate, and leisure activities. From that point to the present, voluntary religious expression has generally declined in all the capitalist societies. On the basis of national survey data collected in 1975, Canadian sociologist Reginald Bibby has estimated that about half of all adults in that country have simply lost interest in their Judeo-Christian heritage: "Rather than turning to religious answers new and old, these Canadians consciously and unconsciously, rationally and non-rationally limit reality to the perceivable (*empiricism*) and in everyday life live out the correlate of *materialism*, whereby the perceivable world becomes the object of their attention and commitment."[14] This is what secularization means above all, and it appears no less in Western Europe and Great Britain than in Canada, and but slightly less in the United States. The following paragraphs summarize four kinds of evidence for this trend.

four signs of secularization: first, dwindling church attendance

First is that church attendance has generally fallen off during the last two decades. This decline is important, but it must be understood in context. Even at the height of Christendom, the average medieval European attended mass less often than once a week, and millions of undeniably religious Latin American men seldom set foot on church steps even today. The reason church attendance is taken more seriously in the United States and other capitalist societies is that once religion is denied a formal, public, political role in social structure, regular participation in voluntary worship services becomes the major quasi-public means of acknowledging the sacred. When the economy insists that nothing is beyond human capabilities, people have to go to church in order to acknowledge their limitations. Only in this light is it significant that as of 1978, a mere 40 percent of Americans attended church weekly, a mere third of Canadians, and even smaller proportions of Western Europeans. Churchgoing itself, moreover, today as in the past, hardly springs from exclusively religious motivation. As in the case of voluntary associations generally, denominational get-togethers may serve such diverse purposes as ethnic solidarity, sociable recreation, neighborhood morale, entertainment of children, political protest, and community betterment, all of these quite distinct from the cult of the supernatural. The actual social significance of going to church varies widely by age, sex, educational level, income stratum, denomination, and other factors. There is always a hint of religion in it and often much more. But church attendance remains in any case almost the only opportunity citizens have to assert religion in public life. That is why the decline in attendance is so worthy of note.

second, the decline of religious institutions

Second, and related to church attendance as a measure of secularization, is membership in the denominations, their overall organizational strength. In both Canada and the United States, many of the smaller, fundamentalist, sectlike religious bodies have actually grown substantially during the last fifteen years. The more important trend, by contrast, is the precipitous decline of the mainline Protestant and Catholic denominations. Between 1965 and 1976, the Anglican and United churches in Canada each suffered a net loss in membership, even as the Canadian population was growing steadily. In the same period, the U.S. population increased by about 11 percent, while the membership of the Episcopal, United Presbyterian, and United Methodist churches declined by 15 percent, 13 percent, and 10 percent respectively. For the Lutheran Church in America, the decline was

3 percent. The U.S. branch of the Catholic church grew during these eleven years by about 7 percent, but the population of Catholic nuns was reduced by more than a quarter, the number of priests declined as well, and there was a net loss of more than 3500 Catholic schools. Another measure of the decline of the denominations is the U.S. government's report that if the effects of inflation are set aside, less than half as much money was spent annually on the construction of new religious buildings in the late 1970s as in the late 1950s and early 1960s. These varied data tend to confirm the casual impressions of everyday life. One need only compare the local church to a nearby bank, and observe which is kept in better repair and bedecked with the more carefully manicured shrubs.[15]

third, encroachments on religious domains

A third kind of evidence for the secularization process is penetration by government agencies, professions, and businesses into fields formerly tinged with religion and controlled by the denominations. Higher education is the clearest example. In 1813, a Protestant commentator reviewed the 23 colleges and universities by then established in the United States. He praised those 8 "which adopt the Bible as the rule of faith without any supplement, and whose system of instruction favours rational and simple Christianity."[16] He deplored the 15 remaining, which additionally impressed upon their students' minds "sectarian pecularities"—whether Presbyterian, Papal, Episcopal, or some other kind. By 1979, only about a quarter of the 1500 colleges and universities in the United States were in any way connected with such peculiarities, and these struggling little schools enrolled fewer than 10 percent of all undergraduate students. The process is even farther advanced in English Canada, where all but a few denominational colleges survive only as adjuncts to large, public, secular universities, free of any rule of religious faith, biblical or otherwise. In neither society nor elsewhere in the capitalist world has the state actively sought to eliminate religious institutions of higher education. It has simply let them fade away for lack of financial support, meanwhile giving tax money to secular alternatives.

But this is not the only area of secular entry into a once religious domain. Psychiatrists and other physicians today hear many of the confessions once told to priests. People take their family problems increasingly to certified counselors instead of ministers. Secular nurses far outnumber nuns in hospitals, and by an ever-increasing margin. Municipal recreation centers serve a purpose once left to church basements, the YM-YWCA, masonic lodges, and Knights of Columbus halls. For wedding dinners people rely steadily more on caterers and less on the ladies at church. If Jewish businessmen have doubts about taxation ethics, they are more likely to let accountants resolve them than to seek out a rabbi. Undertakers and insurance agents provide comfort to the bereaved, thus encroaching on a prime clerical duty. Catholics all across North America used to travel in pilgrimage to shrines; now the shrines compete unsuccessfully with packaged holidays in the Sunbelt. Most of these intruders into the domain of religious denominations barely existed until the last half-century, but day by day they seize more of that domain. What social significance the denominations still have is mainly in those few areas where they have secured governmental recognition and funding for some task they perform. Examples are Jewish and Catholic family and children's services in

Canada and the United States, separate Catholic schools in Canada, and some denominational hospitals in both countries. With such exceptions, secular agencies have steadily taken over purposes once served by people in religious roles and under religious authority.

*fourth, the churches'
identification of divine
with human power*

Fourth and finally, the process of secularization is evident not only in the demise of denominations but also in shifts toward this-worldliness in their own rituals, beliefs, programs, and architecture. Among the innovations are folk-song liturgies, outreach programs, sensitivity sessions and "group raps," drop-in centers and community ministries, conversational homilies, and a variety of other novel activities justified by new theologies that emphasize the "immanence of God," that is, the identification of divine with human power. These new religious practices have appeared in most major Protestant denominations and, all the more remarkably, in the Catholic church. Old-timers tend to resist these reforms, claiming that they dilute the religious substance of Christianity. Proponents of the trendy innovations insist that they only make Christianity more modern. In a sense both sides are right. Modernity, as defined many pages ago, is self-conscious human creativity. Clearly the changes reflect such creativity and proclaim the goodness of an active humanity. But the old-timers are also right, because religion is the converse of modernity. Religion is self-conscious affirmation of the *limits* of human prowess, awareness that something is *beyond* our strength. It is this affirmation, this awareness, that most of the recent modifications to mainline Christianity in the capitalist world have tended to suppress.

*the significance of
Riverside Church*

Perhaps the most striking symbol of the secularization of American religion is a magnificent Protestant edifice overlooking the Hudson River in New York City. It was built in 1931. Riverside Church is remarkable not only because the headquarters of the National Council of Churches stands next door to it, nor because Rockefeller money helped pay for it, nor for the intricacy of its Gothic architecture, nor still for its interdenominational, nondoctrinal status. What makes the church so extraordinary is its celebration of the secular. In the statuary of the chancel screen behind the altar, Jesus and Paul are required to share space with Florence Nightingale, Abraham Lincoln, Booker T. Washington, Johann Sebastian Bach, Sir Joseph Lister, and other heroes of human ingenuity. Graven images of Newton, Pasteur, Kepler, and Einstein perch over the main entrance. Stained-glass windows depict the Declaration of Independence, Kantian philosophy, the invention of the radio, and similar subjects. Scientists are carved into choir-stall armrests, along with singing angels. More dramatically than any book, Riverside Church tells the story of the American denominations, even as its construction foreshadowed by forty years changes in religion across the land. It is not so much a religious building as a temple to the achievements of mere men and women. And in this light the building deserves applause. Celebrating what we humans can do is hardly illegitimate. But this is not religion. Religion means recognizing what we cannot do. Denominations in the capitalist world only reflect the secularization process when they mix steadily more of the former, profane purpose with the latter, religious one.

In summary, Protestantism seems to have created the instrument of its own

Were Riverside Church a less modern edifice, this statue from above its main entrance might be of Albert von Bollstadt (ca. 1193–1280), the teacher of Thomas Aquinas, bishop, theologian, and philosopher, who was called "the Great" even in his lifetime and later canonized. But the statue is instead of Albert Einstein (1879–1955), physicist and author of the general theory of relativity. Einstein was 51 years old when this image was carved and placed. (Randy Matusow)

demise. In the liberal-capitalist social structure it has engendered, people are required to work relentlessly and they are paid for it, but whether they pray or not is up to them and is formally irrelevant to the structure of reward. That is, everyone in a Protestant society is required to ponder his or her capabilities and to exercise them for profit in the market economy. No one is obliged to recognize the fundamental weakness and vulnerability of us all in the face of death, our ultimate uncertainty, our inescapable apartness. Predictably enough, the longer and more successfully the capitalist game has been played, the more religion has been pushed out of human consciousness. Secularization is just the name for this process, the growing celebration of what people have done, what they are doing, and what they can do as part of further economic growth. Protestantism predestined this demise of religion, and thus it has occurred in all the societies where Protestantism took root. It has been a slow and subtle process, with many setbacks and varied in its concrete manifestations across capitalist societies. But in this part of the world, to paraphrase T. S. Eliot, this is the way religion ends, not with a bang but a whimper.

Religion under Nonliberal Regimes

In the eighteenth and nineteenth centuries, while the Protestant world was holding religion in check and making rapid strides in economic advance, societies elsewhere remained relatively static, unmoved from their traditional ways of life. Previous chapters have already pointed up the obvious fact that most of these societies—in southern and eastern Europe, Latin America, Africa, and Asia—are static no longer, that they are now on the move toward development and democracy no less earnestly than Britain and the United States. Their strategies for achieving these goals, however, have been shown generally to diverge from the liberal-capitalist principles legally entrenched in Protestant lands. Their strategies seem mostly to be socialist, entailing extensive public ownership and control of property, restricted internal markets, single-party politics—reflections of a corporatist, group-centered conception of social order. The following few paragraphs briefly outline the effects of the socialist kind of development on religion, especially on organized Christian religion.

effects on religion of the socialist kind of development

In a word, the effects have been negative. Regardless of setting or strategy, self-conscious development cannot occur without a dramatic shift away from the contemplation and cult of limits, the impossible beyond. But the shift is made differently in non-Protestant settings. For while organized Protestant religion stepped aside and saluted the arrival of industrial technology, the Roman church did not, nor did the Orthodox churches. These older Christian bodies resisted both political and economic innovation, allied themselves with traditional monarchies, and discouraged popular awareness of the universal human right to exercise power. By and large they were content to drag their feet into the modern world. As late as twenty years ago, Catholic theologians regularly referred to the thirteenth as "the greatest of centuries." Hence groups favoring development and democracy in traditional Catholic or Orthodox societies had no choice but to rebel pointedly against religion. Representative government and the conquest of nature could not be for them religious duties, as was the case in Protestant lands. Quite on the contrary, only by standing up to religion, denouncing it, frontally attacking it could they hope to accomplish change.

atheism and anticlericalism

Accordingly, two themes have figured prominently in the ideologies of progressive groups throughout the Catholic and Orthodox world. The first is atheism. Activists in Protestant lands did not need to deny the existence of god. The Protestant god had already fled into the privacy of individual conscience and thus lost the legal right to interfere with the actions of people on each other and the earth. Because the older Christian god refused to retreat, it became important not just to deny his existence but to proclaim the denial noisily, shout it loudly, and prove it logically. A second and related theme was anticlericalism. Since popes, bishops, and patriarchs were disinclined to shrink the holy voluntarily, it had to be desecrated. Only by sacking monasteries, burning churches, decapitating kings, and otherwise spoiling the sacred could the realm of the secular be enlarged. In a sense, Protestantism leapt into its own grave; because Catholicism and Orthodoxy refused to do so, they had to be pushed.

No socialist thinker better displays the general emphasis on atheism and anticlericalism than Marx. The dialectics in his social and economic theory did not extend to recognition that there is a limit to human prowess, something beyond the strength of men and women. Marx despised the exploitation of some people by others and for this reason rejected the idea of hired labor no less firmly than he condemned prostitution. But no less than capitalist ideologues, Marx took to heart the biblical mandate to subdue nature and have dominion over it. Equally as much as liberals like Locke, Marx took a one-sided and aggressive attitude toward nature: only by separating themselves from the earth and exploiting it to the full could people achieve the communist utopia. This was for him the positive route to development, the scientifically inevitable course of human history. Marx therefore had no use for religion and defined it as nothing more than a superstitious obstacle in the path of an active, modern human race.

Marxism's appeal in the non-Protestant world

If Marxism fell mostly on deaf ears in the Protestant societies, even in the class of wage laborers, one major reason was undoubtedly the final requiem it sounded for all religious institutions. Protestant activists had no need to condemn religion so completely; far from hindering development, their version of Christianity actually encouraged it. To those seeking change in southern and eastern Europe, by contrast, Marx's theory of religion was one of his most enchanting themes. Thus did his theory become the ideological justification of the almost total annihilation of the Russian Orthodox Church during the Bolshevik revolution, for later assaults on Orthodox churches in the Ukraine, Yugoslavia, Romania, Albania, and the Caucasus, for aggression against the Roman church in Poland, Lithuania, Czechoslovakia, and Hungary, and still later for persecution of Confucianists and Daoists in China. Wherever communist governments came to power in the first half of the twentieth century, religious institutions of all kinds soon felt death-dealing blows from state bureaucracies. Most Western governments were horrified at such virulent atheism and used it to bolster their own hostility toward communism. They generally failed to recognize that given the historical background of Eastern Europe, strident atheism and anticlericalism were virtually inevitable concomitants of the arrival of modernity in those countries. Aghast, moreover, at what communist governments were doing quickly and violently, capitalist ones tended to overlook the fact that they were accomplishing similar purposes slowly and with subtlety.

churches fared poorly also in revolutionary France, Mexico, and elsewhere

But Marx and his disciples were neither the first nor the only ones to build into their strategies of socialist development overtly antireligious doctrines. Nor have communist governments been unique in their persecution of religious institutions. It was in France, a society which geographically and culturally straddles the line between the Protestant, liberal-capitalist European north and the Catholic, corporatist, socialist south, that religion felt its first lethal assault in the quest for self-conscious modern development. In the name of liberty, equality, and fraternity, the revolutionaries of 1789 sought to destroy anything that smacked of Christianity and free France for creative change. Out of that struggle against both cross and crown, the First Republic was proclaimed in 1792. During the nineteenth century, atheism and anticlericalism were major themes in revolutionary movements all across Latin America. In Mexico in the late 1860s, the reform movement of President Benito Juarez confiscated church properties, excluded clerics from public education, affirmed religious liberty, and in general sought to crush the power of the Catholic church. To this day, Mexican law forbids priests to wear the Roman collar in a public place. As of 1971, only five of the Latin American republics—Costa Rica, Bolivia, Colombia, Paraguay, and Peru—still joined their governments in a relationship of patronage to the church of Rome.[17]

It is important to understand that non-Protestant Christian societies, once they embark on the path of political and economic development, cannot just relegate religion to a private sphere formally irrelevant to the rest of life, as happened quite naturally in the United States. People in such societies find it hard to think of anything, much less religion, as so clearly detached from everything else. They have no historical experience of a religion that is not structurally intertwined with all other facets of life, an integral part of an overall structure that also includes government, work, family, education, and virtually everything else. In a sense, these cultures lack a private, individualistic, secluded corner where religion can be made to stand. Almost none of them, moreover, is religiously diverse; a single religious body, the universal church or a national one, embraces the bulk of citizens. Hence it is not surprising that faced with churches which defend social change as intrinsically pernicious, revolutionaries who sought to make change the very essence of the social order defined the churches as pernicious, defined them, in fact, out of existence. It was a matter of shifting emphasis from the humble, dominated side of the human person to the proud, creative side. In this shift religion was by definition on the losing side.

the persistence of religion in socialist societies

Nonetheless, nowhere has religion been eliminated. In most cases, the church has simply lost much of its power and been forced to accept a more minor role in the public order. The Soviet Union has rooted religion out of life perhaps more successfully than other socialist societies, but even there the process of secularization is far from complete. In 1973, the Soviet sociologist, A. A. Lebedev, reported results of a survey on religion in the industrial city of Penza, about a day's drive southeast of Moscow toward the Volga River.[18] Interviews with 6000 people revealed that 43 percent of housewives and 39 percent of pensioners were still religious believers, and only 52 percent of the sample as a whole professed to be atheists. In a nearby rural community, only 39 percent of citizens professed atheism. Nor should too much be made of the official godlessness of Soviet society. It is true that there are no professors of theology at Moscow's prestigious Lomosonov University, but neither are there at the University of California at Berkeley. At the former, religion is studied under the rubric of scientific atheism, at the latter under the name of religious studies or comparative religion. The Russian treatment is admittedly more hostile than the American one, but neither leads very often to student requests to be baptized or confirmed.

In the Eastern European communist societies, especially the Roman Catholic ones, religion remains stronger still. A church full of people is a far more common sight in Warsaw than in Philadelphia, and it is a fair guess that the cardinal-archbishop of Prague is better known in his city than the cardinal-archbishop of Winnipeg is in his. In Latin America, attempts to bar the church from public life have been but partially successful. In Mexico and other Latin republics, marriages can be legally performed only in a secular court, but high percentages of couples repeat the civil ceremony later before a priest and reserve the celebration for the

John Paul II in the slums of Guadalajara, Mexico, 1979. In Latin America and Eastern Europe, the church he leads is a potent force. (Goldberg/Sygma)

second occasion. When the pope visited Mexico in 1979, the Mexican government accorded him its hospitality and ignored its ban on the public wearing of religious garb. Even Cuba, despite the fervor of its revolution and its ties with Moscow, has failed to eliminate the Catholic hierarchy; Fidel Castro himself has episcopal friends. The Polish government is careful to respect the teaching of the Catholic bishops in that land. The Chinese government craves the Dalai Lama's approval for its policies in the Tibetan highlands. In a sense, the demise of religion under socialist or quasi-socialist regimes has been until now less complete than under capitalist regimes. For if a church survives at all in a socialist society, it survives like everything else *in the context of public life.* If it has a voice at all, its voice is heard. In a liberal society, by contrast, the public order is legally soundproofed against religious voices, even while their freedom of expression is guaranteed.

Concluding Words

summary: the general decline of religion in history

Chapter Six sketched the growth of the economy, the progressive pressing of the earth into the service of humankind. This chapter has outlined the corresponding decline of religion, steady withdrawal from the celebration of human limitations. The decline escaped notice in its initial stages—in the separation of the profane from the sacred, in the cultivation of magic and primitive science, in the transition from polytheism to monotheism, and in the spread of the myth of the god-man,

308

Jesus. The contraction of religion has come more clearly to light since the sixteenth century, when the Protestant movement swept through one part of the Christian world. Liberal societies commenced a fervent crusade for the unholy grail of the good life on earth. They reduced Christianity to the Bible and made it a matter of private opinion. They separated their states from their churches, leaving the latter to dwindle away as denominations in ever more secular milieux. As the capitalist crusade progressed, people became more full of themselves and emptier of awe except in the face of their own achievements. More recently, during the last century especially, the rest of the Christian world has also awakened to the fact of human capability. Orthodox and Catholic societies have also conjured up unholy grails and launched crusades in pursuit of them. Influenced by liberal capitalism but also bolstered by their atheistic and anticlerical ideologies, they have sought to secularize quickly, to raise the religious roof right off their social dwelling places. The more enlightened by modern culture people have become, the lower they have turned the once radiant flame of the cult of the beyond.

Should we then take it for granted that the flame will soon go out? Do the data of the sociology of religion suggest that religion can be eliminated? The issue still remains, the issue of whether a society needs to recognize and celebrate the limits of its capabilities, or whether it is enough that people believe in themselves.

THE POSSIBILITY OF IRRELIGION

The evidence suggests that at least in one respect the Marxists are right and the functionalists wrong. Religion is not a necessary means of achieving social integration. People do not have to dream impossible dreams. The possible ones *the sufficiency of civil* held out by materialist ideologies are enough to keep people in line, accepting the *religion for social* tedium of everyday life and working steadily in some plan of political and economic *stability* advance. With its army lurking in the background, the national government of an industrial society can almost surely give its people enough earthly things to celebrate that they need not look beyond the earth at all. A flag, an anthem, martial music, a little fireworks, a civic holiday now and then, Lenin's tomb or Kennedy's, space rendezvous, moon walks, exhibitions, trade fairs, Olympic games, and similar secular rites can excite so much national pride that the bulk of people behave themselves admirably. Some scholars, California's Robert Bellah most famously, call this civil religion, but *religion* is an ill-chosen word. It is the cult of the profane, the celebration of nonlimitation, the worship of human prowess. It is surrogate religion, relieving stress in a manner analogous to that of sex therapists. But there is no reason in principle why it cannot work, as indeed it works even now for millions of people in the urban-industrial world. Ancient societies glued themselves together with much stranger illusions than the myth of human boundlessness.

But what, one may ask, about mortality, uncertainty, and inequality, facts that demonstrate ultimate human weakness? The last two can be falsely explained away as easily as was the fact of human creativity before the dawn of the modern world. Science textbooks can as readily be portrayed as fonts of certain knowledge as holy scriptures were in ages past. Or at least, the scientific method can be culturally defined as an infallible guide to Reality, Truth, the "way things *really* are." In the first chapter of this book, I noted that many sociologists today and in the past have argued that with our strategies of inquiry we actually discover laws inherent in nature. The prevalence of such naive faith in science is evidence enough that people can be one-dimensional on either side of the dialectic of their earthly situation. Among forms of false consciousness, the certainty of self-conceit is no less possible than that of self-contempt. As for inequality, both capitalist and communist governments soothe the pain of present disparities between rich and poor with the tranquilizing ointment of projections and promises. Capitalist regimes explain how further economic growth will make even the poor richer; they urge people to save for their retirement years and plan for their children's future. Communist ideologues regularly insist that just one further five-year plan will bring a glimpse of utopian light at the end of the revolutionary tunnel.

the troublesome reality of death

Mortality is a graver problem. Even the most determinedly secular society neither eliminates death nor explains it away. Still, life can be arranged in ways that delay death and minimize people's awareness of it. Toward these ends the societies of Europe and North America have made great strides in the last half-century. Until recent decades death mingled visibly with life even in the experience of children, imprinting itself on their consciousness the way it did on mine the day after Christmas of 1955. My grandpa had always been someone I could count on. He defended my view of porridge and sugared his even more heavily than I. "Infernal oats," he called it. He had taken me fishing years earlier and told spine-tingling tales of ghosts and leprechauns. But since 1951, he and Grandma had lived in a little house in town. His eyes, his ears—all of him was wearing out. I remember him lying in bed and shining his flashlight over to the mantel clock, the better to see how quickly time passed. Like everyone else, I knew Grandpa was dying. It was a fact so blunt that no one had to say it. Our gathering at his home that cold, snowless afternoon was not in panic but in respect. No strangers were there, only his family—so many grandchildren that we younger ones spilled out into the hall, where we stood motionless studying our shoelaces. One of my cousins, a nurse, closed his eyes when the end came. And then the tall young priest arrived. As he entered the room, his cassock brushed against me, sent a shiver through me, and made a chilly, swooshing sound that seemed to echo in the stillness. We knelt as he crossed Grandpa's forehead with oil and murmured Latin prayers. When the undertaker came, my older brothers helped him lift Grandpa onto the stretcher. Not long after that, my dad came over to me. His eyes were red. "Come on home, boy," he said gently, "there's feeding to be done."

My indelible experience that day, or some variation of it, was, even in the recent past, an integral and normal part of growing up. Unless it happened by accident or to the young, death seemed not a loathsome intrusion into life but its supremely natural if regrettable culmination. I witnessed that day no sense of failure, no frantic effort to *do* something. Grandpa himself had said earlier, "I've been doctored on enough." But today, as the Mexican poet, Octavio Paz, has written, "In New York, in Paris, in London, the word death is not pronounced because it burns the lips."[19] For making the word's pronunciation less necessary, six attributes of the structure of advanced societies are especially important.

six ways by which advanced industrial societies have reduced citizens' awareness of death

First and most obvious is a lengthened life expectancy. In the year of my grandpa's birth, the average baby boy could expect to live no more than forty years.

Today in many societies, a baby boy can count on thirty years more, a baby girl thirty-five. The general principle applies, that the longer a journey is expected to take, the more one's attention turns from the destination to the scenery along the way. Second is the growing segregation of the aged, those nearest death, from younger people. It is a latent function of retirement villages and homes for the aged to shield people from the death of close friends and relatives. For most people death today happens somewhere else, to old folks one remembers knowing years ago. Third is the hospitalization of the terminally ill. Increasingly, a dying person actually expires only after being separated from family, home, and the company of friends in everyday surroundings. The event is usually attended by a mere handful of people, mostly medical professionals who get paid for their presence and for whom death becomes banal.

A fourth attribute of urban-industrial societies in recent years is their routinization and simplification of funeral rites. Could anyone imagine guiding a coffin into the elevator of a high-rise condominium so that the deceased owner of unit 140 might lie in state in his own living area? Yet in the fairly typical rural community I knew as a boy, farmers often built their houses with double doors to ease the carriage of coffins inside for future wakes. The removal of the coffin from home to funeral parlor, the shortening of funeral processions, the practice of dropping by the funeral home instead of attending the funeral, the fixed hours announced for such visits ("2–4 P.M. and 7–9 P.M. only"), the brevity of periods of mourning, the growing popularity of cremation, and even rent-a-coffin schemes and other innovations reduce the significance of death and make it easier to forget. A fifth way of preventing death from burning the lips is to drain away its impact and meaning, to define and study it with the cool, disinterested stance of a scientist. With the help of detailed actuarial charts, people today routinely bet against their living much longer and try to outwit insurance companies; winning the bet means dying soon and leaving a bundle to inheritors. With the same charts, younger people can buy their coffins, tombstones, freight, and embalming costs at budget prices through prepayment funeral plans. A field called *thanatology*, the scientific study of death, has come to be noted on professors' resumes, and the sociology of death has become a popular course in many universities. By thus estranging themselves from death and planning their own, contemporary urbanites minimize concern for the event that concerns them most. It is hard to imagine anything more profane.

But perhaps a sixth attribute of the structure of our status quo insists upon profanity still more. It is the denial of the knowledge of impending death to those who are about to die. Surveys indicate that only a minority of medical doctors feel obliged to inform terminally ill patients of their probably imminent departure.[20] As the moment of expiration approaches, patients are commonly drugged and tranquilized, and they die with little more self-awareness than a lawn mower as it sputters to a stop. Sophisticated hospitals experiment with even bolder programs. Some place their dying patients in therapy groups and encourage them to discuss their feelings about what is soon to happen, as if the power of positive thinking could make death a creative experience. There have also been experiments in the administration of LSD and other hallucinogenic drugs to the dying. Reading such reports in professional journals, I recall the Indians of the British Columbia coast, who used to say that a man soon to die could hear the owl call his name. Therapies and drugs today muffle that spooky bird's cry, and death steals upon us unawares.

Data from numerous advanced industrial societies suggest that the possibility of irreligion is no longer theoretical but empirically obvious. There is no need to overlook the religion that remains. Multinational companies like Marcona in Peru still sometimes ground themselves in Christian symbols, the better to deter worker unrest. Knowing the terror of combat, even the U.S. government gives military chaplains officers' rank and pays them with public funds. Some governments still finance separate denominational schools and welfare agencies. Sizable minorities still go to church. Religious symbolism still crops up in political speeches and holiday parades. Nonetheless, so slight is the supernatural tincture that colors public culture in many societies of both East and West that it could undoubtedly be eliminated completely. Purely secular glue is strong enough to hold a technologically advanced society together.

THE LIKELIHOOD OF RELIGION

continuing religious practice and belief among the poor and powerless

Although the cause of social integration does not require it, some form of religion can be taken as an enduring regularity even in industrialized societies as the process of human history goes on. The most obvious reason is that powerless, poor, and dishonored citizens, along with frustrated individuals in all social strata, will continue voluntarily to seek out the old religions and to be swept up in new ones. However advanced, dynamic, and modern a national economy may become, citizens isolated from creative participation in that economy can be expected to lose faith in human power and muster faith in gods. Probably the best current example in the United States is young men and women still in school, worried about their future in a crowded job market. Aged citizens forced into retirement and having lots of time to ponder their economic irrelevance are also prone to religious activity. So, too, bored housewives, the unemployed and marginally employed, demoted executives and go-getters facing blocked careers, and recent immigrants dislocated from conventional life. Indeed, the exclusion of so many citizens from power in advanced corporate capitalism is reflected in the contemporary groundswell of popular religion.[21] Membership in many fundamentalist religious bodies—like the Southern Baptist Convention, the Church of the Nazarene, and the Churches of God—has increased steadily over the past two decades, even while the mainline denominations have been in decline. Still more striking is the proliferation of new sects and cults, some of them Christian (like the Jesus movement and Catholic pentecostalism), others grounded in Oriental religious traditions (Guru Maharaj-ji's Divine Light Mission, Reverend Moon's Unification Church, the Hare Krishna movement, and transcendental meditation, for example).

Nonetheless, too much should not be made of these kinds of religious revival. Grass-roots cults and sects are indeed evidence of contradictions, inadequacies, and inequalities in the established order of life. They demonstrate that even in the most powerful societies on earth, many citizens are desperate and disheartened. But religious fanaticism seldom has much effect on the structure of economic and

"*However advanced, dynamic, and modern a national economy may become, citizens isolated from creative participation in that economy can be expected to lose faith in human power and muster faith in gods.*" (© *Jim Anderson 1980/Woodfin Camp & Assoc.*)

political life. It serves usually just to assuage personal difficulties, inject meaning into the boring routine of life at the bottom, and help citizens through periods of stress and despair. When fanaticism does spill over into electoral politics, moreover, its results are either silly (like passage of the prohibition amendment to the U.S. Constitution in 1919) or destructive (like government by mullahs and ayatollahs in Iran at the beginning of this decade). Religious excitement on the margins of contemporary Western societies must therefore be considered in the main only a regrettable sign of imperfections in contemporary economic organizations. It is an easy retreat from history for those to whom history is unkind. It is a symbol of present problems, but not of future solutions. Development in the years ahead will depend as it always has on reason, the confident and disciplined use of human power for human purposes. Dogmatic, frenzied religious movements will continue to appeal to citizens left out of the development process, but if history is on course the number of such citizens should decline progressively.

limitation is still a fact, the beyond is eternally real

More compelling evidence for the persistence of religion in the decades and even centuries to come is the simple fact that there *are* after all limits on human capabilities. No matter how persistently we seek to organize earthly life in a reasonable way, reason itself remains inadequate. However effectively the capitalist and Marxian strategies of development have suppressed the recognition and

FOR EXAMPLE

Gary T. Marx's study of religion and black militancy*

Although results of survey research inform all the chapters of the present book, not since the methods chapter have I presented such results systematically in tabular form. This is a good place to do so again, both for shedding further light on survey techniques and for presenting some important findings about religion's political effects. For these purposes the paragraphs below summarize an article by Gary T. Marx on the connection between religious involvement and civil rights militancy among black Americans. The research was based on structured interviews with about 1100 randomly selected black adults in 1964, a time of widespread protest for racial equality in the United States, of new federal civil rights legislation, and of growing resentment among blacks against longstanding prejudice and oppression.

Marx began his report by presenting contradictory views of how religion relates to efforts for political change. Most sociologists have considered the relation negative: religion is a means of social control, a defender of the status quo, preacher of conservatism and discourager of dissidence. The author's famous namesake, Karl Marx, articulated this view forcefully. Sometimes, however, religion seems to inspire courage to dissent. In particular, black ministers in the United States have led movements of protest against domination by whites, and black churches have often served as rallying points for collective action. As prophetic leaders from Nat Turner to Martin Luther King bear witness, religious faith may indeed stimulate activism on behalf of change.

To test these conflicting hypotheses against the survey data, Marx first devised measures of the two variables, religion and militancy, using questions from the interview schedule. He scored respondents as more or less religious depending on how they answered three questions, one on doctrinal orthodoxy, the second on the subjective importance assigned to religion, the third on frequency of attendance at worship services. He considered "very religious" a respondent who had no doubt about God's or the devil's existence, considered religion extremely important, and attended church once a week or more. At the other extreme, he labeled "not at all religious" anyone who rejected the basic doctrines, considered religion personally unimportant, and rarely if ever went to church. Militancy was measured by seven relevant questions—about support for civil rights demonstrations, willingness to take part in them, opposition to racial discrimination, impatience with the speed of integration, and so on. Respondents who gave a militant response to at least five of these questions were labeled "militant."

Having measured both these variables, Marx could then assess the connection

*Based on Gary T. Marx, "Religion: Opiate or Inspiration of Civil Rights Militancy among Negroes," *American Sociological Review 32:* 64–72 (1967). Used by permission of the American Sociological Association and the author. Dr. Marx teaches at the Massachusetts Institute of Technology.

between them by dividing the 1100 respondents into his four categories of the independent variable (from "very religious" to "not at all religious") and then calculating within each category the percentage militant. The results showed clearly which competing hypothesis was the better one. Only 26 percent of "very religious" respondents were militant, 30 percent of the "somewhat religious," 45 percent of the "not very religious," and 70 percent of the "not at all religious." Obviously, people like Martin Luther King who combined religious involvement with social activism were exceptional. Religion's political effect was better typified by a Detroit housewife's comment during the interview: "I don't go for demonstrations. I believe that God created all men equal and at His appointed time He will give every man his portion, no one can hinder it."

Since factors other than religion also affect militancy, Marx took his research a step further and added other factors as control variables in his analysis. Might it be, for example, that education is what makes the difference, that college-educated blacks are more militant regardless of how religious they are? Table 7-1 answers this question. The respondents here are split into twelve categories, the four of religion and then each of these into three categories of education. Of the 26 college-educated, very religious respondents, only 38 percent were militant, compared to 87 percent of the 15 college-educated, not at all religious respondents. The table shows that introducing education as a control variable leaves the basic finding unchanged: whatever the level of schooling, religious involvement relates negatively to activism for civil rights. Analysis with other control variables held a similar lesson. Although younger respondents were more militant than older ones, men more than women, Northerners more than Southerners, and mainline Protestants more than followers of cults and sects, militancy was lower in each category among the very religious. Statistical tests, moreover, indicated significance, that these results could hardly have occurred by chance. The conclusion is clear: if all black Americans had been very religious in the 1960s, there would probably not have been a civil rights movement.

Research at other times and in other political contexts has yielded results similar to Gary Marx's. Frequent churchgoers, citizens for whom religion is very important, are disproportionately (though not necessarily) on the side that prefers to keep human hands off God's world.

Table 7-1 *Proportion militant by religion, controlling for educational level*

EDUCATION	VERY RELIGIOUS	SOMEWHAT RELIGIOUS	NOT VERY RELIGIOUS	NOT AT ALL RELIGIOUS
Grammar school	17% (N=108)	22% (N=201)	31% (N=42)	50% (N=2)
High school	34% (N=96)	32% (N=270)	45% (N=119)	58% (N=19)
College	38% (N=26)	48% (N=61)	59% (N=34)	87% (N=15)

SOURCE: *Based on Marx, op. cit.*

315

celebration of the beyond, the beyond is still there. However deep runs the conviction that science is a positive way of knowing, it remains nothing more or less than a human art. If most people no longer look death in the face then still it captures them, only from behind. Perhaps it was inevitable that in the first few centuries after humans became aware of their strength that they would overestimate it and discourage religious dissent from their schemes to transform the earth. The world at the time could tolerate such illusions. Like an insolent child pounding the arms of its father, the human race was still too weak to do serious damage. It is your fate and mine, however, to have been born too late to entertain illusions. With the accumulated techniques of centuries of work, a few industrial societies now have the power to press the earth beyond its limits and even to end most human life on the planet. If we permit those societies to do so, the reality of limitation will force itself on the minds of survivors. If we prevent such a catastrophe, it will be because we have built into our political and economic structures recognition that the question of human existence has two sides: not just how to act but how not to act, not just how to become but how to be, not just how to rule the earth but how to live with it.

the urgent practical value of the cult of human weakness

This point deserves a stronger formulation. It is unlikely that the advanced societies can develop much further through one-sided affirmation of human capabilities. More than ever before in history, these societies need to recognize the fact of limitation, celebrate the beyond publicly, and let the cult of human weakness have an influence on what they do. Would people's relation to the earth become more salutary if everyone in the Ukraine or in Illinois died in nuclear war? How about if everyone died in the U.S.S.R. or in the United States? Would the human marriage to the earth be healthier if everyone died a radioactive death? Even to ask these questions defines nuclear war as beyond the point where human beings can go. It is a tree of forbidden fruit. Yet in defiance of limits the American, British, Russian, French, and Chinese governments boast of their "nuclear capabilities." So now does India, and other regimes seem likely to do likewise. Or again, would we be like gods on the day the last bit of fossil fuel were burned or exploded into energy? Of course not, we would be irremediably poorer. Yet we hasten that day's arrival, joy-riding in jumbo jets. Or with respect to social ecology, would the world be a better place if we humans doubled our number in the next twenty years, as we did in the last forty? Nuclear war, resource depletion, and unending population growth are but three reminders that development *cannot* mean the unlimited exercise of human capabilities. Sheer indolence is more productive than many schemes for which billions of dollars are spent annually today.

From another eminently practical perspective, too, the advanced industrial societies would do well to fall prey to religious influence. Marx and others have claimed that inequality persists on account of religious justification, that secular societies promote equality for lack of an excuse to permit exploitation. History in this century reveals that plenty of secular excuses can be found: scientifically based doctrines of racism in Nazi Germany, South Africa, the United States, and elsewhere; the supposed law of proletarian dictatorship in the communist countries; laissez faire economic principles throughout the capitalist world; game theory rehearsed on computers and applied to war. Indeed, by now it is clear, or it should

An Islamic cemetery at the tip of the Golden Horn in Istanbul. "It is only at those limits, in the awesome mysteries of birth and death, that our fundamental commonality is dramatized and held out as a dream to strive for. We humans are not of equal strength. We are of equal weakness." (© Luc Bouchage/Rapho/Photo Researchers, Inc.)

be, that equality disappears even as a goal when people cease to contemplate the limits of earthly life. It is only at those limits, in the awesome mysteries of birth and death, that our fundamental commonality is dramatized and held out as a dream to strive for. We humans are not of equal strength. We are of equal weakness. Only the recognition and celebration of our equality in the face of the beyond can sustain a quest for equality of reward within the structures of our own societies. In South America even now, it is not the secular military regimes who champion the cause of the poor, but bishops, priests, and nuns like the one I interviewed in Paraguay.

again, the value of two-sided thinking

Bringing together two great religious traditions, the Catholic Spaniard Miguel de Unamuno once quoted the Unitarian American William Ellery Channing: "None are so likely to believe too little as those who have begun by believing too much."[22] This point is important in two contexts. The first is that of liberation from traditional religion. Having been led by parents and priests to believe too much in the limits on their creativity, the progenitors of the modern world rejected these limits too completely. The cost of their thoughtlessness is the brink of catastrophe to which we cling precariously today. But the same line is relevant also in a second context, that of liberation from materialism and modern science. There is some danger that as the pretense of science reveals itself more and more, people will disbelieve it too much and retreat into the equally false security of religious dogmatism. It is such retreat that the growth of fundamentalist sects in North America today reflects. The spread of charismatic pentecostalism in mainline Protestant and Catholic denominations is further evidence. The hippie flight from the industrial world was an earlier expression of the same excessive disbelief in the magnificent powers of an active, hard-working human race. Bible thumpers and drug freaks on the one hand, and all-knowing scientists and growth-at-any-cost economists on the other have this in common: all are one-sided and none should be trusted to chart the course of development at this point in history. The truth of the human situation is twofold and will ever remain so. We are both powerful and powerless in the face of nature. Our goal must be to bring out the best in both us and it.

What kind of religion can best enhance a contemporary marriage between people and the earth varies, of course, across societies. Symbolic paraphernalia for acknowledging the limits of human action neither are nor should be any more universal than the content of action itself. Nations have no more need to adopt alien religious systems than to follow foreign economic designs. Better that each look first to its own history for the language, myths, music, rituals, and ministries by which it can most authentically celebrate the fact of ultimacy, while not fearing to enrich itself with religious expressions created elsewhere. The late British economist, E. F. Schumacher, wrote enthusiastically of what he called Buddhist economics: "It is a question of finding the right path of development, the Middle Way between materialist heedlessness and traditionalist immobility, in short, of finding 'Right Livelihood.' "[23] But Christianity, Judaism, Islam, and the other ancient traditions also offer symbolic repertoires with which contemporary peoples can enact celebrations of the beyond. None of these deserves to be forgotten in settings where it can compel recognition of what transcends the empirical world. The important thing is not the symbol but the awareness it evokes, the knowledge that every human scheme is a leap in the dark and therefore to be made with care and gentleness.

In the absence of nuclear war or some comparable disaster, no religious system is likely ever to cloud the horizon of human restlessness as completely as all of them did in premodern times. We know better now how far we ourselves can travel. It is just that final step that is ultimately beyond us—the step into eternity, certainty, the unity of all in all. The religion appropriate for the contemporary era is one *the final step* which rests on that final step, leaving people free to climb all other ones themselves. It is a charismatic religion, but one whose charisma dances in step with mundane reason and law. A humble religion, admitting that if the last frontier is beyond the tampering of women and men, depictions of it are not.[24] But a proud religion, too, refusing to be isolated from public life and laughing aloud at any sign of human arrogance. But let my sociologist's pen rest here. For with respect to authentic religion Lao'zi was right: "He who knows does not speak. He who speaks does not know."[25] Or in Paul's words drawn from Isaiah: "Eye has not seen, nor ear heard, nor the heart of man conceived, all that God has prepared for those who love him."[26]

For Reflection

functionalist conception of religion
Marxian conception of religion
religion as response to limitation
death, inequality, uncertainty
silence
alleluia
glossolalia
authentic religion
religion and the status quo
religious evolution
sacred versus profane
magic and science
monotheism
Christianity
routinization of Christianity
Innocent III
Protestantism
priesthood of all believers

church-state separation
universal church
established church
sect
denomination
Catholicism in America
secularization
rates of church attendance
religion and education
this-worldliness
Riverside Church
religion under socialism
atheism and anticlericalism
religion in the U.S.S.R.
civil religion
denial of death
nuclear capabilities
religion and inequality

For Making Connections

With Chapter One: Where can the plainest truth be found, in sociology or in religion? In both equally? Or in neither one?
What differences in method and approach are there between sociology and theology as academic disciplines?

With Chapter Two: What measures can you list of the concept of religion, and how would these measures differ depending on whether you took a functionalist approach, a Marxian approach, or an outlook on religion as response to limits?
Write down the five or six concepts you consider most important for a sociological understanding of religion in your own society.

With Chapter Three: What kinds of religious organization strengthen the division of the world into national societies? What kinds weaken national boundaries?
If you knew nothing about a society except that all its churches were organized as voluntary associations, what further characteristics of that society would you be willing to hypothesize?

With Chapter Four: In what ways does the Christian religion, both as described here and as you have personally experienced it, emphasize the humble side of the human person? In what ways the proud side?
Would deeply religious parents be more or less likely than nonreligious ones to socialize their children to an ethic of modernity and achievement motivation? Or would this depend on the kind of religion they believed in?

With Chapter Five:	Does charismatic authority have a place in a modern society? If so, what kind of place? If not, why not?
	Why have societies on the socialist path to democracy been generally more overtly hostile to religion than societies on the liberal path?
With Chapter Six:	Explain in detail what connection you see between the process of economic development and the course of religious evolution.
	What differences are there between the early and advanced stages of capitalist development?

For Further Reading

Current research in the sociology of religion appears regularly in all the general journals of the discipline but also in those which specialize in this subfield. Among the latter are *Social Compass*, *Sociological Analysis*, the *Journal for the Scientific Study of Religion*, and the *Review of Religious Research*. Of no less value are journals in theology and religion and books by practitioners of these disciplines. Within sociology proper, I can recommend especially the following ten sources:

1 Thomas F. O'Dea, *The Sociology of Religion*, Prentice-Hall, Englewood Cliffs, N.J., 1966. A short, splendid introduction to the field by a student of Parsons who far surpassed his teacher in understanding religion and studying it with reverence. Also worthwhile are O'Dea's books on two major U.S. denominations: *The Mormons*, Univ. of Chicago Press, Chicago, 1957, and *The Catholic Crisis*, Beacon, Boston, 1968.

2 Werner Stark, *The Sociology of Religion*, 5 vols., Routledge & Kegan Paul, Oxon, 1967ff. A monumental appraisal of Western religious history, engrossing and rich in detail. Stark is in that illustrious lineage of sociological thinkers who were born and educated in the Germanic world but who reached intellectual maturity in an Anglo-American milieu—a lineage that includes among many others Marx, Mannheim, Arendt, Schumacher, Fromm, Marcuse, and Berger.

3 Peter L. Berger, *The Sacred Canopy*, Doubleday, New York, 1969. The coauthor of *The Social Construction of Reality* here focuses the earlier and more general analytic framework specifically on the religious institution. See also his *Rumor of Angles*, Doubleday, New York, 1970, a more theological treatment where Berger insists upon the supernatural still more pointedly.

4 Robert Bellah, *Beyond Belief*, Harper & Row, New York, 1970. A lucid and coherent work by the United States' leading civil-religion theorist. Note the difference between this and his later book, *Broken Covenant*, Seabury, New York, 1975. For an antidote see Marie-Augusta Neal, *A Socio-Theology of Letting Go*, Paulist, New York, 1977, which begins with the question of when civil religion is no longer religious but only civil.

5 J. Milton Yinger, *The Scientific Study of Religion*, Macmillan, New York, 1970. A thoughtful and standard textbook, itself a contribution to the subject, by the 1977 president of the American Sociological Association.

6 Emile Durkheim, *The Elementary Forms of the Religious Life*, Macmillan, New York, 1961. First published in 1912, this is the classic example of functionalist analysis of religion. Still worth reading, if only because of Durkheim's influence on such contemporary students of the subject as Harold Fallding, *The Sociology of Religion*, McGraw-Hill Ryerson, Toronto, 1974; Elizabeth Nottingham, *Religion: a Sociological*

320

View, Random House, New York, 1971; Louis Schneider, *The Sociological Approach to Religion*, Wiley, New York, 1970; as well as Parsons, Bellah, Yinger, Tiryakian, and many others.

7   Stewart Crysdale and Les Wheatcroft (eds.), *Religion in Canadian Society*, Macmillan, Toronto, 1976. The first reader on the sociology of Canadian religion, with varied contributions by 30 different scholars.

8   *Canadian Journal of Sociology* 3 (Spring 1978). An issue given over to comparative analyses of religious organization in Canada and the United States; includes contributions by Harold Fallding on mainline Protestantism, O. Kendall White on Mormonism, Harry Hiller on sectarian Protestantism, Stuart Schoenfeld on Judaism, Rodney Sawatsky on Mennonitism, and me on Catholicism. The articles include extensive bibliographies.

9   Patrick H. McNamara, (ed.), *Religion, American Style*, Harper & Row, New York, 1974. This well-chosen collection of articles on contemporary American religion demonstrates in a variety of ways the links between religious, economic, and political life.

10   Bryan Wilson, *Religion in Secular Society*, Penguin, New York, 1969. An excellent presentation of the secularization hypothesis by the dean of contemporary British sociologists of religion. Andrew Greeley offers a contrasting point of view in an article of almost the identical title in *Social Research* 15:226–40, 1974, and also in a book entitled *Unsecular Man*, Schocken, New York, 1972. For every sociologist who accurately describes some wave of the future another writes a book about the undertow; the problem is to decide which is which.

Family

Chapter Eight

*I ask what ties of bed and
blood amount to in societies
of different kinds and how
the Western world is changing
in this regard.*

The Tony Award for best play of 1978 went to a drama whose main character was already dead by the time of the opening scene. Hugh Leonard wrote the play. Barnard Hughes performed the title role of Da, an antiquated Irish gardener recently deceased. But Hughes was anything but lifeless in the role, nor was he supposed to be, for dead or not Da still lived on in the mind of his expatriate son. He followed the son around, intruding into his plans, distracting, bothering, infuriating, and outraging him, never quite leaving him alone. Family members are like that. They do not easily part company. Parents dead or seldom visited, wives and husbands long ago divorced, children runaway, and siblings far removed all have a want of haunting those to whom they once were joined in the stubborn stickiness of domestic life. The family is the thickest of social institutions, congealed from all the happy tears and sad ones shed within it. That makes the study of the family especially important—and difficult.

*the thickest of social
institutions appears to
be wearing thin*

We in the advanced industrial societies have cause even for urgency in the study of family ties, since they seem in general to be loosening. The institution which has traditionally promised to safeguard the deepest and most complete investment of ourselves has in many respects grown soft and thin. Later sections of this chapter detail the evidence. Here I would note only the shifts in vocabulary which affirm a weakening of marital and kinship bonds. We have translated fornication into premarital sex, adultery into an extramarital affair. Homosexuals are no longer queer but positively gay, and divorced mothers are just single parents. *Miss* and *Mrs.* yield steadily to *Ms.* Perhaps more clearly than in any other way, we applaud rebellion against our inherited family values by describing it in words free of stigma or reproach. Yet the applause is hardly without some hesitation. Who of us can fail to be troubled by the family's weakening when our own identities have been sunk so deep within it? Is our quest for individual freedom perhaps more accurately described by the title of Philip Slater's book, *The Pursuit of Loneliness*? Our fear, I think, is that the very trends we welcome will lead to more apartness than humans have yet felt from one another, to the terror of people utterly unstuck to anyone. The family merits study now more than ever, when rapid changes within it stir emotions at once fervent and mixed.

It would be hard to argue that my discipline has given the family the attention it deserves. Our prestigious fields of study are class and politics, rough counterparts to neurosurgery among medical practitioners. The sociology of the family, by contrast, ranks with research on religion in the league of psychiatry and public health. In the prevailing view of sociologists, the family and religion have actually much in common. Unlike government or the economy, both these institutions have a womanly connotation and thus partake of the lower status of the female sex. Both are seen as repositories of traditional values, reminders of the past more than portents of the future, dampers on innovation more than vents for it. Both appear to have shrunk in size and social import over time. And still more to the point, sociologists have tended to take further shrinkage in both cases for granted. Functionalist scholars have argued, for example, that the family best serves its purpose in an industrial society when it is reduced to its nucleus of mother, father, and children still at home. William J. Goode of Stanford University, probably the most influential student of the family in the United States, became famous for this view in the 1960s. For many Marxian scholars even the nuclear family is too much; like denominational religion, it is seen as a lingering historical remnant, expendable as development proceeds. In neither perspective does the family appear as an institution so precious to human existence that even the economy might need to bend on its behalf.

But despite a pervasive tone of resignation to the demise of family life, sociology and the other social sciences offer a rich and voluminous corpus of research in the area. The task of the present chapter is to pull some of the major studies together in such a way that the past importance and present breakdown of the family can be *overview of this chapter* understood in its economic and political context. Toward this end, the first section below analyzes the family in terms of its components, varieties, and types, thus clarifying its definition. The next section focuses on the particular type characteristic of Western Europe and North America until after World War II, the kind of family from which most readers of this book derive their existence and much of their personal identities. Thereafter two forms of deviation from the classic Western family are discussed, first the communal experiments in countercultural utopias, the Soviet Union, and Israeli kibbutzim, then the multifaceted breakdown of family life in the mainstream Western world, especially in the United States, during the last three decades. The chapter concludes with a tentative answer to the most crucial question of all on this subject, how much and what kind of family life we can reasonably take for granted in the decades to come.

A Social Overlay on Biological Ties

The three preceding chapters defined the polity, the economy, and religion, respectively, as *any* structured societal response to a particular problem or task inherent in the human situation. The polity was conceptualized as *whatever* roles and procedures, values and norms, constitute public order, the economy as *whatever* patterns of thought and action relate people to their environment, and religion as *whatever* celebration of ultimate limits a society enacts. The family is also associated with a particular problem or task, that of replenishing the human population, creating new persons to replace aged ones and teaching this younger generation what it must know to continue and improve upon the present structure of social life. Thus it is tempting to define the family as *whatever* system of interaction a society adopts for solving this problem, as *any* set of roles and procedures, values and norms, for accomplishing this task. Such a definition would have the virtue of consistency with those already offered for the other institutions. But it would only confuse our inquiry at its very beginning.

No one can doubt, of course, that the procreation and socialization of children are inescapable requirements placed upon the human race. And it is obvious that the family helps satisfy these demands wherever it is empirically observed. Nonetheless, there are other means of achieving these ends. Procreation can result from a single act of sexual intercourse between strangers. It can happen as well through artificial insemination, the mechanical injection of some named or nameless donor's sperm into a woman's vagina. From Bristol, England, in 1978, came news of the first documented "test-tube baby," conceived in a petri dish and implanted as a fetus in a woman's womb. In sum, procreation can be accomplished in ways no one would include in the idea of the family. So can the socialization of a younger generation. Orphanages and day-care centers exist for this purpose, as do nursery schools, kindergartens, elementary and high schools, colleges and universities, and such voluntary associations as Brownies and Scouts. No one would define these structures of action as part of the family. If children can be conceived, born, and raised outside the family, moreover, the family can also serve purposes quite apart from child-rearing. Many societies entrust to it a host of other tasks, from economic production and political organization to social control and the cultivation of leisure. For all these reasons, the family cannot be conceptualized in the same way as the three institutions earlier reviewed, in terms of problems or tasks inherent in the human situation.

The family is grounded not in an inescapable challenge facing people but in equally inescapable relationships entangling them. We can take it for granted that no human being comes into existence except through the joining of a woman's ovum to the sperm of a man. This is the preeminent fact of life, the most basic and enduring of all empirical truths about ourselves. Because of it two kinds of physical, biological relationship among people are found in all societies. The first ties together the woman and man whose bodies have been joined in the production of new life. This tie of parenthood, though ordinarily realized in **sexual** union, is no less biologically a fact when fertilization occurs through artificial insemination or

why the family is not defined in terms of tasks inherent in earthly life

*the biological family is
composed of procreative
and consanguineal ties*

even outside a woman's womb. Every child born is a sign of the procreative relationship between its parents. But a second kind of tie is equally evident, that of the child to its parents, and through them to everyone else whose existence derives from the procreative actions of some common ancestor. This connection is usually called *consanguinity* or blood relation. In its direct line it links grandparents to parents, parents to children, and so on from one generation to the next. In collateral lines it joins brothers, sisters, aunts, uncles, nieces, nephews, cousins, and so on. These two kinds of relation, procreative and consanguineal, are intrinsic to every human society. They are as real as we ourselves. They are the foremost evidence that all of us are social by nature, that no one is "an island, entire of itself."

In a biological sense, the term *family* refers simply to a collection of people closely tied by procreative and consanguineal relationships. Thus can anyone in any society, given the necessary information, draw his or her biological family tree. Such trees are universal in their structure, with one set of parents for each person, two sets of grandparents, uncle branches, great-aunt branches, and appropriate twigs for all possible procreative, lineal, and collateral connections. The *number* of relatives people have differs, of course, depending on how active in procreation they and their kinsfolk have been, but all biological family trees are structurally identical. There are no illegitimate children in nature, no estranged husbands, no disinherited grandchildren. Nature knows none of these—only procreators and their offspring. But the importance of biological relationships themselves must not be overdrawn. A tree of bodily connections is useful for tracing the genetic inheritance of facial features and the like, in much the same way as a city map helps explain the spread of contagious diseases and exposure to environmental hazards. But because we human beings are more than animals, neither physical kinship nor physical proximity by itself accounts for much of the shape of our lives. In contemporary urban settings, next-door neighbors often do not even know each other's names. And it is socially true though biologically impossible that some children are born without fathers.

For sociological purposes, the family is best understood as an order *imposed upon* procreative and consanguineal relationships, a structure of thought and action which invests natural bodily ties with *meaning*, a group in which physical kinship is a social *role*, with attendant rights and obligations. The family in this sense includes three kinds of role relationship. The first is conjugality, the tie between a woman and a man who have been publicly and legally granted the right to make a habit of sexual intercourse with one another and who therefore ordinarily procreate. This is the marriage bond, which gives meaning and legitimacy to the sexual union of husband and wife and casts a shadow upon such union in other contexts. The second kind of role relationship goes by the name of its biological analogue, consanguinity; it imposes reciprocal rights and duties on people who can trace their origin to the conjugal relations of some common ancestor. Third and finally, the sociological family includes relationships based on affinity, which joins people to the relatives of their own spouses, the spouses of the relatives of their own spouses, and still more distantly, the relatives of the spouses of the relatives of their own spouses. Affinity represents the intersection of conjugal and consanguineal ties, or of two sets of conjugal ties. It connects a woman to her husband's parents, for

*the sociological family is
composed of conjugal,
consanguineal, and
affinal role relationships*

To sociologists, the family is a structure of meaning imposed on relationships of bed and blood, the transformation of these physical ties into social roles, with attendant rights and duties. Participation in family reunions is often such a right—and duty. (© Arthur Tress 1980/Woodfin Camp & Assoc.)

example, a woman's husband to her brother's wife, or a man's parents to his wife's parents. Affinity is the bond between in-laws.

In the context of this book, therefore, the family can be defined as any group in which people are assigned roles by virtue of their location in a common network of conjugal, consanguineal, and affinal relationships. In every society, of course, people tend to regard their particular way of organizing this group as the natural way, that is, to identify their specific sociological family with its universal biological counterpart. And there is some truth in such identification—that is why the family is so thick an institution. Most people who think of themselves as brothers are brothers biologically. Most procreative activity does in fact occur between conjugal partners. Most people called grandma are physically mothers of the caller's own mother or father. But the fit between social and physical realities is

casual impressions notwithstanding, the family is what a society makes of the physical facts of life

never perfect, and there is no reason to expect it to be. Even if it is, moreover, nothing biological requires sisters to loan dresses to each other, wives to cook meals for their husbands, or fathers to pay the tuition fees of their children in university. Such role expectations are mere social conventions, to be taken seriously for reasons of history, culture, custom, or law, not on biological grounds. In whatever society, the family is but a social overlay upon the physical facts of life. It is whatever a society *makes* of the procreative and consanguineal relationships inherent in nature. For clarifying and illustrating the socially constructed character of the family, the paragraphs below review five distinct kinds of evidence.

ILLEGITIMACY

Whatever the society, the creation and maintenance of its system of family relations require discipline upon the sexual habits of its citizens. Marriage by its very definition removes sexual activity from the realm of whim and impulse and sequesters it in the enduring social relationship of specific individuals. The trouble is that no such discipline is ever quite complete. It is only desire that is inherent in nature, not its object or the context of its satisfaction. Thus sexual union regularly happens in all societies between people who lack the public permission of conjugality. And in the nature of things, such deviance is sometimes publicly proclaimed by the birth of children. They are called illegitimate, since they are born in defiance of the conditions formally spelled out for procreation. Latin Americans use an equally accurate but gentler term, *natural* children, thereby distinguishing them from other children for whom nature has been mediated by convention. Nowhere, however, do children born outside of accepted structures enjoy the benefits of those born within them. Usually they suffer relative economic deprivation. Often they are treated with overt or subtle scorn, so much even that they sometimes doubt their worth as human beings.

natural children reveal the family as a social invention

People born outside of wedlock and penalized on that account should be encouraged by the sociological outlook on their circumstance. For illegitimacy is but a socially invented designation. Natural children are intrinsically and really equally as good and beautiful as legitimate ones. The difference is made only by the rules and customs of particular societies. In most parts of the contemporary Western world, a child born a week after its mother's wedding is legitimate, provided her husband calls himself the father, while a child born a week before the wedding is not. In rural areas of northern Europe in the nineteenth century, the firstborn of a young, unmarried woman was scarcely stigmatized at all, so long as she found a husband relatively soon. Often, where the norms of a minority culture clash with those of a nation-state, a child may be illegitimate in the eyes of law but quite legitimate in the context of his or her particular subculture. In the United States before the Civil War, for example, most black children were officially illegitimate, since the law gave scant recognition to marriages between slaves; unofficially, on the other hand, many slave children grew up with a strong sense of lineage and family identity. Similarly, various Caribbean and Central American societies even in the recent past have classed as many as half of all births as illegitimate, since many couples disregard the requirements of legal marriage in favor of indigenous local customs. In sum, to be a legitimate child means nothing more than that one's biological parents procreated according to rules established in their particular time and place.

ADOPTION AND SIMILAR ADDITIONS

The birth of children outside family structures testifies in all societies to the fact that these structures are socially contrived. But so does the incorporation *within* family structures of people who on biological grounds do not belong. Adoption is the most common procedure by which this occurs, appearing in some form in nearly all societies. It is the formal, public assignment of a regular kinship role in a specific family to someone, usually a child, who cannot claim that role by birth or marriage. Orphans, foundlings, children of illegitimate birth, and those rendered homeless by natural or social misfortune are, of course, the prime candidates for adoption. They gain thereby not only such extrinsic benefits of family life as economic support and socialization for adult roles, but also a sense of legitimate identity, a feeling of security and rootedness in the society as a whole. In many societies, moreover, even children with socially real families of their own may be transferred by adoption to other families. A wealthy but childless couple may adopt as their son a nephew, cousin, or even a boy from an altogether separate family, thus creating an heir for their property and name through law and custom rather than by procreation. Adoption may thus serve parents' interests equally as much as children's. In any case it is evidence that the family is a social invention, one grounded in biological facts but not tied to them.

Adoption implies no basic restructuring of the biological family tree, only the assignment of positions in the tree on other bases than birth or marriage. Some societies modify even the tree itself, creating new positions which have no biological referent. One of the best examples is the Latin American institution of *compadrazgo*, which translates literally as *coparenthood*. It is rooted in the Roman Catholic ritual of infant baptism, at which a man and a woman other than the parents act as godparents or sponsors, speaking for the infant in its profession of faith. They are chosen by the parents and their names are recorded in the official church records. This ritual is practiced in Catholicism throughout the world, and in some branches of Protestantism as well. In many parts of Latin America, however, it incorporates the godparents (*padrinos* in Spanish) socially into the child's family, according them rights and duties which endure indefinitely. Their relation to the child is significantly closer than that of an aunt or uncle. They are expected to show an interest in the child's schoolwork and general welfare, to maintain periodic contact, and to give the child presents on birthdays and similar occasions. The child is obliged to show his or her *padrinos* special respect and to respond seriously and politely to expressions of their concern. Further, the godmother now finds herself related to the mother as *comadre* (comother) and the godfather and father refer to each other as *mi compadre* (my cofather). These relationships imply trust, the mutual doing of favors, inclusion in family get-togethers, and a degree of familiarity comparable to that between brothers or sisters. It would be difficult to imagine how any analysis of the Latin American family could fail to treat *compadrazgo* as an integral, albeit totally nonbiological, part of it.

coparenthood: family roles without biological foundation

VARIATION IN LANGUAGE, LINEAGE, AND LOCALITY

A third kind of evidence for the socially constructed character of the family is variety across societies in how relatives are named, how lines of kinship are drawn, and how domestic units or households are constituted. In a biological sense every human being has thousands, even millions of relatives—people to whom he or she

"The godmother now finds herself related to the mother as comadre *(comother) and the godfather and father refer to each other as* mi compadre *(my cofather). These relationships imply trust, the mutual doing of favors, inclusion in family get-togethers, and a degree of familiarity comparable to that between brothers and sisters." Above, the child's first birthday brings parents and coparents together to celebrate. (© Marcia Weinstein)*

is tied by some degree of consanguinity or affinity. Societies differ, however, in which physical relatives they pick from this vast pool, group together, and define to be meaningful company. The variety is evident in language above all, since no society can make much of a relationship without a name for it. In English, for example, we use the single word *uncle* for the brothers and brothers-in-law of both one's parents; other languages might have separate words for one's mother's brothers and father's brothers, and no word at all for their respective brothers-in-law. Similarly, the people I lump together under the label *cousins* could be divided, if the English language gave me words, into numerous distinct categories: my father's sister's female children, my mother's sister's male children, my mother's brother's daughter's male children, and so on. Robert H. Lowie (1883–1957), a student of Franz Boas and long-time professor of anthropology at Berkeley, devoted much of his life to the study of kinship terminologies, especially in various North American Indian tribes. On the basis of his research, he argued that the rules governing behavior with a given kind of relative (mother's brothers, for instance) are more precise and distinct if the language offers a special name for them (like *muncles*) than if they share a label with others (*uncles*). It follows from his argument that the kinship terminology available in a given language determines not just how people behave toward their various relatives but even whom they define their relatives to be. It also follows that the relatively sparse and nonspecific vocabulary for relatives in our own English language discourages us from making more of our extended families than we do.

Closely tied to language is the method by which a society reckons lineage, that is, how it defines lines of descent across the generations. Western civilization for the most part follows rules of *bilateral* descent. Each set of brothers and sisters has a unique set of relatives, those on their mother's side and those on their father's. We use the same set of words—*grandfather, cousin, aunt,* and so on—to describe people

kinship terminologies: tools for deciding who is related to whom

lines of descent: rules by which citizens are given ancestries

in each set. If one set is more important than the other, this is because of local circumstance, not because of public policy or the law. Yet only a minority of societies on earth have shared our bilateral method of tracing ancestry. Yale anthropologist George P. Murdock, in a classic analysis of the structures of more than 300 past and present societies, found that most have been *unilineal*, identifying children with only one set of kin. The majority of traditional societies are *patrilineal*, joining a child socially to the father's relatives but making those on the mother's side socially irrelevant. Societies with *matrilineal* descent discount the father's kin, and let the child inherit name, status, religion, property, and identity from the mother's side. A few societies even divide siblings between the lineages of the father and mother, using sex or birth order as the criterion of assignment. In any case, unilineal rules of descent imply that every legitimate child belongs to a *clan*, that is, a unified and corporate kinship group, a subculture whose members are all related to one another but to no one else. Societies founded on bilateral descent can hardly have such strong and solidary groupings of the extended family, since the children of each marriage have their own particular array of relatives. Thus do rules for determining ancestry and lineage determine how many physically consanguineal kin a person defines as relatives, which ones they are, and how important to social structure they can be.

Conjugal, consanguineal, and affinal relationships make their deepest impression on human life when they imply or require residence in a common household, the most intimate sharing of space and coordinating of time in an everyday routine. Given the diversity across societies in which of these relationships are recognized in language and counted for purposes of lineage, we should not be surprised that rules vary also with respect to the constitution of households. The present norm in the urban Western world is that each pair of newlyweds should move to their own house or apartment, away from both her family and his, and make a new home for themselves and their children. This pattern is termed *neolocal*. In most patrilineal societies, by contrast, the pattern is *patrilocal*: the newlywed wife goes off to live with her husband and his people, and their children are raised in the social order of his clan. Similarly, matrilineal societies are usually *matrilocal* as well, incorporating the husband into the clan organization of his wife. Only rarely, moreover, do a couple and their children live in a clearly distinct domestic unit. More often they share a house, meals, production and consumption tasks with various combinations of additional relatives from one side of their conjugal unit or the other. This is often the case even in societies founded on bilateral descent. There are also documented cases of societies where the husband does not even join his wife's domestic unit, leaving her, her parents, and her siblings to raise the children of their marriage. In sum, the rules of domestic locality established in societies are no more universal than the vocabulary for classifying relatives or the norms of tracing descent. This fact lends further credence to a conceptualization of the family as an overlay upon biological connections, not the connections themselves.

constitution of households: rules about who should live with whom

MONOGAMY AND ITS ALTERNATIVES

Since in the absence of human intervention about equal numbers of boys and girls are born and grow into adulthood, human nature is inherently disposed toward monogamy in family organization, that is, the restriction of a man to one wife at a time and a woman to one husband. Research reveals, moreover, that the majority of marriages in the majority of societies are in fact monogamous. But neither nature nor prevalence justifies anything or makes it good. Remember that without human intervention both you and I would probably be dead by the age of 35, as the majority of people in the vast majority of societies indeed have been until the last century. History is a record of human attempts to improve upon nature, usually for better though occasionally for worse, and the number of people in a conjugal unit has for millennia been a matter of social convention.

Outside Western civilization and the Christian religious tradition, most societies have granted to men at the top of their reward structures the right and even the duty to marry more than one woman, to practice the particular kind of polygamy labeled *polygyny*. Two common attributes of social organization have made the practice attractive. The first is male dominance, the tendency of the physically stronger and nonchildbearing male sex to subjugate the female sex. In societies which place wives under the authority of their husbands, the man with two wives is literally one up on his monogamous fellows. The man with three wives demonstrates his superiority still more. As a prerogative of elite men in male-dominant societies, polygyny is widespread simply as a power trip. A second attribute of such societies further encourages this kind of conjugal structure. It is that their male members, through socialization more aggressive and daring, are more susceptible to early death during travel, by accident, and in war. For this reason, the sex ratio (number of men per 100 women) among adults in most societies is less than 100, and there are enough women that some men can have several wives without reducing other men to celibacy. Male dominance and a low sex ratio are so common across societies that even the second largest religious tradition in the contemporary world, Islam, permits polygyny. Even so, under the impact of Western influence and industrial development, its practice is waning. By now there are only a few national societies in Africa and Asia where some husbands, usually fewer than 5 percent, have more than one wife.

Only a handful of societies known to social scientists have structured the conjugal unit on bases other than monogamy or polygyny. The two other alternatives, polyandry (one wife with several husbands) and group marriage (multiple women married to multiple men), were common among only a few traditional peoples, all of whom have abandoned these marriage forms long ago. Ironically, these societies seem to have been male-dominant as well. Among the Lesu of New Ireland, an island now part of New Guinea, the first husband paid his bride-price to his wife's relatives upon their marriage but the second husband paid his bride-price to the first.[1] It also appears that most polyandrous societies routinely practiced female infanticide, thereby ensuring the high sex ratio necessary in their marriage system. This is gruesome evidence indeed of the incalculable plasticity of the human species with respect to norms governing family life.

EXOGAMY AND ENDOGAMY

One further reflection of the mutability of family structures deserves discussion in the present context: the variety in norms governing the choice of marriage

The right and duty of plural marriage caught up with King Tribhuvana of Nepal in 1918, when he was only twelve and his senior and junior brides (sisters imported from India) were younger still. To all appearances the threesome lived happily together for the next thirty-seven years, until the god-king's death in 1955. Tribhuvana was a rare monarch in this age of constitutional government, since he led a revolution on behalf of it and gained power because of it. For his dynasty, the Shah family, had not actually ruled the impenetrable Himalayan kingdom since roughly 1769. Governance was in the hands of a rival lineage named Rana, within which the supreme role of prime minister was passed along from one generation to the next. The Ranas meanwhile kept a succession of Shah kings in luxurious but isolated captivity in the royal palace in Kathmandu. Tribhuvana, however, managed to smuggle books into the palace and thereby informed himself of the outside world. He hit upon the idea of ousting the Ranas, introducing somewhat democratic government and installing himself as a constitutional monarch. For years his plans came to nought, though in peasant's disguise he regularly escaped his home to conspire with dissidents. Then in 1948, the prime minister granted Tribhuvana a seemingly innocuous request. He allowed the king to bring into Nepal a German physiotherapist to give massages to the senior queen. Between treatments this woman, Erika Leuchtag, gained the king's trust and became his confidante. She informed him further of the outside world, taught him to dance, encouraged his planned revolution, and helped gain the Indian government's support for it. It occurred successfully in late 1950, and for the last five years of his life Tribhuvana was the working king he wanted to be. Leuchtag later recounted her life with the royal family in a poignant memoire, Erika and the King, *published by Coward McCann in 1958. Tribhuvana's son and successor, King Mahendra, presided over the outlawing of polygamy and child marriage in 1963.*

the variable norms governing choice of marriage partners

partners. For nature is of scarcely any help at all in deciding who shall form the tie of conjugality with whom: rules *have* to be invented without biological help. Those rules in any society which forbid marriage between members of the same group or category (members of the same clan, for example) are called *exogamous*; those which require it (as between members of the same religion) are termed *endogamous*. Only one such rule appears to be universal, that which forbids the incestuous union of parent and child. But even this taboo, so deeply entrenched in all cultures, has less to do with instinct or physical realities than with social learning. For as animals bred for show and sport bear witness, procreation by parent and child is indeed biologically possible. It repels and disgusts in the case of our own species, as the aforementioned George Murdock explained, not for biological reasons but because incest strikes at the very core of human social life. If parent-child marriage were permitted, sexual rivalry and jealousy would pit mother against daughter and father against son, while the offspring of such unions would so hopelessly confuse kinship roles that the family itself would disappear—and with it all that separates us humans from beasts.

Beyond this one taboo, rules of exogamy and endogamy vary as much as societies themselves. Presumably for the same reasons as parent-child marriages are taboo, those between brothers and sisters are virtually everywhere banned as well, but they were unashamedly condoned in the royal families of ancient Egypt, Hawaii, and Peru. Many Western governments forbid marriage between first cousins, but cross-cousin marriages were often preferred by parents among the African Ashanti and Thonga, in various parts of China, and elsewhere. Societies with unilineal rules of descent tend to prohibit marriage between members of the same clan, even if no common ancestor can be traced for some prospective bride and groom. Roman Catholic canon law requires a special dispensation before a godparent and godchild can legally wed, even if they are otherwise unrelated. Most societies, moreover, place substantially the same restrictions on adoptive kin as on those who have gained their kinship roles by birth. In sum, who can marry whom is in all societies limited by rules, but the rules change from place to place. In the contemporary Western world they are comparatively loose, except for the incest taboo among members of the nuclear family. Nonetheless, only in the past few decades have some American states become willing to admit black-white intermarriage. Informal norms, moreover, not just about race but also about class, religion, height, ethnicity, education, and other social factors still reduce the freedom of young people in their choice of mates much more than most of them are aware.

SUMMARY

The preceding few pages have placed on a firmer empirical basis the main assertion of this section of the chapter, that the family as it appears in human societies does not arise naturally from physical connections, whether procreative or consanguineal, linking one person to another. The family instead *makes these connections*. It is a human scheme that ties a man and a woman together in a procreative bond and joins them to their children and a range of others according to publicly established norms. Because it is a human scheme, it never encompasses quite all procreative acts, as illegitimate children bear witness. Because people have invented it, they can freely define it to include adoptive kin and even biologically impossible kinship roles. And as a social construct, the family is open to diversity across societies in the language of kinship, the calculation of lineage, the rules on residence, the number of wives and husbands, and the norms of exogamy and endogamy. Many more dimensions of variation could be discussed as well: divorce regulations, authority structures, child-rearing practices, penalties for adultery, economic significance, and so forth. But the discussion given here should be enough to make the point that it is we who are responsible for our family law and family life. Nature deserves neither blame nor credit in this regard.

why purely conventional family ties seem so natural

One final point bears emphasis before we proceed to analyze the Western family in more detail. Doubtful readers might yet wonder why if the family is humanly created its hold on people is so tight. Why should kinship relations be so thick, so sticky, and so everlasting if they rest on mere convention? Why cannot people quit their roles as son, niece, mother, or cousin as easily as they leave their jobs in department stores and factories? If family norms in any society are as idiosyncratic as the evidence reviewed above suggests, why do they seem so natural? Even a sociologist must resort to biology in attempting answers to such questions. For once some kind of family structure is socially in place it does indeed order biological connections. Most people in most societies in fact are born legitimate, and most people socially defined as mothers, brothers, sisters, and so on occupy these roles physically as well. Thus the family of whatever kind succeeds by and large in regulating connections based in nature. And to the extent that it does, it then seems to be justified in terms of those same natural ties. The fact that most American mothers, for example, are the biological mothers of their sons lends a kind of credibility to the purely idiosyncratic mother-son relationship defined by American culture. Or similarly, the fact that Prince Charles is biologically the firstborn son of Queen Elizabeth makes it seem more reasonable that he of all people should succeed her on the British throne. In sum, there is first the laying down of rules about marriage and kinship, but once the rules are followed they gain legitimacy by the physical relations they create. Such is the way a human society encloses itself within its own world and makes that world seem real.

Kinship and Marriage in the West

the hard question: why the Western world excelled

In all of social science few questions cry so loudly for an answer as why the ragged little island-kingdom of Great Britain, along with societies nearby on the European continent, began in the sixteenth and seventeenth centuries to outstrip all others in economic development and to bring on modern times. Was there something special about the medieval Roman civilization of which these peoples had earlier been part? How much does the answer lie in idiosyncrasies of their own? We need answers, especially we Americans, Australians, British, Canadians, Dutch, Germans, New Zealanders, Swedes—all of us for whom the European northwest is a cultural heritage. Without answers we cannot hope to understand ourselves. But people elsewhere need answers, too. For those few little societies on a scrawny northern continent ruled the earth for a while and touched with their colonizing hands the shape of life on every continent. Still today they and their offspring in North America and Australasia are unexcelled in wealth and power. They are culturally the Occident, the Western world. On the whole they are the settings where people speak English without resenting it. And they are the objects of suspicion, distrust, and often warfare by societies elsewhere—in eastern Europe, the Middle East, Asia, Africa, even South America. How could anyone fail to wonder what it was about the peoples of northwestern Europe a few hundred years ago that spurred them to leave so indelible a mark on the history of the human race?

A basic book like this is not equal to a question so big. The three previous chapters have done no more than summarize some partial answers given with much care and thoughtfulness by a variety of scholars. Politically, it seems that Western triumphs have had much to do with the liberal kind of democracy, representative but noninterventionist government, the kind proposed by Locke and Jefferson. Economically, the defense of private property, the quest for profit, wage labor, and other attributes of that bleak strategy called capitalism seem at the root of the Western mind. And with respect to religion, Christianity in general and Protes-

after political, economic, and religious answers, an answer here in terms of family life

tantism in particular seem to underlie the ascendancy of the Western way of life, as Weber argued. Now in the present context the same question deserves to be addressed in connection with the structure of family life. Of all possible ways of ordering marital and kinship ties, what kind of order have these particular societies imposed on their citizens? How if at all has it contributed to their dynamism? What role has this familial order played in their overall ways of life? It is questions like these which this section of the chapter is intended to address, albeit briefly. Our focus first is on medieval Christendom, to which these societies earlier belonged. Then it shifts to the Western family in modern times.

I should acknowledge here in preface the hard work of a dozen or so historians who in recent years have researched the Western family in much detail and studied its role in economic and political development. France has contributed Philippe Ariès to this effort; his 1962 volume, published later in English as *Centuries of Childhood*, has become a classic. At England's Cambridge University Peter Laslett and his colleagues have completed scores of meticulous analyses of early census data and ecclesiastical records. In the United States John Demos has done a book on the family among the Puritans at Plymouth Rock; research he did jointly with Virginia Demos also appears in *The American Family in Social-Historical Perspective*, a book edited by Connecticut sociologist Michael Gordon and published in 1973. Canadian historian Edward Shorter published in 1975 a splendid book entitled *The Making of the Modern Family*; Ariès has called it a "powerful synthesis presented with a logical rigour and grace rare among historians."[2] Thanks to the work of these scholars and some others, most of whom teach in departments of history, the sketch offered here of the family in past centuries is made with much less guesswork than would otherwise be necessary.

THE MEDIEVAL BACKGROUND

What we think of as the Western family is an amalgam of diverse culture traits, many of them traceable even to the ancient Jews, Greeks, and Romans. But for present purposes we need not travel intellectually back so far. For these ancient cultures have left their mark on us mainly through the medium of medieval Christianity. They helped to shape that culture centered in Rome which spread steadily across Europe in the first one and a half millennia after Christ and which impressed upon European tribes a basic order of family life discernible even in the midst of their diversity. It is this medieval Christian conception of the family which we need to understand, since within it the earlier influences were synthesized and upon it most of the Western family even now is based. In basic outline, the Christian family structure amounted to laxity with respect to kinship but severity surrounding marriage. Compared to societies elsewhere at that time, medieval Christian ones seem to have taken consanguineal and affinal ties rather lightly, but the sexual, procreative bond with utmost seriousness. The relative unconcern with kinship is evident especially in three ways.

three signs of the laxity of kinship in medieval Christendom

First, while rules of descent favored the father's line a little more than the mother's, they were generally loose and variable. Christianity did not encourage the sharp division of societies into clans that prevailed, for instance, in some Celtic tribes of Ireland and Scotland. The church's incest taboos applied equally to maternal and paternal relatives, fostering thereby the idea of bilateral descent. Lineage was important, to be sure, since property and position were normally handed down from father to son, usually the eldest son by right of primogeniture. Nonetheless, location in a kinship network was rarely so precise, definite, and socially all-important as among numerous non-Christian peoples. Second, rules of exogamy and endogamy were also relatively loose, permitting the royal families of medieval kingdoms to intermarry and placing few legal barriers to marriage across ethnic or linguistic lines. Few people crossed such lines in choosing mates; then as now most marriages occurred between very similar people. But officially the homogeneity of Christian faith was held to outweigh cultural differences. Third and most important, the preeminent institution of medieval life, the church, was officially cut off from the kinship system. Popes, bishops, priests, monks, and nuns were celibate by law in Western Europe and hence could have no legitimate direct heirs. Ecclesiastical positions, property, and wealth could not therefore be inherited or claimed as a birthright. If kinship sometimes intruded into the church through nepotism or through favoritism toward clerics of noble birth, this was by virtue of sub rosa politics. Roles in the largest, wealthiest, and most powerful institution of the Christian world had formally to be assigned for nonfamilial reasons. Thus nowhere in Western Europe could kinship be the all-encompassing ground of social order.

kinship and social change

But if being some kind of relative meant less in the medieval world than elsewhere, what difference did this make for the course of Western history? Probably quite a lot. If some imaginary wicked king asked social scientists to advise him how best to ensure endless stability in his realm, I suspect he would be told to build kinship into every corner of social structure. Each person would need to receive just by the fact of birth into a specific family a whole lifetime's worth of obligations. No authority could be exercised except on hereditary bases. The rules governing economic exchange would vary from instance to instance, depending on the precise kind of kinship tie between the parties involved. Religion would consist of ancestor worship, or perhaps the cult of household gods. Kinship rules would preselect each man's wife through some kind of cross-cousin scheme. In sum, as actually happens in certain isolated, static societies known to anthropologists, no one could interact with anyone else without knowing the exact familial relationship between them and the norms governing it. The point here is that even the early Christian world was not like that. There was space to move in innovative ways within the kinship web. Christian identity by baptism transcended if only a little the identity inherited from one's parents. Holy orders could not formally be a birthright. The church's celibate functionaries had to interact with one another in purposive, organizational, bureaucratic terms, not in terms of a family tree. Indeed, the Christian scriptures offered Jesus' own family policy: "I have not come to bring peace, but a sword. For I have come to set a man against his father, and a daughter against her mother, and a daughter-in-law against her mother-in-law; and a man's foes will be those of his own household. He who loves father or mother more than me is not worthy of me; and he who loves son or daughter more than me is not worthy of me."[8]

The mythical king desirous of stability would fault Christianity for its irreverence toward kinship norms. But its solemn attitude toward sex and marriage would

"The king would want to encourage the kind of culture once known in Peru and India, where craftsmen painted copulating couples on their pottery and carved them into temple walls."
(Photo by Terese Tse Bartholomew, Curator of Indian Art, Asian Art Museum of San Francisco)

sexuality and social change

distress him even more. For his sociological mentors would urge him, I believe, to inundate his realm with the cult of sensuality, to foster romance and erotic goings on, thus to intoxicate his subjects with the delightfulness of people as they are, not as they might become. The king would want to encourage the kind of culture once known in Peru and India, where craftsmen painted copulating couples on their pottery and carved them into temple walls. He would find no need at all to forbid polygamy or divorce, to count lifelong virginity a virtue, to deny sexual expression to yet unmarried youth, or to castigate adulterers. There would be rules on sexual activity, to be sure, since social order is unthinkable without them and since in the kinship system every child would have to have a clear, legitimate, family-based identity. But the rules would be like those on money-making under capitalism, designed to encourage as much of it as possible. The social environment would maximize everyone's exposure to seductive sights, alluring sounds, ambrosian foods, the aromas of musk and perfume, and the ravishing touch of romantic love. All this for the sake of keeping human consciousness in present time, and not letting it escape into a future creatable through innovative work.

four signs of severity surrounding sex in medieval Christendom

The medieval world was not like that either. It ranks indeed among the more sexually restrictive experiments in social order ever made by the human race. Four of its attributes clearly point this out. First was the idea, deeply entrenched in the theology of Rome, that God is more pleased by sexual abstinence than indulgence, by celibacy for religious motives than by marriage. The New Testament endorses such a view just by portraying Jesus as celibate, his mother as Virgin, and his apostles as uninterested in sex and procreation. More to the point, this view was institutionalized in the requirement of clerical celibacy in the Western church and in the voluntary chastity of members of all religious orders. This view was impressed upon married Christians, too, since only in the presence of a spouseless priest could they legally exchange their vows. Second, Christianity defined monogamy even in early centuries as the only legitimate kind of marriage. Hence even royal and aristocratic men in Christendom, unlike ancient Jewish kings or Moslem sheiks in later centuries, could have but one legal wife at a time. Third, the church made divorce officially impossible. A willful marriage once consummated could never legally be undone. At most it might be annulled, that is, certified to have been void from the beginning, but Rome granted annulments reluctantly and only after detailed investigation. Fourth and finally, Christian moral teaching limited sexual intercourse to marriage, and even there it was not to be enjoyed with dissolute abandon. Fornication and adultery, like masturbation and homosexuality, were considered gravely sinful and deserving of punishment even by civil authority when detected.

the Christian influence on European family life

No scholar today can know the precise extent to which the church's teaching with respect to either kinship or marriage was followed in the everyday life of medieval men and women. History has not yet yielded up the necessary data, and perhaps it never will. Across the hundreds of distinct cultures coexisting in Europe during the roughly 1000 years of the medieval era there must surely have been immense variation in the practical conduct of familial and sexual matters. The values institutionalized in the church of Rome had to compete everywhere with indigenous customs and non-Christian influences. "Carmina Burana," a shamefully delightful rendition of old Latin drinking songs by the contemporary composer Karl Orf, demonstrates that bawdiness was hardly unknown in some sectors of the medieval population. Available evidence suggests that Nordic and Teutonic peasants took premarital sex for granted.[4] The Moorish occupation of southern Spain from the eighth to the fifteenth centuries left an erotic flavor in the culture which persists even now. Clans survived in the British Isles long after Christianity took root there, and the peoples of eastern Europe relaxed the rule of celibacy for parish priests.

Nonetheless, nonchalant attitudes toward kinship and restrictive ones on sex and marriage were emanating from Rome and bearing down on Christendom throughout the medieval era. And if contemporary historians have correctly described the overall quality of life in those centuries, it did indeed reflect the church's attitudes. Courtship and mate selection were relatively free of romance and sexuality. Aristocratic youth generally accepted thier parents' choice of spouse, and peasant youth respected parental preference in making their own choices. In neither case did erotic attraction figure so importantly as matters of health, property, and ability to perform nonsexual roles. Premarital sex in most settings seems to have been far less than half as common as it is today. Illegitimacy accounted for a mere 2 or 3 percent of births. The marriage bond did not normally imply deep affection or sentiment. Intercourse was not so much lovemaking as a husband's sexual release and a woman's impregnation. Fidelity was common, divorce was not. Children were not smothered with love but treated as miniature adults and put to work early. Perhaps most important, popular culture in most parts of Europe does not seem to have been sexually charged. Peasant dress was modest. So was art. Medieval craftsmen carved no copulating couples into church decor. Now admittedly, such generalizations as these are based on fragmentary evidence and conjecture. But since we know what the church was teaching and how powerful it was, and since we lack widespread evidence to the contrary, we might best conclude that people more or less followed the rules. Especially must we guard against the tendency to justify our own more permissive sexual norms by projecting them onto our Euorpean ancestors.

In summary, family life in medieval Europe seems to have been marked by relative moderation with respect to kinship, but severity concerning sex and marriage. This combination of qualities encouraged a dynamism in Western civilization, a propensity to change, what the modern Chinese intellectual Hu Shih has called the most outstanding characteristic of the West, "not to know contentment."[5] Yet the Middle Ages did not give rise directly to modernity and an industrial economy. The tens of thousands of celibate clergy and religious were unfettered by kinship, free enough not to be content, able to challenge the status quo, but their challenges ran mostly in political and religious directions. Medieval energies were aimed above all toward the extension of Christendom, the conquest and conversion of pagan tribes, the amassing of foreign treasure in Christian hands—toward the general aggrandizement of the patrons of the universal church and of the church itself. Crusades to recapture Palestine, war and statecraft within Europe, cathedrals and universities, and the beginnings of trade with the East: these were the innovative schemes of medieval times. It was an otherworldly asceticism, fomenting an enlarged celebration of Christian faith more than an enlarged domain of human action on the earth.[6] The asceticism remained but was redirected toward this world in England and parts of central Europe from the sixteenth century onward, and but slightly later in America. We turn now to family life in these societies, the immediate progenitors of the contemporary Western world.

otherworldly asceticism: springboard of Western dynamism

THE EARLY MODERN FAMILY

England's defeat of the Spanish Armada in 1588 was not just a military victory but a symbol of the northward shift of the European center of power and innovation. Southern Europe remained loyal to Rome and to the high medieval culture it espoused, a situation that was not to change decidedly for the next three centuries. The north by contrast, as earlier chapters have pointed out, became alive with political, economic, and religious novelty. What variation on the Christian family did these societies of the north compose and execute? Beyond relatively lenient kinship norms and stringent ones on sexuality, what attributes characterized the family in England and adjacent societies when they came to the forefront of world history? Three such attributes merit our attention here: the rejection of clerical celibacy, the single-family household, and the idea of companionate marriage.

three marks of the family in Britain and the European northwest: first, an end to clerical celibacy

It would be hard to cite any Roman Catholic norm more uniformly rejected by the various Protestant movements of the sixteenth and seventeenth centuries than the one forbidding the clergy to marry. In one respect the abandonment of clerical celibacy was a step toward greater structural stability: once drawn more closely into the web of kinship ties, organized religion could never again be so free to challenge and criticize the existing order. But the overall significance of this move was quite the opposite. For by permitting their ministers to marry, the Protestant groups renounced the definition of marriage as a second-best state in life. Thereby they symbolically affirmed the goodness in principle of worldly involvement, and in a practical sense they opened the way for more to be made of the conjugal bond. Henceforth in the Protestant world marriage could officially and publicly be more than an institution necessary for the procreation of children. It could evolve, as in fact it did, into a shamelessly deep and exclusive love relationship between husband and wife. This was true especially because the reformers retained the older Christian emphases on monogamy, premarital chastity, and marital fidelity. There is no need to argue that love and passionate lovemaking between husband and wife were unknown in Europe before this time. But the Reformation paved the way for the emotional and physical pleasure of marriage to be freed from any taint of guilt or sinfulness.

second, neolocal residence

Equally important is the fact that in England, America, and northern France, even as early as the seventeenth century, the overwhelming majority of married couples lived with their dependent children in separate domestic units. This fact has been amply demonstrated by the studies in historical demography directed by Peter Laslett at Cambridge. It seems that in the countries which industrialized first, the family was normally neolocal even at that time, and possibly centuries earlier. Children did not as is sometimes imagined grow up in a common household with their grandparents, aunts, uncles, and other relatives. In most communities of English origin for the last three centuries, whether in Britain or America, no more than 10 or 15 percent of households have included both parents and grandparents, the families of two married brothers, or some other kinship group beyond a couple and their children. This finding is especially remarkable for its contrast with corresponding research results for southern and eastern Europe. Even in the nineteenth century, extended- or multiple-family households embraced well over half the total in Russia, Hungary, Latvia, Estonia, and parts of Italy, and a quarter or more in southern France, Ireland, and parts of Germany. In general it appears that where Protestantism, capitalism, and liberal democracy took their first and deepest root, few parents even then shared the intimate, everyday routine of life with relatives other than their own young children, and few children shared it with any kin beyond parents and siblings. In the part of Europe which now is socialist or socialistically inclined, neolocal family residence was much less common.

third, the beginnings of companionate marriage

A third and related attribute of the family in the early modern world is what Laslett and others have called *companionate marriage*. They mean the term a bit more broadly than the man who used it first, Ben B. Lindsey, as the title of a 1927 book. A reformist Colorado judge, Lindsey coined the term for his proposal that a husband and wife should be free to divorce by mutual consent so long as they had no children. Companionate marriage in this specific sense did not exist three centuries ago, since divorce laws still were restrictive. In a broader sense, however, Lindsey's term is usefully applied to that earlier family structure, and not only because it suggests where that earlier structure has led. For at the root of Lindsey's proposal is the idea that the husband and wife as partners are in charge of their marriage, that it is their own voluntary creation to do with as they please. It is this idea that can be discerned in the societies under discussion here even three centuries ago. And it distinguished these societies from other ones. For elsewhere marriage was more firmly locked into the village community and the wider network of kin, just as it was physically located as a rule in a little house shared with other relatives. Few people in such settings could imagine a couple privately sitting down to plan their marriage as if it belonged to them, to ponder how many children they should have or how to organize their own common life. But such thinking can be found in the early industrial societies. The husband was still both literally and figuratively the senior partner in marriage, but he was on average only a year or two older than his wife (an age gap smaller than elsewhere) and even she was typically 26 or 27 years old when they were wed (four or more years older than in eastern Europe). Being mature adults of similar age, they could more easily think of themselves as autonomous partners with authority over their married life. Their neolocal residence encouraged the idea. Letters and literature from that era suggest that many couples in fact saw themselves as loving companions in a social contract of their own.

the nuclear family—legacy of Western history

In summary, the early industrializing societies did not repudiate medieval family values but instead carried them to a specific practical conclusion. Kinship was taken more lightly than ever. Rules of descent remained bilateral and loose, rules of endogamy flexible. But now the social import even of close relatives was reduced; the nuclear, neolocal household gained autonomy from the extended network of kin. Marriage, for its part, was taken still more seriously. Not only was it still to be monogamous, permanent, and the sole legitimate context of sexual activity, but now it could even be enjoyed, invested with unashamed affection, and lived more freely according to the wishes of husband and wife. Thus was created the basic outline of what is today considered the Western kind of family structure. It endured and strengthened through more than two centuries of economic development and modernization. It survived a transplant to New World settings: the American, Canadian, and Australian frontiers. Beginning in the nonaristocratic classes, it also infiltrated family life in the upper echelons and in nonanglophone immigrant minorities. The structure of the Western family spread to other continents, in tandem with Christianity, urbanization, and capitalist development. By now it is often taken for granted as the natural kind of marital and kinship structure. The first definition of *family* in my dictionary is "a father, mother, and their children." The question is what part this kind of family has played in the overall composition of Western societies.

THE NUCLEAR FAMILY IN CONTEXT

as separate as oil from vinegar, but no less necessary

In answer we might liken the family's part to that of the sweeter liquid in a bottle of oil-and-vinegar salad dressing. The oil does not mix with the vinegar even though it shares the same bottle and is important for balanced taste. In the Western model of society, life outside the family has a vinegarish quality. Politicians must compete with each other for the votes of electors, never able to rest on birthright laurels. Business proprietors must constantly try to undercut their adversaries in the marketplace, lest they themselves be driven into the working class. Wage laborers

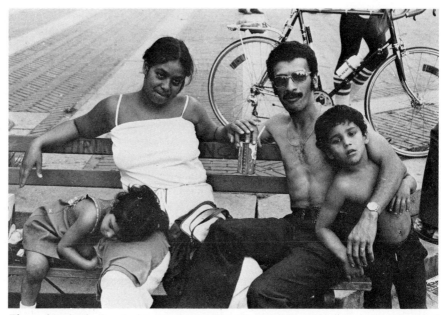

The nuclear family "survived a transplant to New World settings: the American, Canadian, and Australian frontiers. Beginning in the nonaristocratic classes, it also infiltrated family life in the upper echelons and in nonanglophone immigrant minorities." (© Jim Anderson 1979/Woodfin Camp & Assoc.)

know that family connections are seldom enough to ensure a steady and profitable return on the sale of their work. Nor can the churchgoer draw much comfort from his or her baptism as an infant, since most Protestant groups insist upon a mature profession of faith as a condition of Christian worth. In sum, the Western world outside the family resembles a pack of rugged, lonely individuals each trying to achieve more than the rest, each placing self-interest above collective concerns and therefore never finding rest. In this kind of society it is thought aberrant or unfair to vote, to hire, to take a job, or to go to church merely on the basis of family ties. Roles within families are not supposed to spill over very much into roles outside of them. The basic structure of political and economic life has little room for the sticky entanglements of relatives.

The separation of the family from other institutions has not made the family weak or irrelevant, however, at least not until recent decades. The family has continued to be the major instrument for transmission of culture and property from one generation to the next, the place where children "get their start in life." Parentage has remained the preeminent influence upon where a child ends up in the stratification system. But the major function left to the family in the modern *the main function of the* Western world is to serve as a "haven in a heartless world," to quote the title of a *Western family: to be a* 1977 book on the subject by Christopher Lasch, an historian at the University of *haven of love* Rochester. For with the passing of traditional ways of life, some kind of refuge from the harsh, impersonal, uncaring pressures of the marketplace became a desperate necessity. Until then people could take some comfort from the changelessness of life, poor though it was. Serfs might be tied by law to their little plots of land, but then the land was also tied to them. In England until the seventeenth century there were public lands, the commons, where landless peasants could freely graze their sheep. But the coming of capitalist modern times changed all that. English landlords enclosed the commons and made them private property. Wage laborers found themselves untied to any means of production. The standard of living rose, but so did the sense of precariousness about everyday life. *Fiddler on the Roof*, until 1979 the longest-running Broadway play in history, dramatized with poignant success the terror and uncertainty of a peasant as he watches life lose its predictability. He tries to control his children, but he cannot. He rages in anger at his wife, but to no avail. What is he to do? How can he assuage his deep anxiety? With stark honesty and historical accuracy, Tevyev then sings to his wife, "Golda, do you love me?" For people caught in the Western strategy of development, family is nearly all they can count on. It is the sweet oil that makes bitterness outside the home even taste good.

This split between the family and other institutions is more than just a mechanical separation of roles. It is the wrenching apart of the dimensions of pride and humility within the human person, as these terms were discussed in Chapter Three. The capitalist economy and the liberal polity require and reward an attitude of aggressive self-assertion, shrewd calculation, dispassionate innovation, the seizure of power and opportunity for the furtherance of individual ambition. Western societies encourage their workers to be go-getters, people who can make hard decisions and get results. The attitude that pays is one that keeps distance from other people, holds them at arm's length, guards secrets from them, and manipulates them for extrinsic purposes. But what of the dimension of humility, the side of whimsy, gentleness, openness, passion, trust in other people, love for them, admission to them of one's own weakness? In the modern West this side of human nature is banished mainly to the family; only there can it freely be expressed. Consider that weighty sentence with which a nuclear family customarily begins: "I have fallen in love with you." This is the admission of weakness *par excellence*, the supreme negation of the guardedness and impersonality in public life. It is thought odd that a man truly in love with his wife should work with her in the same enterprise—productivity might suffer and the marriage, too. The Western mentality is to keep the dimensions of the person apart and to sequester love in the confines of the family home.

The progressive separation of the family from economic and political life, its transformation into a refuge from the insecurities outside, has therefore not disrupted but actually bolstered the general course of liberal-capitalist development. But there have also been more particular consequences, especially on the roles of women and children. Traditionally, in Europe, women were not primarily wives and mothers. Their roles were defined by their sex, not their sexuality. It was taken for granted that a woman would satisfy her husband in bed and bear and raise numerous children. But her life was not expected to consist in or even revolve around these tasks. She had work to do: cooking, cleaning, raising vegetables, carrying wood, feeding chickens, preserving foods, pitching hay, and so on. She was subservient to her husband but still involved in the tasks of production. In most regional cultures there was a customary division between a man's work and a woman's work, and both were seen as integral parts of the overall economy. Women were not free, but neither were men. Each sex had its accustomed place in a routine of life that seemed always to have been the same.

As Western development progressed, however, economic production took place increasingly away from the home in factories and businesses. The family farm began to embrace fewer and fewer families. Husbands left home to work in that outside world, but pregnancies and infant care prevented their wives from doing so. Women often tried to retain a role in production by "taking in work" or raising gardens on city lots, but they were steadily squeezed out of the market. Their situation worsened as household gadgetry increased and housework eased. Even the housework that was left, since it was unpaid and outside the market economy, came to be redefined as outside the production process—it neither is nor can be, for example, included in the calculation of a gross national product. This is to say that the work of women was redefined as consumption. Women were left with completely private lives, the one-dimensional half-people of Western industrial societies. Increasingly their role was just to assuage the pain inflicted by an outside world which they themselves were not part of: to be good lovers for their hard-working husbands, comforters for their children after school, and occasional participants in voluntary charities and women's clubs. There were exceptions to this pattern, of course, in the early decades of this century: the roughly 10 percent of women who never married, many of whom had careers outside the home; the 5 to 10 percent of married women who also held outside jobs; the working-class women who lacked household appliances and for whom housework remained a heavy burden. But the overall trend until the past few decades was toward the purely private woman's role of loving wife and dutiful mother. Women even came to symbolize all the human goodness, gentleness, and love that industrial capitalism had drained from the rest of life.

As the split between family and other institutions intensified, the role of the child also underwent a transformation. Most important of all, it became more separate and distinct from the role of adult. In premodern Europe, a person moved more gradually from infancy to adulthood, mixing steadily more work and less play into the day's activities. As a rule it seems that children were assigned tasks to the maximum of their capabilities. Rarely were they coddled or protected from the blunt realities of life on earth. For several reasons this changed as Western development advanced. Work roles came to require literacy and schooling, as did the principles of democracy. First 4 or 6, then 8, then 12, and now even more years of education have come to be expected of every child. The brutalizing of young wage laborers led to passage of restrictive child-labor laws early in the twentieth century. Parents sought to delay their children's entry in the labor force until they had the education to enter on an economically higher plane. Children could still work at home after school, of course, but gadgets and machines steadily eliminated children's chores. By the 1950s childhood in the advanced societies had become a long and often boring period of waiting to grow up, a kind of prolonged postnatal incubation. This boredom became a major threat to social order, expressing itself in various forms of juvenile delinquency and "behavior problems" at school. Mothers had to busy themselves entertaining their children, chauffering them to recreational activities, desperately trying to keep them occupied until they gained enough

in the course of Western progress, women's work was redefined as consumption

the period of childhood dependency lengthened

FOR EXAMPLE

Philippe Ariès, "The Family and the City"*

Sociology consists in making connections. Here Ariès connects the ascendancy of the nuclear family (and the stress upon it) to changes in city life. People crave "free areas," he argues, frontiers, places outside the controlling presence of external authority. Neighborhood pubs and cafes were important free areas in nineteenth-century cities, but no longer. Now family homes are almost the only free areas left. Ariès doubts that homes are enough.

Neighborhoods are segregated not only by social class but also by function. Thus, just as there are rich, bourgeois neighborhoods and poor, working-class ones, so, too, there are business districts and residential ones. Offices, businesses, factories, and shops are found in one location, houses and gardens in the other.

The means of transportation most often used to get from one place to the other is the private car. In this scheme of things there is no longer room for the forum, the agora, the piazza, the corso. There is no room, either, for the cafe as meeting place. The only thing there is room for is the drive-in and the fast-food outlet. Eating establishments are to be found in both business and residential districts; depending on their location, they are busy at different times of the day. In business and industrial districts, they are humming with activity at lunchtime; in residential neighborhoods they do most of their business at night. During the off-hours, in both places, they are empty and silent: the only sign of life amidst the furniture and electric lights is the bored face of the cashier.

What is truly remarkable is that the social intercourse which used to be the city's main function has now entirely vanished. The city is either crowded with the traffic of people and cars in a hurry or it is totally empty. Around noontime, office workers in business districts sometimes take an old-fashioned stroll when the weather is nice, and enjoy a piece of cake or an ice cream cone in the sun. But after five o'clock the streets are deserted. Nor do the streets in residential neighborhoods become correspondingly crowded, except around shopping centers and their parking lots. People return to their homes, as turtles withdraw into their shells, At home they enjoy the warmth of family life and, on occasion, the company of carefully chosen friends. The urban conglomerate has become a mass of small islands—houses, offices, and shopping centers—all separated from one another by a great void. The interstitial space has vanished.

This evolution was precipitated by the automobile and by television, but it was well underway before they had even appeared, thanks to the growth of the

---

*Reprinted from Philippe Ariès, "The Family and the City," in *The Family*, Alice S. Rossi, Jerome Kagan, and Tamara Hareven (eds.), by permission of the author and W. W. Norton and Co., Inc. Copyright © 1978, 1977, by the American Academy of Arts and Sciences. Born in 1914, Philippe Ariès is a French social historian.

cult of privacy in the bourgeois and middle classes during the nineteenth century. To people born between 1890 and 1920 (now between 50 and 80 years old), the green suburb represented the ideal way of life. They wanted to escape from the bustle of the city and to live in more rural, more natural surroundings. This shift to the suburbs, far from the noise and crowds of city streets, was caused by the growing attraction of a warm private family life. In those areas where private family living was less developed, as in the working-class areas along the Mediterranean, i.e., in societies dominated by obstinate males, community life fared better.

During the nineteenth and early twentieth centuries, the results of the increased privacy and the new family style of living were kept in check, it seems, thanks to the vitality of community life in both urban and rural areas. A balance was achieved between family life in the home and community life in the cafe, on the terrace, in the street. This balance was destroyed and the family carried the day, thanks to the spread of suburbia as a result of the unexpected help it received from the new technology: the automobile and television. When that happened, the whole of social life was absorbed by private, family living.

Henceforth, the only function of the streets and cafes was to enable the physical movement between home and work or restaurant. These are no longer places of meeting, conversation, recreation. From now on, the home, the couple, the family claim to fulfill all those functions. And when a couple or a family leave the house to do something that cannot be done at home, they go in a mobile extension of the house, namely, the car. As the ark permitted Noah to survive the Flood, so the car permits its owners to pass through the hostile and dangerous world outside the front door. . . .

Although people today often claim that the family is undergoing a crisis, this is not, properly speaking, an accurate description of what is happening. Rather, we are witnessing the inability of the family to fulfill all the many functions with which it has been invested, no doubt temporarily, during the past half-century. Moreover, if my analysis is correct, this overexpansion of the family role is a result of the decline of the city and of the urban forms of social intercourse that it provided. The twentieth-century post-industrial world has been unable, so far, either to sustain the forms of social intercourse of the nineteenth century or to offer something in their place. The family has had to take over in an impossible situation; the real roots of the present domestic crisis lie not in our families, but in our cities.

seniority to call themselves adults. By and large, this condition of young people persists to the present day. The invention of television has made it perhaps more bearable. In the United States this machine accounts for about three hours of every day in a schoolchild's life, four hours for preschoolers.

SUMMARY

Few readers need to be reminded that the attributes reviewed above of the modern Western family are general ones, admitting of variation and exception across the millions of specific families in the various Western societies. The structure described here emerged as more typical of the Anglo-Saxon majority than of ethnic minorities, especially those originating outside Western Europe. It appeared more clearly in the large middle-income strata than among the very rich or very poor. It was more urban than rural, since vestiges of traditional life persisted longer on farms. But even today, despite the changes to be discussed in the following pages, this structure remains the culturally most acceptable kind of family life in the Western world, especially the anglophone part of it. It is thought both normal and proper that a man and a woman should fall into romantic love sometime in their early twenties; that they should marry and begin their sexual lives together; that they should be faithful to each other and never get divorced; that they should keep in touch with both her family and his but live together in a separate home with their dependent children; that the husband should find a job by which to support his wife and children; that his wife should be a good partner to him, sexually and otherwise, and make the care of the children and the home her major or even only work; that the children should enjoy a happy and carefree childhood as they progress through school; and that they should eventually grow up to repeat the cycle themselves. This more than anything is what family life has meant in the Western world. It is our only home, as Robert Frost described it, "the place where, when you have to go there, they have to take you in, . . . something you somehow haven't to deserve."[7]

the conventional norms of Western family life

For to appreciate the family in Western capitalist societies and the deep regard in which it is held by citizens one has to understand that without it they are homeless. Their neighborhoods and communities are not home; people move too often. Their jobs cannot be home except for the few who are securely self-employed; it is too easy to be fired, laid off, squeezed out, transferred, or attracted to a better job elsewhere. Even their friends are not home; they, too, are on the move, and in any case they never *have* to take anyone in except members of their own families. And certainly the government is not home; welfare offices may dispense a little money but never self-esteem or worth. Nor do the churches qualify as home; rituals, ministers, and members change. There is no friendly constant in capitalist societies except one's parents, siblings, spouse, and children. Only the family can truly be counted on. The rest of life may often be pleasant enough, but then no one can be blamed for trying to make money. That after all is how the system works. Except in the family. The family is supposed to be pure, unadulterated love, smiling faces recorded on Polaroid film and treasured for keeps in an album. If that were all there is to it we could end the chapter here. But there is more.

Dissent from the Western Family

No one, least of all university students, needs to be reminded that the family structure just described is showing signs of wear. But before trying to make sense of the sexual revolution and related changes in the West, a few pages are in order on the family in modern, contemporary societies outside the Western mainstream. For as previous chapters have stressed repeatedly, the world reveals multiple paths of economic and political progress. West is not the only way to go. And if developing societies elsewhere have avoided liberal democracy, the free-market economy, and Protestantism, we should not be surprised that they have also declined to structure their family life in the Western way. In general, the goal outside the core capitalist nations has been to create economic and political orders humane enough, secure enough, even gentle enough that citizens need not run to their spouses for refuge nor to their parents for a start in life. The clean split between the proud and humble dimensions of human life is fairly much a Western phenomenon. Most peoples elsewhere do not divide themselves in half the way we have learned to do. Love in their societies is perhaps never present so purely as in the Western conjugal relationship, but then neither is it absent so completely from the political and economic realities of life. Three modern alternatives to the Western family structure deserve brief description here: those of various utopian communities, of the Soviet Union, and of Israeli kibbutzim.

outside the West, the split is never so clean

FAMILY-FREE UTOPIAN COMMUNITIES

For at least the last four or five thousand years, groups of dissenters have occasionally arisen who, for want of opportunity or inclination, choose not to revolutionize their own societies but to create just for themselves insular subsocieties where their ideals can be realized more quickly and fully. Such subsocieties are often called utopian communities or countercultures. Monasteries and religious orders have been the commonest kind in the Christian world: today in the United States alone about 150,000 Catholics live their lives as monks, brothers, sisters, or religious priests in such communities. The Lubavitcher and other Chassidic Jewish sects provide another example. So do the Hutterites and Old Order Mennonites, communal Protestant groups dating from the Reformation who have settled in various rural areas of North America, especially on the Canadian prairies. The Doukhobors, a flamboyant Russian sect best known for their occasional public nudity, number more than 20,000 in British Columbia. Many other utopian communities founded with lofty aspirations have ceased to exist: the Shakers, for example, the Owenites of New Harmony, Indiana, and the Oneida community in upstate New York, which survives only as a trademark for silverware. The decade of the 1960s saw an upsurge of interest in countercultural life among North American youth. The Manson cult in California and the ill-fated Jonestown experiment in Guyana are the most famous examples, but hardly representative. Many communal experiments founded in that era survive happily and peacefully without publicity in the backwoods of the continent.

Basic to a utopian community is the idea that the good life consists not in the

the mentality that underlies utopias pursuit of individual self-interest but in collective commitment to common goals. All of the founders of such communities have expressed this view, people like Benedict (480–543), whose rule is followed by many Catholic monasteries, Theresa of Avila (1515–1582), who established the Carmelite order of nuns, Robert Owen (1771–1858), the Scottish cotton magnate who financed the New Harmony experiment, John Humphrey Noyes (1811–1886), the Protestant theologian who set up the Oneida colony, or the contemporary Stephen Gaskin, who led some 300 followers from San Francisco to a Tennessee farm in the late 1960s. In accordance with this view, and in sharp contrast to the principles of capitalism, members of utopian communities hold much or all of their property in common. Whatever a member may personally possess is only a trust to be used unselfishly for the welfare of all. Once elected or otherwise agreed upon, leaders have broad authority, often extending to the assignment of work, living quarters, and the schedule of everyday life. Government within the community is socialist and interventionist, quite the opposite of a liberal regime. Members are usually expected to wear a standard uniform, to take at least some meals in common, to attend group meetings faithfully, to be wary of contact with outsiders, to criticize one another—in sum, to identify their wills as much as possible with the general will of the community. Individual achievement is not counted a virtue, but only loyal and unswerving dedication to the common goals. To the extent that there is inequality of reward among members, and there is usually not much, it reflects a communal decision to honor exceptionally unselfish service to the community.

Yale sociologist Rosabeth Moss Kanter has been both creative and meticulous in her research on past and present utopian communities, and on the fate of the family *the survival of utopias depends on their minimization of marriage* within them.[8] She concludes, as do most other students of the subject, that a community's very survival depends to a great extent on how completely it eliminates or debilitates the Western kind of family. It is as if the community as a whole must become the family. Particular kinship and marital ties serve only to weaken the egalitarian, communal bond among all members and to divert commitment away from the goals of the group. Communities vary widely in how they prevent such divisiveness. In the Catholic religious communities, members take a lifelong vow of chastity. New members are not reproduced but recruited from the outside world. Thus the sexual, procreative bond is simply eliminated. And if perchance two members are consanguineally related in the outside world, they are expected to treat one another no differently than their other brothers or sisters of the community. The Shakers organized themselves in much the same way, even with both men and women in the same group. The Perfectionists at Oneida, by contrast, practiced what they called *complex marriage*. Any man and woman in the community were free to have sexual intercourse so long as they had permission from the authorities and did not develop an exclusive sexual or love relationship with one another. By thus rotating sexual partners, the procreative bond was enlarged to coincide with the community itself; children were raised communally, without special attachment to their biological parents.

The roughly 15,000 Hutterites in Western Canada exemplify yet another pattern. They follow the mainstream Western norm of faithful, lifelong, monogamous marriage, but structure life in such a way that husband and wife do little more in one another's exclusive company than share the same bedroom. Land and property are owned by the particular colony and regulated by an elected committee.

Members take meals in a common dining room, with men and women seated at separate tables. From the ages of 3 to 15, children spend their days in the colony school and eat together as a group, while their respective mothers work at whatever tasks have been assigned to them. The Amish and Old Order Mennonites are more flexible, permitting families to live on separate, privately owned farmsteads (though often in kin groups larger than the nuclear unit). Men and women are expected to do much of the farm work with other members of the colony, however, and to practice a wide variety of forms of mutual aid.

Utopian communities are clear evidence, albeit on a micro level, that family life varies across societies not only in kind but also in degree. The Catholic religious orders have flourished for 1500 years as vibrant, productive, intensely social communities from which sexual, procreative ties are absent and in which any consanguineal ties are irrelevant. The Perfectionists permitted sexual activity but prevented conjugality, and the roughly sixty children born during Oneida's thirty-three years of existence were defined as communal progeny. There are husbands, wives, brothers, and sisters among the Hutterites, but imagine how empty of meaning these family identities must be in the egalitarian common life of a colony. But what is perhaps more important, utopian communities demonstrate that any society's family life, however much of it there is and whatever kind it may be, can be understood only in relation to that society's political, economic, and religious institutions. Only because the members of a communal group can all look to it for support, direction, secure and satisfying work, and meaning in their lives are they then willing to forego the experience of falling deeply and romantically in love and retreating to the private happiness of a family home. Contrariwise, we in the Western mainstream cannot depend much on our distant governments and profit-oriented employers for support, direction, secure and satisfying work, or indeed for the meaning in our lives. That is why, among other things, so many conventional, hard-working citizens have family pictures on their office desks or in their wallets.

family life is understood only in economic, political, and religious contexts

SOVIET COLLECTIVISM

Had Karl Marx and Friedrich Engels been wealthier and less politically inclined, they might well have migrated to Indiana or someplace like that and founded a utopian community on the principles of communism. Robert Owen, their fellow socialist in Britain and a major influence on their thought, had done just that in 1824. But Marx and Engels chose a different tack. In his 1880 pamphlet, *Socialism: Utopian and Scientific*, Engels scorned the idea of "model experiments" and proposed instead that communist revolutions would overtake whole societies. Even so, the family would fare no better in the new classless order than it had in small-scale utopias. In 1884, Engels published his treatise on *The Origins of the Family, Private Property and the State*, relying mainly on historical research by the U.S. anthropologist Lewis Henry Morgan (1818–1881). Engels argued, as Morgan had earlier, that monogamous marriage and private property were closely intertwined and were both destined to disappear. He noted in particular the "domestic slavery of women" in conventional Western marriage and portrayed the communist order as one in which such exploitation of one sex by the other would be eliminated.

When a victorious Bolshevik party began to implement the ideas of Marx and Engels in Russia in 1917, a revolutionary family policy was high on its list of priorities. For the new Russia would not be a place from which people would have to take refuge in isolated families on separate plots of land. Unlike bourgeois liberal society, it would not be grounded in an ethic of divisiveness and exploitation. People would find security and meaning in the public order itself and hence the family would lose its significance. By the Family Code of 1918, people became free to marry and divorce at will, recording these decisions if they chose in a governmental office; illegitimacy was officially eliminated, and all children born were accorded equal rights; women were guaranteed the right to work and to be paid the same as men; a vast network of nurseries, day-care centers, camps, and schools was set up for children while their mothers were at work; abortion clinics were built and women permitted to patronize them freely. The idea was that every man, woman, and child would be an equal citizen of the common order, unshackled by ties of marriage and kinship which encourage inequality. As for sex, some dauntless Bolsheviks propounded the "glass-of-water theory": Sexual desire would be quenched as casually as thirst with no implication of possessive love between sex partners. More seasoned revolutionaries disagreed. In a memorable comment Lenin called the theory un-Marxian and unsocialist. "Of course thirst cries out to be quenched," he said. "But will a normal person under normal circumstances lie down in the dirt on the road and drink from a puddle? Or even from a glass with a rim greasy from many lips? . . . Drinking water really is an individual concern. Love involves two, and a third, a new life, may come into being. That implies an interest on the part of society, a duty to the community."[9]

As implied earlier in Chapter Six, Marxian communism must today be understood not as some ultimate stage in political and economic development but as a strategy for progressing toward the ever-elusive paradise that beckons to us all. Hence no one should have expected that the Soviet Family Code of 1918 would endure forever unchanged. The immense freedom it gave with respect to marriage in fact turned out to permit continued exploitation of women—men could too easily refuse any responsibility at all for the children they fathered. The initial code also had the effect of depressing the birthrate—women became more interested in pursuing careers than having babies. Hence a variety of new laws have been passed
in the last half-century, the general effect of which has been to strengthen somewhat the nuclear family. Marriage is taken more seriously and often contracted solemnly in so-called wedding palaces. Divorce is more difficult, though it remains about as common as in the Western world. Abortion is also more difficult, and women with many children have at least until recently received both monetary subsidies and civic honors. Nonetheless, the family in the Soviet Union remains dramatically less significant in social life than it is in the Western world. An estimated 85 percent of married women are in the labor force, and a "career" as housewife is a curious anomaly. The children of parents in the upper strata do tend to get a more advantageous start in life, but the importance of parentage in this respect is less than in the West. Fewer than half of newlywed couples live in separate households, and the nuclear family lacks the autonomy and isolation taken for granted in English-speaking parts of the world. Newspapers seldom report events in the family life of public figures. Since productive property is under

governmental authority, inheritance means little. Many Soviet leaders and scholars today insist that they would not even want to eliminate the special love between husband and wife or parents' special concern for their own children. In the structure of Soviet society, however, such values are secondary to the collective welfare of all citizens, as served by public, governmental agencies.

ISRAELI KIBBUTZIM

Probably the single major obstacle to the elimination of family life in the Soviet Union has been size. People cannot easily relate to a society of 260 million people, nor to one of 10 million, nor even to one of 10,000. A national government may provide employment, housing, protection, and basic income security, but a person still feels most at home in a group where he or she is known by name as a complex, multifaceted being who can laugh and cry. That is why the Soviet Union has transcended marital and kinship ties perhaps most effectively on the *kolkhozy*, collective farms larger than an extended family but still small enough to provide an ambiance of intimacy and reciprocal concern. This is to say that no national society can ever substitute itself for family life, though possibly it can replace the family with small communities centered on common farms, factories, or other productive enterprises. This hypothesis gains empirical support from the experience of the kibbutzim in Israel, collectively owned farm settlements each with a few hundred members. The first of these were founded by Jewish immigrants from eastern Europe in the 1920s, more than two decades before the state of Israel came into existence. By now nearly 250 kibbutzim count a combined membership of over 100,000, roughly 3 percent of the national population. Kibbutzniks have been a vanguard of the Zionist movement and account for a vastly disproportionate share of Israel's military and political leadership.

The family means even less on the kibbutzim than it does among the Hutterites. As in the latter setting, members take meals and hold nearly all possessions in common, children are cared for in a common nursery and school, and work assignments are made with minimal regard for kinship ties among members. The kibbutzim go even further, however, toward *draining the biological family of social significance*. They espouse an explicit ethic of sexual equality, and women are not separated from men in the dining room or workplace. Once having graduated from high school, young people are free to pair off in temporary sexual liaisons. The sign of long-term commitment to an exclusive sexual relationship is a request for a double room. Such roommates thereafter are publicly known as a couple (*zug*), a young man (*bachur*) and young woman (*bachura*), or simply each other's friend (*chaver*). Conventional terms like *marriage, husband,* and *wife* are not ordinarily used, though in conformity with national law the couple now usually have a simple wedding before the birth of their first child. A *zug* may be dissolved as easily as it is formed, by relinquishing the common room and requesting separate ones. During recent decades many kibbutzim have been assimilated to mainstream family norms of Israeli society and have allowed the *zug* relationship to become more like a conventional marriage. It also appears that, despite formal norms to the contrary, men predominate in the leadership and in certain occupations of most kibbutzim. Nonetheless, these communities are vivid contemporary evidence of how irrele-

draining the biological family of social significance

The nursery of an Israeli kibbutz, 1978: evidence of just how irrelevant the family can be. (© Marvin E. Newman 1978/Woodfin Camp & Assoc.)

vant to social life procreative and consanguineal ties can be in an enduring, self-sufficient, self-reproducing, and obviously successful order of life.

WHAT THE ABSENCE OF WESTERN FAMILY LIFE IMPLIES

Almost as a daily refrain in the United States or Canada, hard-working adults can be heard to say, "I would like to spend more time with my family, but I have to work." That brief sentence overflows with insight into the oil-and-vinegar structure of Western societies. Work is thought to be something people would avoid if they could, a burden which only the hope of wealth and the fear of poverty can induce people to accept. The truth of this idea is vindicated, moreover, by the actual circumstance of work in advanced industrial capitalism, by the lack of control most workers have over what they do, by the prevalence of goldbricking and strikes for higher pay. Life becomes then a routine of "going out" to play roles in a merciless world and then "running home" to be oneself. Perhaps the key quality about the alternative social orders described above is the absence of such an oil-and-vinegar mentality. Benedict's rule, Marx's sociology, Hutterite opinion, and kibbutz ideology all agree on this point: work is not just necessary but good, humanizing, and worthwhile in itself. Hence there is no need for a family haven into which members of these societies can retreat. Nor is there hope that one's work will yield personal wealth which then can be lavished on one's personal family. Nor yet is there fear that mishap or miscalculation on the job will cause especial suffering to one's immediate family. To be sure there is the taste of vinegar in monastic life, in agrarian utopias, and in contemporary Russia. But it is mixed with the sweet, secure sensation of being part of a larger, greater good than the nuclear family.

As to the effects on children of an absence of the Western kind of family life, the research literature is ample enough. Especially noteworthy are Melford Spiro's 1958 book, *Children of the Kibbutz*, and a volume published by Urie Bronfenbrenner in 1970, *Two Worlds of Childhood: U.S. and U.S.S.R.*. Both of these and other studies suggest that growing up outside the family has demonstrable effects. Communal nurseries and schools seem to have a leveling effect on children: fewer students either fail miserably or excel brilliantly. Peer-group pressures are strong and encourage conformity to the goals and standards set forth by adult authorities. Independence, competition, and individual achievement are valued much less *how children should be* than in the Western childhood experience, especially that of U.S. society. In sum, *raised depends on what* the kind of upbringing children are given in most societies corresponds more or less *is expected of adults* to the kind of behavior the societies expect of their adults. Western youth grow up with a sharper, more aggressive sense of self, readier to face—as they need to be—a marketplace governed by the rule of selfishness. Youth in Russia or on kibbutzim emerge from childhood less confident of themselves as individuals, shyer perhaps, more prepared—as they should be—for the cooperative values embodied in a planned economy. Hence the question of which is better, socialization in close-knit families or in some wider group, is substantially the same as a question of the relative merits of capitalist and socialist strategies of development. There are no universal answers. The making of history is a chancy enterprise.

Family Breakdown in Advanced Capitalism

For the sake of understanding recent changes surrounding marriage and kinship in the West, a general point made in Chapter Five bears repeating. It is that liberal-capitalist societies are inherently dynamic, and change is intrinsic to their structures. This is not the case of any socialist or corporatist society, no matter how modern, democratic, or industrialized it may be. Progressive, revolutionary governments in Russia, China, Cuba, and elsewhere have indeed transformed the shape of life in these countries and will probably continue to do so. But they have done it intentionally, thoughtfully, by public design. They have sought to control change, to plan it, to plot the future of their societies deliberately, weighing carefully the probable effects of proposed innovations. It is taken for granted in such lands, as it has been in most of the world for most of history, that any important new idea must first win the approval of common political authority before it is implemented. The same applies also in a monastery, a Hutterite colony, or a kibbutz. But not in the mainstream Western world. Governments in Washington, Ottawa, and similar capitals have tried in recent decades to control change more carefully, but most of it seems just to happen naturally. The reason is that free economic actors are obliged by the capitalist market to keep conjuring up new ideas, expressing them in commodity form, and selling them at a profit. Now obviously governmental policies affect this process and the kind of innovations that result. The important point remains that change in the capitalist world happens constantly and inevitably by virtue of market forces, often even without governmental knowledge until after the fact.

The relevance here of this general point is that family life in the Western world has been intensely vulnerable to events and trends in the economy. Western governments did not ordain deliberate family policies and then manage or control economic change in accordance with those policies. Instead they left the economy free to follow its profit-minded nose and left the character of family life to be shaped by the ongoing process of capitalist development. Governments did set down in law some basic norms like monogamy, fidelity, the exceptional nature of divorce, and restrictions on overt sexuality. But no government decreed the neolocal pattern of residence, the late age at marriage, the separation of work from the household, the withdrawal of women from the labor force, the depth of romantic love, or the intense concern of parents for their children's welfare. The ardent, autonomous, intimate nuclear family "just happened." It was by and large a voluntary and spontaneous creation, a raft built hastily and clung to desperately in the fast-moving stream of economic change. But what an uncontrolled economy encourages at one stage of development, it can also weaken or destroy at a later stage. This seems to be the case even now for the kind of Western family structure described earlier. Indeed, Christopher Lasch has convincingly argued that "from the moment the conception of the family as a refuge made its historical appearance, the same forces that gave rise to the new privacy began to erode it."[10]

a deliberate family policy versus letting the family be shaped by ongoing economic trends

What the erosion or breakdown of the nuclear family means empirically is the weakening or trivializing of the conjugal and consanguineal relationships of which it is composed. This section begins its discussion of this process with two ways in which the conjugal tie has become less significant: first the steady loss of its claim to sexual exclusiveness, second the steady increase in divorce. Thereafter our focus shifts to the consanguineal bond between parent and child and the way that bond has diminished in force. I need hardly emphasize in preface that it is general trends in the Western world that are at issue here. There are still millions of close, even vibrant nuclear families left, a multitude of virginal brides, husbands who never commit adultery even in their hearts, and children who call their parents "sir" and "ma'am." By looking mainly at continuities between family life in the past and now, it is possible even to conclude that nothing has changed. Mary Jo Banes does just that in her little book published in 1976, *Here to Stay: American Families in the Twentieth Century*. Edward Shorter calls her the leader of "a Polyanna school of sociologists."[11] As I look at the data, I am inclined to agree with Shorter. But readers should be aware that there is another point of view.

THE SEXUAL BREAKOUT

Perhaps the main reason for the intense and special place of marriage in modern Western civilization has been the confinement within it of all legitimate sexual enjoyment. No one was supposed to stimulate or satisfy anyone's sexual desire except that of husband or wife. Sexual arousal outside the conjugal bond, even between a boy and girl on a date, was supposed to be denied or concealed. Laws mandated punishment for fornication, adultery, homosexuality, and other forms of sex outside of marriage. They also forbade prostitution, pornography, public nudity, and various kinds of sexually exciting entertainment. During the last twenty years, however, both in Europe and North America, laws restricting sexual enjoyment have mostly gone up in smoke. Pierre Trudeau, then Minister of Justice of Canada, pointedly expressed the new mentality in 1967: "There's no place for the state in the bedrooms of the nation."[12] That was to say that political authority should no longer defend the confinement of sex to marriage. Trudeau's remark caused a stir even then, but the idea behind it has been steadily gaining favor throughout the Western world. Many laws against premarital, extramarital, and homosexual sex have been repealed. Many more are ignored. Still others, like those against pornography, are loosely applied. People have become legally free to enjoy sex almost however and with whomever they choose, provided that only consenting adults are involved.

But the change is not just a formal one. Laws are not suddenly unmade, ignored, or reinterpreted without signifying change in what people do with their time. And the evidence suggests that during the past few decades people in Western societies have been spending more and more of their time enjoying sex, almost certainly more than in the nineteenth or early twentieth centuries and quite possibly more than ever before in Western history. Now this is a hard point to prove conclusively to those who prefer to believe otherwise. The farther back the student of sexuality goes, the less reliable and more obscure the data become. It is not hard to find records from the past of prostitutes, adulterers, Don Juans, and Lady Godivas, as well as of husbands and wives who loved one another with unbridled passion. Neither is it hard to find records of people who lived to be 80 years old. But the data suggest that sexual voluptuaries like octogenarians were quite a small minority.

Most of the hypothesized increase in sexual activity has occurred, as might be expected, within the fully legitimate context of marriage. Until the 1970s, when premarital sex became extremely common, both men and women in North America were rushing to get married at ever earlier ages. The median age at first marriage for men in the United States in 1970 was 23, for women 20, in both cases about two years earlier than late in the nineteenth century. The average age for Canadian men was 24 in 1970, for women 21, about three years earlier even than in 1950. Once married, moreover, contemporary couples find far fewer obstacles to an active sex life than did their ancestors. There are fewer periods of prenatal and postnatal abstention from intercourse, since the typical wife today gives birth only twice in her lifetime, as compared to eight or ten times in mid-nineteenth century, when the birthrate in North American first began to decline. Both smaller families and larger homes afford couples more privacy for sexual play. The ever-greater effectiveness, availability, and use of birth control techniques during the last fifty years, first condoms and diaphragms and later IUDs and pills, have allayed fears of unwanted pregnancies. The steady strengthening of the ideology of romantic love and companionate marriage has also, one might guess, encouraged a more active sex life. When couples view intercourse as lovemaking, a symbol of their affection and concern for one another, they can hardly help but seduce one another more often.

Only since World War II have survey researchers been gathering detailed, systematic data on sexual practices within marriage, and randomly selected husbands and wives even now often decline to answer questions about such intimate matters. Alfred C. Kinsey (1894–1956), a biologist at the University of Indiana, directed the first major studies on this topic. His famous book, *Sexual Behavior in the Human Male*, appeared in 1948, the companion volume on females in 1953. Dozens of scholars since then have been updating and expanding upon his research. In his review of much of this literature over the past three decades, Edward Shorter has concluded that a "thoroughgoing eroticization"[13] of the lives of married people has occurred. Whatever their age, couples now have intercourse at least a third more often than couples of the same age in the late 1940s—currently about every other day for couples under 25, down to about once a week for couples over 55. About two-thirds of both wives and husbands, moreover, now masturbate occasionally, double the proportion Kinsey found. Couples now spend more time in foreplay, too, and report greater variety in techniques and positions for enjoying sex. The percentage of wives who report trouble achieving orgasm has declined over time. Now in all these respects there is immense variation across couples, and exact statistics are in any case impossible to come by, but the overall trend is unmistakable. Nor is it present only in the United States. Research elsewhere in the Western world has yielded similar results.

If the upsurge of eroticism were confined to marriage it might actually strengthen the conjugal component of the modern Western family. Such is not the case. The major social importance of the new sexual enthusiasm is that it has broken out of the conjugal bond, escaped from the relationship which was earlier its only legitimate target. There is no need here to review the scores of studies of unmarried youth, especially of university students, showing the rising rate of premarital sexual expression since the 1960s. The major increase has been for single women in their late teens and early twenties: 80 percent or more reported virginity in Kinsey's day, 40 percent or fewer in the late 1970s. Similarly, the 1970 U.S. census reported 29,000 unmarried couples living together; the figure for 1978 was 236,000.[14] More startling evidence is the rise in illegitimate childbirth in both Canada and the United States since World War II. Because of the earlier age at marriage and an improved technology of contraception, illegitimacy rates might have been expected to decline during this period, whatever the sexual habits of youth. But instead these rates dramatically *increased*. In 1950, about 4 of every 100 American or Canadian births were illegitimate; by 1973, this number had reached 9 in Canada, 13 in the United States. Or to express the same trend differently, for every 1000 unmarried U.S. women aged 15 to 44 in 1950, there were 14 illegitimate births; in 1973, this number was 25, almost double. There is no more tangible symbol of the prevalence of premarital sex during this period than the roughly 5 million children born during it in the United States alone to unwed mothers, most of them still teenagers. We can expect, of course, that the increase in contraceptive use will soon catch up with the increase in premarital intercourse, causing rates of illegitimate childbirth to decline. The easing of abortion laws in the United States since 1973 can be expected to have the same effect.

As in the past, Western societies continue to value marital fidelity much more highly than premarital chastity. Nonetheless, if the current trend toward hyperac-

rising rates of premarital sex and illegitimate births

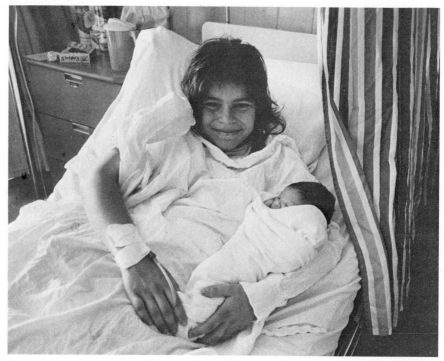

This mother is only fifteen years older than her daughter. She has no husband. "When you have all planned something," she told an interviewer in 1979, a year after her child was born, "then it can blow up in your face and spoil the whole thing. I don't want to plan. If something good happens, it happens." Currently in the United States, over a million teenage girls get pregnant each year. About a third get abortions. Some miscarry. More than half a million give birth. (© Mary Ellen Mark/Magnum Photos, Inc.)

tive sexuality has thoroughly undermined the latter, it would be anomalous if the former were not also weakened, at least a little. The much publicized mate-swapping groups and couples' clubs are evidence that such weakening has occurred, though no more than 1 or 2 percent of married couples have engaged in such *growing tolerance of sex* activities. Public opinion research reveals that while the vast majority of people *outside of marriage* continue to disapprove of adultery, their disapproval is not so absolute or vehement as that reported in surveys ten or twenty years ago. With respect to adulterous behavior, the overall percentages do not seem to have changed much during the last three decades: roughly 50 percent of married men and 20 percent of married women have had extramarital intercourse by the age of 45. It seems likely, however, that among young husbands and wives adultery has become more common. In his relatively careful study of 1972, Morton Hunt found that about a third of married men under 25 years of age admitted to extramarital intercourse, as compared to only a quarter in Kinsey's study in the 1940s.[15] The counterpart figures for women under 25 were 24 percent in Hunt's study, 8 percent in Kinsey's. Numerous research projects have documented the correlation between premarital sexual experience and extramarital sex later on. If this correlation persists in the future, and if premarital sex remains as popular as it is, we can expect that the Western value on marital fidelity will be compromised steadily as time goes on.

the eroticization of everyday life

But for understanding the sexual breakout from marriage, our attention should not rest too much on rates of premarital and extramarital intercourse. There are other indications, too, that sexual arousal has been transformed from a private, exclusive, even secret prerogative of husband and wife into a kind of public free-for-all. *Playboy* and *Penthouse* magazines, for example, each have a larger circulation than either *Time* or *Newsweek*, and rank among the fifteen most popular periodicals in the Western world. "Three's Company" was the third most popular American TV program in 1978; "Charlie's Angels" ranked fifth, "M.A.S.H." was sixth, and "Soap" was also among the top twenty. Erotic beats and lyrics in popular songs, the electric motion of discos, the tempting plots and scenes of most successful movies, and the suggestive *double entendres* of advertisements all contribute to an overall atmosphere—public, legal, and legitimate—of sexual stimulation. Its effect is to put a strain on marriage. For one lone person, husband or wife, is expected somehow to satisfy all the sexual desire induced and heightened by the stimuli of everyday life. And more than that—to transform the cheap, exploitative quality of sex in the public media into gentle, caring, private romantic love. The provision of sexual fulfillment becomes indeed the major purpose of marriage, now that it has lost most of its importance as an economically productive and biologically reproductive institution. No wonder sexual recipe books sometimes make the best-seller lists. Husbands and wives must cultivate their sexual skills lest they doom their marriages to breakup for a reason earlier generations would scarcely understand.

why Western culture has become so sexually charged

Just why Western culture has become so sexually charged is a complicated question and no answer in these pages can aspire to adequacy. The best clues to an explanation probably lie in the correlates of deviance in the past from the traditional ascetic morality. Most such deviance appears to have been concentrated

One regrettable consequence of the sexual revolution of the 1960s and 1970s has been higher incidence of venereal diseases—illnesses transmitted through sexual intercourse. The French physician Alfred Fournier was among the pioneers, late in the nineteenth century, in efforts to cure VD—syphilis and gonorrhea mainly—and to increase public understanding of the problem. France honored him with a stamp in 1946, issued to raise funds to fight these potentially debilitating illnesses. The fight was nearly won by the late 1950s, through improved techniques of treatment (penicillin and other antibiotics) and prevention (condoms), and through large-scale programs of public education. Some experts predicted the eradication of syphilis and gonorrhea by 1975. Instead the incidence of the latter roughly doubled in the United States between 1959 and 1969; other Western societies reported comparable trends. In the early 1980s, possibly as many as 5 million Americans will be infected each year by some form of VD—gonorrhea principally, but increasingly a virus called herpes simplex type 2 and more rarely syphilis. The increase is usually attributed to greater variety of sexual partners among young men and women, and to the switch from condoms to pills and IUDs for contraceptive purposes. Barring a return to sexual asceticism (as in China, where VD rates are low), the problem of venereal disease will be solved only as citizens learn to overcome embarrassment, take precautions, seek medical advice at the first suspicion of infection, and speak frankly with sex partners about any concerns in this regard.

in the highest and lowest social strata: among wealthy and secure aristocrats, who worked very little, and in the impoverished class of unskilled wage laborers, who worked a lot but without autonomy or hope. People in the middle, those who owned and worked their farms and businesses, conformed more closely to the restriction of sex to marriage. But as Chapter Six pointed out, this old middle class has all but disappeared. The new middle class is a little like the old elite, in the amount of leisure time it has at its disposal and in the range of commodities it can buy. But it is even more like the old working class, since roughly 90 percent of people in the U.S. or Canadian labor force today sell their labor for pay and lack much control over what they do on the job. That is to say that in contemporary advanced capitalism most people are well off but not in control. For them life is a matter of responding appropriately both as producers and as consumers to studied manipulation by corporate overlords. It is perhaps this basic economic condition more than anything that explains the so-called sexual revolution. Out of boredom and for want of challenge in their working lives, people shift their thinking away from the future toward the present and become more content to take pleasure just in one another's bodies. This tendency is exacerbated by the growing corporate use of sex as a manipulative tool, the sprinkling of it carefully throughout the media in order to capture people's attention for the sake of profit. Effective contraceptive techniques, of course, also encourage the trend.

THE POPULARITY OF DIVORCE

Some sociologists downplay the significance of today's rising divorce rates. All marriages come to an end, they say, some of them by death and others voluntarily. Or they observe that marriage is today no less popular than before, only now more people change partners once or twice in a pattern labeled *serial monogamy*. Such statements are true enough, but they belittle what is actually a profound transformation of Western family life. Divorce would be less serious if Western societies were like kibbutzim or Hutterite colonies and provided larger, nonfamilial structures within which citizens could find meaning, a sense of personal identity, income security, child care, and a basic framework for daily life. But in the mainstream Western world the nuclear family is supposed to serve these ends. It is the oil that is supposed to balance a vinegarish economy, the place where people should find the security of mutual giving. Hence there is cause for concern when the U.S. Census Bureau estimates that half of all children born in 1979 will spend some portion of their childhood with only one parent. Nor is it trivial that between 1971 and 1978, according to the census, the number of U.S. men and women over 35 years of age living alone increased three times over.[16] In a society where home is defined as husband, wife, and children, it is a serious matter that the proportion of homeless people has begun to soar.

the seriousness of divorce in the Western world

For the most part, divorce is a twentieth-century phenomenon. Most societies of the past (though not medieval Christian ones) permitted it to elite males for serious and specific reasons, like a wife's adultery or childlessness, but at most 2 or 3 percent of marriages were actually dissolved and the partners permitted to remarry. Even the United States, which has led the world in marital breakup for most of the last two centuries, reported only 8 divorces for every 100 marriages in 1900. By this measure and by others used in social science, divorce became slowly more popular in America until the late 1940s, when in the aftermath of the war it became more common. In 1946, there were 27 divorces for every 100 marriages. A slight decline followed during the 1950s, but there have been huge increases since 1968. By 1975, there were 46 divorces for every 100 marriages. It is impossible to translate this or other rates into the exact odds that a marriage contracted today will or will not end in divorce. Nonetheless, a fair guess in light of current trends is that close to half the couples wed in 1980 in the United States will not wait for death to end their conjugal bond. In other Western societies the odds favoring divorce are somewhat lower, about one-third to two-thirds lower in Canada, Britain, Germany, and Scandinavia than in the United States. Still, the rates in all of them have increased so rapidly since the 1960s that it is safe to say that the trend is general throughout the Western world. In the Catholic countries, by contrast, like Mexico, Argentina, Ireland, or Spain, divorce remains either illegal or difficult and in either case uncommon. It is also rare in Japan, where the rates are roughly what they were in the United States in 1900.

legal change as explanation for rising divorce rates

A search for explanations of the increase in divorce leads inevitably to the actions of government, to laws and court decisions. As might be expected, the trend in almost all Western jurisdictions has been toward lenience in this respect. The state of California took a dramatic step in 1969, passing legislation which permits "no-fault" divorce, the dissolution of marriage by a couple's voluntary decision, with no necessary implication of misbehavior on the part of either spouse. Most other states have by now enacted similar laws. Their significance is immense, even beyond the fact of making divorce easier. For effectively the no-fault laws redefine the conjugal bond as a purely private relationship, a contract which can be voided just by mutual consent. No longer must there be proof of some kind of wrongdoing on the part of husband or wife. In a sense, the new laws deinstitutionalize marriage, transforming it from a building block of social structure into a supplementary prop, one which two individuals may set up and take down freely, with minimal regard for public authority. In this respect the new laws are similar to the Soviet Family Code of 1918. But in another and crucial respect they are not. For the Soviet law was an integral part of a package of reforms, one that included massive construction of agencies for collective child-rearing and the strengthening of all kinds of nonfamilial groups wherein people might find security and meaning, economic roles and personal identities. The new U.S. laws, by contract, reflect the absence of family policy in the Western model of development. They have been passed simply in response to popular demand as piecemeal adaptations of family life to more advanced stages of the dynamic capitalist economy.

the impact of women's economic emancipation on divorce

But the question then is what underlying principles or trends in recent Western history have had the unintended consequence of undermining the permanence of the conjugal bond. Two general ones seem especially noteworthy, the first of which is the steady progress of women's economic emancipation. As noted some pages back, women in all but the lower classes were mostly squeezed out of production as industrial capitalism advanced and were left in the private roles of wife and mother. In these roles they depended utterly on their husbands not only for their livelihood but also for their prestige in the wider society. They assumed even the first names of their husbands, as etiquette still ordains, prefixing them with "Mrs." Tied to their

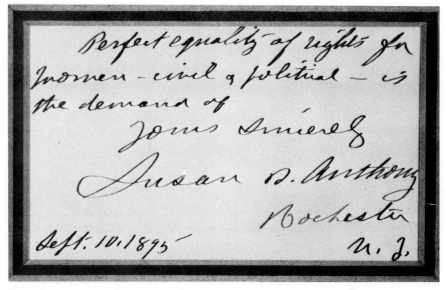

Rising divorce rates are due in part to the movement toward women's economic emancipation. Susan B. Anthony (1820–1906) was one of the pioneers in this effort, combining her fight for women's suffrage with a campaign for laws to make divorce easier. Another pioneer was Lucy Stone (1818–1893), whose activism led to the word Lucy Stoner being applied to anyone in favor of women retaining their maiden names after marriage.

usually numerous children, excluded from the labor market and ill-prepared for it in any case, most such wives could accurately conclude that divorce would mean "losing everything." They therefore had little choice but to remain with their husbands, no matter how ornery, obnoxious, overbearing, or cruel these men might be. Burdened with an exploitative man, a wife might threaten, cajole, argue, and run away occasionally, but fundamentally she was trapped. Ordinarily she would prefer to exploit him herself for his paycheck, in the meanwhile relying for moral support on women friends and relatives.

This explanation for the low divorce rates of the past is unflattering to men, but it seems a fair interpretation to place upon various kinds of data. Why else, for example, have more than twice as many husbands as wives felt free to commit adultery and give their partners a legal ground for divorce? Or similarly, why else have divorce rates been higher by and large in those social strata where wives are less dependent on their husbands? The major finding here is that divorce occurs from two to five times more often in the low-income strata of urban wage workers than in the affluent upper middle class. Poorly paid and often unemployed husbands lacked the wherewithal to enforce economic domination of their wives. Indeed, even years ago they often had to permit their wives to work outside the home, typically as domestic servants, to keep food on the family table. But even such meager employment gave these women a measure of dignity and independence at home, a trump card to play if their husbands became burdensome. Divorce rates have also been high for decades in the tiny category of wealthy working women, mainly in the arts, whose husbands serve no vital economic role.

the link between marital permanence and social stratification

But the major evidence for what may be called the exploitation hypothesis of marital permanence is that the overall divorce rates have steadily increased, the more married women have joined the labor force. Especially since the late nineteenth century, women have been rebelling against their enforced restriction to private life and seeking to become active in the capitalist economy. The desperate need for labor during World War II gave them their first big opportunity to show both themselves and their husbands their ability to work in economically productive roles. Now more than 50 percent of married women in the United States are in the labor force, up from about 5 percent at the turn of the century. Such employment has lessened wives' economic dependence on their husbands, as has the availability of various kinds of social welfare, especially governmental aid to women with dependent children, and the smaller average number of children women have. In sum, probably the main reason divorce rates have risen is that fewer women today are economically trapped in the hell of a mutually exploitative marriage.

The bondage of wives in an earlier era was hardly the only thing that kept marriages together, of course, and wives' relative emancipation in the present day is not all that pulls marriages apart. Lifelong wedlock is not by definition an instrument for the domination of women. Indeed, it can endow both wife and husband with a singular kind of happiness unmatched by any more transient relationship. Millions of couples found such happiness in the past, even in a milieu of gross sexual inequality. Why then do not still more couples find it today, when marital commitment need not be so sullied by constraint? Why do so many marriages just "not work out" despite the fervent determination with which they are begun? In answer I would propose a second general trend in the Western world, a steady decline in how much a husband and wife share besides a sex life. The evidence suggests that the physical and emotional enjoyment of romantic love is by itself quite inadequate to ensure marital permanence. The fun of making love, dining by candlelight, cuddling beside a January evening fire, or strolling along an August morning beach—this is to Shakespeare's marriage of true minds what a keystone is to an arch, the thing that brings all the rest together, the apex, the crowning triumph. But a keystone by itself does not make an arch. Instead it falls flat. So does a sex life unsupported by sharing in other aspects of everyday life.

the insufficiency of sexual love for marital permanence

Probably nothing can bind a couple together so closely as work in common, shared involvement in some kind of productive labor. The farm couple joined in the seasonal rhythm of agricultural production exemplifies what was traditionally the most common form of sharing in this respect. Divorce rates even now are only about half as high in the farm population of Canada and the United States as among city dwellers. Another kind of sharing involves religious beliefs, ethnic background, and class and wealth of the respective families of origin. Numerous studies show that the more similar a husband and wife are in these respects the less likely is their marriage to end in divorce. A third common ground beneath a marriage can be the work of raising children, the multifaceted task of parenthood in the nuclear family. The likelihood of divorce generally declines the more children a couple have. I should emphasize, however, that it is not children themselves that keep a marriage together but shared parental involvement in their upbringing. In particular, marriages hastily arranged because of a young woman's pregnancy have a high risk of divorce. A fourth basis of permanence in marriage is simply a couple's common past. The more years a husband and wife spend together, joining their respective biographies into a single marital history, the less likely are they to break up. Divorce rates spread themselves more or less evenly over the first five years of marriage, during which more than half of divorces currently occur, after which the rates progressively decline. In sum, the evidence refutes decisively the ancient adage that love conquers all. Love is most likely to endure when instead of having to conquer differences it can celebrate similarities, when it crowns the joint investment of husband and wife in a broad range of quite ordinary activities.

the decline of shared commitments as explanation for divorce

The long-term trend in the Western world, however, is toward shrinking the extent of commonality of which marriage is composed. So long as married women remained housewives they could not share in their husbands' work except in an informal, unpaid, and often servile way. The recent entry of more wives into the labor force has not in most cases changed that. Few couples have enough capital to set up joint economic enterprises in which both spouses might work together, even if they chose to. This is common today only in farming, in professional private practice, and in some small retail businesses like franchised variety stores. It is much more typical for spouses to sell their labor to separate employers, often in wholly unrelated production processes. Thus is work often even a divisive influence on marriage, as the demands of separate occupations and divergent career interests come into conflict. The responsibilities of parenthood, moreover, have tied husband and wife together with diminished force during recent decades, as the average number of children has declined and as nonfamilial socialization agencies have gained in importance. Still further, encouraged by a belief that "love is what really matters," young couples increasingly marry across religious, ethnic, and other status lines, reducing the extent of their commonality still more. This last trend should not be overstated—about 75 percent of Catholics and 85 percent of Jews in anglophone North America still marry within their own faiths. The proportions, however, seem to be in decline. Finally, because roughly 85 percent of divorced men and women remarry, a high divorce rate has a self-multiplying effect. More and more couples at any point in time are in the first years of marriage, whether it is their first, second, third, or a later one, the early years when for lack of a common history couples are most likely to divorce. Spouses previously divorced, moreover, have to overcome the difference between them that their prior marital backgrounds constitute. For them the divorce rates are higher than for spouses in a first marriage.

summary hypotheses about divorce, and two qualifications

In summary, more marriages today fall apart because there is less to keep them together. Fewer wives are trapped in wedlock by sheer economic dependence on their husbands. Fewer couples invest themselves together in shared productive work. Parenthood commands less of a couple's joint effort and attention. The conjugal unit is less embedded in a shared community of ethnic, religious, and local values. More husbands and wives are newlyweds to each other, working to create a common life from scratch; fewer know the joy of building on decades of shared experience. The progress of Western history has dislodged all these supports for marital permanence, leaving the marital relationship to consist ever more simply in sexual, romantic love. Marriage has come to be understood in popular culture almost as a kind of leisure activity whose worth depends on how skillfully and pleasantly the spouses turn each other on after they both get home from work. As such it must compete with the more temporary turn-ons available in a sexually permissive milieu. The evidence suggests that in such conditions lifelong marriage competes rather poorly. So long as feelings and orgasms are nearly all that is involved, people can fall in and out of love in quick succession.

Finally two qualifying comments are in order. First, the majority of men and women, even in the United States, still remain with their initial spouses until death. In some highly industrialized societies—France, Japan, or Norway, for example—divorce is even now as rare as it was in the United States in 1900. The general process of economic development neither requires nor rules out high rates of divorce. The paragraphs above have done no more than review certain aspects of the Western *kind* of development which make divorce more likely. Second, I should emphasize that every marriage in every society remains in some respects unique. Whether it endures or breaks up depends not only on the general trends reviewed here but on the particular personality traits of the spouses and all the influences that bear upon their specific situation. The future of any marriage depends as well on willpower, how committed each spouse is to the building of a common life. If love cannot conquer everything, it nevertheless can undo numerous impediments.

THE DECLINE OF PARENTAL AUTHORITY

A common principle underlies the discussion above about husbands and wives and the discussion below about parents and children. It is that family relationships, whether conjugal or consanguineal, neither mean much nor last long when they are founded only on affection. The bridge between individual solitudes is common, collective, cooperative *action*: working, cooking, cleaning, eating, conversing, dancing, singing, picnicking, traveling, worshipping, playing, planning, budgeting, *together*. From a cultural point of view, probably the main source of family breakdown in Western civilization is the empirically unfounded idea that human relationships are somehow stronger, deeper, purer, and more genuine when they are removed from the domain of work and the other less glamorous aspects of life. A satisfying and enduring relationship cannot be built simply on a principle of "let nothing come between us." If there is nothing between people they will eventually get bored with the sound and sight and touch of one another. A relationship thrives and strengthens when all kinds of concerns come between the people involved, but concerns which they jointly can share and grapple with. *Being* together for a moment of eternity delights the most when tedious hours of *becoming* together have gone before. That is why marriage begins to dissolve when mediocre things like shared work and parenthood no longer intrude upon it. And by the same principle, parent-child relationships begin to melt away when they are drained of economic, disciplinary, and didactic action and reduced to friendliness. No self-respecting 6-year-old, much less a teenager, wants a 40-year-old playmate. Parenthood must mean more than that if it is to mean anything at all.

During the nineteenth and early twentieth centuries, consanguineal ties in the Western family derived most of their strength from parents' near-monopoly of the economic resources their children needed for a start in life. Few sons in that era

like husband-wife relations, those between parents and child rest on social and economic bases

Despite the concentration of capital and spread of wage labor, some parents still have economic and even political positions to bequeath to their children. In these increasingly exceptional cases, parent-child relationships tend to be strong even today. Can you imagine Charles Windsor renouncing his parentage and settling with Diana in some faraway land, the better to be accepted for "who they really are"? As they say in Great Britain, "Not bloody likely."

aspired or expected to spend their lives selling their own labor to somebody else. Well-paid wageworkers in white collars still were scarce and the average worker was poverty-stricken. The typical ambition of a young man was to own and operate some kind of profitable enterprise in the market economy, possibly a business employing others but more probably a petit bourgeois farm, sawmill, bakery, haberdashery, restaurant, shoe shop, hotel, grocery, saloon, or whatever. To achieve that goal a young man needed capital. His father was the most likely source, for the vast majority of fathers were themselves petit bourgeois, independent producers. They held economic positions which they could, by the laws of inheritance, pass down to a son. They could also give or lend their sons money to set up their own farms or businesses. And their sons had almost nowhere else to turn. Even a friendly banker willing to lend a young man money on a farm or store would typically require his father's signature on the note. In the upper echelons, moreover, whose young men sought to attend universities, parents once again held the purse strings—governments gave no educational grants or loans to students. As for daughters, their dependence on parents was even greater. Custom forbade a young woman to look for work on her own. Ordinary fathers and mothers placed a daughter as a servant or mother's helper in some respectable family until she arrived at marriageable age. Wealthy parents might send her to a finishing school and sweeten a young man's interest in her with the prospect of a capital donation. As late as 1952, 52 percent of a sample of married German women reported having brought a dowry to marriage.[17]

an inheritance not just of property but of skills

It was not just productive property that once was handed down on a large scale from parents to children, but also an immense variety of occupational and household skills. Most children grew up spending most of every day physically near to one or both parents, learning their work with a casualness that is today hard even to imagine. Children on farms, who were still the majority in North America at the turn of this century, tagged along after their fathers in barnlots and their mothers in vegetable gardens. As they grew older they learned to work alongside their parents in the varied tasks of the rural household. Fathers taught their sons to handle a team, fix machinery, build fences, and so on, while mothers introduced their daughters to the complexities of starching shirts, sewing dresses, darning socks, preserving foods, and baking a cake from scratch. Nor was the parent-child relationship much different for most urban children, at least those whose fathers controlled the conditions of their work and whose mothers were still tied to an unmechanized household. The shoemaker's children could often be found working or playing in his shop, and so could the blacksmith's, the cabinetmaker's, the grocer's, the druggist's, and the merchant's. Or if not there the children were usually somewhere around the house, where mothers kept an eye on them. Such a way of growing up should not be romanticized. Parents justifiably complained that their children were always underfoot, and children that they had too little time for themselves. Nonetheless, this way of life nourished a deep and intimate relationship between parent and child. Parents were more than providers. They were teachers, moral guardians, disciplinarians, employers, exemplars, ever-present standards against which children had no choice but to measure themselves. I remember often in youth getting a haircut at Vic's Barber Shop under the gaze of the eight or ten old tobacco chewers who always loitered there. "This is John Westhues's boy," Vic would say, never mentioning my name. It was not that my father was especially well known, rather that parentage was the prime locator of a child's identity in that earlier kind of capitalist community.

the effects of monopolization of capital on parents' importance to their children

On the Great Plains of North America, in other rural regions of the continent, and even in some old city neighborhoods there still are settings where children grow up as thoroughgoing social products of their parents' marriages. But the proportion has declined and so has the intensity of parent-child interaction almost everywhere in the Western world. The underlying reason is the concentration of capital in fewer hands, the fact that today fewer than 15 percent of Canadian or American parents own and work some kind of economic establishment which their children could conceivably inherit. Many of these establishments, moreover, are small, unprofitable, antiquated farms or businesses with no future in them. Family ties remain strong to be sure in the famous lineages of wealth—the Du Ponts, Fords, Rockefellers, Bronfmans, Kennedys, and others on a smaller scale. Their children have something to inherit: a name, a tradition, and directorships on corporate boards. For the children of the upper middle class, however, inheritance means nothing more than money for a house and a stock portfolio. Children of parents in the lower wage-laboring strata can look forward to even less. This is to say that only a tiny percentage of parents are now able to bequeath to one or more of their children a position in the economic order. The vast majority of fathers and mothers sell their labor to firms they do not own. Their children will have to do the same. It is the reality of advanced corporate capitalism.

The steady concentration of capital has not eliminated, of course, the impact of parental income on the educational, occupational, and income attainment of their children. A 1971 survey of Ontario high school students showed that bright children of high-income parents were roughly twice as likely to plan on a university education as equally bright children of low-income parents.[18] The pattern is similar elsewhere in Canada, in the United States, and in other Western societies. Children, therefore, still depend significantly on their parents for a start in life. But increasingly the dependence is indirect. Parental income determines where a family can afford to live. Neighborhood then determines in great part who the children's friends will be, which school they will attend, and how they will think of themselves. The main benefit children of upper-income families today enjoy is a milieu in which they are assumed to be winners, on their way to a degree and a high-paying job for some growing corporation. The main cost to children of the poor is an environment of parents, teachers, neighbors, friends, and the media which tells them they are second-rate, best suited perhaps for hourly work. Money matters directly, too, and no one can gainsay the positive effect of having parents who can afford to be generous. But what matters more is the consumer lifestyle parents offer their children. What makes the lifestyle possible is largely irrelevant. Many children today scarcely know what their fathers and mothers do for a living except "travel a lot," "go to the office," or "work at the plant."

parenthood as leisure activity

No matter what kind of work parents do, moreover, it normally takes them away from home into a setting where children are not welcome. Plant managers and office supervisors ordinarily want their workers as free of distractions as possible. Children thus come to be considered part of a private world formally irrelevant to the workplace. They should get to know their parents after hours. Parenthood becomes like conjugal love a leisure-time activity. If the mother is a full-time housewife, children have indeed more contact with her, but she has less to teach and to expect of them than formerly. Household conveniences have eliminated most of the physically and mentally complex tasks of maintaining a home. What, then, is it that parents and children can share? They can eat together, though common family dining seems to have declined in popularity. They can pursue hobbies together, and to the extent that strong parent-child relationships exist it is usually on this basis. There is always the television to watch in common, provided everyone can agree on the channel. But overall it is hard for parents and children to find a basis on which to interact. When a mother or father says to a child almost beseechingly, "Please tell me what is new in your life, what your problems are," I imagine the response is thought more often than it is said, "Why should I tell you? What earthly difference does it make?" Sheer friendliness is not much reason to talk to anyone.

four trends that weaken parents' influence outside the home

While the direct authority of parents over children has declined during recent decades, so has their influence over other agents of socialization. Parents were once locked in relatively small and stable communities with their children's teachers and bus drivers, the school principal and the board members, the owners of the local drugstore and candy shop, constables and policemen, and the parents of their children's schoolmates. In many respects this community extended parents' own authority. It appeared to children as a kind of conspiracy, a united front of adults aimed at keeping youth under control. Four trends in particular have weakened such communities and thereby parents' main collateral support. First is the increased size of cities and of schools: today's urban children grow up in settings more anonymous simply by force of the larger numbers of people within them. Second is the geographical mobility of families under the pressure of a dynamic economy: in typical suburban neighborhoods, parents are personally acquainted with only a fraction of their children's friends. Third is the professionalization of teachers, guidance counselors, recreation supervisors, child-care workers, social caseworkers, police officers, and others involved in the socialization process. These caretakers of youth increasingly feel themselves qualified to act quite irrespective of parental expectations. Their accountability is mainly to higher-ups in their respective occupations and bureaucracies, relatively little to the parents of their charges. Parents have little power over such professionals. The fourth trend is the spread of such technological innovations as the automobile, television, radio, stereo, and telephone. All of these have helped emancipate youth from parental supervision, whether by facilitating physical escape from the home or by enabling children to tune their parents out. All these trends leave most parents in an awkward situation. Few have the time, capital, or circumstance of work necessary to be in fact the overriding influence on their children's upbringing. They must therefore choose between forcing their children to sit at home, bored and resentful, and surrendering their children to the drift of outside influence. The latter choice comes easier.

SUMMARY

The past dozen pages may well have ruffled the feathers of some readers who count themselves progressive. "What would he have us do," they might ask, "resurrect puritan morality, deny oppressed wives their right to a divorce, and subjugate children to the tyranny of parental rule?" The answer is no, but that is beside the point. The purpose here is neither to denounce nor to defend the ongoing process of family breakdown in the Western world, the United States especially, but to insist that a breakdown is in fact underway. Awareness of overall current trends is our prime objective. It is a little sneaky to affirm the continuing relaxation of norms surrounding sex, marriage, and the home, all in the name of individual rights and freedom, while at the same time denying that one thereby undermines the family as a social institution. Recall the definition of the family offered earlier: the investment of procreative and consanguineal physical ties with *social meaning*, a set of *rights* and *duties* grounded in biological relationships. Then consider the extent to which sexual intercourse happens today outside the conjugal bond, the stupendous rise in rates of premarital sex, the greater acceptance of homosexuality and extramarital sex, the doubling or even tripling of illegitimacy rates in twenty years, the fact that most governments now permit men and women to couple and

the contemporary Western family is not just changing but also lessening

uncouple at will, the near doubling of divorce rates in ten years, and the steady diminution of parents' power over their children's upbringing. The conclusion cannot be escaped that the family has become not just different but less. Citizens today need not and do not take conjugal, consanguineal and affinal ties as seriously as before. Marriage bequeaths fewer rights and imposes fewer duties—not least the right and duty of permanence. The relationship between parent and child on average simply amounts to less. Roles in families have fewer inescapable consequences. Wife, husband, mother, father, son, and daughter can still be counted on, taken for granted, but in various ways not quite so much as forty years ago.

This decline of the family's significance need not be attributed to a simple shift of the human will, as if people nowadays choose more libertine lifestyles than formerly. For the extent and character of family life in the Western world have not been a matter of conscious political decision, of public policy and planning. Liberal democratic governments have not organized their economies toward the end of bolstering certain politically defined values concerning sex, marriage, and kinship. They have instead unleashed the dynamics of capitalist development and let the family be shaped in reaction and response, as a by-product of economic trends. So long as most workers still held title to their own productive resources and controlled the conditions of their work they could temper the market economy for the sake of preserving traditional family values. Even in defiance of economic efficiency and profit maximization, independent farmers and shopkeepers could bring their little children with them to the workplace, hire their relatives, take pride in supporting their wives at home, and look forward to handing enterprises down to the next generation. It was the family haven, so they said, that made work in a heartless economy worthwhile. And it justified sexual austerity, for work could be taken as seriously as play.

the root source: processes inherent in a dynamic capitalist economy

By the normal workings of capitalism, however, ever-larger corporations have dispossessed more and more individuals of their capital. The latter have lost control of their work and with it the chance to limit the profit motive for familial purposes. The vast majority of fathers can no longer give their wives and children much but money and leisure time. Wives increasingly have taken employment, too, gaining incomes of their own from jobs unrelated to their husbands'. The progress of women's liberation from traditional subservience has thus occurred in a way that tends to weaken the conjugal unit. With both wives and husbands on the treadmill of the labor market, moreover, children are increasingly on their own, left to be raised by one another, the mass media, and nonfamily professionals. In short, advanced corporate capitalism forces individuals to choose more sharply than ever between economic well-being on the one hand and family life on the other. One cannot move half a continent for a job, take the night shift as required, work overtime, take evening courses to upgrade oneself, accept transfer or promotion to another city, entertain obnoxious associates in one's home, or otherwise do what employment today routinely requires without straining or neglecting family relationships. The never-ending pursuit of economic security in a crowded, constantly changing labor market thus renders home life insecure. It is this fact above all that explains the breakdown of the family and the hyperactive sexuality by which people compensate for the lack of depth in personal relationships.

the breakdown is an obvious trend, not yet an accomplished fact

I had best conclude this section of the chapter, nonetheless, by acknowledging that the breakdown of the Western family is far from complete. It is but an ongoing trend, not yet an accomplished fact. The same economic forces that pull families apart have an uncaring quality that prolongs and even intensifies citizens' yearning for the surety of husband-wife and parent-child relationships. Surveys document the desire of most Americans, indeed of most citizens of the Western World, to live their lives in strong and vibrant nuclear households. When most young men and women fall in love they mean it to be forever and completely. Most parents crave strong and enduring ties with their children. And a majority of citizens still achieve permanence in marriage and reasonable stability in family life. Often this costs the wife and mother a productive role in the economy, the husband and father occupational advancement, and the children acceptance in today's youth subcultures. But literally millions of husbands and wives even now are lucky enough to share productive work and economic well-being with each other and with their children. The point of this section has not been to challenge the Western family or to deny any evidence of it in everyday reality. But the evidence has shrunk and is shrinking. The reason, so it seems, is that the economic vinegar which makes the oil of family life so sweet tends in the course of time to destroy it.

Concluding Words

If the family were merely a biological phenomenon, this chapter could have come to an end much sooner. For as a network of procreative, lineal, and collateral connections, the family is universal, inescapable, and structurally identical for all human beings. Biological differences from one family to the next in themselves matter little in social life, moreover, and progressively less the further economic development proceeds. But the family that has commanded our attention here is not just biological. It is a social overlay upon physical relationships, a human invention that encloses procreation within conjugality and transforms physiological consanguinity into role expectations. Biological ties are but raw material out of which societies manufacture the groups labeled *family, relatives,* and *kin.* The reason for all the pages in this chapter is just that some societies have manufactured more and others less, that they have crafted from a common physical reality widely divergent social realities. The family is a sociological universal only in the banal sense that no society has yet completely ignored the ties of bed and blood. Our purpose here has been to go beyond banalities, to sketch the structures of family life as found in existing contemporary societies and to understand those structures in their political and economic context.

the diminishing place of kinship in the process of development

Consecutive sections of this chapter have made the historical direction of family relationships clear enough. It has been toward the reduction of their social import. Western civilization, the one that has outstripped all others in its domination of the earth, was remarkable for its apathy toward kinship even in medieval times. Indeed, one can attribute the success of the West in part to its readiness to forsake family roles for more transient, explicitly purposive ones in such organizations as the church, elected government, public bureaucracy, voluntary association, and profit-seeking corporation. It bears remembering that the intimate, bilaterally constituted nuclear family, however strong it has been in Western Europe and North America, is itself but a vestige of the all-embracing clans and lineages of most nonindustrial societies. And with the twentieth century has come a barrage of attacks on even the nuclear household. In the East, the communist world especially, it has been assailed politically as an exploiter of women and preserver of inequality. In the West it has fallen prey to a dynamic economy and grown emptier even while its virtues continue to be proclaimed. Some scholars depict the overall trend as away from ascription toward achievement: away from roles that individuals cannot do anything about toward roles over which they can exercise control and choice. Being of the former kind, family roles should gradually disappear. We are moving, so the argument runs, toward a world in which every man is recognized just for who he is, not for who his father was or who his wife and children are, a world where every woman is free to make it on her own, irrespective of parents, husband, daughters, or sons. Thus will the constrictive ties of marriage and kinship be left farther and farther behind.

Young hikers in Austria: "Aloneness is a bad dream . . . the identity of every person is a social process, created in the give and take of relationships with other people."

But such a theory of history is ill-conceived. No man can ever be recognized for who he is, nor can any woman make it on her own. Aloneness is a bad dream. As Chapter Four pointed out, the identity of every person is a social process, created in the give and take of relationships with other people. Everybody is and needs to be from somewhere. Most of anyone's identity can accurately be ascribed to certain other people. The question is just which ones. Even if we were all conceived in petri dishes, gestated in incubators, and raised in communal nurseries there still could be discerned for each of us the particular nurses and upbringers involved in the shaping of our respective personal identities. And citizens hatched in more highly rated hives would probably put on airs. It is a mistake, in short, to imagine that people ever can or should be unshackled from each other. Such chaos would completely thwart the process of societal development. The process requires instead a social structure at once tight enough that people know who they are and loose enough that they can freely become something more. Thus *any* role that leaves a person trapped is destructive, whether it is held by reason of biology (serf's daughter, for example) or some other circumstance (like a political hostage or captured slave). But equally abhorrent is a condition of such detachment from roles, such lack of rootedness in present order, that a person does not know who he or she is—in the extreme, the case of a child who has never received a name from other people. Thus conjugal, consanguineal, and affinal ties are not in themselves obstacles to the betterment of life on earth. Marital and kinship roles can be in fact a boon to the human race, provided only that they leave people room to assert themselves and innovate.

the need for social structures tight enough to let people be, loose enough to let people become

In the long haul of history the development process has indeed implied a loosening of family ties, even as it also has entailed an increase in the division of labor, an enlargement of societies, a shrinking proportion of the labor force in agriculture, and the growth of cities. But none of these trends is or ought to be thought interminable. Each step in the development process demands reassessment of goals, reformulation of theories, and redefinition of what constitutes the good life on earth. The realization of our human nature requires each generation to inspect its location in history and to ask, "Where shall we go from here?" This question is urgent today in the Western world with regard to family life. No responsible thinker proposes a return to the kinship-saturated structures of past centuries, when lineage was the supreme basis for distributing rewards across individuals. Nor can anyone mindful of women's humanity want to reverse the trend toward absolute equality in power, wealth, and honor between the roles of wife and husband. Nor is there any need, given today's effective means of contraception, to revert to an ethic of sexual repression. But babies still have to be conceived and born, children still have to be invested with identities, and adults still need to be anchored in intimate groups. Such ends as these could be accomplished quite apart from marriages and families. This has already been shown in Israeli kibbutzim. It could become the case in the mainstream Western world. But if the thickest of social institutions is allowed more and more to disappear, this should at least be by our reasoned and conscious choice, not by default of human ingenuity.

For Reflection

procreative tie
physical consanguinity
lineal and collateral kinship
biological family tree
conjugality
social consanguinity
affinity
illegitimacy
natural child
adoption
compadrazgo
language of kinship
unilineal, matrilineal, patrilineal
clan
bilateral descent
neolocal, matrilocal, patrilocal
monogamy, polygyny, polyandry
exogamy, endogamy
incest
Western societies
medieval family norms
clerical celibacy
medieval sexual austerity
single-family household

companionate marriage
nuclear family
haven in a heartless world
falling in love
lengthening of childhood
family in utopian communities
complex marriage
Hutterite colonies
Soviet family life
Israeli kibbutzim
Western family breakdown
rates of marital sex
rates of premarital sex
rates of extramarital sex
illegitmacy rates
eroticism
divorce rates and correlates
no-fault divorce laws
women's liberation
women in the labor force
bases of marital permanence
decline of parental authority
inheritance

For Making Connections

With Chapter One: How would a psychologist have written this chapter differently?
What enduring regularities about the family are you willing to take for granted in coming decades, and why?

With Chapter Two: How important are historical methods for understanding contemporary forms of marriage and kinship?
Do sociologists who say they study adultery and fornication thereby betray their personal values? How about those who say they study extramarital and premarital sex?

With Chapter Three:	In light of data on family life in the contemporary world, how much difference do national borders make?
	How do changes in the structures of power, wealth, and honor relate to changes in the Western family?
With Chapter Four:	In what ways has the weakening of kinship ties made people more able to express their creative sides, and in what ways less able?
	Have recent changes in Western family life resulted in a more or less effective system of child socialization?
With Chapter Five:	What differences in family life can in general be expected between liberal-democratic and socialist societies?
	Relate the weakening during recent decades of husbands' authority over wives and parents' authority over children to the overall trend in Western history away from traditional toward rational types of authority.
With Chapter Six:	To what extent is it inevitable that family ties loosen in the course of economic development?
	To what extent can changes in the Western family during the last hundred years be traced to changes in the dynamic capitalist economy?
With Chapter Seven:	In contrast to the polity and economy, the institutions of religion and the family seem to have declined over time. Are the reasons similar in both cases?
	Which could a society more easily do without, religion or family life?

For Further Reading

The best-known periodical for the sociology of the family in North America is the *Journal of Marriage and the Family*, but there are numerous others, and many of the best articles on the subject appear in the general sociological, anthropological, historical, and social work journals. Following are eleven exceptionally valuable sources I can recommend:

1 Philippe Ariès, *Centuries of Childhood*, Knopf, New York, 1962. A detailed and engrossing account of child-rearing practices and family life during France's ancien régime, the book that in some respects spearheaded the thrust of contemporary historians into family research.

2 Edward Shorter, *The Making of the Modern Family*, Harper & Row, New York, 1977. A beautifully unpedantic survey of change in the Western family from traditional Europe to present-day North America. Amply documented, this inexpensive paperback reads as if its author is both careful and caring.

3 Christopher Lasch, *Haven in a Heartless World*, Harper & Row, New York, 1979. Another excellent paperback, this one organized as a history of how social scientists have treated—and mistreated—the family in America. The author deserves to be ranked among the twenty most perceptive living commentators on contemporary American society.

375

4 George P. Murdock, *Social Structure*, Macmillan, New York, 1949. A classic depiction of the variety in kinship structures across human societies. Of similar relevance is William N. Stephens, *The Family in Cross-Cultural Perspective*, Holt, Rinehart & Winston, New York, 1963, a concise compendium of selections from studies of almost all aspects of marriage and family life in diverse cultures, smoothly interwoven by Stephens's commentary.

5 William J. Goode, *World Revolution and Family Patterns*, Free Press, New York, 1963. A classic systematic comparison of Western, Arabic-Islamic, sub-Saharan African, Indian, Chinese, and Japanese family structures; makes a strong pitch for the Western-style nuclear family.

6 Michael Young and Peter Wilmott, *Family and Kinship in East London*, Routledge & Kegan Paul, Oxon, 1957. Three years after publishing this insightful, easy-to-read study of a working-class suburb, the same authors and the same publisher released a counterpart volume on a middle-class suburb, *Family and Class in a London Suburb*. Thirteen years later came *The Symmetrical Family: A Study of Work and Leisure in the London Region*. All are worth reading, both as depictions of contemporary British family life and as lessons in how to do community research.

7 William F. Kenkel, *The Family in Perspective*, Goodyear, Santa Monica, Calif., 1977. Among the more thoughtful and comprehensive texts on the American family, recommended especially for its attention to Western history and its concise portrayals of family life in non-Western settings.

8 Michael Gordon (ed.), *The Nuclear Family in Crisis*, Harper & Row, New York, 1972. A collection of thirteen well-chosen articles on societies and groups which minimize the importance of the nuclear family; the kibbutz, hippie communes, and the Oneida community are among the cases discussed.

9 K. Ishwaran, *The Canadian Family*, Holt, Rinehart & Winston, New York, 1976. Nearly 700 pages of articles on contemporary Canadian family life, with admirable concern for the diversity among classes and ethnic groups. Useful for qualifying the necessarily general statements made in a book like the one you are reading now.

10 Peter Laslett, *Family Life and Illicit Love in Earlier Generations*, Cambridge Univ. Press, New York, 1977. Useful if pedantic essays on the history of the family in Europe and North America by the author of *The World We Have Lost*, Methuen, New York, 1965, and *Household and Family in Past Time*, Cambridge Univ. Press, New York, 1972. Laslett demonstrates the rich potential of historical-demographic methods of research.

11 Herman Lantz et al., "The Changing American Family from the Preindustrial to the Industrial Period: A Final Report," *American Sociological Review* **42**:406–21 (1977). The last of a series of reports by a professor at Southern Illinois University and his students. Their research not only chronicles the evolution of companionate marriage but also illustrates how much is to be learned from the content analysis of dusty old magazines on library shelves.

Chapter Nine

Education

Chapter Nine

*I ask how culture is handed down
and passed around, especially in
universities and schools, and how
schooling relates to occupational success.*

Like many boys whose fathers work with their hands, I grew up in awe of the higher learning. But I understood it poorly. As a college freshman I once asked an upperclassman why it is that almost no matter what you study, whether chemistry or French, statistics or history, if you keep at it long enough you get a doctorate in philosophy, a Ph.D. The logic of this nomenclature escaped me, but my more experienced friend had a ready explanation. In graduate school, he told me, you study so long in so much depth with such intensity that regardless of your particular field, it reveals to you a whole philosophy of life. Wow, I thought to myself, satisfied and inspired by this new insight into the academic world.

Alas, awe dwindled as experience increased. The great expectations with which I began higher studies at a leading university unraveled term by term, credit by credit, computer card by computer card. My respect for M.A.s and Ph.D.s sank so low that I declined even to attend the ceremonies where my own advanced degrees were conferred. Such solemn events by then seemed to me exercises in pretense and priggery. Few of my courses had offered or required much depth. Few of my professors had displayed or demanded intensity of effort. And we graduate students had taught each other more philosophy of life over noncredit beers than ever we learned in class. I finished my studies wishing my father knew how little more than he my teachers knew.

Yet I was content to keep the diplomas the university sent me in the mail. I listed them, moreover, on the curriculum vitae (academic language for résumé) by which I declared myself a candidate (that is, an applicant) for a university appointment (in simpler terms, a teaching job). And eventually those diplomas combined with time, work, and publications to bring me to an afternoon of irony. As department chairman in a fine university on May 27, 1976, I donned for the first time ever a gown and hood and fell into line with other administrators and faculty for the graduation procession. As we shuffled along amidst the crescendos of Elgar's *Pomp and Circumstance*, I watched the parents watching us in our many-colored robes. Lots of mothers touched Kleenex to their eyes. The fathers, too, seemed deeply moved—some in their coats and ties stood uncomfortably, respectfully erect, as if they spent most afternoons working with their hands. But what was worst of all, I felt in myself an unmistakable hint of rapture, a sense of deference at being part of that noble enterprise called education.

the hold schools have on citizens

Such is the grip that this institution—the fifth and last to be treated in this book—has not just on me but more or less on all of us citizens of contemporary industrial societies. We who have dwelt in the hallowed halls of academe know well enough their hollowness, the paucity of knowledge and wisdom that cowers within a panoply of detailed degree requirements and hoary formalities. People without much formal education notice the same thing. Blue-collar workers often joke about incompetent graduates and learned fools. But still the grip of schooling holds. Hollow or not, academic institutions dispense a livelihood to teachers, professors, and school administrators, about one of every twenty members of the labor force in contemporary Western societies. And to their graduates these institutions grant diplomas and degrees of measurable worth: the letters (or lack thereof) after a person's name predict reasonably well the numbers (or lack thereof) on that person's paycheck. Unlettered people know this side of the story, too. That is why many working-class parents who sneer at the higher learning also encourage their young to get a piece of it. And apart from these mundane considerations, education commands our trust also for its own sake. Wasn't the Greco-Roman stoic, Epictetus, at least partly right when he observed that only the educated are free? It is for me a sobering fact, imparted by computer analysis no less, that few high-school dropouts could even read and criticize the ideas I set down in this book. How could any writer not be loyal to the institution that teaches women and men to read?

The purpose of this chapter is to make sense of the mixed emotions commonly felt toward education, through concrete analysis of the schools, colleges, and universities that occupy so large a place in contemporary societies. The goal here, as in earlier chapters, is to subject a major dimension of our common life to disciplined empirical reflection, to pool the results of relevant sociological research, and thus intellectually come to grips with another of the hands of history upon us. This chapter will succeed if at its conclusion readers are drained of awe for the higher learning, and the lower, too, and gain instead a deeper understanding of what learning is about. Toward these ends the first three sections below review and reconcile some conflicting definitions of education itself. The next two sections treat schooling or formal education in the past and present, respectively, of the structure of Western societies.

An Agreeable Place to Start

the importance of initial conceptualizations

One example after another in earlier chapters of this book has reinforced an exceedingly important point: that everything a scholar says about any phenomenon depends in great part on how that scholar conceptualized it in the first place. What is a society understood to be—a self-sufficient little community, social life in general, or the order ruled by a nation-state? Or how does some social psychologist commence research—by imagining the person as an outcome of external forces, as a creator of surprise, or as some dialectical mixture of the two? Is the economy defined by some analyst in terms of market exchange, or in broader terms that leave the market only one of several options? Is religion basically a defense against anomie, an enforcer of alienation, both at once, or something still more basic? Again and again we have seen how huge a difference the conceptual starting point makes for what a sociologist can learn about the reality of contemporary life. And in each chapter I have tried to argue for that particular starting point, outlook, definitional leap into the area under study, that will keep us as open as possible to the varied data at hand, and thus as likely as possible to come up with good ideas. To discuss the most fruitful beginnings, the most promising conceptual foundations, can indeed be counted a major purpose of this basic book. The following paragraphs pursue this purpose in the case of education.

No scholar or reader will object, I think, if education is defined here for a start simply as the process by which one or more people learn something from one or more other people. Or conversely, the process by which somebody teaches something to somebody else. In this general sense, education is just the communication by a giver to a receiver of some idea, skill, value, desire, awareness, or other cultural property that the receiver until then did not possess. But even so plain and commonsensical a definition as this serves as a warning against three pitfalls into which the scholarly analysis of education can easily slip, often through sheer thoughtlessness. For the sake of steering the present inquiry in a sound direction, these three pitfalls should be marked and noted here at the outset.

three pitfalls to avoid: first, identifying schooling and education

The first and most common is to identify education with elementary schools, high schools, colleges, universities, and similar organizations. Indeed, the content of some journals and textbooks leaves the impression that the sociology of education is synonymous with the sociology of schools and schooling. It is not. Education is a *process*, a transmission of knowledge by no means limited to those structures formally and specifically charged with inducing it. There are few families in any society, and few churches, television studios, or newspaper offices in societies today which cannot accurately be called educational agencies. To some degree every parent, minister, news reporter, scriptwriter, songwriter, every wife or husband, every friend is in fact an educator: someone who puts new ideas into the head of someone else. If education is not restricted to schools, moreover, neither are schools to education. Today's schools accomplish far more than their official task. They keep youth off both the labor market and the streets, easing at once the problems of unemployment and crime. And many universities devote at least as much energy to researching new ideas as to conveying them to students. Now to be sure, an adequate sociology of education must include analysis of what goes on in classrooms. But schools are no more the sum and substance of education than marriages are of sex, churches of religion, corporations of the economy, or governments of political life. Our goal in the study of any institution is to discern the enduring empirical principles surrounding it, not just to describe transient arrangements in a particular time and place.

"Education is a process, a transmission of knowledge by no means limited to those structures formally and specifically charged with inducing it." Hence the sociology of education in our time can properly focus on television programs equally as much as on school curricula. These two divergent forms of educational experience occupy roughly the same number of hours in the life of today's North American child. (Vivienne/Photo Researchers, Inc.)

second, forgetting that adults learn, too

A second pitfall we had best avoid here is to limit our concern to the education that happens to children, the learning they acquire in the course of growing up. Such a limitation would be less costly were our focus solely on isolated, static, peasant communities of the past. New ideas in such settings were hard to come by. By the time boys and girls reached maturity they knew nearly all of what they were ever going to learn. The major transmission of knowledge that occurred was simply from one generation to the next, from the wise elderly to the ignorant young. This linear, vertical kind of education is still vital, of course; no society endures unless its adults hand down their culture to its children. But the more complex, diverse, and dynamic societies have become, the more education has gained a lateral, horizontal dimension—that is, the more education has come to involve adults teaching and learning from other adults. Empirically, adult education today includes literacy campaigns, high school equivalence programs, job training and retraining, and all manner of continuing education courses offered by colleges and universities. But the schooling of mature students is not the half of it. Simply in order to hold one's job, almost everyone in the labor force constantly has to pick up new skills, learn to operate new machines, master new forms and operating procedures, and keep up with new developments. Much of this learning happens at work and consists simply in reading directives, hearing sales presentations about the latest equipment, attending meetings and seminars, and so on. But much of it also goes on at home, through reading magazines and newspapers, watching television and talking to friends. In sum, education could be limited to children only in an utterly static society, one where nothing new ever happened. Because our industrial capitalist societies thrive on novelty and change, adults within them are constantly teaching and learning, as new ideas spread across the population. An adequate sociology of education can hardly ignore this fact.

third, taking self-education literally

The third and final warning to be sounded here in preface is against taking literally the idea of self-education. For no one learns unless another teaches. Education happens between people, not within an isolated individual—a point made by Pliny the Elder in the first century after Christ. Among all creatures, he wrote, "Man is the only one that knows nothing, that can learn nothing without being taught. He can neither speak nor walk nor eat, and in short he can do nothing at the prompting of nature only, but weep."[1] *Self-education* is thus a malformed word. The better one is *self-schooling*, learning outside the classroom and without a teacher's bodily presence. In the loneliness of his cell the birdman of Alcatraz did indeed learn ornithology. Abraham Lincoln mastered law and politics without amassing credit hours. Teenagers discover how to fix cars just by reading *Mechanix Illustrated* and tinkering with old jalopies. Children gain most of their education just by keeping their eyes and ears open to what adults are accomplishing. Self-schooling indeed happens all the time, whenever a person learns outside of organizations explicitly designed for this purpose. But this is not the same as learning single-handedly. Other people still are involved, if only in the lessons implicit in their behavior and in the products of their work. Somehow, some way, every educational event includes both giver and receiver. Like all institutions, education is a necessarily collective enterprise.

The review below of disparate outlooks on education can therefore be structured around a nucleus of thought on which, I believe, all those who have studied the area agree. It is that education is a process between people, the transfer by one to another of some sort of new idea. The process occurs in schools, from people formally assigned roles like principal, teacher, professor, lab instructor, tutor, or textbook writer to others in roles called pupil, trainee, or student. But it also occurs as an often unnoticed facet of many other speaker-listener, writer-reader, and doer-observer role relationships. Education happens most basically in a vertical way, in the handing down of knowledge from adults to children. But in dynamic societies it assumes also a horizontal dimension, whenever new ideas are passed among adults. In either case the process is necessarily social, involving in some way two people at a minimum; thus *self-education* is a misbegotten word, though *self-schooling* accurately describes a common kind of educational experience. But enough of these initial generalities. The sociology of education becomes more interesting with inspection of divergent views. They are grouped here into two categories, to which the following two sections correspond.

Education as Dispensing and Drinking Truth

the common, traditional imagery

The bulk of theory and research in this area, also most everyday discussions of it, are rooted in an image of a font of true knowledge made available by nature or some god to human beings. The picture is of a finely sculpted fountain set in a garden where flower-bordered pathways intersect. The more knowledge one sips from this source, the more qualified one becomes to live on earth. The font has three remarkable attributes. First, it brims full no matter how many individual humans partake of its bounty. Regardless of how much truth one person is able to digest, there is still the same incalculable amount left to others. The font's second unusual attribute is that it swirls and bubbles with many different kinds of enlightening liquid. One person may imbibe a lot of biology, for example, but never even take a taste of public speaking. Indeed, cultures differ according to which particular currents their citizens set their lips to. Thus were some ancient tribes expert in building with stone, others in using bricks. Our own Western societies are distinguished, however, by how much more knowledge of all different kinds we citizens have consumed. Nevertheless, and this is the font's third exceptional quality, there is no end to the waters surging forth and awaiting human consumption. The more knowledge one takes in, the more one sees how inexhaustible is the still untouched supply, how much remains even undiscovered until now.

Far from being just my own device, this watery metaphor appears often in discussions of knowledge and its transmission in the educational process. For how often one hears that Michael or Judy has a genuine *thirst* for knowledge. Or that Deborah has an immense *capacity* for learning, that she *plunged* into her studies, *waded* through the material, and is now *overflowing* with ideas. Or that Kevin is in a French *immersion* course, though he also *dabbles* in music. Philosophers are said to have *deep* discussions. Marxist students refuse to *swallow* capitalist ideas. *Muddy* or *dry* lectures turn students off. No one likes to be accused of *shallow* thinking. By the end of a term most professors feel *drained*. They wonder how much knowledge students have *absorbed*. But if in an oral exam the examinee's head seems *empty*, the professors will usually *prime the pump* by offering some clues.

one-sidedness in educational thought

Such imagery illustrates dramatically the common, one-dimensional view of education, a perspective narrowly focused on the humble side of the human person. For from this point of view, education happens only to the extent that those receiving it are passive, submissive, acquiescent, open receptacles into which ideas can be poured. Innovative, creative students, the unpredictable and squirmy ones, subvert the whole process. The expectations attached to the learner role are docility, obedience, diligence, respect for the teacher, and zeal in completing assignments. Students should not talk back. They should never surprise their mentors, except perhaps by the speed and thoroughness with which they soak up the ideas given them. The ideal pupil is a guzzler of truth, an insatiable creature with boundless capacity. But mere swallowers of concepts cannot express the active, inventive side of their persons, what was called in Chapter Four the dimension of pride. The latter aspect of human nature should surface only after graduation, once the role of learner has been left behind. You may recall from Chapter Six that from one outlook on the industrial capitalist economy, employees should not expect the chance to be creative in their work, but rather fulfill their need for self-actualization after hours. The outlook on education now being considered holds quite a similar lesson for students: humility is the stance required of them, and pride can wait until school is out or over.

Nor are teachers from this point of view imagined to realize very much the active, creative side of their nature. Givers of knowledge have more discretion and freedom than receivers, of course, but still not much. For they are supposed to carry, bottled as it were inside of them, water from the font of knowledge. The important thing for them is to "have their material down pat," to "know their stuff." And nowadays they are expected also to have imbibed that particular liquid called pedagogy, the teaching techniques by which to stimulate students' thirst and serve them the requisite material in attractive packages. Thus teachers must also be humble. They, too, must knuckle down, buckle down, surrender to the wonders of the font of knowledge. For them equally as for the students, true knowledge is an extrinsic thing, something outside and independent of mere humans, an object for people to consume and then transfer among themselves. Proud creativity hardly enters this outlook on education at all except in the roles of researcher and scientist, the geniuses off in some distant place who write in their reports the new ideas which gradually filter down through various levels of textbooks to students in school. Even such geniuses, however, are thought only to discover new currents and streams in the font of knowledge or to explore its depths. The idea seems preposterous that human beings actually *make* the font and all the water in it.

SOME EXAMPLES

Within the common but one-sided outlook just summarized fall thousands of different books and articles on education, many more than can or need be reviewed here. By way of example, however, I should at least mention the first systematic theory of education ever written, and then some pertinent research emphases in contemporary sociology. It was Plato who spelled out that first comprehensive body of thought about 2400 years ago in Greece. His thinking influenced the whole course of Western education and is still respected today. Plato believed that in some ethereal, supernatural realm there exists a truly just and good society, an eternal, ideal world of which social life on earth is but a pale, distorted reflection, a poor copy. But he also believed that through rational thought philosophers could put inside their heads knowledge of that timeless, perfect reality existing outside and independent of them. These philosophers should therefore be allowed to set up a universal, compulsory school system where boys and girls could be taught as much of this knowledge as their various capacities would permit. Students would be sorted into three classes depending on their abilities, and only those able to understand the ideal *Forms*, thus to become philosophers themselves, would be graduated into the lawmaking, ruling class. From such a position of power these philosopher-kings could then set about restructuring earthly life to fit more and more closely the supernatural Reality, thereby giving rise to a good and just society. Now even this briefest summary of Plato's thought suggests themes which recur in much contemporary writing: placing students according to ability in different streams or tracks, for example, or entrusting government to those who know better than the rest of us how things ought to be. Aristotle's teacher's foremost legacy, however, is the idea that out, up, or down there somewhere is an immutably true Reality that can be known and then communicated in the educational process.

Contemporary educational researchers, not least those labeled sociologists, differ from Plato in many respects. By and large, they place less trust in armchair

Plato's theory of philosopher-kings

philosophers than in upstanding scientists for getting in touch with the truth. But much recent and current research seems still to rest on Plato's assumption that truth exists, thus that education amounts to the inculcation in young minds of such true knowledge as we have so far accumulated and stored in our libraries, computer memories, and teachers' heads. Many scholarly reports seem to take for granted that at the core of every educational effort is a fixed, predetermined bottle of ideas, skills, or values which the teacher must somehow empty into the student. In their much-quoted book, for instance, Talcott Parsons and Robert Bales listed as one of five critical ingredients of education the "denial of reciprocity" between teacher and student.[2] These functionalist authors urge teachers to be supportive, of course, and permissive enough to let students work through their own frustrations. But in the Parsons and Bales perspective, a teacher's happy face is like a nurse's just before giving a shot of penicillin—contrived to facilitate a nonnegotiable injection. The denial of reciprocity means that the educational needle points in just one direction, from a giver who possesses knowledge to a receiver who needs a dose of it. Such a concept is congenial to the functionalist perspective, which views education as a means of ensuring a society's continued existence, as a structure "in which the higher-level patterns of normative culture and systems of objects are internalized in the personality."[3]

functionalism and the denial of reciprocity

A conception of education as simply a humbling experience pervades also the vast literature on the effects of different amounts and techniques of schooling.[4] The dependent variable of such research is normally formulated as an intended educational outcome, a preconceived and measurable result: SAT scores, for example, or ratings on some test of mathematical or reading skills. Sometimes the dependent variable is not cognitive but normative: scores on a test of honesty, for instance, civil libertarianism, rationality, religiosity, or political awareness. But in any case the empirical question is which procedures or conditions most effectively achieve the desired goal. Do children learn more in open classrooms or traditional ones, in large classes or small ones, in public or in private schools, with or without certain audiovisual aids? What is the effect of racially integrated schools on prejudice, or of sexually integrated schools on achievement? Is a Jewish child who was sent to Hebrew school now more likely to be attending synagogue? For each of these and hundreds of similar questions the journals hold dozens of often conflicting research reports. I myself once investigated whether requiring high school boys to wear blue blazers would have a positive or negative impact on how much they learn. Such studies tend to convey an image of students as passive objects who are processed in various ways toward educational outcomes specified in advance.

the preoccupation with IQ

Much the same one-dimensional view is apparent in the continuing preoccupation of many educationists with the concept of intelligence quotient, or IQ. Surely few concepts are more indicative than this one of an image of education as the dispensing and imbibing of truth. For only to the extent that knowledge is something to be swallowed need anyone worry about the learner's capacity. But already Plato worried about it. And early in this century, Alfred Binet (1857–1911) of the French Education Ministry and Lewis Terman (1877–1956) of Stanford University set about developing tests to measure capacity in just this sense. Terman's Stanford-Binet Intelligence Scale became the first IQ test widely used in North America, though by now there are many others as well. IQ has indeed been institutionalized in our culture. In the 1970s, both Arthur Jensen at Berkeley and Richard Herrnstein at Harvard became famous for writing books that posited genetically inherited intelligence as the key predictor of both achievement in school and later success in the stratification system.[5] The much-publicized debates surrounding these books, especially as they touched on racial differences in IQ, need not concern us here. For simply to conceptualize IQ and try to measure it, and to envision school reform grounded in the idea of students' varying personal capacities to learn, imply acceptance of the educational orientation under discussion here.

So much for this outline of an educational outlook focused rather one-sidedly on the humble side of human nature. Often relying on the imagery of a font of true knowledge, people who take this perspective conceptualize ideas as extrinsic things which flow from giver to receiver, provided the former knows how to administer them and the latter has the capacity to take them in. Plato's writings, functionalist thought, the ample research on teaching techniques, and the continuing interest in IQ are but four examples of this perspective. Every reader of this book can think of more examples still: the application to education of B. F. Skinner's experiments with pigeons, for instance, or the programmed learning done in language laboratories, or even true-false tests and those items on exams that have just "one correct answer." A conception of education as dispensing and drinking truth in fact dominates the schools, colleges, and universities of probably all contemporary societies.

Education as Becoming More

Two-dimensional conceptions of education promise more understanding, I believe, than the one-dimensional conceptions just described. It seems to me more fruitful at the very outset of research to recognize that human beings are not just humble, passive, and programmable but also proud, active, and surprising. The paragraphs below review educational research founded on such a dialectical view. But I should note here that this viewpoint does not so much negate the one described above as *not rejecting one-sided views, but transcending them* encompass it, place it in context. The font-of-knowledge outlook does after all make partial sense of the data of our experience. No one who has ever held and loved a mentally retarded child can doubt that however much we might wish otherwise, some humans have greater capacity to learn than others. And the contemporary sad results of certain experiments in unstructured schooling during the late 1960s remind us all that discipline, memorization, drills, homework, and similar humbling practices are indeed necessary to the educational process. Creativity has little place in the spelling of words. Multiple-choice tests do not in themselves undervalue human nature. There is even a sense in which all must agree that knowledge *is* a thing apart from us, to be taken as it comes, accepted, and swallowed irrespective of our preferences. For even if no knowledge is really true and all of it is human handiwork, even if it is all mere invention rather than discovery, still we today have to confront and take seriously into ourselves the knowledge given by history to our time and place. Our education has no springboard but the legacy of ideas, skills, norms, and values handed to us by our forebears. But this is only half the story.

Retarded Children
Can Be Helped

The other half of the story, the one included in dialectical conceptions, can usefully be summarized in four points. First, the content of education is understood to be not something independent of the people involved but the product of their interpersonal activity. There is no notion here of a quantity of knowledge to be inculcated, but only of a set of ideas (skills or whatever) which the teacher believes in and wants to communicate. These ideas may be similar to those of some other teacher, but never identical. No subject, neither organic chemistry nor British history nor carpentry, ever comes out quite the same from any two teachers' mouths or textbook writers' pens. A teacher gives not the truth but only his or her version of it. And a student does not just swallow that version but instead picks it apart and interweaves some of it with the knowledge derived from his or her previous experience. Thus education implies an encounter between two persons, the giver actively expressing some part of his or her own self, the receiver actively responding and deciding how if at all to accept that gift. Teacher and learner could not detach themselves from the content of education even if they chose. For the content is in fact the always uncopied connection the two of them make with each other.

A second, corollary point is that the desired outcome or goal of an educational effort can never be exactly specified in advance. Committed teachers do indeed plan and prepare the lessons they will give: "On Wednesday I will review the geography of Mexico." But no one can know what any student will do with that review—that will depend on what the student already knows of Mexico, of geography, and of anything else to which this lesson might relate. Learning requires that a *connection* be made, an integration of the teacher's ideas into those the student already holds. A quiz, a so-called objective test the next week or month cannot measure this connection. A quiz shows only whether the teacher's gift has arrived; a high score is like a postal return receipt from a registered letter. But the quiz may in fact be the occasion for the student to return the gift to its sender and be done with it. There is no evidence that the goal of an educational effort has been achieved or even that education has in fact occurred until the student expresses some connection he or she has personally made. "Remember what you said about the Sierra Madre Mountains? Aren't they an extension of the Rockies in our own country?" "My parents visited Mexico City last winter, and my dad says tall buildings there tilt just as you said." Not simple recall but only comments like these confirm the meeting of minds in which education consists. Such meetings are the goal of education, their forms cannot be predetermined, and they vary immensely across students in a class, readers of a textbook, or watchers of a demonstration.

Third, a dialectical conception of education implies disinterest in variation across students in innate intellectual capacity, the quality IQ tests are intended to measure. The question is instead how much and what kind of ideas and skills the student has gained by any point in time, since this is the inescapable context in which all further learning must take place. A low educational ceiling is recognized, of course, for individuals born with Down's syndrome or certain kinds of brain damage. But these account for at most 3 percent of the human population. Most of the remaining 97 percent, whatever their differences in genetic endowment, have each a mental capacity sufficient to fill any of the roles, from astronaut to zoologist, in contemporary societies. None has cause to lord it over another intellectually on genetic grounds. Remember that each of us descends from illiterate ancestors who believed the earth was flat. The differences among us humans today, like those between us and our ancestors, are a matter very little of the size of brains but very much of their cultivation. Such a perspective lends a sense of urgency to education, especially in societies so advanced as ours. For we cannot rely on our children's "basic intelligence" to see them through our status quo to a brighter day. Instead we must teach them, every one of them, providing early on a framework of reading, writing, spelling, grammar, arithmetic, methodical problem solving, history, geography—the standard subjects to which they will be able to tie all sorts of ideas later on. And if later on, at the age of 12 or 15, some child appears physically normal but mentally stupid, we dare not be deceived by appearances, and must instead find and teach some ideas the child can learn and then demand the effort required to learn them. For the sake of the future of our race, no child or adult should be allowed to internalize a mentality of "I can't."

fourth, a sense of biography and history

Fourth and finally, a two-sided outlook on education is informed by a sense of history, movement, process, growth at both the individual and societal levels. A person's identity is never regarded as final and fixed but always as a process back and forth between prior experience and new knowledge, the two of them connecting over and over in ever-changing ways, each connection both enlarging the constancy of one's personal past and quickening one's interest in still more newness. To be fully human means not being this or that but day by day becoming something more. The role of an educator is to facilitate that movement, to provide a disciplined, stimulating milieu in which students can thrive, blossom, grow. And this role expectation applies to teachers not just of philosophy or literature but also of agriculture, engineering, even typing—any body of knowledge, exposure to which expands students' horizons and further enlivens their own identities. Education in this sense has a multiplier effect: the richer in ideas one becomes, the more capable of further enrichment, since there are now more hooks onto which new ideas can be hung. Such a dynamic conception of individual biography, moreover, implies similar dynamism in outlook on social history. Social change is not, as Plato believed, for the sake of fitting life on earth to some external standard but instead an intentional back and forth between past experience and novelty. The good society, like the healthy individual, does not just stand on its own feet. It is off and running.

The four points just reviewed do not, of course, exhaust what education means to those who recognize both the humble and proud dimensions of the human person, but they capture at least the fundamentals of this point of view. The font-of-knowledge metaphor is not so much denied by this outlook as it is transcended. The content of education is seen not just as subject matter but as the connection between subject matter and the learner's mind. The goal of education is not just a predictable acceptance of new ideas but the necessarily unpredictable manner of incorporating new ideas into those already held. The target of education is more than a receptacle to be filled; rather it is an almost limitless being to be cultivated. Teachers and students are not mere players in nature's game but active

Functionaries in today's school systems still spend a huge amount of time and money testing children's innate intelligence and making decisions on the basis of IQ scores. Yet already in 1950, the United Nations Statement on Race proclaimed: "It is now generally recognized that intelligence tests do not in themselves enable us to differentiate safely between what is due to innate capacity and what is the result of environmental influences, training and education. . . . The scientific material available to us at present does not justify the conclusion that inherited genetic differences are a major factor in producing the differences between the cultures and cultural achievements of different peoples or groups. It does indicate, however, that the history of the cultural experience which each group has undergone is the major factor in explaining such differences. The one trait which above all others has been at a premium in the evolution of men's mental characters has been educability, plasticity. This is a trait which all human beings possess." The statement had been drafted initially by a committee consisting of the following sociologists and anthropologists: Ernest Beaglehole (New Zealand), Juan Comas (Mexico), L.A. Costa-Pinto (Brazil), Franklin Frazier (United States), Morris Ginsberg (United Kingdom), Humayun Kabir (India), Claude Levi-Strauss (France), and Ashley Montagu (United States). (George Roos/Peter Arnold, Inc.)

creators of their respective biographies and collective history. To amplify further what these points mean, the following paragraphs describe three thinkers about education, widely separate in time and place, whose writings nonetheless reflect a common dialectical perspective. All three are noteworthy, especially because they implemented their ideas in concrete programs of action.

SOME EXAMPLES

Dewey: the goal of continuing capacity for growth

The first is John Dewey (1859–1952), a philosophy professor first at Michigan, later at Chicago, and finally at Columbia, the most influential educational theorist America has yet produced. Like Marx, Dewey created out of an early absorption in Hegelian idealism a body of thought no less dialectical than Hegel's but far more concrete, empirical, and practical. Dewey's approach can be inferred from his friendship at Chicago with George Herbert Mead, the author of the I-me formulation discussed in Chapter Four and the father of symbolic interactionist social psychology. All four points reviewed above are expounded with magnificent simplicity and clarity in Dewey's major treatise, *Democracy and Education*, published in 1916. Therein he railed against static views of education as mere job-training or as indoctrination in the ideas of an outdated, dead past. Democracy implies, he argues, "that the aim of education is to enable individuals to continue their education—or that the object and reward of learning is continued capacity for growth."[6] He expressed distrust for anyone who knew exactly what students should be taught. "What is sometimes called a benevolent interest in others," he wrote, "may be but an unwitting mask for an attempt to dictate to them what their good shall be, instead of an endeavour to free them so that they may seek and find the good of their own choice."[7] Regrettably, thousands of teachers in what came to be called progressive schools misconstrued Dewey's thought and used it to justify the elimination of discipline, books, standards, and requirements from the classroom. Clearly annoyed, Dewey complained in 1938 about *"either-or"* educational philosophies, those which consider only the funded experience of the past (what the teacher gives) or the immediate propensities of students, without realizing that education happens only in the *interaction* between the two. "There is no discipline in the world so severe," he wrote on that occasion, "as the discipline of experience subjected to the tests of intelligent development and direction."[8]

Coady: cooperative methods in extension education

Although no match for Dewey in sheer profundity, Moses Coady (1882–1959) can serve well as a second example of the dialectical outlook on education. A native Nova Scotian, Coady spent his entire career as a professor at St. Francis Xavier University in Antigonish. But he was less concerned with the education of youth than of adults. Already in 1862, the U.S. government had passed the Morrill Act, providing land grants to states for the establishment in each of a college specializing in agriculture and the applied sciences. Most of these institutions can today be recognized by the word *state* in their names: Iowa State, Mississippi State, or Kansas State, for example. And from these schools the idea of *extension education* had spread across the United States and Canada. It was understood mostly in a one-sided way: university experts should extend to unlettered farmers and shop-keepers the rudiments of science, thereby improving the efficiency of production. But Coady invested the concept of university extension with two-sided meaning.

The starting point would be thorough acquaintance by university teachers with the immediate, work-related problems facing ordinary people—problems ranging from ignorance of technology to exploitation by big business and betrayal by politicians. These teachers would then organize and lead discussion groups wherein ordinary people would not only learn together new and helpful ideas but also act cooperatively to put these ideas into effect, thus gaining greater control of their own lives. Coady's extension department, where he taught such principles and techniques of cooperative education, has graduated thousands of this special kind of educator since its founding in 1928. Some have remained to work with fishermen and miners in the Maritime provinces; others have made the word *Antigonish* the prime symbol of Canada in disparate regions of Africa and Asia. "Up to now," Coady wrote in 1943, "education for the masses has meant an exit through which the highly energetic and ambitious escape to the most desirable jobs in the nation. It is an escape mechanism by which the lowly can rise from their class and join the elite. It is the instrument which creates classes in a supposedly classless society. . . . Any profound concept of education would look upon it as an instrument to unlock life to all the people."[9]

Freire: dialogical modes of teaching literacy

The dialectical method is explicit in the work and writings of the third educational thinker in this painfully brief review. He is Paolo Freire, a contemporary Brazilian who began his career at Recife, studying methods of teaching literacy. The methods he devised became so popular and effective in northeastern Brazil that the generals who seized power in the 1964 coup sent Freire into exile in Chile. Later he worked at Harvard and for the World Council of Churches in Geneva before returning to his native land in 1979. The gist of Freire's outlook, developed most fully in *Pedagogy of the Oppressed*, lies in the distinction between antidialogical and dialogical modes of teaching. In the former mode arrogant oppressors, representatives of the power-holding class, seek to conquer their students with "a series of methods precluding any presentation of the world as a problem and showing it rather as a fixed entity, as something given—something to which men, as mere spectators, must adapt."[10] For dialogic teaching, by contrast, teachers must be genuinely in love with the world and their students, humble enough to admit ignorance and learn from students, and possessed of faith in the power of every human to create and re-create, to participate actively in making history. Lofty words, to be sure, but the principles of dialogic education had remarkable results once implemented in concrete literacy programs. The teachers "tuned in" to their students' vocabulary and drew from it the first key words students would learn to read and write—words meaningful and discussible like *slum, work, land, rain,* and *bicycle*. Discussions revolved around these words, especially as they helped students learn to distinguish nature (the world as given) from culture (the world as shaped by men and women). The process of learning to read and write became then a way for peasants to become conscious of their own actions as makers of culture. Literacy was taught as a tool for reflecting, an instrument of liberation from the myth of personal powerlessness. And the students did learn through these techniques—not just to read and write but also to demand a say in the conditions of their lives. For this Freire was jailed and then exiled.

Many other scholars than John Dewey, Moses Coady, and Paolo Freire might have been described here to illustrate recognition in educational theory of not only passive, humble docility in the student role but also active, proud, distinctly human liveliness. But together these three men dramatize the fact that a dialectical or dialogic outlook can be applied to education in any setting or context—from urban American schools to rural Canadian extension programs to literacy projects for Brazilian peasants. For none of these activist scholars defined the content of learning as mere textbook knowledge or its goal as the simple internalization of abstract ideas. None worried much about exceeding students' intellectual capacities, and all three conceptualized education as a dynamic facet of the process of making history. Only economies of space in this book prevent me from adding to this review the profound variations on these same themes that appear in the writings of still other educators. The British philosophers Alfred North Whitehead (1861–1947) and Bertrand Russell (1872–1980) both wrote with immense insight on education, and the latter was much involved in experimental schools.[11] So, too, A. S. Neill, who applied his educational ideas in the much-discussed and widely copied Summerhill school.[12] Few writers about higher education have described it so well as Robert Hutchins, Chicago University's president from 1929 to 1945.[13] Also worth reading are such contemporary critics as Edgar Friedenberg, Paul Goodman, John Holt, and Ivan Illich, each of whom takes contemporary schools to task for stifling students' creativity.[14] But there is no need here to make a lengthy review of this literature. It is enough for present purposes to know that the best educational thinkers of our day understand education to mean more than pouring true knowledge into students' heads.

<aside>dialectical outlooks apply to all educational contexts</aside>

A PRACTICAL SUMMARY

Quite a few pages have by now been spent on distinguishing between two generic outlooks on education. The one sees it as dispensing and drinking truth, the other as a process of becoming more oneself and more able to become still more. Both consider education a necessarily social transfer of cultural items, but in the first perspective the transfer is all one-way, as if learners were alpine canyons to be filled with echoes of true yodels. In the second, more dialectical perspective, learners not only repeat but also respond, voicing and enacting their respective unique mixtures of new ideas with previous experience—and teachers listen, thereby discovering what to offer next, thereby also becoming more themselves. The difference between these two outlooks has been explained and illustrated here in various ways, but with few explicit references to sociology. Plato and Dewey are known as philosophers, after all, Jensen and Herrnstein as psychologists, Coady and Freire as reformist educators. One might ask what their theories have to do with the discipline named in the title of this book. But here, as in earlier chapters, the frailty of boundaries between disciplines reveals itself. The distinction between one-sided and two-sided outlooks has in fact everything to do with the task of a sociology of education, namely to understand this institution in the empirical context of contemporary societies.

For one cannot imagine sociological research on education without some kind of operational definition, concrete measures that enable the researcher to say, "Yes, education is happening here," or "No, it is not." And the basic concept or outlook determines fairly much which measures will be used. Suppose, for a simple example, that a sociologist observed two young women learning to punch coded

<aside>measuring educational outcomes</aside>

393

interview responses onto computer cards. Similar to typing, this skill involves using a keyboard to transform numbers written on paper into holes punched in cardboard. Now the one woman is a sociology student learning to punch up data she herself collected for her honors thesis. The other woman is a secretary newly hired by the university, assigned to sociology, and now expected to learn to operate a machine whose purpose remains a mystery to her. Suppose three days later the sociologist measured which woman has learned more. From a one-sided outlook, the measure to be used is easy: just calculate who is faster, who has better absorbed the skill, who can turn out the most error-free computer cards per hour. From a humanist, dialectical perspective such calculation is only part of the test. The greater part consists of talking to the two women, asking each to explain the purpose of her work, to relate keypunching to other knowledge and skill she has, and to say how keypunching has expanded her horizons. This larger test quite possibly reveals that the secretary punches 45 cards per hour but can say only, "It's not bad, but I like typing better." The sociology student might punch only 30 cards per hour but have much to say. "There's nothing to it," she responds. "I thought it was going to be hard. But now I can see what the control cards are about. I just want to finish punching these stupid things so that I can start my computer runs and analyze my data." From a one-sided point of view, the secretary is 50 percent better-educated in keypunching than the student. From a dialectical viewpoint, the results are mixed but tend to favor the student, who despite her slowness has better incorporated this new skill into the process of her own becoming.

The point of this example applies also to operational measures of education in other contexts. From a two-sided outlook, multiple-choice tests in calculus, chemistry, or English are by themselves inadequate, since they tap only a student's humble side. The same goes for the recitation of capitals, lakes, and rivers as evidence of competence in geography. Nor do passing grades on standardized tests in thirty or forty courses at a high school or university demonstrate an education gained. They show it better, of course, than failing grades, but a dialectical view of education demands harder evidence. It is not enough that a student be a walking dictionary; everyday printed ones are easier to use and cost less. The student must instead create in his or her own uncopied way evidence of having sorted through ideas given and having joined them to prior experience. In the case of cabinet-making this means transforming a pile of wood into a piece of one's own line of furniture. In the case of most academic subjects, it means writing a cogent, coherent paper with a style, content, and organization of one's own design. Only in such difficult ways can learners proclaim the fullness of their humanity and the completion of some educational experience.

training versus
education   A dialectical approach to the sociology of education permits a clear, measurable distinction between mere training and education. This is not the difference between concrete manual skills and abstract nonmanual ideas. Even learning to operate a keypunch or build cabinets can be educational, and one can be trained in chemistry. Training is truncated education, a learning process cut short of a requirement that the learner respond, reflect, and incorporate creatively the new subject matter into personal biography. Trainers differ vividly from educators in the way they treat learners. Trainers discourage questions, ridicule self-expression,

respect only work done "by the book," and never prod learners into making their own links between what is taught and what they already know. That is why we readily speak of training dogs or pigeons. Their creativity is minimal anyway. Fragmented, discrete skills exhaust their capabilities. To train people means to treat them as animals, one-sidedly humble beings to be dominated, conquered, manipulated by others. The slaves of the Old South were carefully trained, though laws actually forbade their education. For to educate people means to train them, yes, but constantly to go beyond training: to foster discussion and debate, field questions and encourage independent work, counter fragmentation by demanding wholeness, thus to enable people to become still more, thus to set them free. Of course, some skills like reading or arithmetic yield by themselves so much potential for further learning that to teach them is almost by definition educational.

*assessing the worth of
educational techniques*

The outlook of Dewey, Coady, Freire, and similar scholars suggests also more adequate empirical standards by which to assess the worth of educational devices and techniques. For of each can be asked not just how much knowledge it communicates and how effectively but also how strongly it encourages learners to make their own connections, think back and forward, express their respective reactions, and thus humanize themselves. Compare, for instance, the nightly news on television and the daily newspaper as tools for instruction in current events. The former teaches more graphically and immediately, the latter in greater detail. But the crucial difference between them is that newspaper readers have the chance to think one story over before proceeding to the next, to skip around, to reread items especially relevant to personal experience, or even to cut them out for mailing to a friend or pasting in a scrapbook. Television viewers, by contrast, are simply fed the news. They cannot reflect or comment on one story without missing the next one—except during brief commercial breaks, which viewers often seize upon for this purpose. Or compare the educational merit of taking a packaged tour to Italy versus traveling there on one's own. The former typically exposes tourists to more sights in less time—today the Vatican, tonight the clubs, tomorrow Pompeii. But following one's own itinerary forces tourists to articulate hour by hour their own preferences, thus to face up to their own identities and relate themselves to new experiences. Still a third example is study through correspondence. Textbooks may be identical to those used in a classroom, and taped lectures even superior in content to those hastily prepared for personal delivery. But the correspondence student misses the ongoing interplay of minds that underlies discussion in class and afterwards in coffee shops and dormitories. These are the kind of concrete issues a two-sided, dialectical outlook on education makes it possible to research. The basis of evaluating any educational medium is not just how well it conveys new ideas but how relentlessly it requires learners to create still newer ideas in response.

Finally and most important, the comprehensive outlook favored in these pages frees us to assess contemporary structures of formal education against an independent yardstick. For the main concern of sociologists must rightfully be those sets of roles and procedures called schools to which the lofty purpose of education is explicitly entrusted in our own societies. But thanks to Dewey, Coady, Freire, and many others of like mind, we have now an outlook that permits us to question just how educational our school systems are. We can take a measure like IQ, years of school completed or degrees held, systematically investigate its significance in social structure and culture, but still leave empirically open the question of what it has to do with education. For from the learner's position, education is above all a process of personal growth, nourished through the absorption of knowledge given by history to our time and place, but propelled by steady, disciplined, creative effort to incorporate this knowledge into one's own unique, ever-lengthening biography. And from the teacher's position, education is the process of giving knowledge for absorption, but also of stimulating, demanding, and affirming each learner's hard work of connecting new ideas to prior experience. Teaching necessarily becomes thereby itself an opportunity to learn. Equipped with such an outlook, we proceed now to the study of schools in our own civilization, first in its past and then in the present day.

The Social Origins of Schooling

Of the five institutions treated in this book, education appears as the last in Western history to have been formalized, spelled out in specific roles and organizations. Even the architectural remains of the past bear this out. Athens and Rome still exhibit the public buildings of ancient politics, the temples of pre-Christian religion, family homes 2000 years old, and all manner of economic relics, from marketplaces and roads to terraces and aqueducts. But libraries, lecture halls, and student dormitories of comparable age are hard to find. Our distant ancestors managed to create huge, efficient bureaucracies for war and statecraft, worship and work, long before they organized school systems. They imposed grandiose methods and plans on civic order, on relations with the earth and the beyond, and even on kinship, both earlier and more carefully than they did on the transmission of culture. Plato's dream of a universal compulsory system of education came to fruition only in the late nineteenth century in Europe and America, barely a hundred years ago.

education has been formalized only recently

Education was happening all the while, of course. Otherwise we would have no history: each generation would have had to start over from scratch, and none could have gone beyond the one before. But until the fourteenth and fifteenth centuries very little of the knowledge underlying European life was written down. No scrolls of agricultural know-how helped peasants till their fields. Written directions simply did not exist for any but a few of the skills on which medieval societies rested. Nowhere did grammars exist by which to learn to read and write one's native tongue. How then was education accomplished? Mostly as a by-product of raising children in families and little communities. Then as now, children watched and copied adults in the varied tasks of the household and local area. Then more than now, children were compelled early in life to try their own hands at these tasks. Children learned more directly and concretely than vicariously and symbolically: they were tossed into successive pools of adult experience and expected to swim. Work was their trade school, worship their Sunday school, and the living reality of traditional authority their civics class. The few children who learned to read and write did so by practicing the habits of literate adults. And any further education after maturity was given and acquired in similar informal ways. Now this unscholastic mode of cultural transmission did not leave the populace well-educated by contemporary standards. Older generations could not transmit what they did not yet have themselves: an awareness of the goodness of human inventiveness, a sense of purposeful history, the spirit of modernity. But most medieval cultures managed to survive and even develop, albeit slowly. Witness the spread of windmills and watermills across the continent. All this without reliance on systems of formal education.

two early kinds of teacher

Specialists in teaching were not unknown, however, either in medieval Europe or in the earlier Greek city-states and Roman Empire. Indeed, most premodern societies included people called *teacher*. But these were mainly of two kinds. First was the individual creative thinker, the preacher of novelty—a philosophic Socrates or Aristotle, a prophetic Jesus or Paul. Teachers like these attracted pupils by their personal charisma, compelling logic, extraordinary experiences, or some kind of gift for words. Their purpose in life was not at all to give their disciples the knowledge necessary to replicate the status quo. They took such knowledge for granted in their listeners. These teachers could hardly be described as agents of entrenched culture, experts in dispensing it to thirsty listeners. They were instead cultural innovators, self-proclaimed harbingers of change, wandering critics with students in tow. The other main kind of full-time teacher was the tutor for children of the ruling classes. In medieval times monks often played this role, dividing their time between transcribing manuscripts and teaching rich men's sons to read them. Other tutors, usually also clerics, were attached to royal courts and noble families for the purpose of acquainting youth with knowledge beyond local experience. Charlemagne was well known for encouraging this practice in the ninth century.[15] More than the philosophers and prophets, such tutors resembled the professional teachers of our day. But they were not certified or invested with degrees. Their classrooms were schools only in embryo. There was as yet no school *system* for teachers to be part of.

THE HIGHER LEARNING

universities preceded lower schools

Sometimes it is imagined that formal education began in the distant past with perhaps a two-year basic course, which then lengthened as knowledge increased to the twelve, sixteen, or more years expected today. The evidence of history shows otherwise. Schooling made its debut in Western civilization not at the elementary level but on the lofty plane of universities. The first ones appeared in the twelfth century in cities like Paris, Toulouse, and Montpellier in France, Oxford in England, Bologna and Salerno in Italy. At the start they were nothing more than guilds or trade unions of master teachers, loose associations of clerics whom the local bishop had recognized as fit to teach. In most cities the master teachers began voluntarily to come together on the same principle as master artisans in various crafts, the principle that unity gives strength to resist state authority, to enforce more uniform standards of work, and to obtain higher pay. The term *universitas* could initially be used for any such guild. Only gradually was its use restricted to a group of master *teachers* giving organized instruction in a single city. Each university was expected to have two divisions, a faculty of arts for beginning students and at least one of the higher faculties of law, medicine, and theology. To earn the first, or bachelor's, degree was to complete an apprenticeship in the academic craft. The higher student was a journeyman, closer to the status of master and thus qualified to help teach beginners. From this model of the guild derives the common contemporary practice of entrusting first-year university students to graduate assistants.

Good sense is easy to see in the medieval youth apprenticed by choice to a master carpenter or stonemason—thereby learning skills of obvious value. But why would young men, mainly sons of nobles and free townsmen, want so much to earn academic degrees that in some cities, Bologna for one, they hired masters and founded universities of their own?[16] Or similarly, why would a king like Frederick Barbarossa, Holy Roman emperor from 1152 to 1190, publicly invite students into his realm and promise them immunity from the civil courts? The fact is that the nascent universities struck a chord that harmonized as perfectly as polyphonic chants with the character of medieval life. Popes and kings promulgated charters guaranteeing protection to these new intellectual groups and granting them a measure of autonomy, charters which inaugurated the norms of academic freedom still in force today. The universities did what every successful school anywhere must do: they taught something students wanted to learn and rulers considered valuable. The following paragraphs explain what this something was, what the masters offered that so captured the fancy of their students and of the privileged classes in general.

classical learning was detached from lived experience

The content of what was taught was remarkable first of all for its detachment from everyday experience. The masters made no effort to build upon students' prior knowledge of the society and culture at hand—they forbade students even to speak in their native tongues. Nor did the masters try very hard to come up with new ideas relevant to the practical issues of the day. They had little interest in the data of mere sensory experience, the natural and social events of mundane life. They sought instead to retrieve from manuscripts copied and preserved by monks the philosophic knowledge of the ancient Greeks and Romans, to forsake the foul, unwashed reality of their own societies in favor of Plato's kind of true Reality. From the park where Plato lectured, in fact, derived the medieval and contemporary synonym for school, *academy*. The arts curriculum involved learning what he, Aristotle, and similar worthies had written more than a thousand years earlier. It was divided into seven subjects: the *trivium* of grammar (Latin and Greek), rhetoric, and logic, and the *quadrivium* of arithmetic, geometry, astronomy, and music. The idea was to turn from the crass existing world toward the font of knowledge that bubbled in the heydays of Athens and Rome. An educated man (educated women came later) was one who had successfully separated himself from immediate economic and political affairs and entered into the higher world of the intellect. Such separation took time. To be admitted to university at all an applicant had to be able to parse the Latin authors and possibly the Greek ones, too—hence he would have to have been tutored beforehand, often by his parish priest. The course for the bachelor's degree took four to six years, for the master's two to ten years more. Some universities added still higher degrees like the licentiate and doctorate. But the prime requirement for any degree, however named, was to internalize the knowledge philosophers in the distant past had once acquired.

If we can imagine how dull, boring, changeless, and hopeless life was for our medieval ancestors, then their craving for the knowledge of a dead but glorious past is easily understood. Besides, the seven liberal arts were far more humanist and hopeful than many religious myths by which other premodern peoples sought refuge from a dreary existence. Almost from their inception, moreover, the medieval universities began in fact to connect the classical learning to their own time and place. Anselm in the twelfth century, Thomas Aquinas in the thirteenth, and other scholastic philosophers sought to reconcile in their own writings Aristotelian and other classical thought to the then current teachings of the Christian church. Popes insisted that faculties of law, usually the most popular with students, give instruction not just in the Roman classics but in recent papal decrees. And gradually the ancient authors themselves came to be read less than professors' codifications and summaries of their work, treatises which inevitably reflected the professors' own historical situations. Even in the thirteenth century, universities pressured political régimes and the papacy to limit the practice of law and medicine to graduates of properly chartered faculties.[17] And rulers began even then to rely on professors for the speeches and books that would make their rule seem reasonable and just. In these and other ways the universities became involved in the world around them, while continuing to justify their existence in terms of a past intellectual golden age. If nothing else, universities could promise their graduates at least the public distinction of having imbibed the lofty truth of a bygone halcyon era. It was a scarce distinction, costly in effort and money, yielding an air of superiority and of membership in a cultural elite. Thus did many young men aspire to university degrees, even as they do today.

the modernization of universities

Chapters Five and Six of this book outlined the process of modernization respectively in political terms (from traditional rule by divine right to democratic self-rule) and in economic ones (from a static peasant mentality to the dynamic spirits of capitalism and socialism). The same process can be observed in the history of universities from the sixteenth century on. In this case the shift has been away from detached, ivory-tower contemplation of a dead past toward the disciplined, empirical study of a living present. It has meant an admission, at once terrifying and exhilarating, that there is no exit from present structures of life except into future ones we humans ourselves create. There is no need here to review all the steps taken in this process of academic modernization, but the most obvious ones have been in the content of knowledge itself as taught by philosophers. The Reformation, for its part, emancipated philosophers in the Protestant parts of Europe from slavish adherence to church-defined dogmas and freed them to think creatively on their own—beyond Plato and Aristotle and beyond Christian orthodoxy. Out of the Reformation came that dramatic intellectual shift of the seventeenth and eighteenth centuries, what is often called the Enlightenment or Age of Reason, when philosophers became conscious that nature is good, that progress is possible, and that through reasoned analysis of the data of sensory experience humans can indeed learn something new.[18] Indeed, to some extent the universities caused the sun to rise on the modern world, since it was mostly professors within them—John Locke, Isaac Newton, Immanuel Kant, David Hume, and others—who first articulated in words the kind of awareness we now call modernity.

William and Mary in
1727 versus Virginia in
1800

Modernization also meant changes in university curricula, a shifting away from Greece and Rome toward the here and now. Let one example suffice. By 1727, the College of William and Mary in Williamsburg, Virginia, had a program of study clearly more modern than medieval ones. Latin and Greek still constituted, of course, the basis of the grammar school. And the two professors in the only other division, the philosophy school, were to teach respectively "rhetorick, logick and ethicks" and "physicks, metaphysicks and mathematicks." But the trustees were willing to let some contemporary writings be used, "for as much as we see now daily a further progress in philosophy, than could be made by Aristotle's *Logick* and *Physicks*, which remained so long alone in the other schools, and shut out all other."[19] Further, "we allow the schoolmaster the liberty, if he has any observations on the Latin and Greek grammars, or on any of the authors taught in his school, that with the approbation of the president, he may dictate them to the scholars."[20] Now compare to this the curriculum proposed in 1800 by Thomas Jefferson, an alumnus of William and Mary, who eventually gave up trying to reform his alma mater and instead founded the University of Virginia. Jefferson wanted "an University on a plan so broad and liberal and *modern*, as to be worth patronizing with the public support, and be a temptation to the youth of other states to come, and drink of the cup of knowledge and fraternize with us. . . . I will venture even to sketch the sciences which seem useful and practicable for us, as they occur to me while holding my pen. Botany, Chemistry, Zoology, Anatomy, Surgery, Medicine, Natural Philosophy, Agriculture, Mathematics, Astronomy, Geology, Geography, Politics, Commerce, History, Ethics, Law, Arts, Fine-arts."[21] It is no accident that the same disciple of Locke and Rousseau who wrote the thirteen colonies' declaration of independence and who championed creative economic enterprise should also want university students to be steeped in knowledge of the real, existing world surrounding them.

Change in universities since Jefferson's time can also be understood in part as the continuing penetration of the modern spirit into academic curricula and organization. The abandonment of Latin as the medium of instruction in favor of vernacular languages was part of this trend. So was the invention and spread of sociology, that discipline which forces people to look at and analyze even their own behavior toward one another. But so, too, the shift earlier described within sociology, away from the search for natural, eternal social laws toward naked awareness of the humanly constructed character of human life. The popularity in universities throughout the world of John Dewey's two-sided conception of education was a further step in the process of academic modernization. But perhaps the clearest sign of this process has been the increased study of history itself, both as a distinct discipline and as an orienting framework in all disciplines. For the medieval curriculum had no place for history in the sense of connecting the past to the present. The ancient epoch impressed on medieval students was taught not as a stepping-stone to the present but as a disconnected island away from it. Only gradually has history crept into universities as the study of *our story*, the empirical tale of how the human race has moved through time to the specific arrangements that mark the present day. The study of history in this dynamic sense is indeed essential to the purpose of any modern university, which must teach students not only the practical culture of the society at hand but also the hard truth that humans are responsible for it.

By way of concluding this brief review of how the first major kind of formal education began, two comments are appropriate. First, the further Western universities departed from mere classical learning and the more they faced up to their respective historical situations, the more diverse they became in curriculum and organization. Universities two centuries ago, like Catholic parishes two decades ago, remained relatively united on standard Latin texts thought to contain ideas of timeless worth. But with integration into diverse cultural contexts came diversity among universities themselves, most notably in the language of study: British students came to read mainly English authors, Italian students Italian authors, and so on. Diversity arose as well in where various disciplines prospered most—psychology in the individualistic United States, for example, much more than in Iberia or South America. Universities came to contrast sharply also in their forms of organization: witness the huge status gap between professors and junior faculty in Germany versus the more egalitarian structure in the United States. But the differences across increasingly modern but still autonomous universities resulted also from their divergent responses to quite similar culture contexts. Throughout North America, for instance, Catholic universities tended to emphasize humanistic disciplines like literature, philosophy, and law, while those founded under Protestant auspices delved earlier and more aggressively into the natural sciences. Montreal and McGill, St. Louis and Washington, Detroit and Wayne State, Fordham and New York—each pair is a study in contrasts within a single city. The rich variety among universities both within and across national societies, both today and even a century ago, can only be noted here, not described. Each reader of this book can investigate and ponder how the university (or college) he or she knows best has used its autonomy to enter into the dynamics of its particular milieu.

The second concluding comment I should make is that despite their institutionalization in nearly all national societies, also despite their modernization in the past few centuries, universities have never come close to monopolizing the tasks of transmitting and creating culture. The importance of universities should not be overblown. Until this century, no more than 3 percent of any generation in any society earned so much as a bachelor's degree. Even these few graduates, moreover, furthered their education probably more through travel, reading, discussion, and the direct experience of work in a changing world than through the fulfillment of degree requirements. Such learned modern philosophers as Rousseau, Benjamin Franklin, and Herbert Spencer never attended university at all. Marx and Engels, those most influential of teachers, never held university chairs. The great inventions of the nineteenth century—the telephone, the automobile, the telegraph, the radio, the light bulb, hydroelectricity—were almost all made off campus. Professors of literature account for a remarkably small proportion of great works of literature. In sum, universities survived until quite recent decades mainly, to use blunt words, by snob appeal: by conferring on elite youth the expensive distinction of having imbibed an obscure, uesless, but allegedly deeper kind of truth. It was because of its lingering cult of the classics that Thorstein Veblen poked brutal fun at the higher learning at the turn of this century. "Indeed," he wrote, "there can be little doubt that it is their utility as evidence of wasted time and effort, and hence of the pecuniary strength necessary in order to afford this waste, that has secured to the classics their position of prerogative in the scheme of higher learning."[22] The higher learning has changed some since Veblen's time, of course, but a brief glance at the origins of lower schools had best precede a specific focus on formal education in the present day.

PRIMARY AND SECONDARY SCHOOLS

As a rule in today's Western world, a child first spends a year in kindergarten, six to eight more in elementary school, a further four to six years in secondary school, and only then becomes eligible for admission to the higher learning. This rule is of recent origin, dating only from the nineteenth century. Early universities like Paris and Oxford were more than 700 years old before lower-level school systems were worked out. It appears that our structure of formal education was built backwards, top floors first and foundation eventually. In empirical fact, however, even the idea of an overall educational system, extending all the way from kindergarten through graduate school, has taken root in Western cultures only in the past two decades. The ladder of school attainment youth today are obliged to climb, trying not to jump off until high enough to make a big splash in the economy, has only recently been pieced together from two very different kinds of school. On the one hand were those bent on cultivating classical knowledge apart from everyday life: universities old and new, along with America's colleges of liberal arts and preparatory schools, England's grammar schools, Quebec's *collèges classiques*, Germany's *gymnasia*, and other similar academies. These were financed mainly from private funds, managed mostly by nongovernmental boards, restricted to an elite minority, and voluntary. On the other hand were primary and secondary schools created in the nineteenth

lower schools arose in century for the teaching and learning of more practical knowledge. These latter
the nineteenth century, were funded by local or national governments, controlled by public authorities,
apart from academe intended for all girls and boys, and often compulsory to the age of fourteen or sixteen. It is schools of this second kind whose origin the paragraphs below briefly explain. To understand them is especially important, since they were the first schools ever, at least of any consequence, to teach vicariously in classrooms what was actually happening outside of them. They arose slightly earlier in Europe, Prussia especially, than in English-speaking North America, which nonetheless remains the principal frame of reference for the present discussion.

One reason for the foundation of public schools can be discounted straightaway: it was not in order to teach the masses reading, writing, and arithmetic. Historians of education estimate that already in 1840, the percentage literate of American adults was double the percentage in school of American children—about 75 percent versus 38 percent.[23] Most citizens of the young republic already knew how to read and write before schooling became widespread. They had learned these skills along with the others necessary for adult life informally at home, at church, at work, often also during occasional winter months in makeshift classrooms. Theirs

the main problem:
keeping wageworkers'
children occupied

was an unmethodical and erratic version of what Freire has more recently called dialogic education: asking questions, getting answers, taking orders, talking back, reflecting on real-life experience, and being helped to make sense of it. No one can claim that this kind of education, so little reliant on schooling, was ideal. But no one can doubt that it worked. During the middle decades of the nineteenth century, however, governments became steadily more concerned about the education of youth and more willing to legislate public schools into existence. Horace Mann, appointed secretary of the new State Board of Education in Massachusetts in 1837, became America's foremost crusader for schools. In 1839, his state opened the nation's first school for teachers, called a "normal school" after its counterpart in France, the *école normale*. In 1852, Massachusetts passed America's first compulsory attendance law. By the end of the century, children in almost every state were legally required to spend at least six years in school. The trend was similar in English Canada. Egerton Ryerson, appointed superintendent of education for Upper Canada (present-day Ontario) in 1846, performed a role much like Horace Mann's and established the school system later adopted also in the western provinces. But how can this burgeoning of mandatory, publicly funded classroom learning be explained? Two factors are especially worth noting.

First and most important was the growing proportion of the population in the wage-laboring class. Previous chapters of this book have already described this growth, tracing it to the normal workings of the capitalist economy. But the steady shift of more and more people from the status of independent producer or trader to that of hireling or employee undermined the traditional ways of socializing youth. Work became more separate from the family, as fathers daily left their homes for jobs in city factories where children were not welcome. These fathers owned no businesses, moreover, where they could put their children to work and invite them to learn in anticipation of later inheritance. Indeed, working-class parents could hardly wish their young to grow up like themselves. Better for the children to acquire somewhere else skills useful for obtaining higher-paying jobs or, better still, for succeeding in businesses of their own. Hence to wage laborers in the growing industrial communities of the nineteenth century, public schools offered hope for their children, a possible way out of poverty and sweatshop drudgery. As Horace Mann proposed in Massachusetts, "Education is not only a moral renovator and a multiplier of intellectual power, but . . . also the most prolific parent of material riches. . . . It is not only the most honest and honorable, but the surest means of amassing property."[24] And to factory owners and others in the capitalist class, the schools promised not only to control youth and keep them out of trouble but also to instruct them in the values and skills that would make them later more productive employees. Egerton Ryerson argued forcefully that schooling would reduce the problems of crime and pauperism among juveniles.[25] Thus public schools prospered wherever the industrial capitalist economy was in full swing. They encountered stiff resistance, by contrast, in the rural parts of the continent. Because most farmers still controlled their work and believed in it, they could also control their children and socialize them at home. They had little use for book-learning. But the urban industrial classes, not farmers, carried the day and legally imposed compulsory systems of public schools.

A second major stimulus to mass public education on this side of the Atlantic

"A second major stimulus to mass public education on this side of the Atlantic was the steady influx of immigrants during the second half of the nineteenth century. . . . Public, mandatory, state-controlled schools came to be seen as valuable instruments for assimilating immigrant children to the ways of their new society, for teaching them in English what patriotism means, and assuring their conformity to established norms." (The Library of Congress)

a further problem: non-WASP immigrants

was the steady influx of immigrants during the second half of the nineteenth century—about 16.6 million to the United States, 1.8 million to Canada. Consider what this meant. For every 4 Americans in 1850, 3 immigrants arrived between 1850 and 1900; for every 3 residents of British North America, 2 immigrants arrived. It is no wonder that the native populations of both countries, especially the ruling elites, feared this incursion of foreigners and looked to public schools as a means of teaching native values at least to the second and subsequent generations. This problem weighed less heavily on Canada, where the bulk of immigrants were from Britain and the United States, and thus brought with them an Anglo-Saxon heritage. But most immigrants to the United States came from such countries as Germany, Poland, Ireland, Austria, Norway, Italy, Hungary, and French-speaking Canada—lands of alien language and custom. And after the turn of the century, they came in still greater numbers. Most settled into the urban wage-laboring class, moreover, an economic status easily inclined toward anticapitalist thinking and leftist politics. Public, mandatory, state-controlled schools thus came to be seen as valuable instruments for assimilating immigrant children to the ways of their new society, for teaching them in English what patriotism means, and for assuring their conformity to established norms.

These two interconnected problems—wage workers' children and immigrants' children in increasingly swollen cities—go far toward explaining not only the establishment of public schools but also the primacy of moral, normative education within them. The main thing children had to learn, once corralled in classrooms for most of the year, was that urban industrial capitalism is a good and godly kind of life. Hence the emphasis in these schools on punctuality, daily attendance, a cooperative attitude, obedience, orderliness, diligence in completing assignments, and general deportment. For these were the virtues pupils would have to practice in their later lives as employees. Children had also to be taught civics or good citizenship, a moral discipline they might miss in their informal education in tenement houses and the streets. The intellectual content of the curriculum, by contrast, was of less concern. The school day could easily be filled with drills, exercises, and classes in reading, writing, spelling, arithmetic, health, history, geography, singing, drawing, all taught year after year at increasing levels of difficulty. Pupils, of course, being fairly isolated from the industrializing economy, often showed little interest in these subjects, especially as represented in sanitized, idealized textbooks. Laziness, insolence, orneriness, and daydreaming plagued classrooms then even as today. It was to dispel these plagues and make public schools more educational that John Dewey's progressive movement urged in the first decades of this century a more experiential curriculum, school activities more direct and less vicarious, classrooms that would be veritable microcosms of the society at large. But notwithstanding modest changes in their intellectual offering and teaching techniques, public schools remained basically custodial and normative in character, a required rite of passage enforced by truant officers. And these schools were a world apart from those of the higher learning.

an emphasis on moral education in lower schools

Two further points should be made about mass public schooling in its first decades of existence. First, it ended initially with the elementary level, after which most young men and women entered the labor force—as helpers to their parents or other relatives in homes and businesses, as apprentices in various trades, or increasingly as paid employees in factories and stores. As late as 1890, public high schools accommodated only about 4 percent of American youth aged 14 to 17. By 1942, however, almost half the teenagers of appropriate age were earning secondary school diplomas; by 1960, more than 80 percent. But no less striking than this huge increase in high school enrollment was the change in high school curricula. In the late nineteenth century, the few public high schools in existence emulated the private, preuniversity academies. The emphasis was on mathematics and on languages—Latin especially, but also German, French, and English. As the proportion of youth enrolled in high schools increased, however, curricula came to be divided more and more into an humanistic, classical stream for the college-bound minority and technical, vocational streams for the rest. Courses in typing, sewing, cooking, and shorthand became popular for girls; for boys there were industrial arts, shop, and vocational agriculture. The high schools thus evolved in a way that answered the changing requirements of the labor market. For as Chapter Six of this book explained, the expansion of the wage-laboring class involved also a growing stratification within it, from the unskilled common laborer to the skilled

the slow growth of secondary schools

artisan on to various levels of manager. Employers welcomed the expansion of technically oriented secondary schools, since thereby they gained a pool of better trained, more mature job applicants. And students earnestly pursued their diplomas, even beyond the age of compulsory attendance and even if classes were boring, since graduation offered hope of an above-average job.

cross-national variation in public schooling

Finally I should note that the organization of public schools, both elementary and secondary, has differed substantially both across and within Western societies. In the United States, a deeply rooted value on grass-roots democracy resulted in a vast network of small, highly autonomous school systems, each supported by locally set property taxes and controlled by a locally elected school board. State governments limited themselves initially to enforcing attendance, training and certifying teachers, and setting basic curricular standards; only since World War II have they, and Washington as well, become much involved in the financing and control of public schools. The American value on church-state separation, moreover, has denied tax support to church-sponsored alternatives to the public schools; the latter, maintained by the Catholic church and by various non-Catholic denominations, have been obliged to meet legal requirements while relying on tuition fees and voluntary contributions for financial support. In most provinces of Canada, by contrast, provincial law has permitted two distinct public school systems, both tax-supported, the one for Catholic children and the other for children of other faiths (schools in the Netherlands are organized similarly).[26] And while the Canadian federal government even now remains uninvolved in public schooling, provincial governments have generally been more interventionist than state governments in the United States. In France, to cite still another variant, the national government has sought, through the University of Paris, to enforce a more uniform national school system. There is, in sum, much more variation in public schooling than can be described here. But during the last 150 years all Western societies have established some kind of elementary and secondary schools for all their children. And in all of them the basic reason was the same: to control urban youth in the wage-laboring class, teach them the three R's, train them in the ways and virtues of industrial capitalism, and in the upper years give marketable skills to those not bound for university.

Schooling Today

Whatever else might be said about schools today in North America, there certainly are lots of them. Just six or seven generations ago, the majority of children in the United States escaped school altogether, not even 40 percent completed the elementary course (which at that time meant 6 or 8 six-month school years), and fewer than 5 percent tasted the higher learning. Today, by contrast, about 99

the extensiveness of schooling today

percent of children between the ages of 5 and 15 spend almost ten months of every year in school. Almost 90 percent of young men and women get high school diplomas, and roughly half of these graduates go on to some form of postsecondary schooling. Between 1960 and 1975, as the postwar babies matured, the college-age population in the United States nearly doubled; but during this same period, college and university enrollment *tripled*, rising from 3.8 to 11.2 million. By now, therefore, most youth both in the United States and in other Western societies celebrate their twentieth birthdays still in the peripheral status of full-time student, still isolated except for part-time and summer jobs from the productive economy. About one of every three young Americans earns a bachelor's degree in the course of growing up. About one of every three B.A. graduates goes on for a master's degree. In any given year about 15 percent of adults enroll in some kind of continuing education program. Any observer has to ask why this boom in schooling has occurred.

The answer most often heard, that youth today have more to learn than formerly, simply will not do. The "amount" of knowledge has admittedly increased—there are more books, more fields of study, and more distinct ideas and skills circulating now than in the past among the citizenry. But no individual student learns all this knowledge anyway, only some portion that is different from but probably no bigger than the portions young men and women learned outside of school a century and a half ago. Besides, our understanding of today's world is not improved by thoughtless identification of schools with education, as if the former were necessary for the latter to occur. There is evidence, moreover, that the expansion of schools at least in recent decades has coincided with declines in educational success. Daily newspaper circulation in the United States, for example, has fallen by about 25 percent since 1950, relative to population. Average scores on the SAT, the standard test used for college admissions, fell steadily during the 1970s. Professors complain that they must "water down" their lectures, and college texts tend to be written more simply than in the past. Even so, absenteeism and cheating are by all accounts more popular among students than ever. And it is a rare graduate who, once settled in a job, does not report that many courses he or she took were irrelevant, a waste of time. In sum, the extension of more and more schooling to more and more citizens by no means explains or justifies itself. Culture can be transmitted, after all, with minimal reliance on schooling. Such was the case for many thousands of years. Yet we choose to keep our youth in school until the first quarter of their lives is spent. The question is why.

why schools have grown

The answer lies at root in the continuation of the same trend which brought the first public elementary schools into existence: the enlargement of a wage-laboring class wherein parents could no longer transmit to their own children the knowledge and productive resources that would give them secure niches in the market economy. Every society faces the task of sorting: how to allocate its economic roles among the younger generation as the older one approaches death. Until the last century virtually all societies relied on kinship to accomplish this task. The vast majority of citizens enjoyed the security of some means of supporting themselves, even if only a small patch of land or the skills and equipment of a trade. Parents bequeathed this security routinely to as many of their children as possible, simply by putting their young to work in the domestic enterprise. The progress of capitalism, however, as previous chapters have explained at length, implied the loss of such security by more and more parents, the loss of ownership of anything beyond consumer goods. Thus the kinship system became progressively less able to perform the necessary task of sorting. Fathers employed in businesses and factories were not even physically present to their children on working days. Being powerless to arrange their children's future, parents could hardly prepare them with confidence for specific occupations. Increasingly the younger generation came to resemble what it is today, a relatively rootless, unsettled mass of young men and women eager to find rewarding adult roles in their society but unable to secure the necessary education, much less the actual roles, from their respective families. The school system expanded basically in order to organize this mass in a reasonable way, to keep youth occupied until they were needed in the labor force, meanwhile teaching them basic skills and channeling them toward the various kinds of employment available in the economy.

from parents to schools: a transfer of power

The expansion of schooling therefore represents a transfer of control over children's education, a shift from parents to public authorities (like teachers and school boards) of responsibility for deciding what should become of a particular child. Parents have resisted this loss of power, to be sure—socialization of their own offspring is probably the single major way ordinary citizens can make a difference in the world. Some parents, especially in the lower strata, oppose the schools head-on, urging their sons and daughters not to cooperate with teachers or yield to scholastic expectations. Parents who can afford it sometimes send their young to private schools, thereby asserting parental authority and securing a kind of schooling more congenial to parental values—about 10 percent of U.S. children attend nonpublic elementary and high schools. Most parents, however, are neither angry enough to challenge public schools directly nor rich enough to patronize private alternatives. Aware that schooling is by now the institutionalized, compulsory bridge to rewarding employment in adult life, most parents consider it their duty to help their children do well in school. By locating in neighborhoods with reputable schools, encouraging homework, rejoicing at high marks on report cards, supporting school discipline, and saving money for college tuition, most parents translate their love for a child into pressure on him or her to "get a good education." It is the most they can do. Only those few parents who can bequeath to their children substantial wealth can afford to laugh at poor performance of their children in school. And for their part, most children now grow up taking school for granted. The first ten years are required in any case. Moreover, given their exclusion from the workplace, children find few opportunities except at school to learn in a systematic way. Still further, most expect that one day some prospective employer will inspect their scholastic credentials. Hence, however tedious or irrelevant their studies may seem, they do what they can to earn high marks.

More lay behind the spread of schools, of course, than the inability of an ever-larger proportion of parents to see to the establishment of their own offspring in the adult working world. This trend, an integral part of the monopolization of capital and rise of a corporation-dominated economy, implied an extension of elementary and secondary schooling but not necessarily any increased enrollment in colleges and universities. To account more precisely for the latter increase in the United States, a single historical event was uniquely important: the G.I. bill of rights passed by the Congress in 1944.[27] World War II was nearly over, and the Roosevelt government was worried about how the veterans' homecoming would affect the U.S. economy. The fear was that sudden reduction of the armed forces from more than 8 million to less than 2 million would cause massive unemployment and a return to the depression of the 1930s. The solution recommended by federal economic planners was to give financial support to veterans willing to return to

the singular importance of the G.I. bill

school and thus stay off the labor market. This proposal was implemented in the G.I. bill, a law formally entitled the Servicemen's Readjustment Act. Veterans of modest means jumped at this opportunity by the thousands, eager to enroll in institutions until then generally restricted to the children of the rich. Between 1945 and 1952, the federal government spent more than $13.5 billion on veterans' educational benefits. Thus began the large-scale funding of mass higher education by federal and state governments in America. During the 1950s and 1960s this funding continued and increased—in the form of research money, building grants, student scholarships, fellowships, and loans, and operating grants sufficient to keep tuition costs low. Governments welcomed the chance to spend more on education —to do so was not only fiscally sound but politically astute. For year by year the proportion of high school graduates choosing to delay employment and go on for higher studies increased. Academic degrees symbolized to middle-income youth upward mobility, a partaking of the envied distinctions of the old elites. Degrees also promised in the end higher-paying jobs in managerial or technical strata of the labor force. The expansion of higher schools, in short, proceeded less from lofty educational ideals than from the concrete economic and political challenges facing the United States and other Western societies.

why schools of some kind are here to stay

However crass and unseemly the reasons may be for the growth of schools in our particular history, they are undoubtedly here to stay. All evidence suggests that even apart from the logic of capitalism, schools serve better than kinship networks for educating and preparing young people for their respective statuses in adult life. The formal, scholastic kind of education can be more disciplined and systematic than the informal kind in everyday domestic settings. It can also be more diverse, acquainting youth with far more ideas and skills than their respective parents could give them. Schools can enlarge the range of occupational choices to which youth are exposed, far beyond what any specific family could provide. Further, they can inculcate a sense of national awareness and identity, the culture upon which every national society depends. Most important of all, schools can disseminate modernity, the consciousness of human freedom and the acceptance of responsibility. Hence the relatively new institution of formal education, this novel intermediary between childhood and adult life, can reasonably and profitably be taken for granted as attempts at earthly progress go on. Indeed, virtually all developing societies on earth, capitalist and socialist alike, today give schooling a central and important place in social organization. But to accept schools as desirable in principle by no means implies acquiescence to the content, organization, or duration of schooling evident now in the United States or in other Western societies. The goal, after all, is to educate youth speedily, effectively, and thoroughly—both for capable performance of adult roles as currently defined and for creative action that will improve upon current arrangements. An adequate sociology must investigate critically just how the present school system works.

To serve this purpose at least in brief, the rest of this chapter concerns how schooling today connects with the world of work, the occupations which more than anything define citizens' respective statuses in adult life. The paragraphs immediately below discuss this connection for professional, managerial, and technical workers, a category which by now embraces nearly 30 percent of all working citizens in the United States and Canada. On this same topic, some further paragraphs assess the educational pros and cons of linking colleges and universities to such occupational purposes.

THE STRATEGIC WORTH OF CERTIFIED EXPERTISE

for neither capitalists nor workers is schooling economically worthwhile

The relevance of schooling to occupational success is slight for what were until recently the two major classes of economically active citizens in capitalist societies. First are the capitalists themselves, whether large industrialists or small farmers, owners of big companies or little ones. For them there are far more direct and straightforward ways of demonstrating expertise than scholastic credentials. They have only to observe their success in the market, how well their products sell, how much money they bring home. Their performance in the world of competitive business speaks for itself. Diplomas hanging on the wall do not change red ink to black on a balance sheet. And so long as the ink is black and profits are high, owners of companies readily forgive themselves for not having spent years studying for some academic degree. A degree may be valued, of course, for social purposes, as a sign of cultivation in the finer things of life, but independent business people have more reliable measures of their abilities than framed documents. Their success requires education, to be sure, but whether it was gained in a graduate school or a school of hard knocks is mostly irrelevant. Performance, as they say, is what counts. How much a capitalist knows is answered by the results that the capitalist gets. It is a practical, no-nonsense kind of economic circumstance, one to which most of the achievements of capitalism can be attributed.

Nor is schooling of much practical consequence to ordinary members of the working class, citizens paid by the hour to do blue-collar jobs. Their circumstance, though much less rewarding than that of business proprietors, shares a similarly stark, direct, unvarnished quality. They are hired to do specific jobs at the lowest wage rates employers can get by with paying. Whether a worker flunked the eighth grade or not, acquired the requisite skills in school or out, has a bachelor's in physics or not—all this is beside the point. The question is how well the worker gets his or her job done—assembling parts, laying bricks, operating some machine, or whatever. That job performance depends on know-how and previous learning is obvious. But as in the case of old-fashioned capitalists, it is the expertise itself that counts, much more than any certificate that the expertise exists. Nor does schooling gain relevance when workers unionize for higher pay, more fringe benefits, and better working conditions. A union is not a genteel kind of group. Its strategy is not subtle; its tactics do not rest on academic arguments. Workers admit that they sell their time for money, that they work for extrinsic rewards, that they are basically commodities on the labor market. They make no pretense of doing their jobs as a public service. Their collective action, they concede, is for the purpose of gaining by the threat of a strike a higher return on their self-investment. Unions are the honest voice of a working class that is aware of how the capitalist system runs and ready to bring the system to a halt unless hirelings get a better deal. Now this is not to disparage the educational level of blue-collar workers. Many are highly educated, knowledgeable, reflective, and thoughtful. The point is only that schooling is in itself of little relevance to their working lives.

It is for a third class of economically active citizens that schooling, especially beyond high school, has explicit occupational relevance. This class is composed of workers who earn their bread selling some allegedly extraordinary skill, ideally in private practice but otherwise as employees of public or private bureaucracies, and who are in some degree organized for the sake of common occupational interests. For this class as a whole there is no generally accepted name beyond vague designations like *middle class* or *upper middle class*. But to specific occupations that typify this class the word *profession* is ordinarily applied. Like craft unions, professions are composed of the practitioners of some trade or skill—whether carpentry or medicine, printing or law, plumbing or dentistry, tailoring or engineering. Also like unions, professions seek to protect and increase the power, income, and prestige practitioners derive from their work. Unlike unions, however, professions serve these goals through a distinctly cultural or ideological strategy. This indeed is the principal difference between the two kinds of group. While the union twists the public's arm to win favors, the profession whispers persuasively in the public's ear. Its strategy is to convince governments and citizens that its particular skill is desirable, worth more than common or even skilled labor, and beyond the competence of everyone except certified members of the profession. Instead of taking the artisan's approach, "What you see is what you get," the professional insists, "There is more to me than meets the eye." More than just a skill, also a complex theoretical body of knowledge underlying it. More than just selfish interest, also a working commitment to the common good. And instead of mercenary intent, rigorous adherence to an ethical code. Consumers of the skill are called not customers or bosses but patients, clients, or patrons, and they are asked to pay not an hourly wage but a fee for service, retainer, or at least a monthly salary. A profession, in sum, seeks to gain citizens' trust, to win such legitimacy in law and custom that its members are respected sincerely, remunerated amply, and left free to control the conditions of their work. Ideally, the profession would win a governmentally enforced monopoly on the exercise of its particular skill (something like the closed shop that unions often seek), along with legal requirements on citizens to make use of the skill. In this way the profession would circumvent the harsh realities of capitalist economics and provide its members with relatively assured prosperity.

Because professional status excels the status of most other workers, even those aided by powerful unions, members of nearly all occupations aspire to it. Even prostitutes like to call their trade the "oldest profession." But neither individuals nor groups secure professional recognition just by claiming it. The claim has to be credible, believable. For this purpose a formal program of education or professional school is essential, as the classic cases of medicine and law illustrate. Both these professions tied themselves to universities even centuries ago, adorning their skills with the prestigious mantle of the higher learning. Both physicians and lawyers had the bearing that comes with university experience, an air of acquaintance with some higher realm of truth. Much of their know-how was expressed in Latin (*cum aqua, corpus juris*), a language incomprehensible except to those schooled in it. The belief, therefore, was gradually institutionalized that no one could competently heal illnesses or plead cases without having studied for the prescribed number of years in the appropriate faculty, passed its examinations and received from it a degree. Through the collective efforts of physicians, lawyers, and universities, this belief gained such credence that most Western governments during the last century

schooling suits the new middle class

why professional education must be formalized

passed laws forbidding anyone without the degree even to offer medical or legal services for sale. These professions have thus become models for organized practitioners of many other skills perfected in the course of economic development —skills ranging from planning sewer systems (civil engineering) to filling and pulling teeth (dentistry), from mixing and bottling medicines (pharmacy) to designing buildings (architecture), from sorting out finances (accountancy) to talking with people who feel mentally distressed (clinical psychology), from mapping out cities (urban planning) to treating animals (veterinary medicine). In each of these professions, as in medicine and law, committed practitioners argue that even if their work looks simple, in fact it is not, that it can effectively and safely be done only by those who have appropriate scholastic credentials. Because their argument is generally believed, not least by public authorities, these occupations enjoy professional status. Their members have incomes and prestige higher than skilled artisans. They enjoy relatively high autonomy in their work, even when they are employed in bureaucracies, since laypeople do not feel themselves competent to understand and criticize. Such is what is meant by the phrase "rights and privileges attached hereto," which customarily appears on academic diplomas.

Professions were few a century ago. Medicine, law, theology, and university teaching were the main ones—occupations populated in great part by moneyed young men who were not chosen or did not choose to inherit their fathers' businesses. Being expensive to enter but prestigious and reasonably lucrative to practice, the old professions made appropriate careers for surplus sons of propertied parents. The main alternatives for daughters were nursing and public-school teaching, subordinate professions for which training and certification were generally acquired in distinct schools apart from the university world. As capital became

the proliferation of professions in recent decades

more concentrated, however, and a larger proportion of youth faced lifetimes of selling skills for a living, more and more occupations became targets of professionalization. New kinds of expertise were invented, fields which could plausibly be taught, learned, and marketed as extraordinary skills, elevating their practitioners above the ranks of ordinary workers. Universities incorporated many of these fields—like agronomy, business administration, social work, and various kinds of engineering—as distinct departments, faculties, or schools, thereby fostering the legitimacy these fields enjoy today. By now there are many more. The old normal schools have been transformed into colleges or faculties of education wherein students are certified as expert in special education, elementary education, continuing education, and other kinds of it. The same goes for the old schools of nursing, nearly all of which are now attached to universities. Degrees are given today in secretarial science, library science, military science, actuarial science, poultry science, soil science, aerospace science, computer science, and household science; in hotel administration, hospital administration, public administration, family planning administration, parks administration, and transportation administration; also in nutrition, recreation, journalism, and statistics; and in penology, criminology, epidemiology, and museology. The list goes on and on. Each field is an aspirant profession, a group of practitioners, teachers, and students trying to carve out for themselves a secure niche in an uncertain labor market on the basis of their allegedly extraordinary and distinctive skill.

These fields vary, of course, in their autonomy, income, and prestige—in how

*some conditions for an
aspirant professions's
failure or success*

much professional recognition each has achieved. Some are taken more seriously than others. The reason lies not in their respective skills or amounts of expertise, except as these relate to law and popular culture. The prerogatives and reverence accorded ministers of religion, for example, have declined over the last century not because the clergy are less well-schooled than formerly but because (as Chapter Seven explained) religion itself has on the whole declined. Catholic priests are no less skilled at forgiving sins than they ever were, but the skill is no longer so much in demand. Or to cite a different case, army and navy officers in all societies find their credentials from military academies respected less in times of peace than during wars. Similarly, aerospace engineers had a field day in the late 1960s, when the U.S. space program was going strong, but many found their talents nearly unmarketable a decade later. The status of any profession goes up and down in tandem with political and cultural priorities in its milieu. But a profession can also influence its own status. Through its professional organizations it can lobby for legislation to preserve its autonomy and prevent competing occupations from encroaching on its domain. The American Medical Association, for example, has secured for its members more independence and prosperity than physicians enjoy in probably any other society. The same is true of osteopathic physicians in the United States, though in Canada they are forbidden even to prescribe drugs or do surgery. Newer and more marginal professions, like library science and hotel administration, have much farther to go in proving themselves. The longer the period of training a profession requires, the more abstruse the lingo it develops for its work, the more unique its mastery of even some simple skill, the more astute its manipulation of the media, the more rigid the discipline it imposes on its members, the farther from routine and manual work it keeps them, and the higher the intellectual standards it sets for them, the more credibility it is likely to have before lawmakers and the public at large. In the world of professions success tends to breed success. High-status fields attract high-achieving applicants from high-status families. An aspirant profession that admits "just anybody," by contrast, can expect its practitioners to be treated as "just anybody" on the labor market.

*why not everyone can
be granted professional
status*

A further condition for a profession's success is that it refrain from glutting the market with properly certified practitioners. Admissions to the professional degree program (or at least graduations from it) must be kept low enough that persons deemed qualified to perform the relevant service are always slightly scarce. Otherwise the skill begins to seem common and ordinary, prestige and rates of pay decline, and the very purpose for which the profession exists is lost. The most successful professions, medicine and engineering most clearly, are well known for their wariness of overexpansion. Some other professions—education in the United States and nursing in Canada during the 1970s—were less prudent, with predictably damaging results for their practitioners. But the proliferation of professional programs in universities over the last two decades, combined with generally restrictive admissions policies in each, has had an important implication. It has diminished the prestige and market worth of young adults approaching the job market with first degrees in history, philosophy, literature, political science, and other older academic disciplines. In the postwar decades an undergraduate degree itself promised a rewarding place in the managerial or technical strata of the labor force. Still possessing the value that Veblen attributed to conspicuous waste, such degrees won employers' respect. They benefited, moreover, from their scarcity. Now, however, young professionals capture employers' first attention, making holders of the academic B.A. or B.S. look rather like leftovers. Now this point should not be overblown. Employers in some fields, the publishing industry for one, still seek out liberal-arts graduates. Many such graduates go on for higher-level training in law, medicine, policy analysis, social work, or some other profession. Still others go to graduate school, intent on careers in university teaching or research. And graduates from the most prestigious colleges and universities, whatever their major fields, tend to find good jobs. Some can even return to positions in family-owned businesses. On the whole, however, the more jobs are taken by holders of credible professional degrees, the fewer jobs are left for holders of the traditional academic degrees. The latter currently settle for markedly lower average salaries in their first full-time positions after graduation.

Professional aspirations are not confined to occupations whose training culminates in bachelor's, master's, or doctoral degrees. Morticians, hair stylists, and airplane pilots are among those fields with schools of their own, apart from the world of universities. These schools in many cases have high credibility. Laws in most jurisdictions, for example, currently prevent anyone not formally trained and certified from selling the skill of embalming bodies, cutting hair, or flying planes.

two-year colleges and the lower professions There is also by now a vast network of what are variously called two-year, junior, or community colleges, which prepare youth for jobs generally less rewarding than those requiring four or more years of postsecondary schooling. Some students, of course, use the junior college as a step toward further formal education. For most, however, the two-year diploma or degree is a certificate of eligibility to work in a paraprofessional or semiprofessional occupation—for example, laboratory technologist, day-care worker, photographer, fashion expert, florist, cook, secretary, travel agent, drafter, estimator, programmer, dental assistant, or police officer. These colleges constitute in effect a more modest stratum of schooling designed for youth whose finances, ambitions, or high school marks (often all three combined) fail to qualify for four-year or longer programs. Junior or community colleges are thus a means of "cooling out" a large segment of youth, eliminating them from competition for the better jobs while channeling them into a variety of fields some notches above common labor. Since 1960 colleges of this kind have been the fastest growing sector of the overall system of schools. Their combined enrollment in the United States rose from less than half a million in 1960 to nearly 4 million in 1976. A similar trend occurred in Canada—Quebec's classical colleges, for example, were transformed into "colleges for general and professional instruction." Graduates of two-year postsecondary programs know well enough that their status pales beside that of the "higher professions." Their paychecks and working conditions remind them pointedly. They can take comfort, however, from knowing that at least *some* kind of scholastic credential stands between them and unskilled wage labor. Their professional status may be impugned by holders of doctorates, but seldom by shipping clerks, file clerks, or janitors.

FOR EXAMPLE

Everett C. Hughes, "The Stratification of Teachers"*

The word teacher *applies to roles that vary greatly in the power, money, and prestige attached to them. The selection below describes the ladder of teachers' prestige in today's advanced Western societies.*

The most prestigious professions have been those which could keep their aspirants longest in school before formally admitting them to professional school, then longest in professional school itself, and then longest in postgraduate apprenticeship—and all this without a break. This situation is most nearly approached in medicine. Graduate schools in the physical sciences are not far behind; post-Ph.D. fellowships are the counterpart of postgraduate residencies in medicine. This long, unbroken course of study depends upon the prospect of high income, backed up by income and credit of the student's family and by subsidies. The highest prestige among teachers goes to those who teach the upper and terminal years of this long sequence. One may still gain prestige by teaching the sons of some social, intellectual, or financial elite, but that modicum of prestige is to be found rather more in private preparatory schools than in colleges and universities. Even there, the teacher is judged by the number of his pupils who win places in selective colleges. The colleges being bulwarks of meritocracy, plus parity, tend to mix the social breeds. There are, to be sure, even among the high scorers in college entrance examinations, some students who will bury themselves to esoteric depths in branches of learning which have no obvious professional application. The upper reaches of teaching and of learning offer more than that, at least in the eyes of the professional and learned world. Some of the people of those upper reaches have attained a sort of suprauniversity status, as in the Rockefeller University or in certain government and industrial research enterprises. A certain number of teachers of undergraduates (choice undergraduates) can acquire a national or international charism as culture critics. They have a college base but a larger audience, as physicians of similar repute do, but they are subject to the accusation of quackery. (The true sociological definition of a quack is one who has a greater reputation with laymen than with his colleagues and who is even proud of it.)

The regular prestige rank of teachers is still related to place in the sequence of study of one's students. The second-level professions have established as their basic credential a two-year master's degree taken in a professional school which is attached to a multiversity. Their teachers have this credential and may even have proceeded to a Ph.D. But generally, they have not gone directly from college to a professional master's program, or from there to the Ph.D.

*From E. C. Hughes, "Higher Education and the Professions," in *Content and Context: Essays on College Education*, C. Kaysen (ed.), McGraw-Hill, New York, 1973, pp. 288–90. Reprinted by permission of the author and publisher. Dr. Hughes is professor emeritus of sociology at Brandeis University.

One might construct a model of the teaching prestige ladder thus:

1   It is better to be teaching those who are destined to stay in school a long time and thus to attain membership in a prestigious profession.
2   It is best to teach the prospective elite at any age, but the further along and the older the students, the greater the prestige.
3   While much prestige has attached to pure and liberal subjects taught without thought that the student will follow the subject professionally, in fact greater prestige is associated with teaching those who will follow the subject professionally.

In effect this means that teaching in a community college is more prestigious than teaching in a high school; that teaching in a four-year college is more prestigious than teaching in a community college; that still more prestige is associated with teaching in a graduate school or postbachelor professional school; and that the most prestige of all is attached to some sort of postcurricular teaching designed to develop unusual levels of knowledge and skill or to add to the stock of knowledge. The curve turns downward a bit when the students are being recycled to enter a new phase of their careers, as in the case of the business executive back in school to study management and the high school principal or the librarian back to get a Ph.D. in anticipation of moving into a bigger league.

Teaching the youngest children in kindergartens and the first year of reading carries with it some prestige of experiment and the magic of seeing young children learn. Teaching the disabled and the retarded may be regarded as especially meritorious. Education for rehabilitation is a special social service. Bringing those who left school at an earlier age back into school and to the labor force in the early middle years of life is coming to be a regular function of the community college. Teaching the chronically ill and handicapped to look after themselves and teaching those retired because of age to develop alternative interests are features of a society that keep people alive, whether they are needed by the economy or not. All these activities have become professionalized, and the universities train the people who perform them. They do not fit clearly into the model I have outlined. In the main the model does fit; at one age or stage or another, the teaching takes on a more professional turn. The specifically professional study tends to follow the more general and to come later for those who are headed for the elite positions in the elite professions. And the prestige system of the academic professions reflects this scheme of things. (A curse be upon it.)

Sociologists have written much more about professions in the advanced capitalist economy than the preceding paragraphs reflect.[28] Numerous articles and books concern conflict between "the company and the craft," between rules laid down by bureaucratic employers and standards set by professional bodies. Researchers have also analyzed why members of an occupation sometimes cast aside a finely honed image of high-minded public service, become blunter and more militant, even to the point of calling a strike—nurses, teachers, social workers, and intern physicians are all examples. It is worth noting, too, that for all the time, effort, and expense young men and women invest for the sake of acquiring professional identities, they often abandon these identities later, "moving up" to less professional but more rewarding statuses, usually in management. But the main point for present purposes is simply that the professional mentality underlies the expansion, lengthening, and restructuring of formal education during recent decades. Indeed, postsecondary schooling is increasingly understood to be training for employment in some occupation that requires extraordinary skill. Today more than two-thirds of the two-year diplomas and degrees annually awarded in the United States are in effect certificates of specific marketable expertise. The same is true for at least half of all bachelor's degrees—the stupendous recent growth of programs in accounting and management sciences illustrates the trend. But it is a trend supported on almost all sides. Corporate and governmental employers welcome it, since they gain thereby workers already trained for specific technical and managerial jobs. Students flock to professional programs, aware that in today's economy ability and effort are unlikely to yield returns unless they are scholastically certified. And parents tend to encourage the professional training of their children; to do so is the contemporary version of bequeathing an inheritance, a means of saving sons and daughters from the unvarnished realities of wage labor. Colleges and universities have in the main responded positively to these economic pressures, adding new paths to graduation almost as fast as new occupational destinations can be discerned. Taxpayers, finally, have at least until recently footed the bill without much complaint—roughly one-third of the budget of a typical American state is spent on schooling, as of 1980. For in the hopeful, prestigious name of education almost any expense has seemed to be justified.

professionalization is in part a modernizing trend

The transformation of higher learning into professional training is in some respects a modernizing trend, one which has drawn colleges and universities further into the ongoing process of humans making history. Few of these schools any longer style themselves retreats from the social order at hand. Fewer degrees are today conferred as mere ornaments, honorable badges of time wasted in the study of bygone splendors and useless obscurities. Administrators and students alike routinely subject courses to the harsh but intensely humane criterion of practical relevance. More than ever before, universities have become centers of technical invention. As a means of maintaining professional credibility, professors in each field feel pressures to engage in original theorizing and research and to publish articles in journals which demonstrate their profession's worth. The professional expertise celebrated today in academe is not therefore just a strategically useful bluff. The buildings that house us at work and play do indeed rest on extraordinary knowledge of architecture and engineering. Our long lives are due to medical and nutritional expertise. Our planes would not get off the ground were it not for aerospace science. Our entire way of life depends, in short, on diverse kinds of complex knowledge, and colleges and universities have become the major settings where this knowledge is made available to the coming generation. Students, moreover, learn much in their professional programs. One can hardly blame chicken producers for preferring to hire graduates of poultry-science programs over applicants with degrees in biology, nor newspapers for preferentially giving jobs to young men and women with degrees in journalism. At the university where I have taught since 1975, 8000 students are in so-called cooperative programs, alternating terms of paid employment in their intended occupation with terms of on-campus study for mostly professional degrees. It is a down-to-earth, enlivening way of progressing through school, and it opens the chance for higher schooling to many youth who could not otherwise afford the expense. No one familiar with so intensely modern a form of academic organization could possibly long for a return to the classical curricula whose empty pretensions Veblen long ago exposed.

professionalization is in part antieducational

In other respects, however, the professionalizing of postsecondary schools retards the education of youth in our time, the adequate transmission of our culture from one generation to the next. This is so even from a one-sided view, from an outlook on education simply as dispensing requisite knowledge. The goals of education and of the professions in fact collide at critical points. The former would have every young man or woman learn as much as each can of the knowledge underlying our way of life. But the latter make all knowledge irrelevant except that needed in the lifelong, jealously guarded practice of some occupation. Education in a modern society calls for a versatile labor force, one wherein citizens shift easily from one kind of work to another as some jobs become obsolete and others more in demand. Professions build rigidities into the labor force, as each corps of practitioners seeks to guard its occupational turf. The educational ideal is that know-how be taught quickly, recognized as soon as it is learned, and given the chance to be applied in work. The professional ideal is to extend scholastic training over as many years as possible and withhold the right to practice until the end of this period, in order to bolster the profession's status and increase its rewards. Education implies expressing knowledge as simply and clearly as possible, so that it can be learned easily. A profession finds strategic value in using jargon and making its knowledge seem complicated, difficult to acquire, and therefore deserving of awe and respect. Education, finally, focuses as directly as possible on what people can and cannot do. Professions disregard people's abilities except insofar as they are confirmed by scholastic credentials. In sum, the demise of the classics has by no means banished pretense from the corridors of academe. The professions ensure an ample supply of snobbery, pomposity, protectionism, and other qualities inimical to the educational process.

The professionalization of colleges and universities falls still farther short of educational requirements, when these latter are understood in their full, modern, dialectical meaning. From the outlook of Dewey and others discussed some pages back, education means more than students swallowing the ideas teachers dispense. It means students making their respective unique connections of new ideas with prior experience, and then expressing these connections creatively in an ongoing

In a sense, Ferdinand Demara has made his whole life a damaging critique of the world of professionalism and school credentials. He served in the Korean war as a naval surgeon for the Canadian Armed Forces. Later he was a science teacher at a boys' school in Arkansas, a psychology professor at Gannon College in Pennsylvania, a deputy warden at the maximum-security prison in Huntsville, Texas, a monk of Gethsemane Abbey in Kentucky, and in other settings a Latin teacher, cancer researcher, and hotel auditor. In all these occupations he was reasonably competent, effective, and successful. But he was scholastically qualified for none of them, having dropped out of school in his hometown of Lawrence, Massachusetts, at the age of 16. Thus was he labeled The Great Imposter, *to cite the title of his biography by Robert Crichton, published in 1959, when Demara was 37 years old. What are the implications of this man's life for the degrees, diplomas, and licenses legally required today for the performance of most occupations? (United Press International Photo)*

process of autonomous personal growth. Professional departments and schools, however, tend not to encourage such creative expression or autonomy. The desired outcome of schooling is almost entirely predefined. Teachers know in advance how they want students to turn out. There is a carefully planned package of skills and norms, the relevant professional image, which students must acquire. Multiple-choice and so-called objective tests are enough to measure whether the goals of professional schooling have been met. Nor are students taught their profession's history in a way that encourages them to transform or redirect that history. Founders and early thinkers of the profession tend to be canonized, heroized, endowed with almost superhuman genius. Innovation is the prerogative only of godlike "leading scientists" in an intellectual sphere beyond ordinary practitioners, let alone students.[29] Professional schooling tends to approximate, in fact, what it is commonly called—*training*, more complex than the training dogs or horses get, but training nonetheless. This is especially so now that few students of few professions can any more look forward to independent practice later on, the circumstance small-town physicians, lawyers, and ministers once enjoyed. Most graduates of professional programs, even lawyers, today spend their working lives as employees of corporations or public bureaucracies—privileged employees, to be sure, but salaried workers even so. Their prior professional training prepares them for this economic reality, one in which the chance to assert personal difference is relatively slim. No wonder students in professional programs often become bored and cynical, even to the point of plagiarizing assignments or cheating on exams. Too many of their courses stop short of the uniquely human, personal, reciprocal quality intrinsic to the educational process.

why criticizing professions is so hard

The poverty of professional schooling is a truth hard to understand, much less accept, in societies like our own. Professionals and would-be professionals have become the majority of the labor force. Most of us spent most of our youth acquiring scholastic credentials and rely on them still for our jobs and self-concepts. Diplomas and degrees have become indeed the principal form of personal riches, substitutes for the land, buildings, and machinery the majority of citizens once owned. Threats to professions seem therefore like threats to our very selves. So dear to us is the professional ideal that we shield it from criticism by the way we use words. *Unprofessional* is a synonym for *bad* or *reprehensible*. The word *amateur*, opposite of a professional, is seldom used in its original meaning ("one who works for the love of it," like Olympic athletes) and is applied now more often to bunglers, fumblers, and dilettantes. Still it is possible to examine the professional mode of schooling and work with a critical eye. One has but to shift focus from the security and comfort felt in the practice of one's own narrow area of certified expertise to the insecurity, anxiety, fear, and resentment felt when one sits waiting to be treated by a professional of some other kind. Reflection on the jealously guarded prerogatives of professions other than our own tends to stimulate the imagination, to set the mind working toward a way of life that would allow more people to learn and exercise more skills. The trouble with a professionalized labor force is not the certification of a citizen's ability in some little field, but the implication of that citizen's inability in all the rest. While exaggerating competence in one respect, the professional ideal denies it in all others. At its worst, a society arranged in terms of specialized credentials yields the kind of helplessness John McKnight described in a book entitled *Disabling Professions*: "My world is not a place where I do or act with others. Rather, it is a mysterious place, a strange land beyond my comprehension or control. It is understood only by professionals who know *how* it works, *what* I need and *how* my need is met. I am the object rather than the actor. My very being is as client rather than citizen."[30]

Concluding Words

To sum up what education is about, it can usefully be compared here, finally, to computer programming. For a computer is in some respects the closest thing to a human yet seen on the earth. It can take information in, store it in a memory, and later spew it out. It can assimilate new facts, solve complex mathematical problems, plot the effects of alternative courses of action, ask questions, give answers, and all in a variety of languages. The more highly skilled computers of our time can checkmate champions at chess and catch spelling mistakes in the prose of leading journalists. But no computer can do such things when first its components are assembled into a whole—its moment of birth, so to speak. Computers know nothing except what programmers teach them. The pedagogical techniques are much like those used in teaching humans. One first must make sure the power is one, that the learner has enough energy to function. Then one has to use language the learner understands, lest the new knowledge fail to be retained. Care must be taken to go step by step, never introducing a symbol or concept unless it builds directly on what the learner already knows. And it must not be fed garbled or mistaken information at the start, lest there be still more errors and confusion later on. Periodic quizzes and tests can assess how effective the learning process so far has been. Computer programming is indeed much like the one-dimensional kind of education discussed at this chapter's beginning. It is a nonreciprocal, one-way activity. The programmer dumps an extrinsic quantity of skill into a docile, humble receptacle that swallows it up. Depending, of course, on its capacity—programmers refer to so many bytes of storage space just as teachers speak of high or low IQ. But once the requisite skills have been instilled, the target of instruction can competently perform a wide range of tasks to be assigned from day to day. For many tasks, as by now is common knowledge, a well-programmed computer far excels a well-trained human in speed, accuracy, and endurance, not to mention cost efficiency.

how education transcends computer programming

Yet education transcends computer programming, even as humans surpass computers in ability. Our species has what machines lack: an autonomy, a dynamism, an impetus, an élan, a will to create newness on the earth. The most computers can do is perform predictably; this is all a programmer can expect. But people can do more; they can be contrary on purpose. Computers can give back only what programmers have put in, but students can give their teachers a surprise. Granted, this unique power of humans is not always obvious in the short run. A colleague of mine claims he has had but two new ideas in his life, and he is past 50, a more accomplished and honest sociologist than most. But over the long haul the power of people glistens like sunlight in snow: people make history. Not only do they reproduce themselves but each generation leaves some unprogrammed novelty to the next. The novelty of Dewey, Coady, Freire, and others has been to spell out in words how these novelties are handed down and passed around in such a way that history keeps on happening. Scholars like these portray education of whatever kind and at whatever level as necessarily a two-sided process: not only stuffing ideas into a learner but urging him or her to voice and act out still newer ideas in response. Indeed, once this reciprocal action is underway, learners do not wait to be stuffed. They seize knowledge and skills of their own accord, ingest oldness willingly and voluntarily for the sake of improving their own creative work. Thus educators do not so much work *on* their students as *with* them—facilitating and speeding a learning process in which students themselves cooperate, provided serious opportunities for autonomous expression are at hand. The goal of programming is to bend the computer ever more completely to the programmer's will. The goal of education is to bend students to the teacher's will, but as a means of setting students free.

the main problem today: lack of follow-through The main fault with the scholastic mode of education entrenched today in the Western world is simply the lack of follow-through. Never in history have books been so abundant or libraries so accessible. Never has travel been easier. Never have schools been so comfortable or well equipped with teachers, laboratories, and audiovisual aids. Never have so many youth been left free for so many years to imbibe new knowledge and skill, away from the drudgery of routine work. Now to be sure the technology for exposing youth to our culture and impressing it upon their minds can still be improved. But the main problem does not lie in the lack of such improvement or anywhere in the first dimension of education, the side of programming and domination. The problem is instead that youth have too little chance to respond creatively in a serious way, to act back upon the adult world, to make a difference according to their respective unique inclinations. Our school system seems premised on the belief that children will humbly submit while we pump ideas into their brains for fifteen years. Such submission is in the nature of a computer, not a human being. The human child is more likely to react with some kind of donkey power, to dawdle, daydream, be disruptive, or otherwise find a way of saying no. At every moment of the school day a child asks, "Why should I learn this?" No answer is enough except the assurance that learning this will open new opportunities for leading a full and autonomous life. Some teachers go to heroic lengths giving such assurance. By occupation they are full of promises. Rightly so. But most children nonetheless grow up in scholastic isolation from actual productivity, from work that makes a difference. They can expect in the end, moreover, only employment for a wage or salary in workplaces owned by somebody else. Such a future awaits graduates even of most professional degree programs. Now no one should disparage the buoyancy of young people today. Like their ancestors, they are on the lookout for opportunities to become more than they are. But also like their ancestors, they seize a chance to learn only when it promises a chance to do. It is lack of this latter chance that weakens the otherwise wondrous structures of formal education now in place.

Finally I should briefly note the place of sociology in this vast system of schools.[31] This discipline will continue to serve those few students intending to study, research, write, and teach it as a professional career—mainly in colleges and universities. But most sociology students, indeed most of you readers of this book, will not be labeled *sociologists* in later life. You will work in a long series of jobs, only the first of which can at this point be foreseen with any accuracy. But in your various positions, in how you handle them and in the ones you choose, you will make decisions that affect in small but serious ways the whole future of humanity on earth. And not only in your work but in your married or unmarried life, your political involvements or lack of them, your voting or failure to vote, your hobbies and purchases, your smiles and frowns. The purpose of sociology for you is the main *the educational purposes of sociology* purpose of the discipline itself: to help citizens transcend their little professional identities, the niches in history where they find themselves deposited, and to act responsibly as free citizens. If this book of sociology deserves its name, it is not a burden to read, not something to plow through and memorize for a test. Students today as always crave an understanding of the world that awaits them—not just in order to get a job but to come alive as human beings. The task of sociology is to help satisfy that craving, even in schools aimed mainly at training youth for the job market. There is more to life than a high-paying job, hard as this may be for jobless students to realize. Most jobs, indeed much of life itself, is dull, repetitive, boring, and routine. The most we humans can hope for is awareness of our unfreedom and an explanation of it that permits creative action for reducing it in some small way. This awareness and this explanation are the substance of sociology, whether studied in a required course, an elective one, or none at all. But so long as our scholastic structures permit such awareness and explanation, this substance of sociology (and other kinds of humane learning) to be taught, even if only as a supplement to professional training, surely there is hope.

For Reflection

education versus schooling
vertical versus horizontal dimensions of
   education
self-education
self-schooling
font-of-knowledge outlooks
Plato's theory
the denial of reciprocity
intelligence quotient
dialectical outlooks
Dewey's theory
extension education
dialogic versus antidialogic teaching
multiple-choice tests
education versus training

how to evaluate educational techniques
origins of higher learning
modernization of universities
origins of primary schools
the G.I. bill of rights
schooling and the capitalist class
schooling and the working class
schooling and the middle class
union versus profession
professionalization
two-year colleges
professional training versus education
credentials
education versus computer programming

For Making Connections

With Chapter One: Would sociologists of a positivist bent be more likely to take a dialectical view of education than humanist sociologists? Why or why not?
In what sense or to what degree is sociology a profession?

With Chapter Two: If you were teaching a university course, what kind of tests and measures would you use for assessing how much your students had learned?
How might you operationalize Freire's concepts, *dialogic* and *antidialogic*, as applied to ways of teaching courses in your major field?

With Chapter Three: What difference does schooling make in the structure of rewards in Western capitalist societies, and how has this changed since a century ago?
What does it mean to say that professions adopt an explicitly cultural strategy of occupational advancement?

With Chapter Four:	Could you infer from the way a researcher studies education and schooling the kind of social psychology that researcher believes in? How so?
	What limitations would there be in educational programs grounded in a one-sided focus on the humble side of the person?
With Chapter Five:	How can youth be most effectively educated in the values of modern, legal-rational politics?
	If you were working for political development in some traditional peasant society, what specific techniques of adult education would you try to use?
With Chapter Six:	How has the character of universities changed in the course of economic development?
	Is the professionalization of occupations intrinsic to economic development or only to the capitalist kind of development?
With Chapter Seven:	What effects has the secularization trend in Western societies had on the clergy as a profession?
	What differences would you expect to find between universities affiliated with Protestant denominations and those affiliated with the Catholic church?
With Chapter Eight:	Relate changes in family life in the Western world to changes surrounding elementary and secondary schooling.
	In what ways does the status of a child's parents still affect his or her own eventual class position?

For Further Reading

For better of worse, writers tend to dwell upon themselves. There are lots of novels about novelists, plays about playwrights, and news stories about newspeople. For the same reason, I suspect, dozens and dozens of scholarly journals are concerned with schools and scholars. The *Sociology of Education*, the *Harvard Educational Review*, the *History of Education Quarterly*, the *NEA Research Bulletin*, and the *Comparative Education Review* are especially noteworthy. Analyses of education appear regularly also in the general journals of sociology, politics, and economics, and in such literary magazines as the *Atlantic Monthly*, *Saturday Review*, and *Saturday Night*. Among the thousands of books on the subject, I recommend especially the following:

1 Samuel Bowles and Herbert Gintis, *Schooling in Capitalist America*, Basic, New York, 1976. Two political economists at the University of Massachusetts offer here their engrossing interpretation of the structure of American education in terms of the requirements of the national economy. It is an irritating book, partially because the authors tend to overstate their case and polemize. But even more, I think, because they discredit through meticulous research many of our most deeply cherished platitudes about the social role of schooling.

2 Christopher Jencks and David Riesman, *The Academic Revolution*, Univ. of Chicago Press, Chicago, 1968. An intelligent and readable analysis of the history of higher

education in the United States, detailing the diverse functions colleges and universities have served and chronicling shifts in their control structures. Written by scholars on the Harvard-Berkeley circuit in the heyday of academic expansion, this book does not flow in a critical vein. It is a venerable reference all the same.

3   Christopher Jencks et al., *Inequality: A Reassessment of the Effect of Family and Schooling in America*, Basic, New York, 1972. This book's main theses, amply supported by analyses of census and survey data, are that educational attainment is but weakly related to income, and thus that a widening of educational opportunity by no means implies a leveling of class differences. On this same issue see *Education, Opportunity and Social Inequality*, Wiley, New York, 1974, by the French sociologist Raymond Boudon. Both books demonstrate the value of quantitative methods in sociology.

4   Stephen B. Withey et al., *A Degree and What Else?* McGraw-Hill, New York, 1971. A useful summary of research on the correlates and consequences of a college education. This is one of about twenty-five excellent and influential monographs on education published in the late 1960s and early 1970s by the Carnegie Commission on Higher Education under the chairmanship of sometime Berkeley president Clark Kerr.

5   Alexander F. Laidlaw (ed.), *The Man from Margaree*, McClelland & Stewart, Toronto, 1971. A compendium of the writings of Moses M. Coady, an educational reformer based at St. Francis Xavier University in Antigonish, Nova Scotia. From the early 1930s until his death in 1959, Coady championed the cause of cooperative education and university extension, a cause later institutionalized in the Coady Institute.

6   Paolo Freire, *Pedagogy of the Oppressed*, Herder & Herder, 1972. Even those who feel untouched by oppression can profit greatly from this little book by an outstanding Brazilian educator, exiled after the military takeover of his country's government. Freire's distinction of dialogic and antidialogic methods of teaching is no less relevant in advanced industrial settings than in the hinterlands of Brazil. See also his earlier essays published in English, *Education for Critical Consciousness*, Seabury, New York, 1973.

7   Ivan Illich, *Deschooling Society*, Harper & Row, 1970, *Disabling Professions*, Burns & MacEachern, Don Mills, Ont., 1977, and other works. Reading Illich (or worse yet, listening to him) rankles many people, myself included. But he describes with profound insight how schools serve institutionalized values and keep people down. And he writes in a way that strikes home.

8   Joel H. Spring, *Education and the Rise of the Corporate State*, Beacon, Boston, 1972. A brief, well-thought-out, and readable history of American education, connecting the spread of schooling to the rise of corporate capitalism. Spring belongs to a promising breed of critical historians of education, a breed that also includes Colin Greer, Clarence Karier, and Carl Kaestle, among others.

9   John Dewey, *The School and Society*, Univ. of Chicago Press, Chicago, 1899, *Democracy and Education*, Macmillan, New York, 1916, and *Experience and Education*, Macmillan, New York, 1938. Most of what we see, we who live late in history, has a human theory behind it. Behind much of what we see in contemporary education lie the misconstrued theories of this most influential of American philosophers. At least the first two of Dewey's books listed here have been reissued as inexpensive paperbacks.

10   Geraldine J. Clifford, *The Shape of American Education*, Prentice-Hall, Englewood Cliffs, N.J., 1975. A thoughtful study of the school system of the United States, organized around the four key values of publicness, diversity, universality, and breadth. Also includes a concise analysis of teaching as an occupation.

Chapter Ten

Liberation

Chapter Ten

*I ask by what means people try to
be free and how much unfreedom
lurks in the means they choose.*

A lot of ground has been covered in the nine chapters past. There was first a précis of sociology itself, the discipline and its origins. Its methods of research were surveyed next. Then seven hefty chapters gave substantive sociological knowledge of social order as it currently appears: organized in national societies, enacted by achievement-minded citizens, partitioned into the major institutions of polity, economy, religion, family, and education. Much more could be written under each of these headings, indeed *has been* written by scholars concentrating on one facet or another of our common life. Not every relevant study has been cited here, nor every research finding reported. Many carefully investigated subjects have been slighted or even skipped. I have intentionally sought not to cram as many facts and figures, names and dates, concepts and theories as might be made to fit within the covers of one book. For the classic promise of sociology is a vision of how things connect, a grasp of the conspiracy of order which circumscribes our individual lives. It is this promise the preceding chapters have been written to fulfill in brief and for our time and place. Presenting information was only part of their purpose. The greater part has been to nourish a sense of the connectedness of things, the sense C. Wright Mills called the sociological imagination. No reader should think that by now he or she "knows" sociology—as if this discipline were just a list of rubrics or facts. The worth of a book like this is to facilitate and speed a process of awareness that begins even before birth and lasts as long as life.

But what now for this final chapter, whose title already asserts a departure from the book's main theme? Liberation is not an institution, not part of the structure in our lives, not a component of the sociocultural system at hand. It is instead a process, a transition from the present situation to another of our own design. Liberation means breaking out of present constraints, transcending conformity to the prevailing system and beginning to act in the context of a newer one. That is what revolutionaries in dozens of colonies have done over the past two centuries, in wars of national liberation. What millions of Americans have taken part in more recently, the struggle for black liberation. What the meetings and protests mean in that movement called "women's lib." To speak of liberation is to affirm that the status quo is not forever, that people have power to make change and history. More than this, the word means using power toward the end of giving power, exercising freedom to make people still more free. Should this chapter then be a plan for liberation in our time, a how-to-do-it guide for deliverance from the confinements and restrictions we feel from day to day? That would indeed be a comforting conclusion to this book, a soothing dessert after so many pages of a heavy main course.

To propose here at last a solution to present ills would also please at least some readers of this book. Many students these days display what might be called the "Ann Landers syndrome": an inordinate hunger for advice, an attitude of dependency, a longing for someone to tell them what to do. They have been raised to doubt their own abilities and to look for "the answer" outside themselves—in a textbook or holy book, maybe in a scientific report, perhaps from the lips of a psychiatrist, guidance counselor, career planner, or expert of some other kind. They think the path of liberation has already been mapped and cleared, at least in principle, and that their task is just to find it. They are wrong. To live in history means to go uncertainly where no one yet has gone, and to take personal responsibility for going there. There is a place for maps and guides, to be sure, a need for advice, since none of us ever gets anywhere alone. No sociologist would ever deny the worth of books, articles, and speeches which propose a political direction, urge a starting point for change, or make a call for action of some kind. But the task of our discipline is more basic: to equip citizens with the tools for drawing their own maps, making their own plans, and regaling one another with their own respective proposals for creative change. The goal of sociology is not to say, "Go this way," or "Do that," but rather to inform people of where they stand in history and to remind them of their ability to move on. Hence to end this book with some kind of manifesto would defeat its purpose and muffle its affirmation of faith in the people who read it.

This final chapter therefore keeps closer to the theme of preceding ones than might initially be inferred from its title. The purpose here is not to propose a specific form of liberation but first simply to sketch the variety of forms available, the different kinds of nonconformity in which people can engage. The section immediately following provides such a sketch, a typology or classification of the escape routes from conventional order most commonly traveled. Thereafter the main point of this chapter can be made, that the existing order determines in great part which of its participants will defy its rules and what form their defiance will take. Few if any conclusions of sociological inquiry are as sobering as those outlined in the second section below—the explanations of how history regulates our efforts even to escape or remake history. There and throughout this chapter the worrisome question looms large: Is liberation possible for us in this late twentieth century? If not just our behavior but even our misbehavior is socially, externally induced, then what are we fighting for? What is left when ignorance of our servitude to history is lost?

The Forms of Liberation

The place to begin is with conformity, which means fitting one's actions to those in which a given role consists, meeting the expectations that surround some position in an established society. To conform is to abide by the laws and customs applicable to one's place in the social structure, to give one's personal performance according to the relevant script. Conformity is life as usual, particular individuals living up to the general ideas of how they should behave. These general ideas allow, of course, for incidental variation across role players. In no society is the pattern clear-cut for how a citizen, mother, student, secretary, bus rider, or whatever should behave. The boundaries of acceptable behavior are never precise. How late a 16-year-old girl can appropriately come home from a date, how often a homeowner should mow the grass, how much time a father should spend with his children—questions like these are matters of debate. Lawyers in court present varying interpretations of what the law allows. So do judges. Seldom, moreover, is a person fully aware of what is expected of him or her in roles recently acquired. The first weeks or months one spends as a husband or wife, an employee in some capacity, a resident of a city, university student or whatever, are often a long series of misunderstandings, oversights, faux pas, and embarrassments. Only gradually do we learn by our mistakes the behavior expected in our respective roles. Yet for all the fuzziness of definition and despite abundant faults, role expectations nonetheless are real in our experience. Each of us can sense from day to day the limits of behavior we are not supposed to cross. To stay within those limits is to conform—at least outwardly. Complete conformity forbids even entertaining thoughts of behaving otherwise.

to conform is to toe the line

For any role in a given society or group, the opposite of conformity is deviance: actions or ideas which do not fit the legal and customary expectations attached to that role. To deviate is to go beyond the limits of acceptable behavior, to break a law or contradict a norm that governs some role one occupies, to depart from the script in giving one's personal performance. Deviance is a breach of normal conduct, an irregularity, a particular individual's dissent from the general idea of what he or she should do. Needless to say, deviance is no more exactly specifiable than conformity. The line between the two is fuzzy on both sides. All contemporary societies have more laws on their books than their police and courts could possibly enforce. Jaywalking in many jurisdictions is deviant in a formal sense but normal in practice. The same goes for prostitution, various kinds of gambling, and petty thievery in offices. Both lawmakers and citizens at large tend to espouse far more rigorous codes of behavior than their actions reflect. Yet deviance is no less real in our experience than conformity. It is less common, else there would be no order in our lives. But being less common, it is also more noteworthy and interesting. Conventional, law-abiding citizens often stare at derelicts on the street and relish news reports of crime. Courses in the sociology of deviance attract relatively large enrollments. Conformist people everywhere are curious about those who misbehave.

to deviate is to step out of line

If there were a single, ideal, natural order for human life on earth, an order mirrored in the laws and customs of our own society, then our task as citizens and social analysts would be tidier. Conformity to roles as currently defined could be identified with goodness, and deviance with wickedness. Conformity could be our ultimate goal in life. Research on deviance could be designed toward the end of erasing the last bit of it from human experience. But alas, we know too much history to take so childish a view. Charging interest on loans was once deviant even in our civilization, and accepting challenges to duel exemplified conformity. Today the reverse is true. That a wealthy man should marry half a dozen wives was a routine expectation in most societies of the past; in ours it is a crime. The idea of electing rulers by popular vote was just a few centuries ago enough to land a person in jail; by now the contrary idea merits scorn. Indeed, most of our heroes from the past were deviants in their time. We need not think back so far as Jesus or Socrates. Just twenty-five years ago Martin Luther King was a convicted criminal, an agitator, fanatic, and fit object of close police surveillance. What history asserts, moreover, cross-national diversity today confirms. Communists are conformists in the U.S.S.R., but deviants in the U.S.A. Eating steak is admired in Uruguay, condemned in most of India. The examples need not be multiplied here. But knowing them, we cannot assume, as premodern peoples did, that history stops with us, that ours is *the right* way, that our society has captured human nature once and for all. Unlike our traditional ancestors, we cannot equate conformity with goodness. We bear the awful burden of recognizing vice in some conformity and virtue in some deviance.

the burden of seeing vice in conformity, virtue in deviance

That is why this section is entitled *forms of liberation* and not *forms of deviance*. Although the latter title would be just as accurate, the former one emphasizes that rejection of prevailing norms is not necessarily bad. Or more precisely, that the process of liberation implies behavior and ideas which are deviant. If no one in a society ever rebelled against the status quo, that society would have no history. There would be no change. And if a person never did anything but live up to others' expectations, then that person would never know a dialectical, fully human life. Liberation happens, history happens, only when by word or deed one person says to the rest of the world, "I know what you expect of me but sorry, that's not quite what you get." Now to be sure, few acts of liberation have effects of much consequence. We should be glad. The fruits of creative genius often taste worse than the stale bread of conformity. Most novel behaviors are simply ignored, hardly noticed by anyone except the initiators, who thereafter mend their ways and return to conformity. We humans graciously permit one another to act strangely now and then and do not take such action seriously. Other novel behaviors, especially those repeated too often to be overlooked, are rejected as worse than conformity. Examples include everyday assaults and burglaries. Only occasionally can any of us do something a little out of line and see in response some slight reshaping of the line itself. Even then, as will be explained some pages later on, what we did was probably not half so original or surprising as at first we thought. But before attempts at liberation are explained, they might best be sorted into the four broad categories set forth in Table 10-1.

The primary distinction is between those types of liberation which amount to withdrawal or retreat from role expectations and those which constitute some kind

Table 10-1 *Four generic forms of liberation, or deviance*

DEGREE	WITHDRAWAL		ATTACK	
	INDIVIDUAL	COLLECTIVE	INDIVIDUAL	COLLECTIVE

Mild	Sleeping on the job
	Daydreams, fantasies
	Loafing
	Media opiates
	Occasional drunkenness
	Marijuana smoking
	Many illnesses
		Escapist entertainment
		Sectarian religion
		Cults
			Personal twists and
			  new wrinkles in the
			  performance of
			  conventional roles
			"I'll do it my way"
			Minor innovations
				Fads, crazes
				Under capitalism,
				  marginally new
				  products of private
				  companies
				Reformist social
				  movements

Severe	Refusing to settle
	  down
	A hermit's life
	Habitual drunkenness
	Narcotic addiction
	Psychosis
	Suicide
		Countercultural
		  movements
		Utopian communities
			Invention in science
			  and technology
			Boldly original art
			New philosophic work
			New forms of human
			  organization
			Religious prophecy
				Under capitalism,
				  major new products
				  of private companies
				Revolutionary social
				  movements
				Mass migrations

of attack upon those expectations or an attempt to change them. Second is the difference between deviant actions a single individual can take and those done collectively. Joining these two variables or dimensions of difference results in four broad categories, the four columns in the table. Then within each column particular deviant acts can be classed as mild or severe, depending on how far they diverge from conformity. Now admittedly, all these categories shade off into one another—lines are always fuzzier in lived experience than in books. But for analytic purposes the paragraphs below treat the basic categories one by one.

INDIVIDUAL WITHDRAWAL

Like other organisms, humans cannot be pressed beyond biological limits. Denied sleep and rest long enough, a person simply dies. Hence every society builds into its own structure of demands permissible periods and techniques of withdrawal from those demands. Office breaks, school recess periods, vacations, and holidays are examples of a temporal kind. Moderate drinking, smoking, and various kinds of hobbies, sports, and leisure are among acceptable techniques. To take advantage of legitimate opportunities for escape from routine expectations is not deviance, but often an expression of commitment to the existing order. "I think I'll have a nightcap and go to bed; I've a busy day tomorrow." "Let's go for a swim and finish this later, when we feel fresh." Everyday comments like these are signs of conformity, not dissent. But when people find themselves bored, confused, degraded, or otherwise displeased by their roles, they often withdraw more than is allowed or in ways that are forbidden. This common form of liberation is seized upon by everyone to some extent. Few students have not slept through a dull lecture or spent the hour mentally replaying or rehearsing some romantic escapade. Employees often just go

Prevent
drug abuse

United States Postage 8c

through the motions of their jobs, whiling away time in reveries and private preoccupations. Husbands, wives, sons, and daughters sometimes retreat from family life to hour after stupefying hour before the television screen, next to the stereo speakers, or in the pages of skin magazines. Occasional drunkenness and marijuana use are other examples of mild but deviant withdrawal. So, too, the prolonged use of tranquilizers or stimulants, which lessen one's vulnerability to pressures from the outside world. Research shows also that many illnesses—colds, flu, headaches, back pain, ulcers, allergies, and so on—occur less frequently to people who enjoy their work and family roles than to those who are dissatisfied. Like drowsiness, illness can often be explained in physiological terms alone. But just as often it is best understood as a physically real method of escape from behavior others expect but oneself abhors.

some of the loneliest retreats: drunkenness, addiction, psychosis, suicide

Individuals pursue more kinds of retreat from routine expectations than can be mentioned here. Even a persistent pattern of quitting, a debilitating restlessness, a refusal to settle down exemplifies retreat. So does a hermit's defection from conventional life. But among examples of severe withdrawal, four deserve attention for their prevalence in the contemporary Western world. First is habitual or chronic drunkenness, the consumption of alcohol in such quantity that continuing to work and to maintain family duties is impossible or nearly so. By current estimates about 7 percent of U.S. adults (roughly 9 million) illustrate this kind of flight from current order. Addiction to narcotic drugs like opium or heroin is a second alternative. Although more widespread in Oriental than in Western societies, it remains the escape route for an estimated 300,000 Americans. A third category of severe withdrawal includes the behaviors customarily grouped under the label of mental illness. Especially the functional psychoses, biologically unexplained types of insanity which about 1 percent of people in North America manifest sometime in their lives. Schizophrenia is the principal psychosis, accounting for about a quarter of people admitted to psychiatric hospitals and (because schizophrenics are not easily restored to normality) about half the residents of these hospitals. The very definition of this disorder is withdrawal from interaction with others, dissociation from one's environment, retreat into one's own idiosyncratic and usually chaotic reality. Another mental illness, anorexia nervosa, involves refusing to eat, starving oneself even to the point of death. Fourth and finally is the ultimate withdrawal of suicide, an action taken by about 27,000 Americans each year. Many so-called natural deaths, moreover, are affected by how much the person involved wants to stay alive. Demographers have evidence that people are more likely to die just after their birthdays than just before, and that the death rate for Jews falls before Yom Kippur but rises once this holiest day of the year is passed.[1]

the undesirability of retreat

To apply the word *liberation* to drunkenness, schizophrenia, suicide, and other kinds of withdrawal from current order is not at all to praise these alternatives. Among all forms of liberation, these are indeed the least desirable. The reality we find in history, however hopeless it might seem, is all we have. The person who tunes it out or loses touch with it has nothing left but the pain of loneliness. The point here is only that these options are available and that millions of people take

As a technique of liberation, withdrawal into a private world of bizarre behavior is troublesome to societies and often hurtful to individuals. The question is what to do about it. In the past many people behaving in strange ways were diagnosed as mentally ill and locked up in insane asylums (later called "psychiatric hospitals"). But during the last fifteen years in North America, treatment of people diagnosed as mentally ill has changed dramatically. The population of patients in psychiatric hospitals has been cut in half. The more common treatment today is a daily regimen of tranquilizers or other mood-altering drugs, often administered by nurses in outpatient clinics. (Ken Karp)

them, even all of us in some degree. It is a mistake to count any kind of individual withdrawal as some kind of curse, a fated malady outside of human control. Physical and social factors make a difference, to be sure. Some people are never tempted to get drunk, while for others (called alcoholics) one drink foreshadows months or years of drunkenness. Some people do drive their respective spouses mad, while others keep them sane. Some citizens are in roles especially hard to tolerate, and the chemistry of their bodies may predispose them to withdrawal. Sometimes a person's whole self crumbles before that person even knows what is happening. But external explanations should not be pressed too far. History does not reward the denial of personal responsibility. Whether mild or severe, withdrawal must be seen in part as an assertion by creative beings of their ability to resist conformity, a genuine expression of what was earlier called donkey power. Willfulness may be hard to see in the withdrawal itself but seldom in the process of recovery or return. Psychotics do not regain sanity nor alcoholics sobriety without fighting and struggling within themselves. People who have strayed to the edge of suicide but dragged themselves back from it—they know better than anyone that the power to say no is at once the power to say yes.

COLLECTIVE WITHDRAWAL

Every society incorporates within itself legitimate opportunities for collective as well as individual withdrawal. Houston's Astrodome, New Orleans' Superdome, and comparable stadiums, coliseums, and arenas in other cities are evidence

enough. So, too, the theaters, cinemas, skating rinks, race-tracks, nightclubs, and parks—places of reprieve from the everyday routine. Our interest here is not in these legitimate outlets, respites, and escapes but in deviant ones, in collective ways of losing touch with conventional expectations. But I should point out in preface that laying aside the rare case of collective suicide, as of the Reverend Jim Jones's followers in Guyana in 1978, a group's withdrawal from a society is not so complete as an individual's. The fact of interaction, the shared practice of behavior and belief, is itself a holdover from the mainstream order dissidents are trying to leave behind. Inevitably, moreover, they carry away with them innumerable properties of the order they reject: vocabulary, grammar, meanings, memories, and more little folkways and mannerisms than they ever could slough off. Nor is a group's withdrawal typically so innocuous as an individual's. When an individual "flips out," the action can usually be chalked up to private weakness or personal pathology. When hundreds of people withdraw en masse, as in the Jonestown experiment, conformist citizens can hardly help but be shaken, feel threatened and reproached. Indeed, as workers who go out on strike illustrate, groups sometimes withdraw strategically in order to force change upon the status quo. Their action is thus appropriately placed in the category of "attack" rather than of "withdrawal" among forms of liberation. Our focus for now is on groups whose movement away from the mainstream order is without much intention of inducing change and without much plan for an eventual return. This kind of effort to be free can be considered as before, first in its milder expressions, then in those more severe.

In a sense, mild collective withdrawal appears in any crowd or assemblage engaged in an acceptable kind of recreation but to an unacceptable or fanatic degree. Golf "nuts," football "addicts," and compulsive gamblers are examples. So are those adolescent fans of various entertainers who get "carried away" at rock concerts and festivals. But these are not the best examples to cite here. A crowd obsessed with some sport or star is not quite a group, but only individuals nursing their private obsessions simultaneously. Collective withdrawal is more precisely evident in those offbeat religious denominations commonly called sects and cults, the organized adherents of unorthodox doctrines concerning what is beyond experience. Some sects center on a predicted date for Jesus' return, the world's end, or California's slide into the Pacific ocean. Others revolve around snake handling, miracle working, or faith healing. In many sects, the Jehovah's Witnesses for example, members try earnestly to make converts. In others, Christian Science for one, there is less effort to proselytize. The beliefs themselves may be Christian (fundamentalist and pentecostal congregations), Jewish (various Chassidic groups),

a group's withdrawal is less complete, more threatening

sectarian religion—taking the sting from the status quo

or outside Western traditions (Black Muslims, Baha'is, spiritualists, theosophists, or practitioners of transcendental meditation). Denominations like these obviously differ greatly among themselves. They share, however, a certain detachment from the cultural mainstream, a partial mental and emotional withdrawal from dominant interpretations of everyday experience. Most sectarians hold ordinary jobs and seem conventional in most aspects of their lives. But they have shaken a little loose the grip of the status quo, knowing as they do that it is soon to end, that God's judgment is upon it, or that some higher reality exists alongside it. Beliefs like these, reinforced and celebrated in frequent meetings for study and prayer, are a form of liberation, though without much observable effect on the social order at hand. Usually it is just some little sign—refusal to pledge allegiance to the flag, a distinctive uniform, a pocket Bible, a whispered mantra, or abstention from some beverage or food—that lets ordinary people know that here is one for whom routine rewards and punishments have lost their sting.

countercultures—a more decisive break

The logical extreme of sectarian religion is what has come to be called a *counterculture*: a group which breaks with the mainstream order more sharply, detaches itself more completely, and establishes its own relatively self-contained way of life.[2] This is what the Reverend Jim Jones and his disciples did, in the foundation of the People's Temple in the Guyanese jungle. But there are many less ruinous examples: the several thousand farm communes founded during the hippie era, the Krishna people and the "Moonies," Catholic monasteries and convents of contemplative nuns, and the various utopian communities discussed earlier in the chapter on family life. Countercultures differ widely in the alternatives they pose to conventional life. They have in common, however, a radical and usually dogmatic rejection both of the existing order and of attempts to change it. The counter-cultural technique of liberation is indeed to flee history itself, to abandon the ethic of worldly progress, to forsake the uncertain, fractious work of economic and political development. All this for the sake of living up collectively to some lofty, unchanging, timeless ideal—in purposeful isolation from ordinary people, the ones still caught up in transitory, evanescent concerns. But this is too easy a way out. The data of experience demonstrate that no ideal is timeless, much less is it captured in an unchanging way of life. What "perfection" meant to the Perfection-ists at Oneida contrasts sharply with what it means to Trappist monks, while Hutterites, hippies, dervishes, and Doukhobors have each a definition of their own. In other words, evanescent concerns are all we humans have. History does not cease when small, self-righteous groups run away from it. Instead it passes them by.

The countercultures that last nonetheless are part of history, even if reluctantly. Survival requires coming to terms with the outside world: conforming to its laws at least enough to stay out of jail, possibly recruiting new members from its youth and establishing with it mutually beneficial trade relationships. Whoever has sipped Chartreuse or B and B knows something of what monks have done for Western history. Indeed, the Catholic religious orders have endured these past 1500 years as an integral, albeit exceptional, element of Christendom. The same is true of Buddhist monks in the context of Thai, Burmese, or Laotian societies, and of Chassidic enclaves in the larger Jewish community. Thus as a form of liberation countercultures are not merely escapes. At the very least they are signs of transcendence, reminders to conventional citizens that conventional life is not all there is. Just outside the city where I live are several colonies of Old Order Mennonites, a rural people who in some respects pulled out of Western history some four centuries ago. They wear outdated clothes, speak an obsolete German, ride buggies to market and church, and refuse electricity. By any standard except their own, their deviant, unmodern life is a sorry alternative to mainline conformity. Yet like most others in this city, I rejoice that the Mennonites are here, and not only for the appetizing foods they sell us or the relief work they perform when floods and other disasters strike. Some years ago I took a group of students out to talk with an old Mennonite farmer and his family. In the car afterward one typical undergraduate remarked, "That was the most goddam peaceful man I've ever seen." Symbolizing peace is no mean historical accomplishment. It is one we worldlings can be grateful for—whether done by Mennonites or monks, Krishna chanters or Salvation Army bellringers, flower children or others who have forsaken respectability for sectarian or countercultural ways of life.

INDIVIDUAL ATTACK

As used here, the word *attack* refers to any thought or action directed toward change of the established structure of social life. It does not necessarily imply violence. Indeed many violent acts, like those of police officers in the line of duty,

do not qualify as attacks in this sense at all, since their aim is to enforce compliance with prevailing values and norms. When a bank robber threatens or strikes or fires upon a teller, by contrast, this violent deed is properly considered an attack, since it challenges the normal, acceptable, legal mode of conduct in a bank. The most noteworthy attacks on routine expectations, however, occur without physical force being used against anyone. Charles Lindbergh's flight from New York to Paris in 1927 was a more memorable offense against then-customary life than the kidnapping and murder of his son five years later. Martin Luther King's leadership of a nonviolent movement for civil rights challenged convention in the United States far more than did the assassination of King by James Earl Ray. For to attack the status quo means to inject newness into it, to defy role expectations in a way that prevents life from going on as usual. It means entering history, intruding one's own self upon the arrangement of people and nature in a given time and place and thus leaving some little mark of one's own upon the shape of this planet. As a form of liberation an attack is the opposite of withdrawal. Instead of retreating from the world one tries to change it. Rather than abandoning a role one undertakes to perform it in an uncustomary way. Unwilling either to conform or to quit, one stays and fights. As has been remarked often in this book, saying no is a creative exercise of power. But not half so much as saying yes to something fresh, untried, and new. Attacks are surprises inflicted upon the status quo, attempts to bend it somehow to one's personal will.

The seriousness of an attack is not measured by the response it gets in either the

438

short or the long run. For more than ten years Germany embraced and implemented Hitler's innovative plan, but there and almost everywhere this plan is now repudiated and condemned. The gospel of Jesus, on the other hand, earned its author crucifixion at an early age but the worship of untold millions ever since. It is not the immediate or delayed reaction that defines the seriousness of an attack but how much the existing order would have to change if the attack became routine. By this criterion the attacks most citizens make are exceedingly mild, not even a tenth so grave as those of Hitler or Jesus. We play our conventional roles at work and at home, twisting them but slightly according to personal inclination. No husband, no boss, no receptionist, no student is quite like any other. There is in each performance some little wrinkle that distinguishes it from all others and identifies it with a unique human person. Whenever anyone insists, "I'll do it may way," he or she is claiming the right reserved among all creatures to our own species, the right to break with convention and redefine the structure of earthly life. But the break is seldom radical, the redefinition rarely bold. Few citizens play their roles even so innovatively as the baker in one of the more popular doughnut shops hereabouts. Every other time I go into the place, a trayful of some strange new kind of doughnut beckons alongside the standard dutchies, lemon-filled, crullers, and honey-dipped. Most of these new varieties seem never to be tried a second time. Even if one of them caught on and swept the industry our world would be little changed. But the waitress tells me the baker experiments to ease the boredom of his job. Given the chance, so do millions of other people in their various roles. Thereby they free themselves a little and add to the piecemeal history of our race.

As a rule, the more serious an individual's attack on prevailing norms the more probably it will be rebuffed. The forgotten past is full of instances of newness that diverged too far from the oldness at hand, novelties whose adoption at the time would have required a more thorough overhaul of existing structures than power holders were willing to allow. Indeed, a tragic but common failing of intensely creative humans is refusal to face up to the status quo and to respect it as the sole context for testing the worth of any creative act. Yet history does not always inch along. Sometimes it takes a leap, spurred by a new idea which, however radical, is simply too attractive and compelling to pass up. The people behind such ideas, the initiators of severe but irresistible attacks, appropriately tend to be remembered by name. In the first category fall religious prophets, those who entrenched new myths about the ultimate meaning of earthly life: Moses, Jesus, Guatama Buddha, Muhammad, Joseph Smith. One can think also of those who imprinted themselves on the history of the expressive arts: Beethoven, Shakespeare, Picasso, and so on. Some of the most critical attacks in modern times have come from social theorists and philosophers like John Locke, Adam Smith, Karl Marx, and John Dewey, among many others. Liberation has come in part from severe attacks on prevailing scientific thought (Galileo, Newton, Einstein, Bohr) and on established modes of technology (Franklin, Edison, Bell, Diesel). And also from the design of new kinds of human organization toward unprecedented achievements: Henry Ford's assembly line, for example, Frank Woolworth's department stores, or Alfred Fuller's corps of brush salesmen.[3] For our century, perhaps the single best list of assailants of routine life is of recipients of the prize endowed by Alfred Nobel, the Swedish inventor of

prophets, great artists, philosophers, and inventors make severe attacks

dynamite. The prize is today's best evidence that some mighty blow on behalf of change has found its mark.

As a means of freeing themselves and humanity as a whole, nothing excels the varied attacks individuals make day by day upon established expectations. This is in a sense the only authentic kind of liberation, since withdrawal has meaning only by the novel effect it has on what is withdrawn from and to, and since collective attacks are composed of individual ones. We become free, this is to say, only by doing to others what has not yet occurred to them. To be sure, many such deeds fail to win applause. Many are met with reminders to "behave," "shape up," and "settle down." Properly so. "My way" is seldom better and often significantly worse than the routine, accepted way. The biography of every inventive woman or man is in great part a chronicle of failed experiments. There is always more bad news than good. But if the goal be freedom, the worst news is none at all, an absence of adventure and surprise in earthly experience. There are students who try only to give professors what they want, wives who think of nothing but self-surrender to their mates, role players of all kinds whose sole ambition is to live up to what others have in mind. The tragedy is that such people are not free. Freedom means coming up against another and saying or doing something fresh, something that makes the other cry out, "You're really something else. I've never met anyone quite like you before." What risk there is in provoking such a cry! What insecurity and fear! But history has never been made in any other way. Nor has love.

*in a free society, no
news is bad news*

COLLECTIVE ATTACK

The canons of disinterested scholarship forbid a sociologist to declare openly which category of a typology or list he or she considers to be best. It is permissible and usual, however, to save the favored category for last in a textbook discussion. So it

is in the present case. From a narrowly psychological point of view, the process of liberation can be reduced to the creative acts of ingenious individuals—as in theories which credit history to the triumphs of a few "great men." Yet no individual's attack on the status quo succeeds unless other people accept it, join it, make it a collective enterprise. No individual persists, moreover, in a novel course of behavior or belief except with aid and encouragement from comrades of like mind. For these reasons the main focus in sociology is on collective rather than individual attempts at change: on the American revolution instead of just George Washington, on the Chinese Communist party in preference to the person of Mao Zedong, or on today's multifaceted campaign for sexual equality rather than such leading proponents as Bella Abzug or Betty Friedan. This focus does not belittle the contributions of specific individuals but puts them in context. The point was made early in this book that social order is necessarily a joint effort, something more than a mass of citizens with orderly selves. Here can be added that the same is true of social change—that it requires explictly collective action, not just a horde of go-getters intent on freeing their respective selves. It may be soothing to imagine that progress comes from a tiny gifted minority of people, those

Running and jogging in one sense are fads, but they have become something more: "a rebellion against the lack of physical exercise inherent in today's automobile-centered form of urban life." (Arthur Grace/Stock, Boston)

possessed of exceptional creative genius. The allure of this notion is that it relieves the rest of us of responsibility. But we cannot get off the hook so easily. No headway has ever been made in science, no improvement in technology, no advance in the arts or progress in politics without what is called in sociology *collective behavior*: tens, hundreds, or thousands of people unshackling themselves in unison, sharing the risk of change, combining their attacks on the status quo, and together trying to give newness to the earth.

Sects and countercultures derive from collective behavior, too, but our concern here is with concerted efforts to transform an existing society, not to withdraw from it. In their mildest variant these appear as a fad or craze: a new behavior, product, or style of little consequence, but one that briefly captures the fancy of large numbers of people. When I was in seventh grade the fad was polished cotton pants with a buckle on the back. Because my friends and I owned two pairs each we counted ourselves in the avant garde of humanity's forward march. Our perception was just as true as that of youth more recently, swaggering about in designer jeans. Fads like these—or the hula hoop, pet rock, Crock-pot, cowboy hat, hit recordings, or whatever—are defined by the enthusiasm with which they are embraced and the speed with which they are dropped. About all they signify is the human craving for togetherness and novelty at once. Of greater significance are fads enduring and serious enough to qualify as cultural trends. Health-food stores had a faddish quality when they began to multiply in the early 1970s, but by now they deserve to be seen as part of widespread collective attack on dietary convention, especially on the use of additives and preservatives. The same goes for jogging, which has become in some respects a rebellion against the lack of physical exercise inherent in today's

fads and crazes—trivial forms of collective behavior

automobile-centered form of urban life. Similarly, in the varied fashions and fads surrounding women's clothing over the past two decades can be discerned a general trend toward eroticism and what was once called immodesty, a trend which coincides with rising rates of sexual activity.

Whether faddish or sustained, most collective attacks on the established way of life in a capitalist society are made according to principles of market economics. Critics of capitalism often overlook this point, confining their attention to explicitly political attempts at social change. But as was explained in the latter part of Chapter Six, capitalism is an inherently dynamic strategy of development, one that fosters the unceasing overturn of convention in favor of novelty. Most innovations—from designer jeans to Crock-pots, from jogging shoes to new kinds of doughnuts—appear as products in the marketplace, designed, manufactured, advertised, sold, and purchased by people willing to take a risk. Hence in a capitalist society like the United States, the most common organizational expression of collective behavior is the profit-seeking firm. It is in or to a private company that some citizen first spells out a new idea, hoping listeners will not think it ridiculous. If the innovator's enthusiasm proves sufficiently contagious, the company gets behind the idea, criticizes and revises it, and begins the process of translating it into a salable piece of merchandise. In due course the innovation is introduced into some promising market, where it either displaces products already available or suffers rejection. In the former case, the shape of life is in some degree transformed. In the more frequent latter case, the status quo endures and the innovative company takes a loss. This process applies not only to trifling novelties. Light bulbs, telephones, automobiles, air conditioners, televisions, computers, and most of the other great inventions of the last century and a half have gained a place in our world because profit-minded firms were pushing them. And these inventions have transformed human experience far more profoundly (and beneficially) than any revolutionary war. Nor is the dynamism of the capitalist market limited to items of technology. Cubism prospered not only because Picasso, Braque, and others painted in a certain style but because art dealers, galleries, magazines, newspapers, and other businesses chose to back that style. Innovative books become best-sellers through the efforts not just of their authors (for whom profit maximization is seldom a priority) but of their publishers (for whom the bottom line is what matters most of all). In sum, the principal medium by which groups make change in the Western world is the profit-seeking firm. But there are other media.

the profit-seeking firm as agent of change

As was also explained in Chapter Six, capitalism exists within a political frame. It is not the natural mode of economic organization (no such mode exists) but a set of socially constructed, governmentally enforced rules about how citizens should behave toward one another and the earth. These rules, like those of any sociocultural system, are always open to revision and renegotiation. Attempts to do this, whether to a slight or drastic degree, comprise the expressions of collective behavior most commonly studied in sociology. They are usually called *social movements* or sometimes, to distinguish them more clearly from countercultural and religious expressions, *political movements*. They occur whenever citizens articulate some common grievance or demand and voluntarily rally together for the sake of furthering this common cause. The most noteworthy example in United States

political change by means of social movements

history has been the labor movement: workers in particular crafts, companies, or industries joining to bargain collectively for a better return on the sale of their work. Many other social movements have arisen from disadvantaged minorities intent on improving their lot: the women's movement, extending from the suffragists of the nineteenth century to contemporary advocates of the equal rights amendment; the movement for gay liberation; comparable efforts by and on behalf of youth, the aged, or the handicapped; and, of course, the civil rights campaigns of blacks, Jews, Hispanics, and other ethnic or racial minorities. Many social movements are defined by specific issues like abortion, nuclear arms, nuclear power plants, acid rain, fluoridation of water, student power in universities, or a war like that in Vietnam. In some cases the demand is for unprecedented change—for example, the Women's Christian Temperance Union and the Anti-Saloon League, whose efforts resulted in a ban on alcoholic beverages in the United States during the 1920s. In other cases the goal is restoration of some previous state of affairs—like the drive to end prohibition, successful in 1933. What defines a movement as political is just the redefinition it seeks of the public order within which individuals pursue their private purposes. Political movements are thus a staple of life in all modern societies, those whose citizens are aware of their power to rewrite laws and redirect the course of history. Not all such movements succeed, of course. Most fizzle at the start, and few achieve their goals more than partially.

Most social movements, including all the examples just listed from American history, aim only at reform. Their goal is to perfect, refine, revive, modify, or patch up the existing order, not to replace it outright. This is so even when violence erupts between defenders of the status quo and proponents of change. Indeed it is uncanny how modest a proposed innovation can provoke established power holders to the use of force. Violence is all but inevitable, however, in the case of movements espousing not just reform but revolution, a drastic or fundamental *the continuum from reform to revolution* change in the structure of the society at hand. Revolutionary movements are the severest kind of collective attack. Their purpose is a massive transformation of the shape of life and a wholesale transfer of power from one set of elites to another. The most important revolutionary movements have been those aimed at destroying regimes based on traditional authority or military might in favor of legal-rational, democratic self-rule: the American Revolution of 1775–1782, the French Revolution of 1789–93, the Russian Revolution of 1917, the rebellion culminating in Irish independence in 1922, and scores of comparable attempts at national liberation in other parts of the world. The term *revolutionary* is properly applied also to other efforts at large-scale social reorganization: the Chinese Communist party, which came to power in 1949; the Nazi party in Germany, which ushered in the Third Reich; or more recently, the Sandinista rebellion in Nicaragua in 1979 or the Solidarity movement in Poland in the early 1980s. More loosely still, there is a revolutionary quality about mass migrations (like European settlement of the Americas) and even the spread of certain items of technology (the automobile or television, for example). In all these instances, of course, the attempt at liberation through severe collective attack achieved to significant degree its stated goals. Any list of failed revolutionary efforts would be much longer. The wider the gap between what a movement proposes and what currently exists, the greater the prospect of defeat.

Reflection on the great examples of collective behavior from decades and centuries past, examples like those in the paragraphs above, concludes too often with a melancholy sigh. Would it not have been fun, we imagine, to have shared the excited sense of movement and common cause that united those who introduced heroic inventions, carried out illustrious reforms, brought off revolutions, or otherwise compelled the shape of life to change? Studying history as a boy and listening to adults' reminiscences, I regretted being born so late—after the West had already been settled, the telephones installed, the Nazis defeated, and the cars mass-produced. The important windmills seemed all to have been tilted at. Then, of course, came television, computers, polyester shirts, expressways, suburbs, freedom marches, antiwar protests, student sit-ins, the Beatles, race riots, bra-burners, dual-career marriages, and all kinds of people singing "We shall overcome." The truth is that modern societies are defined by the steady fabrication of windmills for tilting at. Freedom is not so much a condition people live in as a process they enact, with every new assault they make on the way things are. These forays are not cut and dried. In retrospect scholars like me conceptualize a fad here, a social movement there, and the ones that fail we seldom talk about. But to the change-minded people involved, collective behavior is never a matter of marching certainly in step toward the next milestone of history. People fumble and grope their way into collective attacks, wondering whether the distant drummer they hear is real or not, mustering what show of confidence they can to conceal their inward doubts. Like all forms of liberation, collective attack implies uncertainty and risk. But it is happening now as in the past. Students in the twenty-first century will wistfully reflect on those of their ancestors in the 1980s who joined for the sake of progressive change. Those future students are unlikely to appreciate what a confusing, dubious enterprise it is.

freedom is the process of renewing life on earth

SUMMARY

As noted at the start of Chapter Two in this book, the first step toward understanding any phenomenon is to label different parts of it with words, to sort it out into conceptual categories. To do precisely this for the phenomenon of contemporary social life has been a major purpose of all the chapters since those preliminary ones. In the main our emphasis has been on discerning the order in our experience, the kind of arrangement of people in roles that distinguishes our society today from those elsewhere and in the past. That is the worth of concepts like *legal-rational authority, capitalism, denomination, nuclear family,* or *professional schooling.* This section on the forms of liberation, however, has added a different and further dimension to the understanding we seek. For it has put labels on the disorder in our experience, the deviance from role expectations that appears steadily mixed in with the dominant conformity. This deviance has been viewed not like static on a radio or snow on a television screen, as bothersome interference to be removed if possible, but as the variously good or not so good expression of the human will to be free. As such, it was divided into four main conceptual categories, *individual withdrawal, collective withdrawal, individual attack,* and *collective attack.*

conceptualizing deviance is the first step toward understanding it

Within each of these a number of more specific expressions were labeled and discussed. Equipped with this vocabulary, a person intent on understanding, say, a university can look at it and see more than an ongoing structure of demands and rewards, with deans, professors, students, and so on all performing their respective roles in harmony with established purposes. Besides such evidence of prevailing values and norms, the better-equipped observer sees also that some students and professors are cutting class, others popping tranquilizers, still others languishing in chronic drunkenness or unproductive loneliness. And that a clique of nonconformists here, another there, has partially withdrawn from mainstream academic life into some guru's cult or counterculture "on the fringe." And that some creative scholars are writing papers that go beyond the conventional wisdom of their fields (or at least depart from it). And that dissidents within and across departments have formed movements on behalf of new policies, new courses, new programs, and (not infrequently) new leadership. Even in the microcosm of a college or university, indeed in every family, community, company, or church, whoever looks can find people retreating from and rebelling against their assigned roles. All the more is this the case at the level of national societies and other large-scale systems of action and belief. These disorderly aspects of what we see and hear are not signs of pathology, not evidence of some kind of sickness to be cured. They are the stuff of history, what separates human life from its animalic counterparts. Whoever would understand a human group or organization must somehow grasp the current process of abandoning or overhauling it. The discussion here of the forms of liberation is intended to make the grasping easier.

common crime—neither welcome nor very new

But nothing written here, I should repeat, implies that all attempts to break out of established structures deserve to be welcomed, emulated, tolerated, or even overlooked. Clearly they do not. Most of us in the contemporary Western world agree that in our societies we can do without any deviant behavior that involves physically forcing an adult to do something he or she would otherwise not do. We forego whatever benefits might result from citizens taking the law into their own hands in this respect, preferring to place our hope in nonviolent kinds of deviance. Thus we generally applaud the jailing of people convicted of murder, rape, kidnapping, hijacking, hostage taking, assault, robbery—offenses defined by the unauthorized use of force against persons. There is general agreement, too, on the undesirability of various unimaginative but deviant techniques of seizing another's money or property against that person's will. Common auto theft, burglary, and larceny are examples. The basic rules of the capitalist marketplace, so we hope, provide ample room for citizens to conjure up beneficial new schemes for capturing one another's wealth. But it is a grave mistake to think of deviance mainly in connection with these and other common crimes. To dwell only on the sorriest alternatives to conformity is to set one's face against progressive change. Besides, common crime is a poor example of innovative or creative thought. "The man who is admired for the ingenuity of his larceny," John Kenneth Galbraith has observed, "is almost always rediscovering some earlier form of fraud. The basic forms are all known, have all been practiced."[4] That is why in this review I have called to mind some relatively genuine and hopeful instances of deviance, while acknowledging that there are other instances.

Naming a phenomenon and labeling different parts of it are but the start of understanding it. What remains is empirically to connect variation in one part with variation in other parts, to demonstrate the interdependence of different aspects of our experience, to make hypotheses and theories which somehow explain what is going on and render it predictable. Such an effort rankles less, of course, as Comte himself pointed out, when the object of study is subhuman phenomena rather than our own selves. Even if stars, levers, and fruit flies are locked in their environments and helplessly tied to external forces, we prefer to think that humans are or can be free. Each of us wants to be in some sense unconnected, independent, able to make up his or her own mind and to act out of inner conviction and will. The science Comte founded has succeeded, nonetheless, in showing how little this is the case. If preceding chapters of this book have done nothing else, surely at least they have documented how much each of us is a pawn of forces outside our control. But is there not some limit to this humiliating brunt of sociology? A limit, in truth, defined by the forms of liberation? Is not freedom obvious in suicide and psychosis, sects and utopias, invention and prophecy, revolution and reform? If people's power to surprise lies often hidden in ruts of conformity, does it not burst into view when they swim against the tide? Why can't we just say people step out of line because they *want* to, and respectfully end the discussion there?

sociology extends to the explanation of surprise

There is indeed a limit to external explanations of human action, but this is not quite it. Accounts of why people misbehave in fact fill thousands of social scientific articles and books. One of the first systematic quantitative investigations ever done was Emile Durkheim's book on suicide, published in 1897, where he showed how this ultimate act of defiance depends on religious, ethnic, and economic circumstance. For well over a century researchers have been cataloging empirical correlates of madness, inventiveness, and crime. Scholars as far back as de Tocqueville and even farther have made theories about why riots and revolutions happen. By now one can cite hardly a single instance of collective behavior for whose origin some expert has not given an account. It seems almost that sociologists have sought in the explanation of deviance the vindication of their own worth, not only as scientists but as prospective healers of whatever ills might infect the body politic. Not all the hypotheses and theories can or need be presented here. Many of them, like Cesare Lombroso's (1835–1909) attribution of criminal behavior to innate organic defects, fit the data so poorly as to deserve no more than this passing word. Many other research reports are so narrowly focused on some specific type of misbehavior that they are properly passed over in a general and basic book like this one. Still others betray a bias against deviance, a fear of nonconformity which must be filtered out of a review that would nourish the promise of change. The paragraphs below therefore do no more than summarize the clearest and most plausible explanations sociologists have yet devised for the disorder in our experience. The summary is in three parts, corresponding to three sets of conditions or factors which breed behavior that seems strange.

CONFORMITY TO DEVIANT WAYS

Sociologists have enlarged our understanding of deviance first and foremost by pointing out that much of it is in fact conformity, but conformity to a deviant set of values and norms. Often enough, the person who defies role expectations does not do so independently, on his or her own initiative, but out of fidelity to contrary expectations learned and internalized in a different social context. This principle applies to deviance of both laudable and reprehensible kinds. The new employee who seems intensely creative and ingenious might not have much inventiveness at all, but only an ability to carry into a new workplace skills learned in previous employment or at school. Contrariwise, the immigrant who appears to be a cold-blooded murderer, having strangled publicly his sister's boyfriend, may just have performed a duty taught him in his native land, a brother's duty to avenge his sister's loss of virginity. Now the fact that much deviance is learned does not make it immune to reward or punishment. Employers grant raises and promotions, judges mete out sentences and fines, indeed all holders of authority respond to deviance in light and on behalf of the groups they respectively represent, mostly irrespective of the perpetrators' personal merit or blameworthiness. External explanations matter little in the face of judgment. They seem but lame excuses for villainous deeds or signs of modesty for heroic ones. The response an action gets depends on characteristics not of the actor but of the people responding. Yet for understanding the action itself, why it was taken in the first place, nothing deserves closer inspection than the career of learning in the actor's own past. Research has shown four contexts of previous learning to be especially important for understanding deviance in the present day.

four contexts for learning deviance: first, the ethnic group

First is the ethnic group, a subset of a national population bound together by a common culture, usually many centuries old. It can be thought of as a national society minus its own government and economy. Some ethnic groups (called *aboriginal* or *native*) formerly constituted autonomous societies, but their homelands were conquered and they themselves incorporated as minorities into the society of the conquering people. Examples are the Maori in New Zealand, the Quechua in Peru, and all the Eskimo and Indian tribes of Canada and the United States. Other ethnic groups are composed of foreign immigrants to a society and their descendants, so long as they resist complete assimilation and retain parts of their culture of origin. In a sense all Americans of non-WASP origin belong to an immigrant ethnic minority, since the political, economic, and legal foundation of the United States was laid by people of a culture different from theirs. But whether aboriginal or immigrant, the ethnic population's sense of peoplehood is realized not in a sovereign, autonomous structure of life but in distinctive subcultural attitudes, behaviors, and beliefs. Conformity to these ethnic ways constitutes deviance from the mainstream national culture. In the context of the United States one can cite the refusal to fight in war (a proscription taken for granted among the Amish and Mennonites), occasional public drunkenness (almost legitimate withdrawal in Ireland, Finland, and Bavaria), the poaching of fish and game (Indian tribes have

Conformity to one's own ethnic past is often enough to get a person labeled deviant in the powerful national societies of our time. (Omikron/Photo Researchers, Inc.)

their own rules in this respect), favoritism toward relatives in public life (a duty in most Mediterranean cultures), and of course, all kinds of exotic styles of cookery, clothing, architecture, music, and art. There are indeed few techniques of liberation anyone ever chooses which are not holdovers from an ethnic past or to which the person is not predisposed by cultural ancestry. Young militants of the Irish Republican Army made headlines round the world in 1981 with hunger strikes to the death against the British presence in Ulster. Yet a thousand years ago it was an Irish custom to fast outside the house of a neighbor by whom one felt aggrieved. Ethnicity allows no easy escape.

second, the family   A person's family of origin, the immediate domestic unit in which he or she was raised, is a second basic source of nonconformity. Everyday experience and common sense so amply confirm this point that belaboring it here is almost asking for a yawn. After all, parents and older siblings are the earliest models children have, and among their most intimate and enduring ones. Small wonder that so many of the great composers grew up in music-centered families, or that the children of common criminals disproportionately embark on lives of crime. Yet one task of sociology is to drive familiar lessons home by spelling them out in fresh and timely ways. This is what Richard Flacks did in the mid-1960s, in his research on Chicago youth.[5] Antiwar protests, civil rights demonstrations, and sit-ins for student power were common then and were often viewed as expressions of young citizens' dissent from the values their parents stood for. Flacks, however, hypothesized that perhaps student activists were only living out and practicing the very values they had been taught at home. He therefore interviewed fifty such activists, selected from the membership lists of radical organizations, along with fifty other students chosen at random from college directories. Then he interviewed the parents of students in both these samples. To all his respondents, students and parents alike, he asked the same set of questions abour moral and political values and attitudes. His findings confirmed afresh a lesson that is ages old. For on most indices, the student activists were more like their own parents than like the run-of-the-mill students picked from college directories. For example, 91 percent of the activists opposed the U.S. bombing of North Vietnam. So did 73 percent of their fathers. Only 27 percent of the nonactivists opposed the bombing; for their fathers the figure was 20 percent. The pattern was the same for other issues ranging from civil disobedience to socialized medicine. Indeed, in a memorable table Flacks showed that the students most willing to break with convention by dropping out of school or moving in with a friend of the opposite sex were those whose parents were unlikely to intervene if they did so. Flacks concluded that the student movement signified rebellion not so much against parents as against those aspects of American society that contradicted the values certain upper-middle-class parents had taught their daughters and sons. Dozens of other researchers have reached the same conclusion for other kinds of deviance. There is truth in the adage "Like father like son," even in efforts to do something new.

Learning happens most effectively in what the early sociologist Charles H. Cooley called primary groups—intimate, face-to-face associations in which the members are personally involved. After the family, the type of primary group Cooley talked most about was the peer group, an association defined by some identical role or status each member occupies. Classmates, playmates, roommates, workmates, and agemates are all examples, groups whose members think of themselves as buddies or partners. It is hardly surprising, then, that the third main *third, the peer group* setting wherein deviance is learned is the peer group. This context has been the focus of a long lineage of theories of juvenile delinquency and common crime. One of the first was Edwin H. Sutherland's theory of differential association, set forth in 1924 and refined through successive editions of his classic criminology text.[6] What he argued, in brief summary, was that prolonged friendly contact with people who condone some form of deviance makes one likely to behave in that particular deviant way. Sutherland used his theory in research on thieves and on white-collar criminals—people in respectable occupations who mislead customers, misrepresent products, pilfer funds, conceal information, take bribes, or otherwise violate established moral norms in the course of their work. Such misdeeds were shown to result at least in part from personal involvement in groups that considered the misdeeds acceptable. In a similar vein, numerous studies of delinquency document the peer groups to which delinquents look for justification of their vandalism, muggings, burglaries, and similar acts.[7] Articles and monographs detail the normative structures of diverse deviant subcultures: card sharks, prostitutes, bikers, nudists, embezzlers, and so on.[8] But it is not only the more routine kinds of deviance that rely on learning and reinforcement from peers. Research on sectarian and political movements shows that people seldom join simply out of independent reasoned conviction, but only after personal contact and involvement with committed members. In sum, a person's network of friends is an excellent predictor of whether he or she departs from convention, and of which way out of conventional life he or she is wont to choose.

fourth, the mass media

The fourth context for instruction in nonconformity, and the last in this overview, is of a different order than the ethnic minority, family, and peer group. It is not so much a kind of organization to which citizens may belong as an influence to which nearly all of them are subject in contemporary urban-industrial societies. For since about two centuries ago a new institution has been strengthening, in great part replacing relatives, friends, teachers, and the clergy as source of information and moral guidance. This institution is the mass media, comprising wire services and daily newspapers, popular magazines, motion pictures, trade paperbacks, and theme amusement parks, and above all the radio and television networks. Exposure to these media occupies hours of every day in the life of the average adult or child in today's Western world. Increasingly, moreover, in capitalist as in socialist societies, control of these media has become concentrated in fewer hands. It is not uncommon to find a single event, person, or story sensationalized at once in a movie, a book, a television series, newspaper stories, magazine articles, popular songs, and on T-shirts and toys as well. Readers may recall the international suspense in the summer of 1980 over the fictional question of who shot J. R., a lead character in a soap opera on TV. It would take a book larger than this one to review all the ways in which the people who control the media shape the lives of the rest of us. Here let me cite just one scholar's research on how one mass medium helps explain one vitally important kind of nonconformity. In painstaking research published in 1974, David P. Phillips showed that between 1947 and 1968 in the United States, the number of recorded suicides increased by as much as 12 percent in the month following front-page newspaper coverage of cases of suicide. The greater the publicity, moreover, the larger the increase in suicides.[9] Not content with this finding, Phillips wondered if many suicides induced by media publicity do not go unreported, committed discreetly as by causing one's car to crash. He therefore related the day-by-day incidence of automobile fatalities in California between 1966 and 1973 to the news of suicide in the state's two largest newspapers. Sure enough, he found that three days after a publicized suicide, automobile fatalities increased on average by 31 percent.[10] More of these deaths were from single-car crashes than usual, they occurred mainly in that part of the state where the suicide got the most coverage, and the victims tended to be similar in age to those whose suicides were publicized. What Phillips so carefully documented in the case of taking one's own life, of course, undoubtedly also applies to other forms of deviance—murder, assassination, robbery, as well as participation in all kinds of fads and social movements. The mass media, it appears, do more than decide what news citizens find out about. The media also help citizens decide what kind of news they themselves should try to make.

summary: seeing deviance in the context of conflicting groups

The disciplined study of where and how deviance is learned, a study that assuredly goes far beyond the few pages here, has the effect of making much disorder in our experience disappear. For so long as our attention remains fixed on some specific structure of behavior and belief, typically the dominant one in which we find ourselves, then the disorder we see and hear looks like deviance and nothing more. To the extent that we like the structure of focal interest, the disorder plaguing it is puzzling, unsettling, intriguing perhaps in some voyeuristic sense, but fundamentally noxious, objectionable, a fit target of moral crusades. To the extent that we resent the structure at hand, the disorder is exciting, promising, scary perhaps for the mystery in it, but still a fit object of applause, since it offers hope for something new. But in the perspective of the paragraphs above, disorderly conduct appears not very disorderly at all. It is revealed instead as nothing more than the expected performance of roles, but according to a different script from the one we first were thinking of. In the face of some deviant act, we neither hiss nor applaud but investigate how the actor has been conditioned to behave—by his or her ethnic heritage, family of origin, peer associations, the mass media, and whatever other socializing agents we can discern. And the farther our investigation proceeds, the less deviant the actor seems to be. The end result is a view of the world more adequate and complex, recognizing as it does the competing, conflicting structures and scripts that coexist in our experience. But it is a view of the world more sobering, too, for much of the surprise and mystery has been drained from it. Our awareness of the human person is enhanced, and our faith in freedom is reduced.

AROUSAL OF THE URGE TO INNOVATE

For all their explanatory worth, theories of deviance in terms of learned conformity do not fully satisfy our craving to understand. Their usefulness indeed seems to decline the more genuinely deviant are the actions beneath our gaze. Theories like those just reviewed may account fairly well for a wave of suicides, but how about the one with which the wave began? Principles of socialization may illuminate why monasteries and Hutterite colonies persist through time, but what gave countercultures like these their start? Modeling, suggestion, and imitation go farther toward explaining why a new product catches on than why it was initially conceived and made. In the case of social movements, we want to know not just why followers follow but why leaders lead. Everyday experience and still more the data of the past reveal that humans are not merely copycats. If they were, you and I would be as illiterate as everyone was a few millennia ago. But in fact change is real. No one can study how life was a few centuries or even decades ago without laughing at the notion that humans do only what they are taught. History may be heavy but it moves, and the question is why. For this motion through time, this incessant leaving of the past behind, is the truest kind of deviance, the kind that is our only proof and instrument of liberation. If we separate out all the novelty people pick up secondhand, how do we explain the novelty that remains? When the explanatory power of learning theories is spent, what do we do then?

explaining the novelty that is not second-hand

At this point people often abandon sociology and resort to religion or individual psychology. In the absence of a discernible model for someone's nonconformity the response comes easily: "She's gifted," "He is a prophet sent by God," "She just has the devil in her," "He's nuts," or "You're mean." Deviance is thereby chalked up to personal qualities independent of social influence. Newness, whether welcome or not, is considered a matter of will, luck, fate, chance, a diabolic curse or God-given grace, but in any case a phenomenon unprovoked by the conditions of life at hand. Established authorities and others loyal to the status quo often have this kind of conception of the leaders of radical movements for religious or political change.

They think that by eliminating the instigator, the ringleader, the crazed or wicked prophet from whom people are learning to misbehave, the offending movement will disappear. The strategy seldom works, as the killing of Jesus, Joseph Smith, Che Guevara, Martin Luther King, and many others demonstrates. We are thus better off admitting that when an individual innovates, and all the more when a movement for change breaks out, social forces are at work. Attempts at liberation are in part predictable, even when they are genuinely new. For history shows that they do not occur randomly. Some societies have endured almost unchanged for a thousand years. Others, England for one, have been seedbeds of all kinds of novelty, from technical invention to messianic sects. Some eras, like the late nineteenth century in the United States, offer lots of news. Others, like recent decades in the United States, offer mainly more of the same. Sociology by no means stops where innovation starts. A wealth of scholarship connects the act of stepping out of line to the social situation of the person stepping out.

I want to offer here just a single fundamental proposition in this regard, but I should note in preface that no list of material conditions, however detailed, can explain why people retreat and rebel. A businessman does not turn to drink just because his career is on the skids and his marriage on the rocks. Youth in the 1960s did not form communes in the backwoods of this continent because their society was impersonal, imperialistic, or corrupt. The epidemics of polio that used to occur do not explain why Jonas Salk invented his vaccine. No revolution ever stirred anywhere because people did not have enough to eat. It is not material circumstance that gives rise to dissidence but rather the relationship between material circumstance and what is going on in people's minds. The basic

the basic condition: when previous learning and present experience clash

proposition can be formulated as follows: what arouses people's urge to break with convention and innovate is a clash between what they have been taught and what they find in their experience. A businessman who took for granted that his career would advance and his marriage prosper may indeed become a drunk when they do not. Youth who learned personal autonomy at home but then encountered draft boards and academic bureaucrats after moving away from home often enough did "freak out." A society plagued by disease but confident that disease can be rubbed out will surely produce scientists as imaginative as Salk. And when poor people by whatever means become convinced that they should not be so, there is trouble in the wind. These are cases not of mechanical response to objective social ills, nor of learned conformity to deviant ways. They are cases of confusion, unsettledness, of a perception that the world is crazy and mixed up, that things are not making sense. This state, which Durkheim labeled anomie and for which he saw little use, is the necessary source of creativity and change. It is what makes people feel discontented, restless, and ready to exercise the freedom that is theirs.

Humans are not free and cannot innovate except insofar as they feel torn between opposing ways of life to which they have been exposed. They must see in the conventional routine a problematic quality, a quality that comes only from friendly contact with some alternative. Now obviously, most people in most societies even now, and all the more in premodern societies of the past, go to their graves untouched by the instability such exposure and contact bring. In the summer of 1965, some classmates and I moved into the black ghetto of a segregated Southern town to launch a program of community development in cooperation with a local black minister. Being anxious to enlist the support of whites as well, we visited the city fathers. Sitting on the broad, cool veranda of his home, one of them explained to us in all sincerity, "There is no racial problem in this town; we've got good niggers here." This is the mentality of those who have never known or felt inclined toward anything but the status quo. Things just are the way they are. One may be vaguely aware that things are different elsewhere, but elsewhere is an alien, dangerous land. The ideology of one's own society explains alternatives away—as enemies (think of how Russia is envisioned in the United States) or as inferiors (think of how the United States is regarded in France). Not even traveling abroad guarantees the kind of exposure and contact that jar one's commitment to the way of life back home. Tourists often shrink fearfully from native hotels, restaurants, and other services, preferring those which guarantee, as the Holiday Inn company has advertised, "no surprises." Yet today as in the past, reluctantly at first and later eagerly, some people do find themselves caught between the rock of the society at hand and the hard place of some alternative cherished deep inside. Not all the conditions that breed such novelty-inducing tension can be listed here, much less described in depth. But a capsule list of ten can at least summarize what research has shown. Readers might want to rate themselves on these ten indices, to gauge their own susceptibility to creative deviance.

Migration.[11] To move far away but with one's family and to friends, school, workplace, occupation, church, neighborhood, and ethnic associations much like the ones left behind, is an onerous but not jarring experience. It may even confirm the goodness of a status quo spread over so large a space. But to migrate, especially alone, to an alien environment full of people with strange ways, and to be forced to integrate oneself—that is the kind of move that sets the mind working inventively. Mental illness, cults and sects, entrepreneurship in business enterprise, and collective uprisings for political change are all more common among people who have pulled up stakes and settled in some markedly different locale.

Membership in a deprived class.[12] The elite classes of a society are not prone to think critical thoughts. From the top of the structure of rewards, the world tends to look remarkably reasonable and just. The same goes for the middle classes, the ones looking toward the top. And the same for the lower classes, too, in static, traditional societies where the poor think God wills their poverty. But in dynamic, modern societies, those whose ideologies proclaim that everyone can get ahead, the citizens left behind perennially show discontent. Their everyday experience conflicts with the ethic preached to them. Crime rates are higher in the lower strata, even laying aside the fact that lower-class crooks are more likely to be caught and penalized. Rates of mental illness are higher, too. So also the appeal of unconventional religious movements, at least in North America. In England the lower strata of the working class are less radical religiously, more so politically.

Class mobility.[13] Even within a single society, each class inhabits very much a separate world, with its own values, manners, tastes, folkways, and routine of daily life. To edge one's way up in the class hierarchy by no means undermines a person's faith in the way things are. This is the standard expectation in today's Western world. But people who suddenly, incomprehensibly go from rags to riches or, what is worse, from riches to rags—they are people to watch out for. Their exposure to conflicting styles of life raises questions in their minds and nourishes a sense of uncertainty.

Intermarriage.[14] A marriage between people of the same racial, national, linguistic, ethnic, class, religious, and geographic backgrounds tends to reinforce in both the spouses and their children a stable, coherent set of values and beliefs. Conformity is the probable result. But the more different in these respects the marriage partners are, the less can be taken for granted in their domestic life. Not only the spouses but also the children of marriages mixed in some respect are more likely to feel the urge to experiment and to venture out along untried paths.

Social dislocation.[15] Idleness, so the saying goes, is the devil's workshop. It may also be God's, depending on whether one welcomes or deplores the content of the resultant deviance. In every society people who are out of gear and have time on their hands drift easily into the contemplation of nonconformity. Youth are the best example, especially those who have left their parent's home and are not yet tied down to houses, marriages, children, and occupations of their own. Currently in the United States, persons between 18 and 24 years old account for roughly twice the percentage of criminal arrests as of the adult population. Other examples of social dislocation include workers who have lost their jobs or who have recently retired, housewives with much wealth and few responsibilities, and veterans recently returned from military service. People in situations like these easily fall prey to depression, drug use, and other forms of individual withdrawal, and they are also prime candidates for membership in dissident movements of whatever kind.

Jewish identity.[16] To be raised as one of Yahweh's chosen people implies an anxiety and rootlessness, an estrangement from conventional life no Christian in the Occident can share. Fundamentally, Western history has not made sense to Jews for the last 2000 years. A tiny minority of barely 1 percent of the Western population, they have continued to wait for a messiah whom nearly everyone else believes has already come. Until 1948, moreover, they had no place to wait but in the homelands of Christian and Islamic peoples who persecuted them steadily. The constant contradiction of living as a Jew in a world dominated by Christians is the best explanation for why Jews have made such vastly disproportionate contributions to social change. Not only in commerce and economic enterprise but in philosophy, social reform, music, literature—in virtually every field one can name.

Liberal schooling.[17] There is much less truth than is commonly thought in the idea that advanced schooling makes one critical and disposed to creative thought. The norms of professional training, as explained in the preceding chapter, indeed encourage docility, conformity, and loyalty to conventional economic and political structures. Schooling of a liberal or humanistic kind, however, often has the contrary effect. Studying history, anthropology, mathematics, languages, art, and similar subjects (sociology not least) can be a means of distancing oneself from the society at hand and of seeing it in a larger perspective that includes alternatives. The result is growth of a sense of self that transcends the boundaries of one's own place and time. This in turn kindles a willingness to tamper with the status quo and try to improve on it. University students have been in the forefront of most social protests ever since universities began. The same will be true in coming years, so long as nonprofessional programs and courses continue to be taught.

Intellectual occupations.[18] For the same reason as students are inclined to be malcontents, so are people whose jobs consist mainly of studying, reflecting, writing, teaching—working, that is, in the world of ideas. University professors, journalists, teachers, ministers of religion, artists, musicians, researchers and planners of various kinds, architects, editors, novelists, and actors are all examples. They are people predisposed by occupation to the creation and entertainment of new ideas, especially when their administrative tasks are few. If *right* means love for the status quo and *left* means fickleness, people with careers like these fall disproportionately on the left.

A *diverse environment*.[19] To live surrounded by people like oneself is the surest means of keeping in check one's urge to innovate. A closed, agrarian little community left to itself can persist unchanged for centuries. Sameness breeds more of the same, while diversity stimulates innovation of all kinds. That is the importance of cities like Hong Kong, Paris, or New York, places where disparate languages, aromas, costumes, ideas, and purposes mingle in the streets. Crime is common in cities like these, and so is loneliness. Bizarre cults flourish. Political schemes, however improbable, attract ardent followers. But from such cities has come also most of the novelty people elsewhere are now grateful for. Diversity, of course, is not ensured by urban residence. Some urban and suburban neighborhoods are almost as homogeneous as primitive tribes. And a small-town youth who makes friends with outsiders can be aroused to unheard-of mischief.

Catastrophe.[20] Citizens in every social context assume for practical purposes that it will endure forever, or at least that its evolution will be orderly and indigenous. A catastrophe is a sudden challenge to that assumption, a crumbling of all that was before sturdy and secure. If the catastrophe is natural and brief, like an earthquake or typhoon, people usually grieve for a while and then return to their accustomed ways. But if it is humanly caused and long-lasting, as when Europeans descended upon tribes in the South Pacific and the Americas, ripping the fabric of custom irretrievably apart, novel forms of rebellion and withdrawal are a common consequence. Anthropologists have written much about the exotic social movements that have arisen in such situations, calling them variously cargo cults, millennial and revitalization movements.

Here ends the list of conditions that arouse the urge to innovate. It could be longer but there is hardly need, since all the circumstances named are but variations on the basic one: a clash between the structure of life at hand and an opposing structure to which one feels attached. Scholars have discussed this predicament in a variety of terms. Georg Simmel wrote an essay about a type of person he called the *stranger*. Robert Park (1864–1944), an influential sociologist at the University of Chicago, conceptualized a type he called the *marginal man*. Marginality in Park's sociology resembles in some respects what Marx called *alienation*, what Durkheim labeled *anomie*, and what other scholars have described as *angst, stress,* or *structural strain*. For present purposes the distinctions among these terms matter less than the theme running through them, the feeling of having one foot in and one foot out of what is going on. It is from this emotional and mental state that unlearned innovation springs. A new idea does not strike quite like a flash of light or a bolt of lightning from a clear blue sky. It happens along only after one's very self has been jostled by incongruous experiences. But I should repeat here finally that the resultant nonconformity, the assertion of freedom in some act of deviance, is only rarely welcomed, indeed only rarely something of which the actor later on feels proud. Probably the single most common nonconformity is withdrawal into oneself, personal malaise wherein one feels unable to do anything

the stranger, the marginal man

worthwhile. Few people whose inventions, prophecies, original art, or progressive leadership have brought them fame did not often feel despair. Perhaps it takes a lot of people deviating in unproductive ways for one or two of them just occasionally to make history.

OUTLETS FOR DISCONTENT

Although acquaintance with contrasting ways of life arouses the urge to liberate oneself from the way of life at hand, the question remains of what form the attempt at liberation will assume. Will the marginal scientist invent a cure for cancer or commit suicide? Will the stranger write a wondrous book or lapse into chronic drunkenness? Will widespread alienation breed a reformist movement that advances history or some irrational crusade that sets it back? Questions like these to a great extent define the limits of empirical knowledge. There is no sure way of knowing beforehand whether deviance will be to good or bad effect. Innovation necessarily implies uncertainty and risk. Whoever would rule out all but beneficial nonconformity must rule out all of it. No sociologist nor anyone can forecast precisely how people will respond to the angst or stress they feel inside. That is part of the enchanting mystery of life. Yet even in this regard sociological research has yielded some relevant principles, with a few of which this section on the origins of deviance can conclude. These principles reflect the more general one offered in early chapters of this book, that we humans cannot walk except from where we stand. Creative energy, this is to say, is drawn to whatever outlets or opportunities are available. The way people deviate depends on how they are equipped by their past experience and present environment. Now some applications of this principle are just common sense. A society where the wheel is unknown can hardly progress to novel kinds of machinery. A person who has no training in carpentry nor any tools cannot build a conventional house, much less a new and unusual one. A person who cannot read and write is deprived of all expressions of creativity that involve the written word. But some applications of the basic rule are less commonly recognized. The paragraphs below present three of them.

three principles: first, people withdraw when they cannot attack

Perhaps the most important is that those forms of liberation grouped under the label of withdrawal occur mainly in the absence of resources required for attacks upon the status quo and the making of some kind of change. Discontented people do not opt out of history unless they lack the means of redirecting it. They forswear donkey power unless deprived of power in its more uniquely human forms. Sleeping on the job, daydreaming, loafing, drug use, suicide, and indeed sectarian and countercultural religious activity are not first-choice alternatives. They are what people do when they cannot make a difference in the world confronting them. Women, for example, whose power on the whole is less than men's and whose opportunities are fewer, are vastly underrepresented in those forms of liberation classified as attacks. They are about five times less likely than men to be arrested for crime. Their participation in political movements (excepting, of course, those which concern the status of women) is generally less common. They account for much less invention and innovative scholarship than men. About the only forms of liberation equally or more evident in the female half of contemporary populations are mental illness and involvement in deviant cults and sects. In this respect women resemble black Americans and members of some other minorities deprived of economic and political outlets for their creative energies. Or to cite a different example, it appears that the incidence of retreatist forms of deviance declines in most societies during periods of political upheaval and civil unrest—as in contemporary Northern Ireland. Given a chance to become involved in movements for transforming public life, people tend not to withdraw into private worlds. There is thus cause for serious concern in the increasing popularity during recent decades in North America of drunkenness, marijuana use, drug dependency, and escapist entertainment. Cause for concern also in the growth, discussed earlier in Chapter Seven, of dogmatic sectarian denominations. These trends, especially obvious among youth, signify a decline of opportunity and the frustration of citizens' desires for social change.

second, signs of softening invite attack

But if the sealing off of opportunities for social change encourages withdrawal, signs of softening, vulnerability, or flexibility in prevailing political structures invite attack. This is a second instance of how the status quo conditions the forms attempts at liberation take. Aroused, enlightened citizens tend not to waste a chance to go on the offensive and innovate politically. Alexis de Tocqueville observed as much already in 1856, in his effort to explain why the French Revolution occurred when it did. He could see from the historical record that this collective attack came during a period of increasing freedom and prosperity. This puzzling fact led de Tocqueville to the formulation of a classic hypothesis: "For it is not always when things are going from bad to worse that revolutions break out. On the contrary, it often happens that when a people which has put up with an oppressive rule over a long period without protest suddenly finds the government relaxing its pressure, it takes up arms against it. . . . The most perilous moment for a bad government is one when it seeks to mend its ways."[21] The French scholar's insight has far-reaching relevance. During the 1960s, departments of sociology were the target of far more than their share of university-student protests. Part of the explanation is that sociology professors and department chairs were more flexible, vulnerable, and open to change than their colleagues in other disciplines. Or again, the Roman Catholic hierarchy has faced more angry dissent from priests, nuns, and lay Catholics since the Second Vatican Council of 1962–1965 than in the preceding hundred years. One major reason is the council's own program of reform, its relaxation of the church's image of unalterable immutability. It seems hardly fair that rigid, oppressive, tyrannical elites, the ones that treat change as unthinkable, encounter less dissidence than those more willing to experiment and more accepting of creative thought. History in some respects is cruel.

third, the available tools condition how people misbehave

One final and quite different implication of the principle of differential opportunity concerns the tools required for certain undeniably harmful kinds of nonconformity. Three examples are of pressing interest in North America, given how common they have become during the last twenty years. The first is homicide, the rates for which have nearly doubled in both the United States and Canada since 1960 (though the Canadian rates are still only about half those in the United States). Why murder takes place is a complex question but one thing is clear: to be attempted with reasonable prospect of success, the crime requires a tool. One of the main reasons for the increase in homicide is undoubtedly the mass production and widespread purchase, especially in the United States, of the most effective murder

FOR EXAMPLE

Jo Freeman's Study of How Women Mobilized*

In this final break from the routine of chapters in this book, an article by political scientist Jo Freeman in the *American Journal of Sociology* can command our attention with two good effects. The first is to recall and amplify a point made hundreds of pages ago in Chapter Two, that the most useful research technique in sociology is the handiest, least costly, and least arcane: disciplined reflection on data at one's own fingertips. Freeman wrote her insightful analysis of the women's movement mainly from her own working experience within it. Here is how she described her method of research.

As a founder and participant in the younger branch of the Chicago women's liberation movement from 1967 through 1969 and editor of the first (at that time, only) national newsletter, I was able, through extensive correspondence and interviews, to keep a record of how each group around the country first started, where the organizers got the idea, who they had talked to, what conferences were held and who attended, the political affiliations (or lack of them) of the first members etc. Although I was a member of Chicago NOW [National Organization for Women], information on the origins of it and the other older branch organizations comes entirely through ex post facto interviews of the principals and examination of early papers.

Beyond illustrating that ingenuity counts for more than money in the research enterprise, Freeman's study is also of substantive worth. What it shows is that the women's movement did not arise simply from discontent or even from shared commitment to reform. Its origin lies also in the availability to women in the late 1960s of resources for large-scale mobilization, resources which they could seize in reaction to concrete precipitating crises. Freeman's three general conditions for the formation of social movements merit quoting.

Proposition 1: The need for a preexisting communications network or infrastructure within the social base of a movement is a primary requisite for "spontaneous" activity. Masses alone don't form movements, however discontented they may be. Groups of previously unorganized individuals may spontaneously form into small local associations—usually along the lines of informal social networks—in response to a specific strain or crisis, but if they are not linked in some manner, the protest does not become generalized: it remains a local irritant or dissolves completely. If a movement is to spread rapidly, the communications network must already exist. If only the rudiments of one exist, movement formation requires a high input of "organizing" activity.

Proposition 2: Not just any communications network will do. It must be a network that is co-optable to the new ideas of the incipient movement. To be co-optable, it

*Jo Freeman, "The Origins of the Women's Liberation Movement", *American Journal of Sociology* **78**:792–811 (1973). Quotations by permission of the author. Dr. Freeman has recently completed her law degree at New York University.

must be composed of like-minded people whose background, experiences, or location in the social structure make them receptive to the ideas of a specific new movement.

Proposition 3: Given the existence of a co-optable communications network, or at least the rudimentary development of a potential one, and a situation of strain, one or more precipitants are required. Here two distinct patterns emerge that often overlap. In one, a crisis galvanizes the network into spontaneous action in a new direction. In the other, one or more persons begin organizing a new organization or disseminating a new idea. For spontaneous action to occur, the communications network must be well formed or the initial protest will not survive the incipient stage. If it is not well formed, organizing efforts must occur; that is, one or more persons must be skilled and must have a fertile field in which to work.

In the context of these general statements, the core of Freeman's article is an analysis of the two main branches of the women's liberation movement, the one best embodied in NOW and the other composed of younger, more radical feminists, Both branches, Freeman argues, grew out of preexisting communications networks. The National Commission on the Status of Women appointed by President Kennedy in 1961, and the fifty state commissions associated with it, put into contact many of the women who would later join Betty Friedan in establishing NOW. The meetings, conferences, and protests of the campus-based youth movement of the late 1960s drew together dissident women who would later organize as feminist activists. Both these communications networks, moreover, were co-optable to the ideas of the women's movement, predisposed to its purposes—unlike such conventional organizations as the Business and Professional Women's Clubs. Finally, Freeman points to key crises that galvanized feminist opinion and precipitated efforts to organize. A major stimulus to the formation of NOW was the Equal Employment Opportunity Commission's refusal to enforce the provisions of the 1964 Civil Rights Act against sexual discrimination. Mobilization of younger women was prompted by a series of flagrantly sexist public statements by male leaders of the New Left. In light of factors like these, the women's movement is revealed not as a sudden burst of anger out of nowhere but as an organized effort possible only because resources and precipitants for mobilization were at hand.

By reviewing earlier research on social movements and imaginatively relating to it the data of her own experience, Freeman reinforced a fundamental social truth. Effective spontaneity is never altogether spontaneous. Historical moments are never quite discrete. The social movements that get results build on communication networks already in place, networks receptive to the new ideas and usable by organizers when critical events occur. Nothing new and special is made except with old and ordinary tools.

"Why murder takes place is a complex question but one thing is clear: to be attempted with reasonable prospect of success, the crime requires a tool. One of the main reasons for the increase in homicide is undoubtedly the mass production and widespread purchase, especially in the United States, of the most effective murder weapon ever invented, the handgun. Simple, portable, concealable, cheap, and quick, it is the instrument by which about two-thirds of murders are done." (Christopher S. Johnson/Stock, Boston)

weapon ever invented, the handgun. Simple, portable, concealable, cheap, and quick, it is the instrument by which about two-thirds of murders are done. No one can say by how much the murder rates would fall if the public sale and possession of handguns were prevented by law. In that minority of murderers who premeditate the act, some would surely find another instrument. Perhaps the rates would fall by only a third, perhaps by half. The important point is that tools make a difference. The same point applies to drunkenness, arrests for which nearly tripled through the 1970s for youth under the age of 18. One reason for this increase is almost certainly the lowering of the drinking age in most jurisdictions just before or during the same decade, forcing downward the age at which a boy or girl can legally or illegally get access to alcohol. Still a third noxious kind of deviance is addiction to such narcotic drugs as heroin or cocaine. Not only is addiction destructive of the addict, but the need to feed a habit accounts for a substantial proportion of crimes against property and persons in American cities. Just as drunkenness assumes the presence of alcohol, so drug addiction requires a supply of drugs. No program to combat drug abuse holds even a tenth the promise of one which would break up the highly profitable organizations which import, manufacture, and distribute drugs throughout the United States. Now to be sure, other factors are involved in the increase in homicide, adolescent drunkenness, drug addiction, and related crimes than the

*section summary:
freedom rules a very
small domain*

mere availability of the means for deviating in these particular ways. But the fact is that humans under stress take advantage of whatever tools their environment affords for reducing stress. A society that on the one hand heightens stress and on the other hand permits the proliferation of destructive tools for relieving it cannot expect to prosper.

Whether the deviance we confront delights or distresses us, we humans persistently attribute it to somebody's willfulness and discount the extent to which the situation invited this particular deviant act. It is a technique for flattering ourselves. If we need a hero we say something like, "She would not have kept silent even if she had had to go to jail for speaking out." If we want a villain we insist, "He would have found a way to kill his wife even if he hadn't had the gun." Long bookshelves lined with works of sociology militate against such facile explanation of nonconformity. The paragraphs above suggest that the likelihood of a term in jail, the availability of a gun, and thousands of other aspects of the opportunity structure in a person's milieu make a huge difference in what kind of deviance, good or bad, he or she enacts. This point supplements the two made earlier in this section, that much deviance is simply learned conformity to deviant ways, and that more genuine deviance depends on exposure to conflicting ways of life. The effect of this section, if it has presented well the results of relevant research, is to narrow further the domain of freedom. With the perspective and hypotheses given here, readers should be able to look at deviant actions, their own or other people's, and reflect systematically on how little freedom those actions embody. They should be able to search back into a deviant person's past and discern the ethnic, familial, peer, and other influences which taught and reinforced behavior that in the context at hand seems deviant. They can investigate the eye-opening, incongruous experiences that have stimulated the person's ability to innovate. And they can inspect the particular outlets for restlessness that inhere in his or her environment. Such an exercise need not breed despair. There still is room for willfulness. However complete the explanations of today, tomorrow still will come. Tomorrow people like you and me will strain beneath the burden of free choice, and some of them will surprise the status quo. Their surprises will be happier if they remember how unfree they are.

Concluding Words

*how traditional societies
dealt with deviance*

Now that the forms of liberation have been outlined and their social origin discussed, one last question needs to be addressed—summarily, of course, as have been all the topics in this chapter and indeed in this book. The question is what to do with deviance. Given everything we know about people's ability to innovate, what are the possible ways of handling it? The answer given and institutionalized in traditional societies was to squelch that ability. Those little communities were depressingly homogeneous. Everybody spoke the same language, ate much the same foods, wore similar clothes, worshipped the same gods, and did similar kinds of work. Everyday life reinforced the ways in which human minds were set. Nor did people have much acquaintance with alternatives. Everything outside one's own locale was enemy territory—foreign, alien, dangerous, and out of bounds. Having almost no empirical knowledge of the past, people thought the past and present were alike, and so would the future be. The situation was not one that jostled the mind or aroused creative energies. Yet people did occasionally engage in deviance, and when they did the wrath of gods and humans fell upon them. For by cultural definition deviance was wickedness. Superhuman forces were believed to have ordained the status quo and appointed those ruling it. This was the truth. All else was error, and error had no rights. Only a bad ruler would give his people opportunities to experiment or act upon the few stirrings of pride they might feel within themselves. There was not in most such communities even the idea of freedom. Miscreants were thought to be ill starred or diabolically possessed. When in the Judeo-Christian era an ethic of freedom did evolve, it was an ethic that posed two alternatives: knuckle under and be saved or deviate and be damned. Not just be damned but also stoned, crucified, hanged, pilloried, shunned, or otherwise paid in an earthly way the wages of sin. Only by seizing charismatic power, as described earlier in Chapter Five, might a person get by with deviance. But it was deviance without self-consciousness.

the classic American way of handling deviance

For a contrasting example of how a society can handle deviance, there is no better choice than the United States of America in the late nineteenth century. This society was equally as much a sociocultural system as traditional societies had been. There were laws, norms, customs, and a discernible difference between deviance and conformity. But here was a case where deviance, acting out in strange new ways, was counted a virtue. Or to make the same point differently, conformity to American values was understood to imply openness to nonconformity. By the liberal theory of government, every male citizen was entitled to vote and even to run for public office, no matter how bizarre his politics might be. Everyone was allowed to own property and to do with it what he pleased, whether this made sense to anyone else or not. The rules of capitalism, as described in the latter half of Chapter Six, rewarded those who delighted their compatriots with new things to buy, and punished those who clung to economic practices that progress had rendered out of date. The weight of culture was on the side of individual human rights, above all the right to conjure up a new idea and try to convince others of its worth. This was the meaning of the freedoms laid down in the Bill of Rights: freedom to speak error if one thought it true, to worship false gods if one believed in them, to print absurdities in magazines and books, and to gather friends for discussion of tomfoolery. The Constitution made it hard for the courts to crack down even on murderers, thieves, and others whose deviance was clearly intolerable. Anyone accused of breaking a law was held to be innocent until proven guilty. No one, however obviously guilty of some heinous crime, could be punished for it if in an initial trial he or she had mistakenly been judged innocent. But deviance was encouraged not only by the political, economic, and judicial frameworks. Everyday life had the same stimulating effect. Immigrants were streaming into the land. A walk through New York, Philadelphia, Chicago, or St. Louis was like a tour through all the disparate countries of Europe. Vestiges of traditionalism remained, of course, notably in the restrictions placed on women and black citizens. But it would be hard to find in history any society where the rules were looser, the restrictions fewer, or the opportunities for deviance more numerous than the United States about one century ago. Other societies of the

in the nineteenth century, the United States provoked lots of the deviance that helps

liberal-capitalist world were similar but not quite so free of traditional inhibitions.

American society got the deviance it asked for. Much of it was detestable: the fraud, larceny, brigandage, assaults, and murders done not only by outlaws on the frontier and immigrants in city slums but by captains of industry intent on getting rich. Then as now, the United States was a world leader in crime. But common crime was not the only form of liberation in which Americans engaged. In local communities and nationwide, citizens' movements of all kinds fought over the issues of the day. There were campaigns to persecute blacks and to grant them equal rights, to preserve immigrants' ethnic identities and to assimilate them to WASP values, to get children into school and to keep them out of school. Collective bargaining in industry, temperance, women's suffrage, child labor, and all manner of other issues got citizens involved. But most important, the era was what has been called the heroic age of American invention. Entrepreneurs all across the land were steadily inventing things. Traveling salesmen were thinking up new lines by which to peddle wares their customers had never seen before. Farmers eagerly adopted whatever new machines might help them increase production and thus stay in business. Proprietors in every sector of commerce and industry were thinking hard to come up with ways of eliminating their competitors. In sum, the United States was a place that not only compelled creativity but provided outlets for it that on the whole enhanced the quality of citizens' lives. Immigrants would not have poured into the United States, and to a lesser extent other societies of the New World, had they not seen here the promise of being free to innovate and of enjoying the innovative fruits of the freedom of their compatriots. They were willing to put up with the deviance that hurts for the sake of the deviance that helps.

Resolving the question of how to handle deviance would be easy if the choice were between any traditional society and late nineteenth-century America. For by now in history we are aware of the human power to innovate and we know that it is good. But for us the choice is not between old alternatives. The United States, indeed all the Western world, has changed. In a material sense it has improved, at least until very recent years. Life spans have lengthened and the standard of living has in general gone up. But in the provision of opportunities for people to deviate in beneficial ways, our whole civilization seems to have declined. The process of monopolization of capital has deprived most citizens of ownership of productive property. Few have the chance to innovate in their work. Most have jobs described in policy manuals written by committees somewhere out of sight. Nor does the consumption side of the economy give one much chance for originality. Today's consumer seldom negotiates with the manufacturer over the shape or style of some economic good. Even haggling over the price has become exceptional. Consumers must simply choose between prepackaged goods whose prices are fixed. The occasion to make some creative difference in the world comes to fewer and fewer citizens. Yet the value on creativity persists. People still feel the restlessness of modern times. The persistence of this feeling in the absence of legitimate opportunities for doing something about it is probably the single best explanation for increases in so many hurtful kinds of deviance. It is as if we teach our children to be go-getters but offer them nowhere to go except to shopping malls and employment agencies. Then when they misbehave we send them to some kind of specialist for a diagnosis of their "behavior problem."

the present problem: shrinkage of opportunity

Beyond the shrinkage of opportunity that has come with capitalist development, we today are in trouble on another count. We are not as naive as our ancestors a

a further problem: despondency

century ago. They knew enough history to be convinced of the virtue of their way of life, but not so much as to raise doubts. A sociologist like William Graham Sumner could analyze with illuminating detachment religions and polities other than his own, but Christian America was in a class by itself. It was generally believed that God or fate had willed Europeans' conquest of the Americas and the civilization they had planted here. It was a matter of the progress or evolution of the human race. Capitalism was considered not just a development strategy but the natural strategy. Christianity was not one religion among many but the true one. To us such certainties are denied. Noncapitalist and non-Christian peoples all over the world have shown that they can make change too, sometimes better change than we. Every drop of acid rain, every breath of polluted air, every thought of nuclear war makes us wonder if our own achievements have not boomeranged. Perhaps worst of all, sociology and the other social sciences have made us feel smaller than our ancestors felt. In some respects we are glad for external, historical explanations of ourselves, but they make our steps into the future hesitant. Whatever we do or think, we wonder whether it is not just an instance of some scientist's general rule. Awareness shakes our confidence.

That this problem, too, is soluble is the premise beneath all the pages of this book. Retrogression is possible but not assured. If we put our minds and hands to the task, we will find a way of organizing ourselves that gives all and each of us the chance to become more than we are. Humans have outdone themselves before. So can we in our time and place. That is the faith with which Karl Polanyi closed his masterwork:

Karl Polanyi's promise

Resignation was ever the fount of man's strength and new hope. Man accepted the reality of death and built the meaning of his bodily life upon it. He resigned himself to the truth that he had a soul to lose and that there was worse than death, and founded his freedom upon it. He resigns himself, in our time, to the reality of society which means the end of that freedom. But, again, life springs from ultimate resignation. Uncomplaining acceptance of the reality of society gives man indomitable courage and strength to remove all removable injustice and unfreedom. As long as he is true to his task of creating more abundant freedom for all, he need not fear that either power or planning will turn against him and destroy the freedom he is building by their instrumentality. This is the meaning of freedom in a complex society; it gives us all the certainty that we need.[22]

For Reflection

conformity	collective withdrawal
deviance	sectarian religion
forms of liberation	countercultures
individual withdrawal	individual attack
drunkenness	invention
drug addiction	prophecy
psychosis	collective attack
suicide	collective behavior

fads, crazes	marginality
social movements	stress
reform versus revolution	migration
common crime	class mobility
learning deviance	social dislocation
ethnic group	Jewish identity
primary group	intellectuals
deviant subcultures	catastrophe
mass media	the principle of differential opportunity
incongruous experience	gun control
anomie	tradition
the stranger	human rights
alienation	freedom

For Making Connections

With Chapter One: In which approach to sociology would you think deviance is looked upon more favorably, a positivist approach or some humanist one?
To what extent do you think sociological and psychological outlooks on deviance complement one another, and to what extent do they conflict?

With Chapter Two: One part of this chapter spelled out a conceptual scheme for the study of deviance, while another part offered propositions. Which parts were they? Could one have been written without the other? Explain your answer.
The hypothesis that the experience of catastrophe stimulates various kinds of nonconformity can be applied to both societal and individual levels of analysis. How would your techniques differ between tests of this hypothesis at these two levels?

With Chapter Three: How does the distribution of power, wealth, and honor differ between a static society and one where there is lots of innovation and change?
Must a sociologist observe and analyze some sociocultural system in order to understand withdrawal from and attacks upon it? Why or why not?

With Chapter Four: In what ways has the present chapter confirmed or qualified the research reviewed in connection with what was called the dimension of humility?
Who has more cause for pride, a person who generally conforms to the social order at hand or one who often deviates?

With Chapter Five: How do conditions that give rise to political kinds of dissidence differ from those that stimulate religious or countercultural dissent?
How does the response to nonconformity differ between traditional and legal-rational forms of government? How about between liberal and socialist forms of government?

With Chapter Six: How does capitalism encourage deviance? What kind of nonconformity does this strategy of development favor?

What connection would you suggest between the trend toward monopolization of capital and crime rates in the United States?

With Chapter Seven: What implications do you find in Gary Marx's study of black religion and civil rights militancy for the more general relationship between churchgoing and deviance in contemporary societies?

Recent studies in North America have found that in many respects ministers and priests are more activist and reform-minded than the members of their congregations. How would you explain this finding?

With Chapter Eight: Which kind of family organization would you expect encourages nonconformity more, a unilineal system or one based on bilateral descent? Strict rules of endogamy or loose ones? The extended family in domestic life or the nuclear family?

Do the perspectives in this final chapter help explain why the sexual revolution has occurred? If so, how?

With Chapter Nine: Which kind of school is more likely to produce graduates willing to try something new, one founded on the font-of-knowledge view of education or one that takes a dialectical approach? Explain.

Which students in today's colleges and universities would you expect to be more inclined to deviance and innovation, those studying in professional programs or those taking liberal-arts programs?

For Further Reading

This chapter draws on theory and research in a variety of subfields of sociology and related disciplines, especially on literature in criminology, deviant behavior, collective behavior, social movements, and social change. The list below offers a smattering of good books from these too often separated fields.

1 John Hagan, *The Disreputable Pleasures*, McGraw-Hill Ryerson, Toronto, 1977. There is a static, sybaritic cast to the title and perspective of this book, but it remains an excellent text on crime and delinquency. It is carefully and thoughtfully written, and Hagan's deviants are livelier and more human than those of most criminologists. The author is a very reputable professor at the University of Wisconsin.

2 Ian Taylor, P. Walton, and J. Young, *The New Criminology: For a Social Theory of Deviance*, Routledge & Kegan Paul, Boston, 1973. A reasoned call by three British sociologists for more attention to politics and less to individual pathology in the explanation of crime and deviance. If one measure of a book's worth is how stridently it is denounced, then this book is worthy indeed. For a critique of the new criminology see David Downes and Paul Rock (eds.), *Deviant Interpretations*, Robertson, 1979.

3 Richard Quinney, *The Social Reality of Crime*, Little, Brown, Boston, 1970, and later works. An exceedingly balanced and thoughtful theory of what constitutes crime by a sociologist now at Brown University. Quinney relates the conceptions of crime propagated by elites to the incidence of criminal behavior and to criminals' own self-conceptions.

4 Edwin Lemert, *Human Deviance, Social Problems and Social Control*, Prentice-Hall, Englewood Cliffs, N.J., 1967, and Thomas Scheff, *Being Mentally Ill: A Sociological Theory*, Aldine, 1966. Two works that explain the importance of others' reactions to a person's persistence in some kind of deviant behavior. The implication, widely discussed in sociology during the last decade, is that once a person is labeled as some kind of deviant (like "bad boy" or "schizophrenic"), the label itself acts to encourage the person to continue the deviant mode of conduct.

5 Ralph Turner and Lewis M. Killian, *Collective Behavior*, Prentice-Hall, Englewood Cliffs, N.J., 1972, and Neil J. Smelser, *The Theory of Collective Behavior*, Free Press, New York, 1962. Two of the standard general theories of why humans come together and set off in new directions.

6 John Wilson, *Introduction to Social Movements*, Basic, New York, 1973. A lucid and intelligent text centered on the most important form of collective behavior. One of the standard related anthologies is Joseph R. Gusfield, *Protest, Reform and Revolt: A Reader in Social Movements*, Wiley, New York, 1970.

7 Samuel D. Clark, J. Paul Grayson, and Linda M. Grayson (eds.), *Prophecy and Protest: Social Movements in Twentieth-Century Canada*, Gage, Toronto, 1975. Valuable not only as the sole collection of readings yet published on the exceedingly interesting forms of political dissent in Canada, but for Sam Clark's concise summary of research on social movements in the introduction.

8 Erich Fromm, *Escape from Freedom*, Rinehart, New York, 1941. A really splendid book, written in the context of the rise of Nazism but informed by the keenest sense of the history of freedom in Western civilization and of the threats to it posed by capitalist development.

9 George Gilder, *Wealth and Poverty*, Basic, New York, 1981. An engaging, masterful, important, but overly coherent treatise. It combines the uncombinable, namely a paean to freedom, creativity, and risk with a defense of male supremacy and monopoly capitalism. Among ideologists for contemporary rightist political forces in the United States, Gilder is unexcelled.

10 Franklin L. Baumer, *Modern European Thought*, Macmillan, New York, 1977. A lucid and deeply enriching analysis of how Western philosophic and artistic ideas have changed over the past four centuries—a change the Yale professor summarizes with the phrase, "from Being to Becoming." Baumer presents in historical relief the world view that permits a chapter like the one preceding to be written and read.

Notes

Footnotes for Chapter 1, Discipline

[1] Quoted in Richard Hofstadter et al., *The American Republic*, vol. 2, Prentice-Hall, Englewood Cliffs, N.J., 1970, p. 79.

[2] "Reflections upon the Sociology of Herbert Spencer," *American Journal of Sociology* **26:**129, (1920).

[3] *Careers in Sociology*, American Sociological Association, Washington, D.C., 1977, p. 19. The booklet is especially worth quoting because it reflects the collaboration of a number of sociologists and was released as a publication of the association itself rather than of a particular author.

[4] Literal translation from the original German of the *Eighteenth Brumaire of Louis Bonaparte*; see Karl Marx and Friedrich Engels, *Selected Works*, International Publishers, New York, 1964, p. 97.

[5] What I call Second Sociology here is substantially the same thing as described in my earlier article, "Social Problems as Systemic Costs," *Social Problems* **20:**419–31 (1973). I had not yet read Professor Titmuss's work when I wrote that article, but no one better exemplifies the kind of scholarship I had in mind. I think not only of his widely acclaimed *The Gift Relationship*, Allen & Unwin, Winchester, Mass., 1971, but of his more general, theoretical statement, *Social Policy: an Introduction*, Allen & Unwin, Winchester, Mass., 1974.

[6] The title of a bitter article by David Heaps, a former Ford Foundation official, in *The New York Times*, March 13, 1979.

[7] The reference is to R. W. Hodge et al., "Occupational Prestige in the United States, 1925–1963," *American Journal of Sociolgoy* **70:**286–302 (1964). The findings are similar for Canada and other national societies. The tendency I am criticizing in this paragraph is

much the same as what C. Wright Mills called "abstracted empiricism" and inveighed against in *The Sociological Imagination*.

[8]This is the sole reference to sociology in *Bartlett's Familiar Quotations*, 14th ed., Little, Brown, Boston, 1968, p. 870.

[9]*Newsweek*, December 25, 1978, p. 72.

[10]*Newsweek*, December 18, 1978, p. 112.

[11]Jean-Jacques Rousseau, *The Social Contract and Discourse on the Origin and the Foundation of Inequality among Mankind*, Pocket Books, New York, 1967, p. 177.

[12]For a splendid and readable case study of this difference, see Joseph Helfgot, "Professional Reform Organizations and the Symbolic Representation of the Poor," *American Sociological Review* **39**:475–91, (1974).

[13]Allen Ginsberg, *Howl*, part 1, line 1, *Howl and Other Poems*, City Lights, San Francisco, Calif., 1956.

[14]David Barrett, quoted in *Colombo's Canadian Quotations*, Hurtig, Edmonton, 1974, p. 36.

[15]Albert Pepitone, "Toward a Normative and Comparative Biocultural Social Psychology," *Journal of Personality and Social Psychology*, **34**:641–53 (1976).

Footnotes for Chapter 2, Methods

[1]W. I. Thomas and Dorothy S. Thomas, *The Child in America*, Knopf, New York, 1928, p. 572.

[2]C. Wright Mills, *The Sociological Imagination*, Grove, New York, 1959, p. 212.

[3]*Alice's Adventures in Wonderland & Through the Looking-Glass*, New American Library, New York, 1960, p. 187.

[4]Max Weber, *The Protestant Ethic and the Spirit of Capitalism*, Scribner's, New York, 1958, p. 29.

[5]Ibid., pp. 48f.

[6]R. H. Tawney, *Religion and the Rise of Capitalism*, Smith, 1963. (First published 1926.)

[7]C. T. Jonassen, "The Protestant Ethic and the Spirit of Capitalism in Norway," *American Sociological Review* **12**:676–86 (1947).

[8]Herman Israel, "Some Religious Factors in the Emergence of Industrial Society in England," *American Sociological Review* **31**:589–99 (1966).

[9]A. R. M. Lower, "Two Ways of Life: The Primary Antithesis of Canadian History," in C. Berger (ed.), *Approaches to Canadian History*, Univ. of Toronto Press, Toronto, 1967.

[10]Edward A. Tiryakian, "Neither Marx nor Durkheim . . . Perhaps Weber," *American Journal of Sociology* **81**:1–33 (1975).

[11]Dorothy Dohen, *Nationalism and American Catholicism*, Sheed & Ward, New York, 1967.

[12]E. Digby Baltzell, *The Protestant Establishment*, Random House, New York, 1964.

[13]John Porter, *The Vertical Mosaic*, Univ. of Toronto Press, Toronto, 1965.

[14]Charles H. Anderson, *White Protestant Americans*, Prentice-Hall, Englewood Cliffs, N.J., 1970, p. 144.

[15]Robert Redfield and Villa Rojas, *A Village That Chose Progress*, Univ. of Chicago Press, Chicago, 1953.

[16]Liston Pope, *Millhands and Preachers*, Yale Univ. Press, New Haven, Conn., 1943.

[17]Horace Miner, *St-Denis: A French-Canadian Parish*, Univ. of Chicago Press, Chicago, 1939.

[18]G. L. Gold, *St-Pascal*, Holt, Rinehart & Winston, Toronto, 1975.

[19]Sidney Goldstein, "Socioeconomic Differentials among Religious Groups in the United States," *American Journal of Sociology* **74**:658–71 (1969).

[20]Gerhard Lenski, *The Religious Factor*, Doubleday, New York, 1963.

[21] Andrew Greeley, "Influence of the 'Religious Factor' on Career Plans and Occupational Values of College Graduates," *American Journal of Sociology* **68**:658–71 (1963).

[22] J. D. Photiadis, "The American Business Creed and Denominational Identification," *Social Forces* **44**:92–100 (1965).

[23] Norval Glen and Ruth Hyland, "Religious Preference and Worldly Success: Some Evidence from National Surveys," *American Sociological Review* **32**:73–85 (1967).

[24] Alfred M. Lee, "Sociology for Whom," *American Sociological Review* **41**:925–36 (1976).

[25] Quoted in G. M. Vernon, *Sociology of Religion*, McGraw-Hill, New York, 1962, p. 257.

[26] Robert Bellah, *Tokugawa Religion*, Free Press, New York, 1957.

Footnotes for Chapter 3, Society

[1] I have sketched the fascinating relationship between transnational churches and national societies in my articles: "Stars and Stripes, the Maple Leaf, and the Papal Coat of Arms," *Canadian Journal of Sociology* **3**:245–61 (1978); and "Foreign Gods and Nation-States in the Americas," *Canadian Review of Studies of Nationalism* **7**:351–71 (1980).

[2] Peter Newman, *The Canadian Establishment*, McClelland & Stewart, Toronto, 1975. Additional information on John McDougald was gleaned from various issues of *Maclean's*, the weekly newsmagazine of which Peter Newman is editor.

[3] Karl Marx, *The Economic and Philosophic Manuscripts of 1844*, International Publishers, New York, 1964, p. 165.

[4] Thorstein Veblen, *The Theory of the Leisure Class*, New American Library, 1953, p. 70.

[5] Thomas Gray, *Elegy Written in a Country Churchyard*, stanza 9. (First published 1750.)

[6] Kingsley Davis and Wilbert Moore, "Some Principles of Stratification," *American Sociological Review* **10**:244 (1945).

[7] Not entirely, but mostly. See Melvin Tumin, "Some Principles of Stratification: A Critical Analysis," *American Sociological Review* **18**:387–94 (1953); and Dennis Wrong, "The Functional Theory of Stratification: Some Neglected Considerations," *American Sociological Review* **24**:772–82 (1959). The complaint of too much tidiness can be directed as well at the functional theory of social change, at least as Wilbert Moore presents it in his book, *Social Change*, Prentice-Hall, Englewood Cliffs, N.J., 1963. There is no need to incarcerate the source of change in the structure of demands, to suggest that change arises naturally from some kind of mysterious interinstitutional tension. I suppose change happens most frequently because some society somehow invades some other society. There is nothing wrong with structural functionalism except when one becomes inextricably entangled in this one conceptual web. On this point see Robert Nisbet, *Social Change and History*, Oxford Univ. Press, New York, 1969, p. 283.

[8] Wallace Clement, *The Canadian Corporate Elite*, McClelland & Stewart, Toronto, 1975. Note especially John Porter's introduction.

[9] Newman, op. cit., p. 156.

[10] James Gibson, quoted in *Colombo's Canadian Quotations*, Hurtig, Edmonton, 1974, p. 217.

[11] No single piece of research demonstrates this point more clearly than Raymond Breton, "Institutional Completeness of Ethnic Communities and the Personal Relations of Immigrants," *American Journal of Sociology* **70**:193–205 (1964). I suppose the basic point is that a subculture by itself cannot exist any more than the cultural dimension alone of any sociocultural system; there has to be some kind of visible, audible interaction to reinforce and embody the particular norms, values, and beliefs.

[12] This is the title of William Sumner's best-known book, *Folkways*, published in 1907 and reprinted by New American Library, New York, 1960.

[13]Robert MacIver "Sociology," in the *Encyclopedia of the Social Sciences*, Macmillan, New York, 1934, p. 244. He was referring to German as well as to American sociology.

[14]See Howard Odum, *Folk, Region and Society*, University of North Carolina Press, Chapel Hill, N.C., 1964.

Footnotes for Chapter 4, Person

[1]Graham Greene, *The Human Factor*, Avon, New York, 1979, 181–82. First published by Simon & Schuster, New York, 1978. Copyright © by Graham Greene. Used by permission.

[2]H. H. Gerth and C. W. Mills (eds.), *From Max Weber: Essays in Sociology*, Oxford Univ. Press, New York, 1946, p. 155.

[3]Quotations in this paragraph are from pages 60, 107–8, 108 and 296, respectively, of W. O. Mitchell, *Who Has Seen the Wind*, Macmillan of Canada, Toronto, 1972. Copyright © 1947 by W. O. Mitchell. Used by permission.

[4]John Kunkel, *Behavior, Social Problems, and Change*, Prentice-Hall, Englewood Cliffs, N.J., 1975, p. 175.

[5]George Woodcock, *Anarchism: A History of Libertarian Ideas and Movements*, New American Library, Meridian, New York, 1962.

[6]Charles Reich, *The Greening of America*, Bantam, New York, 1971, p. 241.

[7]On the jacket of *Back Here on Earth*, United Artists, 1968.

[8]Max Weber in Gerth and Mills, op. cit., p. 246.

[9]Not to multiply footnotes, but Werner Stark has written an analysis both brief and brilliant of Weber's dialectical or dualistic view of human beings: "The Agony of Righteousness: Max Weber's Moral Philosophy," *Thought* **43**:380–92 (1968).

[10]George Herbert Mead, *On Social Psychology*, Anselm Strauss (ed.), Univ. of Chicago Press, Chicago, 1964, p. 233.

[11]Ibid., p. 229.

[12]Ibid., p. 233.

[13]Jean-Jacques Rousseau, *The Social Contract*, Pocket Books, New York, 1967, p. 7.

[14]See John Clammer's article on Europeans and the Pacific in Volume 8 of E. Evans-Pritchard (ed.), *Peoples of the Earth*, Grolier, Danbury, Conn., 1973.

[15]David McClelland's *Achieving Society*, D. Van Nostrand, New York, 1961, is the classic work; see also B. C. Rosen et al. (eds.), *Achievement in American Society*, Schenkman, Cambridge, Mass., 1969.

[16]See Myron Weiner (ed.), *Modernization: The Dynamics of Growth*, Basic, New York, 1966, and Alex Inkeles's later article, "Making Men Modern," *American Journal of Sociology* **75**:208–25 (1969).

[17]See his article in the *Journal of Cross-Cultural Psychology* **2**:365–71 (1971), and his report with S. Ariella in *Developmental Psychology* **3**:16–20 (1970).

[18]Charles Cooley, *Social Organization*, as reprinted in T. Parsons et al. (eds.), *Theories of Society*, Free Press, New York, 1961, p. 315.

[19]See Albert Bandura and Richard Walters, *Social Learning and Personality Development*, Holt Rinehart & Winston, New York, 1963, and Albert Bandura, *Aggression: A Social Learning Analysis*, Prentice-Hall, Englewood Cliffs, N.J., 1973.

[20]Stanley Milgram, "Behavioral Study of Obedience," *Journal of Abnormal and Social Psychology* **67**:371–78 (1963).

[21]S. K. Padover (ed.), *Thomas Jefferson on Democracy*, New American Library, Mentor, New York, 1939, p. 170.

[22]Erving Goffman, *Asylums*, Doubleday, 1961.

[23]Rom. 13:14.

[24]Solomon Asch, "Opinions and Social Pressure," *Scientific American*, Nov. 1955. Reprint no. 450.

[25]Richard Henshel, *The Future of Social Prediction*, Bobbs-Merrill, Indianapolis, 1975.

[26]Compare the retrospective statement by John Porter shortly before his death: "I wrote of freedom as a condition necessary to be creative, and of power as the capacity of some to monopolize creativity," *The Measure of Canadian Society*, Gage, Toronto, 1980, p. 208.

[27]Lucan, The Civil War, book 2, line 10.

[28]Thomas Hobbes, *Leviathan*, part 1, C. B. Macpherson (ed.), Penguin, New York, 1968. The quotation comes from Chapter Thirteen, "Of the NATURAL CONDITION of Mankind, as concerning their Felicity, and Misery," which nicely captures Hobbes's bleak view of our species, especially in the Penguin edition, which retains the original spelling.

[29]Dennis Wrong, "The Oversocialized Conception of Man in Modern Sociology," *American Sociological Review* **26**:183–93 (1961).

[30]For a broad introduction to competing factions in contemporary sociology, with lucid summaries and a useful annotated bibliography, see Scott McNall (ed.), *Theoretical Perspectives in Sociology*, St. Martin's, New York, 1979.

[31]Dante, the Divine Comedy. Purgatorio, canto 16, line 79. Albeit more timidly in these timid times, Seymour Martin Lipset makes a similar point in concluding his report of the multiple failures of social scientists to predict events in recent decades. The report, he writes, "may be viewed as a declaration of independence, of autonomy, of insistence that people can still feel free to make their own history, that the future is not so determined that we should feel helpless about our ability to affect it. We are still far from having a Calvinist social science, from having to accept predestination. Social science can help us, can trace relations, but the future still remains an uncharted sea waiting for the venturesome," *Predicting the Future of Post-Industrial Society: Can We Do It?*, Univ. of Chicago Press, Chicago, 1979, p. 35. For Lipset's adverb *still* I should prefer *forever*.

Footnotes for Chapter 5, Polity

[1]Margaret Walker, *Jubilee*, Houghton Mifflin, Boston, 1966, p. 125.

[2]H. H. Gerth and C. W. Mills (eds.), *From Max Weber*, Oxford Univ. Press, New York, 1946, p. 296.

[3]Bernard Marchland (ed.), *Two Views of Man*, Ungar, New York, 1966, p. 56; this book enshrines in a single binding both Innocent's dreary appraisal ("On the Misery of Man") and an attempt to refute it by the fifteenth-century Renaissance Italian, Giannozzo Manetti ("On the Dignity of Man").

[4]Gerth and Mills, op. cit., p. 295.

[5]Matt. 8:22.

[6]Gerth and Mills, op. cit., p. 297.

[7]John Locke, *Two Treatises on Government*, Peter Laslett (ed.), New American Library, New York, 1965, p. 316.

[8]Gerth and Mills, op. cit., p. 299.

[9]The concluding words of John Kennedy's inaugural address, published in *Vital Speeches* **27**:227 (1961).

[10]Quoted in P. E. Trudeau, *Federalism and the French Canadians*, Macmillan of Canada, Toronto, 1968, p. 110.

[11]The data are available in publications of the U.S. government; for an analysis see Miles D. Wolpin, *Military Aid and Counterrevolution in the Third World*, Lexington Books, Lexington, Mass., 1972. I can also recommend I. L. Horowitz' article on the military in S. M. Lipset and A. Solari (eds.), *Elites in Latin America*, Oxford Univ. Press, New York, 1967.

[12]The best-known book on the politics of mass society was written by Berkeley's William Kornhauser and published with that title by the Free Press, New York, in 1959. My discussion in this chapter differs somewhat from that book but less so from Kornhauser's more recent thinking—at least as I understood it one evening in 1977 over much wine and a little cheese.

[13]Harry Eckstein, quoted in S. M. Lipset, *The First New Nation*, Doubleday, New York, 1967, p. 269. I hope the line of argument in these paragraphs capably reflects the lessons I took from many discussions with two of my senior colleagues, Walter B. Simon, now at the University of Vienna, and Luiz A. Costa-Pinto, now at Waterloo. I especially recommend Simon's article, "Motivation of a Totalitarian Mass Vote," *British Journal of Sociology* **10**:338–46 (1959), a study of the rise of Nazism; and Costa-Pinto's "Pueblo y Populismo," *Revista de Estudios Políticos* No. 3, 39–53 (1978), an analysis of demagoguery in Latin America.

[14]William Eustis, quoted in *Colombo's Canadian Quotations*, Hurtig, Edmonton, 1975, p. 185.

[15]Adam Smith's *Inquiry into the Nature and Causes of the Wealth of Nations*, 2 vols., Irwin, Homewood, Ill., 1963, remains worth reading even 200 years after it first appeared. One should read the book with the same interest as one would study the original surveys for a city like London or Paris: not as analysis of something eternal but as an initial plan for something which was later realized.

[16]Statistics like these are presented in round numbers throughout this book as of 1980. They are not usually footnoted because of their ready accessibility in the *World Almanac*, the *Statistical Abstracts of the United States*, the *Yearbook of the United Nations*, the *Yearbook of Labour Statistics*, and similar standard compilations of governmental reports.

[17]Jean-Jacques Rousseau, *The Social Contract*, Pocket Books, New York, 1967, p. 111.

[18]Joseph Schumpeter, *Capitalism, Socialism and Democracy*, Harper & Row, New York, 1962, p. 82.

[19]On the effects of foreign investment, see Kari Levitt, *Silent Surrender*, Macmillan of Canada, Toronto, 1970, and Celso Furtado, *Obstacles to Development in Latin America*, Doubleday, New York, 1969.

[20]V. I. Lenin, *Imperialism: The Highest Stage of Capitalism*, International Publishers, New York, 1939.

[21]Norman Cantor, *Medieval History*, Macmillan, New York, 1969, p. 544.

Footnotes for Chapter 6, Economy

[1]Gen. 1:28.

[2]*The Way of Lao Tzu*, Wing-Tsit Chan (trans.), Bobbs-Merrill, Indianapolis, 1963, Sec. 10.

[3]Julius K. Nyerere, *Ujamaa—Essays on Socialism*, Oxford Univ. Press, London, 1968, pp. 32–33.

[4]For details of this remarkable story see the articles in M. L. Fowler (ed.), *Explorations into Cahokia Archaeology*, Illinois Archaeological Survey Bulletin no. 7, Univ of Illinois, Champaign, 1977. An important difference between Mexico and the United States is evident in the contrast between the reverent restoration of pre-Columbian ruins near Mexico City and in the Yucatàn and the tiny museum at Cahokia, a site bisected by Interstate Highway No. 70 and encroached upon by suburban developments. Mexican society respects and celebrates its myriad indigenous roots; the United States ignores the few indigenous roots it has.

[5]Robert Nisbet, *Social Change and History*, Oxford Univ. Press, New York, 1969.

[6]The reference is to a classic article by D. F. Aberle et al., "The Functional Prerequisites of a Society," *Ethics* **60**:100–111 (1950).

[7]Gen. 1:20.

[8]Emile Durkheim, *The Division of Labor in Society*, Free Press, New York, 1933, p. 372.

[9]Marcel Mauss, as quoted in Steven Lukes, "Marcel Mauss," *International Encyclopedia of the Social Sciences* vol. 10, Macmillan, New York, 1968, p. 81.

[10]John Law, *Law, Money and Trade Considered with a Proposal for Supplying the Nation with Money*, Kelley, Fairfield, N.J., 1966. This truly remarkable treatise was originally published in 1705.

[11]A thoughtful though I believe neglected book in this connection is Kenneth E. Boulding's *The Meaning of the 20th Century*, Harper & Row, New York, 1965, especially his discussion of the second law of thermodynamics as applied to social systems, the principle of diminishing potential—that is, the ever present danger of entropy.

[12]Kahlil Gibran, *The Procession*, Philosophical Library, 1958, p. 57.

[13]As quoted in Murray Melbin, "Night as Frontier," *American Sociological Review* **43**:17 (1978).

[14]Mark Twain, *Life on the Mississippi*, chap. 1.

[15]Stephen P. Robbins, *The Administrative Process*, Prentice-Hall, Englewood Cliffs, N.J., 1976, p. 308.

[16]Letter to DuPont de Nemours, April 24, 1816.

Footnotes for Chapter 7, Religion

[1]My research on religion in Peru and Paraguay is reported in a series of articles: "American Catholicism in a Latin Setting," *Missiology* **3**:265–85 (1975); "The Established Church as an Agent of Change," *Sociological Analysis* **34**:106–23 (1973); and "Curses versus Blows: Tactics in Church-State Conflict," *Sociological Analysis* **35**:1–16 (1975).

[2]This conception of religion relates closely to Thomas O'Dea's, as presented in Chapter Two of his *Sociology of Religion*, Prentice-Hall, Englewood Cliffs, N.J., 1966; therein may be found more complete discussion of and references to the scholars named in this paragraph. I should also caution readers here against identifying religion simply with what was earlier described as the humble dimension of human nature. Emmanuel Percival, you may recall from Chapter Four, was well aware of human limitations and thus could appropriately illustrate the dimension of humility. But he did not respond to the fact of transcendence. Instead he wallowed in the hell of cynical despair. Religion does indeed assume recognition of human limitations, the beyond, all that transcends human hands; thus it assumes a posture of humility. But it implies also an action of surrender to what is beyond us, a joyful, playful celebration of our own incapabilities, an intentional leap into ultimacy, a willful acceptance of the mystery in earthly life.

[3]William Blake, *Auguries of Innocence*, Ms. line 1 (First published about 1800.)

[4]Quoted in Dorothy Dohen, *Nationalism and American Catholicism*, Sheed & Ward, New York, 1967.

[5]See Robert Bellah, "Religious Evolution," *American Sociological Review* **29**:358–74 (1964). My analysis of later stages in the process, however, contrasts sharply with his.

[6]See Ralph Underhill, "Economic and Political Antecedents of Monotheism: A Cross-Cultural Study," *American Journal of Sociology* **80**:862–69 (1975) Underhill's "Economy, Polity and Monotheism: Reply to Swanson," Ibid. **82**:418–21 (1976); and Swanson's "Comment on Underhill's Reply," Ibid. **82**:421–23 (1976).

[7]See Charles Y. Glock and Rodney Stark, *Christian Beliefs and Anti-Semitism*, Harper & Row, New York, 1966. Far better, it seems to me, to focus on what Randall Stokes has called *operant* religion in his article "Afrikaner Calvinism and Economic Action: The Weberian Thesis in South Africa," *American Journal of Sociology* **81**:62–81 (1975).

[8]Acts 9:4–6, 18.

[9]There is more to be learned from the study of the religious orders than sociologists generally

recognize. See, for example, Leo Moulin, "Policy-Making in the Religious Orders," *Government and Opposition* 1:25–54 (1965); E. K. Francis, "Towards a Typology of Religious Orders," *American Journal of Sociology* 55:437–49 (1950); and the first three chapters of my *Society's Shadow*, McGraw-Hill Ryerson, Toronto, 1972.

[10]Typologies of religious organization abound (see the references in my "The Church in Opposition," *Sociological Analysis* 37:299–314 [1976]); which one is best depends on what one is trying to explain or predict. In the present context I draw mainly on Werner Stark's five-volume *Sociology of Religion*, Routledge & Kegan Paul, Oxon, 1967ff. H. R. Niebuhr's *Social Sources of Denominationalism*, Holt, New York, 1929, remains a classic for understanding religious organization in liberal-capitalist societies.

[11]These and most other contemporary church statistics cited herein are taken from Constant Jacquet (ed.), *Yearbook of American and Canadian Churches*, Abingdon, Nashville, Tenn. This exceedingly useful compilation is published annually for the National Council of Churches.

[12]See my "Public versus Sectarian Legitimation: The Separate Schools of the Catholic Church," *Canadian Review of Sociology and Anthropology* 13:137–51 (1976).

[13]Bryan Wilson, *The Sacred Canopy*, Doubleday, New York, 1969, p. 107.

[14]Reginald Bibby, "Canadian Commitment: A Preview," *Yearbook*, op. cit., 1978, p. 246. Bibby reports his research more fully in a 1979 article in the *Canadian Review of Sociology and Anthropology*.

[15]Data from the *Yearbook*, op. cit., 1979.

[16]An anonymous author, "The Sectarian Status of American Colleges in 1813," cited in R. Hofstadter and W. Smith (eds.), *American Higher Education*, Univ. of Chicago Press, Chicago, 1961, p. 187.

[17]See the articles by Harry Kantor and Thomas G. Sanders in Donald E. Smith (ed.), *Religion and Political Modernization*, Yale Univ. Press, New Haven, Conn., 1974.

[18]A. A. Lebedev, "The Secularization of the Population of a Socialist City," *Soviet Sociology* 12:77–106 (1973).

[19]Octavio Paz, quoted by Christopher Derrick in "The Mexican Soul—as Interpreted by Octavio Paz," *Peoples of the Earth*, vol. 4, E. Evans-Pritchard, Grolier, 1973, p. 27.

[20]See, for example, Juanne Clarke, "Medicalization in the Past Century in the Province of Ontario," Ph.D. thesis, University of Waterloo, Waterloo, 1979.

[21]See the review article by Thomas Robbins et al., "Theory and Research on Today's New Religions," *Sociological Analysis* 39:95–122 (1978); that issue of the journal includes five other articles on various expressions of the contemporary religious revival. See also Dean Kelley, *Why the Conservative Churches Are Growing*, Harper & Row, New York, 1972; and Charles Glock and Robert Bellah, *The New Religious Consciousness*, Univ. of California Press, Berkeley, 1976.

[22]Miguel de Unamuno, *The Tragic Sense of Life*, Dover, New York, 1954, p. 78.

[23]E. F. Schumacher, *Small Is Beautiful*, Abacus, London, 1974, p. 51.

[24]The idea of conquering frontiers is, of course, integral to American culture, as the historian Frederick Jackson Turner (1861–1932) so perceptively pointed out. More recently, Murray Melbin has picked up on the same idea and given it a new twist; see his "Night as Frontier," *American Sociological Review* 43:3–22 (1978). But these are reachable frontiers. There is one that is not. American society, and all societies, might best admit it—or so it seems to me.

[25]The Way of Lao Tzu, Wing-Tsit Chan (trans.) Bobbs-Merrill, Indianapolis, sec. 56.

[26]1 Cor. 2:9.

Footnotes for Chapter 8, Family

[1]Hortense Powdermaker, *Life in Lesu*, W. W. Norton, New York, 1933.

[2]Edward Shorter, *The Making of the Modern Family*, Basic, 1977, Ariès is immodestly quoted on the cover of Professor Shorter's book.

[3]Matt. 10:34–37.

[4]See the fine article by Richard F. Tomasson, "Premarital Sexual Permissiveness and Illegitimacy in the Nordic Countries," *Comparative Studies in Society and History* **18**:252–70 (1976).

[5]Quoted in W. T. DeBary et al., *Sources of Chinese Tradition*, vol. 2, Columbia Univ. Press, New York, 1960, p. 191.

[6]I do not want to press this point too far. Monasteries, especially Cistercian ones, led in the mechanization of production during the later Middle Ages. See Jean Gimpel, *The Medieval Machine*, Holt, Rinehart & Winston, New York, 1977.

[7]Robert Frost, "Death of the Hired Man," first published by Henry Holt in 1914. The poem is stark illumination for the Western problem of mixing oil and vinegar.

[8]I recommend especially Rosabeth Moss Kanter, "Commitment and Social Organization: A Study of Commitment Mechanisms in Utopian Communities," *American Sociological Review* **33**:499–517 (1968). Part of that article is reprinted in my *Society's Shadow: Studies in the Sociology of Countercultures*, McGraw-Hill Ryerson, Toronto, 1972, which also includes numerous additional references.

[9]V. I. Lenin, quoted in W. F. Kenkel, *The Family in Perspective*, Goodyear, Santa Monica, Calif., 1977, p. 114.

[10]Christopher Lasch, *Haven in a Heartless World*, Basic, New York, 1979, p. 168.

[11]Edward Shorter, *The Making of the Modern Family*, Harper & Row, New York, 1977, p. xviii.

[12]*Colombo's Canadian Quotations*, Hurtig, Edmonton, 1974, p. 595.

[13]Edward Shorter, op. cit., p. 251.

[14]U. S. Bureau of the Census, "Marital Status and Living Arrangements: March 1978," *Current Population Reports*, ser. P-20, no. 338, 1979.

[15]Morton Hunt, *Sexual Behavior in the 1970s*, Playboy, New York, 1974.

[16]"Marital Status," op. cit.

[17]Cited in W. J. Goode, *World Revolution and Family Patterns*, Free Press, New York, 1963.

[18]Marion Porter, John Porter, and Bernard Blishen, *Does Money Matter?* York Univ. Institute for Behavioural Research, Toronto, 1973.

Footnotes for Chapter 9, Education

[1]Pliny the Elder, *Natural History*, bk. 7, sec. 4.

[2]Talcott Parsons and Robert Bales, *Family, Socialization, and Interaction Process*, Free Press, New York, 1955.

[3]Talcott Parsons, "An Outline of the Social System," in T. Parsons et al. (eds.), *Theories of Society*, vol. 1, Free Press, New York, 1961, p. 58.

[4]A wide variety of education journals regularly publish contributions to this literature. The following articles are only suggestive: J. M. McPartland and J. L. Epstein, "Open Schools and Achievement: Extended Test of a Finding of No Relationship," *Sociology of Education* **42**:133–44 (1969); Nancy Karweit, "A reanalysis of the Effect of Quantity of Schooling on Achievement," *Sociology of Education* **49**:236–46 (1976); Harold S. Himmelfarb, "The Non-linear Impact of Schooling: Comparing Different Types and Amounts of Jewish Education," *Sociology of Education* **42**:114–29 (1977); and Lee M. Wolfle, "The Enduring Effects of Education on Verbal Skills," *Sociology of Education* **53**:104–114 (1980). See also Burton Clark's review-article, "Development of the sociology of higher education," *Sociology of Education* **46**:2–14 (1973), wherein he notes the "relatively massive but trivial literature" in the study of college impact.

[5]Arthur Jensen's book was entitled *Educability and Group Differences*, Harper & Row, New York, 1973, and Richard Herrnstein's was *IQ in the Meritocracy*, Little, Brown, Boston, 1973. For a defense of their lines of argument against people like me, believers in nurture more than nature, see the lucid and feisty collection of essays by Antony Flew, *Sociology, Equality and Education*, Harper & Row, New York, 1976.

[6]John Dewey, *Democracy and Education*, Macmillan, New York, 1916, p. 100.

[7]Ibid., p. 121.

[8]John Dewey, *Experience and Education*, Macmillan, New York, 1977, p. 90.

[9]Moses Coady, quoted in A. F. Laidlaw (ed.), *The Man from Margaree: Writings and Speeches of M. M. Coady*, McClelland & Stewart, Don Mills, Ont., 1971, pp. 57–59. The lines are from "The Antigonish Way," a radio series for the Canadian Broadcasting Corporation.

[10]Paolo Freire, *Pedagogy of the Oppressed*, Seabury, New York, 1970, p. 135.

[11]See Alfred North Whitehead, *The Aims of Education*, Macmillan, New York, 1929, and Bertrand Russell, *Education and the Social Order*, Allen, 1938.

[12]See Especially A. S. Neill, *Summerhill*, Hart, 1960, and *Freedom, Not License*, Hart, 1966.

[13]See Robert Hutchins, *Education for Freedom*, Louisiana State Univ. Press, Baton Rouge, 1943, and *The Conflict of Education in a Democratic Society*, Harper & Row, New York, 1953.

[14]Among others: Edgar Friedenburg, *The Dignity of Youth and Other Atavisms*, Beacon, Boston, 1965, Paul Goodman, *Growing Up Absurd*, Vintage, House, 1965, New York, John Holt, *Freedom and Beyond*, E. P. Dutton, New York, 1972, and Ivan Illich, *Deschooling Society*, Harper & Row, New York, 1971.

[15]I can recommend Walter Horn and Ernest Born, *The Plan of St. Gall*, 3 vol., Univ. of California Press, Berkeley, 1980, a study of a monastery in Charlemagne's empire. The blueprint for the monastery indicates two classrooms, accommodation for about thirty students, and fourteen toilets for their use.

[16]The classic history of early higher education is Rashdall Hastings' multi-volume work, *Rise of the Universities*, published in 1895. A. B. Cobban published an update, *The Medieval Universities: Their Development and Organization*, Methuen, New York, 1975, a book I found meticulous but dry as dust. I am more inclined to recommend Nathan Schachner, *The Medieval Universities*, Frederick Stokes, 1938, a genuinely delightful book to read.

[17]A little point but an important one. See Vern L. Bullough, "Education and Professionalization: An Historical Example," *History of Education Quarterly* 10:160–69 (1970).

[18]For a brief but splendid description of the Enlightenment see Crane Brinton's article under that title in the *Encyclopedia of Philosophy*, vol. 2, Macmillan, New York, 1967, pp. 519–525.

[19]"Statutes of William and Mary, 1727," in *American Higher Education: A Documentary History*, vol. 1, Richard Hofstadter and Wilson Smith (eds.), Univ. of Chicago Press, Chicago, 1961, p. 44.

[20]Ibid., p. 43.

[21]"Jefferson Plans the University of Virginia," in Hofstadter and Smith, op. cit., pp. 176–77. See also in the same volume, "The Plan of Studies at the University of Virginia," pp. 230–31.

[22]Thorstein Veblen, *The Theory of the Leisure Class*, New American Library, Mentor, New York, 1953, p. 255. The entire last chapter of the book merits reading in this connection.

[23]The statistics are from S. Bowles and H. Gintis, *Schooling in Capitalist America*, Basic, New York, 1976, chap. 6, the major reference for this and the following paragraphs.

[24]Ibid., p. 164.

[25]See John Porter, *The Measure of Canadian Society: Education, Equality and Opportunity*, Gage, Toronto, 1979, p. 261.

[26]For the Canadian case, see my "Public versus Sectarian Legitimation: The Separate Schools

of the Catholic Church," *Canadian Review of Sociology and Anthropology* **13**:137–51 (1976). Robert J. Havighurst's *Comparative Perspectives on Education*, Little, Brown, Boston, 1968, is a compilation of articles on the school systems of various societies.

[27]For further discussion see David Nasaw, *Schooled to Order*, Oxford Univ. Press, New York, 1979, chap. 12.

[28]Eliot Friedson at New York University has written wide-ranging, careful, and critical analyses of professions. See his edited volume, *The Professions and Their Prospects*, Sage, Beverly Hills, Calif., 1973, also his *Professional Dominance: The Social Structure of Medical Care*, Aldine, 1970. Among other standard works are Amitai Etzioni, (ed.), *The Semi-professions and Their Organization*, various articles by Everett Hughes in his *The Sociological Eye*, Aldine-Atherton, 1971, and Harold Wilensky's seminal article, "The Professionalization of Everyone?" *American Journal of Sociology* **70**:137–58 (1964).

[29]This alienating arrangement holds even in the social sciences. Neil Smelser has written that "recent trends in higher education have worked to accentuate this distinction between those who make and those who teach the disciplines and to separate those who make the disciplines from the undergraduate students who take courses in them;" in "The Social Sciences," *Content and Context*, C. Kaysen (ed.), McGraw-Hill, New York, 1973, p. 139. One can hardly expect that teachers in such a system will urge students to think creatively, when even for the teachers creative thought is considered out of bounds.

[30]John McKnight et al., *Disabling Professions*, Burns & MacEachern, Don Mills, Ont., 1977, p. 87. Professor McKnight teaches communications and urban affairs at Northwestern University.

[31]For an alternative viewpoint see Peter H. Rossi, "The Challenge and Opportunities of Applied Social Research," *American Sociological Review* **45** (1980).

Footnotes for Chapter 10, Liberation

[1]A specific point that deserves specific reference: D. P. Phillips and Kenneth A. Feldman, "A Dip in Deaths before Ceremonial Occasions: Some New Relationships between Social Integration and Mortality," *American Sociological Review* **38**:678–96 (1973).

[2]The most authoritative recent discussion of countercultures is J. Milton Yinger's 1977 presidential address to the American Sociological Association, published as "Countercultures and Social Change," *American Sociological Review* **42**:833–53 (1977).

[3]See James S. Coleman's perceptive article, "Social Inventions," *Social Forces* **49**:163–73 (1970).

[4]John Kenneth Galbraith, *The Age of Uncertainty*, Houghton Mifflin, Boston, 1977, p. 75.

[5]Richard Flacks, "The Liberated Generation: An Exploration of the Roots of Student Protest," *Journal of Social Issues* **23**:52–75 (1967).

[6]The seventh and posthumous edition was under the joint authorship of Edwin H. Sutherland and Donald R. Cressey, *Principles of Criminology*, Lippincott, New York, 1966.

[7]For four contrasting treatments of delinquent subcultures, otherwise called subcultures of delinquency, see A. K. Cohen, *Delinquent Boys*, Free Press, New York, 1955, Richard Cloward and Lloyd Ohlin, *Delinquency and Opportunity: A Theory of Delinquent Gangs*, Free Press, New York, 1960, David Matza, *Delinquency and Drift*, Wiley, New York, 1964, and Elliot Liebow, *Tally's Corner*, Little, Brown, Boston, 1967.

[8]My colleague at the University of Waterloo, Robert C. Prus, has published two such ethnographies, one with C. R. D. Sharper, entitled *Road Hustler*, Gage, Toronto, 1979, the other with Styllianoss Irini, entitled *Hookers, Rounders and Desk Clerks*, Gage, Toronto, 1980. The bibliographies of these books offer numerous other examples.

[9]David P. Phillips, "The Influence of Suggestion on Suicide: Substantive and Theoretical

Implications of the Werther Effect," *American Sociological Review* **39**:340–54 (1974). I am grateful to Metta Spencer for calling my attention to Phillips's work.

[10]David P. Phillips, "Suicide, Motor Vehicle Fatalities, and the Mass Media: Evidence toward a Theory of Suggestion," *American Journal of Sociology* **84**:1150–74 (1979).

[11]Two excellent and relevant articles are Thomas F. O'Dea and Renato Poblete, "Anomie and the 'Quest for Community': The Formation of Sects among the Puerto Ricans of New York," *American Catholic Sociological Review* **21**:18–36 (1961; and Erdmann Beynon, "The Voodoo Cult among Negro Migrants in Detroit," *American Journal of Sociology* **43**:894–907 (1938).

[12]See [7]. For the class bases of religious sects one good source is Werner Stark, *The Sociology of Religion. Vol. 3: Sectarian Religion*, Fordham Univ. Press, New York, 1967; another is Liston Pope, *Millhands and Preachers*, Yale Univ. Press, New Haven, Conn., 1942. The class bases of social movements are discussed in virtually all systematic treatments of the latter, among them the books by Wilson and by Clark, Grayson, and Grayson in the suggestions for further reading at the end of this chapter. Yet one should never underestimate the extent of the status quo's hold upon the disadvantaged social strata. The classic research report to this effect is Ely Chinoy, "The Tradition of Opportunity and the Aspirations of Automobile Workers," *American Journal of Sociology* **57**:453–59 (1952).

[13]An old but venerable reference is August Hollingshead, R. Ellis, and E. Kirby, "Social Mobility and Mental Illness," *American Sociological Review* **19**:577–83 (1954). Collective mobility, of course, has similar unsettling consequences. This is essentially the basis of discussions about "revolutions of rising expectations." See, for example, James Davies, "Toward a Theory of Revolution," *American Sociological Review* **27**:5–19 (1962).

[14]The situation of half-castes is a major theme in research on the "marginal man" spearheaded by Robert Park at the University of Chicago during the 1930s. See, for example, E. V. Stonequist, *The Marginal Man*, Scribner's, New York, 1937.

[15]I can recommend in this regard Bennett M. Berger, "On the Youthfulness of Youth Cultures," *Social Research* **30**:319–42 (1963).

[16]In his introduction to the Stonequist book cited in [14], Park exaggerated only slightly: "He [the marginal man] occupies the position which has been, historically, that of the Jew in the Diaspora. The Jew, particularly the Jew who has emerged from the provincialism of the ghetto, has everywhere and always been the most civilized of human creatures" (op. cit., p. xvii).

[17]See the review of literature in Stephen B. Withey et al., *A Degree and What Else?* McGraw-Hill, New York, 1971.

[18]The classic reference here is Karl Mannheim, *Ideology and Utopia*, Harcourt, Brace & World, New York, 1936.

[19]I can recommend Lewis Mumford, *The City in History*, Harcourt Brace Jovanovich, New York, 1961.

[20]Analyses and accounts of millennial movements make fascinating reading. Here are four to choose from: Sylvia Thrupp (ed.), *Millennial Dreams in Action*, Schocken, New York, 1970; Norman Cohn, *The Pursuit of the Millennium*, Harper & Row, New York, 1961; Kenelm O. L. Burridge, *New Heaven New Earth*, Copp Clark Pitman, Toronto, 1969; and Peter Worsley, *The Trumpet Shall Sound*, MacGibbon, 1967.

[21]Alexis de Tocqueville, *The Old Regime and the French Revolution*, Stuart Gilbert (trans.), Doubleday, New York, 1955, pp. 176–77. Sulamita de Britto Costa-Pinto's unpublished paper, "Crisis and Rising Expectations," York Univ., Toronto, 1980, has served to remind me of the contemporary relevance of de Tocqueville's work.

[22]Karl Polanyi, *The Great Transformation*, Rinehart, New York, 1944.

Name Index

Aberhardt, W., 181
Aberle, D. F., 474
Abzug, B., 440
Adorno, T., 153
Agger, B. N., 200
Albert the Great, 188, 304
Alfonso, king of Spain, 167
Alger, H., 243
Allende, S., 175, 187, 194
Anderson, C. H., 52, 470
Anselm, 399
Anthony, S. B., 363
Aquinas, T., 188, 294, 399
Archibald, W. P., 155
Arendt, H., 21, 320
Ariès, P., 336, 346-347, 375, 477
Aristotle, 161-162, 397
Arius, 292
Asch, S., 141-142, 144-145, 473

Bach, J. S., 303
Bales, R., 386, 477
Baltzell, E. D., 51-52, 470
Bandura, A., 136, 145, 472
Banes, M. J., 356
Baran, P. A., 274

Barralet, J. J., 75
Barrett, D., 28, 470
Baruch, B., 110
Baumer, F. L., 467
Beaglehole, E., 390
Bechtel family, 253
Beethoven, L. van, 439
Bell, A. G., 439
Bellah, R., 65, 278-279, 288, 309, 320,
    321, 471, 475, 476
Benedict, 350
Benedict, R., 53
Bensman, J., 115
Benton, T. H., 243
Berger, B., 480
Berger, C., 470
Berger, P. L., 20, 32, 33, 300, 320
Berlin, I., 75
Beynon, E., 480
Bibby, R., 301, 476
Binet, A., 386
Black, C., 101
Blake, W., 282, 475
Blishen, B., 477
Blumer, H., 123, 146, 155
Boas, F., 53, 330
Bohr, N., 439

Bordaberry, J., 175
Born, E., 478
Bottomore, T., 33
Boudon, R., 426
Boulding, K. E., 21, 475
Bowles, S., 425, 478
Braque, G., 442
Braudel, F., 106
Braverman, H., 206, 274
Bredemeier, H., 155
Breton, R., 471
Brinton, C., 478
Bronfenbrenner, U., 355
Bronfman family, 368
Broom, L., 1-2
Buber, M., 124-125, 282
Buchanon, J., 281
Bullough, V. L., 478
Buonarroti, M., 165
Burridge, K. O. L., 480

Calvin, J., 90, 229, 295-296
Camus, A., 122
Cantor, N., 197, 200, 474
Carnegie, A., 6, 271
Carroll, L., 41

Carter, J., 260
Castro, F., 187, 308
Cather, W., 243
Channing, W. E., 317
Charlemagne, 397
Charles I, king of England, 170
Charles II, king of England, 170
Chinoy, E., 480
Chirot, D., 115
Churchill, W., 165
Clammer, J., 472
Clark, B., 477
Clark, J., 79
Clark, S., 467, 480
Clark, S. D., 275
Clarke, J., 476
Clement, W., 104, 471
Clifford, G. J., 426
Cloward, R. A., 275, 479
Coady, M. M., 391–392, 395, 422, 426, 478
Cobban, A. B., 478
Cohen, A. K., 479
Cohn, N., 480
Coleman, J. S., 479
Columbus, C., 165
Comas, J., 390
Comte, A., 3–4, 24, 64, 279, 446
Cook, J., 127
Cooley, C. H., 6, 135, 449, 472
Coolidge, C., 260
Copernicus, 4, 288
Coser, L., 152
Costa-Pinto, L. A., 390, 474
Costa-Pinto, S., 480
Cotton, J., 295
Couette, R., 181
Cressey, D. R., 479
Crichton, R., 420
Cromwell, O., 170
Crysdale, S., 321
Curtis, J. E., 115

Dahl, R., 200
Dalai Lama, 308
Daniel, 163
Dante, 153, 473
Darwin, C., 5, 289

Davies, J., 480
da Vinci, L., 165, 229
Davis, K., 102, 155, 471
DeBary, W. T., 477
Debs, E., 248
Demara, F., 420
Demos, J., 336
Demos, V., 336
Derrick, C., 476
Descartes, R., 217
Dewey, J., 12, 391–395, 401, 406, 419, 422, 426, 439, 478
Dickey, J., 158
Diesel, R., 439
Djilas, M., 37
Dohen, D., 51–52, 470, 475
Domhoff, G. W., 200
Downes, D., 466
Dumont, F., 200
DuPont de Nemours, E. I., 475
DuPont family, 253, 368
Durkheim, E., 4, 24, 55, 64, 123, 221–223, 275, 278–279, 290, 320, 446, 452, 455, 475

Eckstein, H., 180, 474
Edison, T., 439
Einstein, A., 303–304, 439
Eisenhower, D. D., 65, 101, 165, 167, 260
Eliot, T. S., 304
Ellis, R., 480
Emerson, R. W., 209
Engels, F., 5, 171, 279, 351, 402, 469
Epictetus, 380
Epstein, J. L., 477
Etzioni, A., 20, 115, 479
Eustis, W., 186, 474
Evans-Pritchard, E., 155, 472, 476

Fallding, H., 155, 278, 320, 321
Feldman, K. A., 479
Feuerbach, L., 279
Flacks, R., 448, 479
Flew, A., 478
Ford, E., 263
Ford, G., 79
Ford, H., 263, 266, 439
Ford family, 253, 368
Fournier, A., 360
Fowler, M. L., 474
Fox, G., 295
Francis, E. K., 476
Franco, F., 248

Franklin, B., 42, 402, 439
Franklin, B. J., 68
Frazier, F., 390
Frederick Barbarossa, 398
Freeman, J., 458–459
Frei, E., 187
Freire, P., 392, 395, 422, 426, 478
Freud, S., 123, 155
Friedan, B., 28, 440
Friedenberg, E., 393, 478
Friedman, M., 21, 187, 274
Friedman, R., 274
Friedrichs, R. W., 33
Friedson, E., 479
Fromm, E., 153, 155, 320, 467
Frost, R., 348, 477
Fuller, A., 439
Furtado, C., 206, 474

Galbraith, J. K., 21, 38, 90–91, 99, 205, 274, 445, 479
Galilei, G., 165, 217, 439
Gandhi, I., 230
Gandhi, M. K., 163
Gaskin, S., 350
Gaugin, P., 127
George I, king of England, 240
George III, king of England, 166
Gerth, H. H., 33, 472, 473
Getty family, 253
Gibran, K., 229, 475
Gibson, J., 471
Giddings, F., xiv, 7
Gilder, G., 467
Gimpel, J., 477
Ginsberg, A., 27–28, 470
Ginsberg, M., 390
Gintis, H., 425, 478
Glenn, N. D., 62, 471
Glock, C. Y., 475, 476
Goffman, E., 140, 155, 472
Gold, G. L., 54, 56–57, 470
Golding, W., 158
Goldstein, S., 55, 470
Goode, W. J., 324, 376, 477
Goodman, P., 393, 478
Gordon, M., 336, 376
Gouldner, A. W., 2, 13, 19, 33
Gray, T., 101, 471
Grayson, J. P., 467, 480
Grayson, L. M., 467, 480
Greeley, A., 61, 321, 471
Greene, G., 117–119, 121, 128, 472
Greenfield, M., 18
Greer, C., 426

Guevara, C., 452
Gusfield, J., 467
Gutenberg, J., 165

Habermas, J., 153
Hagan, J., 466
Hagedorn, R., 68
Haile Selassie, emperor of Ethiopia, 167
Hareven, T., 346
Harrington, M., 200
Hastings, R., 478
Havighurst, R. J., 479
Heaps, D., 469
Heffner, R. D., 182
Hegel, G. F., 5, 152
Heilbroner, R. L., 258-259, 274
Helfgot, J., 470
Henry VIII, king of England, 295
Henshel, R., 144-145, 473
Heraclitus, 164
Herrnstein, R., 387, 393, 478
Hiller, H., 321
Himmelfarb, H. S., 477
Hitler, A., 139, 150, 163, 170, 180-181, 195, 248, 439
Ho Chi Minh, 187, 193
Hobbes, T., 151, 157-158, 473
Hodge, R. W., 469
Hofstadter, R., 33, 199, 469, 476, 478
Hollingshead, A., 480
Holt, J., 393, 478
Homans, G. C., 28-29, 155
Hoover, H., 260
Hope, B., 75
Horkheimer, M., 153
Horn, W., 478
Horowitz, I. L., 473
Hostos, E. de, 8, 20
Hu Shih, vi, 12, 340
Hughes, B., 323
Hughes, E. C., 416-417, 479
Hume, D., 399
Hunt, M., 359, 477
Hunt family, 253
Hus, J., 295
Hutchins, R., 393, 478
Hyland, R., 62, 471

Illich, I., 393, 426, 478
Inkeles, A., 131, 472
Innis, H. A., 8, 205, 275
Innocent III, pope, 162, 294, 473
Irini, S., 479
Isaiah, 318
Ishwaran, K., 376
Israel, H., 50, 470

Jacquet, C., 476
James, W., 282
Jefferson, T., 140, 166, 187, 229, 269, 272, 335, 401, 472
Jehoiakim, 163
Jencks, C., 425-426
Jensen, A., 387, 393, 478
Jeremiah, 163
Jesus, 163-164, 286, 292, 303, 337, 397, 439, 452
Joan of Arc, 163
John, king of England, 164, 169
John Paul II, pope, 308
Johnson, L.B., 260, 286
Jonassen, C. T., 50, 470
Jones, J., 153, 436-437
Juarez, B., 306-307

Kabir, H., 390
Kaestle, C., 426
Kagan, J., 346
Kant, I., 399
Kanter, R. M., 350, 477
Kantor, R., 476
Kaplan, A., 69
Karier, C., 426
Karweit, N., 477
Kaysen, C., 416, 479
Kelley, D., 476
Kenkel, W. F., 376, 477
Kennedy, J., 170, 181, 186, 260, 473
Kennedy family, 52, 253, 368
Kepler, J., 303
Kerr, C., 426
Keynes, J. M., 267
Khomeini, R., 163
Kierkegaard, S., 123, 282
Kilian, L. M., 467
King, M. L., 149, 163, 281, 314-315, 438, 452
Kinsey, A. C., 358
Kipling, R., 175
Kirby, E., 480
Kluckhohn, C., 82, 115
Kornhauser, W., 474

Kropotkin, P., 122
Kuhn, T. S., 33
Kunkel, J., 122, 155, 472

Labovitz, S., 68
Laidlaw, A. F., 426, 478
Landers, A., 430
Lantz, H., 376
Lao-zi, 203, 318
Lasch, C., 343, 356, 375, 477
Laslett, P., 336, 341, 376
Laurier, W., 171
Law, J., 224-225, 475
Lebedev, A. A., 307, 476
Lecky, W. E. H., 25
Lee, A. M., 63, 471
Leger, J., 79
Leiss, W., 206, 275
Lemert, E., 467
Lenin, V. I., 5, 187, 193, 195, 474, 477
Lenski, G., 59-62, 470
Leo XIII, pope, 299
Leonard, H., 323
Leonardo da Vinci, 165, 229
Leuchtag, E., 333
Levesque, G.-H., 8
Levesque, R., 172, 195-196
Levi-Strauss, C., 390
Levitt, K., 474
Liebow, E., 479
Lightfoot, G., 123
Lin, N., 68
Lincoln, A., 218, 303
Lindbergh, C., 438
Lindsey, B. B., 341-342
Lipset, S. M., 167, 199, 473, 474
Lister, J., 303
Locke, J., 166, 170, 187, 192, 199, 229, 306, 335, 399, 401, 439, 473
Lombroso, C., 446
Long, H., 181
Louis XIV, king of France, 166
Louis XVI, king of France, 167
Lower, A. R. M., 50, 52, 470
Lowie, R. H., 330
Lucan, 150, 473
Luckmann, T., 33
Lukes, S., 475
Luther, M., 229, 295-296

McCarthy, E., 28
McCarthy, J., 181
McClelland, D., 131, 472

McDougald, J. A., 88-89, 92-107, 111, 253
McGovern, G., 28
Machiavelli, N., 150
MacIver, R. M., xiii-xv, 112, 472
McKnight, J., 479
McLuhan, M., 205
McNall, S., 473
McNamara, P. H., 321
MacNeill, H. A., 130
McPartland, J. M., 477
Macpherson, C. B., 21, 187, 199, 473
Madsen, M., 132-133, 143, 145
Maharaj-ji, 312
Mahendra, king of Nepal, 333
Malinowski, B., 278
Manetti, G., 473
Mann, H., 404
Mannheim, K., 24, 82, 115, 320, 480
Manoel, king of Portugal, 167
Mao Zedong, 187, 193, 440
Marchland, B., 473
Marcuse, H., 153, 155, 320
Maritain, J., 187
Marx, G. T., 314-315
Marx, J., 5
Marx, K., 4-5, 24, 82, 99, 149, 152, 171, 187, 235, 247, 248, 269-270, 272, 279, 306, 314, 316, 320, 351, 402, 439, 455, 469
Maslow, A., 123
Mather, C., 295
Matza, D., 479
Mauss, M., 222, 275, 475
Mead, G. H., 123, 126, 146, 155, 391, 472
Mead, M., 53
Melbin, M., 475, 476
Mellon family, 253
Melville, H., 127
Merton, R. K., 84, 115, 151
Merton, T., 282
Michelangelo Buonarroti, 165
Milgram, S., 138-139, 143-145, 472
Miliband, R., 21, 206
Mill, J. S., 187
Mills, C. W., 13, 24-25, 33, 38, 200, 253, 275, 470, 472, 473

Milquetoast, C. (fictional character), 150
Miner, H., 54, 200, 470
Mishan, E. J., 206
Mitchell, W. O., 119-121, 128, 472
Montagu, A., 53, 390
Moon, S., 312
Moore, W. E., 102, 471
Morgan, L. H., 351
Moses, 439
Moulin, L., 476
Mugabe, R., 187
Muhammad, 163-164, 286, 439
Mumford, L., 480
Murdock, G. P., 331, 333, 376
Mussolini, B., 248

Napoleon, 170
Nasaw, D., 479
Nasser, G. A., 110
Neal, M. A., 320
Nehru, J., 110
Neill, A. S., 393, 478
Newman, P. C., 88, 471
Newton, I., 165, 217, 303, 399, 439
Nicholas Romanov II, czar of Russia, 161, 167
Niebuhr, H. R., 476
Nightingale, F., 303
Nisbet, R. A., 208, 471, 474
Nixon, R. M., 79, 84, 167
Nobel, A., 439
Nottingham, E., 278, 320
Noyes, J. H., 350
Nyerere, J., 187, 192, 205, 474

O'Connal, B., 119-121, 128
O'Dea, T., F., 115, 282, 320, 475, 480
Odum, H., 112, 472
Ohlin, L., 479
Orf, K., 339
Osborne, H. W., 68
Otto, R., 282
Owen, R., 350, 351

Padover, S. K., 472
Palavi, M. R., 169-170
Park, R., 455, 480
Parsons, T., 20, 33, 78, 82, 84, 87, 115, 151-153, 199, 208, 278-279, 321, 386
Pasteur, L., 303
Paul, 293-294, 303, 318, 397
Paz, O., 310, 476
Pearson, L. B., 165

Pepitone, A., 28-29, 470
Percival, E., 117-119, 121, 128
Peron, J., 181
Phillips, D. P., 450, 479, 480
Phipps family, 253
Photiadis, J. D., 61, 471
Picasso, P., 439, 442
Pipes, R., 200
Piven, F. F., 275
Plato, 161-162, 385-386, 393, 396, 398, 399
Pliny the Elder, 383, 477
Poblete, R., 480
Polanyi, K., 205-206, 222-224, 275, 464, 480
Polo, M., 165
Polsby, N., 200
Pope, L., 54, 470, 480
Porter, J., 20, 51, 104, 115, 470, 473, 477, 478
Porter, M., 477
Powdermaker, H., 476
Proudhon, P. J., 122
Prus, R. C., 479

Quinney, R., 466

Ranas family, 333
Rand, A., 133
Ray, J. E., 438
Reagan, R., 78-79, 260
Redfield, R., 53-54, 77, 115, 200, 470
Reich, C., 122, 472
Riel, L., 163
Riesman, D., 425
Riley, M., 68
Rinehart, J. W., 206, 275
Robbins, S. P., 475
Robbins, T., 476
Robertson, J., 206
Rock, P., 466
Rockefeller, J. D., 6
Rockefeller family, 253, 368
Roosevelt, F. D., 167, 181, 260, 409
Roosevelt, T., 167
Rosen, B. C., 472
Ross, E. A., xiii, 13, 24
Rossi, A. S., 346
Rossi, P. H., 479
Rotstein, A., 275
Rousseau, J.-J., 23, 126-127, 151, 166, 170, 187, 192, 193, 200, 229, 279, 401, 402, 470, 472, 474
Russell, B., 393, 478
Ryerson, E., 404

Salk, J., 452
Sanders, T. G., 476
Sapir, E., 282
Sartre, J.-P., 122, 123
Sawatsky, R., 321
Schachner, N., 478
Scheff, T., 467
Schmidt, H., 79
Schoenfeld, S., 321
Schreyer, E., 79
Schumacher, E. F., 206, 261, 274, 318,
    320, 476
Schumpeter, J., 25, 194, 474
Scott, W. G., 115
Selltiz, C., 68
Selznick, P., 1-2
Shah family, 333
Shakespeare, W., 5, 439
Shapiro, K., 282
Shils, E., 115
Shorter, E., 336, 356, 375, 477
Sihanouk, N., 161
Sills, D., 33
Simmel, G., 8, 12, 123, 152, 455
Simon, W. B., 474
Sinclair, P. R., 115
Sinclair, U., 248
Singer, I., 17
Skinner, B. F., 121-122, 135, 148,
    152-153, 155, 387
Slater, P., 324
Small, A., 7
Smelser, N. J., 467, 479
Smith, A., 187, 189, 193, 269, 439, 474
Smith, D. E., 476
Smith, J., 163, 296, 439, 452
Smith, M. E., 94
Smith, W., 476, 478
Socrates, 397
Solari, A., 473
Solomon, 162
Sousa, J. P., 75
Spellman, F., 101, 281
Spencer, H., xv, 5-6, 24, 64, 82, 187,
    279, 402, 469
Spencer, M., 480

Spengler, O., 22
Spiro, M., 355
Spring, J. H., 426
Stalin, J., 150, 195
Stark, R., 475
Stark, W., 320, 472, 476, 480
Stephens, W. N., 376
Stevenson, R. L., 127
Stokes, R., 475
Stonequist, E. V., 480
Stroessner, A., 181
Sumner, W. G., 6-7, 112, 464, 471
Sutherland, E. H., 449, 479
Suzuki, D. T., 282
Swanson, G. E., 278, 290, 475
Sweezy, P. M., 21, 206, 274

Tawney, R. H., 22, 50, 470
Taylor, F. W., 247
Taylor, I., 466
Tchaikovsky, P. I., 36
Tell, W., 90
Terman, L., 386
Thatcher, M., 79
Theresa of Avila, 350
Thomas, D. S., 470
Thomas, W. I., 37, 470
Thrupp, S., 480
Thurow, L. C., 274
Tiryakian, E. A., 50, 123, 321, 470
Titmuss, R., 14, 469
Tito, J., 110
Tocqueville, A. de, 182-183, 221, 457,
    480
Tomasson, R. F., 477
Tribhuvana, king of Nepal, 333
Trudeau, P. E., 79, 181, 200, 357, 473
Tumin, M., 471
Turnbull, C. M., 155
Turner, F. J., 243, 476
Turner, N., 314
Turner, R., 467
Twain, M., 243, 475

Unamuno, M. de, 17, 317, 476
Underhill, R., 290-291, 475

van den Berghe, P., 155
Veblen, T., 24, 100, 205, 402-403,419,
    471, 478
Vernon, G. M., 471
Victor Emmanuel, king of Italy, 167
Vidich, A. J., 115

Villa Rojas, A., 53-54, 470
Vogt, E. Z., 115
von Bollstadt, A., 304

Walker, M., 158, 473
Wallace, G., 181
Wallerstein, I., 106, 115
Walters, R., 136, 145, 472
Walton, J., 200
Walton, P., 466
Wangchuk, J. S., 161
Ward, L. F., xiii, 7, 13
Washington, B. T., 303
Washington, G., 36, 75, 440
Wayne, J., 75
Weber, Marianne, 40
Weber, Max, 8, 25, 40-49, 64-66, 102,
    119, 123, 161-166, 199, 235, 281,
    294, 336, 470, 472, 473
Weiner, M., 472
Wesley, J., 295
Wheatcroft, L., 321
White, O. K., 321
White, T. H., 75
Whitehead, A. N., 393, 478
Wilensky, H., 479
Wilhelm, kaiser of Germany, 167
Williams, R., 297
Williamson, J. B., 68
Wilmott, P., 376
Wilson, B., 300, 321, 476
Wilson, J., 467, 480
Wilson, W., 167, 260
Windsor, C., 335, 367
Wing-Tsit Chan, 474, 476
Withey, S. B., 426, 480
Wolfle, L. M., 477
Wolpin, M. D., 473
Woodcock, G., 122, 472
Woolworth, F. W., 439
Worsley, P., 480
Wrong, D., 152, 155, 471, 473
Wycliffe, J., 295

Yahweh, 163, 203, 216
Yinger, J. M., 278, 320-321, 479
Young, J., 466
Young, M., 376

Zijderveld, A., 123
Zorba the Greek (fictional character),
    283

Subject Index

Abortion, 231-232, 352
Absolutes, vi, 286, 464
Achievement and ascription, 372
Achievement motivation, 131-133
Addiction, 460
   (*See also* Alcoholism; Drug
      addiction)
Adoption, 328-329
Adult resocialization, 140-141
Adultery, 323, 339, 358-359
Advertising, 243, 267
Affinity, 326-327
Age:
   and deviance, 454
   drinking, 460
   at marriage, 342, 357
Aged, the, 112
   in labor force, 228
   and religion, 312
   social segregation of, 311
Aggression:
   of adults, 138-140
   of children, 136
Agricultural work, 215
Agriculture:
   and domestication of nature,
      208-209

Agriculture (*Cont.*):
   and economic development, 226-228
   mechanization of, 227
   monopolization in, 244
Alcoholism, 435
   (*See also* Drunkenness)
Alienation, 158
   economic, 178-185
   effects of, 179-186
   (*See also* Powerlessness)
Alleluia, 282
Amen, 282
American Sociological Association, 7, 10
Anarchists, 122-123
Anarchy:
   politics as safeguard against, 157-158
   religion as safeguard against,
      278-279
Ancestry, determination of, 331
Animal husbandry, 208-209
Ann Landers syndrome, 430
Anomie, 157, 221, 452, 455
Anorexia nervosa, 434
Anthropology, 7, 29, 53-54, 63,
     124-125
Anthropomorphism, 206
Anticlericalism, 305-306

Anti-Semitism, 292, 294
Antitrust legislation, 246
Art:
   innovation in, 439
   and religion, 282-283
Artists, 149-150
Ascription and achievement, 372
Atheism, 305-307
Authority:
   charismatic, 162-164, 293
   defined, 98, 174
   legal-rational, 164-168
      sources of, 165-166
      threats to, 170-185
   in medieval times, 160-162, 197
   vs. military power, 174
   of parents, 366-370
   political, expansion of, 218
   vs. power, 98, 159-160, 174
   traditional, 160-162, 164
Automation, 215-216, 228
Automobile crashes, 450
Automobiles, 262-263

Balkanization, 220
Behaviorism, 121, 146

487
SUBJECT INDEX

Being and becoming, 123
Beyond, the, 281-287, 313, 316-318
Bilateral descent, 331, 336-337
Biography, 24-25
    dehumanizing view of, 128
    as research technique, 49
    sense of, 389
Biological basis of the family, 325-326, 335
Birthrates, 230-232
Blood, sale of, 238
Boundaries, national, 74
Bourgeoisie, 104
    (See also Middle class; Ruling class)
Bureaucracies:
    functionalist analysis of, 96-97
    private (see Corporations)
    public, 89, 248-250, 253, 256-257
    reward structure in, 105

Calvinism, 41
Capital, monopolization of (see Monopolization of capital)
Capitalism, 92, 234-272
    characteristics of, 236-241
    and class conflict, 238, 247-255
    vs. communism, 109-110
    contemporary problem of, 269-271
    and crime, 445, 462-463
    and cultural organization, 93-94
    defined, 241
    dynamism of, 194, 237, 355-356, 442
    and family life, 94-95, 342-348, 355-372
    future of, 258-259, 271-272
    ground rules of, 271
    and inequality, 238, 247-255
    international, 105-109, 194-195, 235
    and liberal democracy, 188-189, 197, 234-235
    and market mode of exchange, 226
    in nineteenth century, 242-243
    one-sidedness of, 235-241, 300
    planning, 258-259
    political aspects of, 89
    products of, 265-268
    and Protestantism, 41-66
    as reason for socialism, 194-195

Capitalism (Cont.):
    and religion, 295-304
    resilience of, 259
    and rights of labor, 247-250
    and role of government, 237, 256-260
    and schooling, 403-412
    social stratification in, 250-255
    as strategy vs. stage, 235
    and trend toward monopoly, 242-246
    and urbanization, 260-265
    welfare, 248-250
Cars (see Automobiles)
Case studies, 50
Catastrophe, 455
Catholicism, 41-42, 46, 50-57, 60-62, 65-66, 277-280, 299, 305-309
    and birth control, 230
    and dissent, 457
    family patterns in, 329
    and monotheism, 291
    and public schools, 407
    and schooling, 44
    and universities, 402
Celibacy, 338-341
Census data, 54-55
Change, social (see Dynamism; Economy; Education; Family, the; History; Innovation; Liberation; Polity; Religion)
Charisma, 123
    as basis of authority, 162-164, 180-181
    in religious evolution, 293-294
    and religious revival, 312-313
    routinization of, 164
Child-of-nature hypothesis, 128
Childhood:
    in medieval Europe, 339
    in modern Western world, 345, 355
Christianity, 287
    and family life, 336-340
    medieval, 294
    religious significance of, 292-293
    (See also Religion, Christian)
Church attendance, 301
Church-state separation, 297-300
Churches and sects, 298-299
Cities:
    and family life, 346-347
    and innovation, 455
    size of, 261-262
    (See also Urbanization)
Civil religion, 309
Clan, 331, 336, 339
Class (see Social class)

Class conflict, 238, 247-255
Clergy, the, 289, 302, 414
Clocks as sign and measure of work, 215
Cold war, 109-110, 176
Collective bargaining, 248-249
Collective behavior, 440-444, 458-459
    origins of, 451-461
Collectivism vs. individualism, 124-125
Colleges and universities (see Universities and colleges)
Commodities, 92, 236
    defined, 224-225
    of doubtful worth, 267-268
Common sense, 19-20, 46
Communications networks, 458-459
Communism:
    vs. capitalism, 109-110
    and family life, 350-355
    as stage of development, 235
Compadrazgo, 329
Comparative studies, 50, 82
Competitiveness, 132-134
Complex organizations, 96
    (See also Bureaucracies; Corporations)
Computer programming vs. education, 421-422
Computers:
    and money, 225
    in research, 63
Concentration of capital, 243-247
Concepts:
    formation of, 35-39
    key, 45, 380-381
Conceptual schemes, 39-43, 62, 380-381, 444
Conflict theorists, 152
Conformity, 431-432
    as deviance, 447-451
Conjugality, 326-328
    (See also Marriage)
Consanguinity, 326-328
    (See also Kinship)
Conspicuous consumption, 100
    and the higher learning, 402-403
Constitutional government, 164-170
    threats to, 170-185
    ways to strengthen, 184
Consumer loans, 267
Consumer spending, 266-267
Contemporary records, 51-52, 62, 458
Content analysis, 376
Contextual imperative, 149-150
Contraceptives, 230-232, 357-360
Contradictions in everyday life, 84, 86, 452-455

Control variables, 44-45
  in demographic analysis, 55
  in survey research, 60-61, 314-315
Conversion, religious, 293-294
Cooperative education, 392, 419
Coparenthood, 329
Corporations, 92
  as agents of change, 442
  and arms industry, 268
  defined, 238-241
  early, 240
  increasing size of, 244-247
  largest, 106, 246
  multinational, 106-109
  need for, 239
  need to control, 257, 260
  size of, 257
Correlation, 55
Correspondence schools, 395
Countercultures, 349-351, 437-438
Coups d'etat, 175-178
  means of preventing, 178
  prerequisites for, 176-177
Crazes, 441-442
Crime, 445
  capitalism and, 445, 462-463
  defined, 84
  organized, 460
  urban, 264
  white-collar, 449
Crowds, 436
Cultural relativism, 234
Culture, 78-86
  agencies of, 93-94
  Christian, 292-293
  erotic, 337-338
  and family life, 326-335
  and individual rights, 462-463
  legal aspects of, 80
  mass, 178-180, 266-267
  modern: economic, 228-230
    political, 165-168, 196-197
  national, 75
  vs. nature, 392
  sacred vs. profane, 288-289
  secularization of, 300-304
  and social class, 250-255
  and social structure, 78-80
  of socialism, 191-193

Culture (*Cont.*):
  traditional: economic, 42-43,
    206-207, 214, 216, 233
    political, 160-162, 171-174
  transmission of, 129-137, 382-387,
    396-397, 403-409
  and universities, 402-403
Custom, 81
  in traditional societies, 160-162
  (*See also* Traditionalism)

Dance, 83
Data, defined, 46
Databanks, 59
Death, 101
  denial of, 310-312
  personal control of, 434
  rates, 230-232
  as reason for religion, 278-279, 281,
    316
  by suicide, 434-435, 450
Deficit spending, 267
Delinquency (*see* Deviance)
Demagoguery, 180-181
Demands (*see* Structure of demands)
Democracy:
  in Aristotle's theory, 162
  conceptions of, 185-196
  degrees of, 170-185
  kinds of, 185-196
  vs. legal-rational government,
    169-170
  liberal, 186-191
  little evidence of, 185
  slow path to, 170
  socialist, 187, 191-196
Demographic techniques, 54-55, 62
Demographic transition, 231
Denomination, religious, 298-299
Dependent variables, 44-45
  in demographic analysis, 55
  in survey research, 58-61, 314-315
Descent, rules of, 331
Despotism in democracies, 182-183
Detachment from nature, 224, 236
Development (*see* Economic
  development)
Deviance, 84-85, 96
  from ascetic morality, 360-361
  conceptual scheme for, 444
  as conformity, 447-451
  defined, 431-432
  and family, 448-449
  helpful vs. harmful, 463
  from norms about sex, 328
  types of, 433-444

Deviance (*Cont.*):
  from Western family, 349-372
  and youth, 454
  (*See also* Liberation)
Deviant subcultures, 449
Dialectic:
  and art, 155
  defined, 121
  of economic development, 207-208
    and capitalism, 235-236
  Marxian, 4
  of person, 117-128
    and deviance, 432
    and education, 383-396
    and family life, 344, 373
    misapplications of, 126-128
    and outlook on politics, 157-158
    and religion, 316-318
    and sociologists, 151-153
    and theories of religion, 278-279
Dialogic vs. antidialogic education,
  392, 403-404
Differential association theory, 449
Dimension of humility, 121, 126-128
  contemporary evidence, 129-142
  defined, 121
  and family life, 344
  and religion, 316-318
  (*See also* Dialectic, of person)
Dimension of pride, 121, 126-128
  in capitalist economy, 344
  contemporary evidence, 142-150
  defined, 121
  (*See also* Dialectic, of person)
Disarmament, 178
Discipline:
  of sociology, 19-20
  work and, 214
Discontent, 451-461
  mobilization of, 458-459
  outlets for, 456-461
Diversification, 246
Division of labor, 29
  under capitalism, 251-252, 413-421
  in economic development, 220-222
  in sociology, 10-12
Divorce, 339, 361-366
Domestication of nature, 208-209
Donkey power, 146, 435, 456-457
Dowries, 367
Draft animals, 211-212
Drug addiction, 434, 456, 460
Drunkenness, 434, 447, 460
Dynamism:
  of capitalist economy, 194, 237,
    355-356, 442

Dynamism (*Cont.*):
  in educational thought, 389
Dysfunctional phenomena, 96

Eastern Orthodoxy, 295, 305–307
Economic development, 206–234
  and agricultural production, 226–228
  and birth control, 230–232
  capitalist mode of (*see* Capitalism)
  defined, 207
  and the division of labor, 220–222
  and domestication of nature, 208–209
  and energy, 210–214
  and eroticism, 338
  and family, 337, 342–345, 372–374
  geological constraints on, 212–214, 258–259
  and gift giving, 222–224
  and history, 207–208, 233–234
  imbalanced, 217–218
  literacy and, 216–218
  and market economics, 224–226
  mistaken path of, 213–214
  and modernization, 228–230
  and modes of exchange, 222–226
  one-sided theories of, 234–242
  principles of, 208–232
  and progress, 233–234
  and religion, 287–293
  and size of societies, 218–220
  socialist kind of, 305–308
  stages of, 235
  technological aspects of, 209–210
  topsy-turvy kind of, 269
  variety in, 207–208, 226–227, 233–234
  work and, 214–216
  (*See also* Communism; Socialism)
Economic growth, 241, 258–259
Economics:
  as dismal science, 204–206
  vs. sociology, 21
  substantive vs. formal, 205
Economy, 202–275
  capitalist (*see* Capitalism)
  defined, 203
  functionalist outlook on, 87, 89, 92–93

Economy (*Cont.*):
  hunting and gathering, 206–209
  impact on politics of, 196–197
  primitive, 222–224
  of scale, 219–220
Education, 378–426
  adult, 382, 391–392, 408
  as becoming more, 387–396
  Coady's theory of, 391–392
  vs. computer programming, 421–422
  content of, 383–384, 388
  cooperative, 392, 419
  through correspondence, 395
  defined, 381, 383–393
  Dewey's theory of, 391
  dialectical outlooks on, 387–396
  dialogic vs. antidialogic, 392, 403–404
  as dispensing truth, 383–387, 393–396
  extension, 391–392
  Freire's theory of, 392
  functionalist outlook on, 87, 95, 386
  one-sided outlooks on, 383–387, 393–396, 419–420
  origins of formal, 396–407, 409–410
  Plato's theory of, 385
  political, 184
  in primary and secondary schools, 403–409
  professional (*see* Professions)
  vs. schooling, 381, 395–396, 408
  self-, 383
  and sociology, 423–424
  vs. training, 394–395, 420–421
  in universities, 397–403, 409–410, 412–421
  vertical and horizontal dimensions of, 382
  (*See also* Schooling; Universities and colleges)
EEC (European Economic Community), 108
Electricity, 212–213
Elephantiasis, social, 220
Elites, 104, 253–254
Empires, 76–77
  colonial policies of, 174–175
Empiricism, 23
Endogamy, 365
  (*See also* Exogamy and endogamy)
Enemies of legal government, 170–185
  alienation in everyday life, 178–185
  lingering traditionalism, 171–174
  militarism, 174–178

Energy, 210–214
  nonrenewable sources of, 212–214, 316
  renewable sources of, 211–212
  and urban renewal, 265
Enlightenment, the, 399
Environment:
  adaptation to, 203
  control of, 134, 144–145
  effects of diverse, 455
  pollution of, 257–259
Equal rights amendment, 27
Equality, 317
Eroticism, 337–338
Eroticization:
  of everyday life, 360
  of marriage, 358
Established church, 298, 307
Ethnic groups, 111–112
  aboriginal vs. immigrant, 447
  and deviance, 447–448
  and public schools, 404–406
  and social movements, 443
Ethnocentrism, 234
Evaluation research, 14
Evolution, religious, 287–294
Exchange, economic, 222–226
Existential philosophy, 122–123
Exogamy and endogamy, 333–334
  in medieval Christendom, 337

Fads, 441–442
Family, the, 322–376
  attempts to minimize, 347–355
  biological basis of, 325–326, 335
  biological vs. sociological, 326–327
  breakdown of Western, 355–374
  under capitalism, 94–95, 342–348, 355–372
  in Christendom, 336–340
  under communism, 350–355
  decline of, 323–324, 355–372
  defined, 327
  and deviance, 448–449
  early modern, 340–342
  and economy, 342–346, 355
  extended, 341
  functionalist outlook on, 87, 94–95, 324–325
  on kibbutzim, 353–354
  Marxian perspective on, 324, 351–353
  medieval, 336–340
  neolocal, 331, 341
  nuclear, 342–346
  persistent value on, 371–372

Family, the (*Cont.*):
  policy and ideology of, 355–356
  reward structure in, 105
  socially constructed character of,
    326–335
  as sociocultural system, 85–86
  in utopian communities, 348–351
Family planning (*see* Birth control)
Farming (*see* Agriculture)
Federal political structure, 89
Fieldwork, 52–54, 56–57, 62, 458
Firms (*see* Corporations)
First New Nation (Lipset), 167
First Sociology, 14
Folkways, 112
Font-of-knowledge outlook, 383–384
Forms of liberation, 431–445
Fornication, 323, 339, 358
Fossil fuels, 212–214, 316
Freedom, 30, 143–144, 153, 440, 444, 464
  conditions for, 452
  vs. determinism, 122–123
  enemies of (*see* Enemies of legal
    government)
  of religion, 297
Frontier, last, and religion, 318
Fueros, 165
Functional needs, 87
Functionalism (*see* Structural
  functionalism)
Funeral rites, 311

General will, the, 191–193
Gentrification, 265
G.I. bill of rights, 409–410
Gift giving, 222–226
Glossolalia, 282
GNP (gross national product), 92, 241
Go-getter, 131, 344
Government:
  charismatic, 162–164
  and corporations, 240–241, 257, 260
  defined, 159
  and economic development, 222–226
  growth of, 253, 256–260
  of law, 164–170
    kinds of, 186–196
    threats to (*see* Enemies of legal
      government)

Government (*Cont.*):
  metropolitan, 265
  national, 73–74
  role in capitalist economy, 237,
    256–260
  and schooling, 403–407, 409–410
  separation from religion, 288–289,
    297–300
  traditional, 160–162
Gross national product (GNP), 92, 241
Gun control, 460

Hare Krishna, 282
"Haven in a heartless world," family as,
  343
Higher learning, 397–403, 409–421
  (*See also* Schooling; Universities and
    colleges)
Historical records, 49–51, 62
Historicism, 207–208
History:
  and biography, 24–25
  and countercultures, 437–438
  dehumanizing view of, 126–128
  in education, 389, 401–402, 420
  escape from, 313
  and idea of progress, 207–208,
    233–234
  intrusion of self on, 432, 438
  life, 49
  outlooks for grasping, 97–99
  vs. sociology, 21–22
  theories of, 15
  traditional ignorance of, 160–164
Hobbes's question, 151–152
Holism, 20–21
Holy words, 282–283
Home, meaning of, 348
Homicide, 457, 460
Homo duplex theorem, 123
Homosexuals, 112, 323
Honor, 100–105
  (*See also* Occupational prestige;
    Social class; Social stratifi-
    cation)
Households, constitution of, 331–332
Housing, 252
Humanist sociology, 12–14, 15–18
Humility (*see* Dimension of humility)
Hunting and gathering societies,
  206–207, 214
  religion in, 287–288
Hypotheses, 43–46
  key, 45
  methods of testing (*see* Methods of
    testing hypotheses)

I and *me*, 123
I and *Thou*, 125
Id, 123
Identity:
  national, 74–75
  personal, 117–128
    and family, 323, 373
    Jewish, 454
    looking-glass self, 135
    and power, 146
Ideology, 82, 197
  (*See also* Values)
Illegitimacy, 328, 358–359
  in medieval times, 339
Illness, 434
Immigration and schooling, 404–406
Imposters, 420
Incest, 333
Income supplements, 249
Income tax, 256
Incongruous experience, 84, 86,
  452–455
Independent variables, 44–45
  in demographic analysis, 55
  in survey research, 58–61, 314–315
Individualism:
  vs. collectivism, 124–125
  possessive, 189
Industrialization, 209–210, 234
  and Christianity, 292–293
  (*See also* Economic development)
Inequality:
  in capitalist societies, 238, 247–255
  in division of labor, 222
  explanations for, 102
  in honor, 100–105
  in income, 99–100, 252–253
  international, 107–108
  political, 169
  of power, 98–105, 147–148
  of power vs. income, 252–253
  among prostitutes, 253
  and religion, 278–279, 281, 309–310,
    316–318
  sexual, 332–333, 344–345, 362–366
    and deviance, 456–457
    and women's movement, 458–459
  among slaves, 250
  in Third World, 217
  in wealth, 99–105
  (*See also* Social class; Social
    stratification)
Infallibility, 286, 309
Infant mortality, 234
Infanticide, 332
Infrastructure, 89

Inheritance, 366-370
Innate intelligence, 388
Innovation, 147-149, 438-444
    under capitalism, 267, 463
    as deviance, 432
    and play, 215
    religious, 293-294
    and role of teacher, 397
    and rule of selfishness, 237
    and social-contract theory, 165-166,
        171-172
    in socialist societies, 193
    sources of, 85, 451-456
Institutional school of economists, 205
Institutionalization vs. change, 152
Institutions:
    defined, 87
    formalization of, 396
    functionalist definition of, 325
    (See also Economy; Education;
        Family, the; Polity; Religion)
Insult in social science, 17-18, 143
Insurance plans, public, 249
Intellectuals, 22-23, 454-455
Intelligence (IQ) tests, 386-388, 390
Intermarriage, 453-454
Intermittent reinforcement, 122
Internalization, 135
International capitalism, 105-109,
    194-195, 235
International Sociological Association,
    8
Interviewing, 47, 57, 59-60
Inventors, 439-440
Investment:
    direct, 194
    indirect, 195
Investment money, 99-100
IQ (intelligence) tests, 386-388, 390

Jewish identity, 454
Jogging, 441
Jonestown (Guyana), 153
Journalism, 22
Judaism, 41, 55, 60, 62, 65, 365, 480
    ancient, 163
    and innovation, 454
    as religion, 286-287, 291
Just price of a good, 188

Kibbutzim, 353-354
Kinship, 326-335
    and incest taboo, 333
    and social change, 337
    in utopian communities, 350-351
    in Western world, 335-346
    (See also Family, the; Marriage)
Knowledge, 383-396
Kolkhozy, 353

Labor:
    division of (see Division of labor)
    skilled vs. unskilled, 215-216
    wage (see Wage labor)
    (See also Work)
Labor force, the:
    in agriculture, 227
    children in, 345
    contemporary, 215-216, 227-228
    rigidities in, 419
    self-employed in, 244-245
    women in, 345, 352, 364
Labor unions (see Unions)
Language, 37, 81
    anthropomorphic, 206
    and economic development, 216-218
    of family breakdown, 323-324
    of kinship, 329-330
    in national societies, 75-76
    and prestige of professions, 421
    in university instruction, 401
Latent functions, 151
Law:
    child-labor, 345
    of corporations, 238-241
    vs. custom, 81
    defined, 80-81
    divorce, 341, 362
    family, 328, 341
    government of (see Government,
        of law)
    labor, 248-249
    natural, 3-5, 162
    of natural selection, 5-6
    profession of, 399, 414, 421
    and professionalization, 414-415
    and sexual behavior, 357
    of three stages, 3
Leisure, 214-216
    marriage as, 365-366
    parenthood as, 369
Level of analysis, 47-48, 71-72
Liberalism:
    and capitalism, 188-189, 197,
        234-235
    origins of, 188-189

Liberalism (Cont.):
    and religion, 295-304
Liberation, 428-467
    attack as, 438-444
    collective, 436-438, 440-444
    defined, 430, 432
    and deviance, 432
    explanation of attempts at, 446-461
    forms of, 431-445
    individual, 433-435, 438-440
    possibility of, 464
    withdrawal as, 433-438
Life expectancy, 230-231, 310
Limits:
    of behavioral science, 143-144
    biological, 433
    of human population, 230-232
    religious response to, 281-287, 313,
        316-318
    of sociology, 456
Lineage, calculation of, 331
Literacy, 130, 195
    and economic development, 216-218
    and origin of schooling, 403-404
    programs for teaching, 392
    rates of, 217
Little communities, 77, 218
    and deviance, 461
Looking-glass self, 135
Love:
    falling in, 344
    in medieval family, 338-339
    and sex, 352, 357, 364

Magic, 289-290
Manifest functions, 151
Manufacturing, 227
Marginal man, the, 455
Marginal strata, 251-252
Market, 224-226
    (See also Capitalism)
Marriage:
    analogy with politics, 186
    companionate, 341-342
    complex, 350
    defined, 326
    eroticization of, 358
    group, 332, 350
    and increase in divorce, 361-366
    on kibbutzim, 353-354
    mate selection for, 333-334
    minimization of, 350-351
    monogamous vs. polygamous, 332
    political aspect of, 159
    and rules of endogamy, 333-334
    sex in, 357

Marriage (*Cont.*):
  sharing in, 364–365
  across status lines, 453–454
  in Western world, 335–349
  (*See also* Family, the)
Marxian outlook:
  on capitalism, 235, 247–248,
    269–270
  on economy, 306
  on family, 324, 351–352
  on inequality, 104
  on peasant class, 171
  on police, 11
  on politics, 194–195
  on religion (*see* Religion, Marxian
    outlook on)
  on social psychology, 152–153
Mass culture, 178–180, 266–267
Mass media, 450
  (*See also* Newspapers; Television)
Mass production, 266
Mass society, 180–181
Masturbation, 339, 358
Mathematics:
  for economic development, 217, 227,
    231, 234
  in social research, 58–59, 63–64,
    68
Matrilineal family, 331
Matrilocal family, 331
Me and *I*, 123
Measurement:
  of concepts, 38
  of economic development, 217, 227,
    231, 234
  of educational outcomes, 393–396
  in money terms, 224–225, 236
  of status, 103–104
Mechanical solidarity, 221
Mechanization of industry, 251–252
Media, mass, 450
Medical profession, 399, 414
  and death, 311
  and magic, 289–290
Mental illness, 434–435
Mental retardation, 388–389
Mercantilism, 188
Mercenaries, 238
Metaphysical stage of knowledge, 3

Methods of research, 34–69
  concept formation, 36–39
  conceptual schemes, 41–43
  hypotheses, 46–62
  testing hypotheses, 46–62
Methods of testing hypotheses, 46–62
  analysis of contemporary records,
    51–52, 458–459
  analysis of historical records, 49–51
  demographic techniques, 54–55
  fieldwork, 52–54, 56–57, 458–459
  surveys, 58–62, 314–315
Metric system, 110
Middle class, 250–252
  from old to new, 38
  and schooling, 411
  and youth movement, 449
Migration, 453
Militancy and religion, 314–315
Militarism, 174–178
  of European empires, 175
  in Latin America, 175–178
Military aid, 176–178
Minimum wage laws, 248
Minority groups, 111–112
  and illegitimacy, 328
  (*See also* Ethnic groups)
Mobility:
  geographical: and deviance, 453
    and parental authority, 369
  social, 453
Mobilization of discontent, 458–459
Models in child socialization, 136
Modernity:
  defined, 229
  economic, 228–230
  and education, 389–393
  individual, 131
  political, 165–168, 196–197
  and professional schooling, 418–421
  and religion, 303–304
  and universities, 399–403
Modernization, defined, 229
Modes of economic exchange, 222–226
Monarchy, decline of, 167, 169–170
Monasticism, 282–284, 294, 296,
    437–438
  and family life, 349–350
Money, 99–100
  in capitalist economy, 236
  study of, 205
  types of, 224–225
Monogamy, 332–333, 339
Monopolization of capital, 243–247
  and divorce, 365
  efforts to halt, 246

Monopolization of capital (*Cont.*):
  and family breakdown, 371
  and freedom, 463
  and parent-child relations, 366–370
  and spread of schooling, 404–418
  and urbanization, 261–262
Monotheism, 290–291
Mounds, Amerindian, 207
Multinational corporations, 106–109
Multiple-choice tests, 387, 388, 394,
    420
Murder, 457, 460

Naming things, 35–39, 216–217
  in religious doctrine, 284, 288
Nation, 74
National societies, 72–78
  defined, 76
  diversity of school systems among,
    407
  diversity of universities among, 402
  international constraints on, 105–111
  modern, 228–230
  population densities of, 260–261
  size of, 90–91
  socialization in, 134
  as sociocultural systems, 78–86
  as structures of demands, 86–89,
    91–97
  as structures of rewards, 97–105
Native-born population, 74
Natural children, 328
Nazism, 180–181, 292
Neolithic age, 208–210
Neolocal family, 331, 341
Newspapers, 3, 115, 199, 274, 395
  circulation of, 408
  and suicide, 450
No-fault divorce laws, 362
Noble-savage hypothesis, 126–128
Nonaligned nations, 109–110
Nonverbal indicators of group life, 52
Norm, defined, 78–79
Novelty (*see* Dynamism; History;
    Innovation)

Occupational prestige, 16
  and professionalization, 411–418
  of teachers, 416–417
Occupational specialization, 220–222
  (*See also* Division of labor)
Oil-and-vinegar analogy, 342–344
Oil shortage, 213, 265
Om, 282
One-sidedness:
  of capitalism, 300

One-sidedness (*Cont.*):
  in economic development, 235–241
  in educational thought, 383–387,
    393–396, 419–421
  of Marxism, 306
  and religion, 317–318
  in social psychology, 121–122
Operant conditioning, 121
Organic solidarity, 221
Organizations:
  typology of religious, 298–299
  (*See also* Bureaucracies;
    Corporations)
Orthodoxy, Eastern, 295, 305–307
Otherworldliness, 41–42, 340
Overpopulation, 230–231, 316
Overproduction, 267
Oversocialized conception of man,
  152
Ownership, 99
  concentration of, 243–247
  declining significance of, 250–251
  foreign, 106–108
  home, 252
  inequalities in, 100
  private, 236–237

Paradise:
  fool's, 213
  nonexistence of, 127–128
Parental authority, 366–370, 408–409
Partial societies, 192
Participant observation, 52–54, 56–57,
  458
Patrilineal family, 331
Patrilocal family, 331
Peasants, 171
Peer groups, 135, 449
Pentecostalism, 312–313, 317–318
Percent of variation explained, 143
Percentage tables, 55, 60–61
Perception, 141–142
Perquisites, 99–100
Persons:
  artificial (*see* Corporations)
  real, 116–155
    and education, 383–396
Philosopher-kings, 385
Philosophy, 23

Planning:
  of change, 355–356
  economic, 258–259
  family, 230–232
  and freedom, 464
  rejection of, 359
  urban, 264–265
Plato's theory of education, 385–386
Play:
  and innovation, 215
  in social research, 38
  socializing aspects of, 136
  vs. work, 214
Police, 10–12, 73
  need for, 178
Political movements (*see* Social
  movements)
Political parties, 189–190, 260
Political science, 21
Political subdivisions, 88
Polity, 156–200
  change of, 442–444, 458–459
  defined, 158
  and family life, 343–344
  functionalist outlook on, 87–89
  and multinational corporations, 108
  relation to economy, 196–197
  and religion, 288, 297–300, 305–308
  (*See also* Government)
Polyandry, 332
Polygyny, 332–333
Polytheism, 290–291
Population:
  control of, 230–232
  densities, 260–261
  explosions, 231–232
  horse, 212
  limits on human, 316
  native-born, 74
  in school, 407–408
  world, 230–231
Positive stage of knowledge, 3
Positivism, 10–18
Postal service, 256
Potlatch, 222–224
Power, 98–105
  vs. authority, 98, 159–160, 174
  and creativity, 146
  defined, 98
  in division of labor, 222
  donkey, 146, 435, 456–457
  economic: political importance of,
    184
    variation in, 147
  and history, 99
  military, 174–178

Power (*Cont.*):
  and modernity, 229–230
  of nature, 206–207, 235
  of parents, 408–409
  as precondition for humanness,
    144–149
  shortage of, 252–253
  straw-boss, 251
  through work, 147–148
Powerlessness:
  in advanced capitalism, 253
  and religion, 312–313
  and sexual behavior, 361
  (*See also* Alienation)
Predictability, sources of, 145
Premarital sex, 323, 339, 358–360
Prestige (*see* Honor)
Pride (*see* Dimension of pride)
Priesthood of all believers, 296
Primary groups, 135, 449
Prisons, 140
Private consumption, 252–255, 266–267
Private property, 236–237
Probability theory, 58–59, 143
Products of capitalism, 265–268
Profane vs. sacred, 288–289
Professions, 411–421
  conditions for success of, 414
  vs. education, 418–421
  and parental authority, 369–370
  proliferation of, 413
  and schooling, 412–413
  vs. unions, 411–412
  (*See also specific professions, for
    example*: Law, profession of;
    Medical profession; Teachers)
Progress, idea of, 206–208, 233–234
Proletariat, 104
  (*See also* Working class)
Property (*see* Ownership)
Prophets, 163, 180–181, 439
Propositions (*see* Hypotheses)
Protection rackets, 218
Protestantism:
  and capitalism, 41–66
  and family life, 340–342
  history of, 295–296
  religious significance of, 291,
    295–304
  and universities, 399
  value on work in, 229
Psychology:
  social: defined, 117
    reviewed, 117–155
  vs. sociology, 26–29, 38–39, 451–452
Psychoses, 434

Public bureaucracies, 89, 248-250, 253, 256-257
Public order, defined, 159

Quack, defined, 416
Quadrivium, 398
Quantitative research methods, 54-55, 58-63
Quantophrenia, 63
Questionnaires, 47, 59-60

Random sample, 58
Reciprocity:
  denial of, 386
  in economic life, 206-208
  in education, 386, 388-396, 422
  in gift giving, 223
  in human relations, 124-125, 149-150
Records:
  contemporary, 51-52, 62, 458
  historical, 49-51, 62
Redistribution, 224-226
Reform vs. revolution, 443
Religion, 276-321
  authentic, 282-283
  Christian, 292-308
    (*See also* Christianity)
  civil, 309
  and civil rights militancy, 314-315
  and death, 310-312
  decline of, 287-312
  defined, 282, 286
  and economy, 41-66
  evolution of, 287-295
  and family values, 336-342
  functionalist outlook on, 87, 93-94, 277-279, 284, 290-291, 309
  future of, 309-318
  under liberal capitalism, 295-300
  likelihood of, 312-313, 316-318
  vs. magic, 289-290
  Marxian outlook on, 277-279, 284, 290-291, 306, 309, 314
  monotheistic, 290-291
  under nonliberal regimes, 305-308
  possibility of eliminating, 309-312
  rebellious, 280-281, 284-285
  as response to limits, 281-287, 313, 316-318
  sectarian, 436-438

Religion (*Cont.*):
  and social class, 284-285, 312-313
  socially constructed character of, 285-286
  (*See also specific religions, for example:* Catholicism; Judaism; Pentecostalism; Protestantism)
Research methods (*see* Methods of research)
Resocialization, 140-141
Resources:
  nonrenewable, 212-214
    and religion, 316
  renewable, 211-212
  of violence, 73
    improvement of, 174, 177-178
    spending on, 174-178, 268
Revolutions, 167, 443-444
  causes of, 451-457
  proletarian, 247
  and religion, 306
Reward, selective, 134-135
Rewards (*see* Structure of rewards)
Riverside Church (New York City), 303-304
Role conflict, 86
Roles:
  defined, 78-79
  deviant, 447-451
  in family vs. economy, 343-344
  fixed in custom, 81
  legal definition of, 80
  and personal identity, 139
  power attached to, 98-99, 147-148
  of women, 344-345
Roman Catholicism (*see* Catholicism)
Routinization of charisma, 164
  in Christianity, 294
Rule of selfishness, 237
Ruling class, 104, 253

Sacred vs. profane, 288-289
Sacred words, 282-283
Safecracking, 225
Sampling, 58-59
SAT (Scholastic Aptitude Test), declining scores on, 408
Schizophrenia, 434
Schooling, 396-421
  and civil rights militancy, 315
  desirability of, 410
  and deviance, 454
  vs. education, 381, 395-396, 408
  elite, 95
  higher, 397-403, 409-421
  inadequacies of, 419-420, 423
  and IQ tests, 386-388, 390

Schooling (*Cont.*):
  and parentage, 368-369
  in Plato's theory, 385
  primary and secondary, 403-409
  private, 95
  and professionalization (*see* Professions)
  public, 403-411
  and religion, 299, 302
  secondary, 406
  self-, 383
  and social class, 411-412
  social origins of, 396-407
  and teachers' prestige, 416-417
  techniques of, 386
  in two-year colleges, 415
  (*See also* Education; Universities and colleges)
Science:
  of man, 125
  pure, 217
  as working language, 216-217
Scientific management, 247
Scientific tidiness, 102
Second Sociology, 14
Sects, 298, 312-313, 436-438
Secularization, 300-304
Self, the, 126, 128
  (*See also* Identity, personal)
Self-actualization, 253, 384
Self-education vs. self-schooling, 383
Self-employed workers, 242-245
  party preference of, 260
  and risk taking, 271
Self-interest, 131-133
  in capitalist economy, 237
  vs. socialism, 191-192
Selfishness:
  capitalist use of, 270
  rule of, 237
Separation, church-state, 297-300
SES (socioeconomic status), 103-105
  (*See also* Occupational prestige; Social class; Social stratification)
Sex differences:
  in age at marriage, 342, 357
  in civil rights militancy, 315
  in deviance, 456-457
  in politics, 172
  in socialization, 136-137
Sex ratio, defined, 332
Sexual behavior:
  and countercultures, 350
  glass-of-water theory of, 352
  illegitimate, 328
  increases in, 356-361
  and love, 352, 357, 364

Sexual behavior (*Cont.*):
  in medieval Christendom, 337–339
  premarital, 323, 339, 358–360
  Protestant norms about, 341
  rules on, 326, 333
  and social class, 360–361
Sexual inequality (*see* Inequality, sexual)
Significance, statistical, 59
Silence as form of religious expression, 282–283
Single-family households, 341
Size:
  of cities, 261–262
  of corporations, 243–247, 257
  family, 231, 364
  of government, 255–260
  of production units, 261–262
  of societies, 218–220, 250
Slavery, 238–239
  education and, 395
  and illegitimacy, 328
Sleep as form of liberation, 433
Small businesses, 242–245
SMSAs (Standard Metropolitan Statistical Areas), 261
Social change (*see* Dynamism; Economy; Education; Family, the; History; Innovation; Liberation; Polity; Religion)
Social class, 250–255
  and attitude toward work, 61
  and chance for humanness, 147–148
  and deviance, 84–85, 453
  and divorce rates, 363
  and family life, 342, 347
  and longevity, 101
  and mate selection, 334
  mobility in, 453
  and parentage, 352, 366–370
  and party preference, 260
  and place of residence, 264
  and religion, 284–285, 312–313
  ruling, 104
  and school attainment, 368–369
  and schooling, 95, 392, 409, 411–415
  and sexual behavior, 360–361
  shrinkage of capitalist, 242–245
  and socialization, 133–134, 137
  study of, 103–104

Social class (*Cont.*):
  and university education, 402–403
Social-contract theory, 166
Social movements, 440–444
  origins of, 451–461
Social psychology, 117–155
  and inequality, 147
Social security, 249
Social status (*see* Status, socioeconomic)
Social stratification, 104, 250–255
  and consumer spending, 252
  graphic representation of, 254–255
  and suburbs, 264
  of teachers, 416–417
  (*See also* Inequality; Social class)
Social welfare, 248–250, 256–257
Social work, 22, 28
Socialism, 66, 187, 191–196
  and child socialization, 355
  fear of, 259
  origins of, 191–194
  and redistributive mode of exchange, 226
  and religion, 305–308
Socialization:
  of adults, 137–142
  of children, 129–137, 355, 366–370
  cognitive, 130, 141–142
  content of, 129–134
  defined, 129
  to deviant ways, 447–451
  outside the family, 325
  moral, 130–133, 406
  among Pygmies, 132
  techniques of, 134–141, 386, 395–397
Society:
  defined, 77
  humanist outlook on, 13
  hunting and gathering, 206–207, 214
    religion in, 287–288
  mass, 180–181
  modern, 228–230
  national (*see* National societies)
  overview of, 70–115
  size of, 218–220
Sociocultural system, 78–86
Socioeconomic status (SES), 103–105
  (*See also* Occupational prestige; Social class; Social stratification)
Sociological imagination, 24–25
Sociologism, 123
Sociology:
  vs. anthropology, 7, 29
  applied, 27–28
  vs. common sense, 19–20, 46
  contemporary diversity in, 8–10, 151–153

Sociology (*Cont.*):
  contrasting psychological views in, 151–153
  defined, 29
  vs. economics, 21
  and family research, 324
  vs. history, 21–22
  humanist, 12–14, 15–18
  vs. journalism, 22
  main focus of, 72
  in modernization of universities, 401
  origins of, 2–8
  vs. philosophy, 23
  vs. political science, 21
  positivist, 10–12
  vs. psychology, 26–29, 38–39, 451–452
  purposes of, 423–424, 430
  research priorities in, 112–113
  scope of, 446, 451–452, 456
  vs. social work, 22
  vs. theology, 23
Solidarity, mechanical vs. organic, 221–222
Sovereignty, 73
Specialization (*see* Division of labor)
Standardization, 266
State, defined, 159
Stateways, 112–113
Status, socioeconomic (SES), 103–105
  (*See also* Occupational prestige; Social class; Social stratification)
Stranger, the, 455
Straw-boss power, 251
Stress, 455
Strikes, 248, 271
Structural functionalism:
  defined, 86–87
  and education, 386
  and family research, 324–325
  and inequality, 102
  limits of, 96
  psychological basis of, 151–152
  and religion (*see* Religion, functionalist outlook on)
Structural strain, 455
Structure of demands, 86–97
  and structure of rewards, 100–102
Structure of rewards, 97–105
  in advanced capitalist societies, 250–255
Subcultures, 111–112
  deviant, 449
  ethnic, 447–448
Subsystem, 88
Suburbanization, 262–265
  and family life, 346–347

Trivium, 398

Suicide, 434–435, 450
  and religion, 64
Superego, 123
Superpowers, 109–110
Surplus, 218, 241
Surprise, 124, 142, 146, 149, 461
Survey research, 58–62, 314–315
Symbolic analysis of nature, 216–218
Symbolic interactionism, 123, 146, 391
System:
  defined, 86
  mechanical vs. social, 97

Taxation, 218–219
  increase and change in, 256
Teachers, 384–385, 397, 409, 414,
    416–417
  schooling of, 404
Technology, 209–210
  and education, 386, 395
  of warfare, 176–178
Television, 179, 346–348, 360, 381,
    382, 395, 450
Test-tube babies, 325
Thanatology, 311
Theological stage of knowledge, 3
Theology, 23
Theory building, 21
Third Sociology, 14–15
This-worldliness, 296, 303
Tidiness in social science, 101–102
Time, structuring of, 215
Tools and machines, 209–210
Total institutions, 140–141
Tourism, 395, 453
Towers and mountains, scaling, as
    symbol for human control, 269
Traditionalism:
  and birth control, 230
  economic, 42–43, 206–207, 214, 216,
    233
  end of, 343–344
  and freedom, 452–453, 461–462
  in politics, 160–162, 171–174
  in religion, 41–42
  among women, 172
Training vs. education, 394–395,
    420–421

Ujamaa, 192
Uncertainty and religion, 278–279, 281,
    309–310
Unemployment, 228, 267
  and higher learning, 409–410
  and religion, 312
  and withdrawal, 454
Unions, 248–249
  vs. professions, 412
  and school credentials, 411–412
Unitary political structure, 88–89
Universal church, 298, 307
Universalism, 82
Universities and colleges, 391–392,
    397–403
  diversity among, 402
  liberal arts in, 415, 423–424
  liberation in, 445
  modernization of, 399–403
  origins of, 397–403
  and professionalization (*see*
    Professions)
  and social class, 402–403
  as sources of dissent, 448–449, 454
  two-year, 415
Urban renewal, 265
Urbanization, 260–265
  automobiles and, 262–264
  and parental authority, 369
Usury, 188
Utility, maximization of, 92
Utopian communities:
  and family life, 349–351
  (*See also* Countercultures)

Validity, problem of, 48–49
Values:
  on achievement, 131
  on competition, 131–133
  defined, 82
  of sociologists, 12, 38
  in Western world, 131–134
  on work, 229
Variables, 44
  in analysis of data, 55, 60–61
  in survey research, 58–61, 314–315
Venereal disease, 360
Violence, resources of (*see* Resources of
    violence)
Voluntary associations, 93–94
  Protestant churches as, 296–298
Voting:
  by sex, 172

Voting (*Cont.*):
  and social class, 260

Wage labor, 238
  in nineteenth century, 242–243
  and public schools, 404
  reason for hiring, 243
  rights of, 247–250
  spread of, 242–247
  stigma of, 250
  (*See also* Labor force, the)
War:
  nuclear, 316
  tools of, 174–178, 268
Water power, 212
Wealth, 99–105
Welfare, social, 248–250, 256–257
Western world:
  basic characteristics of, 335–336
  defined, 335
  family patterns in, 335–349
Wind power, 212
Withdrawal:
  collective, 436–438, 456–457
  individual, 433–435, 456–457
Women:
  economic emancipation of, 362
  in labor force, 345, 352, 364
  mobilization of, 458–459
  power of, 456–457
  role of, 344–345
  and traditional authority, 172
Women's movement, the, 72, 362–364,
    458–459
Work, 214–216
  agricultural, 215
  capitalist way of encouraging, 237
  manual vs. nonmanual, 215–216
  vs. play, 214
  in primitive economies, 220
  in religious ritual, 296
  value on, 229
  (*See also* Division of labor;
    Wage labor)
Working class:
  and dissidence, 453
  growth of, 242–245
  and schooling, 404, 411
  stratification within, 250–255
  and welfare capitalism, 247–250
  (*See also* Social class)
World:
  as level of analysis, 47–48, 62
  as a whole, 109–110
World population, 230–231